MICROSOFT®

Excel 2002

Comprehensive Course

Mastering and Using

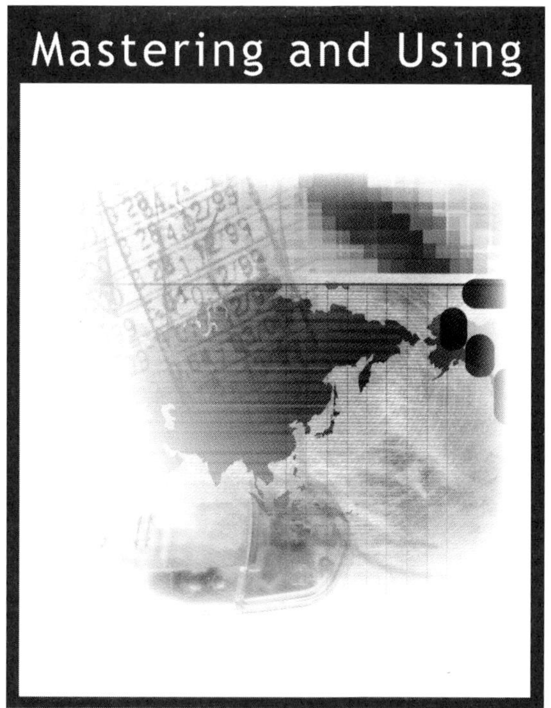

H. Albert Napier
Philip J. Judd
Benjamin Rand

Australia • Canada • Mexico • Singapore • Spain • United Kingdom • United States

Mastering and Using Microsoft® Excel 2002 Comprehensive Course

by H. Albert Napier, Ph.D. & Philip J. Judd, Benjamin Rand

Managing Editor:
Melissa Ramondetta

Development Editor:
Robin M. Romer, Pale Moon Productions

Product Marketing Manager:
Kim Wood

Product Manager:
Robert Gaggin

Associate Product Manager:
Jodi Dreissig

Production Services:
GEX Publishing Services

Copy Editor:
GEX Publishing Services

Cover Design:
Steve Deschene

Compositor:
GEX Publishing Services

Printed in the United States of America

3 4 5 6 7 8 9 BM 04 03

For more information, contact Course Technology, 25 Thomson Place, Boston, Massachusetts 02210.

Or find us on the World Wide Web at: www.course.com

ISBN 0-619-05832-3

Mastering and Using

Microsoft® Excel 2002 Comprehensive Course

The Future Is Now…

Our Napier & Judd series, *Mastering and Using Microsoft Excel 2002 Comprehensive Course*, is the most comprehensive, instructional tool designed for the user who wants to master and use the application software. This expertly written product provides all the instruction necessary to become certified as a Microsoft Office User Specialist (MOUS) Expert user of Excel.

Mastering and Using Microsoft Excel 2002 Comprehensive Course

◆ Text	0-619-05832-3
◆ IRK (Instructor's Resource Kit)	0-619-05807-2
◆ Review Pack	0-619-05809-9

The Instructor's Resource Kit (CD-ROM) includes lesson plans, SCANS correlations, scheduling charts, PowerPoint presentations, and much more!

Mastering and Using Microsoft Access 2002 Comprehensive Course

◆ Student Text	0-619-05814-5
◆ IRK (Instructor's Resource Kit)	0-619-05807-2
◆ Review Pack	0-619-05809-9

Mastering and Using Microsoft Word 2002 Comprehensive Course

◆ Student Text	0-619-05820-X
◆ IRK (Instructor's Resource Kit)	0-619-05807-2
◆ Review Pack	0-619-05809-9

Mastering and Using Microsoft PowerPoint 2002 Comprehensive Course

◆ Student Text	0-619-05826-9
◆ IRK (Instructor's Resource Kit)	0-619-05807-2
◆ Review Pack	0-619-05809-9

Mastering and Using Microsoft Office XP Advanced Course

◆ Student Text	0-619-05808-0
◆ IRK (Instructor's Resource Kit)	0-619-05801-2
◆ Review Pack	0-619-05809-9

COURSE TECHNOLOGY™
THOMSON LEARNING

For more information about these Course Technology products and others:
Join us On the Internet at www.course.com/masteringandusing

What's New in Excel 2002

Office XP

- Streamlined, flatter look
- Multiple task panes containing command shortcuts
- Ask A Question Box Help tool
- Smart Tags
- AutoCorrect Options
- Revised Office Clipboard
- Paste Options
- Route documents for review with tracked changes via e-mail
- Speech Recognition
- Improved "crash" recovery features
- Search task pane
- Digital signatures for documents routed over the Internet

Excel 2002

- Query data directly from Web pages and XML files
- Import data from a variety of sources, including databases, OLAP data sources, and SQL Server
- Function arguments displayed in ScreenTips as functions entered
- Function Wizard uses natural language query to help find best function available
- Cut-and-paste function examples from Help into a worksheet
- Expanded AutoSum functionality includes commonly used functions such as MIN, MAX, and AVERAGE
- Formula evaluator shows results of nested formulas
- Formula error checking
- Color-coded worksheet tabs
- Smart Tags for paste, fill, insert, and formula checking
- Border drawing to create complex outline borders
- AutoRepublish Excel data to the Web
- Open and save XML files
- Speech playback of cell content
- Graphics can be inserted into headers and footers for printing
- Merge and unmerge cells with a Format toolbar button
- Links Management

Napier & Judd

In their over 50 years of combined experience, Al Napier and Phil Judd have developed a tested, realistic approach to mastering and using application software. As both academics and corporate trainers, Al and Phil have the unique ability to help students by teaching them the skills necessary to compete in today's complex business world.

H. Albert Napier, Ph.D. is the Director of the Center on the Management of Information Technology and Professor in the Jesse H. Jones Graduate School of Management at Rice University. In addition, Al is a principal of Napier & Judd, Inc., a consulting company and corporate trainer in Houston, Texas, that has trained more than 120,000 people in computer applications.

Philip J. Judd is a former instructor in the Management Department and the Director of the Research and Instructional Computing Service at the University of Houston. Phil now dedicates himself to consulting and corporate training as a principal of Napier & Judd, Inc.

Philip J. Judd

H. Albert Napier, Ph.D.

Preface

At Course Technology, we believe that technology will change the way people teach and learn. Today millions of people are using personal computers in their everyday lives—both as tools at work and for recreational activities. As a result, the personal computer has revolutionized the ways in which people interact with each other. The *Mastering and Using* series combines the following distinguishing features to allow people to do amazing things with their personal computers.

Distinguishing Features

All the textbooks in the *Mastering and Using* series share several key pedagogical features:

Case Project Approach. In their more than twenty years of business and corporate training and teaching experience, Napier & Judd have found that students are more enthusiastic about learning a software application if they can see its real-world relevance. The textbook provides bountiful business-based profiles, exercises, and projects. It also emphasizes the skills most in demand by employers.

Comprehensive and Easy to Use. There is thorough coverage of new features. The narrative is clear and concise. Each unit or chapter thoroughly explains the concepts that underlie the skills and procedures. We explain not just the *how*, but the *why*.

Step-by-Step Instructions and Screen Illustrations. All examples in this text include step-by-step instructions that explain how to complete the specific task. Full-color screen illustrations are used extensively to provide students with a realistic picture of the software application feature.

Extensive Tips and Tricks. The authors have placed informational boxes in the margin of the text. These boxes of information provide students with the following helpful tips:

- *Quick Tip*. Extra information provides shortcuts on how to perform common business-related functions.
- *Caution Tip*. This additional information explains how a mistake occurs and provides tips on how to avoid making similar mistakes in the future.
- *Menu Tip*. Additional explanation on how to use menu commands to perform application tasks.
- *Mouse Tip*. Further instructions on how to use the mouse to perform application tasks.
- *Task Pane Tip*. Additional information on using task pane shortcuts.
- *Internet Tip*. This information incorporates the power of the Internet to help students use the Internet as they progress through the text.
- *Design Tip*. Hints for better presentation designs (found in the PowerPoint chapters).

End-of-Chapter Materials. Each book in the *Mastering and Using* series places a heavy emphasis on providing students with the opportunity to practice and reinforce the skills they are learning through extensive exercises. Each chapter has a summary, commands review, concepts review, skills review, and case projects so that the students can master the material by doing. For more information on each of the end-of-chapter elements see page ix of the How to Use This Book section in this preface.

Appendices. *Mastering and Using* series contains three appendices to further help students prepare to be successful in the classroom or in the workplace. Appendix A teaches students to work with Windows 2000. Appendix B illustrates how to format letters; how to insert a mailing notation; how to format envelopes (referencing the U.S. Postal Service documents); how to format interoffice memorandums; and how to key a formal outline. It also lists popular style guides and describes proofreader's marks. Appendix C describes the new Office XP speech recognition features.

Microsoft Office User Specialist (MOUS) Certification.
What does this logo mean? It means this courseware has been approved by the Microsoft® Office User Specialist Program to be among the finest available for learning Microsoft Office XP, Microsoft Word 2002, Microsoft Excel 2002, Microsoft PowerPoint® 2002, and Microsoft Access 2002. It also means that upon completion of this courseware, you may be prepared to become a Microsoft Office User Specialist.
What is a Microsoft Office User Specialist? A Microsoft Office User Specialist is an individual who has certified his or her skills in one or more of the Microsoft Office desktop applications of Microsoft Word, Microsoft Excel, Microsoft PowerPoint®, Microsoft Outlook® or Microsoft Access, or in Microsoft Project. The Microsoft Office User Specialist Program typically offers certification exams at the "Core" and "Expert" skill levels. The Microsoft Office User Specialist Program is the only Microsoft approved program in the world for certifying proficiency in Microsoft Office desktop applications and Microsoft Project. This certification can be a valuable asset in any job search or career advancement.
More Information: To learn more about becoming a Microsoft Office User Specialist, visit *www.mous.net*. To purchase a Microsoft Office User Specialist certification exam, visit *www.DesktopIQ.com*.

SCANS. In 1992, the U.S. Department of Labor and Education formed the Secretary's Commission on Achieving Necessary Skills, or SCANS, to study the kinds of competencies and skills that workers must have to succeed in today's marketplace. The results of the study were published in a document entitled *What Work Requires of Schools: A SCANS Report for America 2000*. The in-chapter and end-of-chapter exercises in this book are designed to meet the criteria outlined in the SCANS report and thus help prepare students to be successful in today's workplace.

Instructional Support

All books in the *Mastering and Using* series are supplemented with an ***Instructor's Resource Kit.*** This is a CD-ROM that contains lesson plans with teaching materials and preparation suggestions, along with tips for implementing instruction and assessment ideas; a suggested syllabus; and SCANS workplace know how. The CD also contains:

- Career Worksheets
- Evaluation Guidelines
- Hands-on Solutions
- Individual Learning Strategies
- Internet Behavior Contract
- Lesson Plans
- Portfolio Guidelines
- PowerPoint Presentations
- Solution Files
- Student Data Files
- Teacher Training Notes
- Test Questions
- Transparency Graphics Files

ExamView® This textbook is accompanied by ExamView, a powerful testing software package that allows instructors to create and administer printed, computer (LAN-based), and Internet exams. ExamView includes hundreds of questions that correspond to the topics covered in this text, enabling students to generate detailed study guides that include page references for further review. The computer-based and Internet testing components allow students to take exams at their computers, and also save the instructor time by grading each exam automatically.

Student Support

Data Disk. To use this book, students must have the Data Disk. Data Files needed to complete exercises in the text are contained on the Review Pack CD-ROM. These files can be copied to a hard drive or posted to a network drive.

*The availability of Microsoft Office User Specialist certification exams varies by application, application version and language. Visit *www.mous.net* for exam availability.

How to Use This Book

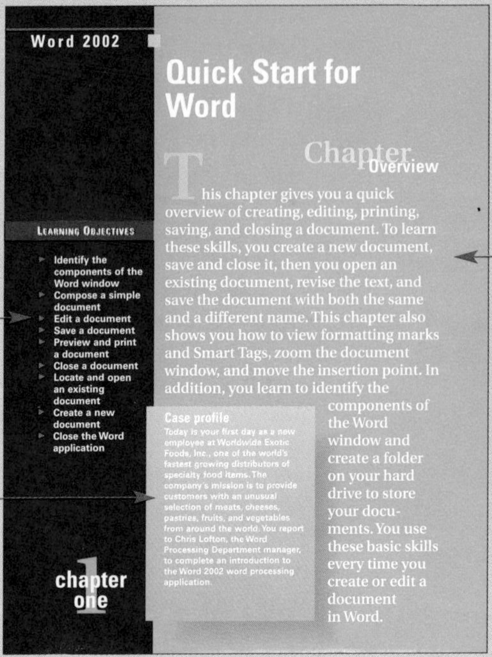

Learning Objectives — A quick reference of the major topics learned in the chapter

Case profile — Realistic scenarios that show the real-world application of the material being covered

Chapter Overview — A concise summary of what will be learned in the chapter

Clear step-by-step directions explain how to complete the specific task

Caution Tip — This additional information explains how a mistake occurs and provides tips on how to avoid making similar mistakes in the future

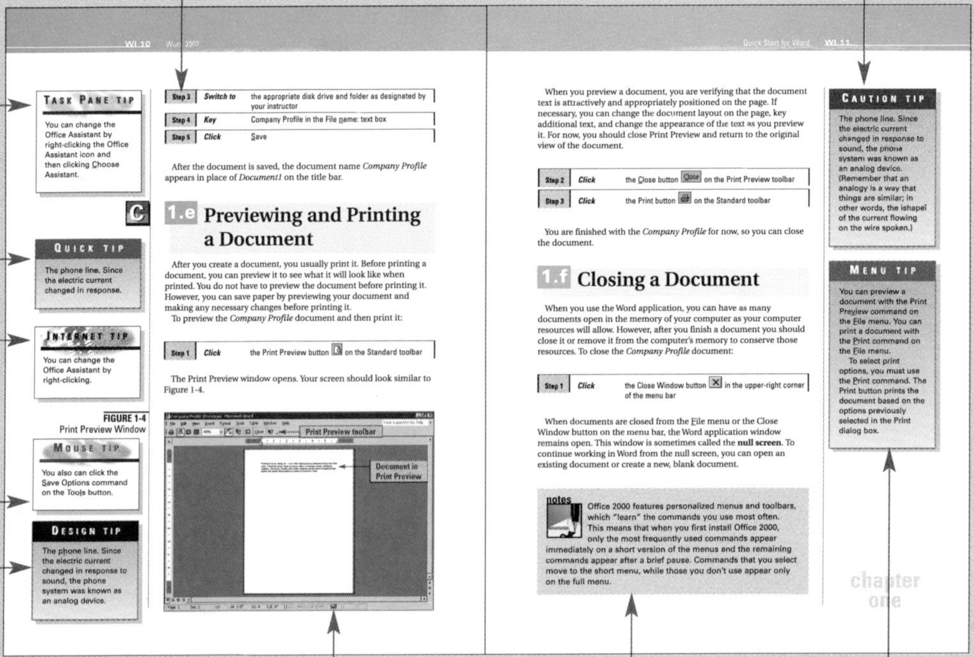

Task Pane Tip — Additional information about using task pane shortcuts

Quick Tip — Extra information provides shortcuts on how to perform common business-related functions

Internet Tip — Information to help students incorporate the power of the Internet as they progress through the text

Mouse Tip — Further instructions on how to use the mouse to perform application tasks

Design Tip — Hints for better presentation designs (found in only the PowerPoint chapters)

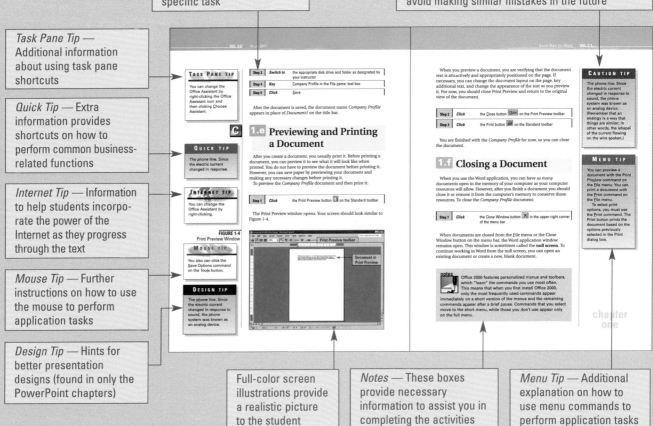

Full-color screen illustrations provide a realistic picture to the student

Notes — These boxes provide necessary information to assist you in completing the activities

Menu Tip — Additional explanation on how to use menu commands to perform application tasks

End-of-Chapter Material

Concepts Review — Multiple choice and true or false questions help assess how well the student has learned the chapter material

Summary — Reviews key topics discussed in the chapter

Commands Review — Provides a quick reference and reinforcement tool on multiple methods for performing actions discussed in the chapter

WI 46 Word 2002

Summary

- The block format is commonly used for business correspondence.
- Word has preset top, bottom, left, and right margins that you can change in the Page Setup dialog box.
- The date and time can be inserted in a document as text or as a field that automatically updates to the current system date when the document is printed.
- You can select characters, words, or groups of words with the mouse or keyboard.
- Selected text can be cut, copied, and pasted using menu commands, a shortcut menu, toolbar buttons, and the Office Clipboard task pane.
- You can collect up to 24 cut or copied selections and then paste them individually or all at one time using the Office Clipboard task pane.
- You can repeat or undo your last action.
- Word has several ways you can view your document, including: Normal view, Print Layout view, and Full Screen view. Use Normal view to key, edit, and format text. Use Print Layout to view and work with margins, headers and footers, columns, graphics, and drawing objects. Use Full Screen view to see more lines of text on the page.

Commands Review

Action	Menu Bar	Shortcut Menu	Toolbar	Task Pane	Keyboard
Set margins	File, Page Setup				ALT + F, U
Insert date	Insert, Date and Time				ALT + I, T
Update a selected date field		Right-click, then click Update Field			ALT + SHIFT + D F9
Cut, Copy, Paste	Edit, Cut or Copy or Paste	Right-click, then click Cut or Copy, or Paste		Click an item or Paste All in the Office Clipboard task pane	ALT + E, T or C or P CTRL + C (copy) CTRL + X (cut) CTRL + V (paste)
Turn on or off Overtype			Double-click the OVR mode indicator		INSERT
Undo or Redo actions	Edit, Undo Edit, Redo				ALT + E, U ALT + E, R CTRL + Z CTRL + Y
Repeat actions	Edit, Repeat				ALT+ E, R CTRL + Y
Cancel an action					ESC
Change editing views	View, Normal, Web Layout, Print Layout, Outline, Full Screen				ALT + V, N or W or P or O or U ALT + CTRL + P ALT + CTRL + O ALT + CTRL + N

Creating and Editing a Word Document WI 47

Concepts Review

Circle the correct answer.

1. You can remove text by selecting the text and pressing the:
   - [a] EXT key.
   - [b] ALT + PAGEUP keys.
   - [c] CTRL key.
   - [d] DELETE key.
2. You cannot add a date to a document by:
   - [a] keying the date manually.
   - [b] inserting a date field that updates automatically.
   - [c] inserting the date as text.
   - [d] pressing the Insert key.
3. The selection bar is:
   - [a] located below the status bar.
   - [b] used to open other Office applications.
   - [c] used to select text in different ways.
   - [d] used to set left and right margins.
4. When you use the block format for a business letter, the:
   - [a] date and complimentary closing are centered on their respective lines.
   - [b] letter address is positioned below the salutation.
   - [c] letter components all begin at the left margin.
   - [d] letter components all begin at the right margin.
5. Margins refer to the:
   - [a] distance from the center of the page to the edge of the page.
   - [b] distance from the top, bottom, left, and right edges of the page to the text.
   - [c] number of lines you can have on a page.
   - [d] size of the text on a page.
6. By default, Word is in the:
   - [a] Overtype mode.
   - [b] Edit mode.
   - [c] Online Review mode.
   - [d] Insert mode.
7. Which of the following is not a selection technique in Word?
   - [a] pressing the CTRL + SHIFT + END keys to select from the insertion point to the end of the document
   - [b] double-clicking the selection bar opposite the paragraph you wish to select
   - [c] double-clicking a word
   - [d] pressing the ALT key and clicking a word
8. Using the mouse to move or copy text is called:
   - [a] cut-and-drag.
   - [b] select-and-cut.
   - [c] copy-and-cut.
   - [d] drag-and-drop.
9. Overtype mode allows you to:
   - [a] select text.
   - [b] key over existing text.
   - [c] move text.
   - [d] copy text.
10. Which of the following is not an editing view?
    - [a] Full Page view
    - [b] Full Screen view
    - [c] Print Layout view
    - [d] Normal view

Circle **T** if the statement is true or **F** if the statement is false.

- T F 1. When you are in the Overtype mode and enter new text, any character you key replaces the character to the right of the insertion point.
- T F 2. Word automatically defaults to the Edit mode.
- T F 3. Word can undo multiple actions.
- T F 4. The mouse and the keyboard can both be used to select text in a document.

chapter two

Skills Review — Hands-on exercises provide the ability to practice the skills just learned in the chapter

Case Projects — Asks the student to synthesize the material learned in the chapter and complete an office assignment

SCANS icon — Indicates that the exercise or project meets SCANS competencies and prepares the student to be successful in today's workplace

MOUS Certification icon — Indicates that the exercise or project meets Microsoft's certification objectives that prepare the student for the MOUS exam

Internet Case Projects — Allow the student to practice using the World Wide Web

WI 48 Word 2002

- T F 5. The EXT mode indicator appears bolded when you are using the Extend mode feature.
- T F 6. You can restore text that has been deleted.
- T F 7. You can maximize the number of lines of text displayed on the screen by switching to Full Screen view.
- T F 8. Normal view displays your document much like it looks when printed.
- T F 9. You can insert the date and the time together in a Word document.
- T F 10. The Office Clipboard is a reserved place in the memory of your computer you can use to temporarily store up to 24 items you have cut or copied.

Skills Review

Exercise 1

1. Create the following document. Use the block style with 2-inch top margin and 1-inch left and right margins. Insert the current date in the format of your choice at the top of the document. As you key the text, use the movement techniques and insert/delete actions you learned in this chapter to correct any keying errors you make. You revise the document in the next exercise.

> Current date
>
> Ms. Gail Jackson
> Corporate Travel Manager
> International Travel Services
> 1590 W. Convention Street
> Chicago, IL 60605-1590
>
> Dear Ms. Jackson:
>
> Thank you for helping plan business trip to London this winter. I am really looking forward to seeing the sites, as well as taking care of some business. This is my first trip to London, and you were quite courteous in answering my questions.
>
> Yours truly,
>
> Kelly Armstead
> Executive Assistant to B. D. Vickers
>
> ka

2. Save the document as *Travel Letter*. Preview, print, and close the document.

Creating and Editing a Word Document WI 53

Case Projects

Project 1

B. D. Vickers is traveling on business to Melbourne, Australia in three weeks. Prepare a letter to Mr. David Melville, Reservations Manager at the Excelsior Hotel, 3500 Wayburne Drive, Melbourne, VIC, 30001, Australia, requesting accommodations for a week beginning three weeks from today. Insert the date as text using the Day, Month (in text), Year format. Save, preview, and print the document.

Project 2

Open the document you created in Project 1 and change the accommodation dates to four weeks from today using the Overtype mode. Save the document with a new name, then preview and print it.

Project 3

Kelly Armstead has asked you to find a list of keyboard shortcuts you both can use to prepare correspondence. Using the Ask A Question Box, search online Help for a list of keyboard shortcut keys for moving the insertion point in a document and selecting text in a document. Print the lists. With your instructor's permission, use the lists to demonstrate the keyboard shortcuts to a classmate.

Project 4

B. D. Vickers is considering ordering several IntelliMouse pointing devices for the Purchasing Department and has asked you to find out how the devices are used to increase productivity in the department. Using the Help menu resources, including Web resources, search for information on the IntelliMouse pointing device. Create a new document containing at least three paragraphs describing how the Purchasing Department employees can improve their productivity by using the IntelliMouse pointing device. Insert the current date as text using the mm/dd/yy format. Save, preview, and print the document.

Project 5

There have been several power failures because of storms in the area and Kelly is concerned that she may lose documents she is working on if the power fails. She has asked you to find out what options Word has to automatically back up documents as she is working and to automatically recover documents lost during a power failure. Using the Help menu, research what backup and document recovery features Word provides. Create a new document containing at least four paragraphs describing how to set backup procedures and recover lost or damaged documents. Insert the date as a field using the format of your choice. Save, preview, and print the document.

Project 6

B. D. Vickers has extended the business trip discussed in Project 1 and now plans to spend two days in Hong Kong and three days in London before returning. Kelly needs a list of possible accommodations in Hong Kong and London and has asked you to search the Web for information on hotels in these cities. She also needs you to review flight schedules and suggest flights from Melbourne to Hong Kong, from Hong Kong to London, and from London to Chicago. Connect to the Internet and search the Web for the information you need. Save at least two URLs as "favorites." Print at least five Web pages. Create a new, blank document and key the title and URL of the pages you printed. Insert the date as text in the format of your choice. Save, preview, and print the document.

chapter two

Acknowledgments

We would like to thank and express our appreciation to the many fine individuals who have contributed to the completion of this book.

No book is possible without the motivation and support of an editorial staff. Therefore, we wish to acknowledge with great appreciation the project team at Course Technology: Melissa Ramondetta, managing editor; Robert Gaggin, product manager; and Jodi Dreissig, editorial assistant. Our appreciation also goes to Robin Romer for managing the developmental editing of this series. In addition, we want to acknowledge the team at GEX for their production work, especially Karla Russell, Kendra Neville, Michelle Olson, and Angel Lesiczka.

We are very appreciative of the personnel at Napier & Judd, Inc., who helped to prepare this book. We acknowledge, with great appreciation, the assistance provided by Ollie Rivers and Nancy Onarheim in preparing and checking the many drafts of the Office unit and the appendices of this book.

We gratefully acknowledge the work of Benjamin Rand for writing the Excel unit for this series.

H. Albert Napier
Philip J. Judd

Thanks go to my wife Erika, who was so supportive throughout the writing of this book (I think her exact words were, "Oh no, not again"). More thanks to my boys who had to wait too many times for Daddy to finish working. Thanks for being so patient—it's wrestle time!

I was extremely fortunate to be paired with Kitty again on this venture. Thanks for all your suggestions, input, help, and hard work. Thanks also to the team at Course Technology for having me back and for their support and encouragement.

Benjamin Rand

Contents

Microsoft Office XP

Getting Started with Microsoft Office XP

Chapter Overview

Microsoft Office XP provides the ability to enter, record, analyze, display, and present any type of business information. In this chapter, you learn about the capabilities of Microsoft Office XP, including its computer hardware and operating system requirements and elements common to all its applications. You also learn how to open and close those applications and get Help.

Learning Objectives

- Describe Microsoft Office XP
- Determine hardware and operating system requirements
- Identify common elements of Office applications
- Start Office applications
- Get Help in Office applications
- Close Office applications

chapter one

This book assumes that you have little or no knowledge of Microsoft Office XP but that you have worked with personal computers and are familiar with Microsoft Windows 2000 or Windows 98 operating systems.

1.a What Is Microsoft Office XP?

Microsoft Office XP is a software suite (or package) that contains a combination of software applications you use to create text documents, analyze numbers, create presentations, manage large files of data, and create Web pages.

The **Word 2002** software application provides you with word processing capabilities. **Word processing** is the preparation and production of text documents such as letters, memorandums, and reports. **Excel 2002** is software you use to analyze numbers with worksheets (sometimes called spreadsheets) and charts and to perform other tasks such as sorting data. A **worksheet** is a grid of columns and rows in which you enter labels and data. A **chart** is a visual or graphical representation of worksheet data. With Excel, you can create financial budgets, reports, and a variety of other forms.

PowerPoint 2002 software is used to create a **presentation**, or collection of slides. A **slide** is the presentation output (actual 35mm slides, transparencies, computer screens, or printed pages) that can contain text, charts, graphics, audio, and video. You can use PowerPoint slides to create a slide show on a computer attached to a projector, to broadcast a presentation over the Internet or company intranet, and to create handout materials for a presentation.

Access 2002 provides database management capabilities, enabling you to store and retrieve a large amount of data. A **database** is a collection of related information. A phone book and an address book are common examples of databases you use every day. Other examples of databases include a price list, school registration information, or an inventory. You can query (or search) an Access database to answer specific questions about the stored data. For example, you can determine which customers in a particular state had sales in excess of a particular value during the month of June.

Outlook 2002 is a **personal information manager** that provides tools for sending and receiving e-mail as well as maintaining a calendar, contacts list, journal, electronic notes, and electronic "to do" list. The **FrontPage 2002** application is used to create and manage Web sites.

QUICK TIP

Office contains a variety of new features designed to minimize the impact of system crashes and freezes, such as one-click save in case of a system crash, timed recoveries, a new document recovery task pane, the Hang Manager, and a new corrupt document recovery feature.

For the remainder of this book, Microsoft Office XP may be called Office. Rather than include the words *Microsoft* and *2002* each time the name of an application is used, the text refers to the respective software package as Word, Excel, PowerPoint, Access, or Outlook.

A major advantage of using the Office suite is the ability to share data between the applications. For example, you can include a portion of an Excel worksheet or chart in a Word document, use an outline created in a Word document as the starting point for a PowerPoint presentation, import an Excel worksheet into Access, and merge names and addresses from an Outlook Address Book with a Word letter.

1.b Hardware and Operating System Requirements

You can install Office applications on computers using the Windows 2000, Windows 98, or Windows NT Workstation 4.0 (with Service Pack 6a installed) operating systems. Office XP applications do not run in the Windows 95, Windows 3.x or the Windows NT Workstation 3.5 environments.

You can install Office on a "x86" computer with a Pentium processor, at least 32 MB of RAM for Windows 98 or 64 MB of RAM for Windows 2000, a CD-ROM drive, Super VGA, 256-color video, Microsoft Mouse, Microsoft IntelliMouse, or another pointing device, a 28,800 (or higher) baud modem, and 350 MB of hard disk space. To access certain features you should have a multimedia computer, e-mail software, and a Web browser. For detailed information on installing Office, see the documentation that comes with the software.

QUICK TIP

Speech recognition features enable users to speak the names of toolbar buttons, menus, menu items, alerts, dialog box control buttons, and task pane items. Users can switch between two modes—Dictation and Voice command—using the Language bar. For more information on using the Speech Recognition features, see Appendix C.

1.c Common Elements of Office Applications

Office applications share many technical features that make it easier for Information Technology (IT) Departments in organizations to manage their Office software installations. Additionally, the Office applications share many features that enable users to move seamlessly between applications and learn one way to perform common tasks, such as creating, saving, and printing documents or moving and copying data.

Office applications share many common elements, making it easier for you to work efficiently in any application. A **window** is a rectangular area on your screen in which you view a software application, such as Excel. All the Office application windows have a similar look and arrangement of shortcuts, menus, and toolbars. In addition, they share many features—such as a common dictionary to check spelling in your work, identical menu commands, toolbar buttons, shortcut menus, and keyboard shortcuts to perform tasks such as copying data from one location to another.

notes

You learn more about the common elements of the Office applications in later chapters of this unit or in specific application units.

Figure 1-1 shows many of the common elements in the Office application windows.

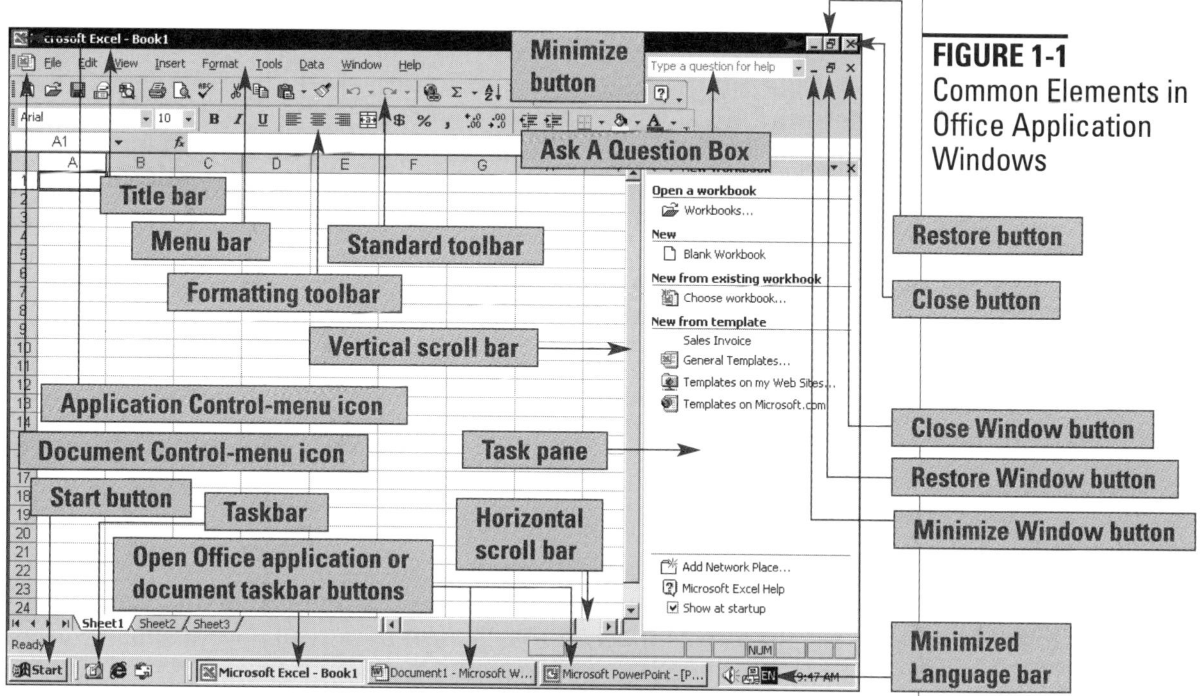

FIGURE 1-1
Common Elements in Office Application Windows

Title Bar

The application **title bar** at the top of the window includes the application Control-menu icon, the application name, the filename of the active document, and the Minimize, Restore (or Maximize), and Close buttons.

The **application Control-menu** icon, located in the upper-left corner of the title bar, displays the Control menu. The Control menu commands manage the application window, and typically include commands such as Restore, Move, Size, Minimize, Maximize, and Close. Commands that are currently available appear in a dark color. You can view the Control menu by clicking the Control-menu icon or by holding down the ALT key and then pressing the SPACEBAR key.

The **Minimize** button, near the right corner of the title bar reduces the application window to a taskbar button. The **Maximize** button, to the right of the Minimize button, enlarges the application window to fill the entire screen viewing area above the taskbar. If the window is already maximized, the Restore button appears in its place. The **Restore** button reduces the application window to a smaller size on your screen. The **Close** button, located in the right corner of the title bar, closes the application and removes it from the computer's memory.

Menu Bar

The **menu bar** is a special toolbar located at the top of the window below the title bar and contains the menus for the application. A **menu** is list of commands. The menus common to Office applications are File, Edit, View, Insert, Format, Tools, Window, and Help. Other menus vary between applications.

The **document Control-menu** icon, located below the application Control-menu icon, contains the Restore, Move, Size, Minimize, Maximize, and Close menu commands for the document window. You can view the document Control menu by clicking the Control-menu icon or by holding down the ALT key and pressing the HYPHEN (-) key.

The **Minimize Window** button reduces the document window to a title-bar icon inside the document area. It appears on the menu bar below the Minimize button in Excel and PowerPoint. (Word documents open in their own application window and use the Minimize button on the title bar.)

The **Maximize Window** button enlarges the size of the document window to cover the entire application display area and share the application title bar. It appears on the title-bar icon of a minimized Excel workbook or PowerPoint presentation. (Word documents automatically open in their own application window and use the Maximize button on the title bar.) If the window is already maximized, the Restore Window button appears in its place.

The **Restore Window** button changes the size of the document window to a smaller sized window inside the application window. It appears in the menu bar to the right of the Minimize Window button in Excel and PowerPoint. (Word documents automatically open in their own application Window and use the Restore button on the title bar.)

The **Close Window** button closes the document and removes it from the memory of the computer. It appears in the menu bar to the right of the Restore Window or Maximize Window button.

Default Toolbars

The **Standard** and **Formatting toolbars**, located one row below the menu bar, contain a set of icons called buttons. The toolbar buttons represent commonly used commands and are mouse shortcuts that enable you to perform tasks quickly. In addition to the Standard and Formatting toolbars, each application has several other toolbars available. You can customize toolbars by adding or removing buttons and commands.

When the mouse pointer rests on a toolbar button, a **ScreenTip** appears, identifying the name of the button. ScreenTips are also provided as part of online Help to describe a toolbar button, a dialog box option, or a menu command.

Scroll Bars

The vertical scroll bar appears on the right side of the document area. The **vertical scroll bar** is used to view various parts of the document by moving or scrolling the document up or down. It includes scroll arrows and a scroll box. The horizontal scroll bar appears near the bottom of the document area. The **horizontal scroll bar** is used to view various parts of the document by moving or scrolling the document left or right. It includes scroll arrows and a scroll box.

Ask A Question Box

The **Ask A Question Box** is a help tool alternative to the Office Assistant that appears on the menu bar of every Office application. The Ask A Question Box is used to quickly key a help question in plain English and then view a list of relevant Help topics.

Task Pane

Office XP includes a **task pane** feature, a pane of shortcuts, which opens on the right side of the application window. The contents of the task pane vary with the application and the activities being performed. For example, task pane shortcuts can be used to create new Office documents, format Word documents or PowerPoint presentations, or perform a Word mail merge. The task pane can be displayed or hidden as desired.

Taskbar

The **taskbar,** located across the bottom of the Windows desktop, includes the Start button and buttons for each open Office document. The **Start button,** located at the left end of the taskbar, displays the Start menu or list of tasks you can perform and applications you can use.

You can switch between documents, close documents and applications, and view other items, such as the system time and printer status, with buttons or icons on the taskbar. If you are using Windows 2000 or Windows 98, other toolbars, such as the Quick Launch toolbar, may also appear on the taskbar.

QUICK TIP

The **Office Assistant** is an interactive, animated graphic that appears in the Office application windows. When you activate the Office Assistant, a balloon-style dialog box opens to display options for searching online Help by topic. The Office Assistant may also automatically offer suggestions when you begin certain tasks. You can customize the Office Assistant by changing the animated graphic image or turning on or off various options. Any customization is shared by all Office applications.

MOUSE TIP

This book uses distinct instructions for mouse operations. **Point** means to place the mouse pointer on the specified command or item. **Click** means to press the left mouse button and then release it. **Right-click** means to press the right mouse button and then release it. **Double-click** means to press the left mouse button twice very rapidly. **Drag** means to press and hold down the left mouse button and then move the mouse on the mouse pad. **Right-drag** means to press and hold down the right mouse button and then move the mouse on the mouse pad. **Scroll** means to use the application scroll bar features or the IntelliMouse scrolling wheel.

1.d Starting Office Applications

You access the Office applications through the Windows desktop. The Windows operating system software is automatically loaded into the memory of your computer when you turn on your computer. After turning on your computer, the Windows desktop appears.

You begin by using the Start button on the taskbar to view the Start menu and open the Excel application. To use the Start button to open the Excel application:

Step 1	***Click***	the Start button Start on the taskbar
Step 2	***Point to***	Programs
Step 3	***Click***	Microsoft Excel on the Programs menu

The Excel software is placed into the memory of your computer and the Excel window opens. Your screen should look similar to Figure 1-1.

notes

You may sometimes use the keyboard to use Office application features. This book lists all keys, such as the TAB key, in uppercase letters. When the keyboard is used to issue a command, this book lists keystrokes as: Press the ENTER key. When you are to press one key and, while holding down that key, to press another key, this book lists the keystrokes as: Press the SHIFT + F7 keys.

You can open and work in more than one Office application at a time. When Office is installed, two additional commands appear on the Start menu: the Open Office Document command and the New Office Document command. You can use these commands to select the type of document on which you want to work rather than first selecting an Office application. To create a new Word document without first opening the application:

Step 1	***Click***	the Start button Start on the taskbar
Step 2	***Click***	New Office Document
Step 3	***Click***	the General tab, if necessary

The New Office Document dialog box on your screen should look similar to Figure 1-2. A **dialog box** is a window that contains options for performing specific tasks.

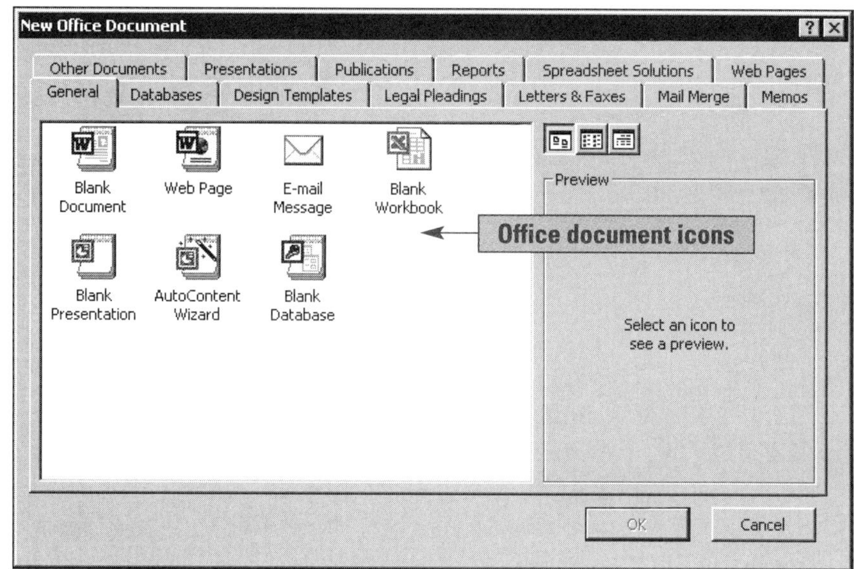

FIGURE 1-2
General Tab in the New Office Document Dialog Box

This dialog box provides options for creating different Office documents. **Icons** (or pictures) represent the Office document options; the number of icons available depends on the Office suite applications you have installed. The icons shown here create a blank Word document, a blank Web page (in Word), an e-mail message (using Outlook or Outlook Express), a blank Excel workbook, a blank PowerPoint presentation, a PowerPoint presentation using the AutoContent Wizard, and a blank Access database. You want to create a blank Word document.

Step 4	***Click***	the Blank Document icon to select it, if necessary
Step 5	***Click***	OK

The Word software is placed in the memory of your computer, the Word application window opens with a blank document. Your screen should look similar to Figure 1-3.

MOUSE TIP

Double-clicking an icon is the same as clicking the icon once to select it and then clicking the OK button.

FIGURE 1-3
Word Application Window

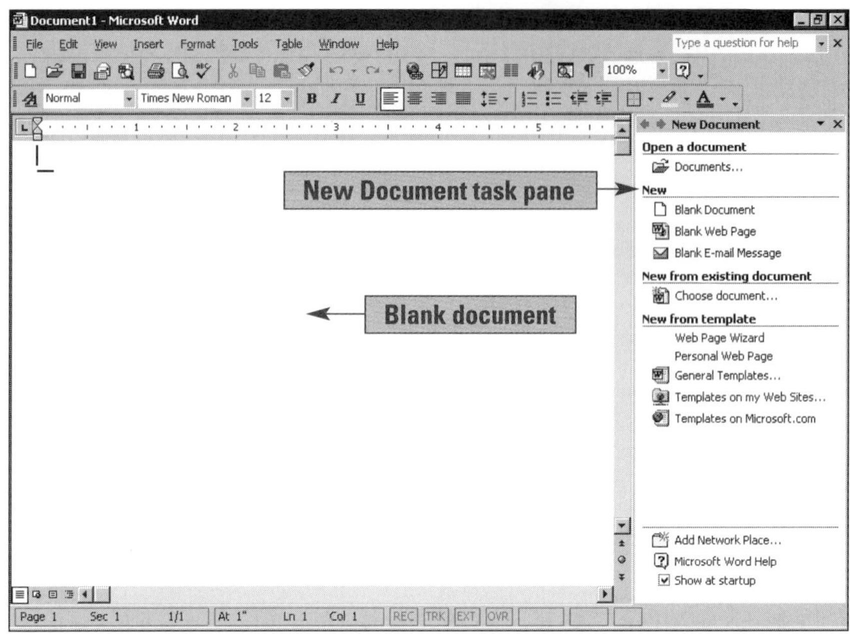

> **MENU TIP**
>
> The task pane containing shortcuts to create new documents or open existing documents opens by default when you launch a Word, Excel, or PowerPoint application. However, if you create or open another document in the same application, the task pane automatically hides. To display it again, click the Task Pane command on the View menu.

Next you open a blank presentation. To open the PowerPoint application:

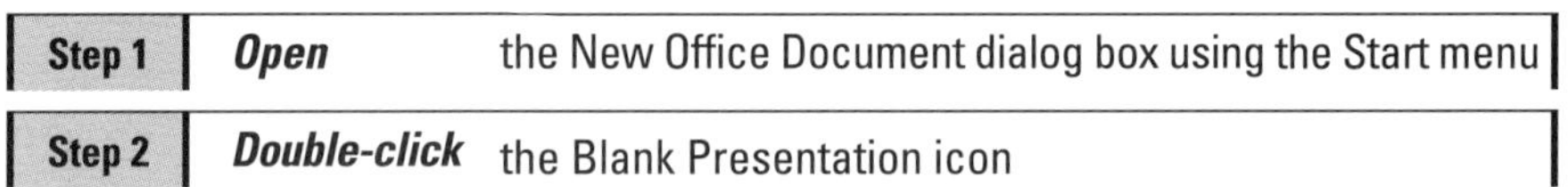

Step 1	***Open***	the New Office Document dialog box using the Start menu
Step 2	***Double-click***	the Blank Presentation icon

Your screen should look similar to Figure 1-4.

FIGURE 1-4
Blank PowerPoint Presentation

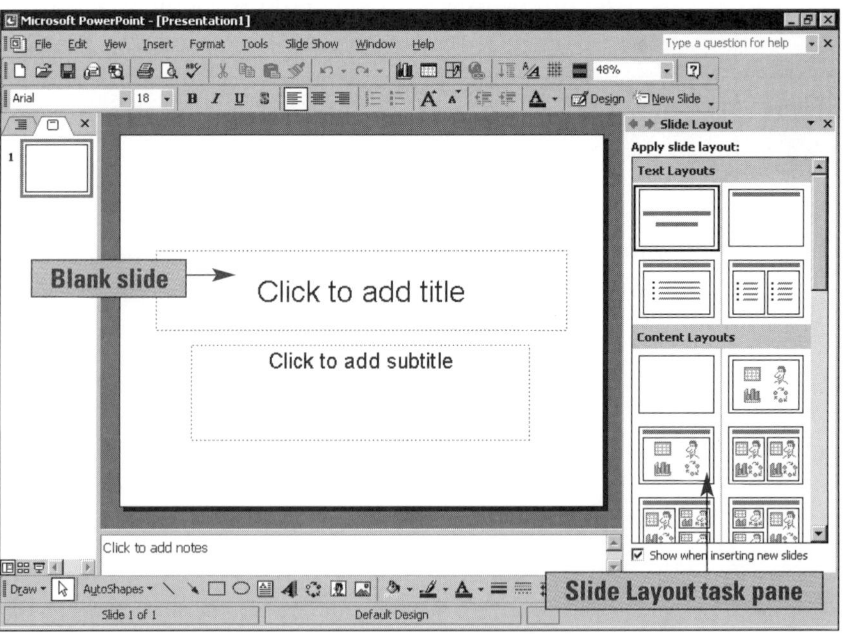

You can also open an Office application by opening an existing Office document from the Start menu. To open an existing Access database:

Step 1	***Click***	the Start button Start on the taskbar
Step 2	***Click***	Open Office Document
Step 3	***Click***	the Look in: list arrow in the Open Office Document dialog box
Step 4	***Switch to***	the disk drive and folder where the Data Files are stored
Step 5	***Double-click***	*International Sales*

The Access application window and Database window that open on your screen should look similar to Figure 1-5.

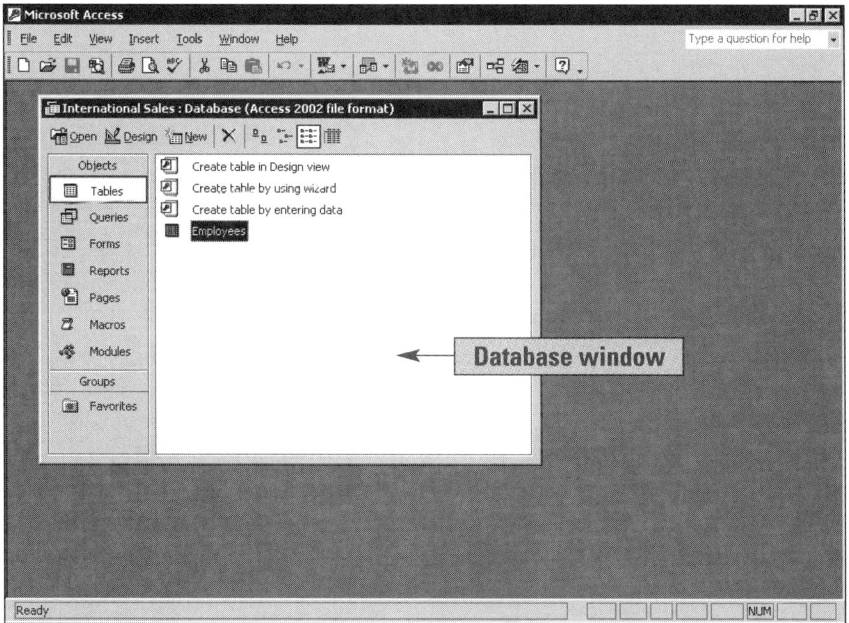

FIGURE 1-5
International Sales Database in Access Window

QUICK TIP

You can have multiple Excel workbooks, PowerPoint presentations, and Word documents open at one time. The number of documents, workbooks, and presentations you can have open at one time is determined by your computer's resources. You can open only one Access database at a time.

You can switch between open Office documents by clicking the appropriate taskbar button. If multiple windows are open, the **active window** has a dark blue title bar. All inactive windows have a gray title bar. To switch to the Excel workbook and then the Word document:

Step 1	***Click***	the Excel button on the taskbar
Step 2	***Observe***	that the Excel application window and workbook are now visible
Step 3	***Click***	the Word Document1 button on the taskbar
Step 4	***Observe***	that the Word application window and document are now visible

1.e Getting Help in Office Applications

You can get help when working in any Office application in several ways. You can use the Help menu, the Help toolbar button, or the F1 key to display the Office Assistant; get context-sensitive help with the What's This command or the SHIFT + F1 keys; or launch your Web browser and get Web-based help from Microsoft. You can also key a help question in the Ask A Question Box on the menu bar.

Using the Ask A Question Box

Suppose you want to find out how to use keyboard shortcuts in Word. To get help for keyboard shortcuts using the Ask A Question Box:

Step 1	*Verify*	that the Word document is the active window
Step 2	*Click*	in the Ask A Question Box
Step 3	*Key*	keyboard shortcuts
Step 4	*Press*	the ENTER key

A list of help topics related to keyboard shortcut keys appears. Your list should look similar to the one shown in Figure 1-6.

FIGURE 1-6
List of Help Topics

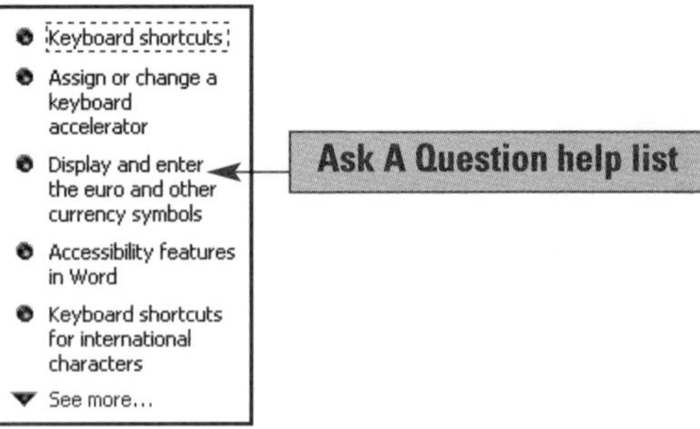

If you want to view the detailed help for any topic, simply click that topic in the list.

Step 5	*Press*	the ESC key
Step 6	*Click*	in the document area to deselect the Ask A Question Box

Using the Help Menu

The Help menu provides commands you can use to view the Office Assistant or Help window, show or hide the Office Assistant, connect to the Microsoft Web site, get context-sensitive help for a menu command or toolbar button, detect and repair font and template files, and view licensing information for the Office application. To review the Help menu commands:

Step 1	*Click*	Help on the menu bar

The Help menu on your screen should look similar to Figure 1-7.

FIGURE 1-7
Help Menu

Step 2	*Observe*	the menu commands
Step 3	*Click*	in the document area outside the menu to close the Help menu

Using What's This?

You can get context-sensitive help for a menu command or toolbar button using the What's This? command on the Help menu. This command changes the mouse pointer to a help pointer, a white mouse pointer with a large black question mark. When you click a toolbar button or menu command with the help pointer, a brief ScreenTip help message appears, describing the command or toolbar button. You can quickly change the mouse pointer to a help pointer by pressing the SHIFT + F1 keys.

To view the help pointer and view a ScreenTip help message for a toolbar button:

QUICK TIP

You can click the Help button on the title bar in any dialog box to convert the mouse pointer to a What's This help pointer.

Step 1	*Press*	the SHIFT + F1 keys
Step 2	*Observe*	the help mouse pointer with the attached question mark
Step 3	*Click*	the Save button on the Standard toolbar
Step 4	*Observe*	the ScreenTip help message describing the Save button

Step 5	***Press***	the ESC key to close the ScreenTip help message

1.f Closing Office Applications

There are many ways to close the Access, Excel, and PowerPoint applications (or the Word application with a single document open) and return to the Windows desktop. You can:

- double-click the application Control-menu icon on the title bar.
- click the application Close button on the title bar.
- right-click the application button on the taskbar to display a shortcut menu and then click the Close command.
- press the ALT + F4 keys.
- click the Exit command on the File menu to close Office applications (no matter how many Word documents are open).

To close the Excel application from the taskbar:

Step 1	***Right-click***	the Excel button on the taskbar
Step 2	***Click***	Close

You can close multiple applications at one time from the taskbar by selecting the application buttons using the CTRL key and then using the shortcut menu. To close the PowerPoint and Access applications at one time:

Step 1	***Press & hold***	the CTRL key
Step 2	***Click***	the PowerPoint button and then the Access button on the taskbar
Step 3	***Release***	the CTRL key and observe that both buttons are selected (pressed in)
Step 4	***Right-click***	the PowerPoint or Access button
Step 5	***Click***	Close

Both applications close, leaving only the Word document open. To close the Word document using the menu:

Step 1	***Verify***	that the Word application window is maximized
Step 2	***Click***	File
Step 3	***Click***	Exit

Summary

- The Word application provides word processing capabilities for the preparation of text documents, such as letters, memorandums, and reports.
- The Excel application provides the ability to analyze numbers in worksheets and for creating financial budgets, reports, charts, and forms.
- The PowerPoint application is used to create presentation slides and audience handouts.
- You use the Access databases to store and retrieve collections of data.
- The Outlook application helps you send and receive e-mail and maintain a calendar, "to do" lists, and the names and addresses of contacts—and perform other information management tasks.
- One major advantage of using the Office suite applications is the ability to integrate the applications by sharing information between them.
- Another advantage of the Office suite applications is that they share a number of common elements such as window features, shortcuts, toolbars, and menu commands.
- You can start the Office suite applications from the Programs submenu on the Start menu and from the Open Office Document or New Office Document commands on the Start menu.
- To close the Office applications, you can double-click the application Control-menu icon, single-click the application Close button on the title bar, right-click the application button on the taskbar, press the ALT + F4 keys, or click the Exit command on the File menu.
- To get help in an Office application, you can click commands on the Help menu, press the F1 key or the SHIFT + F1 keys, or click the Microsoft Help button on the Standard toolbar.

Concepts Review

Circle the correct answer.

1. ScreenTips do not provide:
- [a] the name of a button on a toolbar.
- [b] help for options in a dialog box.
- [c] context-sensitive help for menu commands or toolbar buttons.
- [d] access to the Office Assistant.

2. To manage a Web site, you can use:
- [a] Outlook.
- [b] FrontPage.
- [c] Excel.
- [d] Publisher.

3. The title bar contains the:
- [a] document Control-menu icon.
- [b] Close Window button.
- [c] Standard toolbar.
- [d] application and document name.

4. The Excel application is best used to:
- [a] prepare financial reports.
- [b] maintain a list of tasks to accomplish.
- [c] prepare text documents.
- [d] manage Web sites.

5. A major advantage of using Office applications is the ability to:
- [a] store mailing lists.
- [b] analyze numbers.
- [c] share information between applications.
- [d] sort data.

6. Word processing is used primarily to:
- [a] create presentation slides.
- [b] analyze numbers.
- [c] prepare text documents.
- [d] maintain a calendar and "to do" lists.

7. Right-click means to:
- [a] press the left mouse button twice rapidly.
- [b] place the mouse pointer on a command or item.
- [c] press and hold down the right mouse button and then move the mouse.
- [d] press the right mouse button and then release it.

8. You cannot close Office XP applications by:
- [a] clicking the Exit command on the File menu.
- [b] clicking the Close button on the title bar.
- [c] right-clicking the application button on the taskbar and clicking Close.
- [d] pressing the SHIFT + F4 keys.

Circle **T** if the statement is true or **F** if the statement is false.

T F 1. You use Excel to create newsletters and brochures.

T F 2. Word is used to create presentation slides.

T F 3. The Office Assistant is an interactive graphic used to get online help in Office applications.

T F 4. Access is used to create and format text.

T F 5. You can open and work in only one Office application at a time.

T F 6. When you open multiple documents in an Office application, each document has its own button on the taskbar.

Skills Review

SCANS

Exercise 1

1. Identify each of the numbered elements of Office application windows in the following figure.

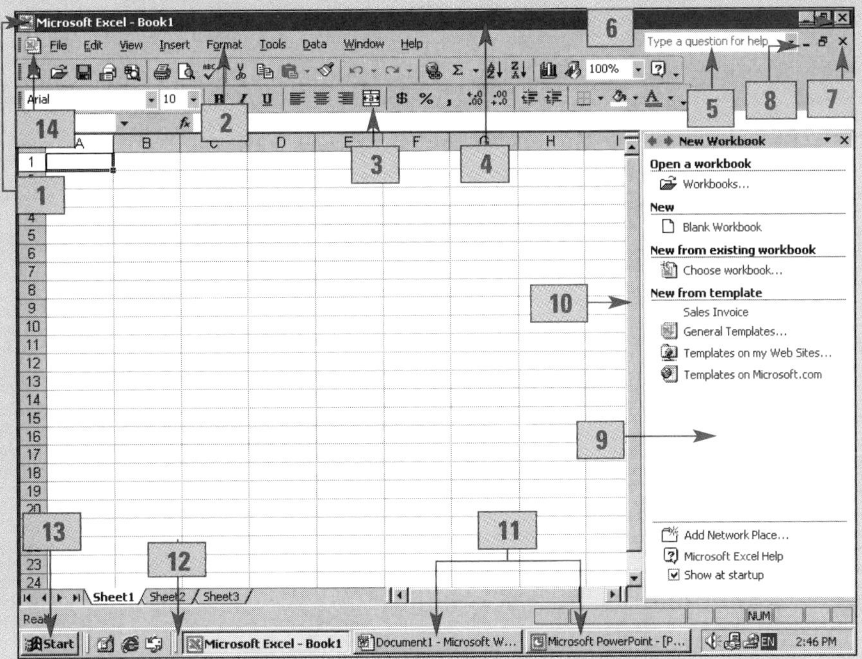

Exercise 2

1. Open the Word application using the Programs command on the Start menu.
2. Close the Word application using the taskbar.

Exercise 3

1. Open the Excel application using the Programs command on the Start menu.
2. Open the PowerPoint application using the Programs command on the Start menu.
3. Open the Access application and the *International Sales* database using the Open Office Document command on the Start menu.
4. Switch to the PowerPoint application using the taskbar button and close it using the Close button on the title bar.
5. Close the Excel and Access applications at the same time using the taskbar.

Exercise 4

1. Create a new, blank Word document using the New Office Document command on the Start menu.
2. Create a new, blank Excel workbook using the New Office Document command on the Start menu.
3. Switch to the Word document using the taskbar and close it using the Close button on the title bar.
4. Close the Excel workbook using the taskbar button.

Exercise 5

1. Open the Word application using the Start menu.
2. Show the Office Assistant, if necessary, with a command on the Help menu.
3. Hide the Office Assistant with a shortcut menu.
4. Show the Office Assistant with the Microsoft Word Help button on the Standard toolbar.
5. Search online Help using the search phrase "key text."
6. Click the "Change typing and editing options" link.
7. Review the Help text and then close the Help window.
8. Show the Office Assistant, and then click the Options command on the Office Assistant shortcut menu.
9. Click the Use the Office Assistant check box to remove the check mark and turn off the Office Assistant.

Exercise 6

1. Write a paragraph that describes the different ways to close the Word application.

Exercise 7

1. Open any Office application and use the Ask A Question Box and the keyword "Office Assistant" to search for online Help for information on using the Office Assistant.
2. Write down the instructions for selecting a different Office Assistant graphic image.

Case Projects

Project 1

You are the secretary to the marketing manager of High Risk Insurance, an insurance brokerage firm. The marketing manager wants to know how to open and close the Excel application. Write at least two paragraphs describing different ways to open and close the Excel application. With your instructor's permission, use your written description to show a classmate several ways to open and close the Excel application.

Project 2

You work in the administrative offices of Alma Public Relations and the information management department just installed Office XP on your computer. Your supervisor asks you to write down and describe some of the Office Assistant options. Display the Office Assistant. Right-click the Office Assistant graphic, click the Options command, and view the Options tab in the Office Assistant dialog box. Click the What's This? or Help button on the dialog box title bar and review each option. Write at least three paragraphs describing five Office Assistant options.

Project 3

As the new office manager at Hot Wheels Messenger Service, you are learning to use the Word 2002 application and want to learn more about some of the buttons on the Word toolbars. Open Word and use the What's This? command on the Help menu to review the ScreenTip help for five toolbar buttons. Write a brief paragraph for each button describing how it is used.

Project 4

You are the administrative assistant to the vice president of operations for Extreme Sports, Inc., a sports equipment retailer with stores in several cities in your state. The vice president wants to save time and money by performing business tasks more efficiently. She asks you to think of different ways to perform common business tasks by sharing information between the Office XP applications. Write at least three paragraphs describing how the company can use Word, Excel, PowerPoint, Access, and Outlook to improve efficiency by combining information.

Working with Menus, Toolbars, and Task Panes

Chapter Overview

Office tries to make your work life easier by learning how you work. The personalized menus and toolbars in each application remember which commands and buttons you use and add and remove them as needed. Office has two new tools—task panes and Smart Tags—that provide shortcuts for performing different activities. In this chapter, you learn how to work with the personalized menus and toolbars and how to use task panes and Smart Tags.

Learning Objectives

- Work with personalized menus and toolbars
- View, hide, dock, and float toolbars
- Work with task panes
- Review Smart Tags

chapter two

2.a Working with Personalized Menus and Toolbars

A **menu** is a list of commands you use to perform tasks in the Office applications. Some of the commands also have an associated image, or icon, which appears to the left of each command in the menu. Most menus are found on the menu bar located below the title bar in the Office applications. A **toolbar** contains a set of icons (the same icons you see on the menus) called "buttons" that you click with the mouse pointer to quickly execute a menu command.

notes

The activities in this chapter assume the personalized menus and toolbars are reset to their default settings. As you learn about menus and toolbars, task panes, and Smart Tags you are asked to select menu commands and toolbar buttons by clicking them with the mouse pointer. You do not learn how to use the menu command or toolbar button, task pane, or Smart Tags to perform detailed tasks in this chapter. Using these features to perform detailed tasks is covered in the individual application chapters.

When you first install Office and then open an Office application, the menus on the menu bar initially show only a basic set of commands and the Standard and Formatting toolbars contain only a basic set of buttons. These short versions of the menus and toolbars are called **personalized menus and toolbars**. As you work in the application, the commands and buttons you use most frequently are stored in the personalized settings. The first time you select a menu command or toolbar button that is not part of the basic set, that command or button is automatically added to your personalized settings and appears on the menu or toolbar. If you do not use a command for a while, it is removed from your personalized settings and no longer appears on the menu or toolbar. To view the personalized menus and toolbars in PowerPoint:

Step 1	***Click***	the New Office Document command on the Start menu
Step 2	***Click***	the General tab in the New Office Document dialog box, if necessary
Step 3	***Double-click***	the Blank Presentation icon
Step 4	***Click***	Tools on the menu bar
Step 5	***Observe***	the short personalized menu containing only the basic commands

The Tools menu on your screen should look similar to Figure 2-1.

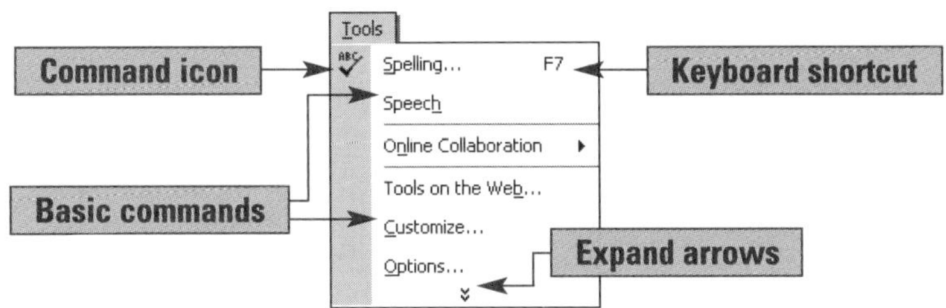

FIGURE 2-1
Personalized Tools Menu

If the command you want to use does not appear on the short personalized menu, you can expand the menu. The fastest way to expand a personalized menu is to double-click the menu command on the menu bar. For example, to quickly expand the Insert menu, you can double-click the Insert command on the menu bar. Another way to expand a menu is to click the Expand arrows that appear at the bottom of the personalized menu when it opens. Finally, after opening a menu, you can pause for a few seconds until the menu automatically expands. To expand the Tools menu:

Step 1	***Pause***	until the menu automatically expands *or* click the Expand arrows at the bottom of the menu to expand the menu

The expanded Tools menu on your screen should look similar to Figure 2-2.

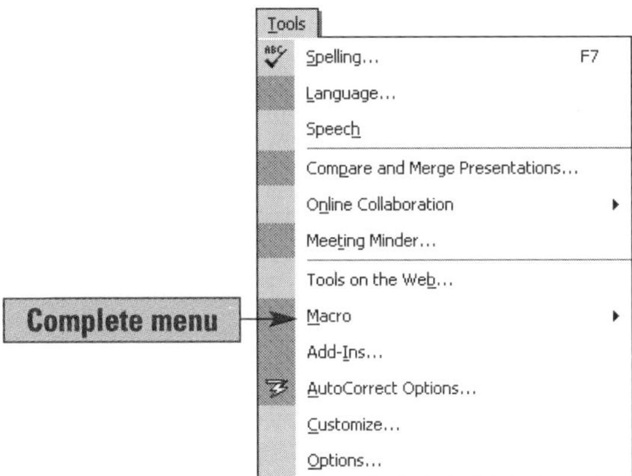

FIGURE 2-2
Expanded Tools Menu

You move a menu command from the expanded menu to the personalized menu simply by selecting it. To add the AutoCorrect Options command to the short personalized Tools menu:

Step 1	***Click***	AutoCorrect Options

Step 2	***Click***	Cancel in the AutoCorrect dialog box to close the dialog box without making any changes
Step 3	***Click***	Tools on the menu bar
Step 4	***Observe***	the updated personalized Tools menu contains the AutoCorrect Options command

The Tools menu on your screen should look similar to Figure 2-3.

FIGURE 2-3
Updated Personalized Tools Menu

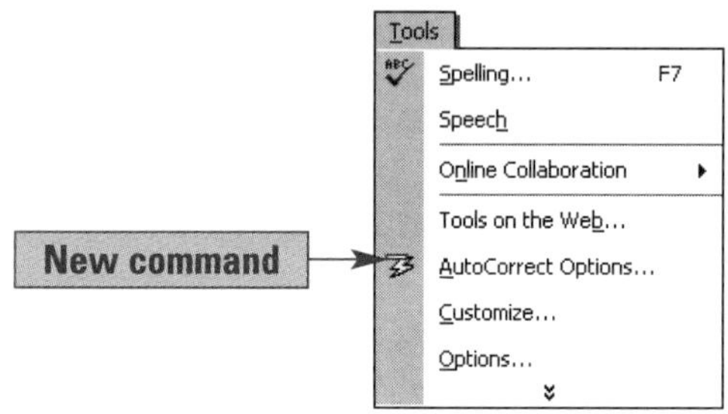

Step 5	***Press***	the ESC key twice to close the menu

The first time you launch most Office applications, the Standard and Formatting toolbars appear on one row below the title bar. In this position, you cannot see all their default buttons. If a toolbar button is not visible, you can resize or reposition one of the toolbars. When the mouse pointer is positioned on a toolbar **move handle** (the gray vertical bar at the left edge of the toolbar), the mouse pointer changes from a white arrow pointer to a **move pointer**, a four-headed black arrow. You can drag the move handle with the move pointer to resize or reposition toolbar. To resize the Formatting toolbar:

Step 1	***Move***	the mouse pointer to the move handle on the Formatting toolbar
Step 2	***Observe***	that the mouse pointer becomes a move pointer

The move pointer on your screen should look similar to Figure 2-4.

FIGURE 2-4
Move Pointer on the Formatting Toolbar Handle

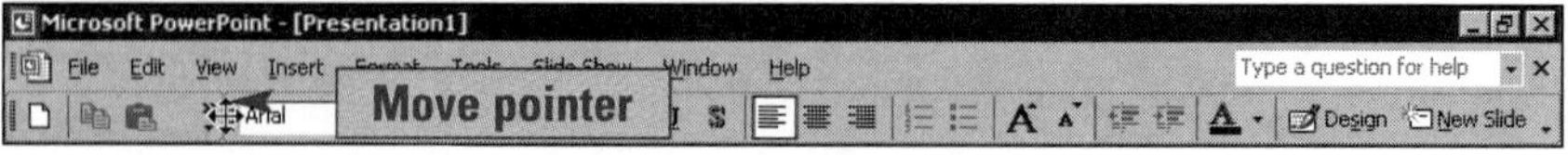

Step 3	***Click & hold***	the left mouse button
Step 4	***Drag***	the Formatting toolbar to the right as far as you can to view the default buttons on the Standard toolbar

Step 5	***Drag***	the Formatting toolbar to the left as far as you can to view the default buttons on the Formatting toolbar
Step 6	***Release***	the mouse button
Step 7	***Observe***	that you now see three buttons on the Standard toolbar

The buttons that don't fit on the displayed area of a toolbar are collected in a Toolbar Options list. The last button on any toolbar, the Toolbar Options button, is used to display the Toolbar Options list. To view the Toolbar Options list:

Step 1	***Click***	the Toolbar Options button list arrow on the Standard toolbar
Step 2	***Observe***	the default buttons that are not visible on the toolbar

The Toolbar Options list on your screen should look similar to Figure 2-5.

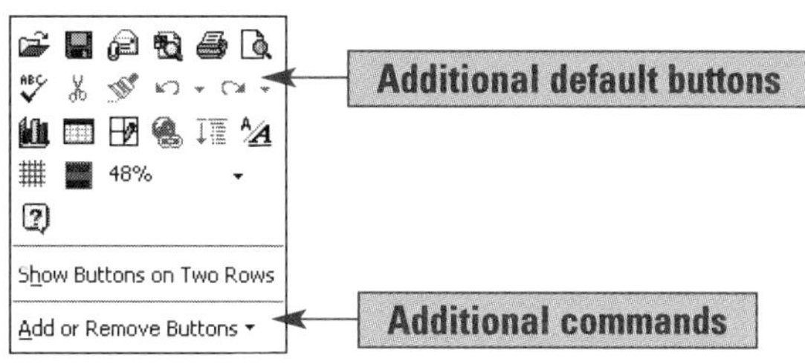

FIGURE 2-5
Toolbar Options List

If you want to display one of the default buttons on a personalized toolbar, you can select it from the Toolbar Options list. To add the Search button to the personalized Standard toolbar:

Step 1	***Click***	the Search button
Step 2	***Observe***	that the Search button is added to the personalized Standard toolbar

When you add another button to the personalized Standard toolbar, one of the other buttons might move out of view. This is because of the limited viewing area of the Standard toolbar in its current position. If you want to view all the menu commands instead of a short personalized menu and all the default toolbar buttons on the Standard and Formatting toolbars, you can change options in the Customize dialog box. To view the Customize dialog box:

Step 1	***Click***	Tools on the menu bar

Step 2	*Click*	Customize
Step 3	*Click*	the Options tab, if necessary

The Customize dialog box on your screen should look similar to Figure 2-6.

FIGURE 2-6
Options Tab in the Customize Dialog Box

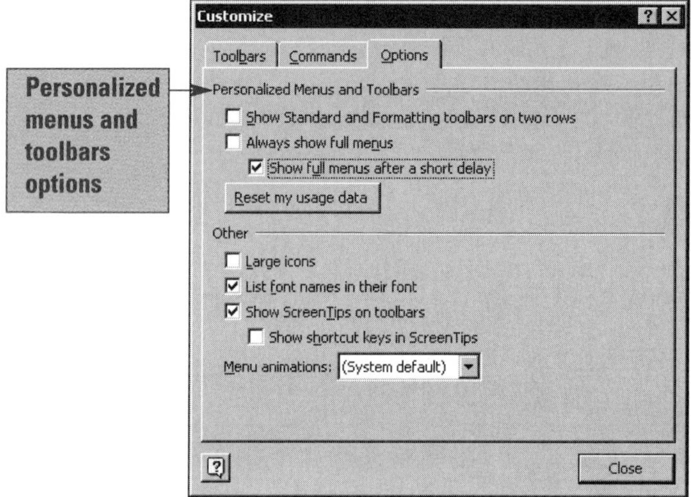

If you reposition the Formatting toolbar below the Standard toolbar, you can view all the default buttons on both toolbars. You can do this by inserting a check mark in the Show Standard and Formatting toolbars on two rows check box. You can insert a check mark in the Always show full menus check box to view the entire set of menu commands for each menu instead of the short personalized menus. If you do not want the short personalized menus to expand automatically when you pause, you can remove the check mark from the Show full menus after a short delay check box. Then, to show the full menu, you have to double-click the menu or click the expand arrows at the bottom of the menu.

You want to show all the Standard and Formatting toolbar buttons and menu commands.

Step 4	*Click*	the Show Standard and Formatting toolbars on two rows check box to insert a check mark
Step 5	*Click*	the Always show full menus check box to insert a check mark
Step 6	*Click*	Close to close the dialog box
Step 7	*Observe*	the repositioned and expanded Standard and Formatting toolbars

Step 8	*Click*	Tools to view the entire set of Tools menu commands
Step 9	*Press*	the ESC key to close the Tools menu

You can return the menus and toolbars to their initial (or **default**) settings in the Customize dialog box. To open the Customize dialog box and reset the default menus and toolbars:

Step 1	*Click*	Tools
Step 2	*Click*	Customize
Step 3	*Click*	the Options tab, if necessary
Step 4	*Remove*	the two check marks you just inserted
Step 5	*Click*	Reset my usage data
Step 6	*Click*	Yes to confirm you want to reset the menus and toolbars to their default settings
Step 7	*Close*	the Customize dialog box
Step 8	*Observe*	that the Tools menu and Standard toolbar are reset to their default settings

MOUSE TIP

You can use a command on the Toolbar Options list to place the Standard and Formatting toolbars that currently appear on one row on two rows. You can also place the Standard and Formatting toolbars that appear in two rows back to one row with a command on the Toolbar Options list.

2.b Viewing, Hiding, Docking, and Floating Toolbars

Office applications have additional toolbars that you can view when you need them. You can also hide toolbars when you are not using them. You can view or hide toolbars by pointing to the Toolbars command on the View menu and clicking a toolbar name or by using a shortcut menu. A **shortcut menu** is a short list of frequently used menu commands. You view a shortcut menu by pointing to an item on the screen and clicking the right mouse button. This is called right-clicking the item. The commands on shortcut menus vary depending on where you right-click, so that you view only the most frequently used commands for a particular task. An easy way to view or hide toolbars is with a shortcut menu.

notes

Although the PowerPoint application is used to illustrate how to customize toolbars, the same techniques are used to customize toolbars and menus in the Word, Excel, and Access applications.

chapter two

To view the shortcut menu for toolbars:

Step 1	***Right-click***	the menu bar, the Standard toolbar, or the Formatting toolbar
Step 2	***Observe***	the shortcut menu and the check marks next to the names of displayed toolbars

Your shortcut menu should look similar to Figure 2-7.

FIGURE 2-7
Toolbars Shortcut Menu

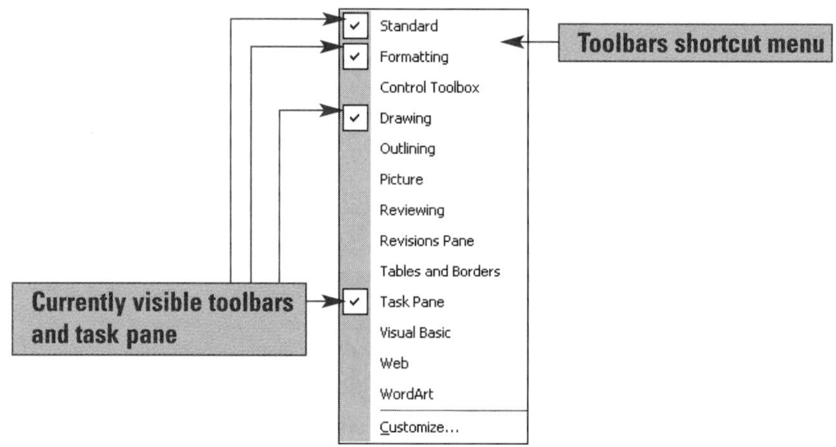

Step 3	***Click***	Tables and Borders in the shortcut menu
Step 4	***Observe***	that the Tables and Borders toolbar appears on your screen

QUICK TIP

Some of the toolbars that appear on the toolbars shortcut menu vary from one Office application to another.

The Tables and Borders toolbar, unless a previous user repositioned it, is visible in its own window near the middle of your screen. When a toolbar is visible in its own window, it is called a **floating toolbar** and you can move and size it with the mouse pointer similar to any window. When a toolbar appears fixed at the screen boundaries, it is called a **docked toolbar**. The menu bar and Standard and Formatting toolbars are examples of docked toolbars because they are fixed below the title bar at the top of the screen. In PowerPoint, the Drawing toolbar is docked at the bottom of the screen above the status bar. You can dock a floating toolbar by dragging its title bar with the mouse pointer to a docking position below the title bar, above the status bar, or at the left and right boundaries of your screen.

To dock the Tables and Borders toolbar below the Standard and Formatting toolbars, if necessary:

Step 1	***Click & hold***	the title bar in the Tables and Borders toolbar window

Step 2	*Observe*	that the mouse pointer becomes a move pointer
Step 3	*Drag*	the toolbar window up slowly until it docks below the Standard and Formatting toolbars
Step 4	*Release*	the mouse button

Similarly, you float a docked toolbar by dragging it away from its docked position toward the middle of the screen. To float the Tables and Borders toolbar, if necessary:

Step 1	*Position*	the mouse pointer on the Tables and Borders toolbar move handle until it becomes a move pointer
Step 2	*Drag*	the Tables and Borders toolbar down toward the middle of the screen until it appears in its own window

When you finish using a toolbar, you can hide it with a shortcut menu. To hide the Tables and Borders toolbar:

Step 1	*Right-click*	the Tables and Borders toolbar
Step 2	*Click*	Tables and Borders to remove the check mark and hide the toolbar

2.c Working with Task Panes

The task pane is a tool with many uses in the Office applications. For example, when you launch Word, Excel, PowerPoint, or Access a new file task pane appears on the right side of the application window. This task pane allows you to create new documents in a variety of ways or open existing documents and replaces the New dialog box found in earlier versions of the Office applications. For example, in the Word application, this task pane is called the New Document task pane and contains hyperlink shortcuts for creating a new document or opening an existing document, creating a blank Web page, sending an e-mail message, choosing an existing document to use as the basis for a new document, and other options. A **hyperlink** is text or a graphic image that you can click to view another page or item. The hyperlink shortcuts in the task pane are colored blue. When you place your mouse pointer on a blue hyperlink shortcut, the mouse pointer changes to a hand with a pointing finger. You can then click the hyperlink shortcut to view the page or option to which the shortcut is linked.

Another way to use a task pane in each of the Office applications is to display the Search task pane and use it to search your local computer

MOUSE TIP

You can dock a floating toolbar by double-clicking its title bar. The toolbar returns to its previously docked position.

You can close a floating toolbar by clicking the Close button on the toolbar's title bar.

QUICK TIP

In Excel, the new file task pane is called the New Workbook task pane; in PowerPoint, it is called the New Presentation task pane; in Access, it is called the New File task pane.

Each Office application also contains specific task panes: for example—you can format text in a Word document, copy and paste data in an Excel worksheet, and apply an attractive design and animation scheme to a PowerPoint presentation—all from special task panes.

system and network for files based on specific criteria such as keywords in the file text, the file's location, the file type, and the file's name. You can also search for Outlook items using the Search task pane.

To view a blank Word document and the Search task pane:

Step 1	***Start***	the Word application using the Start menu
Step 2	***Click***	File on the menu bar
Step 3	***Click***	Search

The Basic Search task pane is now visible. Your screen should look similar to Figure 2-8.

FIGURE 2-8
Basic Search Task Pane in Word

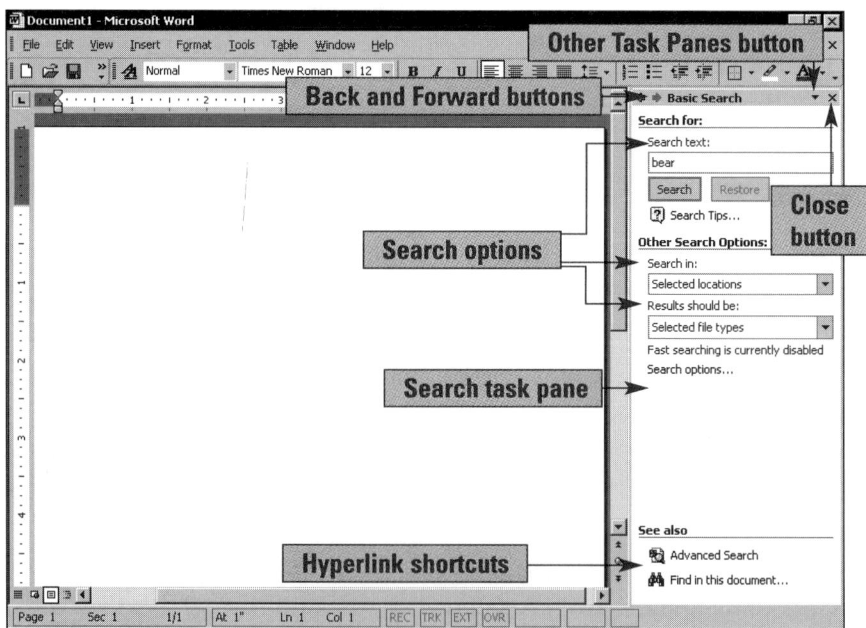

MOUSE TIP

You also can view the Search task pane by clicking the Search button on the Standard toolbar.

When you have multiple task panes open, you can use the Back and Forward buttons on the task pane title bar to switch between the task panes. To switch from the Basic Search task pane to the New Document task pane:

Step 1	***Click***	the Back button in the Basic Search task pane to view the New Document task pane
Step 2	***Click***	the Forward button in the New Document task pane to view the Basic Search task pane

You can key text in the Search text: text box to look for files containing specific text. You can use the Search in: list to select the locations in which to search, and use the Results should be: list to select the file types to search for. If your search criteria are more complex, you can click the Advanced Search link to view the Advanced Search task pane, where you can set additional search criteria such as file attributes called **properties**, or use operators such as "and" to set multiple criteria or "or" to set exclusive criteria.

A task pane appears docked on the right side of the application window by default. You can "float" the task pane in the application window or dock it on the left side of the application window, as you prefer. Like docking a floating toolbar, when you double-click a task pane title bar, it returns to its last docked or floating position. To float the docked task pane:

Step 1	***Double-click***	the Basic Search task pane title bar
Step 2	***Observe***	the task pane's new position, floating in the application window

Your screen should look similar to Figure 2-9.

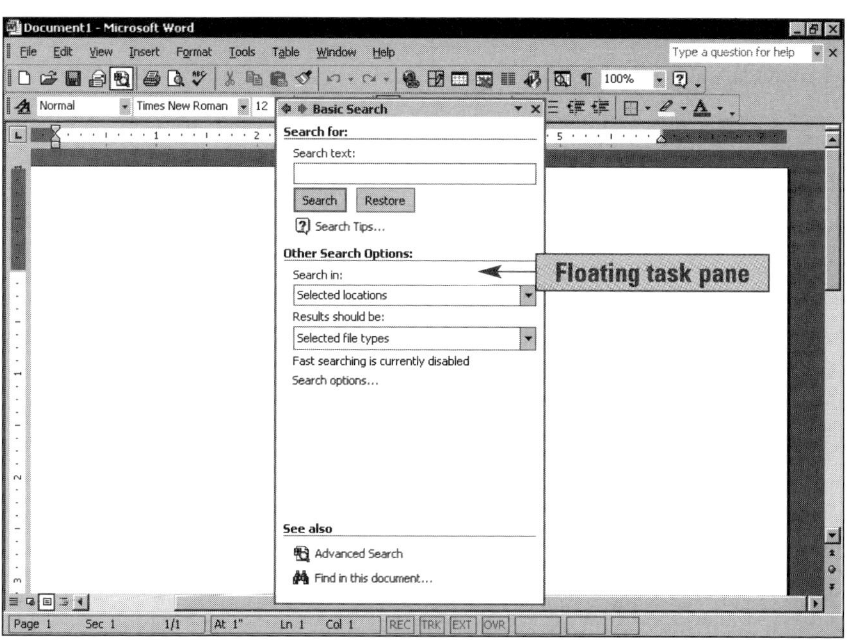

FIGURE 2-9
Floating Task Pane

Step 3	***Double-click***	the Basic Search task pane title bar
Step 4	***Observe***	that the Basic Search task pane returns to its previous docked position

TASK PANE TIP

You can click the Other Task Panes list arrow on the task pane title bar to view a list of different task panes available in the application. Then, you can click one of the task panes in the list to open it. Additionally, some task panes appear automatically as you perform certain activities in an application.

You can also display the last previous visible task pane by using the Task Pane command on the View menu.

MOUSE TIP

You can float a docked task pane by dragging the task pane away from its docked position using the mouse and the task pane title bar. Conversely, you can dock a floating task pane by dragging the task pane to the left or right side of the screen.

You can size a floating task pane by dragging the pane's top, bottom, left, or right borders with the mouse pointer.

You can close the current task pane by clicking the Close button on the task pane title bar. When you close the current task pane, all open task panes are also closed. For example, you currently have the New Document task pane and the Basic Search task pane open. When you close the Basic Search task pane, both task panes are closed. You can view the New Document task pane again with a menu command or toolbar button. To close the Basic Search and New Document task panes and then reopen the New Document task pane:

Step 1	*Click*	the Close button on the Basic Search task pane title bar
Step 2	*Observe*	that neither the Basic Search nor the New Document task pane is visible
Step 3	*Click*	File on the menu bar
Step 4	*Click*	New

The New Document task pane opens at the right side of the application window.

QUICK TIP

The **Office Shortcut Bar** is a toolbar that you can open and position on your Windows desktop to provide shortcuts to Office applications and tasks. The Office Shortcut Bar can contain buttons for the New Office Document and Open Office Document commands you see on the Start menu, shortcut buttons to create various Outlook items, and buttons to open Office applications installed on your computer. You can access the Office Shortcut Bar with the Microsoft Office Tools command on the Programs menu.

2.d Reviewing Smart Tags

Smart Tags are labels used to identify data as a specific type of data. You can use Smart Tags to perform an action in an open Office application instead of opening another application to perform that task. For example, a person's name is one kind of data that can be recognized and labeled with a Smart Tag. Suppose you key a person's name in a Word document and then want to create a contact item for that person in your Outlook Contacts folder. You can use a Smart Tag to create the contact item from Word without opening Outlook.

Smart Tags are represented by an action button and a purple dotted line underneath the text. The Smart Tag options are found in the AutoCorrect dialog box. To view the Smart Tag options in the Word application:

Step 1	*Click*	Tools on the menu bar
Step 2	*Click*	AutoCorrect Options
Step 3	*Click*	the Smart Tags tab in the AutoCorrect dialog box

The AutoCorrect dialog box on your screen should look similar to Figure 2-10.

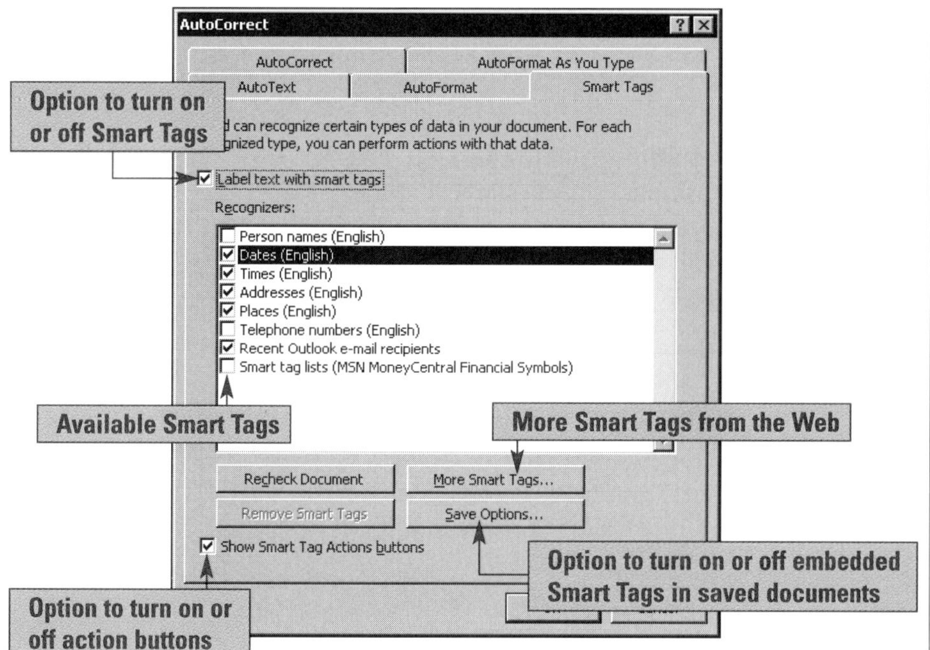

FIGURE 2-10
Smart Tags Tab in the AutoCorrect Dialog Box

You can turn on or off the Smart Tag feature with the Label text with smart tags check box. You can use the Show Smart Tag Actions buttons check box to turn on or off the Smart Tag action buttons. By default, Smart Tags are embedded in a document when it is saved. You can turn off this feature with the Save Options button. You can also remove the Smart Tags or recheck the document using the Remove Smart Tags or Recheck Document buttons. The use of specific Smart Tags and action buttons is covered in more detail in later chapters.

Step 4	***Click***	the Cancel button to close the AutoCorrect dialog box without making any changes
Step 5	***Click***	the Close button on the title bar to close Word
Step 6	***Close***	the PowerPoint application

QUICK TIP

A limited number of Smart Tags are installed with the Office applications. You can access more Smart Tags from the Microsoft Web site by clicking the More Smart Tags button in the Smart Tags tab of the AutoCorrect dialog box.

Summary

- The first time you launch an Office application after installing Office, you see personalized menus that contain basic commands. As you use different commands, they are automatically added to the personalized menu. Commands that are not used for some time are removed from the personalized menus.
- The first time you launch an Office application after installing Office, the Standard and Formatting toolbars share a single row below the menu bar. You can reposition the Formatting toolbar to view more or fewer toolbar buttons. The remaining default toolbar buttons that are not visible on the toolbars can be added from the Toolbar Options list. You can turn off or reset the personalized menus and toolbars in the Options tab of the Customize dialog box.
- You can hide or view toolbars as you need them by using a shortcut menu. Toolbars can be docked at the top, bottom, or side of the screen, or they can be floating on screen in their own window.
- You can open task panes that contain shortcuts to perform various activities; these task panes can be docked at the left or right side of the application window, or they can be floating in the application window. Two examples of a task pane are the New Document and Basic Search task panes.
- Smart Tags are labels that identify text or data as a certain type and provide shortcuts to taking certain actions with the text or data.

Commands Review

Action	Menu Bar	Shortcut Menu	Toolbar	Task Pane	Keyboard
Display or hide toolbars	View, Toolbars	Right-click a toolbar, click the desired toolbar to add or remove the check mark	[X] on the toolbar title bar		ALT + V, T
View the New Document task pane	File, New				ALT + F, N
View the Search task pane	File, Search		[Search button]		ALT + F, H
View the last visible task pane	View, Task Pane	Right-click a toolbar, click Task Pane			ALT + V, K
View the available Smart Tag options	Tools, AutoCorrect Options, Smart Tags tab				ALT + T, A

Concepts Review

Circle the correct answer.

1. A menu is:
- [a] a set of icons.
- [b] a list of commands.
- [c] impossible to customize.
- [d] never personalized.

2. A toolbar is:
- [a] a list of commands.
- [b] always floating on your screen.
- [c] a set of icons.
- [d] never docked on your screen.

3. Which of the following is not an option in the Options tab in the Customize dialog box?
- [a] turning on or off ScreenTips for toolbar buttons
- [b] turning on or off Large icons for toolbar buttons
- [c] adding animation to menus
- [d] docking all toolbars

4. Right-clicking an item on screen displays:
- [a] the Right-Click toolbar.
- [b] animated menus.
- [c] expanded menus.
- [d] a shortcut menu.

5. Double-clicking the menu name on the menu bar:
- [a] resets your usage data.
- [b] floats the menu bar.
- [c] turns off the personalized menus.
- [d] expands a personalized menu.

6. A Smart Tag is:
- [a] a personalized menu.
- [b] displayed by double-clicking an item on your screen.
- [c] automatically expanded when you pause briefly.
- [d] a label used to identify text or data items for shortcut actions.

7. To view all the default buttons on both the Standard and Formatting toolbars at once, you should:
- [a] view the toolbar with a shortcut menu.
- [b] add the View All button to the toolbar.
- [c] reposition the Formatting toolbar on another row below the Standard toolbar.
- [d] drag the Formatting toolbar to the left.

8. The Advanced Search task pane cannot be viewed by clicking a:
- [a] command on a shortcut menu.
- [b] command on the File menu.
- [c] button on the Standard toolbar.
- [d] link on the Basic Search task pane.

Circle **T** if the statement is true or **F** if the statement is false.

T F 1. The Standard and Formatting toolbars must remain on the same row.

T F 2. When updating docked personalized toolbars, some buttons may be automatically removed from view to make room for the new buttons.

T F 3. One way to use a Smart Tag is to create an Outlook contact from a name in a Word document.

T F 4. You cannot add animation to menus.

T F 5. A floating toolbar window can be resized and repositioned using techniques that are similar to those used for any other window.

T F 6. When you open an Office application, the Search task pane is docked at the right side of the application window.

T F 7. You cannot use keyboard shortcuts to run commands in Office applications.

T F 8. You cannot turn off the personalized menus and toolbars options.

Skills Review

Exercise 1

1. Open the Word application.
2. Open the Options tab in the Customize dialog box and reset the usage data; show the Standard and Formatting toolbars on one row, and show full menus after a short delay.
3. If necessary, drag the Formatting toolbar to the right until you can see approximately half of the Standard and half of the Formatting toolbar.
4. Add the Show/Hide button to the personalized Standard toolbar using the Toolbar Options list.
5. Add the Font Color button to the personalized Formatting toolbar using the Toolbar Options list.
6. Open the Customize dialog box and reset your usage data in the Options tab.
7. Close the Word application and click No if asked whether you want to save changes to the blank Word document.

Exercise 2

1. Open the Excel application.
2. Open the Options tab in the Customize dialog box and reset the usage data; show the Standard and Formatting toolbars on one row, and show full menus after a short delay.
3. View the personalized Tools menu.
4. Add the AutoCorrect Options command to the personalized Tools menu.
5. Reset your usage data.
6. Close the Excel application.

Exercise 3

1. Open the PowerPoint application.
2. Display the Basic Search task pane using a menu command.
3. Display the advanced search options.
4. Close the Advanced Search task pane.
5. Close the PowerPoint application.

Exercise 4

1. Open an Office application and verify that the New Document, New Presentation, or New Workbook task pane is docked at the right side of the application window.
2. Float the task pane by dragging it to the center of the application window.
3. Drag the left border of the floating task pane to resize it.
4. Double-click the task pane title bar to dock it in its previous position.
5. Close the task pane.
6. Open the Basic Search task pane using the Search button on the Standard toolbar.
7. Open the New Document task pane using the File menu.
8. Switch between task panes using the Back and Forward buttons on the task pane title bar.
9. Close the task pane.
10. Close the application.

Exercise 5

1. Open the Excel application.
2. View the Drawing, Picture, and WordArt toolbars using a shortcut menu.
3. Dock the Picture toolbar below the Standard and Formatting toolbars.
4. Dock the WordArt toolbar at the left boundary of the screen.
5. Close the Excel application from the taskbar.
6. Open the Excel with the New Office Document on the Start menu. (*Hint:* Use the Blank Workbook icon.)
7. Float the WordArt toolbar.
8. Float the Picture toolbar.
9. Hide the WordArt, Picture, and Drawing toolbars using a shortcut menu.
10. Close the Excel application.

Exercise 6

1. Open the Word application.
2. Turn off the personalized menus and toolbars.
3. Open the Options tab in the Customize dialog box and change the toolbar buttons to large icons and add random animation to the menus.
4. Observe the toolbar buttons and the menu animation.
5. Turn off the large buttons and remove the menu animation.
6. Turn on the personalized menus and toolbars and reset your usage data.
7. Close the Word application.

Case Projects

SCANS

Project 1

As secretary to the placement director for the XYZ Employment Agency, you have been using an earlier version of Word—Word 97. After you install Office XP, you decide you want the Word menus and toolbars to appear on two rows the way they did in the Word 97 application. Use the Ask A Question Box to search for help on "personalized menus." Review the Help topics and write down all the ways to make the personalized menus and toolbars appear on two rows.

Project 2

You are the administrative assistant to the controller of the Plush Pets, Inc., a stuffed toy manufacturing company. The controller recently installed Excel 2002. She is confused about how to use the task panes and asks for your help. Use the Ask A Question Box to search for help on "task panes." Review the topics and write down an explanation of how task panes are used. Give at least three examples of task panes.

Project 3

As administrative assistant to the art director of MediaWiz Advertising, Inc. you just installed PowerPoint 2002. Now you decide you would rather view the complete Standard and Formatting toolbars rather than the personalized toolbars and want to learn a quick way to do this. Use the Ask A Question Box to search for help on "show all buttons." Review the topic and write down the instructions for showing all buttons using the mouse pointer. Open an Office application and use the mouse method to show the complete Standard and Formatting toolbars. Turn the personalized toolbars back on from the Customize dialog box.

Introduction to the Internet and the World Wide Web

Chapter Overview

Millions of people use the Internet to shop for goods and services, listen to music, view artwork, conduct research, get stock quotes, keep up to date with current events, and send e-mail. More and more people are using the Internet at work and at home to view and download multimedia computer files that contain graphics, sound, video, and text. In this chapter, you learn about the Internet, how to connect to the Internet, how to use the Internet Explorer Web browser, and how to access pages on the World Wide Web.

Learning Objectives

- Describe the Internet
- Connect to the Internet
- Use Internet Explorer
- Use directories and search engines

chapter three

QUICK TIP

Large commercial enterprises, colleges, universities, and government institutions may already have a network that is part of the Internet through which users can connect to the Internet. Many public library systems also provide free Internet access.

There are several commercial networks that are separate from the Internet. These commercial networks provide users with features such as online newspapers and magazines, chat groups, access to investment activities, computer games, and special-interest bulletin boards as well as Internet access. Popular commercial networks include America Online and the Microsoft Network.

USENET is another network that is separate from but closely connected to the Internet. A **newsgroup** is an Internet discussion group whose members use e-mail to exchange articles of interest on specific topics. The **USENET** network is a collection of computers that maintain and exchange newsgroup articles.

3.a What Is the Internet?

To understand the Internet, you must understand networks. A **network** is simply a group of two or more computers linked by cable or telephone lines. The linked computers also include a special computer called a **server** that is used to store files and programs that everyone on the network can use. In addition to the shared files and programs, networks enable users to share equipment, such as a common network printer.

The **Internet** is a worldwide public network of private networks, where users view and transfer information between computers. For example, an Internet user in California can retrieve (or **download**) files from a computer in Canada quickly and easily. In the same way, an Internet user in Australia can send (or **upload**) files to another Internet user in England. The Internet is not a single organization, but rather a cooperative effort by multiple organizations managing a variety of different kinds of computers.

You find a wide variety of services on the Internet. You can communicate with others via e-mail, electronic bulletin boards called newsgroups, real-time online chat, and online telephony. You can also download files from servers to your computer and search the World Wide Web for information. In this chapter, you learn about using a Web browser and accessing pages on the World Wide Web. Your instructor may provide additional information on other Internet services.

3.b Connecting to the Internet

To connect to the Internet you need some physical communication medium connected to your computer, such as network cable or a modem. You also need a special communication program called a Web browser program (such as Microsoft Internet Explorer) that allows your computer to communicate with computers on the Internet. The Web browser allows you to access Internet resources such as Web pages.

After setting up your computer hardware (the network cable or modem) and installing the Internet Explorer Web browser, you must make arrangements to connect to a computer on the Internet. The computer you connect to is called a **host**. Usually, you connect to a host computer via a commercial Internet Service Provider, such as America Online or another company who sells access to the Internet. An **Internet Service Provider (ISP)** maintains the host computer, provides a gateway or entrance to the Internet, and provides an electronic "mail box" with facilities for sending and receiving e-mail. Commercial ISPs usually charge a flat monthly fee for unlimited access to the Internet and e-mail services.

3.c Using Internet Explorer

A **Web browser** is a software application that helps you access Internet resources, including Web pages stored on computers called Web servers. A **Web page** is a document that contains hyperlinks (often called links) to other pages; it can also contain audio and video clips.

notes

The activities in this chapter assume you are using the Internet Explorer Web browser version 5.0 or higher. If you are using an earlier version of Internet Explorer or a different Web browser, your instructor may modify the following activities.

To open the Internet Explorer Web browser:

Step 1	***Connect***	to your ISP, if necessary
Step 2	***Double-click***	the Internet Explorer icon on the desktop to open the Web browser

When the Web browser opens, a Web page, called a **start page** or **home page**, loads automatically. The start page used by the Internet Explorer Web browser can be the Microsoft default start page, a blank page, or any designated Web page. Figure 3-1 shows the home page for the publisher of this book as the start page.

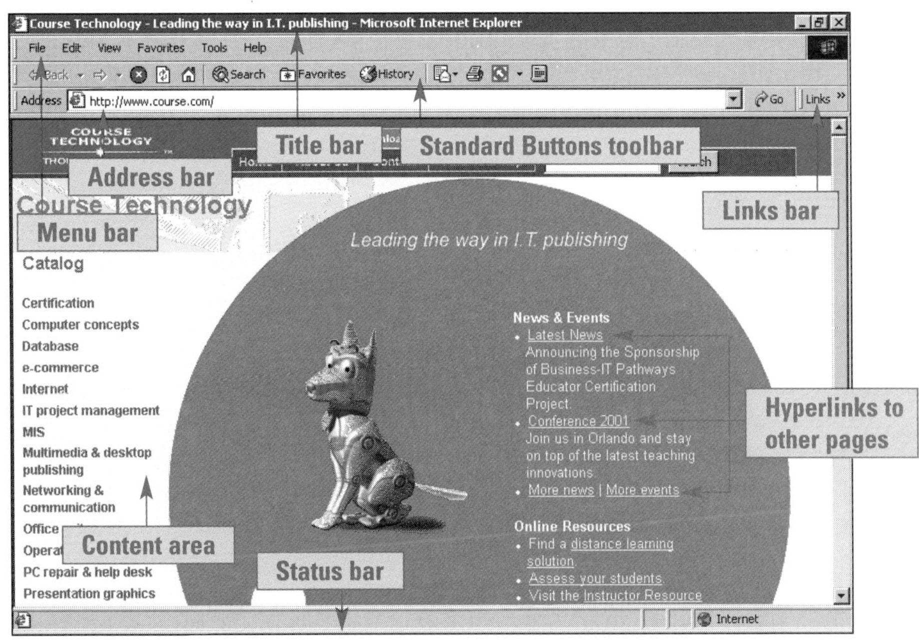

FIGURE 3-1
Internet Explorer Web Browser

CAUTION TIP

During peak day and evening hours, millions of people are connecting to the Internet, and you may have difficulty connecting to your host computer or to other sites on the Internet.

QUICK TIP

Challenges to using the Internet include the amount of available information, communication speed, the dynamic environment, lack of presentation standards, and privacy/security issues. Evaluate the source and author of information from the Internet and confirm business-critical information from another source.

MENU TIP

You can create a favorite by clicking the Favorites command on the menu bar and then clicking Add to Favorites, by right-clicking the background (not a link) on the current Web page and clicking Add to Favorites, or by right-clicking a link on the current Web page and clicking Add to Favorites.

MOUSE TIP

You can click the Stop button on the Standard Buttons toolbar to stop downloading a Web page.

QUICK TIP

Another way to load a favorite is to use the Favorites button on the toolbar to open the Favorites list in the Explorer bar. The **Explorer bar** is a pane that opens at the left side of the Web browser screen.

The **title bar** contains the Internet Explorer Web browser Control-menu icon and application name, the title of the current Web page, and the Internet Explorer Web browser Minimize, Restore, and Close buttons. The **menu bar** contains the menu commands you can use to perform specific tasks when viewing the Internet Explorer Web browser window—such as opening a file from your hard disk or printing the current Web page. The **Standard toolbar** contains buttons that provide shortcuts to frequently performed tasks. The **Address bar** contains a text box in which you key the path and filename of the Web page you want to load and a drop-down list of recently loaded Web pages and files. You can click the Go button to load the Web page after keying the page's address in the Address Bar. The **Links bar** is a customizable bar to which you can add shortcuts Web pages you load frequently. The **status bar** displays information about the current Web page. The security zone indicator on the right side of the status bar identifies the security zone you have assigned to the current Web page.

As a Web page loads, the progress bar illustrates the progress of the downloading process. When you place the mouse pointer on a link in the current Web page, its URL appears in the left side of the status bar. The **content area** contains the current Web page. Vertical and horizontal scroll bars appear as necessary so that you can scroll to view the entire Web page after it is loaded.

Loading a Web Page

Loading a Web page means that the Web browser sends a message requesting a copy of the Web page to the Web server where the Web page is stored. The Web server responds by sending a copy of the Web page to your computer. In order to load a Web page, you must either know or find the page's **URL** (Uniform Resource Locator)—the path and filename of the page that is the Web page's address. One way to find the URL for a Web page is to use a search engine or directory. If you are looking for a particular company's Web page, you might find its URL in one of the company's advertisements or on its letterhead and business card. Examples of URLs based on an organization's name are:

Course Technology	*www.course.com*
National Public Radio	*www.npr.org*
The White House	*www.whitehouse.gov*

You can try to "guess" the URL based on the organization's name and top-level domain. For example, a good guess for the U.S. House of Representatives Web page is *www.house.gov*.

You can key a URL directly in the Address bar by first selecting all or part of the current URL and keying the new URL to replace the selection. Internet Explorer adds the "http://" portion of the URL for you. To select the contents of the Address bar and key the URL for the U.S. House of Representatives:

Step 1	***Click***	the contents of the Address bar
Step 2	***Key***	www.house.gov
Step 3	***Click***	the Go button or press the ENTER key
Step 4	***Observe***	that the home page of the U.S. House of Representatives' Web site opens in your Web browser

Creating Favorites

Web pages are constantly being updated with new information. If you like a certain Web page or find a Web page contains useful information and plan to revisit it, you may want to save a shortcut to the page's URL in the Favorites folder. Such shortcuts are simply called **favorites**. Suppose you want to load the U.S. House of Representatives home page frequently. You can create a favorite that saves the URL in a file on your hard disk. Then at any time, you can quickly load this Web page by clicking it in a list of favorites maintained on the Favorites menu.

The URLs you choose to save as favorites are stored in the Favorites folder on your hard disk. You can specify a new or different subfolder within the Favorites folder and you can change the name of the Web page as it appears in your list of favorites in the Add Favorite dialog box. To create a favorite for the U.S. House of Representatives Web page:

Step 1	***Click***	Favorites
Step 2	***Click***	Add to Favorites
Step 3	***Click***	OK
Step 4	***Click***	the Home button to return to the default start page

One way to load a Web page from a favorite is to click the name of the favorite in the list of favorites on the Favorites menu. To load the U.S. House of Representatives home page from the Favorites menu:

Step 1	***Click***	Favorites
Step 2	***Click***	the United States House of Representatives favorite to load the page

CAUTION TIP

Any Web page you load is stored in the Temporary Internet Files folder on your hard disk. Whenever you reload the Web page, Internet Explorer compares the stored page to the current Web page either each time you start the browser or each time you load the page. If the Web page on the server has been changed, a fresh Web page is downloaded. If not, the Web page is retrieved from the Temporary Internet File folder and you do not have to wait for the page to download. To view and change the Temporary Internet File folder options (and other options that control how Internet Explorer works), click the Internet Options command on the Tools menu.

MENU TIP

You can remove a favorite by displaying the Favorites menu, right-clicking the desired favorite shortcut, and then clicking the Delete command on the shortcut menu. You can also open the Organize Favorites dialog box with the Organize Favorites command on the Favorites menu and select and delete a favorite shortcut.

MOUSE TIP

The Links bar provides shortcuts to various Web pages at the Microsoft Web site. You can also add shortcuts to your favorite Web pages by dragging the URL icon from the Address bar to the Links bar. You can reposition the toolbar, the Address bar, and the Links bar by dragging each one to a new location below the title bar.

Step 3	*Click*	the Home button to return to the default start page

The Back and Forward buttons allow you to review recently loaded Web pages without keying the URL or using the Favorites list. To reload the U.S. House of Representatives home page from the Back button list:

Step 1	*Click*	the Back button list arrow on the toolbar
Step 2	*Click*	United States House of Representatives

3.d Using Directories and Search Engines

Because the Web is so large, you often need to take advantage of special search tools, called search engines and directories, to find the information you need. To use some of the Web's numerous search engines and directories, you can click the Search button on the Standard toolbar to open the Search list in the Explorer bar. To view the Search list:

Step 1	*Click*	the Search button on the Standard toolbar
Step 2	*Observe*	the search list options

Search engines maintain an index of keywords used in Web pages that you can search. Search engine indexes are updated automatically by software called **spiders** (or **robots**). Spiders follow links between pages throughout the entire Web, adding any new Web pages to the search engine's index. You should use a search engine when you want to find specific Web pages. Some of the most popular search engines include AltaVista, HotBot, and Northern Light.

Directories use a subject-type format similar to a library card catalog. A directory provides a list of links to broad general categories of Web sites such as "Entertainment" or "Business." When you click these links, a subcategory list of links appears. For example, if you click the Entertainment link, you might then see "Movies," "Television," and "Video Games" links. To find links to Web sites containing information about "Movies," you would click the "Movies" link. Unlike a search engine, whose index is updated automatically, Web sites are added to directories only when an individual or a company asks that a particular Web site be included. Some directories also provide review comments and ratings for the Web sites in their index. Most directories also provide an internal search engine that can only be used to search the directory's index, not the entire Web. You use a directory when you are looking for information on broad general topics. Popular directories include Yahoo and Magellan Internet Guide.

To search for Web pages containing "movie guides":

Step 1	*Key*	movie guides in the Find a Web page containing text box
Step 2	*Click*	the Search button or press the ENTER key
Step 3	*Observe*	the search results (a list of Web pages in the search list)

The search results list consists of Web page titles displayed as hyperlinks. You can click any hyperlink to load that page from the list. To close the Explorer bar and search list:

Step 1	*Click*	the Search button Search on the Standard toolbar
Step 2	*Close*	Internet Explorer

The Web's many search tools are all constructed differently. That means you get varying results when using several search engines or directories to search for information on the same topic. Also, search tools operate according to varying rules. For example, some search engines allow only a simple search on one keyword. Others allow you to refine your search by finding phrases keyed within quotation marks, by indicating proper names, or by using special operators such as "and," "or," and "not" to include or exclude search words. To save time, always begin by clicking the search tool's online Help link. Study the directions for using that particular search engine or directory, and then proceed with your search.

QUICK TIP

You can reload pages from the History folder, which stores the Web pages you load for a specific period of time. You set the number of days to store pages on the General tab in the Options dialog box. The default number of days to store pages in the History folder is 20 days. Click the History button on the toolbar to open the History list in the Explorer bar.

CAUTION TIP

After you find the desired information, "let the user beware!" Because the Web is largely unregulated, anyone can put anything on a Web page. Evaluate carefully the credibility of all the information you find. Try to find out something about the author and his or her credentials. Many college or university library Web sites have good tips on how to evaluate online information.

Summary

- A network is a group of two or more computers linked by cable or telephone lines, and the Internet is a worldwide "network of networks."
- The World Wide Web is a subset of the Internet from which you can download files and search for information.
- Other external networks related to the Internet are large commercial networks like America Online, CompuServe, Prodigy, the Microsoft Network and USENET.
- To access the Internet, your computer must have some physical communication medium such as cable or dial-up modem, and a special communication program such as Internet Explorer.
- An Internet Service Provider (or ISP) maintains a host computer on the Internet. In order to connect to the Internet, you need to connect to the host computer.
- You use a Web browser, such as Internet Explorer, to load Web pages. Web pages are connected by hyperlinks that are text or pictures associated with the path to another page.
- Directories and search engines are tools to help you find files and Web sites on the Internet.

Commands Review

Action	Menu Bar	Shortcut Menu	Toolbar	Task Pane	Keyboard
Load a Web page	File, Open		Go		ALT + F, O Key URL in the Address bar and press the ENTER key
Save a favorite	Favorites, Add to Favorites	Right-click hyperlink, click Add to Favorites	Drag URL icon to Links bar or Favorites command		ALT + A, A Ctrl + D
Manage the Standard toolbar, Address bar, and Links bar	View, Toolbars	Right-click the Standard toolbar, click desired command	Drag the Standard toolbar, Address bar, or Links bar to the new location		ALT + V, T
Load the search, history, or favorites list in the Explorer bar	View, Explorer Bar		Search Favorites History		ALT + V, E

Concepts Review

Circle the correct answer.

1. A network is:
- [a] the Internet.
- [b] two or more computers linked by cable or telephone wire.
- [c] two or more computer networks linked by cable or telephone lines.
- [d] a computer that stores Web pages.

2. Which of the following is not a challenge to using the Internet?
- [a] light usage
- [b] dynamic environment
- [c] volume of information
- [d] security and privacy

3. The Address bar:
- [a] is a customizable shortcut bar.
- [b] contains the search list.
- [c] contains your personal list of favorite URLs.
- [d] contains the URL of the Web page in the content area.

4. The content area contains the:
- [a] Standard toolbar.
- [b] status bar.
- [c] list of favorites.
- [d] current Web page.

5. You can view a list of recently loaded Web pages in the:
- [a] Channel bar.
- [b] Explorer bar.
- [c] Address bar.
- [d] Links bar.

6. Search engines update their indexes of keywords by using software called:
- [a] Webcrawler.
- [b] HTTP.
- [c] HotBot.
- [d] spiders.

Circle **T** if the statement is true or **F** if the statement is false.

T F 1. Commercial networks that provide specially formatted features are the same as the Internet.

T F 2. USENET is the name of the military Internet.

T F 3. All search engines use the same rules for locating Web pages.

T F 4. Internet users in Boston or New York can access computer files on computers located in the United States only.

T F 5. Spiders are programs that help you locate pages on the Web.

T F 6. A Web page URL identifies its location (path and filename).

Skills Review

Exercise 1

1. Open the Internet Explorer Web browser.
2. Open the Internet Options dialog box by clicking the Internet Options command on the Tools menu.
3. Review the options on the General tab in the dialog box.
4. Write down the steps to change the default start page to a blank page.
5. Close the dialog box and close the Web browser.

Exercise 2

1. Connect to the Internet and open the Internet Explorer Web browser.
2. Open the search list in the Explorer bar.
3. Search for Web pages about "dog shows."
4. Load one of the Web pages in the search results list.
5. Close the Explorer bar.
6. Print the Web page by clicking the Print command on the File menu and close the Web browser.

Exercise 3

1. Connect to the Internet and open the Internet Explorer Web browser.
2. Load the National Public radio Web page by keying the URL, *www.npr.org*, in the Address bar.
3. Print the Web page by clicking the Print command on the File menu and close the Web browser.

Exercise 4

1. Connect to the Internet and open the Internet Explorer Web browser.
2. Load the AltaVista search engine by keying the URL, *www.altavista.com*, in the Address bar.
3. Save the Web page as a favorite.
4. Search for Web pages about your city.
5. Print at least two Web pages by clicking the Print command on the File menu and close your Web browser.

Exercise 5

1. Connect to the Internet and open the Internet Explorer Web browser.
2. Load the HotBot search engine by keying the URL, *www.hotbot.com*, in the Address bar.
3. Save the Web page as a favorite.
4. Locate the hyperlink text or picture that loads the online Help page. Review the search rules for using HotBot.
5. Print the HotBot Help page by clicking the Print command on the File menu and close your Web browser.

Exercise 6

1. Connect to the Internet and open the Internet Explorer Web browser.
2. Load the Yahoo directory by keying the URL, *www.yahoo.com*, in the Address bar.
3. Save the Web page as a favorite.
4. Search for Web sites that contain information about restaurants in your city.
5. Print at least two Web pages by clicking the Print command on the File menu and close your Web browser.

Exercise 7 

1. Connect to the Internet and open the Internet Explorer Web browser.
2. View the Links bar by dragging the bar to the left using the mouse pointer.
3. Click each shortcut on the Links bar and review the Web page that loads.
4. Drag the Links bar back to its original position with the mouse pointer.

Exercise 8 

1. Connect to the Internet and open the Internet Explorer Web browser.
2. Click the History button on the Standard toolbar to load the History list in the Explorer bar.
3. Review the History list and click a hyperlink to a page loaded yesterday.
4. Print the page by clicking the Print command on the File menu, close the Explorer bar, and close the Web browser.

Case Projects

Project 1

Your organization recently started browsing the Web with the Internet Explorer Web browser and everyone wants to know how to use the toolbar buttons in the browser. Your supervisor asks you to prepare a fifteen-minute presentation, to be delivered at the next staff meeting, that describes the Internet Explorer Standard Buttons toolbar buttons. Review the Standard Buttons toolbar buttons and practice using them. Write an outline for your presentation that lists each button and describes how it is used.

Project 2 

You are working for a book publisher who is creating a series of books about popular movie actors and actresses from the 1940s and 1950s, including Humphrey Bogart and Tyrone Power. The research director asks you to use the Web to locate a list of movies that the actors starred in. Use the Explorer bar search list and the Yahoo directory search tool to find links to "Entertainment." Click the Entertainment link and close the Explorer bar. Working from the Yahoo Web page, click the Actors and Actresses link. Search for Humphrey Bogart in the Actors and Actresses portion of the database. Link to the Web page that shows the filmography for Humphrey Bogart. Print the Web page that shows all the movies he acted in. Use the History list to return to the Actors and Actresses search page. Search for Tyrone Power, then link to and print his filmography. Close the Internet Explorer Web browser.

Project 3 

You are the new secretary for the Business Women's Forum, a professional association. The association's president asked you to compile a list of Internet resources, which she will distribute at next month's lunch meeting. Connect to the Internet, open Internet Explorer, and search for Web pages containing the keywords "women in business" (including the quotation marks) using the AltaVista search engine. To load the AltaVista search engine key the URL, *www.altavista.com*, in the Address bar. From the search results, click the Web page title link of your choice to load the Web page. Review the new Web page and its links. Create a favorite for that page. Use the Back button list to reload the AltaVista home page and click a different Web page title from the list. Review the Web page and its links. Create a favorite for the Web page. Continue loading and reviewing pages until you have loaded and reviewed at least five pages. Return to the default home page. Use the Go To command on the View menu and the History bar to reload at least three of the pages. Print two of the pages. Delete all the favorites you added in this chapter, and then close Internet Explorer.

Microsoft Excel 2002 Introductory

Quick Start for Excel

Chapter Overview

Spreadsheet applications, such as Excel, help you organize and analyze information, especially information involving numbers. In this chapter, you learn about the components of the Excel window, and you perform simple tasks to become more familiar with how Excel works. You open a workbook file, navigate a workbook, select cells, work with worksheets, save your work, preview and print a workbook, and create a new workbook based on a predesigned template.

Learning Objectives

- Identify the components of the Excel window
- Locate and open an existing workbook
- Navigate a worksheet
- Select cells, columns, and rows
- Insert, reposition, and delete worksheets
- Save a workbook
- Preview and print a worksheet
- Close a workbook
- Create a new workbook from a template
- Exit Excel

Case profile

Luis Alvarez owns a computer store called Super Power Computers. His business has grown from a single location to a medium-sized chain of outlets spread out over several states. Luis employs several hundred people, and his business is divided into several departments to handle sales, inventory, delivery, technical support, accounting, and personnel. As an administrative assistant, you use Excel to organize and prepare a sales report for Luis.

chapter one

notes

This text assumes that you have little or no knowledge of the Excel application. However, it is assumed that you have read Office Chapters 1–3 of this book and that you are familiar with Windows 98 or Windows 2000 concepts.

The illustrations in this unit were created using Windows 2000. If you are using the Excel application installed in Windows 98, you may notice a few minor differences in some figures. These differences do not affect your work in this unit.

1.a Identifying the Components of the Excel Window

A **spreadsheet** is a computer file specifically designed to organize data by using special containers, called **cells**. Cells are organized into rows and columns to create a **worksheet**. A collection of worksheets is called a **workbook** and is saved as an Excel file.

Before you can begin to work with Excel, you must open the application. When you open the application, a new, blank workbook opens as well. To open Excel and a new, blank workbook:

Step 1	***Click***	the Start button Start on the taskbar
Step 2	***Point to***	Programs
Step 3	***Click***	Microsoft Excel

Within a few seconds, Excel starts. Your screen should look similar to Figure 1-1.

chapter one

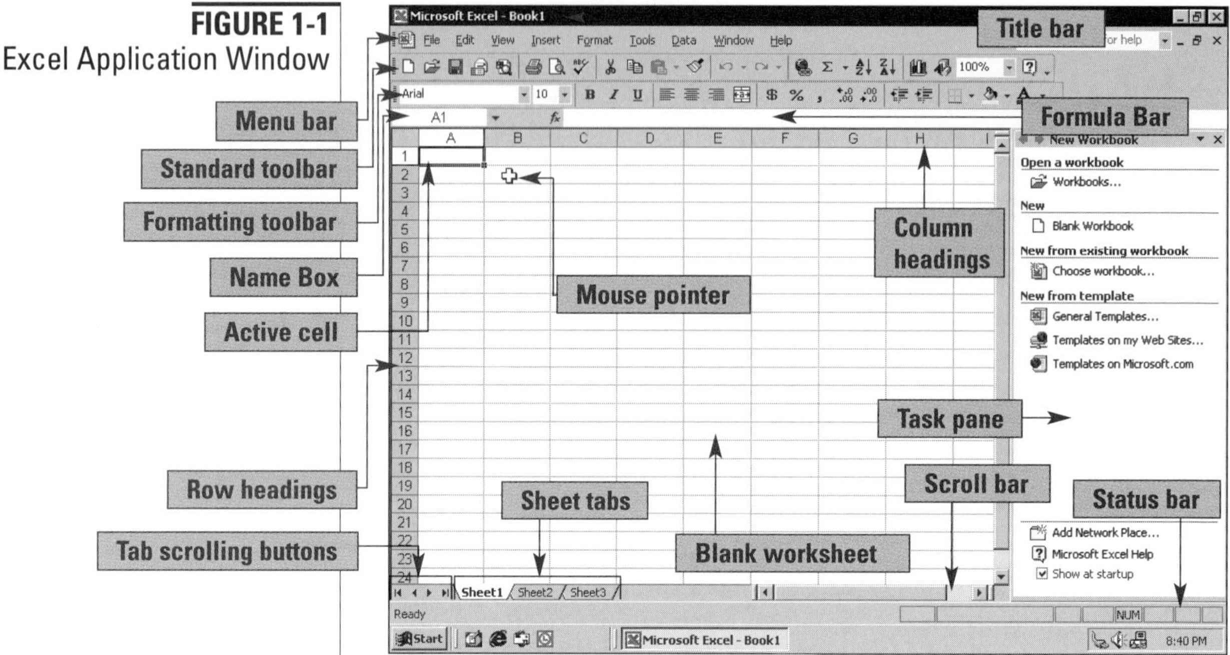

FIGURE 1-1
Excel Application Window

Worksheets

Each new workbook contains three worksheets, similar to pages in a notebook. You switch between worksheets by clicking the **sheet tabs** near the bottom of the Excel window. Each worksheet can be named and color-coded individually. When you click a sheet tab, you make that worksheet the **active worksheet**, and any values you key are entered on that worksheet. The active sheet tab appears to be in front of the other tabs, with the sheet tab name in bold.

Worksheets are divided into columns and rows. **Columns** run vertically up and down a worksheet. **Rows** run horizontally from left to right across a worksheet. Across the top of each worksheet you see **column headings**, which are lettered from A to Z, AA to AZ, and so on to column IV (256 columns in total). On the left side of each worksheet are **row headings**, which are numbered from 1 to 65,536 (the maximum number of rows in a worksheet).

Cells are the containers where values are stored. **Values** include numbers, text, hyperlinks, formulas, and functions. A **cell reference** is the column letter and row number that identifies a cell; for example, cell A1 refers to the cell at the intersection of column A and row 1. Each cell can contain up to 32,000 characters. When you click a cell, it becomes the **active cell**, and a thick border surrounds it. Any values you enter are stored in the active cell.

When you move your mouse pointer over a worksheet, it changes to a large, white cross. This mouse pointer changes shape depending on what you are doing.

Task Pane

The **New Workbook task pane** helps you work faster by providing helpful shortcuts. Using the New Workbook task pane, you can quickly open recently used workbooks, create new workbooks from templates, or search for templates on the Microsoft Web site, *Microsoft.com*. There are other task panes to help you complete specific types of tasks, such as when you need to paste information from the Clipboard or when you need to search your computer for a certain file.

Top of the Window

The **title bar** displays the application name as well as the current workbook name. The default name for the blank workbook that appears when you start Excel is "Book1." On the right side of the title bar are the Minimize, Maximize/Restore, and Close buttons. The **menu bar**, located below the title bar, features drop-down menu commands that contain groups of additional, related commands. The activities in this book instruct you to select menu bar commands with the mouse; if you prefer, however, you can press the ALT key plus the underlined letter in the menu command to open the menu, then press the underlined letter in the command on the menu. In addition, many menu commands have an associated keyboard shortcut. For example, to open a file, you could click the File menu, then click Open; you could press the ALT + F keys, then press the O key; or you could press the CTRL + O keys. The Commands Review section at the end of each chapter summarizes both the mouse and keyboard techniques used to select a menu command.

The **Standard toolbar**, located beneath the menu bar, provides easy access to commonly used commands, such as Save, Open, Print, Copy, and Paste, as well as to many other useful commands. The **Formatting toolbar**, shown below the Standard toolbar in Figure 1-1, provides easy access to commonly used formatting commands, such as Style, Font, Font Size, Alignment, Fill Color, and Font Color. The **Name Box**, located beneath the Formatting toolbar, displays the current cell or cells. Use the **Formula Bar**, to the right of the Name Box, to create and edit values. The Formula Bar becomes active whenever you begin keying data into a cell. When the Formula Bar is active, the Enter, Cancel, and Edit Formula buttons appear.

notes

Office XP features personalized menus and toolbars, which "learn" the commands you use most often. This means that when you first install Office XP, only the most frequently used commands appear immediately on a short version of the menus, and the remaining commands appear after a brief pause. Commands that you select move to the short menu, while those you don't use appear only on the full menu.

The Standard and Formatting toolbars appear on the same row when you first install Office XP. When they appear in this position, only the most commonly used buttons of each toolbar are visible. All the other default buttons appear on the Toolbar Options drop-down lists. As you use buttons from the Toolbar Options list, they move to the visible buttons on the toolbar, while the buttons you don't use move into the Toolbar Options list. If you arrange the Formatting toolbar below the Standard toolbar, all buttons are visible. Unless otherwise noted, the illustrations in this book show the full menus and the Formatting toolbar on its own row below the Standard toolbar.

Bottom of the Window

The **tab scrolling buttons** allow you to navigate through the sheet tabs, or worksheets, contained in your workbook. The right- and left-pointing triangles scroll one tab to the right or left, respectively. The right- and left-pointing triangles with the vertical line jump to the first and last sheet tabs in the workbook, respectively. Scrolling the sheet tabs does not change your active worksheet. The **status bar** at the bottom of the Excel window indicates various items of information, such as whether the NUM LOCK or CAPS LOCK feature is active. If you select a range of cells containing numbers, the sum of the selected cells is displayed on the status bar.

Luis, the company president, would like you to review the workbook he has been using to track regional sales.

1.b Locating and Opening an Existing Workbook

MOUSE TIP

Click the Open button on the Standard toolbar to open the Open dialog box.

When you want to edit an existing workbook, you need to open it from the disk where it is stored. You can open several workbooks at a time. Luis asks you to review the *Super Power Computers – Q1 Sales* workbook he has created.

notes

If you do not know where your Data Files are stored, check with your instructor to find out the location.

To open an existing workbook:

Step 1	**Click**	the Workbooks or More workbooks link in the Open a workbook section of the New Workbook task pane

The Open dialog box on your screen should look similar to Figure 1-2, although your file list might differ.

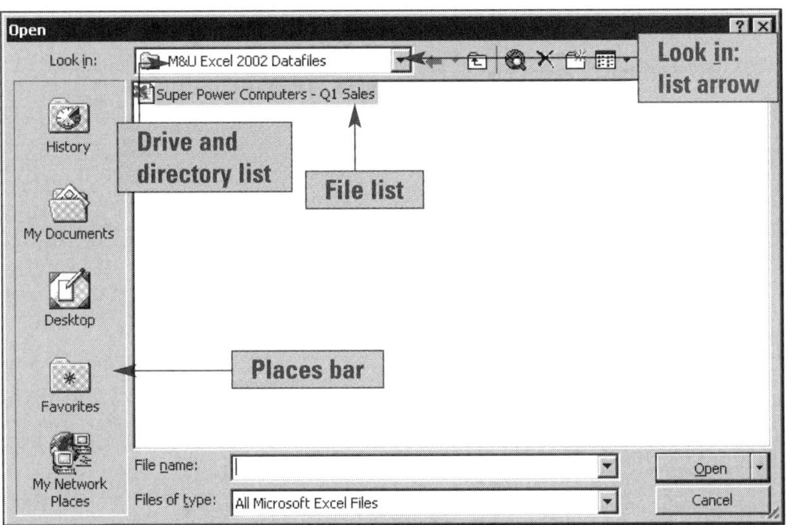

FIGURE 1-2
Open Dialog Box

Step 2	**Click**	the Look in: list arrow
Step 3	**Switch to**	the disk drive and folder where your Data Files are stored
Step 4	**Double-click**	*Super Power Computers – Q1 Sales* in the file list

The *Super Power Computers – Q1 Sales* workbook opens, and the New Workbook task pane closes until you need to use it again. Luis created this workbook to keep track of sales for the first quarter of 2003.

CAUTION TIP

Your system may be set up to show three-letter filename extensions, which identify the file type. The Excel filename extension is .xls. The illustrations in this book do not show filename extensions.

TASK PANE TIP

If you or someone else has opened workbooks in Excel, the New Workbook task pane hyperlink is "More workbooks" instead of "Workbooks."

QUICK TIP

The Places bar on the left side of the Open dialog box provides quick access to commonly used folders on your computer. My Network Places allows you to set up links to folders located on other computers in your network, or even other computers on the Internet.

1.c Navigating a Worksheet

In Excel, data you enter is placed in the active cell. Recall that the active cell is the cell with the thick black border around it. When you want to make a cell active, position the mouse pointer over the cell you want to activate, and then click the cell. To activate a cell using the mouse:

Step 1	*Point to*	cell B6
Step 2	*Click*	cell B6
Step 3	*Verify*	that cell B6 is active by looking in the Name Box

You can use the ARROW keys and other keyboard shortcuts to move the active cell. Table 1-1 summarizes some of the keyboard shortcuts for moving around in Excel.

TABLE 1-1
Using the Keyboard to Navigate a Workbook

To Move	Press
Up one cell	the UP ARROW key
Down one cell	the DOWN ARROW key
Right one cell	the TAB key or the RIGHT ARROW key
Left one cell	the SHIFT + TAB keys or the LEFT ARROW key
To first active cell of the current row	the HOME key
To last active cell of the current row	the END key and then the ENTER key
Down one page	the PAGE DOWN key
Up one page	the PAGE UP key
To cell A1	the CTRL + HOME keys
To last cell containing data in a worksheet	the CTRL + END keys or the END key and then the HOME key
To edge of the last cell containing a value or to the edges of a worksheet	the CTRL + ARROW keys

MOUSE TIP

You can scroll through a worksheet by clicking the scroll arrows to scroll one row or column at a time; drag the scroll boxes to scroll several rows or columns.

You also can move around a workbook using the keyboard. To navigate a workbook using the keyboard:

Step 1	*Press*	the CTRL + HOME keys to move to cell A1
Step 2	*Press*	the CTRL + END keys to move to the last cell containing data in the worksheet
Step 3	*Press*	the HOME key to move to the first cell in the current row

Step 4	*Press*	the CTRL + PAGE DOWN keys to move to Sheet2
Step 5	*Press*	the CTRL + PAGE UP keys to return to the Sales Report Data worksheet

You also can switch to another worksheet by using the mouse. To switch to another worksheet by using the mouse:

Step 1	*Click*	the Sheet2 sheet tab
Step 2	*Click*	the Sales Report Data sheet tab

Throughout the remainder of this book, you are instructed to activate a particular cell or worksheet. Use your mouse to click the cell or sheet tab, or use your favorite keyboard shortcut, whichever you prefer.

MOUSE TIP

With the IntelliMouse pointing device, you can use the scrolling wheel to scroll a worksheet. For more information on using the IntelliMouse pointing device, see online Help.

1.d Selecting Cells, Columns, and Rows

Selecting cells is a fundamental skill used when working in Excel. You select cells for editing, for moving, for copying, for formatting, or as references in formulas. To select cells by using the mouse:

Step 1	*Click*	cell B3, *but do not release* the mouse button
Step 2	*Drag*	the pointer to cell D5
Step 3	*Release*	the mouse button

You have selected a range of cells. A **range** is any group of contiguous cells. To refer to a range, you specify the cells in the upper-left and lower-right corners. In this step, you selected the range B3:D5. As you select the range, the status bar displays the sum of all cells in the selected range containing numerical values, and the Name Box displays a running count of rows and columns in your selected range. In this example, the Name Box indicated 3R x 3C, indicating that three rows and three columns were being selected. As soon as you release the mouse button to close your selection, the Name Box displays the group's active cell reference. The first selected cell, B3, remains unshaded to indicate that it is the active cell in the group. Your screen should look similar to Figure 1-3.

QUICK TIP

The AutoCalculate feature displays the sum of a selected range in the status bar. To display different calculations, such as the average, minimum, or maximum value of a range, right-click the status bar, then click the appropriate calculation in the shortcut menu.

FIGURE 1-3
Selected Range

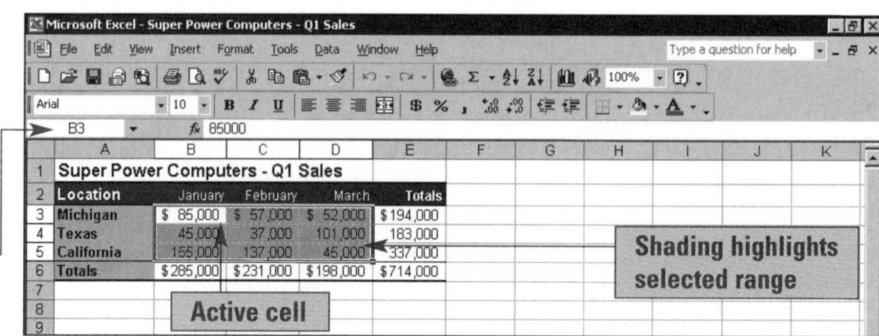

> **QUICK TIP**
>
> While working in a selection, press the ENTER key to move the active cell down one cell. Press the TAB key to move the active cell to the right. Press the SHIFT + TAB keys to move the active cell to the left.

You also can use keys to select cells. Holding down the SHIFT key allows you to select cells by pressing only the ARROW keys. Pressing the CTRL key in combination with the ARROW keys causes the selection to jump to the last cell containing data. If the cells in the direction you specify are blank, the selection moves to the limits of the worksheet. To select cells using keys:

Step 1	***Activate***	cell B4
Step 2	***Press & hold***	the SHIFT key
Step 3	***Press***	the RIGHT ARROW key twice to select cells C4 and D4
Step 4	***Release***	the SHIFT key
Step 5	***Press & hold***	the SHIFT + CTRL keys
Step 6	***Press***	the UP ARROW key
Step 7	***Release***	the SHIFT + CTRL keys to select the range B2:D4
Step 8	***Click***	any cell in the worksheet to deselect the range

> **MOUSE TIP**
>
> Many situations require the use of multiple, nonadjacent ranges. For example, to select cells in columns A and C, select the cells in column A, press and hold the CTRL key, then select the cells in column C.

You often want to apply formatting to an entire column or row, or several columns or rows at once. You can drag to select multiple columns or rows with the mouse, or you click while pressing the SHIFT or CTRL keys. To select an entire row or column, or to select several rows or columns:

Step 1	***Click***	the number 3 in the row 3 heading at the left of the worksheet to select row 3
Step 2	***Drag***	across the column headings for columns B, C, and D to select columns B, C, and D
Step 3	***Click***	the column E heading
Step 4	***Press & hold***	the SHIFT key
Step 5	***Click***	the column B heading to select columns B through E

You can also quickly select an entire worksheet at once. To select an entire worksheet:

Step 1	*Click*	the Select All button  located to the left of column A and above row 1
Step 2	*Activate*	cell A1 to deselect the worksheet

Quick Tip

Press the CTRL+ A keys to select an entire worksheet.

Now that you can easily select cells and navigate a worksheet, you are ready to organize a workbook.

1.e Inserting, Repositioning, and Deleting Worksheets

C

By default, Excel creates new workbooks that contain three worksheets. You can add or delete worksheets from your workbook at any time. You also can change the order of worksheets as you further refine your workbook design.

Menu Tip

You can insert a new worksheet by clicking the Worksheet command on the Insert menu.

Inserting a Worksheet

You need to add a new worksheet to the workbook. To add a new worksheet to a workbook:

Step 1	*Right-click*	the Sales Report Data sheet tab
Step 2	*Click*	Insert
Step 3	*Verify*	that the Worksheet icon in the Insert dialog box is selected
Step 4	*Click*	OK

A new worksheet is inserted to the left of the active worksheet.

Quick Tip

To have Excel insert more or fewer than three worksheets in each new workbook, click the Options command on the Tools menu to open the Options dialog box. On the General tab, enter the number of worksheets in the Sheets in new workbook: text box.

Copying and Moving a Worksheet

You need to create a second copy of the Sales Report Data worksheet for second quarter data. To copy a worksheet:

Step 1	*Right-click*	the Sales Report Data sheet tab
Step 2	*Click*	Move or Copy

The Move or Copy dialog box on your screen should look similar to Figure 1-4.

FIGURE 1-4
Move or Copy Dialog Box

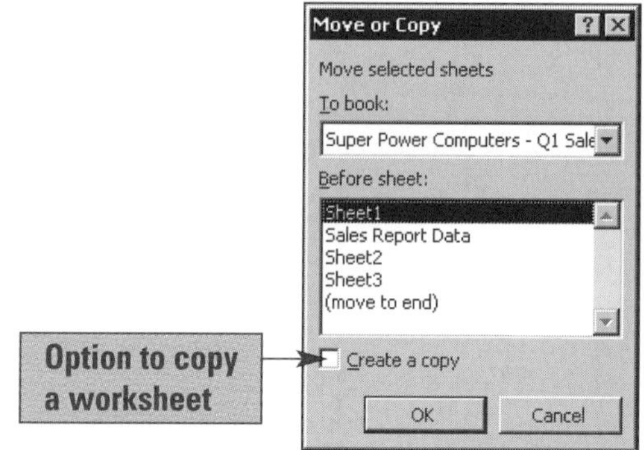

QUICK TIP

To copy a worksheet, press and hold the CTRL key while you drag the sheet tab.

Step 3	*Click*	the Create a copy check box to insert a check mark
Step 4	*Click*	OK

The active worksheet is copied and a new worksheet, called Sales Report Data (2) appears to the left of Sheet1.

You can reorganize your worksheets by dragging sheet tabs to a new location. In your workbook, the Sales Report Data worksheet should appear first, followed by the Sales Report Data (2) worksheet. To move a worksheet:

Step 1	*Point to*	the Sheet1 sheet tab
Step 2	*Press & hold*	the left mouse button

MOUSE TIP

Right-click a tab scroll button to display a menu of sheet tabs. Click any of the listed worksheets to scroll to and activate that worksheet.

The pointer changes to an arrow with a small rectangle attached to it to indicate that you are moving a sheet tab, and a small black triangle appears at the left of the sheet tab to indicate the tab's position.

Step 3	*Drag*	the Sheet1 sheet tab to the right of the Sales Report Data sheet tab

As you drag, the small black triangle moves with the pointer to indicate the worksheet's new position, and the sheet tabs scroll left. Your screen should look similar to Figure 1-5.

FIGURE 1-5
Moving a Sheet Tab

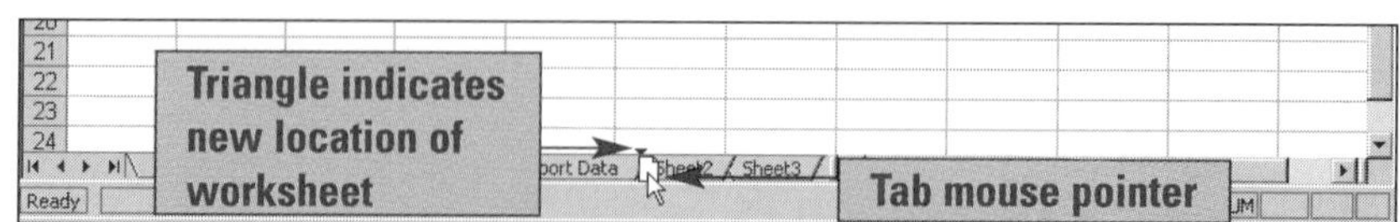

Step 4	*Release*	the mouse button

The sheet tab moves to the new location.

Step 5	*Follow*	Steps 1 through 4 to position the Sales Report Data (2) sheet tab to the right of the Sales Report Data sheet tab

Deleting a Worksheet

You can also delete worksheets that you no longer need. To delete a worksheet:

Step 1	*Right-click*	the Sheet1 sheet tab
Step 2	*Click*	Delete
Step 3	*Click*	the Sales Report Data sheet tab

1.f Saving a Workbook

The first rule of computing is: Save Your Work Often! The second rule of computing is: Follow the first rule of computing. There are two distinct saving operations: Save and Save As.

Managing Files and Folders

To keep your work more organized, you decide to create a new folder. You can do this from the Open or Save As dialog box. To create a new folder:

Step 1	*Click*	File
Step 2	*Click*	Save As
Step 3	*Click*	the Save in: list arrow
Step 4	*Switch to*	the appropriate disk drive and folder, as designated by your instructor
Step 5	*Click*	the Create New Folder button  in the Save As dialog box
Step 6	*Key*	your name as the name of the folder (Example: Kylie)
Step 7	*Click*	OK

MOUSE TIP

You can resize the horizontal scroll bar to view more worksheet tabs. Drag the horizontal scroll bar resize handle, located to the left of the scroll bar, to the right to decrease its size.

CAUTION TIP

Use extreme caution when deleting worksheets. This Excel command cannot be undone. Once you've deleted a worksheet, you cannot get it back.

C

The folder is created in the current location and listed in the Save in: list box.

C

Using the Save As Command

CAUTION TIP

Filenames cannot include the following special characters: the forward slash (/), the backward slash (\), the colon (:), the semicolon (;), the pipe symbol (|), the question mark (?), the less than symbol (<), the greater than symbol (>), the asterisk (*), and the quotation mark (").

When you use the Save As command, you provide a filename and specify the disk drive and folder location where the workbook should be saved. A filename can have as many as 255 characters, including the disk drive reference and path, and can contain letters, numbers, spaces, and some special characters in any combination. If you use the Save As command on a previously saved workbook, you actually create a new copy of the workbook, and any changes you made appear only in the new copy.

You also can use the Save As command to save a workbook file in another format, such as HTML for the Internet, or for use in another spreadsheet or accounting application. First, you save the workbook to a different format to send to someone using a different spreadsheet application. To save a workbook in a different file format:

Step 1	*Verify*	that the Save As dialog box is still open
Step 2	*Click*	the Save as type: list arrow
Step 3	*Scroll*	the list to find WK4 (1-2-3)
Step 4	*Click*	WK4 (1-2-3)

This is the format for Lotus 1-2-3 workbooks.

Step 5	*Select*	All of the text in the File name: text box
Step 6	*Key*	Super Power Computers - Q1 Sales WK4 Format
Step 7	*Click*	Save

INTERNET TIP

To distribute a workbook without personal information (such as your user name): Click the Options command on the Tools menu. On the Security tab, click the Remove personal information from this file on save check box, then click the OK button. The next time you save your document, the personal information will be removed.

A warning message appears telling you that some of the workbook's features may not save correctly in the new format. Although Excel does its best to translate the workbook into another format, not everything transfers correctly. For more information about a specific format's limitations, click Help.

Step 8	*Click*	Yes

You have now created a copy of your Excel formatted workbook. Next, you want to save the workbook back to Excel format. To save the workbook with a new filename in Excel format:

Step 1	*Open*	the Save As dialog box
Step 2	*Key*	Super Power Computers – Q1 Sales Revised in the File name: text box
Step 3	*Click*	Microsoft Excel Workbook in the Save as type: list box

CAUTION TIP

Computers and computer applications are not perfect. Avoid losing data from computer crashes by saving your work every 10 to 15 minutes.

The Save As dialog box on your screen should look similar to Figure 1-6.

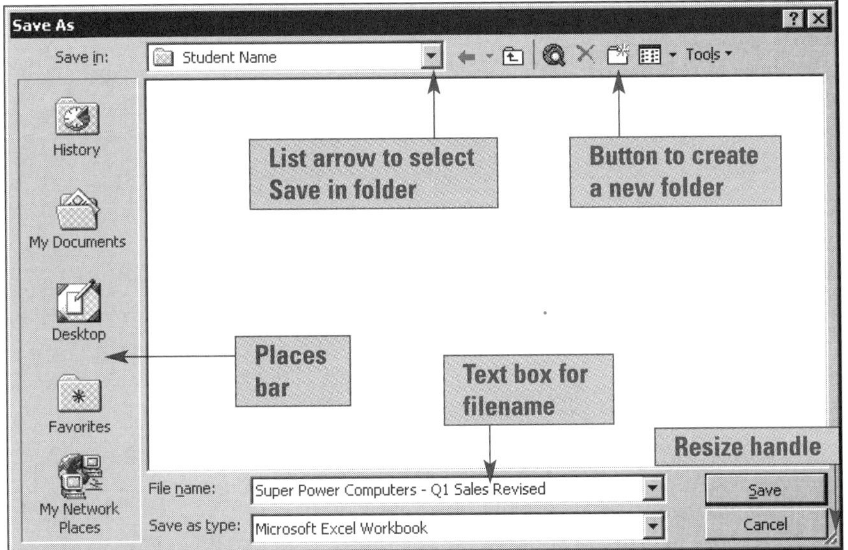

FIGURE 1-6
Save As Dialog Box

MOUSE TIP

You can resize any dialog box by dragging the resize handle in the lower-right corner.

Step 4	*Click*	Save

The workbook is saved to your folder as *Super Power Computer – Q1 Sales Revised*. Notice that the title bar includes the new filename.

QUICK TIP

Press the CTRL + S keys or the SHIFT + F12 keys to quickly save your work. Press the F12 key to open the Save As dialog box.

Using the Save Command

When you want to save changes to a previously named workbook without creating a copy, you use the Save command. No dialog box opens, but the changes are saved to your workbook, and you go back to work. To modify your workbook and save the changes:

Step 1	*Delete*	the Sheet2 and Sheet3 sheet tabs

CAUTION TIP

Once you have completed a Save or Save As operation, you cannot undo it. To avoid inadvertently saving a workbook that you planned to copy, perform the Save As command as soon as you open the file you are going to edit. You can then save frequently without worrying about overwriting your original file.

Step 2	*Click*	the Save button on the Standard toolbar

No dialog box opens because you have already named the workbook.

1.g Previewing and Printing a Worksheet

Luis asks you to print a copy of the Q1 Sales figures. Before you print a worksheet, preview it to ensure that you are printing the right information. To preview the worksheet:

Step 1	*Click*	the Sales Report Data sheet tab, if necessary
Step 2	*Click*	the Print Preview button on the Standard toolbar

Your Print Preview might appear in color or in black and white. The Print Preview toolbar appears at the top of the window. The status bar indicates the number of pages that print. Your screen should look similar to Figure 1-7.

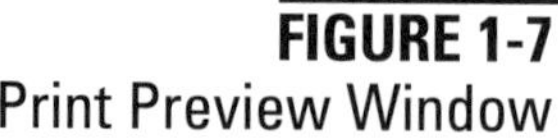

FIGURE 1-7
Print Preview Window

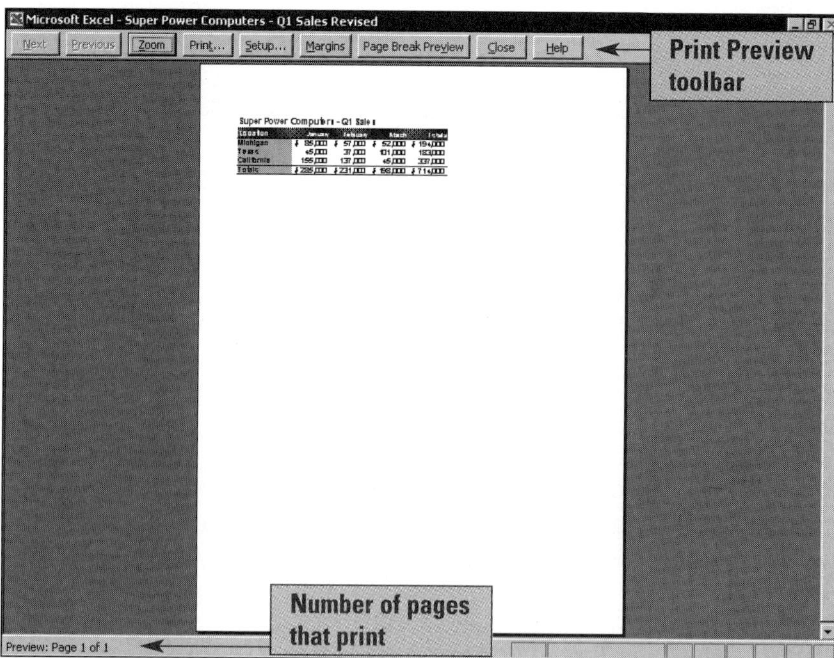

MENU TIP

Click Print Preview on the File menu to preview a document.

Step 3	*Click*	the Print button on the Print Preview toolbar
Step 4	*Click*	OK to send the worksheet to the default printer

1.h Closing a Workbook

When you finish working with a workbook, you can close it without closing the Excel application. If you have modified the workbook you are closing, Excel prompts you to save your work. To close the *Super Power Computers – Q1 Sales Revised* workbook:

Step 1	*Click*	the Close Window button on the right side of the menu bar
Step 2	*Click*	Yes to save any changes, if prompted

Excel displays the next open workbook, if there is one. If no workbooks are open, you see a blank workspace. You can quickly reopen a saved workbook from a folder that you created. To open a workbook from a folder:

Step 1	*Click*	the Open button on the Standard toolbar
Step 2	*Click*	the Look in: list arrow
Step 3	*Click*	the folder with your name (the folder you created in the previous section)
Step 4	*Double-click*	*Super Power Computers – Q1 Sales Revised*

The workbook opens. Next you create a new workbook from a template.

1.i Creating a New Workbook from a Template

A **template** is a workbook into which formatting, settings, and formulas are already inserted. When you create a new workbook, you are actually creating a new workbook based on Excel's default workbook template, which contains three blank worksheets. You can create a new workbook based on another template. You can choose from additional templates provided with Excel, or you can create your own.

CAUTION TIP

Be careful when clicking the Print button on the Standard toolbar. It immediately sends the file to the printer using the current page setup options. You may not be aware of the current print area or even which printer will print the file.

TASK PANE TIP

You can open a workbook by clicking the More workbooks link in the Open a workbook section in the New Workbook task pane.

MENU TIP

Click the Close command on the File menu to close the workbook.

chapter one

CAUTION TIP

You must use the New command on the File menu, which displays the New Document task pane, to access the New dialog box. Clicking the New button on the Standard toolbar opens a new, blank worksheet based on the default template.

You need to create a blank invoice to bill customers of Super Power Computers. To create a new workbook based on the Invoice template:

Step 1	*Click*	File
Step 2	*Click*	New

The New Workbook task pane opens.

Step 3	*Click*	the General Templates link in the New from template section in the New Workbook task pane

The Templates dialog box opens.

Step 4	*Click*	the Spreadsheet Solutions tab
Step 5	*Click*	the Sales Invoice template icon

You should see a preview of the template in the Preview box. Your dialog box should look similar to Figure 1-8.

FIGURE 1-8
Creating a New Workbook from a Template

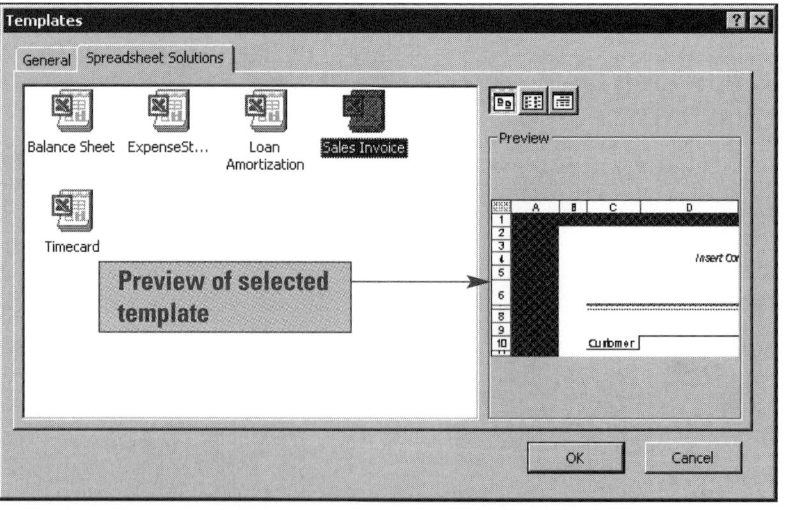

MENU TIP

Click the Exit command on the File menu to close the Excel application.

If you do not see a preview in the Preview box, but instead see instructions on how to install additional templates, insert the Office XP CD-ROM in your CD-ROM drive, click OK, and then skip Step 6 and continue reading.

Step 6	*Click*	OK

A new workbook, based on the Sales Invoice template, opens. The title bar identifies this workbook as "Sales Invoice1." Changes you make to this workbook do not affect the template itself. Your screen should look similar to Figure 1-9.

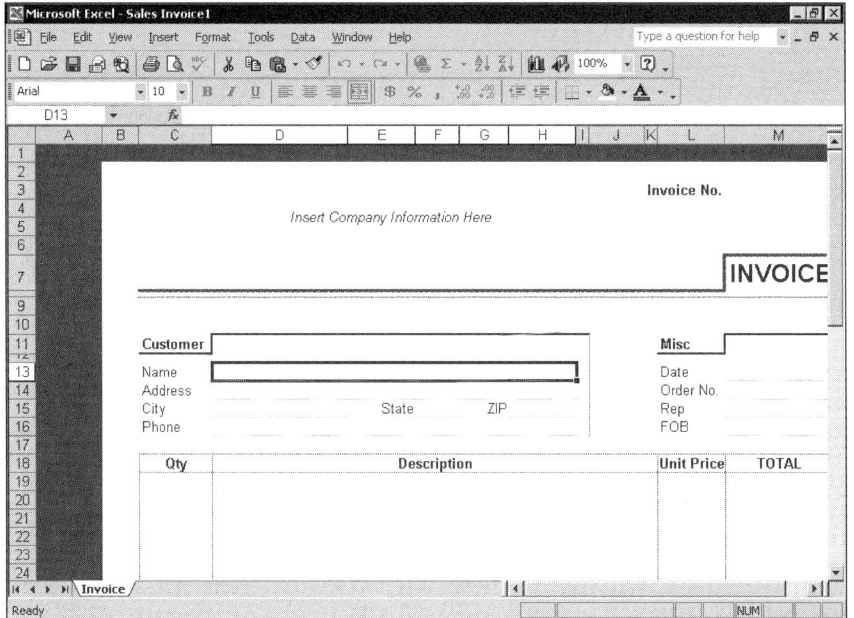

FIGURE 1-9
New Invoice Workbook

> **CAUTION TIP**
>
> Some templates and workbooks contain macros that have been written by other users to automate certain routine tasks in the workbook. Unfortunately, some macros, known as macro viruses, are programmed to do malicious things. Whenever you open a workbook containing macros, you will receive a warning about the possibility of macro viruses. Excel cannot tell you whether the macros will do anything harmful; rather, it simply alerts you to the fact that the workbook contains macros. If you have downloaded a workbook from the Internet and are not sure of its origin, you should take a cautious approach and disable the workbook macros. The data will remain intact, even though the macros are disabled.

The new workbook looks very different from the workbooks you have seen thus far. Gridlines and column and row headings are turned off to reduce the amount of distracting elements in the template.

Step 7	*Scroll*	the worksheet to familiarize yourself with it

Super Power Computers generates many invoices every day. By using this template, you save yourself a lot of time and effort.

1.j Exiting Excel

When you finish working in Excel, you should exit the application. You are prompted to save any modified workbooks that remain open. If you change your mind about exiting, click the Cancel button. To exit Excel:

Step 1	*Click*	the Close button [X] on the Excel title bar
Step 2	*Click*	No if prompted to save any changes to open workbooks

Summary

- A worksheet is an electronic spreadsheet. A workbook is a collection of worksheets.
- Cells are containers in worksheets for text, numerical values, and formulas that calculate data. Cells are organized into rows and columns. A cell reference identifies a particular cell through a combination of the column letter and the row number.
- You can open multiple workbooks in Excel.
- By default, new workbooks are created with three worksheets.
- You can use keyboard shortcuts such as the HOME key, the CTRL + HOME keys, the TAB key, and the SHIFT + TAB keys to navigate around a worksheet. You can also use the mouse to activate a cell or to scroll to other cells.
- You can select cells with the mouse by pressing and holding the left mouse button as you drag across cells. Select cells with the keyboard by pressing and holding the SHIFT key plus the ARROW keys, and other shortcut keys, such as the CTRL, HOME, and END keys. Select columns and rows by clicking the column and row headers.
- You can organize worksheets by inserting, moving, copying, or deleting worksheets.
- You can create new folders to organize your work from within the Open and Save As dialog boxes.
- You can use the Save As command when you want to make a copy of an existing workbook or save a workbook in a different file format.
- You can use the Save command to save a new workbook or to save changes to a previously named workbook.
- You should preview worksheets before you print them.
- Templates are used to start a new workbook with preset formatting, data, and formulas.
- When you close a new or modified workbook, Excel reminds you to save your work.
- When you close the Excel application, Excel reminds you to save any unsaved workbooks.

Commands Review

Action	Menu Bar	Shortcut Menu	Toolbar	Task Pane	Keyboard
Open a workbook	File, Open	Right-click empty Excel workspace, click Open		More workbooks link in New Workbook task pane	CTRL + O ALT + F, O
Create a new workbook	File, New	Right-click empty Excel workspace, click New		Blank workbook link in New Workbook task pane	CTRL + N ALT + F, N
Insert a worksheet	Insert, Worksheet	Right-click sheet tab, click Insert			ALT + I, W
Move or copy a worksheet	Edit, Move or Copy Sheet	Right-click sheet tab, click Move or Copy			ALT + E, M
Delete a worksheet	Edit, Delete Sheet	Right-click sheet tab, click Delete			ALT + E, L
Save a workbook	File, Save				CTRL + S CTRL + F12 ALT + F, S
Save As	File, Save As				ALT + F, A F12
Create a new folder from Open or Save As dialog box		Right-click blank area in dialog box, point to New, click Folder			
Preview a worksheet	File, Print Preview				ALT + F, V
Print a worksheet	File, Print				ALT + F, P CTRL + P CTRL + Shift + F12
Close a workbook	File, Close				CTRL + F4 ALT + F, C CTRL + W
Close multiple workbooks	Press and hold the SHIFT key, then File, Close All				SHIFT + ALT + F, C
Create a new workbook based on a template	File, New	Right-click empty Excel workspace, click New		General Templates link in New Workbook task pane	ALT + F, N
Exit Excel	File, Exit	Right-click application icon, click Close			ALT + F4 ALT + F, X

Concepts Review

Circle the correct answer.

1. Excel worksheets contain:
- [a] 30 rows.
- [b] 256 rows.
- [c] 20,000 rows.
- [d] 65,536 rows.

2. Excel worksheets contain:
- [a] 30 columns.
- [b] 256 columns.
- [c] 20,000 columns.
- [d] 65,536 columns.

3. Excel workbooks use the three-letter filename extension:
- [a] doc.
- [b] txt.
- [c] htm.
- [d] xls.

4. The status bar displays:
- [a] text and formulas you are entering.
- [b] results of the formula you are entering.
- [c] important worksheet and system information.
- [d] the filename of your workbook.

5. The active cell is identified by a:
- [a] thick black border.
- [b] change in the font color.
- [c] shaded cell background.
- [d] thin dashed border.

6. To save changes to a workbook without creating a new copy, use the:
- [a] Save As command.
- [b] Open command.
- [c] More workbooks command.
- [d] Save command.

7. To change the active worksheet:
- [a] click the title bar.
- [b] click the sheet tab.
- [c] press the RIGHT ARROW key.
- [d] click and drag the scroll bar at the bottom of the worksheet window.

8. To select nonadjacent ranges, you drag across the second range while you press and hold the:
- [a] CTRL key.
- [b] SHIFT key.
- [c] CAPS LOCK key.
- [d] ALT key.

9. To select adjacent cells using only the keyboard, you would use the ARROW keys as you press and hold the:
- [a] CTRL key.
- [b] SHIFT key.
- [c] TAB key.
- [d] ALT key.

10. To select an entire column or row:
- [a] key the column letter or row number.
- [b] press and hold the CTRL key, then key the column letter or row number.
- [c] click the column or row header.
- [d] key the column letter or row number in the Name Box.

Circle **T** if the statement is true or **F** if the statement is false.

T F 1. Excel can open many workbooks at once.

T F 2. Cells can contain numbers, text, or formulas.

T F 3. Rows run vertically down the worksheet.

T F 4. You can select menu items using only keyboard shortcuts.

T F 5. The Formula Bar displays the row and column number of the active cell.

T F 6. Columns run vertically down the worksheet.

T F 7. Clicking a tab scroll button changes the active worksheet.

T F 8. Pressing the CTRL + HOME keys closes the Excel application and saves any open workbooks.

T F 9. You cannot open a file unless it is saved on your computer.

T F 10. The Save and Save As commands do exactly the same thing.

Skills Review

Exercise 1 

1. Start Excel.
2. Open the *Sweet Tooth Q1 2003 Sales* workbook located on the Data Disk.
3. Copy Sheet1 to a new worksheet.
4. Save the workbook as *Sweet Tooth Q1 2003 Sales Revised*, and print it.
5. Close the workbook.

Exercise 2 

1. Open the *Region Sales Summary* workbook located on the Data Disk.
2. Save the workbook as *Region Sales Summary Revised*.
3. Change the worksheet order to: East, West, North, South.
4. Activate the East sheet tab.
5. Activate cell A1, if necessary.
6. Save your changes, and print the worksheet.
7. Close the workbook.

Exercise 3 

1. Create a new workbook using the *ExpenseStatement* template.
2. Use Print Preview to preview the printed worksheet.
3. Print the worksheet.
4. Save the workbook as *My Expense Statement*, and print it.
5. Close the workbook.

Exercise 4

1. Open the *2003 Sales Projections* workbook located on the Data Disk.
2. Delete all the sheet tabs for the year 2002.
3. Switch between worksheets to locate the store whose projected sales total will be the greatest.
4. Select the cells containing data for that store.
5. Save the workbook as *2003 Sales Projections Revised*, and print it.
6. Close the workbook.

Exercise 5

1. Open the *Half Marathon Mile Splits* workbook located on the Data Disk.
2. Select cells B3:B9 and D3:D9.
3. Delete the Sheet2 and Sheet3 worksheets from the workbook.
4. Save the workbook as *Half Marathon Mile Splits Revised*, and print it.
5. Close the workbook.

Exercise 6 

1. Create a new, blank workbook.
2. Insert a new worksheet.
3. Move the new worksheet so it is the last worksheet in the workbook.
4. Save the workbook as *4 Blank Sheets* in a new folder named "Practice."
5. Close the workbook.
6. Open the workbook *4 Blank Sheets* located in the Practice folder.
7. Reorganize the worksheets in the following order: Sheet4, Sheet3, Sheet2, Sheet1.
8. Save the workbook as *4 Blank Sheets Revised* in the Practice folder.
9. Close the workbook.

Exercise 7 

1. Open the *State Capitals* workbook located on the Data Disk.
2. Use Print Preview to preview the printed worksheet.
3. Print the worksheet.
4. Save the workbook as *State Capitals WK4 Format* in Lotus 1-2-3 format.
5. Close the workbook without saving any additional changes.

Exercise 8 

1. Open the *2002 Sales Report* workbook located on the Data Disk.
2. On the Southwest Division 2002 sheet tab, select all of the data except the two title lines by using the mouse or keyboard.
3. On the Southeast Division 2002 sheet tab, select column C.
4. On the Northwest Division 2002 sheet tab, select row 9.
5. On the Northeast Division 2002 sheet tab, select cells B8:C8.
6. Save the workbook as *2002 Sales Report Revised*, and print it.
7. Close the workbook.
8. Exit Excel.

Case Projects

Project 1

You work for a large company with many offices spread throughout the United States and Canada. To facilitate information sharing between offices, your company stores many files on an FTP server. Your job is to train new employees how to open files on the company's FTP server. Using the Ask A Question Box, research how to open workbooks on an FTP server, then create a Word document and write at least two paragraphs explaining how to do this. Save your document as *Open an Excel Workbook on an FTP Server* and print it. Close the document and exit Word.

Project 2

You work as an office manager. You decide to reorganize the company's workbook files by date. To do this, you need to create folders for the last five years. Use the Open or Save As dialog box in Excel to create a new folder called "Project 2." Inside that folder, create a new folder for each of the last five years.

Project 3

You would like to find out more about Excel's keyboard shortcuts, particularly as they apply to navigating worksheets. Use online Help to search for keyboard shortcuts, then look for a topic "Move and scroll within worksheets." Copy and paste this list into a Word document and save the document as *Excel Worksheet Navigation Shortcuts*. Print the document, then close it.

Project 4

You work for a mortgage company, and it is your job to calculate amortization tables for clients. You'd like to use a template, but aren't sure how to start. You notice a Templates on Microsoft.com link in the New Workbook task pane, and decide to investigate. Click the link, locate a *Loan Calculator* template for Excel, and download it. Open the template in Excel, then preview and print a copy of the template. Save the workbook as *Loan Calculator*.

Excel 2002

Entering and Editing Data in a Worksheet

Chapter Overview

With Excel, you can store numerical data in a variety of formats. You can also store text data such as names and Social Security numbers. In this chapter, you learn how to enter and edit data in a worksheet. You also learn to use the Undo and Redo commands to help you when you make the inevitable mistake, how to zoom in on a worksheet, and how to name and color sheet tabs.

Learning Objectives

- Create new workbooks
- Enter text and numbers in cells
- Edit cell contents
- Use Undo and Redo
- Change the Zoom setting
- Rename a sheet tab
- Change a sheet tab color

Case profile

To keep track of employees at Super Power Computers, each store uses an employee name list workbook. This workbook stores important information such as the name, hourly wage, and phone number of each employee. A new store has just opened in Kansas City, and you need to provide them with this workbook.

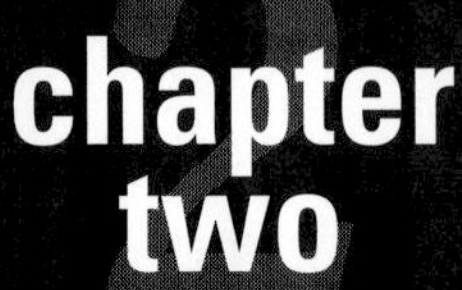

2.a Creating New Workbooks

In Chapter 1, you learned how to create a new workbook based on a template, a special type of Excel file. You also learned that Excel automatically creates a new, blank workbook when you start the application. In this section, you learn to create new, blank workbooks and to create new workbooks from existing workbooks, similar to using a template file.

Creating a New, Blank Workbook

When you start Excel, a new workbook is created for you automatically. However, you may need to create additional workbooks while you are working in Excel. To create a new blank workbook:

Step 1	*Start*	Excel
Step 2	*Click*	the Blank Workbook link in the New Workbook task pane

A new workbook is created in Excel.

Step 3	*Close*	both of the blank workbooks

Creating a Workbook Based on an Existing Workbook

Instead of starting a new workbook, you decide to create the new workbook from an existing workbook file, and then add the data you need to change. The New Workbook task pane provides a quick shortcut for this task. To create a new workbook from an existing workbook file:

Step 1	*Click*	File
Step 2	*Click*	New
Step 3	*Click*	the Choose workbook link in the New Workbook task pane
Step 4	*Select*	*Super Power Computers – Blank Employee List* from the Data Disk
Step 5	*Click*	Create New

A new file is created from the existing workbook. Excel assigns the new workbook the same filename as the original workbook with a "1" at the end of the filename, as you can see in the title bar.

MOUSE TIP

You can click the New button on the Standard toolbar to create a new workbook.

Step 6	*Save*	the workbook as *Super Power Computers – Kansas City Employee List*

2.b Entering Text and Numbers in Cells

You can enter numbers, letters, and symbols into the active cell. When you enter data in a cell, Excel recognizes the type of data you are entering. For example, if you enter your name in a cell, Excel knows that this is a text value and therefore cannot be used in numerical calculations. Date and time values are special cases of numerical data. When you enter this type of data, Excel automatically converts the value you key into a special numerical value, which makes it easier for Excel to use in calculations.

When you've finished entering data in a cell, you need to accept the entry by pressing the ENTER key, the TAB key, or any of the ARROW keys, or by clicking the Enter button next to the Formula Bar or another cell in the worksheet. Before accepting the entry in a cell, you can change your mind by pressing the ESC key, and the cell's content reverts to the way it was before you began entering or editing the data.

Entering Text

You receive the employee information from the new Kansas City store, as shown in Table 2-1. The first row of data has already been entered in the workbook you opened. These values are **column labels**, identifying the data stored in each column.

TABLE 2-1
Super Power Computers Employee Data

Name	Wage	Phone
Jared Wright	$9.00	(816) 555-3456
Kaili Muafala	$9.00	(816) 555-9254
Jenna McGregor	$16.00	(816) 555-0012
Monica Chambers	$11.50	(816) 555-1827
Baka Hakamin	$12.75	(816) 555-4637
Homer Hansen	$14.00	(816) 555-8822

To enter text in a worksheet:

Step 1	*Activate*	cell A2
Step 2	*Key*	Jared Wright

Your screen should look similar to Figure 2-1.

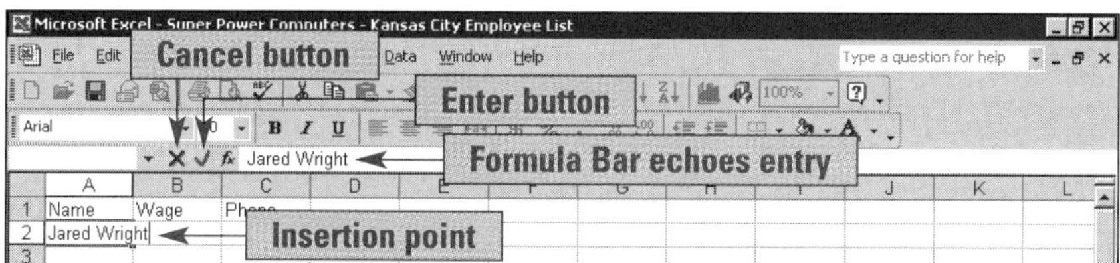

FIGURE 2-1
Entering Data

As you enter data, the status bar displays the word "Enter." The Formula Bar displays the contents of the active cell, while the cell itself shows the results of any formula entered in the cell. In the case of numbers or text, no calculation takes place, so you see exactly what you enter. As you enter or edit data in a cell, the Cancel and Enter buttons appear next to the Formula Bar, the mouse pointer changes to an I-beam pointer to indicate that you are entering a value in a cell, and a blinking **insertion point** appears in the cell to indicate where the next character that you key will go.

Step 3	***Press***	the ENTER key

When you press the ENTER key, the entry is accepted, and the active cell moves down one row by default.

Step 4	***Follow***	Steps 2 and 3 to add each name listed in Table 2-1 to column A of your worksheet

You can use any of the navigation keys to complete data entry in one cell and then move to another.

MENU TIP

You can change the default behavior of the ENTER key by using the Options dialog box. Click the Options command on the Tools menu. On the Edit tab, locate the Move selection after Enter check box. To turn the behavior off, remove the check mark. To force the active cell in a different direction, select a new direction from the Direction: list box.

Entering Numbers

You enter number values directly into the active cell, the same way you enter text values, or date and time values. To enter numerical values:

Step 1	***Activate***	cell B2
Step 2	***Key***	$9.00
Step 3	***Click***	the Enter button on the Formula Bar

Excel recognizes the number you entered as currency. It shows the number in the cell with a dollar sign, but in the Formula Bar, the number is displayed without the dollar sign and the trailing zeros.

You can no longer see the full value in cell A2. The data (Jared's name) is still there; it is just hidden. You learn how to adjust column widths to display more characters in Chapter 4.

Step 4	*Enter*	the rest of the data in the Wage column in Table 2-1

Some types of data, although numeric in appearance, aren't really intended to be used in mathematical calculations. Examples of these special types of numbers include phone numbers and Social Security numbers. When you enter numbers mixed with other characters, such as parentheses, dashes, and so on, Excel automatically treats the cell value as a text value.

Step 5	*Key*	(816) 555-3456 in cell C2
Step 6	*Press*	the ENTER key
Step 7	*Enter*	the rest of the data in the Phone column in Table 2-1

Your worksheet should look similar to Figure 2-2.

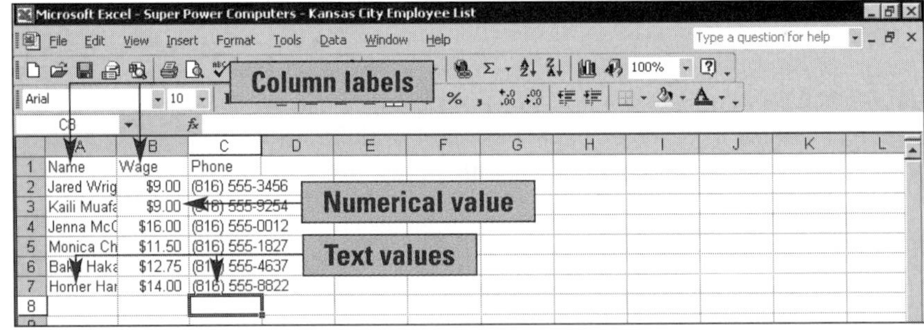

FIGURE 2-2
Super Power Computers Employee Data

In general, entering data into cells is a simple process: activate the cell, enter the data, and accept the entry.

2.c Editing Cell Contents

Excel provides many ways to edit the contents of a cell. You receive updated information from the Kansas City store, and you need to modify your worksheet. To completely replace a cell's value:

Step 1	*Activate*	cell A7
Step 2	*Key*	Ross Phillips

Step 3	*Press*	the TAB key
Step 4	*Key*	$13.00 in cell B7
Step 5	*Press*	the ENTER key

Editing in the Active Cell

Often, you need to revise only part of an entry. To edit in the active cell:

Step 1	*Double-click*	cell B4

The entry in cell B4 changes to display only the number 16 without the dollar sign and trailing zeros, and the blinking insertion point appears in the cell.

Step 2	*Drag*	the I-beam pointer over the 6 to select it

Your screen should look similar to Figure 2-3. The 6 in cell B11 is **selected**. Anything you key replaces the selected text.

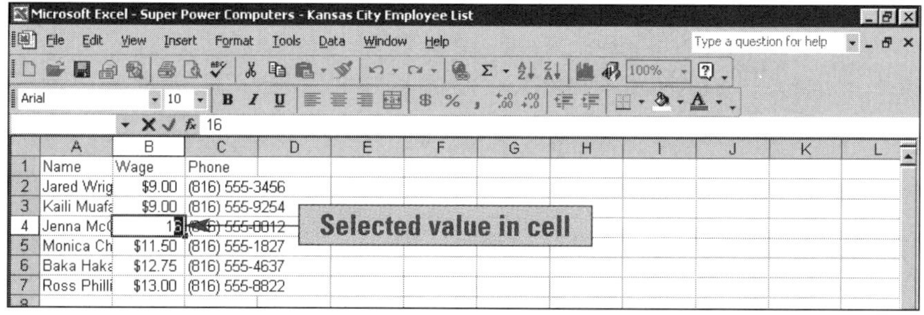

FIGURE 2-3
Editing in the Active Cell

Step 3	*Key*	7.25
Step 4	*Press*	the ENTER key

The wage for Jenna should be $17.25.

Editing in the Formula Bar

An alternative to editing directly in the cell is to use the Formula Bar. You can edit the contents of the active cell in the Formula Bar by either moving the insertion point to where you want to make changes or highlighting the text you want to change and then keying new text.

CAUTION TIP

Although the rekeying method is the fastest way to edit a cell, be careful when taking this approach. The previous contents of the cell are replaced with any new data you enter.

QUICK TIP

Sometimes it is difficult to select text precisely with the mouse. Try this: Click to position the insertion point at the start of your selection, then press and hold the SHIFT key while you press the right ARROW key to move across the text.

> **QUICK TIP**
>
> You can press the F2 key to edit cell contents.
> When editing a cell's contents, press the HOME key to move the insertion point to the start of the data. To move to the end of the data, press the END key.

To edit in the Formula Bar:

Step 1	***Activate***	cell C3
Step 2	***Click***	to the left of 4 in the Formula Bar
Step 3	***Press***	the DELETE key

Pressing the DELETE key deletes the character to the right of the insertion point. Pressing the BACKSPACE key deletes the character to the left of the insertion point.

Step 4	***Key***	8
Step 5	***Click***	the Enter button on the Formula Bar

Your worksheet should look similar to Figure 2-4.

FIGURE 2-4
Modified Worksheet

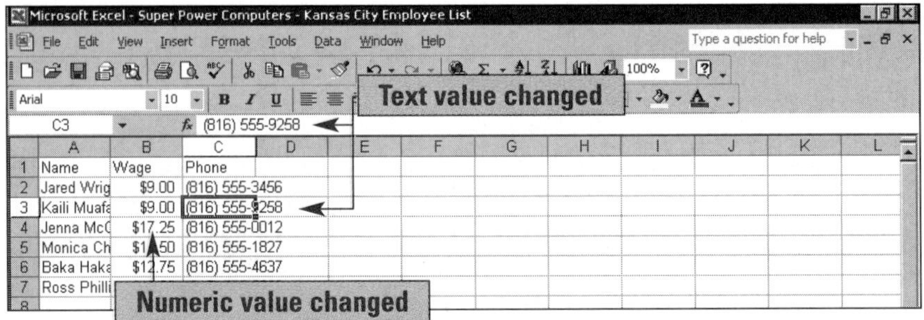

Clearing Cell Content

Sometimes you need to delete all of the contents in a cell. To clear cell content:

Step 1	***Drag***	to select cells A7:C7
Step 2	***Press***	the DELETE key

The contents of cell A7:C7 are deleted. In the next section you learn to use the Undo and Redo tools. Do *not* save your workbook at this point.

2.d Using Undo and Redo

The **Undo** command reverses your previous action or actions. The **Redo** command reinstates the action or actions you undid. You can Undo and Redo one action at a time, or you can select a number of actions to Undo and Redo from a list of up to 16 previous actions. To undo the last action, click the Undo button on the Standard toolbar. The Redo button is not active until you have used Undo. Click the Redo button to undo the last Undo command.

You realize that you changed the value in cell C3 by mistake. Rather than reentering the data, you can use Undo. To use the Undo and Redo commands:

Step 1	*Click*	the Undo button on the Standard toolbar

The contents of cells A7:C7 return.

Step 2	*Click*	the Redo button to change the value back again
Step 3	*Click*	the Undo button on the Standard toolbar to restore the contents again

You can use the Undo list to quickly Undo several commands at once. To use the Undo list:

Step 1	*Change*	the value in cell C4 to (816) 555-1200
Step 2	*Change*	the value in cell A4 to Lori Jones

You have performed two actions, both data entry. The Undo list allows you to select multiple actions to Undo.

Step 3	*Click*	the Undo button list arrow on the Standard toolbar
Step 4	*Move*	the pointer down the list, selecting the top two "Typing" actions
Step 5	*Click*	the second "Typing" action

Cells A4 and C4 return to their previous values. The Redo list functions in the same way as the Undo list.

CAUTION TIP

When you save a workbook, the Undo/Redo list starts over. You cannot reverse any action performed prior to the file save.

QUICK TIP

Press the CTRL + Z keys to Undo the last action. Press the CTRL +Y keys to Redo the last Undo action.

MENU TIP

Click the Undo command on the Edit menu to reverse your last action. Click the Redo or Repeat command on the Edit menu to reverse the previous Undo action.

Step 6	*Save*	the workbook

2.e Changing the Zoom Setting

MENU TIP

Click the Zoom command on the View menu to open the Zoom dialog box, and select the zoom percentage.

If you use a small monitor or worksheets containing a lot of data, it may be hard to read or see the data you want to see. The Zoom setting allows you to **zoom**, to increase or decrease, the viewable area of your worksheet. Zooming in magnifies cells, making them appear much larger. Zooming out makes cells appear smaller, allowing you to see more of the worksheet. You can zoom in to 400% or out to 10%. To zoom in on the worksheet:

Step 1	*Click*	the Zoom button list arrow [100%] on the Standard toolbar
Step 2	*Click*	200%

Your worksheet zooms in to 200%, or twice the default size. You can select any of the preset Zoom options, or key a custom Zoom setting.

Step 3	*Click*	in the Zoom button text box [200%] on the Standard toolbar
Step 4	*Key*	125
Step 5	*Press*	the ENTER key
Step 6	*Save*	the workbook

C

2.f Renaming a Sheet Tab

MOUSE TIP

You can rename a sheet tab by right-clicking the sheet tab, then clicking Rename.

An organized workbook is one in which information is logically grouped and easy to find. Each store's staff comprises sales representatives and technicians. By separating employee data for each group onto different sheet tabs, your workbook will be more organized. Naming each sheet tab makes it much easier to find the data. To name a sheet tab:

Step 1	*Double-click*	the Sheet1 sheet tab
Step 2	*Key*	Sales Reps

Step 3	***Press***	the ENTER key
Step 4	***Rename***	Sheet2 as Technicians

2.g Changing a Sheet Tab Color

To make it even easier to identify sheet tabs, you can color-code the tabs to make them stand out. To change a sheet tab color:

Step 1	***Right-click***	the Sales Reps sheet tab
Step 2	***Click***	Tab Color

MENU TIP

You can rename a sheet tab by clicking the Format menu, then clicking Rename on the Sheet submenu.

The Format Tab Color dialog box on your screen should look similar to Figure 2-5.

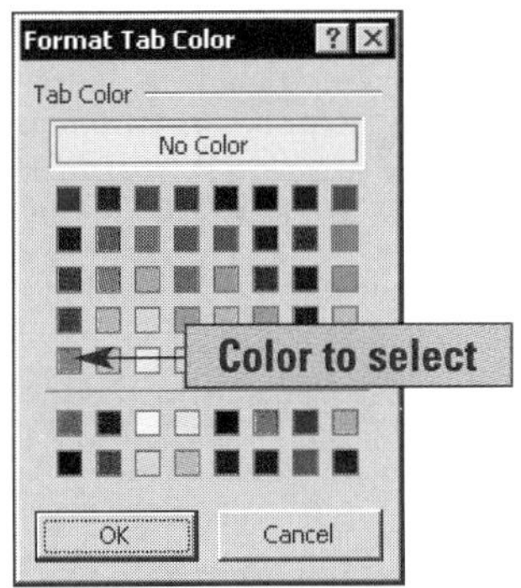

FIGURE 2-5
Format Color Tab

Step 3	***Click***	the pink color
Step 4	***Click***	OK
Step 5	***Change***	the Technicians sheet tab to light orange

Your screen should look similar to Figure 2-6.

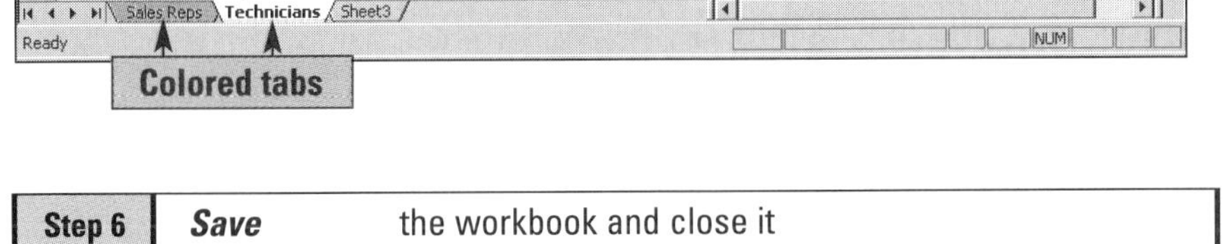

FIGURE 2-6
Workbook with Colored Sheet Tabs

Step 6	***Save***	the workbook and close it

The employee name list workbook for the new Kansas City store is ready to be used.

Summary

- You can create new, blank workbooks by clicking the Blank Workbook link in the task pane.
- You can create a new workbook based on an existing workbook by clicking the New command on the File menu, then clicking the Choose workbook link in the New Workbook task pane.
- You enter data by keying the information directly into the active cell or in the Formula Bar. You can enter text and numbers in a variety of formats.
- You edit data by keying new data in a cell, double-clicking a cell to edit directly in the cell, or pressing the F2 key and using the Formula Bar to edit the cell's contents.
- You can use the Undo list to quickly undo as many as 16 actions at once, including formatting, data entry, editing, and deletion.
- The Zoom command zooms a worksheet in and out, making it easier to read or display more data at one time.
- You can rename and recolor worksheet tabs to make it easier to find data.

Commands Review

Action	Menu Bar	Shortcut Menu	Toolbar	Task Pane	Keyboard
Create a new workbook	File, New	Right-click Null application window, click New		Blank workbook link in New Workbook task pane	CTRL + N ALT + F, N
Create a new workbook based on another workbook				Choose workbook link in New Workbook task pane	
Edit a cell					F2
Accept a cell entry					ENTER
Cancel a cell entry					ESC
Undo the previous action	Edit, Undo				CTRL + Z ALT + E, U
Redo an undo action	Edit, Redo				CTRL + Y ALT + E, R
Zoom	View, Zoom		100%		ALT + V, Z
Rename a worksheet tab	Format, Sheet, Rename	Right-click sheet tab, click Rename			ALT + O, H, R
Change a worksheet color tab	Format, Sheet, Tab Color	Right-click sheet, tab, click Tab Color			ALT + O, H, T

Concepts Review

Circle the correct answer.

1. To cancel an entry in a cell, press the:
[a] TAB key.
[b] ENTER key.
[c] ESC key.
[d] DELETE key.

2. To accept an entry in a cell:
[a] press the CTRL + ALT + ESC keys.
[b] stop keying and wait for the previous value to return.
[c] press the ESC key.
[d] press the ENTER key.

3. You can undo or redo:
[a] as many as 1 operation.
[b] as many as 10 operations.
[c] as many as 16 operations.
[d] an unlimited number of operations.

4. When you activate a cell containing data and begin keying new data, the new data:
[a] is added to the end of the old data.
[b] is added in front of the old data.
[c] is rejected since there is already data in the cell.
[d] replaces the old data.

5. Pressing the DELETE key when the insertion point is blinking in a cell or in the Formula Bar:
[a] deletes the entire value.
[b] deletes one character to the right.
[c] deletes one character to the left.
[d] does nothing.

6. Pressing the BACKSPACE key when the insertion point is blinking in a cell or in the Formula Bar:
[a] deletes the entire value.
[b] deletes one character to the right.
[c] deletes one character to the left.
[d] does nothing.

7. Which of the following values would be treated as a text value?
[a] 111-22-3333
[b] 11,122,333
[c] 111.22333
[d] $111,223.33

8. When you make a mistake while entering data, you should immediately:
[a] save the workbook.
[b] close the workbook without saving your changes.
[c] reopen the workbook.
[d] use the Undo command.

9. Which of the following is not an option when using the Zoom command?
[a] 200%
[b] 50%
[c] Selection
[d] 1%

10. The default action that occurs when you press the ENTER key when entering cell data is to:
[a] accept the entry and move the active cell down one.
[b] accept the entry and move the active cell to the left.
[c] discard the changes and revert the cell's contents back to the way they were.
[d] accept the entry and move the active cell to the right.

Circle **T** if the statement is true or **F** if the statement is false.

T F 1. The Undo command can undo any command in Excel.

T F 2. If you rename a sheet tab, you cannot change its color.

T F 3. To edit a cell entry, you must double-click it first.

T F 4. You cannot use the Undo command until you have first used the Redo command.

T F 5. You can zoom in to 1600% using the Zoom button on the Standard toolbar.

T F 6. When you create a new workbook from an existing workbook, a number is added to the end of the filename.

T F 7. Pressing the ESC key is a valid means of accepting an entry in a cell.

T F 8. The Cancel and Enter buttons do not appear on the Formula Bar until you are entering data in a cell.

T F 9. The insertion point appears while you are editing a cell to indicate where the next character you key will go.

T F 10. Using any of the navigation keys is a valid way of accepting data entry in a cell.

Skills Review 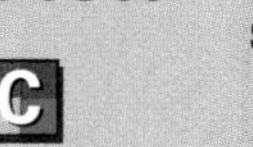

Exercise 1 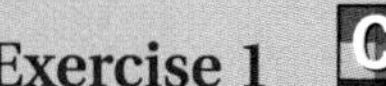

1. Create a new workbook and enter the data below on Sheet1. Enter the text "TIME SHEET" in cell A1. (*Hint:* Enter the dates with forward slashes and the times with colons. Use 24-hour clock times, as shown in the table.)

TIME SHEET		
Date	Start Time	End Time
5/10/2003	8:00	17:00
5/11/2003	8:05	16:30
5/12/2003	8:00	16:55

2. Save the workbook as *Time Sheet,* and print it.

3. Close the workbook.

Exercise 2 

1. Create a new workbook based on the *Employee Time Sheet* workbook located on the Data Disk.

2. Save the workbook as *Employee Time Sheet Revised.*

3. Change the value in cell A2 to your name.

4. Change the start time for 5/10/2003 to 8:15.

5. Change the end time for 5/12/2003 to 17:35.

6. Enter the following data in row 7:

5/13/2003 8:45 17:00

7. Save your changes, and print the worksheet.

8. Close the workbook.

Exercise 3

1. Create a new workbook based on the *Employee Time Sheet Revised* workbook that you created in Exercise 2.
2. Save the workbook as *Multiple Employees Time Sheets.*
3. Rename Sheet2 as "Lori Jones."
4. Rename Sheet3 as "Kaili Muafala."
5. Rename Sheet1 as your name.
6. Change the sheet tab color of each worksheet to a different color.
7. Save your changes, and print the worksheet.
8. Close the workbook.

Exercise 4 

1. Create a new workbook and enter the data below on Sheet1. Enter the label "CHECKBOOK TRANSACTIONS" in cell A1.

CHECKBOOK TRANSACTIONS			
Date	Description	Credit	Debit
10/12/2003	Paycheck	1542.90	
10/14/2003	Groceries		142.57
10/20/2003	Bonus	300.00	
10/21/2003	House payment		842.50

2. Save the workbook as *Checkbook Transactions,* and print it.
3. Close the workbook.

Exercise 5 

1. Create a new workbook based on the *Checkbook Transactions* workbook that you created in Exercise 4.
2. Change cell A1 to read "PERSONAL CHECKBOOK TRANSACTIONS."
3. Save the file as *Personal Checkbook Transactions.*
4. Delete the four transactions found in cells A3 through D6.
5. Save and print the workbook, then close it.

Exercise 6 

1. Create a new workbook and enter the data below on Sheet1. Enter the label "STATE CAPITALS" in cell A1.

STATE CAPITALS	
State	Capital City
Utah	Salt Lake City
Delaware	Dover
California	Los Angeles
Arizona	Tempe
New York	Albany
Florida	Miami
Texas	Dallas
Colorado	Denver

2. Rename Sheet1 as "Capitals."
3. Recolor the Capitals sheet tab to red.
4. Save the workbook as *State Capitals*, and print it.
5. Close the workbook.

Exercise 7  

1. Create a new workbook based on the *State Capitals* workbook that you created in Exercise 6.
2. Save the workbook as *Corrected State Capitals.*
3. Display the Web toolbar, if necessary, by clicking the View menu, pointing to Toolbars, then clicking Web.
4. Search the Web for a list of state capitals.
5. Correct any errors you find in the workbook.
6. Rename the Capitals sheet tab as "Corrected Capitals," and change the sheet tab color to green.
7. Save and print the workbook, then close it.

Exercise 8  

1. Use the Internet to search for movie times in your area.
2. Create a new workbook with column headings for "Movie Title," "Time," and "Theater."
3. Record the start times for at least five different movies you would like to see.
4. Save the workbook as *Movie Times*, and print it.
5. Close the workbook.

Case Projects

Project 1

You are the office manager of a small business. One of your duties is to keep track of the office supplies inventory. Create a workbook using fictitious data for at least 20 items. Include a column for each of the following: name of item, current amount in stock, and estimated price. Save the workbook as *Office Supplies Inventory*, and print and close it.

Project 2

As the payroll clerk at a college bookstore, you must calculate the hours worked by each student employee during the week. Create a new workbook based on the workbook *Employee Work Hours* located on the Data Disk. In row 1 of columns B, C, D, E, and F, list the days Monday through Friday. List the number of hours that each student works each day. Save the workbook as *Employee Work Hours Revised*, and then print and close it.

Project 3

You are a teacher who uses Excel to record student scores. Create a workbook containing 15 fictitious student names with five assignment columns and a total column. Record data indicating each student's scores for the five assignments. Switch to Sheet2 to enter data from another class. Enter 15 more student names and five assignment columns. Record new data as you did before. Rename Sheet1 as "Class 1" and Sheet2 as "Class 2." Change the color of the two sheet tabs to red. Save the workbook as *Student Scores*, and then print and close it.

Project 4

You are thinking of investing money in the stock market. Connect to the Internet and search the Web to find the most current stock price of five companies in which you are interested. Create a new workbook to record the company name, company stock ticker symbol, current share price, yesterday's share price, and the date. Rename the worksheet as "Stocks." Save the workbook as *Stock Prices*, and then print and close it.

Project 5  

You make purchasing recommendations for computer systems to your boss. Connect to the Internet and search the Web to obtain prices for systems offered by at least three different vendors. Create a new workbook to record the vendor name, Web address, system price, processor speed, amount of RAM, hard drive size, and monitor size. When you enter a Web address, Excel automatically formats it with blue text and underline. Rename the sheet tab with today's month and day; for example, Jan 4. Save the workbook as *Computer Prices*, and then print and close it.

Project 6  

You are planning a road trip. Connect to the Internet and search the Web to find the driving distance from your city to at least five other cities you would like to visit. (*Hint:* Search for the keywords "driving directions.") Create a new workbook to record the starting city, destination city, and driving distance. Save the workbook as *Road Trip*, and then print and close it.

Project 7

You are working on a statistics project. Over the next five days, count the number of students attending each of your classes. Create a new workbook. In row 1, enter the dates you used for your survey. In column A, enter the class names. Enter the data you collected each day for each class. Save the workbook as *Attendance Statistics*, and then print and close it.

Project 8

You are a runner training for a marathon. You keep track of your progress by recording the date, mileage, and time of your runs. Create a new workbook to record fictitious data. Rename Sheet1 as "Week 1," Sheet2 as "Week 2," and Sheet3 as "Week 3." Give each sheet tab a different color. On the Week 1 worksheet, record fictitious data for one week. Save the workbook as *Running Log*, and then print and close it.

Building Worksheets

Chapter Overview

Most worksheets do much more than store data. Data needs to be analyzed, calculated, and presented. To perform most of this work, functions and formulas work tirelessly behind the scenes, calculating and recalculating every time data is changed in your worksheets. Reorganizing worksheets by moving and copying data is a regular task. In this chapter, you learn how to accomplish this efficiently.

Learning Objectives

- Create and revise formulas
- Use cut, copy, and paste
- Copy formulas with relative, absolute, and mixed cell references
- Use basic functions
- Use the Insert Function dialog box
- Use 3-D references in formulas

Case profile

One of your duties at Super Power Computers is to calculate sales commissions and bonuses and send this information back to the store managers. Excel makes this simple by allowing you to use formulas to do the calculations. You can also use specialized Excel functions, which help you use your time more effectively. You can then copy and paste the formulas to quickly build your worksheets.

chapter three

3.a Creating and Revising Formulas

Formulas provide much of the true power of a spreadsheet. A **formula** is a mathematical expression that calculates a value. Some formulas are simple, such as those that add, subtract, multiply, and divide two or more values; for example, 2+2. Other formulas can be very complex and include a sequence of **functions**, or predefined formulas. All formulas require **operands**, which can be either values or references to cells containing values. Most formulas require **operators** to indicate the type of calculation that will take place. Common mathematical operators include + for addition, – for subtraction, * for multiplication, / for division, and ^ for exponentiation.

Following Formula Syntax and Rules of Precedence

Formulas follow a syntax. The **syntax** is the proper structure, or order, of the elements (operands and operators) in a formula. Excel follows the **rules of precedence**: it evaluates formulas from left to right, first evaluating any operations between parentheses, then any exponentiation, then multiplication and division, followed by addition and subtraction. Consider the following examples: 5+2*3 and (5+2)*3. In the first formula, 2*3 is calculated first and then added to 5, giving a result of 11. In the second example, 5+2 is calculated first and then multiplied by 3, giving a result of 21.

Entering Formulas

The real power of formulas lies in their ability to use cell references. Using cell references allows you to quickly change values, leaving the formula intact. Sales representatives at Super Power Computers are paid a commission based on the total sales. You need to calculate the sales commission for each employee. To enter a formula:

Step 1	***Open***	the *Super Power Computers - Bonus* workbook located on the Data Disk
Step 2	***Save***	the workbook as *Super Power Computers - Bonus Revised*

This workbook contains sales data from each of the Super Power Computer stores.

Step 3	***Activate***	cell D4 on the Store #1 worksheet

All formulas begin with an equal sign = to indicate to Excel that the following expression needs to be evaluated.

Step 4	*Key*	=c4*0.05

You do not have to capitalize column references. Excel performs this task for you automatically when you enter a formula.

Step 5	*Click*	the Enter button on the Formula Bar

This simple mathematical formula multiplies the value in cell C4 by 0.05 and displays the result, $1,726.55. The Formula Bar displays the formula, not the calculated result. Your screen should look similar to Figure 3-1.

FIGURE 3-1
Formula Displayed in the Formula Bar

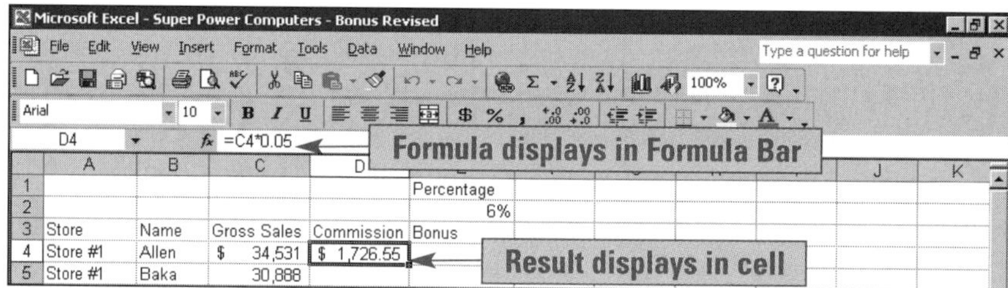

Editing Formulas Using the Formula Bar

Because Super Power Computers has had a good year, the sales commission has been increased to 6%. You can edit the formula to reflect this change. To edit a formula:

Step 1	*Verify*	that cell D4 is the active cell
Step 2	*Drag*	to select 5 in the Formula Bar
Step 3	*Key*	6
Step 4	*Press*	the ENTER key

Cell D4 displays the new result of the calculation, $2,071.86.

Step 5	*Save*	the workbook

QUICK TIP

The blue box that appears around cell C4 is called a **range finder**. It highlights cells that are referenced in a formula.

3.b Using Cut, Copy, and Paste

Moving and copying data helps you organize and prepare worksheets quickly. When data is moved, or **cut**, from a worksheet, it is removed from its original location and placed on the **Clipboard**, which holds data temporarily. To finish moving the data that you cut to another location, you **paste** it from the Clipboard. When data is **copied**, the original data remains in place and a copy of the data is placed on the Clipboard. Data that you cut or copy stays on the Clipboard until you cut or copy more data, or until you exit Excel.

Copying Data Using Copy and Paste

The formula you added to cell D4 needs to be copied for each employee. To copy data using copy and paste:

Step 1	***Activate***	cell D4
Step 2	***Click***	the Copy button on the Standard toolbar
Step 3	***Click***	cell D5
Step 4	***Click***	the Paste button list arrow on the Standard toolbar
Step 5	***Click***	Formulas

This is the default command if you simply click the Paste button. Clicking Values in the list would paste the value from cell D4 instead of the formula.

Step 6	***Press***	the ESC key to end the Copy command

The formula in the Formula Bar has changed to reflect that this cell is in row 5 instead of in row 4. In other words, the formula references cell C5 instead of cell C4.

Copying Data Using the Fill Handle

Using the fill handle, you can quickly copy the contents of a cell to adjacent cells. The fill handle is the small black square that appears in the lower-right corner of a selected cell. To copy a formula using the fill handle:

Step 1	***Activate***	cell D5, if necessary

CAUTION TIP

When you use the Paste button to create copies, you can make multiple copies of the selected cells. It is easy to forget that the Copy command remains active, however. Check the Paste button on the Standard toolbar. If this button appears in color, the Copy command is still active. The Excel status bar also will instruct you to select a destination cell if this command remains in effect.

MOUSE TIP

Click the Paste Options button that appears to the lower right of the pasted item to specify whether formatting is copied from the source cells or copied from the target cells.

> **MENU TIP**
>
> The Cut, Copy, and Paste commands are available on the Edit menu or a shortcut menu.

Step 2	***Drag***	the fill handle to cell D17

Make sure you drag only to cell D17 and not to cell D18.

Step 3	***Release***	the left mouse button

The formula is copied to cells D6:D17. Your screen should look similar to Figure 3-2.

FIGURE 3-2
Formulas Copied Using the Fill Handle

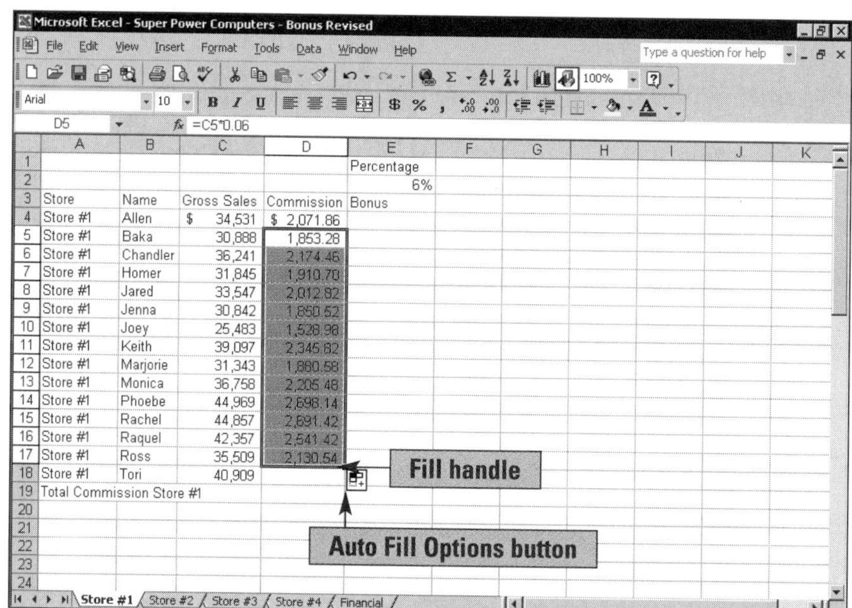

> **MOUSE TIP**
>
> Click the Auto Fill Options button that appears to the lower right of the filled cells to specify whether to copy the contents and formatting of the source cells, only the formatting, or only the contents with no formatting.

Moving Data Using Cut and Paste

When you cut data from cells, a flashing border surrounds the selected area. The status bar provides instructions about how to select a destination cell. The destination can be on another worksheet or even another open workbook. To move data by using cut and paste:

> **QUICK TIP**
>
> The shortcut key combination for cut is CTRL + X, for copy is CTRL + C, and for paste is CTRL + V.

Step 1	***Select***	the range E1:E2
Step 2	***Click***	the Cut button on the Standard toolbar
Step 3	***Activate***	cell F1
Step 4	***Click***	the Paste button on the Standard toolbar

The Cut command in Excel differs from that in other programs, such as Microsoft Word. Excel does not remove the selected text until you take one of two actions: (1) complete the move by selecting a destination and performing the Paste command or (2) press the DELETE key. If you press the DELETE key instead of completing the Paste operation, you do not place the data on the Clipboard; it is removed permanently. If you change your mind before pasting or deleting, press the ESC key to cancel the cut operation.

Using Drag-and-Drop to Cut, Copy, and Paste

Another way to move and copy data is to use **drag-and-drop**. To drag selected cells, click the selection border using the left mouse button. Hold the left mouse button down as you *drag* the cells to a new location. The mouse pointer changes to a four-headed arrow pointer, indicating the cells are being moved. Then *drop* them by releasing the left mouse button. To move data by using drag-and-drop:

Step 1	***Select***	cells A3:E19
Step 2	***Move***	the pointer over the border of your selection
Step 3	***Drag***	the range to cells A1:E17

CAUTION TIP

When moving data with drag-and-drop, Excel prompts you if the move will overwrite data. However, Excel does *not* warn you of this when copying using drag-and-drop, and it overwrites any data in the target cells.

A ScreenTip and a range outline guide you in moving the cells. Your screen should look similiar to Figure 3-3.

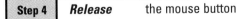

FIGURE 3-3
Dragging and Dropping to Copy Cells

Step 4	***Release***	the mouse button

TASK PANE TIP

If a task pane is already visible, you can click the Other Task Panes list arrow at the top of the open task pane, then click Clipboard to open the Office Clipboard.

You can use a similar process to copy data. To copy data using drag-and-drop:

Step 1	***Select***	cell D15
Step 2	***Press & hold***	the CTRL key
Step 3	***Move***	the pointer over the border of your selection
Step 4	***Observe***	the plus sign in the mouse pointer, indicating that you are creating a copy of the selected data
Step 5	***Drag***	the selection to cell D16
Step 6	***Release***	the mouse button and the CTRL key

Using the Office Clipboard to Paste Data

MOUSE TIP

To move data from one worksheet to another using drag-and-drop, press and hold the ALT key as you drag the range onto the new sheet tab. To copy data to another worksheet using drag-and-drop, press and hold the CTRL + ALT keys as you drag the range onto the new sheet tab.

Every time you cut or copy a piece of data, it replaces the data that was previously on the Clipboard. Office has its own Clipboard, called the Office Clipboard, which holds up to 24 items from any open application. You can then select the item you want and paste it into another Office document. You need to activate the Office Clipboard before you can collect cut or copied items on it. To activate the Office Clipboard:

Step 1	***Click***	Edit
Step 2	***Click***	Office Clipboard
Step 3	***Observe***	that the Clipboard task pane opens
Step 4	***Copy***	the range F1:F2

A portion of the selected data appears on the Clipboard, as shown in Figure 3-4.

FIGURE 3-4
Clipboard Items

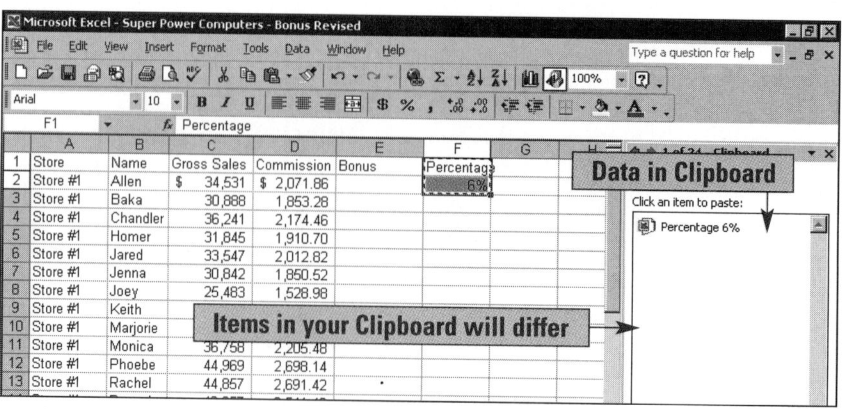

Step 5	*Activate*	cell F1 on the Store #2 sheet tab

The top item on the Office Clipboard is the last item cut or copied.

Step 6	*Point to*	Percentage 6% in the Clipboard task pane

A list arrow appears. If you click the list arrow, a submenu opens with Paste and Delete on it. Clicking the item on the Clipboard is the same as clicking the list arrow and then clicking Paste.

Step 7	*Click*	the Percentage 6% Clipboard item

A copy of your data is placed in cells F1:F2 on the Store #2 worksheet.

Step 8	*Click*	the Close button  on the Clipboard task pane title bar
Step 9	*Save*	the workbook

QUICK TIP

If you paste a new value into a cell referenced elsewhere in another formula, the #REF! error occurs. Rekey the cell reference in the formula to fix this.

MOUSE TIP

To paste all of the items on the Office Clipboard in one step, click the Paste All button. To delete all items from the Office Clipboard, click the Clear All button.

3.c Copying Formulas with Relative, Absolute, and Mixed Cell References

C

Excel uses three types of cell references: absolute, relative, and mixed. When you copy a formula containing a **relative reference**, the references change relative to the cell from which the formula is being copied. If cell C1 contains the formula =A1+B1 and is copied to cell D2, the formula changes to =B2+C2. Cell D2 is one row down and one row over from cell C1; the references B2 and C2 are correspondingly one row down and one row over from cells A1 and B1. When you copied the formulas in column D earlier in this chapter, you copied relative references, so the formulas were automatically updated to reflect the new row they were copied to.

When you need a formula to refer to a specific cell, no matter where the formula is copied, you use an **absolute reference**. Absolute cell references prefix the column and row with a dollar sign ($). A better way to set up the formula in column D is to use an absolute reference to cell F2, so that if the sales commission must be adjusted, it only has to be changed in one place. The formula for cell D2 would be **=C2*$F$2**.

QUICK TIP

To change a relative cell reference to an absolute or mixed reference, position the insertion point within the cell reference in the Formula Bar, then press the F4 key to cycle through the cell references.

When this formula is copied, the first, relative, reference changes, while the second, absolute, reference does not. To edit the formula and add an absolute reference:

Step 1	*Click*	the Store #1 sheet tab
Step 2	*Enter*	=C2*$F$2 in cell D2
Step 3	*Use*	the fill handle to copy cell D2 to cells D3:D16

The formula as well as its format is pasted into cell D3:D16. You don't want to copy the formatting.

Step 4	*Click*	the Auto Fill Options button  on the worksheet
Step 5	*Click*	Fill Without Formatting
Step 6	*Observe*	that the dollar signs disappear from cell D3:D16
Step 7	*Click*	cell D3

Note in the Formula Bar that the relative reference in the formula was correctly updated to the proper row number, while the absolute reference remained fixed on cell F2.

Step 8	*Save*	the workbook

In addition to absolute and relative references, Excel uses mixed references. A **mixed cell reference** maintains a reference to a specific row or column. For example, to maintain a reference to column A while allowing the row number to increment, use the mixed reference $A1. To maintain a reference to a specific row number while allowing the column letter to increment, use the mixed reference A$1.

C

3.d Using Basic Functions

Functions are predefined formulas that reduce complicated formulas to a function name and several required arguments or operands. An **argument** is some sort of data, usually numeric or text, that is supplied to a function. For example, to find the average of a series of numerical values, you must divide the sum by the number of values in the series. The AVERAGE function does this automatically when you supply the series of values as arguments. Arguments can be supplied to functions by keying the value in directly, or by using cell references. You can use formulas, or even other functions, as some or all of the arguments of a function.

To enter a function in a cell, you key the = sign, the name of the function, and then any required and/or optional arguments used by the function enclosed in parentheses. If the function is part of a longer formula, you key the = sign only at the beginning of the formula. The first function you learn about, the **SUM** function, uses the following syntax:

=SUM(number1, number2, ...)

Required arguments are listed in bold. Certain functions, such as the SUM function, allow you to supply as many optional arguments as you like, indicated by the ellipses (...).

Throughout this book function names are capitalized to distinguish them from other text. Function names are not actually case-sensitive, so =count, =Count, and =COUNT are all valid ways to enter the function name.

Using the SUM Function

The SUM function, which adds two or more values, is one of the most commonly used functions. You need to add the total amount to be paid in sales commissions. To start keying the SUM function:

Step 1	***Activate***	cell D17
Step 2	***Key***	=SUM(

The Argument ScreenTip appears with the syntax of the formula you've started entering. You can enter individual values separated by commas, enter a range, or simply select cells. You select a range of cells.

Step 3	***Drag***	to select cells D2:D16

Your screen should look similar to Figure 3-5. The range D2:D16 is the number1 argument of the SUM function.

FIGURE 3-5
Using the SUM Function

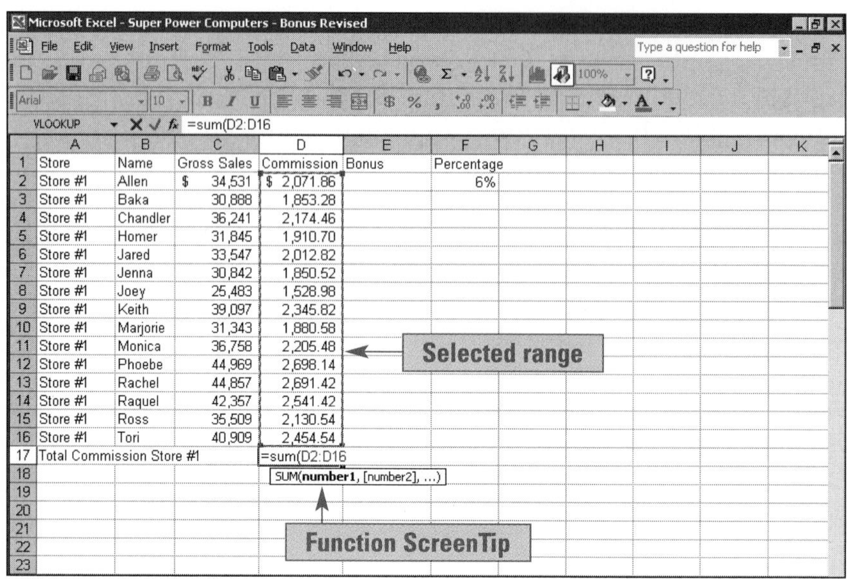

	A	B	C	D	E	F
1	Store	Name	Gross Sales	Commission	Bonus	Percentage
2	Store #1	Allen	$ 34,531	$ 2,071.86		6%
3	Store #1	Baka	30,888	1,853.28		
4	Store #1	Chandler	36,241	2,174.46		
5	Store #1	Homer	31,845	1,910.70		
6	Store #1	Jared	33,547	2,012.82		
7	Store #1	Jenna	30,842	1,850.52		
8	Store #1	Joey	25,483	1,528.98		
9	Store #1	Keith	39,097	2,345.82		
10	Store #1	Marjorie	31,343	1,880.58		
11	Store #1	Monica	36,758	2,205.48		
12	Store #1	Phoebe	44,969	2,698.14		
13	Store #1	Rachel	44,857	2,691.42		
14	Store #1	Raquel	42,357	2,541.42		
15	Store #1	Ross	35,509	2,130.54		
16	Store #1	Tori	40,909	2,454.54		
17	Total Commission Store #1			=sum(D2:D16		

QUICK TIP

Need help in a hurry? Key a question in the Ask A Question Box located on the menu bar.

Step 4	***Click***	the Enter button on the Formula Bar

The total commission for Store #1, $32,350.56, appears in cell D17. Note in the Formula Bar that the end parenthesis was automatically added when you accepted the entry. If you want to sum the values in a second range, separate each range with a comma. For example, to sum the ranges A3:D3 and A14:D14, the SUM function would be written as =SUM(A3:D3, A14:D14).

Entering Functions Using the AutoSum Command

To quickly insert commonly used functions, you can use the AutoSum button on the Standard toolbar. When you use the AutoSum button, Excel inserts the selected function and scans cells above and to the left for arguments. If it detects a continuous series of cells containing values, the reference is selected and added as an argument. To enter the SUM function using the AutoSum button:

Step 1	***Click***	the Store #2 sheet tab
Step 2	***Click***	cell D17
Step 3	***Click***	the AutoSum button list arrow Σ on the Standard toolbar

Five common functions are listed on the AutoSum button list.

Step 4	*Click*	Sum

The range D2:D16 is automatically selected, and the function =SUM(D2:D16) is inserted in cell D17.

Step 5	*Press*	the ENTER key
Step 6	*Observe*	that the result, $35,396.04, appears in cell D17
Step 7	*Save*	the workbook

3.e Using the Insert Function Dialog Box

Excel provides many more functions in addition to the five listed on the AutoSum button. The Insert Function dialog box helps you enter values or cell references for each of the required arguments in the correct order. For convenience, Excel divides functions into categories, such as statistical, date and time, and financial. In this section you preview a few of the many functions available.

Using the Date Function DATE

Date and time values are calculated in Excel by using special values called **serial numbers**. A value of 1 represents the first day that Excel can use in calculations, January 1, 1900. Hours, minutes, and seconds are portions of a day, so 12:00 PM is calculated using a value of .5. Most of the time, you enter the actual date, such as 1/1/1900, and Excel hides the serial value by formatting the cell with a date or time format. At times you may need to convert a given date to its serial number. For example, you need to update your workbook every 60 days, so you want to add the update date to the workbook. You can do this by using the DATE function to change the date to its serial value, and then adding 60 to the result. The **DATE** function returns the serial number value of a date. Its syntax is as follows:

=DATE(year, month, day)

The required arguments, year, month, and day, must be supplied as individual values. To calculate this date using the DATE function:

Step 1	*Activate*	cell C22 on the Store #1 worksheet

MOUSE TIP

You can open the Insert Function dialog box by clicking More Functions on the AutoSum button list.

Step 2	*Key*	Updated
Step 3	*Press*	the TAB key
Step 4	*Click*	the Insert Function button on the Formula Bar

The Insert Function dialog box displays a list of Function categories and function names. Your dialog box should look similar to Figure 3-6.

FIGURE 3-6
Insert Function Dialog Box

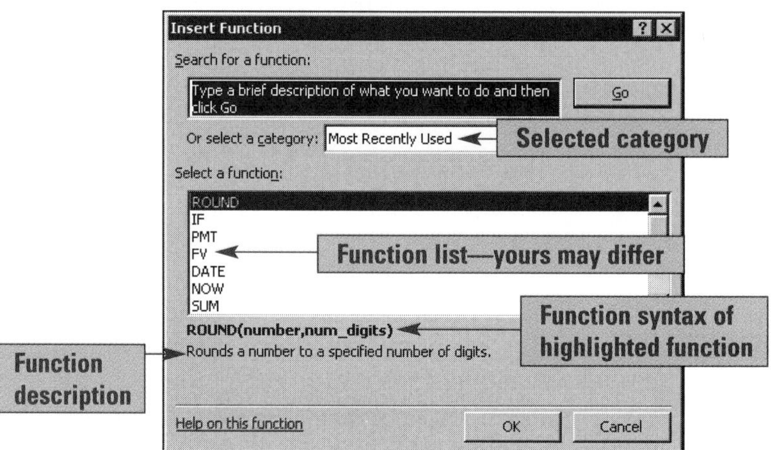

Step 5	*Click*	the Or select a category: list arrow
Step 6	*Click*	Date & Time

The Select a function: list changes to an alphabetical list of all the functions in the Date & Time category.

Step 7	*Click*	Date in the Select a function: list
Step 8	*Click*	OK

The Function Arguments dialog box opens, and guides you through the entry of each argument of the selected function. A description of the function is located in the middle of the dialog box. Each text box is an argument of the function. If the name of the argument is in bold, then it is a required argument. The Year text box is selected, as indicated by the blinking insertion point. A description of the selected argument appears below the function description. See Figure 3-7.

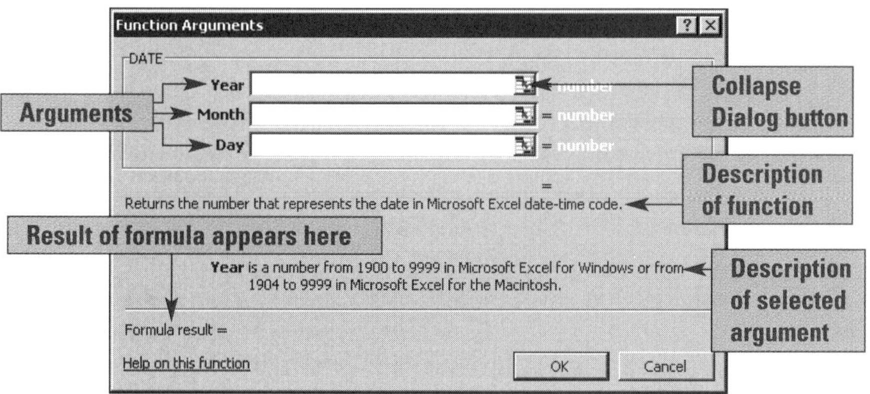

FIGURE 3-7
Function Arguments

Step 9	***Key***	2003 in the Year text box
Step 10	***Press***	the TAB key to move to the Month text box
Step 11	***Key***	5 in the Month text box
Step 12	***Press***	the TAB key to move to the Day text box
Step 13	***Key***	1 in the Day box
Step 14	***Observe***	the formula result at the bottom of the dialog box
Step 15	***Click***	OK

Next, you need to add 60 to the result of the function. To add a formula to a function:

Step 1	***Press***	the F2 key
Step 2	***Key***	+60
Step 3	***Press***	the ENTER key

The result of the formula, 6/30/2003, appears in cell D22.

Using the Financial Function PMT

Financial functions are used to calculate values for all types of investments and loans, as well as to calculate depreciation of assets. The **PMT** function is used to calculate the payment of a loan based on constant payments and a constant interest rate.

Luis Alvarez, the owner of the Super Power Computers chain of stores, is considering borrowing some money to expand its headquarters, and he wants to get his managers' opinions on the loan, so you want to include

QUICK TIP

The name of the function you are working with—in this case, DATE—appears in the Name box in the worksheet.

MOUSE TIP

If you cannot see the cells you want to add as arguments, click the Collapse Dialog button in the text box of the selected argument to shrink the dialog box to a single line. Click the button again to restore the dialog box to its normal size.

CAUTION TIP

When using many financial functions, it is important that the *rate* and *nper* arguments "agree." A loan at 8.5% usually means that you are paying 8.5% interest on the loan over the course of the entire year—not monthly. Because you usually make monthly payments on a loan, the *nper* argument is most likely expressed in months. For a three-year loan, the number of periods, or payments, is 36. To calculate the interest correctly, you must show the interest rate in months, not years. Using a formula, you can divide the interest rate by 12 to bring it into agreement with the number of periods, or payments, on the loan.

this information in the workbook. You need to calculate how much monthly payments on the loan will be. The syntax of the PMT function is:

=PMT(rate,nper,pv,fv,type)

Rate is the interest rate, *nper* is the total number of payments for the loan, and *pv* is the present value of the loan; that is, how much is owed. *Fv* (future value) and *type* (whether the payment is due at the beginning of the month or at the end of the month) are both optional arguments because they have default values of 0 for *fv* and 0 for *type*, indicating payment will be made at the end of the month. To use the PMT function:

Step 1	***Activate***	cell E3 on the Financial worksheet
Step 2	***Click***	the Insert Function button on the Formula Bar
Step 3	***Click***	the Or select a category: list arrow
Step 4	***Click***	Financial
Step 5	***Double-click***	PMT in the Select a function: list

Instead of keying arguments into the Function Arguments dialog box, you can click cells on the worksheet.

Step 6	***Drag***	the Function Arguments dialog box title bar to move the dialog box so you can see row 3
Step 7	***Click***	cell A3

Because the interest rate is expressed in terms of a year, you must divide the rate by 12, and supply this result as the rate argument.

Step 8	***Key***	/12
Step 9	***Press***	the TAB key to move to the Nper text box
Step 10	***Click***	cell B3
Step 11	***Press***	the TAB key to move to the Pv text box
Step 12	***Click***	cell C3
Step 13	***Click***	OK

The monthly payment for this loan is calculated at $3,945.94. It appears in parentheses and in red because it is a negative value (an expense to the company). This is common accounting notation.

Using the Logical Function IF

Logical functions test data using a true/false evaluation. Think of a true/false evaluation is as a yes/no choice. For example, bonuses are paid to a Super Power Computer's sales representative if his or her sales are greater than $37,500. The question "Are the total sales for this employee greater than or equal to $37,500?" has only two answers, "Yes" or "No."

The **IF** function is used to evaluate whether a given statement is true. If the logical test is true, the function returns one value; otherwise, it returns a different value. The IF function has the following syntax:

=IF(logical_test,value_if_true,value_if_false)

The first argument identifies the logical test. The second argument indicates the formula's value if the logical test is true. The last argument identifies the formula's value if the logical test is false. Sometimes it is easier to create logical functions by writing them in statement form first:

If sales are greater than or equal to 37,500, **then** the bonus is 500, **else** (otherwise) the result is 0.

Now, you can put your sentence into something resembling function syntax:

=IF(sales>=37500, then bonus is 500, else bonus is 0)

Finally, create your formula using named ranges, cell references, or values. To use the IF function:

Step 1	***Activate***	cell E2 on the Store #1 worksheet
Step 2	***Click***	the Insert Function button on the Formula Bar
Step 3	***Double-click***	the IF function in the Logical category
Step 4	***Key***	C2>=37500 in the Logical_test text box
Step 5	***Press***	the TAB key
Step 6	***Key***	500
Step 7	***Press***	the TAB key
Step 8	***Key***	0
Step 9	***Click***	OK

Because the value in cell C2 ($34,531) is less than 37500, the value of cell E2 evaluates to 0.

Step 10	***Copy***	the formula in cell E2 to cells E3:E16

MENU TIP

To open the Insert Function dialog box, click the Function command on the Insert menu.

QUICK TIP

If you see #NUM! in a cell, then you used an unacceptable argument in a function requiring a numeric argument. This error also arises if a formula produces a number too large (greater than $1*10^{307}$) or too small (less than $-1*10^{307}$) to be represented in Excel.

3.f Using 3-D References in Formulas

Cell references are used in formulas to ensure that when a data value changes, the formula recalculates and displays the new result automatically. The simple formula =A1+B1, for example, links to cells A1 and B1 to calculate the sum of the values contained in those cells. **Linking** formulas link to the cells on another worksheet. The linked formulas maintain a connection to the worksheet that holds the original formula.

In complex workbooks with many worksheets, you may need to perform calculations that use cell references from several worksheets. This type of cell reference is called a **3-D reference**. 3-D references span not only columns and rows, but worksheets as well.

You need to find the minimum and maximum commissions for all four stores. The syntax of the MAX and MIN functions is similar to that of the SUM function:

=MAX(number1, *number2, ...*)

=MIN(number1, *number2, ...*)

To add the MAX function to a worksheet using 3-D references:

Step 1	***Click***	cell B19 on the Store #1 worksheet
Step 2	***Key***	Maximum commission
Step 3	***Press***	the TAB key twice
Step 4	***Click***	the AutoSum button list arrow Σ on the Standard toolbar
Step 5	***Click***	Max
Step 6	***Press & hold***	the SHIFT key
Step 7	***Click***	the Store #4 sheet tab

This selects all the worksheets from Store #1 to Store #4.

Step 8	***Select***	the range D2:D16

In the formula, you see the 3-D reference =MAX('Store #1:Store #4'!D2:E16). The worksheet names are enclosed by apostrophes (') and separated from the cell references by an exclamation point (!).

Step 9	*Click*	the Enter button on the Formula Bar

The result, 2936.46, is correctly identified as the highest value among the selected cells on the four store worksheets.

To add the MIN function to a worksheet using 3-D reference:

Step 1	*Click*	cell B20 on the Store #1 worksheet
Step 2	*Key*	Minimum commission
Step 3	*Press*	the TAB key twice
Step 4	*Click*	the AutoSum button list arrow on the Standard toolbar
Step 5	*Click*	Min
Step 6	*Press & hold*	the SHIFT key
Step 7	*Click*	the Store #4 sheet tab
Step 8	*Select*	the range D2:D16
Step 9	*Click*	the Enter button on the Formula Bar

The result, 1506.66, is correctly identified as the lowest value among the selected cells on the four store worksheets.

Step 10	*Save*	the workbook and close it

Your workbook is ready for distribution to the four stores.

QUICK TIP

The functions presented in this chapter are only a small sample of the many functions offered in Excel. Take time to explore the functions using the Insert Function dialog box, or use Ask A Question Box to look up detailed help about any function you want to learn more about.

Summary

- You can create formulas to calculate values. Formulas can use cell references to update information whenever the referenced cell's data changes.
- All formulas have a syntax; when Excel calculates results, it follows the rules of precedence.
- Functions are built-in formulas used to perform a variety of calculations. Most functions require arguments, which you can supply as values, cell references, or even formulas.
- You use the cut, copy, and paste operations to move or copy information.
- Use the Office Clipboard to store up to 24 items. These items can be pasted into other workbooks, or even into documents created in other applications.
- You can drag selection borders to move data. Press the CTRL key and drag selection borders to copy data. Press the ALT key to move or copy data to another worksheet.
- Relative cell references change relative to the source cell when copied.
- Absolute cell references always refer to the same cell when a formula is copied. Absolute cell references use the dollar sign ($) in front of the column and row identifiers: $A$1.
- Mixed cell references always refer to a specific row or column when the formula is copied. Mixed references use the dollar sign ($) in front of either the row or column identifier: $A1 or A$1.
- Insert Function and the Function Palette work together as a function wizard, providing helpful information to guide you through the construction of complex formulas.
- Basic functions, such as SUM, MAX, and MIN, can be inserted by using the AutoSum button.
- Date and time functions, including DATE, allow you to perform calculations using dates.
- Financial functions, such as PMT, allow you to calculate values for investments and loans.
- Logical functions, such as IF, test data using a true/false evaluation. The calculated result depends on the result of the evaluation.
- Formulas can use 3-D cell references—cell references from other worksheets or other workbooks.

Commands Review

Action	Menu Bar	Shortcut Menu	Toolbar	Task Pane	Keyboard
Cut	Edit, Cut	Cut			CTRL + X ALT + E, T
Copy	Edit, Copy	Copy			CTRL + C ALT + E, C
Paste	Edit, Paste	Paste		Click item in palette in Office Clipboard task pane	CTRL + V ALT + E, P
Insert common functions using AutoSum			Σ		
Insert Function	Insert, Function		fx		SHIFT + F3 ALT + I, F
Cycle reference type between absolute, mixed, and relative					F4

Concepts Review

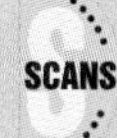

Circle the correct answer.

1. To copy a selection while dragging, press and hold the:
[a] SHIFT key.
[b] END key.
[c] CTRL key.
[d] ALT key.

2. To copy a selection to another worksheet, press and hold the:
[a] SHIFT + CTRL keys.
[b] CTRL + ALT keys.
[c] SHIFT + ALT keys.
[d] CTRL + SPACEBAR keys.

3. Which of the following cell references is an absolute reference?
[a] A1
[b] $A1
[c] $A$1
[d] A$1

4. Copying the formula =A1+B1 from cell C1 to cell E3 would make what change to the formula?
[a] =A1+B1
[b] =A1+C3
[c] =B3+C1
[d] =C3+D3

5. Copying the formula =$A1+B$2 from cell C1 to cell E3 would make what change to the formula?
[a] =$A3+D$2
[b] =$A1+B$2
[c] =$A2+E$2
[d] =$A3+C$2

6. Identify the type of reference for the row and column of the following cell reference: X$24.
[a] absolute, absolute
[b] absolute, relative
[c] relative, absolute
[d] relative, relative

7. The DATE function returns the:
[a] serial value of a date.
[b] current date.
[c] current time.
[d] current system status.

8. The proper syntax for an IF formula is:
[a] =IF(condition,value_if_false,value_if_true).
[b] =IF(condition,value_if_true,value_if_false).
[c] =IF(value_if_true,value_if_false,condition).
[d] =IF(value_if_false,value_if_true,condition).

9. Which of the following formulas returns the value 60?
[a] =10*2+4
[b] =(10*2)+4
[c] =10*(2+4)
[d] =10+(2*4)

10. All formulas start with:
[a] @.
[b] the keyword "Formula".
[c] =.
[d] $$.

Circle **T** if the statement is true or **F** if the statement is false.

T F 1. The Formula Arguments dialog box displays the results of the formula as you add values for each of the arguments.

T F 2. A good way to create a logical formula is to write it out in statement form first.

T F 3. Skipping optional arguments in a function is acceptable.

T F 4. Changing the order of required arguments in a function is acceptable, as long as they are all there.

T F 5. The formula =(5+5)*2 gives the same result as the formula =5+5*2.

T F 6. Formulas are only updated when you press the F9 key.

T F 7. You can use the F4 key to cycle through cell reference options when editing formulas.

T F 8. As soon as you cut data from a worksheet, it disappears, whether you paste it somewhere else or not.

T F 9. A cut-and-paste operation is the same as dragging a selection border to another location.

T F 10. The Office Clipboard provides access to only the last eight items copied or cut.

Several of the following Skills Review exercises introduce functions not covered in the chapter. Use the Insert Function tool to guide you through the use of new functions. For additional information, use online Help.

Skills Review

SCANS

Exercise 1

1. Create a new workbook.
2. Enter "Test Scores" in cell A1.
3. Using the values 100, 121, 135, 117, 143, 122, 125, 118, 111, and 135, use statistical functions (*Hint:* check the Statistical function category) to perform the following tasks:
   a. Determine the minimum value.
   b. Determine the maximum value.
   c. Find the average value by opening the Insert Function dialog box, double-clicking Average in the Statistical category, dragging to select the numbers you entered, then clicking OK.

d. Find the 50th percentile by opening the Insert Function dialog box, double-clicking Percentile in the Statistical category, dragging to select the numbers you entered, typing 0.5 in the K box, then clicking OK.

e. Count the number of items by opening the Insert Function dialog box, double-clicking Count in the Statistical category, dragging to select the numbers you entered, then clicking OK.

4. Save the workbook as *Test Scores*. Print and close the workbook.

Exercise 2 

1. Create a new workbook.
2. Enter "Enter a Date:" in cell A2.
3. Enter "Is it a Friday?" in cell A4.
4. The WEEKDAY function, in the Date & Time category, returns a number indicating a day of the week for a given date, 1 = Sunday, 2 = Monday, and so on. In cell A5, create a formula using an IF statement that determines whether any given date since January 1, 1900 in cell A3 is a Friday. If the date is a Friday, the formula should return "Yes." If not, the formula should return "No."
5. Enter several dates in cell A3 until you find one that is a Friday. Cell A5 should show the value "Yes."
6. Save the workbook as *Day Finder*. Print and close the workbook.

Exercise 3 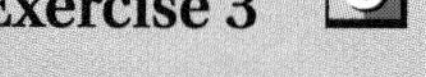

1. Create a new workbook.
2. Enter "The Quick Brown Fox" in cell A2.
3. In cell A3, enter "Jumped Over the Lazy Dog."
4. Use text functions to perform the following tasks:

a. Join the content of cells A2 and A3 in cell A6. To do this, insert the CONCATENATE function from the Text category. Click cell A2 as the first argument, key " " (quotation mark, a space, and another quotation mark) as the second argument, then click cell A3 as the third argument.

b. In cell A8, convert the value of cell A6 to uppercase. To do this, insert the UPPER function from the Text category, and click cell A6 as the argument.

c. In cell A10, locate the character position of the letter "Q" in cell A6. To do this, insert the FIND function from the Text category, enter "Q" as the first argument, and click cell A6 as the second argument.

5. Save the workbook as *Text Practice*. Print and close the workbook.

Exercise 4 

1. Open the *Depreciation Calculator* workbook located on the Data Disk.
2. In cell B12, a financial function called SLN has been entered using relative cell references. This formula was copied to cells C12:K12, resulting in errors. Change the cell references in cell B12 to absolute references.
3. Copy the revised formula in cell B12 to cells C12:K12.
4. In cell L12, total cells B12:K12.
5. Save the workbook as *Depreciation Calculator Revised*. Print and close the workbook.

Exercise 5 

1. Create a new workbook.
2. Enter "Year" in cell A1 and "Roman" in cell B1.
3. Enter the following numbers in column A: 1900, 1941, 1999, 2000, 2010.
4. In column B, use the ROMAN function from the Math & Trig category to convert the numbers to ROMAN numerals by using the cells in column A as the argument.
5. Save the workbook as *Roman Conversion.* Print and close the workbook.

Exercise 6 

1. Create a new workbook.
2. Using the RAND function in the Math & Trig category, generate five random numbers in column A. The RAND function takes no arguments, so simply enter the function in each cell.
3. In column B, create a formula to generate whole numbers between 1 and 100 using the RAND and ROUND functions. To do this, open the Insert Functions dialog box, double-click the ROUND function in the Math & Trig category, type RAND()*100 in the Number argument box, and enter 0 as the Num_digits argument.
4. Save the workbook as *Random Numbers.* Print and close the workbook.

Exercise 7 

1. Enter the following data in a new workbook on the Sheet1 worksheet:

Employee Name	Current Wage	Proposed Wage	Increase per Month
Mark Havlaczek	$7.50	$8.00	
Roberta Hernandez	$8.25	$9.00	
Loren Mons	$12.00	$13.00	
Total Increase (all stores)			

2. Rename the Sheet1 worksheet to "Downtown Store."
3. Enter the following data on the Sheet2 worksheet:

Employee Name	Current Wage	Proposed Wage	Increase per Month
Eric Wimmer	$8.25	$8.85	
Micah Anderson	$7.75	$8.50	
Allyson Smith	$9.50	$10.35	

4. Rename the Sheet2 worksheet "Uptown Store."
5. On the Downtown Store worksheet, create a formula in cell D2 that calculates how much *more* each employee will make per month as a result of the proposed wage increase. Assume that each employee works 168 hours per month. (*Hint:* Subtract the Current Wage from the Proposed Wage, then multiply the result by 168.)
6. Copy the formula to cells D3:D4.

7. Copy the formulas in cells D2:D4 on the Downtown Store worksheet to the same cells on the Uptown Store worksheet.
8. In cell D5 on the Downtown Store worksheet, "enter = sum(".
9. Press and hold the SHIFT key, then click the Uptown Store worksheet.
10. Select cells D2:D4 and press the ENTER key.
11. Save the workbook as *Proposed Wage Increase*. Print and close the workbook.

Exercise 8 

1. Open the *Proposed Wage Increase* workbook you created in Exercise 7.
2. Using drag-and-drop, move cells D1:D5 on the Downtown Store worksheet to G1:G5.
3. Using cut and paste, move cells C1:C4 on the Downtown Store worksheet to E1:E4.
4. Using your choice of move commands, move cells B1:B4 on the Downtown Store worksheet to cells C1:C4.
5. Repeat Steps 2 through 4 on the Uptown Store worksheet.
6. On the Downtown Store worksheet, activate cell G5.
7. Change the cell reference D2:D4 in the Formula Bar to G2:G4.
8. Save the workbook as *Proposed Wage Increase Revised*. Print and close the workbook.

Case Projects

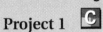

Project 1

You work for an insurance company processing accident claims. One of your tasks is to determine how many days have elapsed between the date of an accident and the date that a claim was filed. You know that Excel stores dates as numbers, so you must be able to create a formula that calculates this information. Use the Ask A Question Box to look up more information about how Excel keeps track of dates. Can you figure out the trick? Create a workbook with column labels for Accident Date, Claim Filed Date, and Elapsed Days. Enter two fictitious accident dates and two corresponding claim filed dates. Save the workbook as *Claim Lapse Calculator,* and then print and close it.

Project 2

You are a college entrance administrator. To gain admittance to your school, a prospective student must score in the 80th percentile on the school's entrance exam. In a new workbook, use the RAND function in the Math & Trig category to generate a list of 100 random test scores between 30 and 100. Once you've generated the random scores, copy and paste the values over the formulas in the scores column to keep them from changing. (*Hint:* Use Copy, Paste Special.) Use statistical functions to find the average test score, the median test score, and the 80th percentile of the scores. Use an IF function with the PERCENTILE function to display "Yes" if the score is higher than the 80th percentile, or "No" if the score is lower than the 80th percentile. Save the workbook as *College Entrance Exam Scores,* and then print and close it.

Project 3 

Connect to the Internet and search the Web to locate a timeline showing major events of the twentieth century. Create a workbook to record the date and a description of the event. Include at least one event from each decade of the twentieth century. Do not include more than three events from any decade. Save the workbook as *20th Century Timeline,* and then print and close it.

Project 4 

Connect to the Internet and search the Web to locate information about current events. Create a workbook to list the date(s) of the event, the place, and a brief description of the event. Save the workbook as *Current Events*, and then print and close it.

Project 5 

The CONVERT function is used to convert units of measurement from one system to another. You work as a lab technician in a bioengineering firm, and you need to convert temperatures from Fahrenheit to Celsius and to Kelvin. Create a workbook with 10 Fahrenheit temperatures in column A. In column B, use the CONVERT function to convert the temperatures to Celsius. In column C, convert from Celsius to Kelvin. Save the workbook as *Temperature Conversion*, and print and close it. (*Hint:* If the CONVERT function is not available, enable it by clicking the Tools menu, then clicking Add-Ins. Click the Analysis ToolPak check box, then click OK.)

Project 6 

You are considering a loan for $8,000 to buy a car. The loan will be paid back in 36 months at an interest rate of 6.5%. Calculate the monthly payment using the PMT function. Then, calculate the amount of interest and principal for each payment of the loan using the IPMT and PPMT functions. Save the workbook as *Car Loan Payments*, and then print and close it.

Project 7

Use the Ask A Question Box to locate and print a list of conversion units.

Project 8 

You are the personnel manager of a large bookstore. Each employee is given one week (five days) of vacation after he or she has been employed for at least six months (180 days). After that time, one day of vacation is added for every 45 days the employee works. Create a new workbook that will calculate the number of vacation days an employee has earned by subtracting the employee's hire date from today's date. (*Hint:* Use the TODAY function to automatically insert today's date.) Save the workbook as *Holiday Calculator*, and then print and close it.

Excel 2002

Enhancing Worksheets

Chapter Overview

Worksheets hold and process a lot of data. The goal of well-designed worksheets is to provide information in a clear, easy-to-read fashion. Thoughtful application of formatting styles can enhance the appearance of your worksheets on-screen and in printed documents. In this chapter, you explore how to format worksheets and cell data, and how to filter a list of data so that only relevant data appears. You also learn to extend the power of pasting far beyond simply copying data from one location to another.

Case profile

One of your jobs at Super Power Computers is to prepare last year's quarterly sales reports for distribution. The workbook must be easy to use and logically present the information so that company managers can quickly summarize the data and report to the president.

Learning Objectives

- Create worksheet and column titles
- Format cells, rows, and columns
- Use Paste Special
- Define and apply styles
- Manipulate rows, columns, and cells
- Filter lists using AutoFilter

chapter four

4.a Creating Worksheet and Column Titles

Titles provide a clear indication of what type of information can be found on the worksheet. You can add titles to a worksheet or column to indicate the type of information in each column.

Merging and Splitting Cells

To add visual impact, titles are often centered at the top of a worksheet. To do this quickly, you can use the Merge and Center command. To merge cells and create a worksheet title:

Step 1	***Open***	the *Super Power Computers - Quarterly Sales Report 2002* workbook on the Data Disk
Step 2	***Save***	The workbook as *Super Power Computers - Quarterly Sales Report 2002 Revised*

This workbook contains a summary of 2002 sales on the Sales Summary worksheet. The Source Data worksheet contains the raw data from the stores. The error message ####### indicates that a numerical value is too long to display using the current column width. You increase the width of the column later in this chapter.

Step 3	***Select***	the range A1:F1
Step 4	***Click***	the Merge and Center button on the Formatting toolbar

CAUTION TIP

If you use the Merge and Center command on multiple cells that contain data, all the data will be lost except that in the upper-left cell in the selected area.

The selected cells are merged into a single cell whose cell reference is the cell in the upper-left corner of the selection—in this case, cell A1—and the contents of cell A1 are centered in the new cell.

Step 5	***Repeat***	Steps 3 and 4 twice to merge and center cells A2 and A3 across the ranges A2:F2 and A3:F3

You didn't mean to center the data in cell A3.

Step 6	***Click***	cell A3
Step 7	***Click***	the Merge and Center button on the Formatting toolbar

The data in cell A3 is no longer centered across cells A3:F3. Your worksheet should look similar to Figure 4-1.

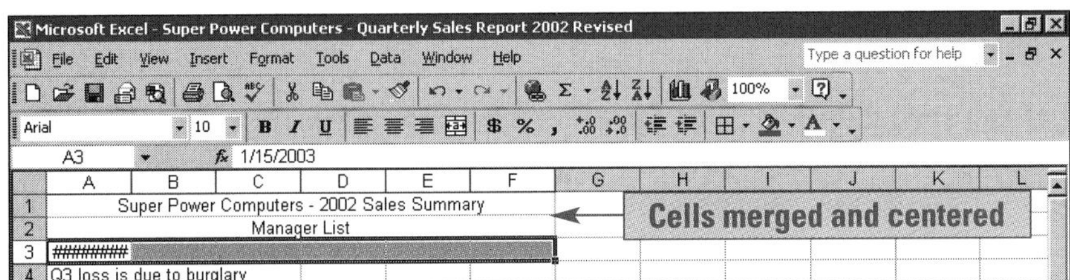

FIGURE 4-1
Merge and Center Titles

Using AutoFill to Create Column Titles

The **AutoFill** command creates a series of values. AutoFill can automatically increment numerical values, cells containing a mixture of text and numbers, days of the week, months of the year, and even custom series you define. To use AutoFill to add column labels:

Step 1	***Activate***	cell B5
Step 2	***Move***	the pointer over the fill handle
Step 3	***Drag***	the fill handle to cell E5

MENU TIP

Not all fill options are available when you drag to use the AutoFill feature. To see additional AutoFill options, use the Edit menu, Fill, Series command to open the Series dialog box.

As you drag the fill handle, a ScreenTip displays the new values being added. Your screen should look similar to Figure 4-2. Excel correctly identifies the quarter numbers and increments them as you drag.

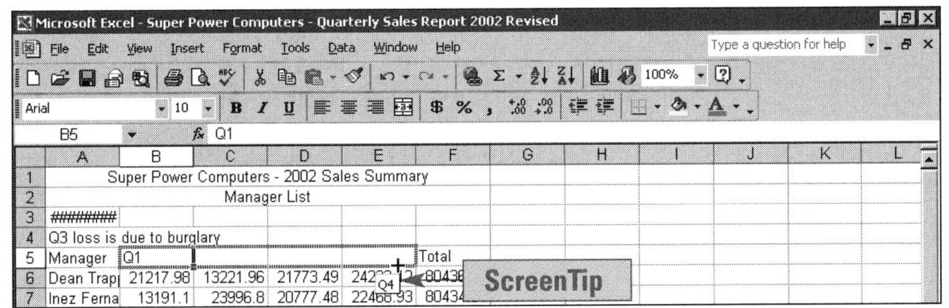

FIGURE 4-2
AutoFill Numbers

Step 4	***Release***	the mouse button

MOUSE TIP

Click the AutoFill Options button on the screen to change how the cells are filled when you drag the fill handle.

When you release the mouse button, the column headings Q1 through Q4 appear in cells B5:E5.

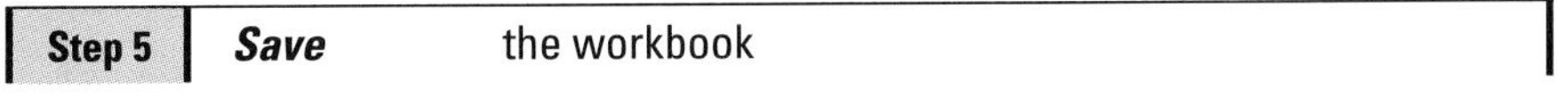

Step 5	***Save***	the workbook

4.b Formatting Cells, Rows, and Columns

Careful application of formatting to rows, columns, and cells transforms a mundane, hard-to-decipher worksheet into a vehicle for sharing information. In this section, you learn about many of the formatting tools available.

Applying AutoFormats to Worksheets

AutoFormats are predefined combinations of shading, cell borders, font styles, and number formatting that quickly give worksheets a stylized look. To apply AutoFormats:

Step 1	***Select***	the range A5:F10
Step 2	***Click***	Format
Step 3	***Click***	AutoFormat

The AutoFormat dialog box displays a list of available AutoFormat styles and should look similar to Figure 4-3.

FIGURE 4-3
AutoFormat Dialog Box

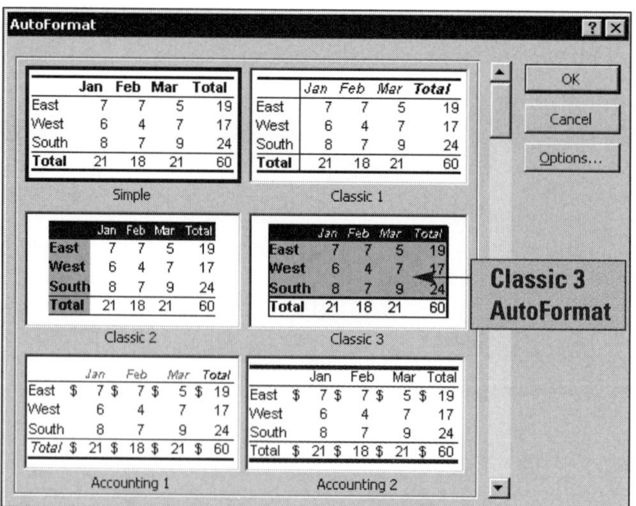

Step 4	***Click***	the Classic 3 AutoFormat
Step 5	***Click***	OK
Step 6	***Click***	any cell in the worksheet to deselect the range

The AutoFormat is applied to the selected area. You don't like the way the AutoFormatted worksheet looks, so you format it yourself.

Step 7	Click	the Undo button on the Standard toolbar

Applying Fonts and Font Styles

A **font** is a set of printed characters that share a common typeface. A **typeface** is the design and appearance of the font in printed form. The **style** refers to whether the font is displayed with *italic*, **bold**, an underline, or normal print. The **point size** refers to the print height. You can also add **effects**, such as strikethrough, superscripts, and subscripts. Some common typefaces include the following:

Arial   Times New Roman   Courier New   Book Antiqua

To maintain consistency in its documents, Super Power Computers has selected the Impact font style, set to point size 14, for worksheet titles. To change the font and font size:

Step 1	Select	cell A1
Step 2	Click	the Font button list arrow Arial on the Formatting toolbar to display the available fonts
Step 3	Click	Impact (or another font if Impact is not available on your system)
Step 4	Click	the Font Size button list arrow 10 on the Formatting toolbar
Step 5	Click	14

Usually, when you increase the font size in a cell, the row height automatically increases to accommodate the larger font; however, when you increase the font size in a merged cell, it does not. You adjust this later in this chapter. You decide to make the Total label stand out more.

Step 6	Change	the font in cell A10 to Arial Black

Another way to add emphasis is to change the font color. To change the font color:

Step 1	Activate	cell A1

CAUTION TIP

To make your worksheets look as professional as possible, avoid using more than three or four fonts. Too many fonts may look comical and detract from an otherwise well-designed layout.

MENU TIP

Click the Cells command on the Format menu, then click the Font tab to choose a font, font size, font style, and font color.

Step 2	*Click*	the Font Color button list arrow on the Formatting toolbar
Step 3	*Point to*	the Blue square (second row, sixth column)

A ScreenTip displays the color name under the pointer.

Step 4	*Click*	the Blue square

You can also use bold, italics, or underlining to draw attention to or emphasize certain cells. To change the font style:

Step 1	*Select*	the range B5:F5
Step 2	*Click*	the Bold button on the Formatting toolbar
Step 3	*Select*	the range A6:A10
Step 4	*Click*	the Italic button on the Formatting toolbar

MOUSE TIP

The Formatting toolbar is extremely helpful when you only need to apply one or two settings to a range. When you need to make several formatting adjustments, use the Format Cells dialog box.

Modifying the Alignment of Cell Content

You can change the alignment of values within a cell. The default horizontal alignment in a cell is for text values to be left-aligned, and numbers, dates, and times to be right-aligned. The default vertical alignment is for data to be aligned at the bottom of a cell. Typically, column labels are centered in the column, while row labels are left-aligned. To change the alignment of cells:

Step 1	*Select*	the range B5:F5
Step 2	*Click*	the Center button on the Formatting toolbar

Applying Number Formats

Understanding how and when to apply number formats is very important. Using the extensive set of number formats in Excel, you can display numerical values such as times, dates, currency, percentages, fractions, and more. When you apply a numerical format to a value, the manner in which the value is displayed may vary dramatically, but the actual value held by the cell remains the same. Table 4-1 illustrates how a common numerical value of 1054.253 would be displayed with different number formats applied.

Category	Description	Default Display (Value = 1054.253)
General	No specific number format	1054.253
Number	Default of two decimal places; can also display commas for thousand separators	1054.25
Currency	Default of two decimal places, comma separators, and $ (the U.S. dollar sign)	$1,054.25
Accounting	Aligns currency symbol, displays two decimal places and comma separators	$ 1,054.25
Date	Displays serial equivalent of date	11/19/1902
Time	Displays serial equivalent of time	11/19/1902 6:00 AM
Percentage	Multiplies value by 100 and displays the result with % sign	105425%
Fraction	Displays decimal portion of value as a fraction	1054 1/4
Scientific	Displays the number in scientific notation	1.05E+03

TABLE 4-1
Comparing Number Formats

The comma format automatically sets the numerical display to two decimal places, inserts a comma when needed for thousands, millions, and so on, and adjusts the alignment of the cell(s) to line up on the decimal. To change the formatting to the comma format:

Step 1	*Select*	the range B6:E10
Step 2	*Click*	the Comma Style button on the Formatting toolbar

The cells are updated to display the new formatting, including a slight, automatic column width adjustment to accommodate the extra formatting. (You format the Total column later in this chapter.)

Currency style is commonly used when dealing with money. There are several ways to adjust currency style, including changing the font color to red for negative numbers. You can also insert other symbols, such as those for the euro (E) and the yen (¥). To use currency style:

Step 1	*Verify*	that the range B6:E10 is still selected
Step 2	*Click*	the Currency Style button on the Formatting toolbar

This looks fine, but you want the negative values to stand out even more. To adjust the currency format, you use the Format Cells dialog box. To change formatting using the Format Cells dialog box:

Step 1	*Click*	Format
Step 2	*Click*	Cells

The Format Cells dialog box opens. Each tab contains a different category of formatting options that you can apply to selected cells.

Step 3	*Click*	the Number tab, if necessary
Step 4	*Click*	Currency in the Category: list

QUICK TIP

When you activate a cell containing a date or time format, the Formula Bar displays the date or time value, not the serial, or number, value. To view the serial value of a date, you must change the cell's format to a number format.

The Number tab in the Format Cells dialog box permits you to change a variety of options for each of the available number formats. When the Currency category is selected, you can choose how negative numbers are displayed. The dialog box on your screen should look similar to Figure 4-4.

FIGURE 4-4
Format Cells Dialog Box

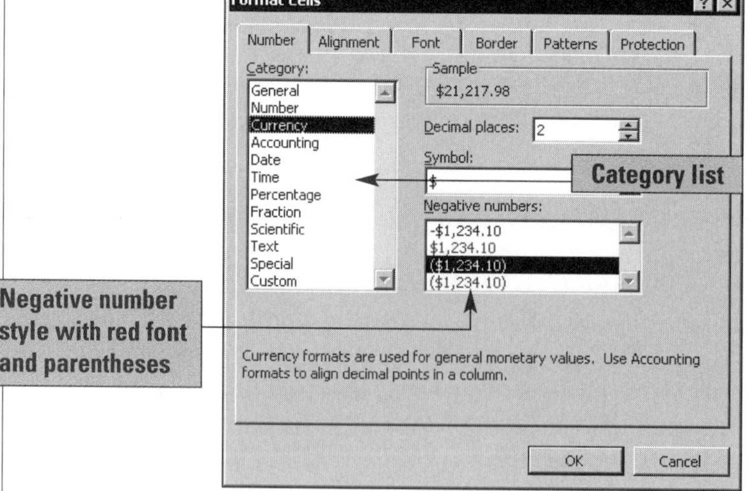

Step 5	*Click*	the fourth item in the Negative numbers: list, red text and parentheses
Step 6	*Click*	OK

The loss in cell D8 is now easy to see.

Adjusting the Decimal Place

You can adjust the number of decimal places displayed in all number formats except General, Date, Time, and Text. To change the number of decimal places displayed in a cell:

Step 1	*Verify*	that the range B6:E10 is still selected
Step 2	*Click*	the Decrease Decimal button on the Formatting toolbar twice

The data in the selected cells is rounded to the nearest whole dollar. Although the cells display rounded numbers, the original value is stored in each cell and appears in the Formula Bar when the cell is active.

Indenting, Rotating, and Wrapping Text in a Cell

To give more visual appeal to your worksheets, you can indent, rotate, or wrap values in a cell. The employee names would be easier to distinguish if they were indented in the cells. To indent cell content:

Step 1	*Select*	the range A6:A9
Step 2	*Click*	the Increase Indent button on the Formatting toolbar

MOUSE TIP

To increase the indent more, click the Increase Indent button on the Formatting toolbar again. To decrease the indent, click the Decrease Indent button on the Formatting toolbar.

Sometimes rotating text is a good way to make it stand out. To rotate text in a cell:

Step 1	*Select*	the range B5:E5
Step 2	*Right-click*	the selected range
Step 3	*Click*	Format Cells
Step 4	*Click*	the Alignment tab

Your dialog box should look similar to Figure 4-5. The Alignment tab is used to control various alignment settings, including rotation.

FIGURE 4-5
Alignment Tab in the Formal Cells Dialog Box

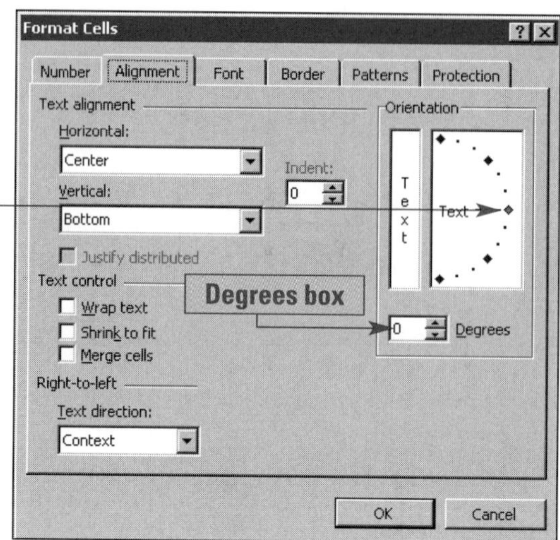

MENU TIP

Data can also be aligned vertically in a cell at the bottom of the cell, at the top, or in the center. To change the vertical alignment, click the Cells command on the Format menu. On the Alignment tab, select an option from the Vertical: list.

Step 5	***Drag***	the red diamond in the Orientation box up until the Degrees box displays 45
Step 6	***Click***	OK

The column labels rotate 45 degrees, and the row height increases to display the rotated value.

When data is too long for the column width, it is displayed as long as neighboring cells are empty. You can adjust the column width, but this isn't always desirable for long entries. Instead, you can use wrapping to maintain column width, while displaying all the data entered in a particular cell. **Wrapping** allows longer cell entries to continue to the next "line" within a single cell. To turn on text wrapping:

Step 1	***Activate***	cell A4
Step 2	***Open***	the Alignment tab in the Format Cells dialog box
Step 3	***Click***	the Wrap text check box
Step 4	***Click***	OK

The text is wrapped to fit within the column width. The row height might adjust automatically. If not, you adjust it later.

Applying Cell Borders and Shading

Cell borders and shading are two of the more dramatic visual effects available to enhance your worksheets. Borders can be used to separate row and column labels from data. Shading can be used to emphasize important cells. Although you see grid lines on your screen, the default for printed worksheets is for no grid lines to appear. If you want grid lines to appear on your printed pages, you need to apply a border. Borders can be applied to a range of selected cells or to individual cells. To add a border:

Step 1	*Select*	the range B6:E9
Step 2	*Click*	the Borders button list arrow on the Formatting toolbar
Step 3	*Click*	the All Borders button

The All Borders command applies a border to all edges surrounding and within the selection. Your screen should look similar to Figure 4-6.

Borders button list arrow

Border around selected range

FIGURE 4-6
All Borders Added to the Selection

One way you can make row 5, which contains the column labels, stand out is to use a "reverse text" effect. To create this effect, you apply a dark fill color to the cells, then change the font color to white. To add shading to a cell:

Step 1	*Select*	cells A5:F5
Step 2	*Click*	the Fill Color button list arrow on the Formatting toolbar
Step 3	*Select*	the Blue square (second row, sixth column)
Step 4	*Click*	the Font Color button list arrow on the Formatting toolbar
Step 5	*Select*	the White square (last row, last column)
Step 6	*Activate*	cell A1 to deselect the cells

QUICK TIP

You are not limited to the 12 choices appearing on the Borders list button. Use the Borders tab in the Format Cells dialog box to select different line styles, change line colors, and choose additional border options, such as inserting diagonal lines and applying borders to only the inside of a selection.

Drawing Cell Borders

You can also draw cell borders exactly where you want them. To draw cell borders:

Step 1	*Click*	the Borders button list arrow on the Formatting toolbar
Step 2	*Click*	Draw Borders to display the Borders toolbar
Step 3	*Click*	the Line Style button list arrow on the Borders toolbar to drop down a list of line styles
Step 4	*Click*	the double-line style
Step 5	*Drag*	across the bottom of cells B9:E9

QUICK TIP

When you select a line style, the Draw Border button is activated, and the mouse pointer changes to a pencil. As long as this button is active, you continue drawing borders.

A double-line is added to the bottom of the cells. To deactivate the Draw Border button, click the button again or turn off the toolbar.

Step 6	*Click*	the Close button on the Borders toolbar

Using the Format Painter

The Format Painter copies formats from one cell to another. To use the Format Painter:

MOUSE TIP

The default behavior for the Format Painter is to allow only one selection. If you need to format multiple ranges, double-click the Format Painter button. When you have finished, click the Format Painter button once more to turn off this tool.

Step 1	*Select*	the range E6:E10
Step 2	*Click*	the Format Painter button on the Standard toolbar
Step 3	*Select*	the range F6:F10

The currency formatting and borders from cells E6:E10 are copied to cells F6:F10.

Clearing Formats

Occasionally, you need to remove formatting from a cell or cells, while maintaining the data in the cell. To clear formatting from cells:

Step 1	*Activate*	cell A10

Step 2	*Click*	Edit
Step 3	*Point to*	Clear
Step 4	*Click*	Formats

All formatting is removed from the cell, and the font is changed to the default style of 10-point Arial.

Step 5	*Save*	the workbook

4.c Using Paste Special

The Paste Special command provides you with extra options when you copy or move data in Excel. The best quarter for each manager is listed in row 12. To create the column labels for this data, you copy and transpose the names listed in column A to row 12. To use the Paste Special command:

Step 1	*Copy*	cells A6:A9
Step 2	*Right-click*	cell B12
Step 3	*Click*	Paste Special

The Paste Special dialog box should look similar to Figure 4-7.

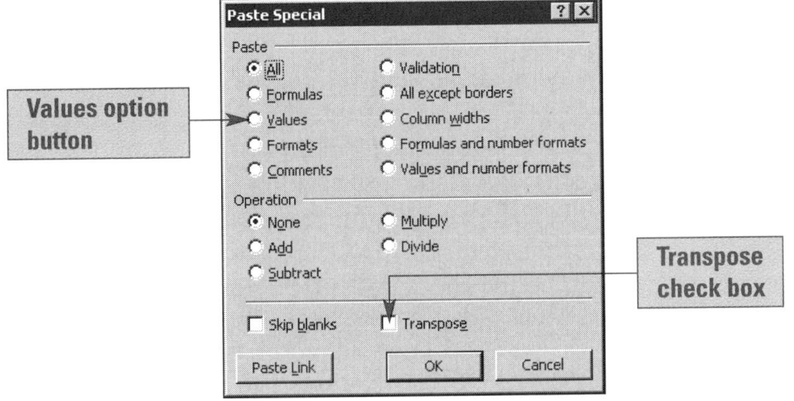

FIGURE 4-7
Paste Special Dialog Box

chapter four

The Paste Special dialog box contains options for pasting data, formulas, and formats in cells. Some of these options are explained in Table 4-2.

TABLE 4-2
Paste Special Options

Paste Option	Description
All	Pastes content and formulas from source cell
Formulas	Pastes only formulas from source cell
Values	Pastes only values from source cell, converting formulas into latest result
Formats	Pastes only formats from source cell, leaving content of destination cell in place
Operation (add, subtract, multiply, divide)	Performs operation on value from source cell with value of destination cell to create new value without a formula

Step 4	*Click*	the Values option button
Step 5	*Click*	the Transpose check box to insert a check mark
Step 6	*Click*	OK
Step 7	*Press*	the ESC key to end the Copy command

The names are transposed to row 12 without the formatting from the source cells.

4.d Defining and Applying Styles

QUICK TIP

To create a style from a previously formatted cell, select the cell, then open the Style dialog box. The format settings for the style of the cell you selected will be listed in the dialog box.

To create a consistent corporate identity, many companies use certain styles whenever a workbook is created. **Styles** can cover a variety of settings, such as number format, alignment settings, font type, cell borders, and cell patterns. You already used some of the built-in styles in Excel when you applied the comma and currency number styles. In addition to numerical styles, you can also define your own styles, which can then be applied to other cells and copied into other workbooks. To create a new style:

Step 1	*Activate*	cell A2
Step 2	*Click*	Format
Step 3	*Click*	Style

The Style dialog box opens, displaying the settings for the Normal style, as shown in Figure 4-8. To create a new style, type a new style name in the Style name: box, then modify the settings as necessary.

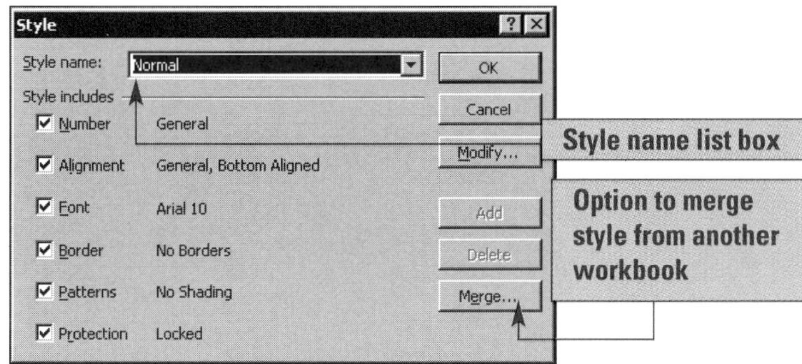

FIGURE 4-8
Style Dialog Box

Step 4	***Key***	Worksheet Subtitle in the Style name: text box
Step 5	***Click***	Modify

The familiar Format Cells dialog box opens.

Step 6	***Click***	the Font tab
Step 7	***Click***	Impact in the Font: list
Step 8	***Click***	12 in the Size: list
Step 9	***Click***	the Color: list arrow
Step 10	***Click***	the Red square (third row, first column)

You can apply alignment options, borders, and numerical formats to your style as well.

Step 11	***Click***	the Alignment tab
Step 12	***Click***	the Horizontal: list arrow
Step 13	***Verify***	that Center is selected

This command centers the value in the cell. It was already selected because you applied the Merge and Center command to cell A2 earlier. When the style is applied to cell A2, it centers, the value in the merged cell. If the style is applied to a cell that isn't merged, it centers the data only in the cell you apply the style to.

MOUSE TIP

You can copy styles from workbook to workbook by using the Format Painter. Open both workbooks. In the source workbook, select a cell with the formatting style you want to copy, and click Format Painter. Switch to the target workbook, then click the cell to which you want to apply the formatting. The style is automatically transferred to the Style list of the target workbook.

QUICK TIP

You can copy styles from workbook to workbook by using the Copy and Paste commands. Open both workbooks, copy the cell in the source workbook containing the desired style, then use the Paste Special command and select the Formats option to paste it into the target workbook.

MOUSE TIP

To remove a style, select the style name in the Style dialog box, then click the Delete button.

Step 14	*Click*	OK to close the Format Cells dialog box
Step 15	*Click*	OK to close the Style dialog box and apply the style to the active cell

To apply this style to other cells in this workbook, activate the cell(s), reopen the Style dialog box, select the style you wish to apply, then click OK. A real advantage of using named styles is that when you modify a named style, all cells with that style applied are updated automatically.

4.e Manipulating Rows, Columns, and Cells

As you organize worksheets, you will find many occasions when you need to insert a few cells into a list—or entire rows or columns—to add new information to a worksheet. You may also need to delete cells, rows, or columns.

MENU TIP

You can insert a new row by clicking Rows on the Insert menu. You can insert a new column by clicking Columns on the Insert menu.

Inserting and Deleting Rows and Columns

You decide to insert a blank row above row 5. To insert a new row:

Step 1	*Right-click*	the row 5 heading
Step 2	*Click*	Insert

The data in row 5 and below is shifted down to accommodate the new row. When a column is inserted, all data is shifted to the right.

Upon reviewing your worksheet, you realize that you don't need the extra row after all. To delete rows or columns:

QUICK TIP

To insert multiple rows, select the number of rows you want to insert, then right-click the row heading and click Insert.

Step 1	*Right-click*	the row 5 heading
Step 2	*Click*	Delete to delete the newly added row

Changing Column Width and Row Height

If the data in a cell is too long for the column width, Excel allows the value to spill over into the next cell, as long as the neighboring cell is empty. If the neighboring cell contains data, Excel shows only the first part of the data. By changing the column width, you can show more or less data.

As you adjusted the font height, or turned on the wrap text feature, you may have noticed that the row height increased to show the data in the cell. Although this change is generally automatic, sometimes you need more precise control of the row height.

You need to resize rows 1 and 2 to accommodate the larger font size. To AutoFit a row to the largest point size:

Step 1	***Double-click***	the boundary between row headings 1 and 2
Step 2	***Double-click***	the boundary between row headings 2 and 3

Rows 1 and 2 increase in height to fit the entries in cells A1 and A2. You also might need to adjust the height of row 4 if it did not automatically resize to accomodate the wrapped text in cell A1.

Step 3	***Double-click***	the boundary between row headings 4 and 5, if necessary

Next you need to adjust column widths to display the widest entries. To manually change the column width:

Step 1	***Right-click***	the column A heading
Step 2	***Click***	Column Width
Step 3	***Key***	15 in the Column width: text box
Step 4	***Click***	OK

You can also use the AutoFit feature to automatically adjust the width to fit the longest entry in the column. To AutoFit a column to the longest entry:

Step 1	***Move***	the mouse pointer over the boundary between the column B and column C headings
Step 2	***Double-click***	the boundary

The column automatically resizes so it is wide enough to display the value in cell B12, the widest entry in column B.

Step 3	***Repeat***	Step 2 to AutoFit columns C, D, and E

QUICK TIP

To change the width of several columns at once, select them before opening the Column Width dialog box.

MOUSE TIP

To change the formatting in a newly inserted row or column, click the Insert Options button that appears after you insert the row or column.

MENU TIP

To adjust the width of a column, click Format, point to Columns, then click Width. To AutoFit the row height, select AutoFit instead of Height.

To adjust the height of a row by using menus, click Format, point to Row, then click Height. To AutoFit the row height, select AutoFit instead of Height.

Now you need to decrease the height of row 4. To manually adjust the height of a row:

Step 1	*Right-click*	the row 4 header
Step 2	*Click*	Row Height
Step 3	*Key*	25.5 in the Row height: text box
Step 4	*Click*	OK

The row height decreases to fit the entry in cell A4.

Inserting and Deleting Cells

In some instances, you may need to insert extra cells without inserting an entire row or column. The Store Data worksheet has an error in column D. The data in rows 27–37 should actually be in rows 28–38. To insert extra cells:

Step 1	*Click*	the Store Data sheet tab
Step 2	*Scroll*	the Store Data worksheet so you can view rows 27–38
Step 3	*Right-click*	cell D27
Step 4	*Click*	Insert

The Insert dialog box opens.

Step 5	*Verify*	that the Shift cells down option button is selected
Step 6	*Click*	OK

The data in column D below row 26 shifts down one cell.

Step 7	*Enter*	1104 in cell D27

Hiding and Unhiding Rows and Columns

You can hide columns and rows when extraneous data does not need to be displayed. To hide a row or column:

Step 1	*Right-click*	the column D heading on the Store Data sheet tab

MENU TIP

To delete cells, select the cells you want to delete, right-click them, and click Delete. The Delete dialog box contains the same options as the Insert dialog box.

QUICK TIP

Click the Insert Options button that appears on screen after inserting new cells to adjuct the formatting of the newly inserted cell.

Step 2	*Click*	Hide

Column E slides left, hiding column D. To unhide a column or row:

Step 1	*Select*	both column headings surrounding column D
Step 2	*Right-click*	either column heading
Step 3	*Click*	Unhide

Column D reappears.

Freezing and Unfreezing Rows and Columns

When working with large worksheets, it can be helpful to keep row and column labels on the screen as you scroll through your worksheet. The Freeze Panes command freezes the rows above and the columns to the left of the active cell and prevents them from scrolling off the screen. The Store Data worksheet contains more data than will fit on the screen at once. To freeze the columns and row headings:

Step 1	*Activate*	cell A5
Step 2	*Click*	Window
Step 3	*Click*	Freeze Panes

A thin, black line appears on your workbook, indicating that the rows above row 5 are frozen and will not scroll with the rest of your worksheet. This black line will not print when you print the worksheet.

Step 4	*Press & hold*	the DOWN ARROW key until your worksheet begins scrolling down

The worksheet scrolls, but the column labels stay fixed at the top of the worksheet. When you no longer need the frozen panes, you can unfreeze them. To unfreeze panes:

Step 1	*Click*	Window
Step 2	*Click*	Unfreeze Panes

MOUSE TIP

You can drag a hidden column into view. Move the mouse pointer to the hidden column boundary by positioning the mouse pointer slightly to the right of the boundary between the two columns on either side of the hidden column. The pointer changes to two black horizontal arrows with a gap between them, indicating that it is on the right boundary of the hidden column. Drag to the right to drag the hidden column into view.

QUICK TIP

To freeze columns, position the active cell to the right of the columns you want to freeze, then use the Freeze Panes command.

Step 3	***Save***	the workbook

The panes are removed, permitting normal worksheet scrolling.

4.f Filtering Lists Using AutoFilter

Excel is often used to store lists of data, similar to a database table. The Store Data sheet tab in your workbook contains a list of sales data. Sometimes, you want to look at data that meets some criteria. **Filtering** a list allows you to screen out any data that does not meet your **criteria**, or conditions that you specify. You can apply more than one filter so as to reduce the list even more. When you apply a filter, only the data meeting the specified criteria are displayed. While the filter remains on, you can format, edit, chart, and print the filtered list. When you have finished, turn the filter off and the rest of the records in the list will appear.

The AutoFilter command offers a fast, easy way to apply multiple filters to a list. To apply AutoFilter:

CAUTION TIP

The active cell must be within the continuous table of data, and not elsewhere in the worksheet for AutoFilter to be able to find the data to filter.

Step 1	***Activate***	any cell in the list
Step 2	***Click***	Data
Step 3	***Point to***	Filter
Step 4	***Click***	AutoFilter

The filter list arrow appears next to each column label. Clicking any of these arrows displays a list of AutoFilter options.

MOUSE TIP

You can filter for a secondary criteria by clicking the list arrow next to a second column label.

Step 5	***Click***	the Filter list arrow next to Store in cell A4
Step 6	***Click***	Store #2

The list is filtered for any entries in column A that contain "Store #2"; your screen should look similar to Figure 4-9. The filter list arrows of the filtered columns and the row headings appear in blue. All other entries are hidden.

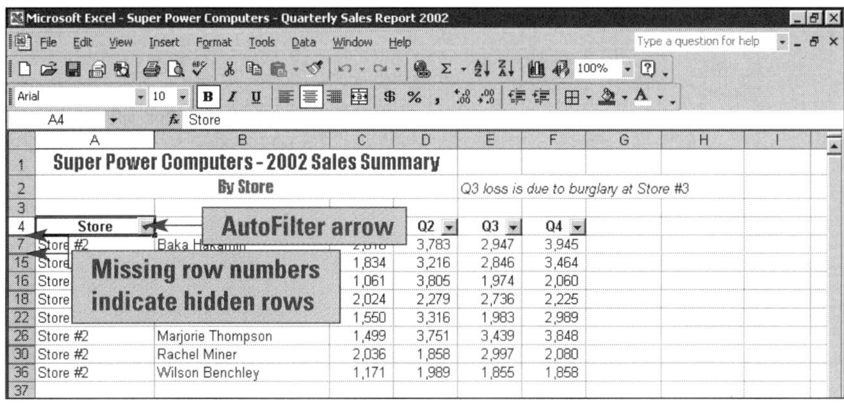

FIGURE 4-9
Applying AutoFilter to a List

When you want to display all of the records again, use the Show all command. To clear the filters:

Step 1	***Click***	the Filter list arrow next to Store in cell A4
Step 2	***Click***	(All) to restore the entries

When you have finished filtering a list, you can turn off AutoFilter. To turn off AutoFilter:

Step 1	***Click***	Data
Step 2	***Point to***	Filter
Step 3	***Click***	AutoFilter
Step 4	***Save***	the workbook and close it

MENU TIP

You can also clear the filters by pointing to Filter on the Data menu, and then clicking Show All.

Your formatted worksheets are much easier to read than the unformatted worksheets were.

Summary

- You can use the Merge and Center command to create worksheet titles.
- AutoFill fills in series of numbers, alphanumeric combinations, and day and month names.
- Judicious use of fonts and font styles can enhance a worksheet's appearance and make it easier to read.
- Align cell contents to enhance visual clarity. The default for text is left-alignment. For numeric entries, such as currency, dates, and times, the default is right-alignment.
- Number formats change how cells' numerical contents are displayed. Excel detects date, time, and currency entries and formats the cell accordingly.
- Rotate text to add visual interest or to decrease the width of a column. Indent text to provide visual breaks or to indicate that a list has a certain hierarchical structure. Use the alignment tab of the Format Cells dialog box to apply these settings.
- Borders and shading can add major visual impact to worksheets.
- Format Painter enables you to copy formats to other cells.
- You can clear cell contents, formats, or both using the Clear command on the Edit menu.
- AutoFormat applies stylized formatting to a selection of cells.
- Paste Special includes many options for pasting. Use Paste Special to paste only formats, to paste only values, to perform calculations automatically, or to transpose data from rows to columns.
- You can create and modify styles to reuse throughout a worksheet and in other workbooks.
- You can insert and delete rows and columns as needed to organize worksheets.
- You can change column width and row height to display more or less data.
- You can insert and delete cells by shifting the remaining cells up, down, left, or right when necessary to maintain surrounding information.
- You should hide columns and rows when extraneous data does not need to be displayed. Unhide them when you want to display the data again.

- You can freeze columns and rows to prevent them from scrolling along with the worksheet.
- You can use AutoFilter to display only data belonging to a certain category.

Commands Review

Action	Menu Bar	Shortcut Menu	Toolbar	Task Pane	Keyboard
Merge and Center					
AutoFill Series	Edit, Fill, Series				ALT + E, I, S
AutoFormat	Format, AutoFormat				ALT + O, A
Format cells	Format, Cells	Right-click selected range, Format Cells			CTRL + 1 ALT + O, E
Font Color	Format, Cells, Font tab				ALT + O, E
Bold	Format, Cells, Font tab				ALT + O, E CTRL + B
Italics	Format, Cells, Font tab				ALT + O, E CTRL + I
Underline	Format, Cells, Font tab				ALT + O, E CTRL + U
Align cell contents	Format, Cells, Alignment tab				ALT + O, E
Apply number formats	Format, Cells, Number tab				ALT + O, E
Rotate text	Format, Cells, Alignment tab				ALT + O, E
Increase/decrease indent	Format, Cells, Alignment tab				ALT + O, E
Add borders	Format, Cells, Borders tab				ALT + O, E
Add shading to cells	Format, Cells, Patterns tab				ALT + O, E
Use Format Painter					
Clear formats	Edit, Clear, Formats				ALT + E, C, F
Apply AutoFormat	Format, AutoFormat				ALT + O, A
Paste Special	Edit, Paste Special	Right-click cell, Paste Special			ALT + E, S
Define or Merge Format Style	Format, Style				ALT + O, S ALT + '
Insert rows	Insert, Rows	Right-click row, Insert			ALT + I, R
Insert columns	Insert, Columns	Right-click column, Insert			ALT + I, C
Delete rows and columns	Edit, Delete	Right-click row or column, Delete			ALT + E, D
Change column width	Format, Columns, Width Format, Columns, AutoFit Selection				ALT + O, C, W ALT + O, C, A

Action	Menu Bar	Shortcut Menu	Toolbar	Task Pane	Keyboard
Change row height	Format, Rows, Height Format, Rows, AutoFit Selection				ALT + O, R, H ALT + O, R, A
Insert cells	Insert, Cells	Right-click cell, Insert			ALT + I, E CTRL + SHIFT + + (plus key)
Delete cells	Edit, Delete	Right-click cell, Delete			ALT + E, D
Hide rows or columns	Format, Row, Hide Format, Column, Hide				ALT + O, R, H ALT + O, C, H
Unhide rows or columns	Format, Row, Unhide Format, Column, Unhide				ALT + O, R, U ALT + O, C, U
Freeze/unfreeze rows and columns	Window, Freeze Panes Window, Unfreeze Panes				ALT + W, F
Use AutoFilter	Data, Filter, AutoFilter				ALT + D, I, F

Concepts Review

Circle the correct answer.

1. Which of the following commands can you use to copy formatting only from one selection to another?
- [a] Copy, Paste Special (Formats option)
- [b] Copy, Paste
- [c] Cut, Paste
- [d] Paste Special, Copy

2. To apply multiple changes to a font, use the ____________ tab of the Format Cells dialog box.
- [a] Font
- [b] Border
- [c] Patterns
- [d] Number

3. To apply custom border styles, use the ____________ tab of the Format Cells dialog box.
- [a] Font
- [b] Border
- [c] Patterns
- [d] Number

4. To insert a cell in the middle of existing data:
- [a] click Format, then click Add Cells.
- [b] right-click the row header, then click Insert.
- [c] right-click the column header, then click Insert.
- [d] right-click the cell where you want a new blank cell to appear, then click Insert.

5. To prevent a row from scrolling, you should:
- [a] hide the row.
- [b] freeze the row.
- [c] insert a new row.
- [d] filter the list.

6. AutoFill can be used to fill series of:
- [a] day names.
- [b] month names.
- [c] alphanumeric combinations.
- [d] All of the above.

7. To maintain a set column width while still displaying all of a cell's content, you must:
[a] indent the text.
[b] rotate the text.
[c] edit the content until it fits.
[d] wrap the text.

8. Using the Font tab of the Format Cells dialog box, you can:
[a] change numerical style settings.
[b] add borders to cells.
[c] change the alignment of text in a cell.
[d] change font settings, such as font, size, style, and color.

9. Cell A1 contains a value of .25. If the currency style is applied to cell A1, the cell displays:
[a] 25%.
[b] 0.25%.
[c] $0.25.
[d] 2.50E-01.

10. Cell A2 contains a value of 45.26 and has been formatted to display 0 decimal places. What is displayed in cell A2?
[a] $45.26
[b] $45.00
[c] 45
[d] 45%

Circle **T** if the statement is true or **F** if the statement is false.

T F 1. To delete a range of cells, you must first delete the rows or columns that contain the cells.

T F 2. You can apply a border diagonally across a cell (or cells).

T F 3. AutoFilter has certain preset categories, but does not automatically add categories based on the data in your worksheet.

T F 4. Increasing the font size automatically increases the row height.

T F 5. Rotating text automatically adjusts the row height.

T F 6. AutoFill cannot fill a series of values containing a mixture of text and numbers, such as "Apollo 11."

T F 7. The Merge and Center command merges only the value in the upper-left cell of your selection.

T F 8. Changing a cell's number format alters the actual value of the cell.

T F 9. You can create your own cell styles.

T F 10. You can copy styles created in one workbook to another workbook.

Skills Review

Exercise 1

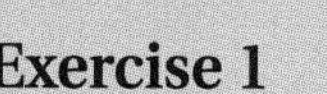

1. Open the *Project Expense Log* workbook located on the Data Disk.

2. Change the numeric format of column A to the MM/DD/YY date format.

3. Change the number format of column C to Currency Style.

4. Merge and center cell A1 across cells A1:C1.

5. Center the column labels in row 3.

6. Turn on AutoFilter and filter the Place column for Phoenix, AZ.

7. Save the workbook as *Project Expense Log Revised*. Print and close the workbook.

Exercise 2

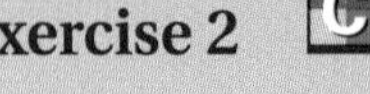

1. Open the *Wage Increase* workbook located on the Data Disk.
2. Use the Format Cells dialog box to format the column labels as follows:
   a. Change the font to Times New Roman.
   b. Increase the font size to 12.
   c. Change the font color to blue.
   d. Change the font style to bold.
   e. Turn on Wrap Text.
3. Center the column labels.
4. Make cells A7:D7 bold and add a Gray-25% shade.
5. Add a thick bottom border to cells A1:D1.
6. Indent cell A7.
7. Adjust the column widths using AutoFit.
8. Hide the row containing Micah Anderson.
9. Delete the range A4: D4.
10. Insert cells above the range A3: D3.
11. Enter the following in row 3: Jared Wright, 8.50, 8.75.
12. Copy the formula from cell D2 to cell D3.
13. Change the format of the range B3: D3 to Accounting with two decimal places and no dollar sign.
14. Save the workbook as *Wage Increase Revised*. Print and close the workbook.

Exercise 3 C

1. Open the *Number Formatting* workbook on the Data Disk.
2. Apply the List 1 AutoFormat to the data.
3. Use the number format indicated by each column label to format the columns. Use the default settings unless otherwise directed.
   a. In the Number column, select the Use 1000 Separator (,) check box in the Number format settings.
   b. In the Date column, set the Date type to 3/14/2001. (Excel converts numbers into dates, starting with 1 equal to 1/1/1900.)
   c. In the Time column, set the Time type to 3/14/2001 1:30 PM. (*Hint:* If you don't have this format, set it as 3/14/01 1:30 PM.)
   d. In the Fraction column, set the Fraction type to Up to two digits (21/25). (*Hint:* Because many of the numbers are whole numbers, no fraction will appear in this column in the worksheet, but the numbers will move to the left side of the cell to allow proper alignment of fractions when needed.)
4. Save the workbook as *Number Formatting Revised*. Print and close the workbook.

Exercise 4 C

1. Create a new workbook.
2. Enter the data as shown in the table below:

Important Dates of World War II	
Date	**Event**
9/1/1939	Germany invades Poland
6/14/40	German troops occupy Paris
7/10/40	Battle of Britain begins
6/22/1941	German troops invade Russia
12/7/1941	Japan attacks U.S. forces at Pearl Harbor, Hawaii
12/8/1941	U.S. declares war on Japan
12/11/1941	U.S. declares war on Germany and Italy
6/4/1942	Battle of Midway starts (turning point of Pacific war)
1/23/1943	Casablanca Conference decides on Cross Channel Invasion of Continental Europe
7/10/43	Allies invade Sicily
6/6/1944	D-Day Allied invasion of Western Europe commences in France
5/7/1945	Germany surrenders to Allies at Reims, France
7/16/1945	U.S. tests 1st atomic bomb in New Mexico
8/6/1945	U.S. drops atomic bomb on Hiroshima, Japan
8/9/1945	U.S. drops atomic bomb on Nagasaki, Japan
8/14/1945	Japan agrees to surrender
9/2/1945	Japan formally surrenders in Tokyo Bay

3. Merge and center the title in the range A1: B1.
4. Bold and center the titles in the range A2: B2.
5. Change the format of the Date column to the Month DD, YYYY format.
6. Format cell A1 with a black fill and white text.
7. Format the text in cell A1 as bold and increase the font size to 16 points.
8. Format row 2 with a dark gray fill and white text.
9. Use AutoFit to adjust the column widths.
10. Save the workbook as *WWII*. Print and close the workbook.

Exercise 5 C

1. Open the *WWII* workbook you created in Exercise 4.
2. Change the width of column B to 45.
3. Turn on wrap text with column B selected.
4. Left align cells A3:A19.

5. Italicize cells A3, A7, A13, A14, and A19.
6. Activate cell A1, then save the workbook as *WWII Revised*. Print and close the workbook.

Exercise 6

1. Open the *New Computer Prices* workbook located on the Data Disk.
2. Change the title in row A1 to 16 point, bold text.
3. Merge and center cell A1 across A1:G1.
4. Bold and center the titles in row 3.
5. Resize columns A–G to fit.
6. Format column C with Currency Style and no decimal places.
7. Change the data in columns E and F to right-aligned. (Do not right-align the column labels.)
8. Save the workbook as *New Computer Prices Formatted*. Print and close the workbook.

Exercise 7 

1. Open the *Employee Time 1* workbook located on the Data Disk.
2. Insert a new column to the left of column A, on the Revised Data worksheet.
3. Move all of the data (including the column heading) under Project to the new column A.
4. Delete the empty column C.
5. Change column C to Number format with two decimal places.
6. Increase the width of column A to show the project names in full.
7. Bold and center the column labels.
8. Move the title in cell B1 to cell A1, make the title bold, then merge and center it across columns A through C.
9. Delete the blank rows 2, 3, and 4 under the worksheet title.
10. Freeze the column labels. (*Hint:* Freeze rows 1 and 2.)
11. Save the workbook as *Employee Time 2*. Print and close the workbook.

Exercise 8 

1. Create a new workbook, and then enter "Title" in cell A1.
2. Change the Font style to Times New Roman, font size 16, and color blue.
3. Fill the cell with the light turquoise color.
4. Create a new style "Title" based on cell A1.
5. Enter "Column Heading" in cell A2.
6. Rotate the text 45 degrees.
7. Change the alignment to center, horizontally and vertically.
8. Add a left and right dashed style border.
9. Create a new style "Column Heading" based on cell A2.

10. Key 1 in cell A5, and key 2 in cell B5.

11. Select A5:B5, then drag the fill handle to cell E5.

12. Save the workbook as *Cell Styles*. Print and close the workbook.

Case Projects

Project 1

You work in a large bank. You are frequently asked about the current exchange rate for U.S. dollars relative to a variety of foreign currencies. Connect to the Internet and search the Web for a site that reports currency exchange rates. Create a new workbook to keep track of recent updates. Include the URL of the site(s) you find in the workbook, which will allow you to access these sites easily later. Record the date and currency exchange rate for converting U.S. dollars into the euro currency and the currencies of at least six countries, including those of Japan, Germany, France, and the United Kingdom. Apply currency formats displaying the appropriate currency symbol for each country (if available). Set up your workbook so that you can monitor the changes in exchange rates over time. Center and bold column labels, and italicize row labels. Make sure your worksheet has a formatted title. Save the workbook as *Foreign Currency Exchange*, and then print and close it.

Project 2

Your mom, a quilter, has come to you with an interesting project. She needs to organize her quilt pattern, but because of the number of pieces, it's very difficult to keep track of everything. You know that Excel can shade cells in different colors. That gives you an idea. Can you use shading and borders to create a fun geometrical pattern? Don't be afraid to modify column widths and row heights to achieve a more artistic pattern. Save your workbook as *Quilt*, and then print and close it.

Project 3

You are an instructor at a community college who teaches working adults about Excel. Several of your students have asked you for additional resources. Connect to the Internet and use the Web toolbar to search for Excel books. Create a new worksheet that lists the title, author name, and ISBN number for each book. Add a fourth column that lists the URL where you found the information about each book. (*Hint:* To copy the URL of the current Web page, click in the Address or Location box in your browser window, click Copy on the Edit menu, then paste this into your worksheet.) Add a title to your worksheet and format it nicely. Save the workbook as *Excel Books*, and then print and close it.

Project 4

You are the manager of a pizzeria. Create a worksheet with fictitious data that shows how many pizzas were sold last month. Calculate the total sales, figuring that each pizza sold for $8.00. Show the following column headings: Overhead, Labor, Ingredients, Advertising, and Profit. Calculate the amount spent in each category, figuring 15% for overhead, 30% for labor, 25% for ingredients, 10% for advertising, and the remainder for profit. Format the column labels to stand out from the rest of the data, and add a worksheet title. Save the workbook as *Pizzeria*, and then print and close it.

Project 5  

You plan on selling your car soon and want to find out how much it is worth. Connect to the Internet and use the Web toolbar to search for used car prices. Try finding a listing for your car and two other cars built the same year. (*Hint:* Search for "Blue Book values.") Create an Excel worksheet listing your car and the two cars you found. List the trade-in value of the cars you selected. Format the workbook nicely. Save the workbook as *Blue Book Values*, and then print and close it.

Project 6  

You are a major sports fan. Create a workbook with column headings for Team Name, City, and Sport, then list as many pro sports teams as you can think of. Use the Internet to help you. When you finish the list, add AutoFilter to the list so you can filter the list by city or sport. Hide the row of the team you dislike the most. Format the worksheet nicely and add a worksheet title. Save the workbook as *Sports Teams*, and then print and close it.

Problem 7 

You are a busy salesperson who is constantly visiting clients in your car, and who therefore, depends on a cellular phone. You want to see if your usage in the last year warrants changing your cellular calling plan. Create a worksheet with columns for local and long-distance minutes. Randomly generate numbers for each month between 0 and 400 for local air time, and numbers between 0 and 150 for long-distance air time. Copy the formula cells, then use the Paste Special command to paste only the values (not the formulas) in the same cells. Add a worksheet title and format the column headings with bold. Change the font color of any monthly total over 400 minutes to red. Save the workbook as *Cell Phone*, and then print and close it.

Project 8

Create a new workbook, enter some data, and then copy the workbook's contents using the Paste Special command. Paste Special provides many ways to copy data from one cell to another. Use the Ask A Question Box to learn about each option. Write a four-paragraph document explaining each of the options. Save the document as *Paste Special Options.doc*, and then print and close it.

Previewing and Printing Worksheets and Workbooks

Chapter Overview

When data needs to be changed or located in a workbook, the Find and Replace commands are at your service. AutoCorrect can simplify data entry and reduce spelling errors by correcting mistakes as you key. Prior to printing, it's a good idea to check for spelling errors. Excel provides many options to help you print exactly what you want. For example, you can print selections, worksheets, or entire workbooks. You also can set up headers and footers using predefined styles, or create custom headers and footers. In addition, you can modify page breaks and margin settings to print sheets to fit every need.

Case profile

Every six months, Super Power Computers holds a long-range planning session. In this meeting, the company president, Luis Alvarez, reviews the accomplishments of the last six months and notes the company's progress toward previously set goals. Goals for the next six months are revised and set. You have prepared a calendar in Excel for 2003 that each participant in the meeting can use for notes.

Learning Objectives

- Use Find and Replace
- Check spelling
- Set print options and print worksheets
- Print an entire workbook

chapter five

5.a Using Find and Replace

The Find command locates data and formats in a cell value, formula, or comment. Your calendars are ready to print, but you reread the worksheet, and you realize that the year displayed on each of your calendars is "02" instead of "03." To find and replace items:

Step 1	*Open*	the *12 Month Calendars* workbook located on the Data Disk
Step 2	*Save*	the workbook as *12 Month Calendars Revised*
Step 3	*Click*	Edit
Step 4	*Click*	Find
Step 5	*Click*	Options >> to expand the dialog box to show search options

CAUTION TIP

If the Options button shows two arrows pointing to the left (Options <<), then the dialog box is already expanded.

The Find tab in the Find and Replace dialog box on your screen should look similar to Figure 5-1. This tab provides many options for finding data. You want to search only this worksheet, by rows, and for data entered directly into a cell; it doesn't matter whether you look in Formulas or in Values. The search options are fine in this case. You enter the search text.

FIGURE 5-1
Find and Replace Dialog Box

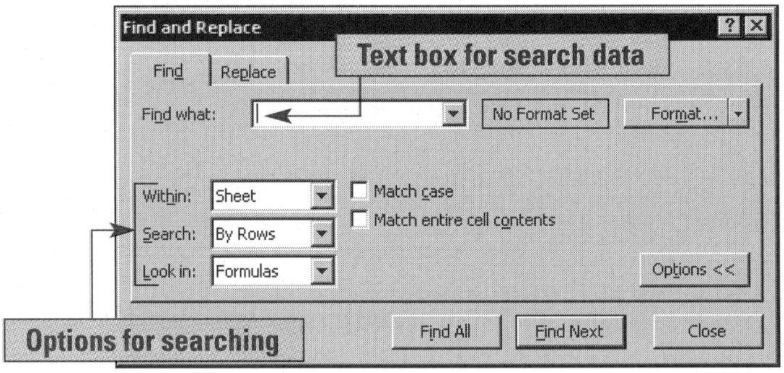

Step 6	*Key*	02 in the Find what: text box
Step 7	*Click*	the Format button list arrow
Step 8	*Click*	Choose Format From Cell
Step 9	*Click*	cell A1

A preview of the format appears to the left of the Format button.

Step 10	*Click*	Find All

At the bottom of the Find and Replace box, a list of cells appears. Each item in this list is a hyperlink to that cell, and you can click any link to jump directly to a cell containing the found item. You want to replace each of these with "03" formatted with bold. The Replace command finds and replaces individual instances or all instances of a given value.

Step 11	*Click*	the Replace tab
Step 12	*Key*	03 in the Replace with: text box
Step 13	*Click*	the Format list arrow in the Replace with: section
Step 14	*Click*	Format
Step 15	*Click*	Bold in the Font style: list on the Font tab
Step 16	*Click*	OK
Step 17	*Click*	Replace All
Step 18	*Click*	OK in the dialog box that opens to tell you that 12 replacements have been made
Step 19	*Click*	Close

The dates are now correct and formatted with bold.

Step 20	*Save*	the workbook

QUICK TIP

The Find and Replace commands do not search comments, chart objects or sheet tabs.

CAUTION TIP

The Replace All button provides a quick way to replace data, but it may make replacements you didn't intend or expect. If you want to verify each item before you replace it, click the Find Next button to locate the data in the worksheet, then click the Replace button to replace each item one at a time.

5.b Checking Spelling

Before you print a worksheet, you should proofread it and check the spelling. Excel provides two ways to check the spelling in a worksheet: AutoCorrect and the spell checker.

Using AutoCorrect

AutoCorrect checks your spelling as you go and automatically corrects common typos, such as "teh" for "the." You can turn AutoCorrect into a powerful helper by adding your own commonly used abbreviations in place of longer words or phrases. You decide to set up an abbreviation in AutoCorrect. To set AutoCorrect options:

Step 1	*Click*	Tools
Step 2	*Click*	AutoCorrect Options
Step 3	*Click*	the AutoCorrect tab, if necessary

Your AutoCorrect dialog box should look similar to Figure 5-2.

FIGURE 5-2
AutoCorrect Dialog Box

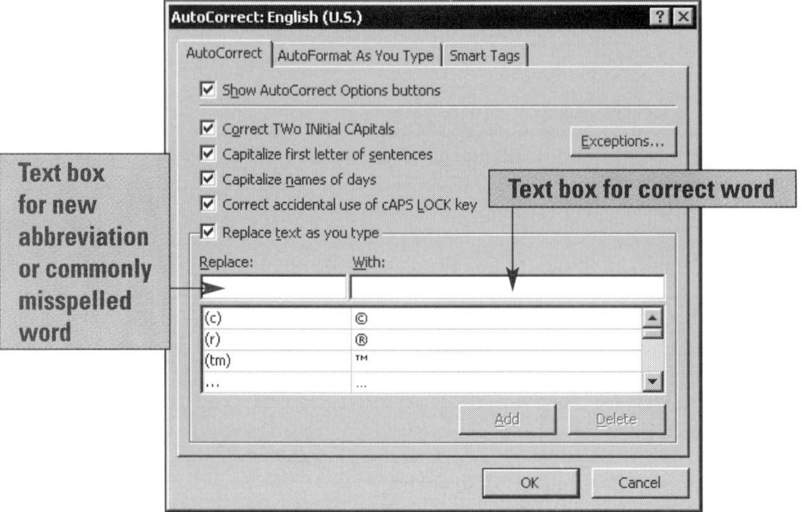

QUICK TIP

Take a quick scroll through the list of AutoCorrect items. You'll be surprised at some handy shortcuts, such as (tm) for the ™ symbol.

CAUTION TIP

If someone has already added "spc" to the AutoCorrect list, the list scrolls to the entry and the Add button is not available. Skip Step 6.

Step 4	***Key***	spc in the Replace: text box
Step 5	***Key***	Super Power Computers in the With: text box
Step 6	***Click***	Add

Now, whenever you key "spc" it will automatically be replaced with "Super Power Computers."

Step 7	***Click***	OK
Step 8	***Insert***	two rows at the top of the worksheet
Step 9	***Key***	spc in cell A1
Step 10	***Press***	the ENTER key
Step 11	***Merge***	and center cell A1 across columns A:O

Another Super Power Computers employee created a style for worksheet titles and copied the style to this workbook, so you can apply it to the title.

Step 12	***Apply***	the Worksheet Title style to cell A1
Step 13	***Save***	the workbook

Checking Spelling

Excel features a powerful spell checker that flags words that are not in the built-in dictionary and suggests alternate spellings. The spell checker does not find words that are spelled correctly but used incorrectly—for example, it will not flag "there" as misspelled when you should have used "their"—so always proofread your worksheets for errors, in addition to running a spell check. To spell check a worksheet:

Step 1	*Click*	the Spelling button on the Standard toolbar

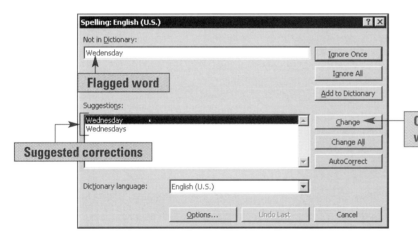

The spell checker starts at the active cell and checks the active worksheet row by row until it reaches the end of the worksheet. If the active cell is not at the top of the worksheet, Excel asks if you want to start at the top. The Spelling dialog box opens when the spell checker locates a word it doesn't recognize. Suggested corrections appear in the Suggestions: list box, as shown in Figure 5-3. Excel locates the misspelled word, "Wedensday" in the March calendar. The first suggestion in the Suggestions: list box is selected and is correct.

FIGURE 5-3
Spelling Dialog Box

Step 2	*Click*	Change to replace the misspelled word with the selected suggestion

There are no more spelling errors in the worksheet, so a dialog box opens, telling you that the spell check is complete.

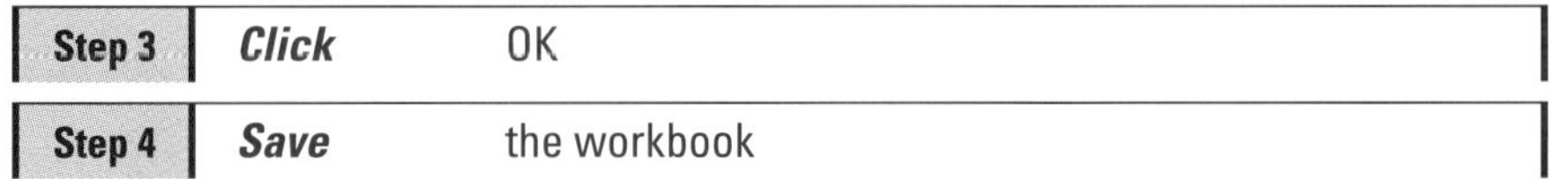

Step 3	*Click*	OK
Step 4	*Save*	the workbook

MENU TIP

You can run the spell checker by clicking the Spelling command on the Tools menu.

QUICK TIP

To spell check multiple worksheets, select the sheet tabs of each sheet you want to check, then click the Spelling button.

CAUTION TIP

Many specialized professions use industry-specific vocabularies that may not be included in the Excel dictionary. Proper names are also not included in the Excel dictionary. Click Ignore Once or Ignore All to skip these items.

5.c Setting Print Options and Printing Worksheets

Excel provides many options for formatting and printing your worksheets. You can change the margins and the orientation, add headers, footers, and print titles, or print multiple ranges or worksheets. You can also set a specific print area.

> **MOUSE TIP**
>
> The Print Preview command may display cell values too small for legibility. In Print Preview, click anywhere on the worksheet page in the window to zoom in and magnify the worksheet. Click again to zoom back out.

Setting the Print Area

By default, Excel prints all data on the current worksheet. If you need to print only a portion of a worksheet, however, you can define a print area by using the Set Print Area command. To set the print area:

Step 1	*Select*	the range A1:011
Step 2	*Click*	File
Step 3	*Point to*	Print Area
Step 4	*Click*	Set Print Area

This action defines a print area covering the worksheet title and the months January-03 and February-03.

Step 5	*Click*	cell A1 to deselect the range

Changing Margins

When the data is not situated properly on the page, you can adjust the margins, or align the data centered on the page. You can change margins in the Print Preview window or in the Page Setup dialog box. To change margins in Print Preview:

Step 1	*Click*	the Print Preview button on the Standard toolbar
Step 2	*Click*	the Margins button on the Print Preview toolbar

Your screen should look similar to Figure 5-4. The dotted lines indicate the margins and the header/footer locations. You can change these margins by dragging the lines.

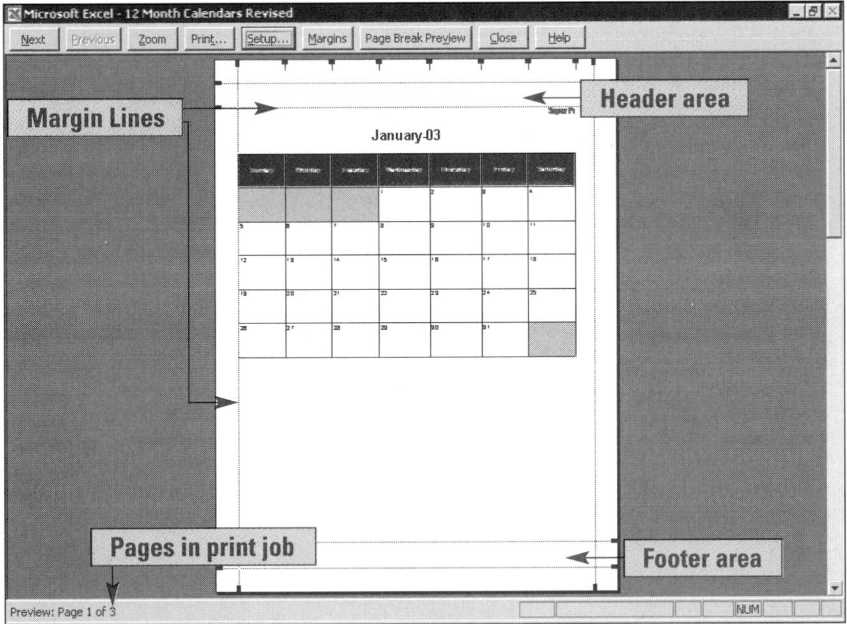

FIGURE 5-4
Adjusting Margins in Print Preview

Step 3	***Move***	the mouse pointer over the left margin line so that it changes to a double-headed arrow
Step 4	***Drag***	the margin line to the right, observing that the status bar indicates the width (in inches) of the margin
Step 5	***Release***	the mouse button when the status bar displays approximately "Left Margin: 1.00"
Step 6	***Click***	the Margins button on the Print Preview toolbar to turn off the margin lines

You also can precisely set margins in the Page Setup dialog box. To adjust the margins using the Page Setup dialog box:

Step 1	***Click***	the Setup button on the Print Preview toolbar
Step 2	***Click***	the Margins tab

MENU TIP

You can click the Print Preview command on the File menu to preview a document.

MOUSE TIP

Drag the scroll box in the vertical scroll bar in the Print Preview window to move to another page.

QUICK TIP

Zoom in to the worksheet to get more precise control.

Your dialog box should look similar to Figure 5-5.

FIGURE 5-5
Margins Tab in the Page Setup Dialog Box

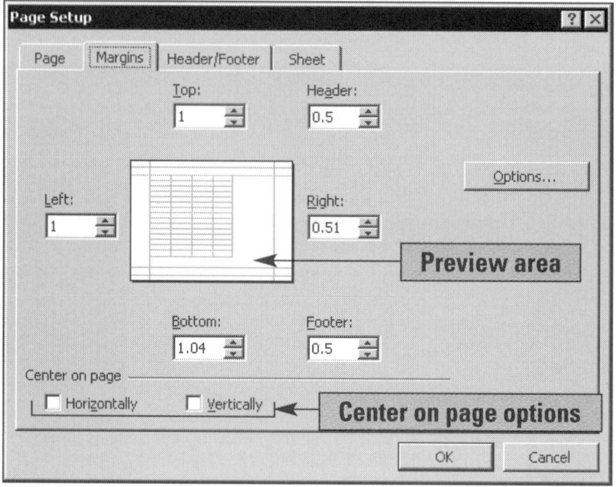

Step 3	***Double-click***	the Right: text box to select the current margin setting
Step 4	***Key***	1
Step 5	***Click***	OK

The right margin is now 1 inch. Luis wants the calendar to print two months to a page and sideways.

Changing Scaling and Page Orientation

The Page Setup dialog box provides many settings through which you can arrange the page, including scaling and orientation. Scaling a document allows you to fit a report to a certain number of pages. To scale the print area:

MENU TIP

You can open the Page Setup dialog box by clicking the Page Setup command on the File menu.

Step 1	***Click***	the Setup button on the Print Preview toolbar
Step 2	***Click***	the Page tab
Step 3	***Click***	the Fit to: option button

The Page tab in the Page Setup dialog box on your screen should look similar to Figure 5-6. The Fit to option automatically fits your print area to the number of pages you specify.

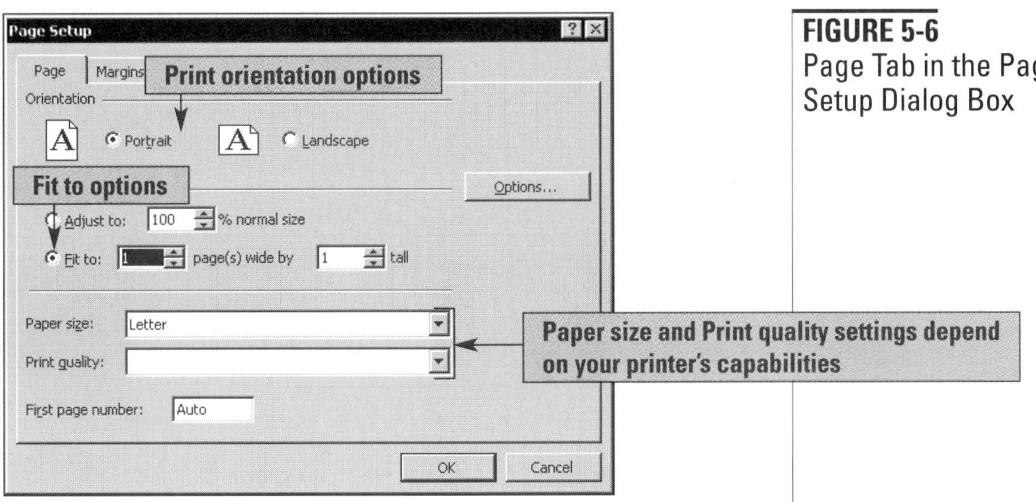

FIGURE 5-6
Page Tab in the Page Setup Dialog Box

Step 4	*Click*	OK

The print job scales to fit on a single page.

Most business documents, including letters, memos, and financial reports, are printed in **portrait orientation**, or across the width of the page. However, in Excel, you may find **landscape orientation** more suitable, because it prints across the length of the page, as if you were holding the paper sideways. To change the orientation:

Step 1	*Click*	the Setup button on the Print Preview toolbar
Step 2	*Click*	the Landscape option button on the Page tab in the Page Setup dialog box
Step 3	*Click*	OK

The print area appears in landscape orientation and all on one page. Your screen should look similar to Figure 5-7.

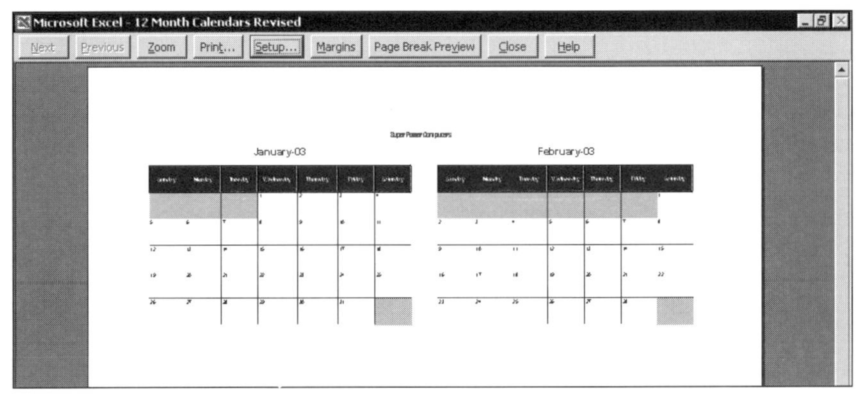

FIGURE 5-7
Calendar in Landscape Orientation

Centering the Page Horizontally and Vertically

You can use the Page Setup dialog box to center the print area vertically and horizontally on the page. To center a print area on the page:

Step 1	*Click*	the Setup button on the Print Preview toolbar
Step 2	*Click*	the Margins tab
Step 3	*Click*	the Horizontally check box to insert a check mark
Step 4	*Click*	the Vertically check box to insert a check mark
Step 5	*Click*	OK to center the print area on the page

Setting Headers and Footers

A **header** appears above the top margin of every page you print. A **footer** appears below the bottom margin of every page you print. Excel has several predefined headers and footers, using common options such as the page number, filename, and date. To add a header:

Step 1	*Click*	the Setup button on the Print Preview toolbar
Step 2	*Click*	the Header/Footer tab
Step 3	*Click*	the Header: list arrow

The Header: list contains preset headers to print the current page number, total number of pages to be printed, worksheet name, company name, date, filename, and user name, as well as several variations and combinations of these elements.

Step 4	*Click*	12 Month Calendars Revised

This choice prints the filename as the header. The mini-preview above the Header: list shows how your header will look. You also can create a custom header and footer. To add a custom footer to your document:

Step 1	*Click*	Custom Footer

The Footer dialog box opens with the blinking insertion point in the Left section: text box. The Header and Footer dialog boxes, which look identical, contain buttons to insert special print codes. See Table 5-1.

QUICK TIP

For more information about options on any tab of the Page Setup dialog box, click the Help button in the upper-right corner to activate the What's This? feature. Click any setting or control in the dialog box to obtain an explanation of the control's function.

TABLE 5-1
Header and Footer Buttons

To	Use	Code Inserted
Change the text font		
Insert a page number		&[Page]
Insert the total number of pages		&[Pages]
Insert the current date		&[Date]
Insert the current time		&[Time]
Insert the workbook path and filename		&[Path]&[File]
Insert the workbook filename		&[File]
Insert the worksheet name		&[Tab]
Insert a picture		&[Picture]
Format a picture		

Step 2	*Key*	your name in the Left section: text box
Step 3	*Click*	in the Right section: text box
Step 4	*Click*	the Date button
Step 5	*Click*	in the Center section: text box
Step 6	*Click*	the Page Number button
Step 7	*Press*	the SPACEBAR
Step 8	*Key*	of
Step 9	*Press*	the SPACEBAR
Step 10	*Click*	the Total Pages button

QUICK TIP

Text you key in the Left section: text box will be left aligned, text in the Center section: text box will be center aligned, and text in the Right section: text box will be right aligned.

The Footer dialog box on your screen should look similar to Figure 5-8.

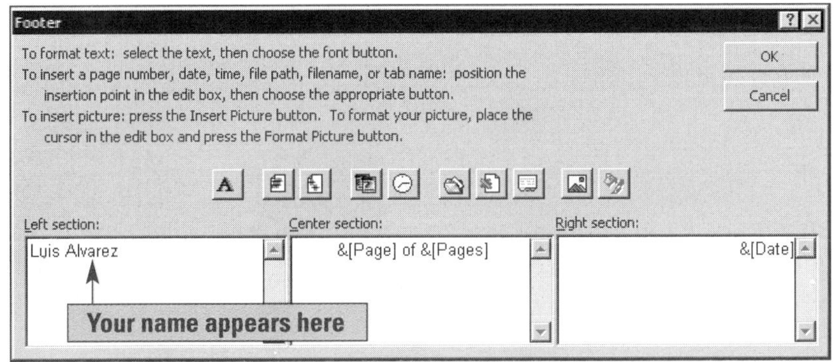

FIGURE 5-8
Footer Dialog Box

QUICK TIP

You can suppress the display of cell errors when printing. In the Page Setup dialog box, click the Sheet tab, then click the Cell errors as list arrow, and choose an option from the list.

Step 11	*Click*	OK

Your footer appears in the Footer: list box, and the mini-preview below the Footer: list box shows what the footer will look like.

Step 12	*Click*	OK to apply the header and footer

The preview shows that one page of the calendar with two months on it will print. However, you need all 12 months to print.

Step 13	*Click*	the Close button on the Print Preview toolbar

MENU TIP

When you open the Page Setup dialog box from the File menu as opposed to the Print Preview toolbar, a few extra options are enabled, such as the Print area: text box and the Print titles section.

Setting Multiple Print Ranges

To print more than one area of a worksheet, you can specify multiple ranges in the Page Setup dialog box. You key a comma between each range to separate them. To set multiple print ranges:

Step 1	*Click*	File
Step 2	*Click*	Page Setup
Step 3	*Click*	the Sheet tab, if necessary

The dialog box on your screen should look similar to Figure 5-9.

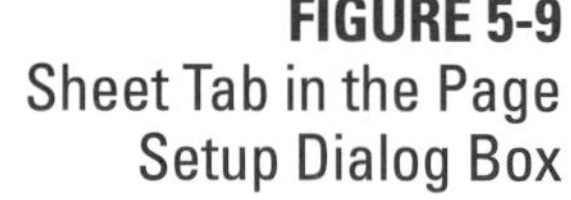

FIGURE 5-9
Sheet Tab in the Page Setup Dialog Box

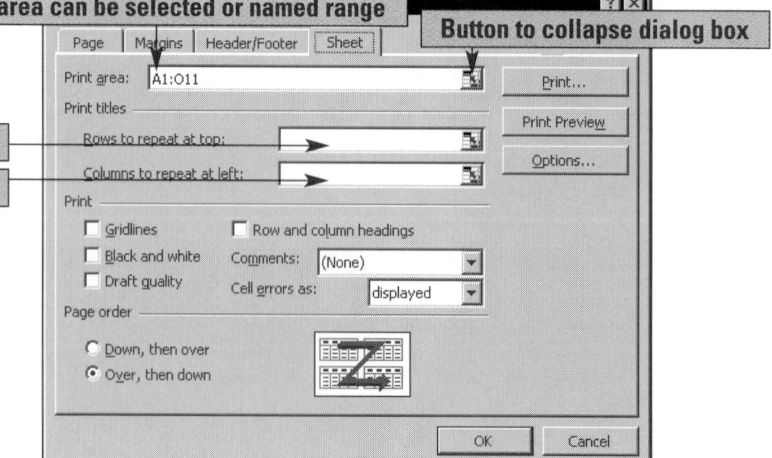

Step 4	*Click*	after the "11" in the Print area: text box

A flashing border in your worksheet indicates the current print area.

Step 5	*Key*	, (a comma)
Step 6	*Click*	the Collapse dialog box button
Step 7	*Select*	A13:O21
Step 8	*Click*	the Expand dialog box button
Step 9	*Click*	Print Preview in the Page Setup dialog box
Step 10	*Click*	the Next button on the Print Preview toolbar
Step 11	*Click*	the Close button on the Print Preview toolbar

Two pages are now set to print. There is another way to print more than one page at a time.

Inserting and Removing Page Breaks

To quickly print all the data on a worksheet, you can use Page Break Preview. When a worksheet contains data that will print on more than one page, you may need to adjust the position of page breaks so that information appears on the correct page. Because you have already defined a print area and set the print setting to Fit to, first you need to clear those settings. To clear the print area and change the Fit to option:

Step 1	*Click*	File
Step 2	*Point to*	Print Area
Step 3	*Click*	Clear Print Area
Step 4	*Open*	the Page tab in the Page Setup dialog box
Step 5	*Key*	6 in the box next to tall
Step 6	*Click*	OK

Your print job fits on six pages, two months per page. To change to Page Break Preview:

Step 1	*Click*	View
Step 2	*Click*	Page Break Preview
Step 3	*Click*	OK to close the Welcome to Page Break Preview dialog box, if necessary

MOUSE TIP

You can print nonadjacent print areas by using the CTRL key and selecting the ranges, then clicking the Selection option button in the Print dialog box.

QUICK TIP

You can select multiple ranges by using the CTRL key, and then setting the print area.

MOUSE TIP

You can insert or remove page breaks by right-clicking in the Page Break Preview window. Click Insert Page Break to insert additional page breaks above and to the left of the active cell. Right-click a cell to the right of a vertical page break or below a horizontal page break and then click Remove Page Break to remove page breaks. You can also click Reset All Page Breaks to return to the default page breaks.

Your screen should look similar to Figure 5-10. Dashed blue lines represent the automatic page breaks in Excel. A light gray page number indicates the order in which pages will print. You can drag the page break to a new location to change how pages are printed.

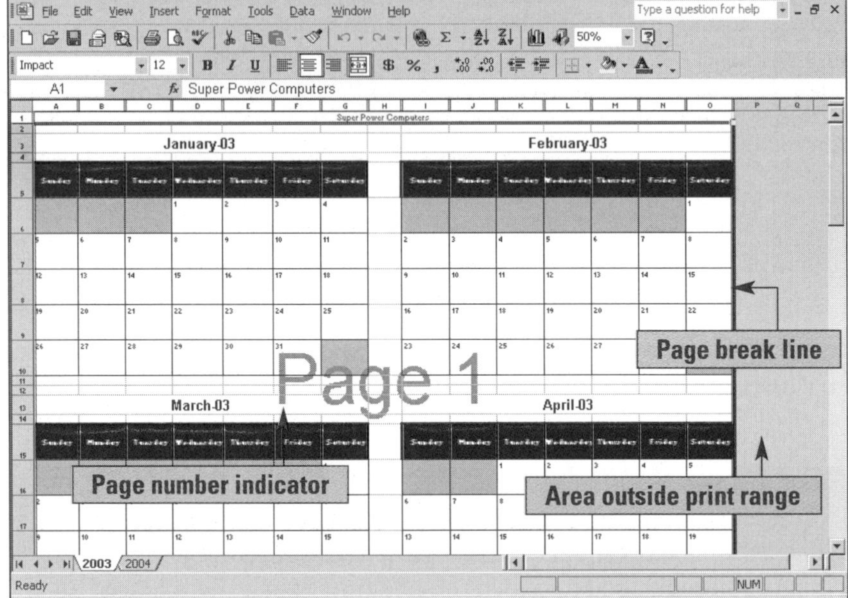

FIGURE 5-10
Page Break Preview Mode

QUICK TIP

You must set page breaks separately for each worksheet in a workbook.

notes

Because of differences in printer margins, the exact row number you use may differ in the steps that follow.

MENU TIP

You can click Remove Page Break on the Insert menu to remove a page break.

Step 4	*Scroll*	the worksheet until you see the dashed line, near row 22
Step 5	*Drag*	the dashed blue page break line from near row 22 to row 11

The dashed blue line changes to a solid blue line, representing a manually adjusted page break.

CAUTION TIP

The dashed blue page break lines may be difficult to see due to the blue heading formatting. View column H as you scroll to observe the lines.

Step 6	*Follow*	Steps 4 and 5 to manually position a page break at rows 21, 31, and 41
Step 7	*Activate*	cell A52
Step 8	*Click*	Insert
Step 9	*Click*	Page Break

In Normal view, the page breaks appear as dotted black lines. To switch back to Normal view:

Step 1	*Click*	View
Step 2	*Click*	Normal

CAUTION TIP

In Normal view, the dotted black page break lines can be turned on and off using the Options dialog box. Click the Options command on the Tools menu, click the View tab, and then click the Page breaks check box in the Window options group to turn this option on or off.

Check to make sure that your calendar will now print two months per page.

Step 3	*Click*	the Print Preview button on the Standard toolbar
Step 4	*Click*	the down scroll arrow five times to scroll through the preview
Step 5	*Drag*	the scroll box back to the top of the scroll bar
Step 6	*Close*	Print Preview

The worksheet title, "Super Power Computers," appears on page 1, but not on the rest of the pages. You can set a print title to appear on each page.

Setting Print Titles

Print titles are useful when you need column or row labels to appear on every printed page. You set print titles from the Page Setup dialog box, but this command is not available when you open the dialog box with the Print Preview window open. To create print titles:

Step 1	*Open*	the Sheet tab in the Page Setup dialog box
Step 2	*Click*	in the Rows to repeat at top: text box
Step 3	*Select*	row 1 in your worksheet
Step 4	*Click*	Print Preview in the Page Setup dialog box
Step 5	*Scroll*	through the pages to verify that the title repeats on every page
Step 6	*Close*	Print Preview

Printing a Worksheet

Now that you have adjusted the page setup options and set the page breaks, you are ready to print. To print a worksheet:

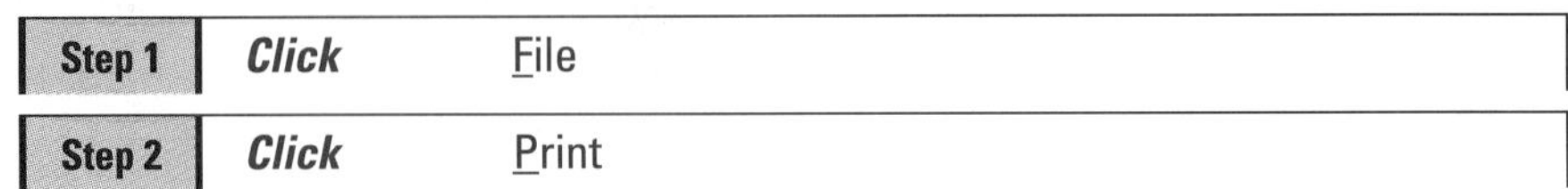

Step 1	***Click***	File
Step 2	***Click***	Print

The Print dialog box on your screen should look similar to Figure 5-11.

FIGURE 5-11
Print Dialog Box

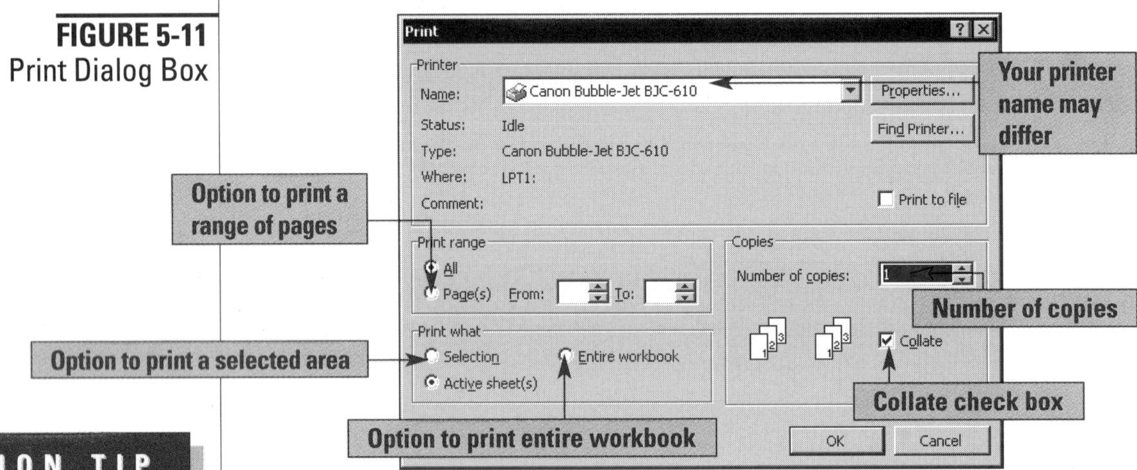

> **CAUTION TIP**
>
> The Print button on the Standard toolbar uses the current page setup options to print your worksheet. Before printing, verify the current print area settings and which printer will print the worksheet.

Step 3	***Verify***	that the Active Sheet(s) option button is selected in the Print what section

By default, the Active Sheet(s) option prints the entire worksheet. However, if you set a print area, or define page breaks, the Active Sheet refers to these manually defined print areas. If you select a region, then click the Print button, that area is printed by default instead of the print areas you may have defined.

Step 4	***Click***	OK

The 2003 worksheet prints, two months per page.

Until now, you have been working with areas on only one worksheet. In the next section, you learn how to print multiple worksheets.

5.d Printing an Entire Workbook

Luis wants everyone to have a 2004 calendar at the meeting as well. It is just for reference, so it can be printed six months to a page. When you print multiple worksheets, each worksheet has its own page break settings. To print the entire workbook:

Step 1	*Click*	the 2004 sheet tab
Step 2	*Switch to*	Page Break Preview
Step 3	*Drag*	the vertical page break line to the right of column O
Step 4	*Drag*	the horizontal page break near row 22 to below row 29
Step 5	*Right-click*	cell A40
Step 6	*Click*	Remove Page Break
Step 7	*Remove*	the other page break at row 50
Step 8	*Switch to*	Normal view
Step 9	*Click*	File
Step 10	*Click*	Print
Step 11	*Click*	the Entire workbook option button in the Print what section
Step 12	*Change*	the Number of copies text box to 2
Step 13	*Click*	Preview
Step 14	*Verify*	that the pages will print as desired
Step 15	*Verify*	that your instructor wants you to print two copies of all eight pages
Step 16	*Click*	the Print button on the Print Preview toolbar
Step 17	*Click*	OK
Step 18	*Save*	the workbook and close it

You're all set for the meeting!

CAUTION TIP

When you print multiple worksheets, remember to check the page breaks on every page.

QUICK TIP

The Collate check box in the Print dialog box organizes the order of your print job. Select it when you are printing more than one copy of a multiple-page worksheet to print a complete copy of the document before starting the next copy.

Summary

- The Find and Replace commands enable you to locate and change data.
- AutoCorrect corrects common spelling errors as you type. Add AutoCorrect entries to replace abbreviations with long words, titles, or phrases.
- You should always spell check workbooks before printing them. Remember that the spell checker does not detect incorrect usage, such as "your" for "you're." Always proofread your document after spell checking it.
- You can define print areas by clicking the File menu, pointing to Print area, and then clicking Set Print Area.
- You can set margins by dragging them in Print Preview or by using the Margins tab in the Page Setup dialog box.
- You can use the Page tab in the Page Setup dialog box to set scaling options and to change the orientation of the page.
- You can use the Margins tab in the Page Setup dialog box to select page centering options.
- You can use the Header/Footer tab to add a header or footer to a printed worksheet.
- You can set multiple print ranges on the Sheet tab in the Page Setup dialog box.
- You can manually adjust page breaks in Page Break view.
- You can select rows and columns to repeat on every printed page on the Sheet tab in the Page Setup dialog box.
- You can print a workbook by clearing print areas, then selecting the Entire Workbook option in the Print dialog box.

Commands Review

Action	Menu Bar	Shortcut Menu	Toolbar	Task Pane	Keyboard
Find	Edit, Find				ALT + E, F CTRL + F
Replace	Edit, Replace				ALT + E, E CTRL + H
Add AutoCorrect entries	Tools, AutoCorrect options				ALT +T, A
Check spelling	Tools, Spelling				ALT +T, S F7
Set print area	File, Print Area, Set Print Area				ALT + F,T, S
Clear print area	File, Print Area, Clear Print Area				ALT + F,T, C
Preview the workbook to be printed	File, Print Preview				ALT + F, V
Set print options	File, Page Setup				ALT + F, U
View page breaks	View, Page Break Preview				ALT +V, P
Switch to Normal view	View, Normal				ALT +V, N
Print	File, Print				CTRL + P ALT + F, P

Concepts Review

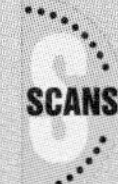

Circle the correct answer.

1. To create multiple ranges for printing, press and hold the:
[a] SHIFT key while selecting ranges.
[b] END key while selecting ranges.
[c] CTRL key while selecting ranges.
[d] ALT key while selecting ranges.

2. To set centering options for a printed report, open the Page Setup dialog box and use the:
[a] Page tab.
[b] Margins tab.
[c] Header/Footer tab.
[d] Sheet tab.

3. To set a page to print in landscape orientation, open the Page Setup dialog box and use the:
[a] Page tab.
[b] Margins tab.
[c] Header/Footer tab.
[d] Sheet tab.

4. When you include the print formula "&[Page]" in a header or footer, it prints:
[a] "&[Page]" on every page.
[b] the total page count on every page.
[c] the current page number on each page.
[d] a box where you can write in the page number by hand.

5. In Normal view, page breaks are indicated by a:
[a] heavy blue line.
[b] heavy black line.
[c] dotted black line.
[d] thin blue line.

6. In Page Break Preview view, default page breaks are indicated by a:
[a] dotted blue line.
[b] heavy black line.
[c] solid blue line.
[d] thin blue line.

7. Replace can replace values in which of the following?
[a] chart objects
[b] comments
[c] formulas
[d] chart objects, comments, and formulas

8. You set up page breaks on Sheet1 of a workbook and select Entire workbook from the Print dialog box. Sheet2 doesn't print correctly. What should you do?
- [a] Click the Print button again to see whether the problem goes away.
- [b] Check to see whether the printer is working properly.
- [c] Clear the print area.
- [d] Use Page Break Preview mode to check the page breaks on both worksheets.

9. To set collating options for a print job, you use the:
- [a] Page Setup dialog box.
- [b] Page Break Preview.
- [c] Print dialog box.
- [d] Options button in the Page Setup dialog box.

10. When you manually adjust page break lines, Page Break Preview displays a:
- [a] dotted blue line.
- [b] heavy black line.
- [c] solid blue line.
- [d] thin blue line.

Circle **T** if the statement is true or **F** if the statement is false.

T F 1. You should always preview before you print.

T F 2. Clicking the Print button on the Standard toolbar opens the Print dialog box.

T F 3. The dotted black page preview lines cannot be turned off.

T F 4. You must select named ranges by opening the Page Setup dialog box from the File menu.

T F 5. Once you change page break locations, you can't undo them.

T F 6. You can see page breaks only in Page Break Preview mode.

T F 7. You should always proofread your worksheet in addition to checking spelling.

T F 8. Headers and footers must use the same font.

T F 9. AutoCorrect can be used to replace a shortcut with a longer word or phrase.

T F 10. You need to set footer options for each page in your printed report.

Skills Review

Exercise 1

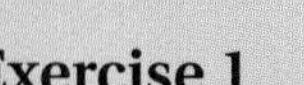

1. Open the *24 Month Calendar* workbook located on the Data Disk.

2. Select the Jan-03, Feb-03, Jun-03, and Jul-03 calendars.

3. Set the print area with these ranges selected.

4. Preview the worksheet.

5. Print the worksheet if instructed to do so.

6. Change the view to Normal view.

7. Activate cell A1.

8. Save the workbook as *24 Month Calendar Revised* and close it.

Exercise 2 C

1. Open the *Sales Rep Data* workbook located on the Data Disk.
2. Add a custom header "Sales Rep Data" using 16-point, bold text, and center it in the header area.
3. Use Page Break Preview to set page breaks after every 30 rows. Pull down the top page break to prevent the two blank rows from printing.
4. Center the print area horizontally, and set row 3 to repeat at the top of each page.
5. Preview your print job, and print the worksheet if instructed to do so.
6. Save the workbook as *Sales Rep Data Revised* and close it.

Exercise 3

1. Open the *Cookie Sales* workbook located on the Data Disk.
2. Replace all instances of the word "chip" with the work "chunk."
3. Use the Replace command to change all cells containing "Totals" to "Total" formatted with 12-point red font.
4. Run the spell checker.
5. Set the print area to cover all the data in the worksheet.
6. Change the print orientation to landscape.
7. Use the Fit to: option to print all of the data on one page.
8. Set the print options to center the data vertically and horizontally.
9. Print the worksheet if instructed to do so.
10. Save the workbook as *Cookie Sales Revised* and close it.

Exercise 4 C

1. Open the *Home Loan* workbook located on the Data Disk (click OK if a dialog box opens warning you about macros).
2. Switch to the Loan Amortization Table worksheet.
3. Use Page Break Preview to print 50 payments per page. Insert new page breaks as necessary.
4. Print the worksheet if instructed to do so.
5. Save the workbook as *Home Loan Revised* and close it.

Exercise 5 C

1. You will be distributing the *24 Month Calendar Revised* to all employees in your company. Write a step-by-step description explaining how to print only the January-03 calendar. Save the document as *Printing a Calendar*. Include the following instructions:
   a. Explain how to add **2003** as the header for the printed report.
   b. Explain how to print the calendar in Landscape orientation.
2. Print your document or e-mail it to a classmate. Have your classmate follow your directions *exactly* and print the report. See how well he or she was able to follow your instructions.
3. Save and close the *Printing a Calendar.doc* document.

Exercise 6 C

1. Open the *Sweet Tooth Q2 2003 Sales* workbook located on the Data Disk.
2. Set print options to print the worksheet centered horizontally and vertically using Portrait orientation.
3. Print the worksheet.
4. Set print options to print the worksheet centered horizontally, but not vertically, using Landscape orientation.
5. Print the worksheet.
6. Save the workbook as *Sweet Tooth Q2 2003 Sales Revised* and close it.

Exercise 7

1. Open the *Sweet Tooth Q3 2003 Sales* workbook located on the Data Disk.
2. Change the top and bottom margins to 3 inches.
3. Create a custom footer displaying the filename on the left, the date in the center, and the time on the right.
4. Print the worksheet.
5. Save the workbook as *Sweet Tooth Q3 2003 Sales Revised* and close it.

Exercise 8

1. Open the *Sweet Tooth 2003 Sales* workbook located on the Data Disk.
2. Add the abbreviation "sw" to the AutoCorrect list. Replace the abbreviation with "Sweet Tooth."
3. Use the AutoCorrect abbreviation "sw" to add "Sweet Tooth" to cell A1 on each of the worksheets.
4. Set the print scale to 150% on all four worksheets.
5. Set the print options on all four worksheets to print in Landscape orientation, with a 2-inch top margin, and centered horizontally.
6. Print the worksheet if instructed to do so.
7. Save the workbook as *Sweet Tooth 2003 Sales Revised* and close it.

Case Projects SCANS

Project 1 

Your job is to train employees in the use of Excel. Search the Internet for Excel tips to include in your weekly "Excel Training Letter." Select one tip and create a Word document of at least two paragraphs describing it. Provide the URL of any sites that you used as references for your tip. Save the document as *Excel Training Letter.doc* and then print and close it.

Project 2 C

As part of your job, you track inventory at a used car dealership. You must record the number of cars sold by type per month. Create a worksheet providing fictitious sales data on at least four different types of cars for a period of four months. Set page breaks to print each month's data on a separate page. Center the data horizontally on each page. Print the worksheet title and column labels on each page. Save the workbook as *Car Sales* and close it.

Project 3 

You're an office manager for a busy construction company. You have a lot of names, phone numbers, and addresses to manage. You keep the data for each state on separate worksheets. Create a new workbook. At the top of each worksheet create the following column headings: Last Name, First Name, Address, City, State, Zip, Phone number. On each worksheet, enter fictitious data for at least five people from the same state. Include a footer on each page with your company's name. Print the entire workbook in landscape orientation. Save the workbook as *Phone List* and close it.

Problem 4 

You are a travel agent. To stay competitive, you use the Internet to find out about your competitors' offers. Connect to the Internet, and use the Web toolbar to locate at least three Web sites offering five- to seven-night packages to Cancun, Mexico. Print pages showing information about each of these packages. Create a workbook listing the name of each package, and enter the Web address where you located the vacation package. Save the workbook as *Vacation to Cancun*. Print it in an attractive format, and then close it.

Problem 5

You are interested in increasing your productivity while using Excel. Using the Ask A Question Box, search for the topic "keyboard shortcuts." Print one of the pages containing keyboard shortcuts for any of the shortcut key categories. Instructions for printing are included on each page in the Help file.

Problem 6  

You need to purchase a workgroup class laser printer (16+ pages a minute, 600 dpi or better) for your publishing company. Connect to the Internet and search the Web for a review of this type of printer. Create a workbook and list your findings on three of the printers. Be sure to include the manufacturer, model, pages per minute, dpi if higher than 600, cost, and the Web address where you found the review. Save the workbook as *Workgroup Printer*, print it in an attractive format, and close it.

Project 7 

In order to be better organized, you decide to create a daily planner. Create a worksheet that breaks the day into one-hour segments, starting from when you get up in the morning and ending when you go to bed at night. Fill in the planner with your usual schedule for seven days. Print the worksheet(s) in an attractive format. Save the workbook as *Daily Planner* and close it.

Project 8

You are the accounts manager of a graphic design company. Create a list of 10 clients who owe your company money. Use fictitious client names and amounts due (between $500 and $2,000). Add a column indicating how many days the account is overdue. Print the worksheet it in an attractive format. Save the workbook as *Overdue Accounts* and close it.

Creating Charts and Sharing Information

Chapter Overview

Charts offer a great way to summarize and present data, providing a colorful, graphic link to numerical data collected in worksheets. Graphics can add visual interest to your worksheet. Creating such an explicit relationship helps other people analyze trends, spot inconsistencies in business performance, and evaluate market share. Sharing information electronically is an essential task. In this chapter, you learn how to create and modify charts, add graphics, add comments to worksheets, use the Web Discussion feature, and save Excel documents as Web pages.

Learning Objectives

- Use the Chart Wizard to create a chart
- Format and modify a chart
- Insert, resize, and move a graphic
- Work with embedded charts
- Preview and print charts
- Use workgroup collaboration
- Use Go To

Case profile

Each quarter, Super Power Computers' regional managers meet with the company president, Luis Alvarez, to review sales figures and set goals for the next quarter. You have collected data from each of the regional offices and are now ready to compile a report for the meeting. You decide to use charts to show the company's final sales figures.

6.a Using the Chart Wizard to Create a Chart

A chart provides a graphical interface to numerical data contained in a worksheet. Almost anyone can appreciate and understand the colorful simplicity of a chart. The data found in the *Super Power Computers - Sales Data Q1 2003* workbook represents Super Power Computers' sales for the first quarter. Your job is to create and format a chart for use in tomorrow's sales meeting. To open the workbook and save it with a new name:

Step 1	***Open***	the *Super Power Computers - Sales Data Q1 2003* workbook located on the Data Disk
Step 2	***Save***	the workbook as *Super Power Computers - Sales Data Q1 2003 Revised*

The Chart Wizard walks you step by step through a series of four dialog box boxes to quickly create a chart. You can create charts as separate workbook sheets called **chart sheets**, or you can place them directly on the worksheet page as **embedded charts**. One type of chart, called a column chart, helps you compare values across categories. To create a chart using the Chart Wizard:

Step 1	***Activate***	cell A5 on the Summary worksheet
Step 2	***Click***	the Chart Wizard button on the Standard toolbar

The Chart Wizard dialog box on your screen should look similar to Figure 6-1. In Step 1, you select the type of chart you want to create from the list of chart types on the left side of the dialog box. You click a chart type on the left to display chart subtypes on the right side of the dialog box. A description of the chart subtype appears below the preview box. You want to create a three-dimensional chart, which is an interesting visual alternative to two-dimensional charts.

QUICK TIP

The fastest way to create a chart is to press the F11 key. This shortcut key creates a default two-dimensional column chart on a separate chart sheet.

MOUSE TIP

The Chart Wizard automatically detects the range you want to include in your chart when you activate any cell within the range.

chapter six

FIGURE 6-1
Step 1 of the Chart Wizard

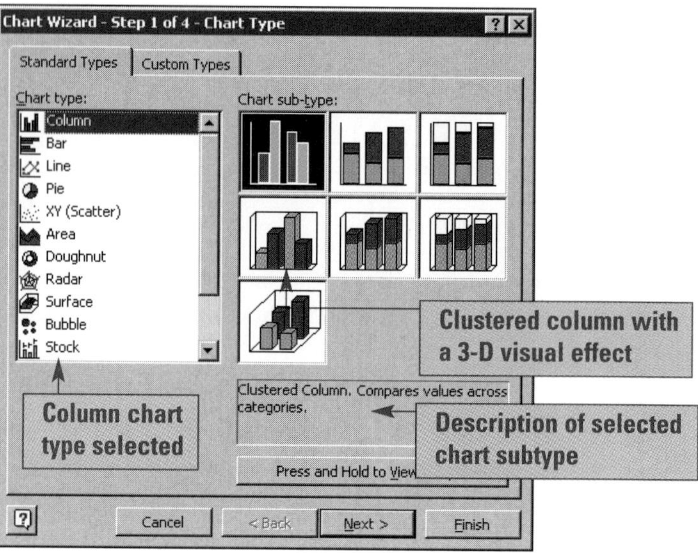

QUICK TIP

By default, data is plotted with the longest edge along the *x*-axis—in this case, the column labels. If the chart doesn't show the data the way you expected, click the other option button in the Series in: section in Step 2 of the Chart Wizard to reverse the way data is plotted in the chart—in this case, by row labels.

MOUSE TIP

You can change a chart to a different type at any time. Right-click the chart you want to change, click Chart type on the shortcut menu, select a new chart type and subtype, then click the OK button.

Step 3	***Verify***	that Column is selected in the Chart type: list
Step 4	***Click***	the Clustered column with a 3-D visual effect from the Chart sub-type: box (first column, second row)
Step 5	***Click***	Next >

In Step 2 of the Chart Wizard, you select or modify the chart's source data. A preview of the selected data appears at the top of the Data Range tab. Notice the flashing border surrounding the chart data in the worksheet behind the Chart Wizard.

Step 6	***Click***	Next >

The Titles tab in Step 3 of the Chart Wizard on your screen should look similar to Figure 6-2.

FIGURE 6-2
Step 3 of the Chart Wizard

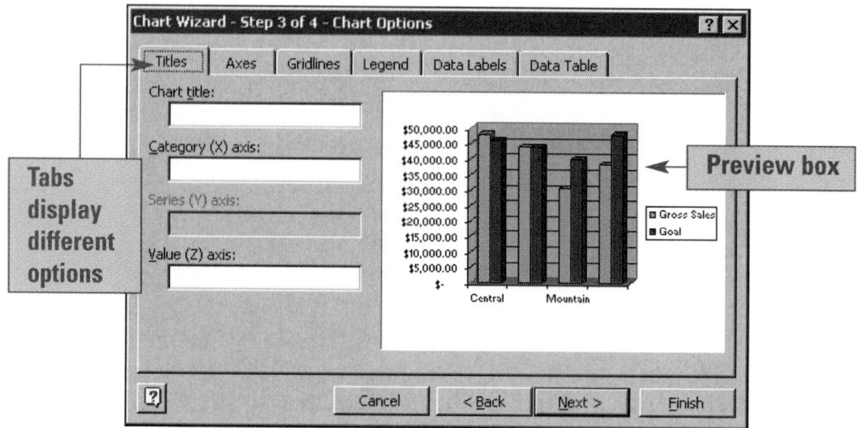

You enter chart options such as titles, legends, and data labels. The tabs vary depending on the chart type you selected.

Step 7	*Click*	in the Chart title: text box
Step 8	*Key*	Gross Sales by Region

The title you just keyed appears in the Preview box after a few seconds.

Step 9	*Press*	the TAB key to move to the Category (X) axis: text box
Step 10	*Key*	Region Name
Step 11	*Click*	the Legend tab
Step 12	*Click*	the Bottom option button
Step 13	*Click*	Next >

The dialog box on your screen should look similar to Figure 6-3. In Step 4 of the Chart Wizard, you specify the location of the new chart. You can create the chart as a new sheet or as an object in another worksheet.

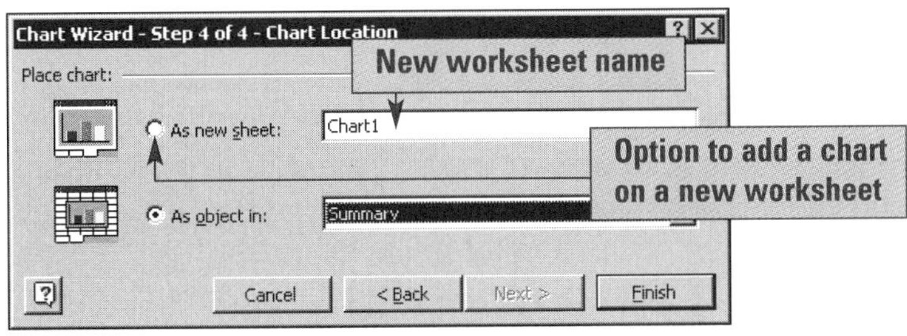

FIGURE 6-3
Step 4 of the Chart Wizard

Step 14	*Click*	the As new sheet: option button
Step 15	*Key*	Gross Sales by Region Chart in the As new sheet: text box
Step 16	*Click*	Finish

The chart appears on a new worksheet in your workbook, and the Chart toolbar appears. Your screen should look similar to Figure 6-4.

MOUSE TIP

Change your mind while using the Chart Wizard? Step backward at any time by clicking the < Back button. Make any changes, then click the Next > button to continue. The wizard leaves all other settings intact.

MOUSE TIP

You can change the location of a chart by right-clicking the chart and clicking Location.

FIGURE 6-4
Chart Created with Chart Wizard

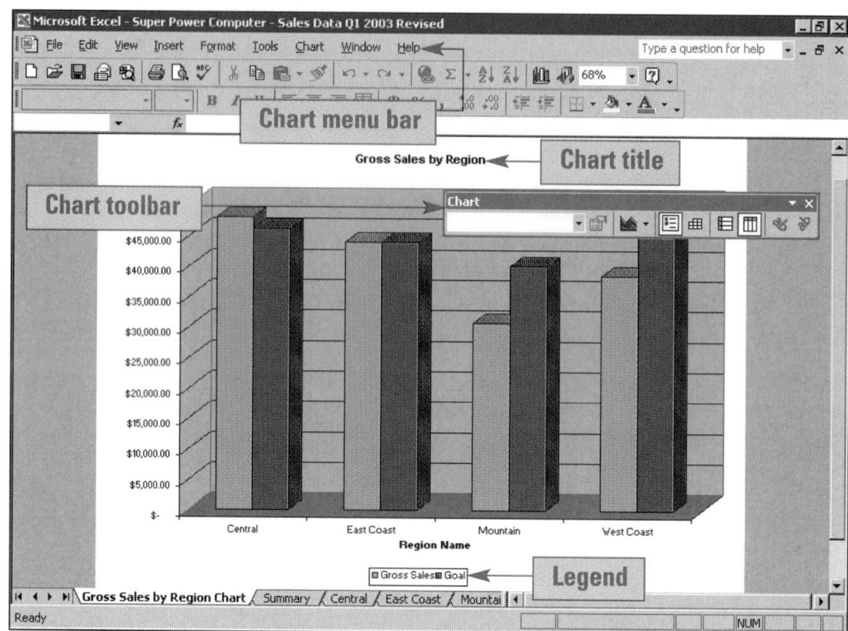

MENU TIP

Do you use a certain type of chart most of the time? You can change the default chart type. First, create a chart. Click Chart Type on the Chart menu, select the type of chart and the subtype that you use most often, then click the Set as default chart button.

When you create a chart, the Chart toolbar appears, and the Chart menu replaces the Data menu in the menu bar. The Chart menu bar and toolbar contain chart-specific tools to help you create and modify charts.

6.b Formatting and Modifying a Chart

MOUSE TIP

To select a data point in a chart, click it, then click it again. Do not double-click the data point.

Every element of a chart, such as the title, legend, and plot area, is considered an object. An **object** is a graphical element added to a worksheet that you can manipulate by moving, resizing, or reformatting it. Each chart object can be formatted by double-clicking or right-clicking the object, then clicking Format *object* (where *object* is the name of the selected object). The Format dialog box displays options unique to each object.

Some of the more important chart objects are defined here. The **legend** is the key used to identify the colors assigned to categories in a chart. **Tick marks** are small marks on the edges of the chart that delineate the scale or separate the data categories. **Data points** represent the numerical data in your worksheet. In the current chart type, the data points are represented by horizontal columns. Data points, however, can also be represented by bars, columns, pie slices, and a variety of other shapes and marks. A **data series** represents all related data points in a set. On your chart, the Gross Sales columns are a data series, as are the Goal columns. A **data label** displays the actual value of each data point on the chart. The **plot area** of a chart is the area that includes only the chart itself.

Changing Chart Fonts

You can change font settings for all text on the chart simultaneously, or you can select individual text objects and then customize their font settings. You want the title to stand out from the other elements of the chart. To change fonts for individual objects:

Step 1	*Move*	the mouse pointer over the Chart Title object at the top of the chart to display the ScreenTip
Step 2	*Right-click*	the Chart Title object
Step 3	*Click*	Format Chart Title
Step 4	*Click*	the Font tab in the Format Chart Title dialog box, if necessary
Step 5	*Click*	Impact in the Font: list
Step 6	*Click*	20 in the Size: list
Step 7	*Click*	the Color: list arrow
Step 8	*Click*	the Blue square (second row, sixth column)
Step 9	*Click*	the Patterns tab
Step 10	*Click*	the Automatic option button in the Border section
Step 11	*Click*	OK
Step 12	*Press*	the ESC key to deselect the Chart Title object

The chart title is now formatted with your selections. Next, you format one of the axes.

Formatting the Axes

You can modify both axes of the chart. The **category axis**, sometimes called the *x*-axis, is the axis along which you normally plot categories of data. This axis runs horizontally along the bottom of many chart types. The **value axis**, or *y*-axis, usually runs vertically along the left side of a chart, and is the axis along which you plot values associated with various categories of data.

Excel gives you full control over the scale of the axes, the number format, and the appearance of the axis labels. You decide to modify the number format of the value axis by dropping the decimal amount. To modify the value axis scale:

Step 1	*Right-click*	the value axis along the left side of the chart
Step 2	*Click*	Format Axis

MOUSE TIP

Double-clicking any chart object opens the Format dialog box for that object.

QUICK TIP

Some types of charts allow you to do interesting things with the data points. For example, you can drag a "slice" of a pie chart away from the rest of the "pie" by clicking the slice once to select the data series, then clicking the slice again to select the individual point. Finally, drag the slice to its new location.

MOUSE TIP

You can quickly format Chart Area fonts. For example, suppose all text on the chart should be bold. Click the Chart Area to select it, then click the Bold button on the Formatting toolbar. All text items are bolded.

Step 3	*Click*	the Number tab in the Format Axis dialog box
Step 4	*Click*	the down spin arrow in the Decimal places: text box twice to set it to 0
Step 5	*Click*	OK

Your screen should look similar to Figure 6-5.

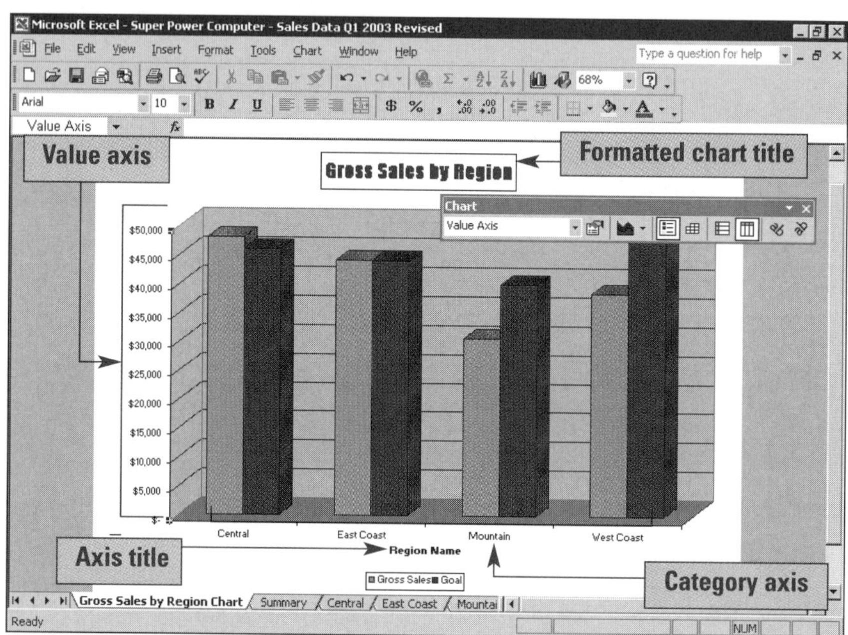

FIGURE 6-5
Changing Value Scale Options

Adding a Data Table to a Chart

A **data table** displays the actual data used to create the chart. For small data sets, you may find it helpful to show this information on the chart worksheet. To add a data table to the chart:

CAUTION TIP

If the Chart toolbar is not displayed, right-click any toolbar, then click Chart.

Step 1	*Click*	the Data Table button on the Chart toolbar

The data table is added beneath the value axis. Your screen should look similar to Figure 6-6.

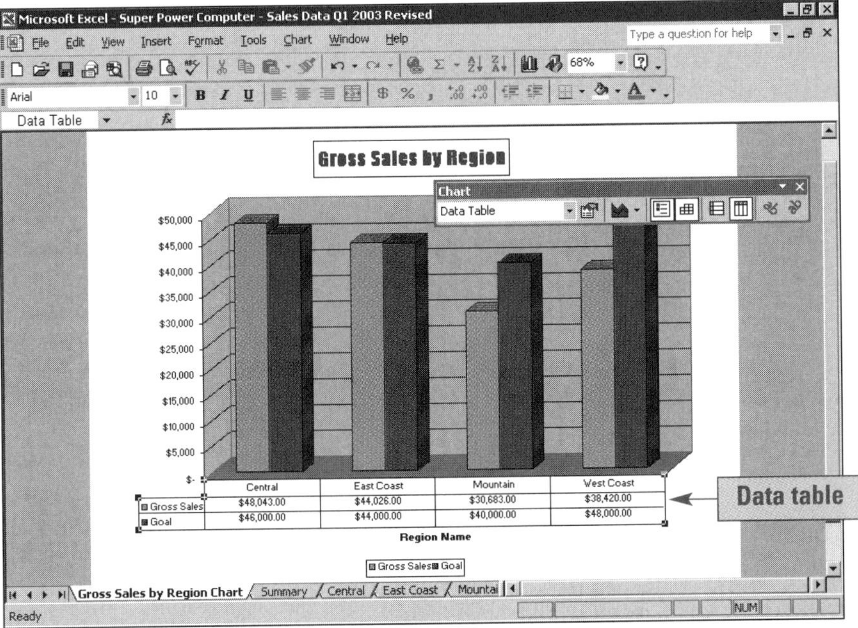

FIGURE 6-6
Adding a Data Table to a Chart

> **MOUSE TIP**
>
> You can add data labels by right-clicking the data series, clicking the Data Labels tab, selecting an option button, then clicking the OK button.

> **QUICK TIP**
>
> When a chart object is selected, you can cycle to other chart objects by pressing the ARROW keys.

Step 2	***Save***	the workbook

The Gross Sales by Region chart is complete. Next, you insert the company logo on the chart.

6.c Inserting, Resizing, and Moving a Graphic

You can insert other types of objects into a chart. For example, you can place text, lines, or pictures to further enhance your chart. To insert an object into a chart:

Step 1	***Click***	the Drawing button on the Standard toolbar to display the Drawing toolbar, if necessary
Step 2	***Click***	the Insert Picture From File button on the Drawing toolbar

The Insert Picture dialog box opens.

QUICK TIP

To insert clip art, click the Insert Clip Art button on the Drawing toolbar. To insert other types of objects, click the Object command on the Insert menu.

Step 3	*Click*	*SPC Logo* on the Data Disk
Step 4	*Click*	Insert

The image object is inserted in your chart. The Picture toolbar might appear. The small circles around the image are **sizing handles**. The image is too large. Pressing the CTRL key while dragging a sizing handle resizes the object uniformly from the center of the object. As you drag the object handle, the Name Box displays a scale percentage.

Step 5	*Press & hold*	the CTRL key
Step 6	*Drag*	the lower-right sizing handle up and to the left
Step 7	*Release*	the mouse button when the object is approximately 45% of its original size

MOUSE TIP

To resize an object proportionally from the edge, press and hold the SHIFT key while you drag a selection handle.

To move the object:

Step 1	*Move*	the mouse pointer over the image object
Step 2	*Drag*	the object to position it to the left of the chart title

The chart on your screen should look similar to Figure 6-7.

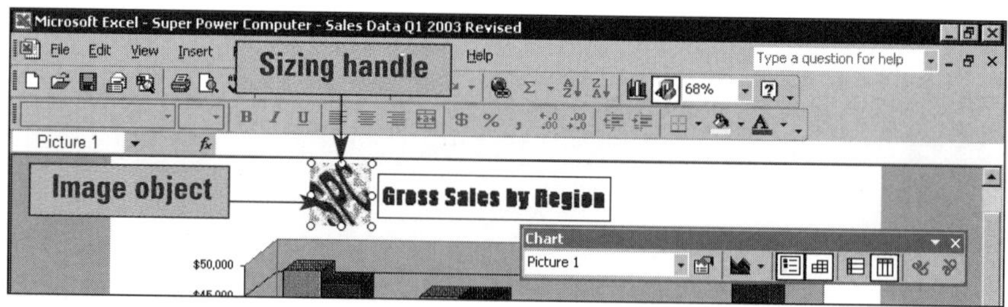

FIGURE 6-7
Inserting and Positioning a Chart Object

QUICK TIP

To delete a chart object, select it and then press the DELETE key.

Step 3	*Press*	the ESC key to deselect the logo
Step 4	*Save*	the workbook

6.d Working with Embedded Charts

Embedded charts are charts placed directly into a worksheet, rather than on a separate sheet tab. You decide to create an embedded chart in your workbook. To create an embedded chart:

Step 1	*Select*	the range A5:B8 on the Central worksheet
Step 2	*Click*	the Chart Wizard button on the Standard toolbar
Step 3	*Click*	Pie in the Chart type: list
Step 4	*Click*	Finish

The default chart type is an embedded chart, so there is no need to click all the way through the Chart Wizard. The chart is embedded in your worksheet, but it needs a little work. To resize and move an embedded chart:

Step 1	*Verify*	that the chart is still selected

Sizing handles appear around the edges of the chart when it is selected.

Step 2	*Drag*	the sizing handle in the middle of the left edge of the chart object
Step 3	*Release*	the mouse button near the divider line between columns D and E
Step 4	*Position*	the mouse pointer anywhere in the white chart area (ScreenTip displays Chart Area)
Step 5	*Drag*	the chart object so that the chart is vertically centered next to the worksheet data

Your screen should look similar to Figure 6-8.

QUICK TIP

To delete an embedded chart, select the chart, and then press the DELETE key.

FIGURE 6-8
Resizing and Moving an Embedded Chart

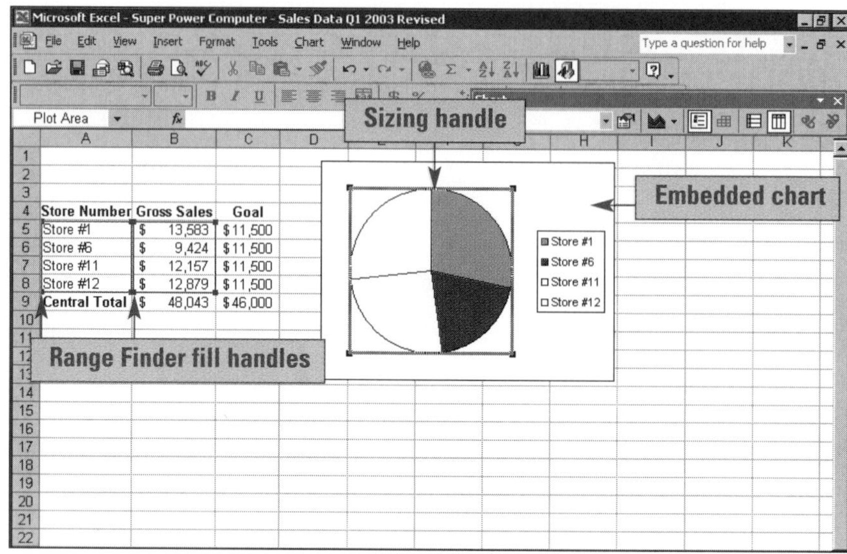

QUICK TIP

If you have an object selected within the chart, you may need to press the ESC key a few times until a cell in the worksheet becomes active.

The data you charted is surrounded by colored boxes, called **Range Finder**. You can use Range Finder to adjust the data used by the chart. You don't want to include the total row in the chart. To modify the chart using Range Finder:

Step 1	*Position*	the mouse pointer over one of the Range Finder fill handles at the bottom of row 8

The pointer changes to a double-headed arrow.

Step 2	*Drag*	the fill handle up to just below row 7

The chart displays only three sets of data.

Step 3	*Press*	the ESC key to deselect the chart
Step 4	*Save*	the workbook

6.e Previewing and Printing Charts

Before you print your chart for the meeting, you should preview it in Print Preview to make sure that everything looks the way you expected. You can preview a chart, change print setup options, and print the chart from the Print Preview window.

Printing Chart Sheets

Printing charts on separate worksheets is very similar to printing any worksheet data. To preview the chart sheet, change chart printing options, and print a chart:

Step 1	*Click*	the Gross Sales by Region Chart sheet tab
Step 2	*Click*	the Print Preview button on the Standard toolbar
Step 3	*Click*	the Setup button on the Print Preview toolbar
Step 4	*Click*	the Chart tab in the Page Setup dialog box

The Scale to fit page option scales the chart until either the height or the width of the chart hits a page margin. The Use full page option scales the chart until both the height and the width touch the page margins on all sides of the page.

Step 5	*Click*	the Scale to fit page option button
Step 6	*Click*	OK
Step 7	*Click*	the Print button on the Print Preview toolbar
Step 8	*Click*	OK

Printing an Embedded Chart

You have a few choices to make when printing embedded charts. One option is to print the chart by itself. Another option is to print the chart as part of the worksheet, and the final option is to exclude the chart from printing at all. By default, an embedded chart prints as part of the worksheet, as long as it is not specifically excluded from a print area. If Print Preview does not show a chart you expected to print, try clearing the print area, or adjusting the page breaks in Page Break Preview. When you select a chart, Excel assumes that you want to print only the chart.

Because of all these print options, it is especially important that you preview the document before printing it when you work with embedded charts. To preview the worksheet with the embedded chart:

Step 1	*Click*	the Central sheet tab

QUICK TIP

You can print an embedded chart by itself or with the data on the worksheet. To print an embedded chart by itself, select the chart by clicking it once, then click the Print Preview button on the Standard toolbar.

Step 2	*Click*	the Print Preview button  on the Standard toolbar
Step 3	*Click*	the Print button on the Print Preview toolbar
Step 4	*Click*	OK
Step 5	*Save*	the workbook

C

6.f Using Workgroup Collaboration

Sharing information electronically is no longer an option; it's an essential part of doing business. To effectively communicate with colleagues and coworkers, you can use comments, engage in Web discussions, and publish pages to a Web server for periodic review.

You need to send the workbook with the finished charts to the regional managers for their comments and suggestions.

Adding and Editing Comments

You can add comments to any cell to provide a simple, effective way to share explanatory information with others. Comments can highlight important cells or explain complex formulas. To add a comment:

MOUSE TIP

To delete a comment, right-click the cell containing the comment, then click Delete Comment on the shortcut menu.

Step 1	*Right-click*	cell C9 on the Central sheet tab
Step 2	*Click*	Insert Comment
Step 3	*Key*	Consider revising goal in Q2 to $52,500
Step 4	*Click*	cell C9 to close the comment

A small red triangle appears in the upper-right corner of cells containing comments. To read comments:

Step 1	*Move*	the mouse pointer over cell C9

The yellow comment note that appears on your screen should look similar to Figure 6-9.

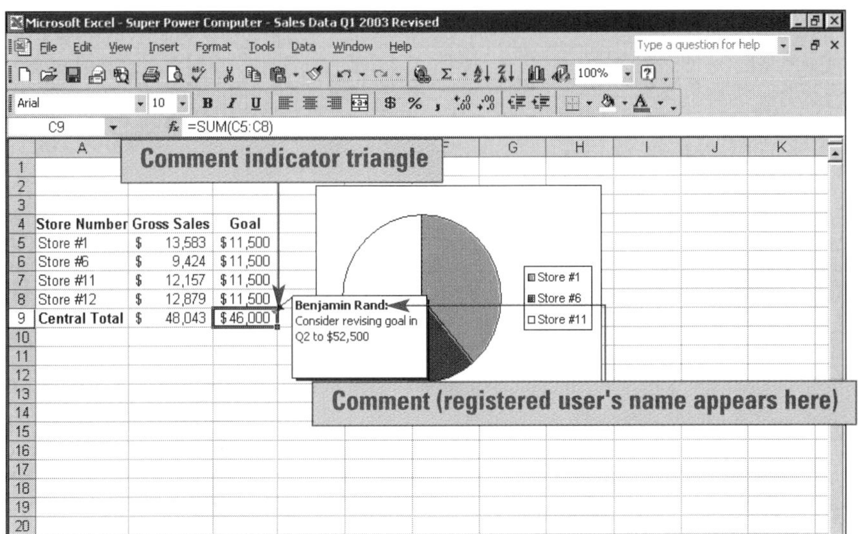

FIGURE 6-9
Reading a Comment

You can add or modify the text in a comment. To edit a comment:

Step 1	***Right-click***	cell C9
Step 2	***Click***	Edit Comment
Step 3	***Select***	$52,500
Step 4	***Key***	$54,000
Step 5	***Click***	cell C9

Inserting Hyperlinks

Another helpful collaboration tool is the ability to insert hyperlinks in a document. A **hyperlink** is a link to another place in the current workbook, to another file on your computer or on your network, or to a Web page, or it can be a mailto link. When clicked, a **mailto link** automatically starts a new message using the user's default e-mail program. To insert a hyperlink in a document:

Step 1	***Right-click***	cell A1 on the Summary worksheet
Step 2	***Click***	Hyperlink
Step 3	***Click***	E-mail Address in the Link to: list

The Insert Hyperlink dialog box on your screen should look similar to Figure 6-10. When you click an option in the Link to: list, the dialog box options change. When you clicked the E-mail Address option, the dialog box provides text boxes to enter an e-mail address and a message subject.

FIGURE 6-10
Insert Hyperlink Dialog Box

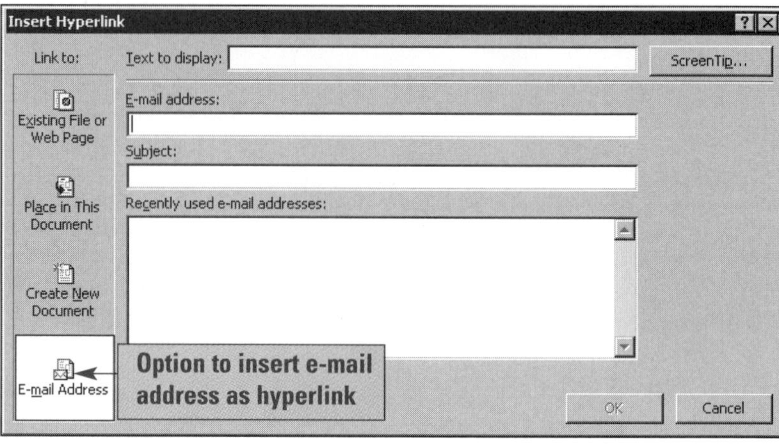

Step 4	***Key***	your e-mail address (or a fictitious e-mail address) in the E-mail address: text box
Step 5	***Key***	Review Chart in the Subject: text box
Step 6	***Select***	the text in the Text to display: text box
Step 7	***Key***	Contact me in the Text to display: text box
Step 8	***Click***	OK

MOUSE TIP

To delete a hyperlink, right-click the link, then click Remove Hyperlink on the shortcut menu.

The hyperlink appears in cell A1 as blue, underlined text. When you click this link, your e-mail program opens with the e-mail address you added in the Insert Hyperlink dialog box in the To text box (in this case, it's your e-mail address). To test the link:

Step 1	***Click***	the Contact me hyperlink in cell A1
Step 2	***Observe***	the message window with your e-mail address in the To text box
Step 3	***Close***	your e-mail program without sending a message or saving changes to the message

Creating and Responding to Discussion Comments

Discussions allow users to post and respond to comments made by other users. For example, one user might post a question about how to perform a certain task in Excel. Other users can then respond to the question.

To use the Discussion feature, you must have access to a discussion server and user rights to view and contribute to discussions.

You display the Web Discussions toolbar to create and respond to topics. For a new topic you enter a subject and message, and then post the topic to the discussion server, where other users can log in, read, and respond to the topic. To create and post a discussion comment:

Step 1	***Click***	Tools
Step 2	***Point to***	Online Collaboration
Step 3	***Click***	Web Discussions to display the Web Discussions toolbar
Step 4	***Click***	the Insert Discussion about the Workbook button on the Web Discussions toolbar
Step 5	***Key***	Review Sales Figures in the Discussion Subject: text box
Step 6	***Press***	the TAB key to move to the message text box
Step 7	***Key***	Please review sales figures for your region and respond with any corrections.
Step 8	***Click***	OK
Step 9	***Click***	the Close button Close to close the Web Discussions toolbar

CAUTION TIP

You may not be able to create a discussion comment if you do not have proper access to a discussion server. If you cannot log on, you cannot complete the steps in this section.

Previewing and Saving a Workbook or a Worksheet as a Web Page

You post the Gross Sales chart on the company's intranet to allow other employees to see the company's progress. You can save a workbook in HTML format for publication on the Web. To preview a workbook as a Web page:

Step 1	***Click***	the Gross Sales by Region Chart sheet tab
Step 2	***Click***	File
Step 3	***Click***	Web Page Preview

A copy of your workbook appears in HTML format in your Web browser. Your screen should look similar to Figure 6-11.

FIGURE 6-11
Previewing a Workbook as a Web Page

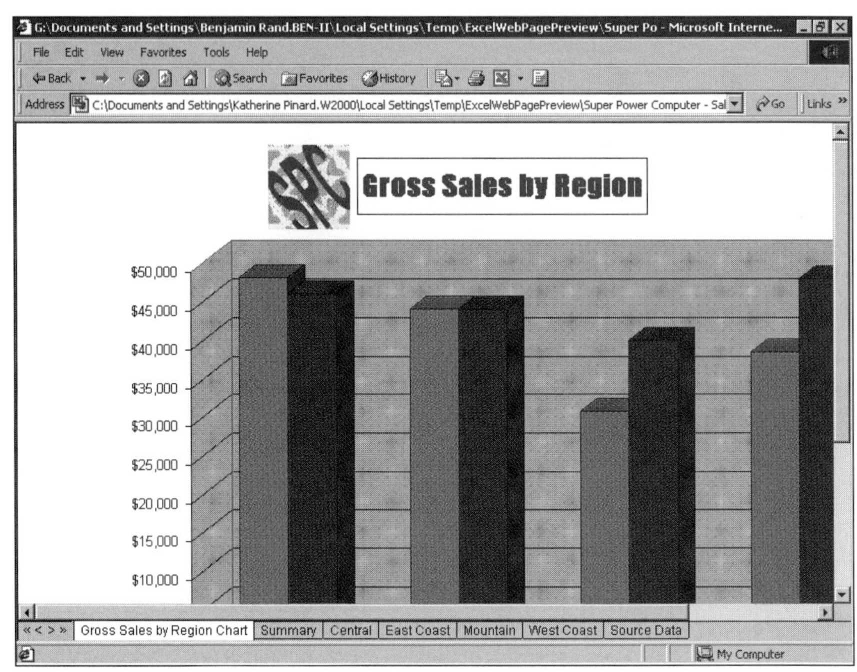

It's a good idea to avoid using spaces and uppercase letters in filenames for pages intended for the Web because many Web servers cannot properly handle them.

Step 4	*Close*	your Web browser

You want to publish only the chart page. To save the chart worksheet as a Web page:

Step 1	*Click*	File
Step 2	*Click*	Save As Web Page
Step 3	*Click*	the Selection: Chart option button
Step 4	*Key*	sales_data_chart in the File name: text box
Step 5	*Click*	Save

The chart is saved and ready to be uploaded to a Web server. You can save your page directly to a Web server by clicking the Publish button instead of the Save button in the Save As dialog box.

6.g Using Go To

A quick way to select cells is to use the Go To command. Using Go To, you can select ranges, named ranges, and cells based on certain characteristics, such as selecting all cells that contain formulas.

To use Go To:

Step 1	*Click*	the Central sheet tab
Step 2	*Click*	Edit
Step 3	*Click*	Go To

The Go To dialog box opens. You can enter a range, select a named range, or click the Special button to locate cells that share common characteristics.

Step 4	*Click*	Special

The Go To Special dialog box on your screen should look similar to Figure 6-12. It provides additional search options.

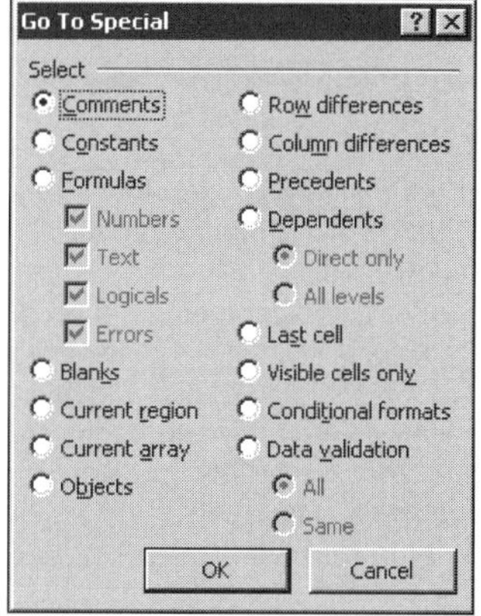

FIGURE 6-12
The Go To Special Dialog Box

Step 5	*Click*	the Formulas option button
Step 6	*Click*	OK

All of the cells containing formulas on the Central worksheet are highlighted.

Step 7	*Save*	and close the workbook

You can use Go To to find and select cells or ranges based on content.

Summary

- The Chart Wizard enables you to create a chart. You can create a new default chart by pressing the F11 key.
- Charts can be placed on a separate chart tab, or they can be embedded in a worksheet. A chart location can be changed at any time.
- Charts contain many types of objects, including titles, legends, data tables, and plot areas. Each of these objects can be formatted independently.
- You can change formatting elements for all chart objects at any time by using the Format dialog box.
- You can add a data table to a chart to show the actual data used to create the chart.
- Drawing objects, such as pictures or text boxes, can be inserted into a chart. Drag selection handles to resize them. Drag entire objects to new locations.
- You can move and resize embedded worksheets as you like.
- It is a good idea to preview charts before printing them so you can set print options. Embedded charts can be printed separately or as part of the active worksheet.
- Comments enable you to highlight important cells or explain formulas. You can edit existing comments.
- Hyperlinks can be added to cell content to provide easy links to Web pages, files, or e-mail addresses.
- Discussion comments can be added to any file if you have a connection to a discussion server.
- Workbooks or worksheets can be previewed and saved as Web pages.
- Go To enables you to find and select cell ranges or cells based on the type of content.

Commands Review

Action	Menu Bar	Shortcut Menu	Toolbar	Task Pane	Keyboard
Use the Chart Wizard	Insert, Chart				ALT + I, H
Create a default chart					F11 ALT + F1
Format a selected chart object	Format, Selected (chart object name)	Right-click chart object, Format (chart object name)	Select object from the Chart Objects list box, ; double-click object		ALT + O, E CTRL + 1
Change chart type	Chart, Chart Type	Right-click chart, Chart Type			ALT + C, T
Change chart options	Chart, Chart Options	Right-click chart, Chart Options			ALT + C, O
Show the Chart toolbar	View, Toolbars, Chart				ALT + V, T
Add a data table to a chart					
Show the Drawing toolbar	View, Toolbars, Drawing				ALT + V, T
Insert a picture	Insert, Picture, From File				ALT + I, P, F
Insert clip art	Insert, Picture, Clip Art				ALT + I, P, C
Insert an object	Insert, Object				ALT + I, O
Preview a chart	File, Print Preview				ALT + F, V
Print a chart	File, Print				CTRL + P ALT + F, P
Add a comment	Insert, Comment	Right-click, Insert Comment			ALT + I, M
Edit a comment	Insert, Edit Comment	Right-click comment, Edit Comment			ALT + I, E
Delete a comment	Insert, Delete Comment	Right-click comment, Delete Comment			ALT + I, M
Insert a hyperlink	Insert, Hyperlink	Right-click text Hyperlink			ALT + I, I CTRL + K
Remove a hyperlink		Right-click hyperlink, Remove Hyperlink			
Insert discussion comments	Tools, Online Collaboration, Web Discussions				ALT + T, N, W
Preview a worksheet as a Web page	File, Web Page Preview				ALT + F, B
Save a worksheet as Web Page	File, Save As Web Page				ALT + F, G
Use Go To	Edit, Go to				ALT + E, G CTRL + G

chapter six

Concepts Review

Circle the correct answer.

1. A data label:
- [a] displays the name of a chart object when the mouse pointer is over that object.
- [b] displays the actual data used to create a chart.
- [c] is a key used to identify patterns, colors, or symbols associated with data points on a chart.
- [d] displays the value of a data point on a chart.

2. A legend:
- [a] displays the name of a chart object when the mouse pointer is over that object.
- [b] displays the actual data used to create a chart.
- [c] is a key used to identify patterns, colors, or symbols associated with data points on a chart.
- [d] can show the value of a data point on a chart.

3. A mailto link opens:
- [a] a Web browser.
- [b] a Web page.
- [c] a new e-mail message and addresses it.
- [d] none of the above.

4. A data point:
- [a] represents a series of data.
- [b] represents a single value.
- [c] identifies the colors assigned to categories in a chart.
- [d] separates the data categories.

5. Which of the following does *not* bring up the Format (chart object) Properties dialog box?
- [a] double-click (chart object)
- [b] right-click (chart object), select Format (chart object)
- [c] select object, click Edit, click Format (chart object)
- [d] click the Chart Objects list arrow on the Chart toolbar to select the chart object, then click the Format (chart object) button on the Chart toolbar

6. The F11 shortcut key allows you to:
- [a] create an embedded chart.
- [b] choose whether to use the Chart Wizard.
- [c] create a default chart sheet chart.
- [d] create either an embedded chart or a chart sheet chart.

7. The Chart Wizard allows you to:
- [a] create either an embedded chart or a chart sheet chart.
- [b] create only an embedded chart.
- [c] create only a chart sheet chart.
- [d] edit an existing chart.

8. If you change your mind while using the Chart Wizard, you can click the:
- [a] Cancel button and start over.
- [b] Finish button, delete the chart, and start over.
- [c] Next button.
- [d] Back button.

9. To change the location of a chart, right-click the chart and click:
- [a] Chart Type.
- [b] Source Data.
- [c] Chart Options.
- [d] Location.

10. The value axis of a chart represents:
- [a] the actual data values of each category.
- [b] the categories of data.
- [c] nothing.
- [d] the chart height and width.

Circle **T** if the statement is true or **F** if the statement is false.

T F 1. Charts make data easier to understand.

T F 2. Embedded charts cannot be moved on the worksheet.

T F 3. A data point is a graphical means of displaying numerical data.

T F 4. The Go To command is one way to select all cells that contain formulas.

T F 5. The Format (chart object) dialog box is the same no matter which object is selected.

T F 6. Hyperlinks cannot be linked to files on your computer.

T F 7. The Use Full Page print option scales a chart in both directions to fill the entire page.

T F 8. You can't print an embedded chart by itself.

T F 9. Web Page Preview is a good way to see what your workbook will look like as a Web page.

T F 10. You do not need access to a discussion server to add comments to a discussion.

Skills Review

Exercise 1

1. Open the *Sales Data* workbook located on the Data Disk.
2. Using the data on the Summary tab, create a new Clustered Column chart with a three-dimensional effect.
3. Title the chart "Sales by Region."
4. Insert the chart on a new chart sheet called "Sales by Region Chart."
5. Print the Sales by Region Chart.
6. Switch to the Source Data worksheet, then use the Go To command to highlight all cells containing a formula.
7. Save the workbook as *Sales Data Revised* and close it.

Exercise 2

1. Open the *Sales Data Revised* workbook that you created in Exercise 1.
2. Look at the embedded chart on the West Coast tab, then find two other types of charts that present the data in a clear manner.
3. Find two types of charts that make it more difficult to understand the data.
4. Using Microsoft Word, write at least two paragraphs describing why certain types of charts worked well to illustrate the data and why others did not. Try to discern from the chart type description what type of information is needed for each type of chart and why your data did or did not work.
5. Save the document as *Chart Types.doc* and then print and close it. Close the workbook.

Exercise 3

1. Open the *Exports by Country* workbook located on the Data Disk.
2. Activate cell A2.
3. Create a line with markers chart using the Chart Wizard.
4. Title the chart "Exports by Country."

5. Add "2003" to the Category (X) axis.
6. Create the chart as an object on Sheet1.
7. Preview and print your chart as part of the worksheet. (*Hint:* Move the chart or change the paper orientation as necessary.)
8. Use Go To to select the last cell in the worksheet.
9. With your instructor's permission, connect to the Internet, and search the Web for a picture of a flag of one of the countries used in your chart. Be sure to verify that the image is one you can use for free.
10. In your Web browser, right-click the picture, then click Save Picture As and save the picture.
11. Insert the picture on your chart.
12. Save the workbook as *Exports by Country Chart,* print the chart sheet, and then close the workbook.

Exercise 4 C

1. Open the *Exports by Country Chart* workbook that you created in Exercise 3.
2. Add the following data to row 5: Japan, $6,438,945.00, $2,345,743.00, $5,098,760.00, $3,198,245.00.
3. Select the chart and use the Range Finder to add Japan's data to the chart.
4. Save the workbook as *Exports by Country Chart Revised,* print the chart sheet, and close the workbook.

Exercise 5 C

1. Open the *Expenses* workbook located on the Data Disk. Activate cell A2.
2. Create a Bar of Pie type chart using the Chart Wizard (in the Pie chart type category). This type of chart uses a selected number of values from the bottom of a list of values to create a "breakout" section. In this case, the breakout section is the category Taxes.
3. Title the chart "Expenses."
4. Show the percentage data labels.
5. Create the chart as an embedded chart.
6. Save the workbook as *Expenses Chart,* print the worksheet, and close the workbook.

Exercise 6 C

1. Open the *Computer Comparison* workbook located on the Data Disk.
2. Create a new chart, using the Line – Column on 2 Axes custom type of chart. (*Hint:* Click the Custom Types tab in Step 1 of the Chart Wizard.)
3. Title the chart "Computer Price/Speed Comparison."
4. Title the *x*-axis "System."
5. Title the *y*-axis "Price."
6. Title the secondary *y*-axis "Speed."
7. Create the chart as a new sheet.
8. Preview the Web page, then save the chart sheet as a Web page called *computer_comparison_chart.htm.*
9. Save the workbook as *Computer Comparison Chart,* print the chart sheet, and close the workbook.

Exercise 7

1. Open the *Computer Comparison Chart* workbook that you created in Exercise 6.
2. Show the data table on the chart.
3. Click the Athlon 1.2 GHz data point two times to select it (do not double-click it). Drag the data point handle at the top-middle of the data point down until the value reads $2,650.
4. Modify the value of the PIII 1 GHz data point to $2,400 by dragging the data point handle.
5. Print the chart.
6. Add comments in cells B3 and B5 indicating that the value of each of these cells was changed.
7. Save the workbook as *Computer Comparison Chart Revised.*
8. Print the chart sheet and the worksheet, and then close the workbook.

Exercise 8

1. Open the *Class Attendance* workbook located on your Data Disk.
2. Create a new chart with the Chart Wizard.
3. Use the Custom Types tab to select the Colored Lines chart type.
4. Title the chart "Class Attendance."
5. Put the chart on a new sheet called "Attendance Chart."
6. Change the area fill of the Chart Area to Automatic (white).
7. On the data page, include a hyperlink to your favorite search engine.
8. Print the chart, save your workbook as *Class Attendance Chart,* and close it.

Case Projects

Project 1  

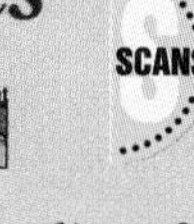

As the entertainment editor for a local newspaper, you publish a weekly chart of the top five films based on their box office revenues for the week. Connect to the Internet and use the Web toolbar to search the Web for information on the top five movies from the last week. Create a worksheet listing each of the titles and showing how much each film grossed in the last week. Add another column to show total revenues to date for each film. Insert comments next to two of the films indicating whether you want to see the film, or what you thought of it if you have already seen it. Create a chart that best illustrates the data. Save the workbook as *Box Office*, and then print and close it.

Project 2

Use the Ask A Question Box to find out how to add a text box to a chart. Create a Word document and use your own words to describe step by step how to accomplish this task. Save the document as *Adding a Text Box to a Chart.doc,* and print and close it.

Project 3  

As the owner of a mall-based cookie store, you want to track your cookie sales by type and month to determine which cookies are bestsellers and what the best time of the year is for cookie sales. Create a worksheet with 10 types of cookies (examples: chocolate chip, oatmeal, walnut, peanut butter). Include fictitious data for cookie sales for each type of cookie during the past 12 months. Create charts showing overall cookie sales by month and overall cookie sales by type. With your instructor's permission, connect to the Internet and search the Web for a picture of your favorite type of cookie. Verify that the file you want to use is an image you can use for free, then save the picture, and then insert it on your chart. Save the workbook as *Cookie Sales,* and print and close it.

Project 4  

Connect to the Internet and use the Web toolbar to search the Web for different types of charts. Look for charts showing sales volume, stock prices, or percentages of sales by category. Create a workbook containing hyperlinks to five different charts. Save your workbook as *Charts on the Web,* and print and close it.

Project 5  

Stock price charts are usually displayed using a high-low-close style chart, which requires three columns of data. Connect to the Internet and use the Web toolbar to search the Web for stock prices for three companies whose products you use. Locate price histories for the last five days for each stock, including the high, low, and closing prices for each day. Create a High Low Close chart (stock category) for each company, showing the price plotted against the date. Save the workbook as *High Low Close,* and print and close it.

Project 6 

Create a worksheet showing one month's expenses for at least 10 expense categories in your household (estimate your expenses or supply fictitious data). Create a three-dimensional pie chart, and separate the largest expense from the pie. Use data labels to display the label and value of each expense. Save the workbook as *Family Expenses,* and print and close it.

Project 7  

As the weather editor of a local newspaper, your job is to create a chart of the five-day forecasts for your city. Connect to the Internet, and locate a Web site that provides a five-day forecast for your area. Enter the data in a new worksheet and create a chart showing the high and low temperatures for each day. Place the chart on a separate worksheet page. Save the workbook as *Temperature Forecast,* print it, save it as a Web page named *temperature_forecast.htm,* and then close the workbook.

Project 8  

You are interested in finding out how the government spends the money in its budget. Connect to the Internet, and search the Web for a site that shows where the government spends tax revenue. Create a new workbook and pie chart showing the information you find. Include at least five categories. If you have access to a discussion server, set up a discussion and include a comment about your budget findings. Have classmates add comments to the discussion. Save your workbook as *Government Spending,* and print and close it.

Microsoft Excel 2002 Advanced

Excel 2002

Linking Worksheets and Workbooks

Chapter Overview

Grouping worksheets can reduce repetitious formatting and worksheet preparation chores. Consolidating data from multiple worksheets is an important task. You do this by using 3-D references in formulas or by using the Data Consolidation command. You can use named ranges to select and identify important cell references. Providing a summary worksheet can help other users understand a complex workbook more quickly. To effectively work with multiple workbooks, you can create hyperlinks between workbooks. You can even save workspaces, which automatically open and arrange workbooks the way you like them.

Learning Objectives

- Group worksheets to share data, formatting, and formulas
- Insert and format a documentation worksheet
- Use named ranges
- Consolidate data from multiple worksheets
- Create 3-D references and links between workbooks
- Work with multiple workbooks

Case profile

With four regional offices and a central office all collecting and combining data, Super Power Computers relies on numerous workbooks to keep track of the stream of information. One of your responsibilities is to combine the information from those various sources and ensure that your data stays up to date, even though the information may be revised daily. You use linked formulas to gather data from other worksheets and other workbooks, and you use hyperlinks to quickly open related documents.

chapter seven

7.a Grouping Worksheets to Share Data, Formatting, and Formulas

A worksheet **group** consists of several worksheets you have selected for editing. When you group worksheets, you can enter data and formulas on one worksheet and have that information appear simultaneously on all of the other grouped worksheets. You also can format cells and perform operations, such as spell checking and printing, across grouped worksheets.

The *Super Power Computers - Central Region* workbook contains most of the data you need to create a company sales summary. None of the formulas or titles that you need for your report has been added to the workbook. You decide to group the worksheets so that you can enter information simultaneously on multiple pages. To group worksheets:

Step 1	***Open***	the *Super Power Computers - Central Region* workbook located on the Data Disk
Step 2	***Save***	the workbook as *Super Power Computers - Central Region Revised*
Step 3	***Click***	the Store #1 sheet tab
Step 4	***Press & hold***	the SHIFT key
Step 5	***Click***	the Store #11 sheet tab

QUICK TIP

Select nonadjacent worksheets by holding the CTRL key down while clicking sheet tabs. You also can use this method to remove worksheets from a group.

Your screen should look similar to Figure 7-1. The store tabs are selected, or grouped, as indicated by the white sheet tabs. The title bar also indicates that a group has been formed. When you group worksheets, any information that you enter and all formatting that you apply, appear on all sheets in the group.

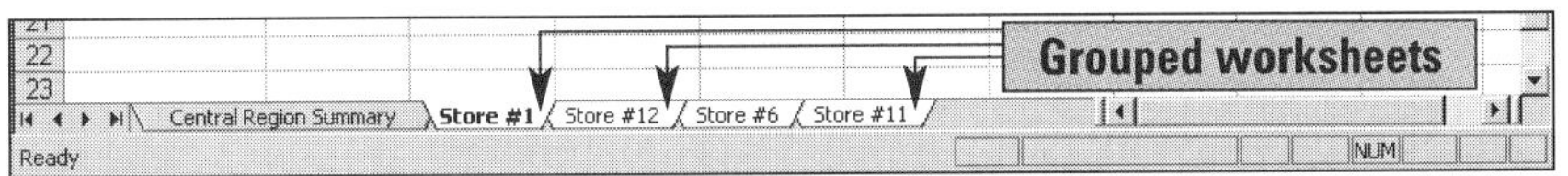

FIGURE 7-1
Grouped Worksheets

Table 7-1 lists the data you need to add to the worksheet group. As you enter the data on the Store #1 sheet tab, the same information is added to the other worksheets in the group. To enter data and format cells on the worksheet group:

Step 1	***Enter***	the data shown in Table 7-1

TABLE 7-1
Data for the Worksheet Group

Cell Reference	Enter
A4	Employee Name
B4	Q1
C4	Q2
D4	Q3
E4	Q4
F4	Total
A9	Total

You can use AutoSum to automatically sum the cells to the left and above a selected range.

Step 2	***Select***	the ranges F5:F8 and B9:F9 using the CTRL key
Step 3	***Click***	the AutoSum button Σ on the Standard toolbar

Now you can apply an AutoFormat to the table.

QUICK TIP

You can also group worksheets for printing.

Step 4	***AutoFit***	columns B, C, D, E, and F to fit the entries in row 9
Step 5	***Format***	the range F6:F8 with no dollar sign symbol
Step 6	***Click***	cell A4
Step 7	***Click***	Format
Step 8	***Click***	AutoFormat
Step 9	***Verify***	that Simple is selected
Step 10	***Click***	OK

Your screen should look similar to Figure 7-2. You can examine the changes to the other worksheets by clicking any tab in the group. The group remains selected as long as you select a tab in the group.

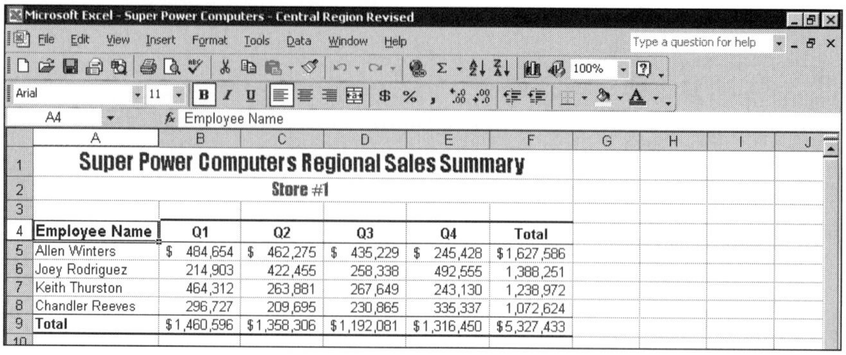

FIGURE 7-2
Data and Formatting Added to Grouped Worksheets

Microsoft Excel - Super Power Computers - Central Region Revised

	A	B	C	D	E	F
1	Super Power Computers Regional Sales Summary					
2	Store #1					
3						
4	Employee Name	Q1	Q2	Q3	Q4	Total
5	Allen Winters	$ 484,654	$ 462,275	$ 435,229	$ 245,428	$1,627,586
6	Joey Rodriguez	214,903	422,455	258,338	492,555	1,388,251
7	Keith Thurston	464,312	263,881	267,649	243,130	1,238,972
8	Chandler Reeves	296,727	209,695	230,865	335,337	1,072,624
9	Total	$1,460,596	$1,358,306	$1,192,081	$1,316,450	$5,327,433

Step 11	*Click*	the Store #11 sheet tab to view the formatting applied to the worksheet data

As you can see, the formatting and data have been applied to this worksheet as well as to the original worksheet. You're finished setting up the table, so you need to ungroup the worksheets to avoid overwriting important data. To ungroup the worksheets:

Step 1	*Right-click*	the Store #11 sheet tab
Step 2	*Click*	Ungroup Sheets
Step 3	*Save*	the workbook

MOUSE TIP

You can click a sheet tab outside the group to ungroup worksheets.

7.b Inserting and Formatting a Documentation Worksheet

Documenting a workbook is very important, especially when you share your workbooks with other people. One way to document a workbook is to provide a documentation worksheet. This page explains the content of the other worksheets in the workbook, and might include the following sections: Identification; Map of the Workbook; and Description, Assumptions, and Parameters.

The **Identification** section includes information about the workbook owner (usually a company name), the developer's name (the person who created the workbook), and the user's name (the person who is using the workbook). In addition, it may indicate the date the workbook was created and the date of the workbook's last revision. The **Map of the Workbook** provides a table of contents, describing the order and contents of the worksheets in the workbook. The **Description, Assumptions, and Parameters** section provides a place to describe the workbook's purpose and details any assumptions or parameters necessary for using it. To create a documentation worksheet:

Step 1	*Insert*	a new worksheet in front of the Central Region Summary worksheet
Step 2	*Name*	the worksheet Documentation
Step 3	*Enter*	the data and format as shown in Figure 7-3

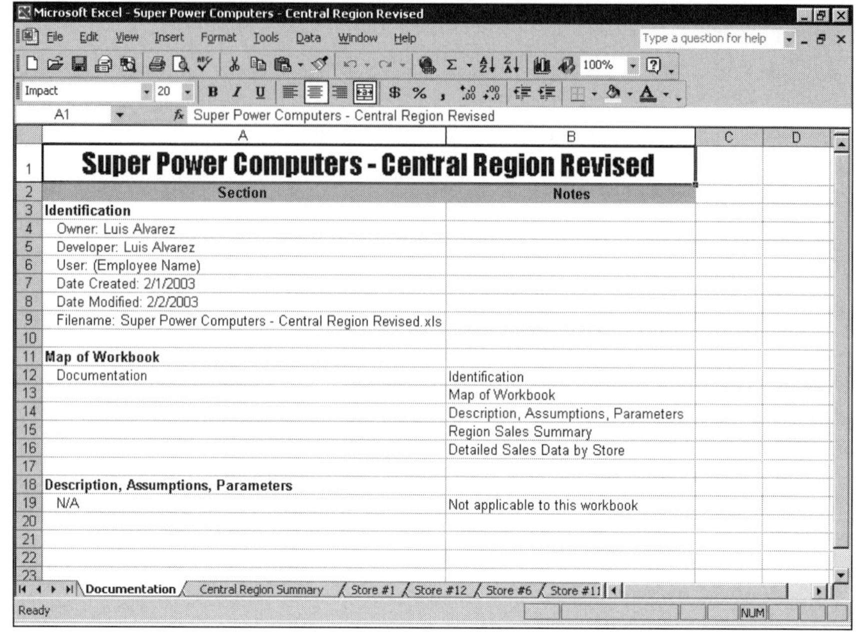

FIGURE 7-3
Data and Format for Documentation Worksheet

> **QUICK TIP**
>
> Before you distribute the workbook to anyone, use the spell check command to check for errors.

Step 4	*Save*	your workbook

7.c Using Named Ranges

A **named range** is a meaningful name given to a cell or a range. You can use the name in place of cell references to help you easily find and reference the cells. For example, the named range Store11Totals is easier to remember than Store #11!B9:E9. Named ranges can be used simply to locate and select cells, or they can be used in formulas to replace cell addresses.

When naming ranges, you can use letters, numbers, and the underscore (_) character, but you cannot use spaces. Named ranges are not case sensitive. SouthTotal, SOUTHTOTAL, and southtotal would all refer to the same range of cells.

Add and Delete a Named Range

The Super Power Computers summary report is a consolidation of data located on many worksheets. To make referencing this data easier, you use named ranges in place of cell references. You can create a named range in the Name Box to the left of the Formula Bar. To create a named range:

Step 1	*Select*	the range B9:E9 on the Store #11 worksheet

Step 2	*Click*	in the Name Box to the left of the Formula Bar
Step 3	*Key*	Store11Totals
Step 4	*Press*	the ENTER key

The named range is added to the Name Box list. You can then use this list to select the named range. To select a named range:

Step 1	*Click*	the Central Region Summary sheet tab
Step 2	*Click*	the Name Box list arrow
Step 3	*Click*	Store11Totals

Excel activates the Store #11 worksheet and selects the cells referenced by the named range. To manage your named ranges, you use the Define Name dialog box. To use the Define Name dialog box to name ranges:

Step 1	*Click*	Insert
Step 2	*Point to*	Name
Step 3	*Click*	Define

The Define Name dialog box on your screen should look similar to Figure 7-4.

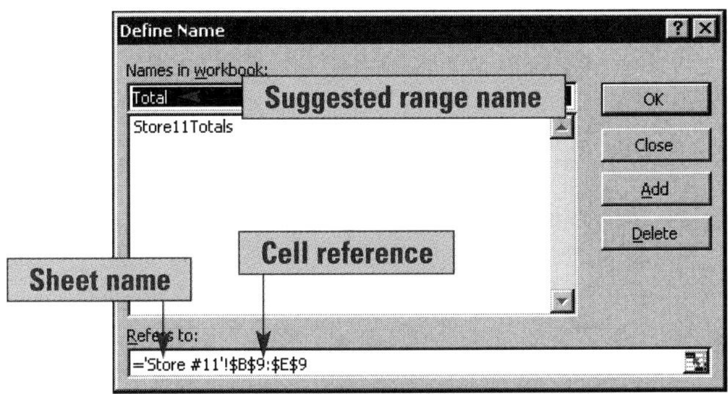

FIGURE 7-4
Define Name Dialog Box

The cell reference in the Refers to: text box begins with an equal sign (=), because the reference is essentially a formula that references the range name you chose. The sheet name appears next, enclosed between single quotation marks. As in 3-D references, an exclamation point separates the sheet name from the cell references. Finally, notice that the cell references are absolute references. You can modify the cell references in the Refers to: text box, select new ones from the worksheet by clicking the Collapse Dialog button, add new named ranges, or delete existing ones. Excel suggests a name for the named range in the Names in workbook: text box. To create a named range using the Define Names dialog box:

QUICK TIP

To delete a named range, open the Define Name dialog box, select the range name in the list, then click the Delete button.

Step 1	*Key*	Store1Totals in the Names in workbook: text box
Step 2	*Click*	the Collapse Dialog button in the Refers to: text box

The dialog box collapses and the title bar changes to Define Range - Refers to: text box, and the status bar prompts you to point to the cells that should be added to your named range.

Step 3	*Select*	the range B9:E9 on the Store #1 worksheet
Step 4	*Click*	the Expand Dialog button in the dialog box
Step 5	*Click*	Add to add the new named range to the Names in workbook: list
Step 6	*Follow*	Steps 1 through 5 to add named ranges for Stores #12 and #6 (the range B9:E9)
Step 7	*Click*	OK to close the Define Name dialog box

Using a Named Range in a Formula

You can use range names instead of cell references in formulas. You need to sum the totals from all the stores on the Central Region Summary worksheet. To create a formula using a named range:

Step 1	*Click*	the Central Region Summary sheet tab
Step 2	*Key*	=sum(in cell B12
Step 3	*Click*	Insert
Step 4	*Point to*	Name
Step 5	*Click*	Paste to open the Paste Name dialog box
Step 6	*Click*	Store11Totals in the Paste name list
Step 7	*Click*	OK
Step 8	*Click*	the Enter button on the Formula Bar

Excel automatically adds the closing parenthesis for the SUM argument and calculates the value as 4778585. Your formula should match the one shown in Figure 7-5.

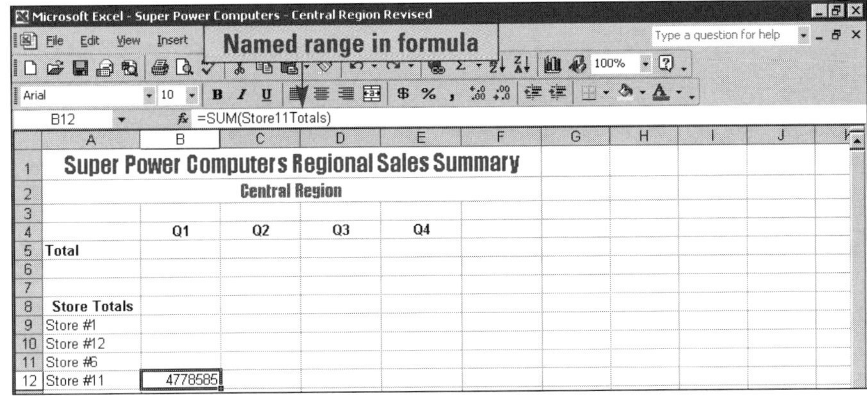

FIGURE 7-5
Named Ranges in a Formula

Step 9	***Follow***	Steps 2 through 8 to add formulas to calculate the remaining stores' totals in cells B9, B10, and B11
Step 10	***Enter***	a formula in cell B13 to sum cells B9:B12
Step 11	***Select***	the range B9:B13
Step 12	***Click***	the Currency Style button on the Formatting toolbar
Step 13	***Click***	the Decrease Decimal button on the Formatting toolbar twice
Step 14	***AutoFit***	column B to show the formatted values
Step 15	***Save***	the workbook

7.d Consolidating Data from Multiple Worksheets

Consolidating data for use in reports is a common business task. One way of consolidating data is to use 3-D references between worksheets. Another way to do this is with the Consolidate Data feature, which helps automate the process. When combined with named ranges, consolidating data can be a fast and effective way to build a summary report.

As part of your summary report, you want to consolidate the data for each quarter. You have already created named ranges for each store's quarter totals. To consolidate data:

Step 1	***Activate***	cell B5 on the Central Region Summary worksheet
Step 2	***Click***	Data
Step 3	***Click***	Consolidate

The Consolidate dialog box on your screen should look similar to Figure 7-6. In this dialog box, you can select the consolidation formula and the ranges to be used in the consolidation.

FIGURE 7-6
Consolidate Dialog Box

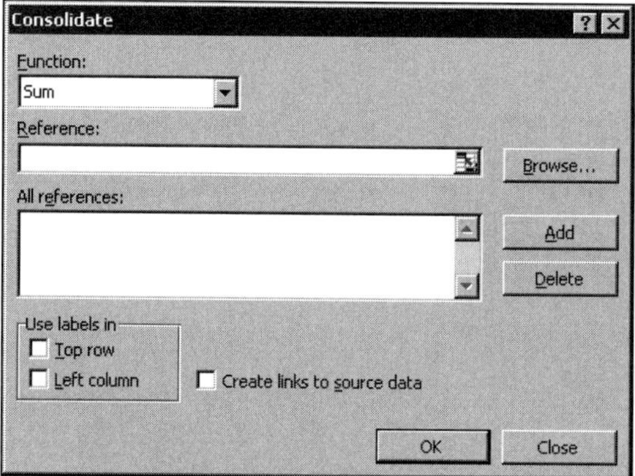

Step 4	***Verify***	that Sum is selected in the Function: list box

Next, you add the named range to the All references: list. As you add the reference, the named range is selected in the worksheet.

Step 5	***Key***	Store1Totals in the Reference: text box
Step 6	***Click***	Add
Step 7	***Follow***	Steps 5 and 6 to add Store12Totals, Store6Totals, and Store11Totals to the All references: list
Step 8	***Click***	OK

The data is consolidated and added in cells B5:E5.

Step 9	***AutoFit***	columns C, D, and E
Step 10	***Activate***	cell B5

Notice in the Formula Bar that a linking formula is not added to the cell by default, just the calculated value. To add linking formulas, formulas that update the calculated values when the cell references used in the formulas are updated, you need to change a setting in the Consolidate dialog box.

Step 11	*Open*	the Consolidate dialog box
Step 12	*Click*	the Create links to source data check box
Step 13	*Click*	OK

When you create links to source data, Excel automatically links to all source data, creates an outline by inserting new rows into the worksheet, adds the SUM function in each column, then hides the data. An **outline** allows you to view data in hierarchies, or levels. To view this data:

Step 14	*Click*	the Expand Outline button [+] to the left of row 9

Your screen should look similar to Figure 7-7. The outline expands to show the sublevel, and the plus outline button changes to a minus sign. All of the data from the Store worksheets is now linked to the Central Region Summary worksheet. Rows 5 through 8 contain the quarterly totals for Stores 11, 12, 1, and 6, respectively.

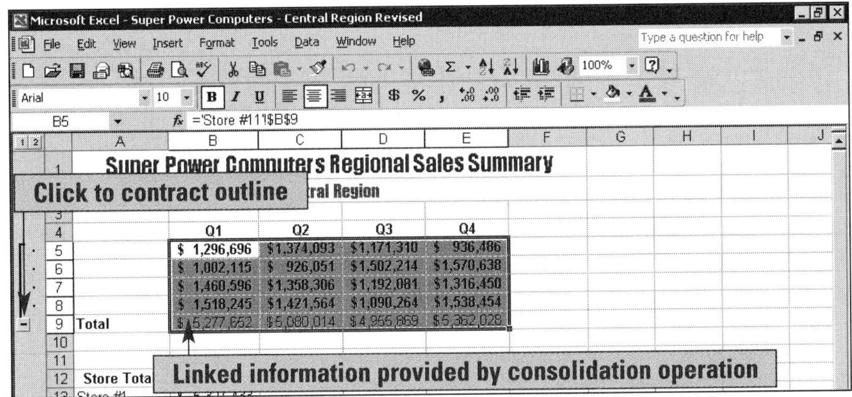

FIGURE 7-7
Summary Created Using Consolidate Data

Step 15	*Save*	the workbook and leave it open

7.e Creating 3-D References and Links Between Workbooks

You know how to create 3-D references between worksheets in the same workbook. A 3-D reference is a link between a cell on one worksheet and a cell on another worksheet. You can also create 3-D references between workbooks. You do this by creating a linking formula or a hyperlink.

Creating Linking Formulas Between Workbooks

You need to combine the summary data in the *Central Region Revised* workbook with the summary data in the *Super Power Computers - East Coast Region* workbook to create a new summary workbook. To create linking formulas between workbooks:

Step 1	***Open***	the *Super Power Computers - Region Summary* workbook located on the Data Disk
Step 2	***Save***	the workbook as *Super Power Computers - Region Summary Revised*
Step 3	***Open***	the *Super Power Computers - East Coast Region* located on the Data Disk

You want to activate the *Super Power Computers - Region Summary Revised* workbook and move it in front of the other workbooks.

Step 4	***Click***	Window
Step 5	***Click***	Super Power Computers - Region Summary Revised
Step 6	***Key***	= in cell B5
Step 7	***Click***	Window
Step 8	***Click***	Super Power Computers - Central Region Revised
Step 9	***Click***	cell B17 on the Central Region Summary worksheet
Step 10	***Click***	the Enter button on the Formula Bar

The formula ='**[Super Power Computers - Central Region Revised.xls]Central Region Summary'!$B$17** is displayed in the Formula Bar. In this case, the formula is just a cell reference to cell B17 on the Central Region Summary worksheet in the *Super Power Computers - Central Region Revised* workbook. The worksheet name is separated from the cell reference by an exclamation point, and the workbook name is in brackets. You want to add a linking formula in cell B6 to cell B12 in the *Super Power Computers - East Coast Region* workbook.

Step 11	***Key***	= in cell B6
Step 12	***Switch to***	the *Super Power Computers - East Coast Region* workbook
Step 13	***Click***	cell B12 on the East Coast Region Summary worksheet
Step 14	***Click***	the Enter button on the Formula Bar

When you link between workbooks, the links are updated as changes are made.

Step 15	***Activate***	the *Super Power Computers - East Coast Region* workbook
Step 16	***Activate***	cell B5 on the Store #2 worksheet
Step 17	***Enter***	425000
Step 18	***Activate***	the *Super Power Computers - Region Summary Revised* workbook

The value in cell B6 has been updated from 17,890,348 to 18,115,348.

Step 19	***Activate***	the *Super Power Computers - East Coast Region* workbook
Step 20	***Close***	the *Super Power Computers - East Coast Region* workbook without saving your changes

Because you closed the *Super Power Computers - East Coast Region* workbook without saving changes, the value you changed was not saved. The *Super Power Computers - Region Summary Revised* workbook was not updated immediately, but will be updated the next time you open the workbook.

MENU TIP

You can create links to cells on other worksheets or workbooks by using the Copy and Paste Special commands. Copy the cell(s) to which you want to link, then switch to the workbook, worksheet, and cell where the new link should appear. Click Paste Special on the Edit menu, then click the Paste Link option to create an absolute reference to the cells you copied.

Creating Hyperlinks Between Workbooks

By adding a hyperlink to the workbooks you just linked, you can quickly reopen the workbooks. You should still have the *Super Power Computers - Region Summary Revised* workbook open. To create a hyperlink:

Step 1	***Right-click***	cell A5 in the *Super Power Computers - Region Summary Revised* workbook
Step 2	***Click***	Hyperlink

The Insert Hyperlink dialog box opens.

Step 3	***Click***	Existing File or Web Page in the Link to: bar, if necessary

The Insert Hyperlink dialog box changes, allowing you to insert a file or Web page name. The list in the middle of the dialog box displays filenames, network drives, and Internet addresses that you've visited recently, depending on which button is selected to the left of the list.

Step 4	***Click***	the *Super Power Computers - Central Region Revised* workbook in the list
Step 5	***Verify***	that Central appears in the Text to display: text box

This text will appear in the cell. Your dialog box should look similar to Figure 7-8.

FIGURE 7-8
Insert Hyperlink Dialog Box

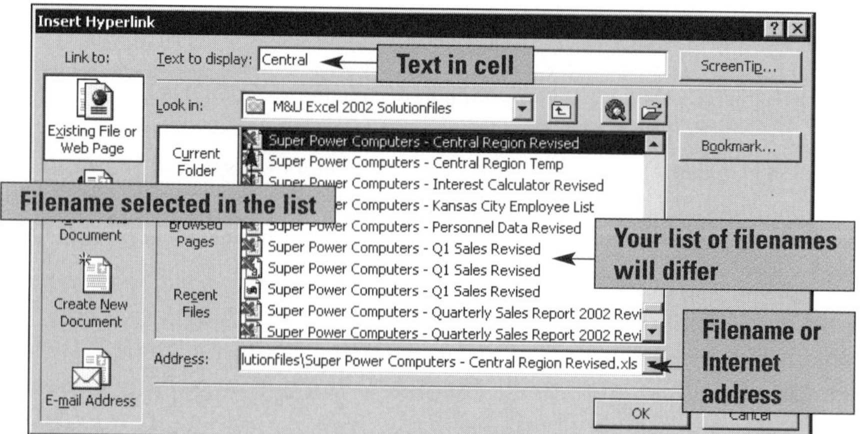

Step 6	***Click***	ScreenTip
Step 7	***Key***	Central in the ScreenTip text: text box in the Set Hyperlink ScreenTip dialog box

MENU TIP

Click Hyperlink on the Insert menu to open the Insert Hyperlink dialog box.

QUICK TIP

When creating hyperlinks to a Web page, you don't have to key the URL. Instead, open the Insert Hyperlink dialog box, then click Web Page on the right to open your browser. Use your browser to find the Web page, click in the address box in the browser, then switch to Excel. The address currently in your browser appears in the Address: text box.

MOUSE TIP

Click the Insert Hyperlink button on the Standard toolbar to insert a hyperlink.

Step 8	*Click*	OK
Step 9	*Click*	OK to change the value in cell A5 to a hyperlink
Step 10	*Follow*	Steps 1 through 9 to add a hyperlink in cell A6 to the Super Power Computers - East Coast Region workbook with the ScreenTip East Coast

Now check your new hyperlinks.

Step 11	*Position*	the mouse pointer over cell A6 to view the ScreenTip with the text "East Coast"
Step 12	*Click*	the East Coast hyperlink

The *Super Power Computers - East Coast Region* workbook opens. The Web toolbar also opens.

Step 13	*Right-click*	the Web toolbar
Step 14	*Click*	Web to close the Web toolbar

Hyperlinks make it easy to connect to a variety of information sources. By creating links to Web pages on the Internet or to other Office documents, you can quickly open documents associated with the workbook(s) with which you are working.

7.f Working with Multiple Workbooks

When working with multiple workbooks, you can arrange them so as to view several workbooks at once. If you must repeatedly manipulate the same workbooks simultaneously, you can save a workspace, which speeds the editing process when you need to work with the same set of workbooks again. **Workspaces** remember which files are open and how the workbooks are arranged.

Arranging Workbooks

When working with multiple workbooks, you may want to display more than one workbook window at a time. Using the Arrange

QUICK TIP

You can modify the formatting of a cell containing a hyperlink by using the normal formatting commands. Altering the formatting does not affect the hyperlink.

CAUTION TIP

If you move a file to which you have created hyperlinks, you must edit the hyperlink to point to the new location. Right-click the hyperlink or object and select Hyperlink, then Edit Hyperlink.

MOUSE TIP

When you add a hyperlink to an object, you cannot click the object to select it, because clicking the object activates the hyperlink. Instead, to select an object with a hyperlink attached, right-click the object. You can then use the shortcut menu to modify the object, or press ESC to close the shortcut menu and move or resize the object.

Windows dialog box, you can create several different arrangements. To arrange the workbook windows:

Step 1	*Click*	Window
Step 2	*Click*	Arrange
Step 3	*Click*	the Tiled option button, if necessary
Step 4	*Click*	OK

Your screen should look similar to Figure 7-9.

FIGURE 7-9
Tiled Windows

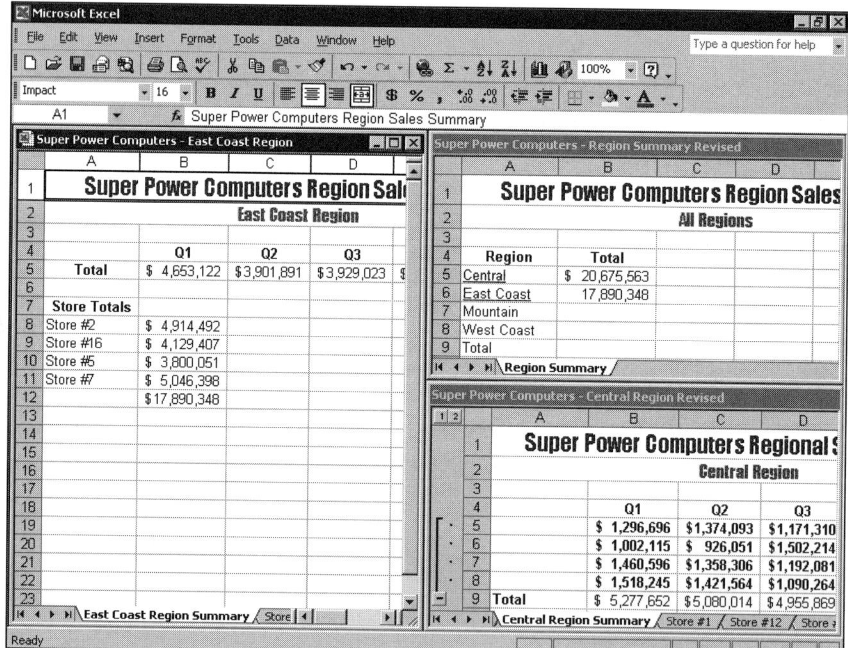

Using a Workspace

Workspaces are great time savers when you frequently use the same files simultaneously. Instead of opening several files and then using the Arrange Windows dialog box every time you need to work with that particular set of files, you can open a workspace, which will automatically open and arrange the desired files. Because you will be using this set of Super Power Computers workbooks frequently, you decide to create a workspace. To create a workspace:

Step 1	*Click*	File
Step 2	*Click*	Save Workspace

The Save Workspace dialog box opens with Workspaces in the Save as type: list box. This is the only option available when you save a workspace. If your computer is set to display file extensions, the Excel workspace file extension, .xlw, also appears.

Step 3	*Save*	the workspace as *Region Summary* to the same location as your Data Files
Step 4	*Click*	Yes To All to save any changes in the workbooks
Step 5	*Press & hold*	the SHIFT key
Step 6	*Click*	File
Step 7	*Click*	Close All

MENU TIP

When you press the SHIFT key before clicking the Close command on the File menu, the command changes to Close All.

Next you open your workspace. Opening a workspace is very similar to opening a workbook. To open a workspace:

Step 1	*Click*	the Open button on the Standard toolbar
Step 2	*Click*	the Files of type: list arrow
Step 3	*Click*	Workspaces (you may need to scroll)
Step 4	*Click*	*Region Summary*
Step 5	*Click*	Open

TASK PANE TIP

You can click the More Workbooks link under Open a workbook in the New Workbook task pane.

Because the *Super Power Computers - Region Summary Revised* workbook contains links to another workbook, Excel prompts you to update the links.

Step 6	*Click*	Update

All of the workbooks are open exactly the way you had them arranged previously.

QUICK TIP

If you change the arrangement of the workbooks, remember to resave the workspace.

Step 7	*Close*	all open workbooks, saving changes as needed

With the links between the workbooks added and the workspace saved, it will be very easy to update this information.

Summary

- To group worksheets, use SHIFT + Click or CTRL + Click. Grouping worksheets makes it easy to add the same data, titles, headings, and formatting to several worksheets at a time. You can also group worksheets for printing.
- Documentation worksheets contain documentation that explains the content of the workbook.
- You can add and delete named ranges to refer to ranges by name instead of by cell reference.
- You can use named ranges in formulas as you would use cell references.
- The Data Consolidation command enables you to automatically include data from the worksheets in a workbook in a formula.
- Use 3-D references when ranges must span multiple worksheets or workbooks. In a 3-D reference, workbook names are enclosed within brackets.
- You can add hyperlinks to cell values or drawing objects in other workbooks or on Web pages. Click the hyperlink to open other files or access an Internet Web site.
- The Arrange Windows command enables you to arrange several windows simultaneously.
- Workspaces enable you to open and arrange several workbooks in the same way each time.

Commands Review

Action	Menu Bar	Shortcut Menu	Toolbar	Task Pane	Keyboard
Ungroup worksheets		Right-click, Ungroup Sheets			
Add named range	Insert, Name, Define				CTRL + F3 ALT + I, N, D
Paste a named range	Insert, Name, Paste				ALT + I, N, P
Consolidate data	Data, Consolidate				ALT + D, N
Add a hyperlink to an object or cell	Insert, Hyperlink	Right-click, Hyperlink	[icon]		CTRL + K ALT + I, I
Arrange workbooks	Window, Arrange				ALT + W, A
Create workspace	File, Save Workspace				ALT + F, W
Close all open workbooks	SHIFT + File, Close All				SHIFT + ALT + F, C

Concepts Review

Circle the correct answer.

1. Hyperlinks can link to:
- [a] other cells.
- [b] other workbooks.
- [c] Web pages.
- [d] other cells, other workbooks, and Web pages.

2. Which of the following formulas contains a valid reference to a range on another worksheet?
- [a] =sum(Totals!A1:B5)
- [b] =sum('Totals'!A1:B5)
- [c] =sum("Totals"!A1:B5)
- [d] =sum(Totals:A1:B5)

3. Which of the following formulas contains a valid reference to a range in another workbook?
- [a] =sum(RegionSales['Sheet1'!A1:B5])
- [b] =sum('[RegionSales]Sheet1'!A1:B5)
- [c] =sum('[RegionSales]Sheet1!A1:B5')
- [d] =sum("[RegionSales]Sheet1"!A1:B5)

4. To simultaneously add data and formatting to multiple worksheets, you must first:
- [a] group the worksheets.
- [b] link the worksheets.
- [c] add the data and formatting, then copy and paste from one worksheet to another.
- [d] join worksheets together.

5. A summary page might include which of the following sections?
- [a] Map of the Workbook
- [b] Identification
- [c] Descriptions, Assumptions, and Parameters
- [d] all of the above

6. 3-D references in formulas:
- [a] cannot be modified.
- [b] allow formatting to be applied across multiple worksheets.
- [c] span worksheets.
- [d] none of the above.

7. An workspace is used to store:
- [a] which workbooks were open but not their arrangement.
- [b] which workbooks were open and their arrangement.
- [c] the arrangement only so you can apply it to currently open workbooks.
- [d] the toolbar arrangement.

8. A referenced workbook name is surrounded by:
- [a] [ ].
- [b] { }.
- [c] ( ).
- [d] < >.

9. You create named ranges by:
- [a] using the name box next to the formula bar or the Define Name dialog box.
- [b] using the Formula Bar.
- [c] right-clicking a selected range and choosing Name.
- [d] double-clicking a range.

10. Hyperlinks can be attached to:
- [a] lines.
- [b] clip art.
- [c] cells.
- [d] lines, clip art, and cells.

Circle **T** if the statement is true or **F** if the statement is false.

T F 1. You can select groups of worksheets only if they are in one continuous group.

T F 2. You can use the SHIFT or CTRL key to create a worksheet group.

T F 3. You can group worksheets for printing, but not for formatting.

T F 4. Hyperlinks between workbooks and linking formulas between workbooks are the same thing.

T F 5. Hyperlinks cannot be made to other types of documents, such as a Word document.

T F 6. You cannot link worksheet text to charts.

T F 7. If linked workbooks are open simultaneously, changes are immediately reflected in both workbooks.

T F 8. Once a workbook is open, you cannot update its links to other workbooks without closing the original workbook and reopening it.

T F 9. Use Paste Link from the Paste Special dialog box to create a quick reference to another cell or cells.

T F 10. Named ranges can be used in formulas in place of cell references.

Skills Review

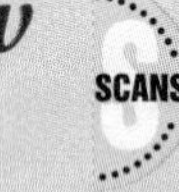

Exercise 1

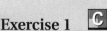

1. Open the *Sweet Tooth Summary* workbook located on the Data Disk.
2. In cells B5:B10 on the Summary worksheet, use a linking formula to link to the total items sold, which is calculated in cell D24 of each item's worksheet.
3. In cells C5:C10 on the Summary worksheet, use a linking formula to link to the total gross sales, which is calculated in cell F24 of each item's worksheet.
4. Activate cell B12 and open the Consolidate dialog box from the Data menu.
5. Enter qty123 in the Reference: text box and click Add. Repeat to add references to qty124, qty125, qty126, qty127, and qty128. Click OK when you are finished.
6. Enter =SUM(in cell C12, then click the Item 123 sheet tab, click cell F24, press and hold the SHIFT key and click the Item 128 tab, then press the ENTER key.
7. Print the Summary worksheet.
8. Save the workbook as *Sweet Tooth Summary Revised,* and then print and close it.

Exercise 2

1. Create a new workbook.
2. Add the name of five Internet search engines in cells A1–A5 (such as Google, Yahoo!, and Northern Light).
3. Add a hyperlink to each of the search engines. Click the Browse the Web button in the Insert Hyperlink dialog box to open your Web browser and locate a Web address. Switch back to Excel, and the address should be inserted into the Address: text box. If it's not, key in the address.
4. Add a ScreenTip and text to the objects to identify the hyperlinks.
5. Save the workbook as *Search Links,* and then print and close it.

Exercise 3

1. Open the *Central Region, Mountain Region, West Coast Region,* and *East Coast Region* workbooks located on the Data Disk.
2. Save the workbooks as *Mountain 1, West Coast 1, East Coast 1,* and *Central 1.*
3. In cell D4 of the *Central 1* workbook, enter "Go to Mountain." Add a hyperlink to jump to the *Mountain 1* workbook with a ScreenTip that says, "Mountain 1 workbook."
4. In cell D4 of the *Mountain 1* workbook, enter "Go to West Coast." Add a hyperlink to jump to the *West Coast 1* workbook with a ScreenTip that says, "West Coast 1 workbook." (*Hint:* Use the Recent Files button in the Insert Hyperlinks dialog box.)
5. In cell D4 of the *West Coast 1* workbook, enter "Go to East Coast." Add a hyperlink to jump to the *East Coast 1* workbook with a ScreenTip that says, "East Coast 1 workbook."
6. In cell D4 of the *East Coast 1* workbook, enter "Go to Central." Add a hyperlink to jump to the *Central 1* workbook with a ScreenTip that says, "Central 1 workbook."
7. Arrange all the open workbooks.
8. Save the workspace as *Region Workbooks.*
9. Save and close all of the workbooks, leaving only the *Central 1* workbook open.
10. Test the hyperlinks, printing the Summary tab of each workbook as it opens.
11. Close all open workbooks.

Exercise 4 

1. Create a new workbook.
2. In cell A1, enter "Jump to Cell."
3. In cell A2, enter "Jump to Worksheet."
4. In cell A3, enter "Jump to Workbook."
5. In cell A4, enter "Jump to Web."
6. Create a hyperlink in cell A1 to another cell on the same worksheet.
7. Create a hyperlink in cell A2 to another worksheet in the same workbook.
8. Create a hyperlink in cell A3 to any of the workbooks you created in the Skills Review Exercises.
9. Create a hyperlink in cell A4 to one of your favorite Web site's address.
10. Include ScreenTips to indicate where the hyperlinks point.
11. Save the workbook as *Jump Around,* and then print and close it.

Exercise 5 

1. ZXY Accounting is a large accounting firm with offices in Orlando, San Diego, Phoenix, and Washington, D.C. Open the *ZXY Accounting* workbook located on the Data Disk.
2. Group all the worksheets.
3. Insert a column in front of column A.
4. Insert a row above row 1.

5. Add the information indicated in the table below:

Cell	Enter
A2	Auditing
A3	Tax Preparation
A4	Consulting
A5	Total
B1	January
C1	February
D1	March
E1	Total

6. Bold and center the titles in the range B1: E1.
7. Bold cell A5.
8. Use the SUM formula in row 5 and column E to sum the data.
9. Ungroup the worksheets and enter and bold the city name (shown on each tab) in cell A1 of each worksheet.
10. AutoFit columns A, B, C, D, and E.
11. Save the workbook as *ZXY Accounting Revised,* and then print and close it.

Exercise 6 C

1. Open the *ZXY Accounting Revised* workbook that you created in Exercise 5.
2. Insert a new worksheet named "Summary" to the left of the Washington, D.C. worksheet.
3. Create a summary table to add the totals for each month across all cities.
4. Create a named range for each city's monthly total cell.
5. On the Summary worksheet, insert a linking formula using the named ranges.
6. Sum each column on the Summary worksheet.
7. Format the data in rows 2 and 6 using the Currency format, no decimal places, and format the data in rows 3, 4, and 5 as Comma with no decimal places.
8. Find the average income for each month by adding a formula in row 8 in each column. Format the data in this row as Currency with no decimal places.
9. Create a chart showing the income by month for each category, on a new worksheet called "Summary Chart."
10. Title the chart "1st Quarter Income."
11. Print the chart.
12. Save the workbook as *ZXY Accounting Summary,* and then print and close it.

Exercise 7

1. Open the *ZXY Accounting Summary* workbook that you created in Exercise 6.
2. Group all the worksheets except the Summary Chart worksheet.
3. Use Page Setup command on the File menu to set print options to center the data vertically and horizontally.
4. Add a centered header "ZXY Accounting" and format it as 20 point and boldface.
5. Preview and print all five worksheets.
6. Ungroup the worksheets.
7. Save the workbook as *ZXY Accounting Summary Print,* and close it.

Exercise 8 

1. Open the *ZXY Accounting Summary Print* workbook that you created in Exercise 7.
2. Group all the worksheets except the Summary Chart and Summary worksheets.
3. Apply AutoFormat style List 2 to the range A1:E5.
4. Use the Page Setup command on the File menu to set print options to landscape orientation and 150% scale.
5. Print the worksheets.
6. Ungroup the worksheets.
7. Save the workbook as *ZXY Accounting Summary Print 2,* and then close it.

Case Projects

Project 1 

You work for the local newspaper. You are currently researching historical weather trends in the United States. Connect to the Internet and use the Web toolbar to search for average monthly temperatures for New York City and Los Angeles in the last year. Create a workbook that includes the temperatures for each city on two separate worksheets. Create a 3-D reference formula on a second workbook to display the average temperature of the two cities for each month of the previous year. Create a chart comparing the average temperatures for each city. Use axis and chart titles to clarify the purpose of the chart. Save the workbook as *Temperature Averages,* and then print and close it.

Project 2

You teach English at a high school. In preparation for the upcoming term, you need to set up a workbook with five worksheets, one for each of five classes. Each worksheet will be used to record five test scores and ten assignment scores. The test scores and the assignment scores must be summed separately. Group worksheets to make your job easier as you input column and row headings, sum formulas, and formatting. Save your workbook as *Fall Semester Scores,* and then print and close it.

Project 3

You work for a small architectural firm that tracks income in one of two categories: contract and consulting work. The firm lumps expenses into four categories: advertising, office, auto, and rent. Create a workbook named *Business Income* showing receipts in both categories for four quarters. Name the worksheet "2002 Income" and remove any unused worksheets. Sum the totals and save the workbook. Create a workbook named *Business Expenses* showing expenses in each category for four quarters. Name the worksheet "2002 Expenses" and remove any unused worksheets. Sum the totals and save the workbook.

Create a workbook named *Business Projection.* Set up separate tables to show both income categories and the four expense categories. Use columns for each quarter. Using a 5% projected growth rate for consulting work, create a formula to link the *Business Income* cells to the *Business Projection* cells, and then add 5% to last year's totals to project this year's consulting income totals. Do the same for contract work, using a projected growth percentage of 7.5%. For expense categories, link the *Business Expenses* figures to the *Business Projection* workbook, and then calculate an inflation adjustment of 4% over last year's totals. Name the worksheet "2003 Projection" and remove any unused worksheets. Print the worksheets in each of the workbooks. Save and close each workbook when you are finished.

Project 4

As a worker in the financial sector, you need to understand the concept of inflation. Connect to the Internet and search the Web for information about inflation. Write a two-paragraph summary explaining what inflation is and how it affects the economy. Save the document as *Inflation.doc*, and then print and close it.

Project 5  

As a small business owner who uses Excel for a variety of functions, you need to use your time effectively. When you need help with Excel, you immediately look for information on the Internet. It takes time to locate useful sites, however. Create a new workbook called *Excel Internet Resources.* Connect to the Internet and search the Web for five useful sites containing tips and other information about Excel. Add hyperlinks to each site in the workbook. When you finish adding the hyperlinks, print the worksheet, and save and close the workbook.

Project 6

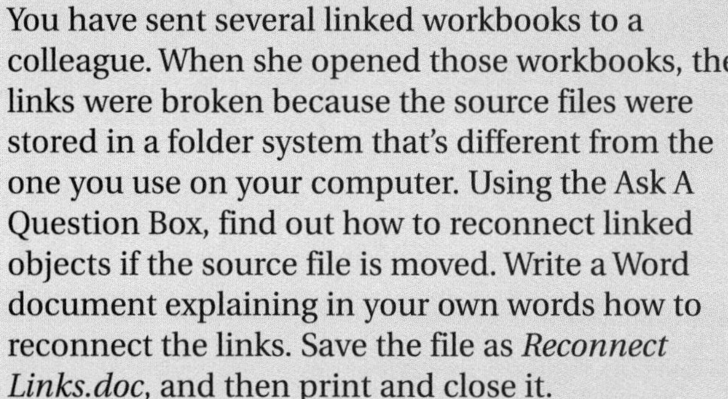

You have sent several linked workbooks to a colleague. When she opened those workbooks, the links were broken because the source files were stored in a folder system that's different from the one you use on your computer. Using the Ask A Question Box, find out how to reconnect linked objects if the source file is moved. Write a Word document explaining in your own words how to reconnect the links. Save the file as *Reconnect Links.doc*, and then print and close it.

Project 7

You work for a distribution company called Sweet Tooth Candy. Create a sample documentation worksheet for use in other workbooks. Be sure to add Identification, Map of the Workbook, and Description, Assumptions, and Parameters sections to the documentation worksheet. Save the workbook as *Sweet Tooth Candy - Documentation Sheet,* and then print and close it.

Project 8  

You would like to set up an Internet e-mail account. Many companies offer free e-mail services. Connect to the Internet and search the Web for at least three companies offering free e-mail. Create a new workbook and insert the company name, the URL, and a brief summary of the terms. Save the workbook as *Free E-mail*, and then print and close it.

Creating, Sorting, and Filtering Lists

Chapter Overview

Some workbooks in Excel are used to store lists of data, much as a database does. In this chapter, you learn about the components of a list. Validation criteria help ensure proper data entry in a list. Using data forms, you can enter, edit, find, and delete records from a list. You can use advanced filters to view subsets of a list. You can sort lists in ascending or descending order. Creating outlines using the subtotal command offers an easy way to summarize data by easily displaying or hiding levels of detail as needed.

Case profile

You need to create a personnel data list for Super Power Computers. You have been asked to make it easy for anyone to enter and find data in this list. By using data validation, you can ensure that other users enter the appropriate data. You can use data forms and filters to locate specific data. You also need to create a sales report, sorted by region and containing subtotals for each region.

Learning Objectives

- Identify basic terms and guidelines for creating lists
- Enter data in a list using data validation
- Use the data form
- Create custom filters
- Perform single and multilevel sorts
- Use grouping and outlines to create subtotals

chapter eight

8.a Identifying Basic Terms and Guidelines for Creating Lists

So far you have seen the capacity for dealing with numerical data in Excel. However, Excel is also adept at handling **lists** of data, in a manner similar to a database. A **database** stores data in a structure called a **table**. Each row in a data table contains a unique record, and each column contains entries belonging to a particular field. A **field** contains a collection of characters or numbers, such as a person's name or a phone number. The **field name** identifies the contents of that particular field. A group of field entries is known as a **record**. At the top of the list, or data table, is a **header row**, which identifies the field names used in the table.

> **QUICK TIP**
>
> Record numbers are often used in large database tables to speed up indexing and data retrieval. They also provide an easy way to sort the list by the order in which the records were entered into the list.

The *Super Power Computers - Personnel Data* workbook contains several records. This list contains fields for each employee's last name, initial of first name, division, salary, and "Rec. No.," a field that stores a unique record number for each record in the list. To open the workbook:

Step 1	***Open***	the *Super Power Computers - Personnel Data* workbook located on the Data Disk
Step 2	***Save***	the workbook as *Super Power Computers - Personnel Data Revised*

The Super Power Computers Personnel list on your screen should look similar to Figure 8-1.

FIGURE 8-1
Typical List in Excel

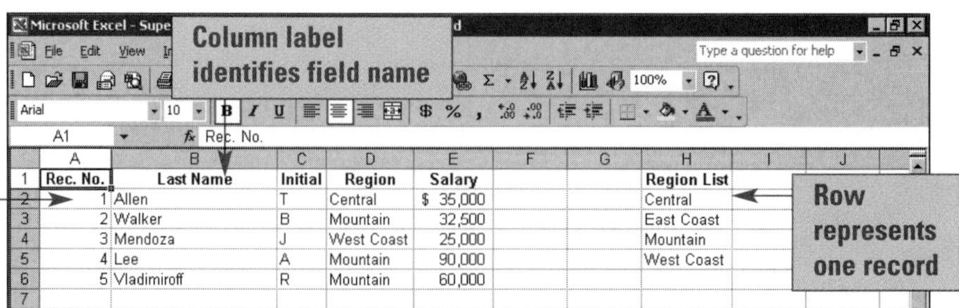

You must remember some important guidelines when creating lists. First, you should format the header row differently from the rest of the data, using bold, italics, or a different font, so that Excel recognizes that it is the header row and not just another record. Second, the header row should appear as the first row of your list. Don't separate the header row from the first row of data by inserting a blank row. If necessary, use borders or the cell fill to distinguish the header row from the data in the list. Third, each field entry in a field must contain the same type of data. For example, don't place a phone number in the Last Name field of a phone directory list. Take note of the following guidelines as well:

- Create only one list per worksheet. If you need more than one list, use a separate worksheet for each new list. This strategy helps you avoid the potential problem of mixing lists when you perform a sort.
- Always leave one column and one row blank on both sides and above and below a list. Excel then can automatically detect the list boundaries, saving you the hassle of selecting the list for sorting, outlining, and AutoFormat operations.
- Avoid using spaces at the beginning of a field entry. Spaces affect the sort order of a list, because the space character comes before alphabetic characters. Entries that have spaces as their first character are placed at the top of a sorted list.
- Format data in a column in a consistent manner. Don't make some names bold and others italic.
- Never place critical data to the left or right of a list. When filters are later applied to the list, you may not be able to see important data.
- Always include a record number field so as to give each record a unique record number. This strategy enables you to return the list to its original entry order after you've performed other sort operations.

CAUTION TIP

The data in the Region field in the Personnel Data file is not considered critical for filtering the personnel list.

8.b Entering Data in a List Using Data Validation

You want to ensure that anyone who uses the *Super Power Computers - Personnel Data Revised* workbook enters the correct data in each field. For example, the Salary field should contain only numerical data. To help the user meet these expectations, you set up data validation for each column. **Data validation** restricts the entry in a field to parameters that you set. You want to limit the entry in the record number field to whole numbers between 1 and 999. To use data validation:

Step 1	*Select*	the range A7:A10
Step 2	*Click*	Data
Step 3	*Click*	Validation

Step 4	*Click*	the Allow: list arrow on the Settings tab

Your Data Validation dialog box should look similar to Figure 8-2. Each choice in the Allow: list restricts the data in the selected cells to a specific type. The options on the Settings tab change for each validation option selected in the Allow: list.

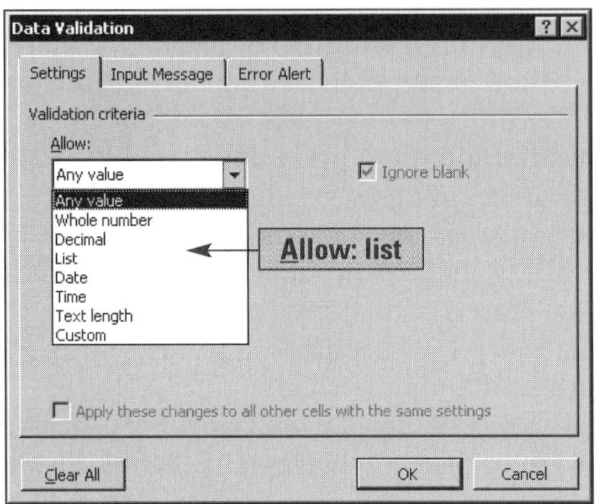

FIGURE 8-2
Allow: List on the Settings Tab of the Data Validation Dialog Box

Step 5	*Click*	Whole number in the Allow: list

For whole numbers, you specify an operator (less than, greater than, between, and so on) along with minimum and maximum values to restrict the range of acceptable values.

Step 6	*Verify*	that between is selected in the Data: list
Step 7	*Key*	1 in the Minimum: text box
Step 8	*Key*	999 in the Maximum: text box

You want to ensure that every new record receives a record number. By default, Excel does not count blank entries as invalid.

Step 9	*Click*	the Ignore blank check box to remove the check mark

Input messages display entry instructions, which make it easier for the user to understand what type of information should be entered into a field. To add an input message to the selected cells:

Step 1	***Click***	the Input Message tab
Step 2	***Key***	Record Number in the Title: text box
Step 3	***Press***	the TAB key to move to the Input message: text box
Step 4	***Key***	A whole number between 1 and 999

Your dialog box should look similar to Figure 8-3.

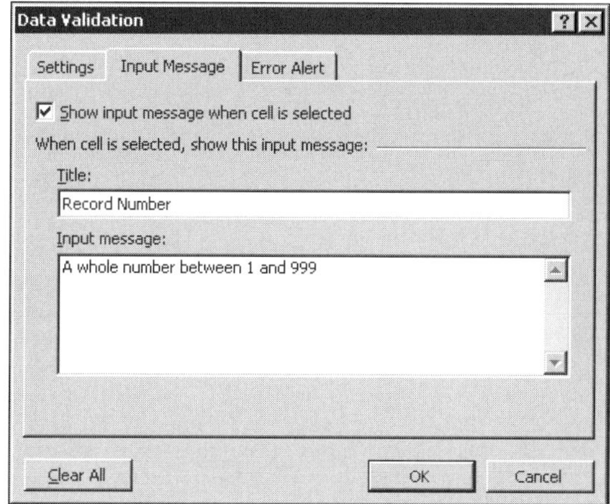

FIGURE 8-3
Input Message Tab in the Data Validation Dialog Box

When a user enters invalid data, you can have the worksheet display one of three types of error messages. Each option produces a different type of error message alert dialog box. The Stop style generates an alert dialog box that contains Retry and Cancel buttons. The Warning style alert dialog box contains Yes and No buttons. The Information style alert dialog box contains OK and Cancel buttons. Because you do not want to allow the entry of invalid data into the worksheet, you will prompt the user to enter the correct entry or cancel the operation. To set the error messages:

Step 1	***Click***	the Error Alert tab
Step 2	***Verify***	that the Show error alert after invalid data is entered check box contains a check mark
Step 3	***Click***	Stop in the Style: list, if necessary
Step 4	***Key***	Record Number in the Title: text box

Step 5	*Press*	the TAB key to move to the Error message: text box
Step 6	***Key***	You must enter a whole number between 1 and 999.

The dialog box on your screen should look similar to Figure 8-4.

FIGURE 8-4
Error Alert Tab in the Data Validation Dialog Box

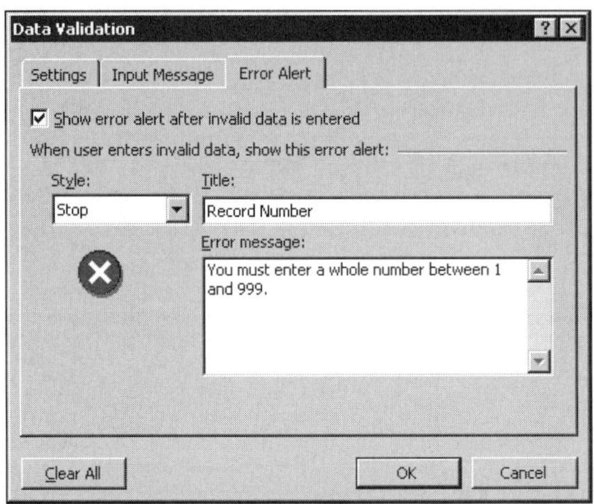

Step 7	*Click*	OK

The dialog box closes, and the input message that you just created appears near the selected cells. Next, you test the new data validation rules. To test data validation:

Step 1	*Activate*	cell A7 to display the information message

Your screen should look similar to Figure 8-5.

FIGURE 8-5
Entering Data with Data Validation

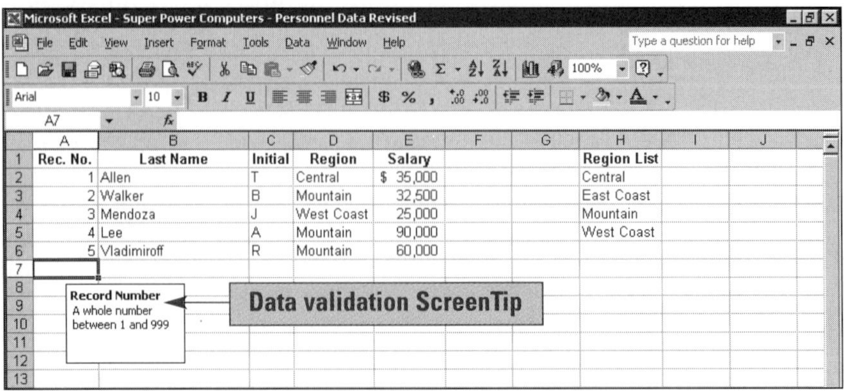

Step 2	*Key*	1000
Step 3	*Press*	the ENTER key
Step 4	*Click*	Retry in the error message dialog box that opens
Step 5	*Key*	6
Step 6	*Press*	the TAB key

This entry is valid and accepted. For the Last Name and Initial fields, you want users to enter only text, and you want to limit the number of characters permitted in each field. To set data validation for the Last Name column:

Step 1	*Select*	the range B7:B10
Step 2	*Open*	the Settings tab in the Data Validation dialog box
Step 3	*Click*	Text length in the Allow: list
Step 4	*Key*	1 in the Minimum: text box
Step 5	*Key*	20 in the Maximum: text box
Step 6	*Click*	the Ignore blank check box to remove the check mark
Step 7	*Key*	Last Name in the Title: text box on the Input Message tab
Step 8	*Key*	Limit last name to 20 characters. Abbreviate if necessary. in the Input message: text box
Step 9	*Verify*	that Stop is selected in the Style: list on the Error Alert tab
Step 10	*Key*	Last Name in the Title: text box
Step 11	*Key*	Please limit last name to 20 characters. Abbreviate if necessary. in the Error message: text box
Step 12	*Click*	OK
Step 13	*Enter*	Rawlins in cell B7

Next, you add the validation criteria for the Initial column. To add the validation criteria for the Initial column:

Step 1	*Select*	the range C7:C10
Step 2	*Open*	the Data Validation dialog box
Step 3	*Set*	the validation criteria to Text length and a minimum and maximum of 1, on the Settings tab
Step 4	*Click*	the Ignore blank check box to remove the check mark

QUICK TIP

If you set data validation for a range of cells but later need to update the validation settings, you can have the update apply to all cells with similar data validation settings. Select any cell that contains the data validation setting you wish to change, then open the Data Validation dialog box to modify the setting. On the Settings tab, click Apply these changes to all other cells with the same settings check box.

Step 5	*Key*	Initial in the Title: text box on the Input Message tab
Step 6	*Key*	Enter initial of employee's first name. in the Input message: text box
Step 7	*Key*	Initial in the Title: text box on the Error Alert tab
Step 8	*Key*	You must enter a one-character initial. in the Error message: text box
Step 9	*Click*	OK
Step 10	*Enter*	J in cell C7

QUICK TIP

To prevent changes to data validation, click Protection on the Tools menu, then click Protect Sheet. Verify that the Contents box contains a check mark before you click OK.

The next field, Region, contains only four valid entries. You can create a list of these valid entries from which the user can select. To set list validation criteria:

Step 1	*Select*	the range D7:D10
Step 2	*Open*	the Data Validation dialog box
Step 3	*Click*	List in the Allow: list on the Settings tab
Step 4	*Click*	the Collapse button in the Source: text box

The dialog box shrinks to just the title bar and input box.

Step 5	*Select*	the range H2:H5
Step 6	*Click*	the Expand button in the Data Validation dialog box
Step 7	*Verify*	that the In-cell dropdown check box contains a check mark
Step 8	*Click*	the Ignore blank check box to remove the check mark
Step 9	*Key*	Region in the Title: text box on the Input Message tab
Step 10	*Key*	Select a region from the list. in the Input message: text box
Step 11	*Key*	Region in the Title: text box on the Error Alert tab
Step 12	*Key*	You must select an entry from the list. in the Error message: text box
Step 13	*Click*	OK
Step 14	*Click*	cell D7
Step 15	*Click*	the list arrow next to cell D7

Your screen should look similar to Figure 8-6.

	A	B	C	D	E	F	G	H
1	Rec. No.	Last Name	Initial	Region	Salary			Region List
2	1	Allen	T	Central	$ 35,000			Central
3	2	Walker	B	Mountain	32,500			East Coast
4	3	Mendoza	J	West Coast	25,000			Mountain
5	4	Lee	A	Mountain	90,000			West Coast
6	5	Vladimiroff	R	Mountain	60,000			
7	6	Rawlins	J					

Drop-down list: Central, East Coast, Mountain, West Coast

cell D7 list arrow

FIGURE 8-6
Using a List to Enter Valid Data in a Field

Step 16	*Click*	East Coast

Salaries over $75,000 at Super Power Computers must be authorized by Luis Alvarez, the company president, so the error alert message for the salary column must be an Information error alert. To set validation with an Information error alert message:

Step 1	*Select*	the range E7:E10
Step 2	*Open*	the Data Validation dialog box
Step 3	*Set*	the validation criteria to Whole number, less than or equal to 75000
Step 4	*Click*	the Ignore blank check box to remove the check mark
Step 5	*Key*	Salary in the Title: text box on the Input Message tab
Step 6	*Key*	Enter salary amount. in the Input message: text box
Step 7	*Click*	the Error Alert tab
Step 8	*Click*	the Style: list arrow
Step 9	*Click*	Information
Step 10	*Key*	Salary in the Title: text box on the Error Alert tab
Step 11	*Key*	Salary must be under $75,000 unless authorized by L. Alvarez. in the Error message: text box
Step 12	*Click*	OK
Step 13	*Enter*	80000 in cell E7

> **MENU TIP**
>
> You can use the Paste Special command to copy data validation criteria to other cells. Once you've set the data validation criteria, copy the cell, click Paste Special on the Edit menu, and select the Validation option button to paste only the validation criteria into the selected cells.

The Information dialog box displays the error alert message. In this case, you have been authorized to add this salary to the list. Clicking the OK button accepts the entry; clicking the Cancel button clears the entry so you can key another value.

Step 14	*Click*	OK
Step 15	*Save*	the workbook

Data validation is not required to enter data in a list. Nevertheless, data validation is important to ensure that the user enters the appropriate type of data in each field. Next, you enter the rest of the data in the list. To enter the data in the list:

Step 1	*Enter*	the records as shown in Table 8-1

TABLE 8-1
Additional Records

Rec. No.	Last Name	Initial	Region	Salary
7	Munns	R	East Coast	45000
8	Greenwood	J	West Coast	30000

Your screen should look similar to Figure 8-7.

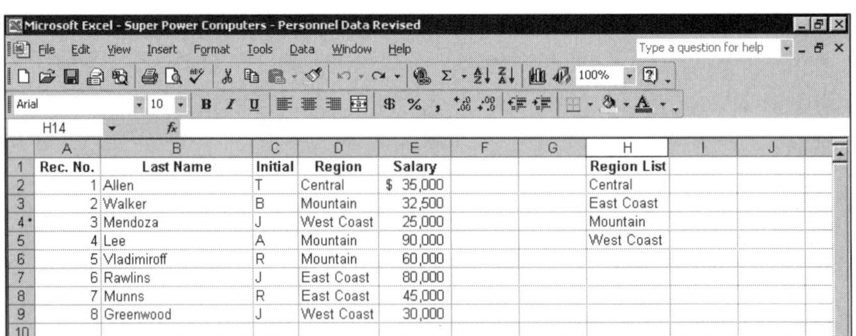

	A	B	C	D	E	F	G	H
1	Rec. No.	Last Name	Initial	Region	Salary			Region List
2	1	Allen	T	Central	$ 35,000			Central
3	2	Walker	B	Mountain	32,500			East Coast
4	3	Mendoza	J	West Coast	25,000			Mountain
5	4	Lee	A	Mountain	90,000			West Coast
6	5	Vladimiroff	R	Mountain	60,000			
7	6	Rawlins	J	East Coast	80,000			
8	7	Munns	R	East Coast	45,000			
9	8	Greenwood	J	West Coast	30,000			

FIGURE 8-7
Completed Data List

Step 2	*Save*	the workbook

8.c Using the Data Form

An alternate method of entering data in a list is to use a data form. A data form simplifies data entry by allowing the user to enter each field of a record using a simple dialog box, rather than the worksheet itself. You also can use the data form to edit and locate specific records in a list.

> **QUICK TIP**
>
> To find out more about data validation options, key "data validation" in the Ask A Question Box.

Entering Data in a List Using the Data Form

You need to add another record to the list. This time, you try the data form. To use a data form to enter a new record:

Step 1	***Activate***	any cell that is part of the list, including the header row
Step 2	***Click***	Data
Step 3	***Click***	Form

The Form dialog box opens, with the worksheet tab name as the title of the dialog box. Your dialog box should look similar to Figure 8-8. You use the scroll bar or the Find Prev and Find Next buttons to scroll through records.

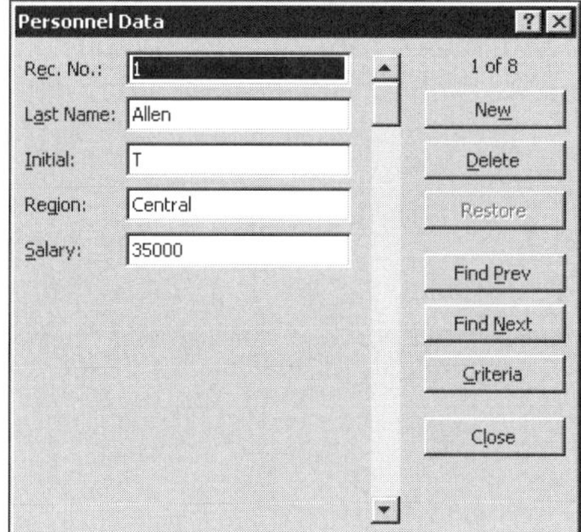

FIGURE 8-8
Form Dialog Box

Step 4	***Click***	New
Step 5	***Key***	9 in the Rec. No.: text box
Step 6	***Press***	the TAB key
Step 7	***Key***	Tate in the Last Name: text box

Step 8	*Press*	the TAB key
Step 9	*Key*	J in the Initial: text box
Step 10	*Press*	the TAB key
Step 11	*Key*	Central in the Region: text box
Step 12	*Press*	the TAB key
Step 13	*Enter*	65000 in the Salary: text box
Step 14	*Press*	the ENTER key

CAUTION TIP

One drawback to using the Form dialog box is that data validation criteria are not active with this method of data entry. In other words, you do not see input messages or error alert messages, and the list option is not available.

The record is added to the bottom of your list, and a new record is started in the Form dialog box. You can enter a new record at this point or close the Form dialog box.

Step 15	*Click*	Close

Finding Specific Records Using the Data Form

The data form allows you to readily locate specific records in a list. Many lists grow to include hundreds, or even thousands, of records. Scrolling through a list of this length to find a certain record would be very time-consuming. You want to review records of employees whose annual salaries are $40,000 or more. Using the data form, you can set criteria for the records you want to see. To search for specific records:

QUICK TIP

You can use the Find Prev button to step back through the records meeting the specified criteria.

Step 1	*Open*	the Form dialog box
Step 2	*Click*	Criteria
Step 3	*Click*	in the Salary: text box
Step 4	*Key*	>40000
Step 5	*Click*	Find Next

The first record meeting the criteria appears in the Form dialog box.

Step 6	*Click*	Find Next five more times

The computer indicates that no more records meet your criteria by making a sound. When you have finished searching for records that meet your criteria, you can clear the criteria. To clear the criteria and view all records again:

Step 1	*Click*	Criteria
Step 2	*Click*	Clear
Step 3	*Click*	Form to return to the Form dialog box

Deleting a Record from a List Using the Data Form

Occasionally, you will need to remove records from a list. To delete a record by using the data form:

Step 1	*Scroll*	to locate the record for J. Rawlins (record number 6)
Step 2	*Click*	Delete

A confirmation dialog box opens, indicating that the record will be permanently deleted.

Step 3	*Click*	OK to remove the record from the list
Step 4	*Click*	Close
Step 5	*Save*	the workbook

MOUSE TIP

You can delete a record by deleting the row in the worksheet or the cells containing the data. Right-click the row number, then click Delete; alternately, select all cells in the record, right-click the selection, click Delete, then choose the appropriate option.

8.d Creating Custom Filters

When you used the Find command in the data form, you filtered the records displayed in the Form dialog box. Alternately, you can filter records in the worksheet. You already know how to filter for one criterion in a field by using the AutoFilter command. You also can create custom filters (also known as advanced filters) to apply conditional operators (AND and OR) and logical operators (greater than, equal to, and less than).

Using AutoFilter to Create a Custom Filter

When you apply AutoFilter to a list, one of the selections on the filter list is (Custom…). When you select this option, the Custom dialog box opens, allowing you to specify criteria for a custom filter. You need to

compile a list of the employees in Super Power Computers' Mountain region who make $50,000 or less per year. To apply an AutoFilter:

Step 1	*Activate*	any cell in the list
Step 2	*Click*	Data
Step 3	*Point to*	Filter
Step 4	*Click*	AutoFilter
Step 5	*Click*	the Filter list arrow in the Region field
Step 6	*Click*	Mountain
Step 7	*Click*	the Filter list arrow in the Salary field
Step 8	*Click*	(Custom...)

The Custom AutoFilter dialog box on your screen should look similar to Figure 8-9.

FIGURE 8-9
Custom AutoFilter Dialog Box

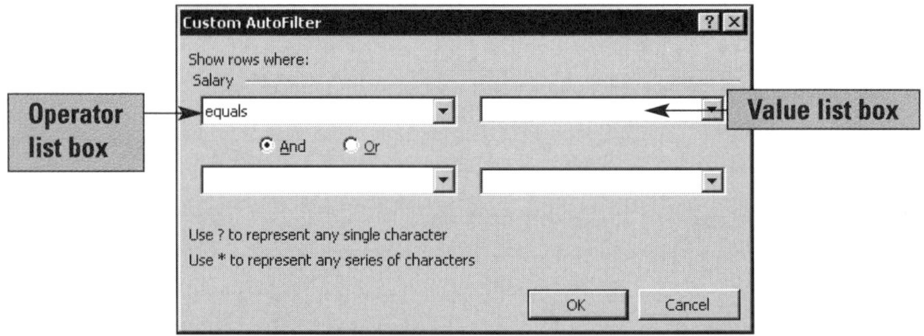

Step 9	*Click*	the operator list arrow on the left side of the dialog box
Step 10	*Click*	is less than or equal to
Step 11	*Key*	50000 in the box on the right side of the dialog box
Step 12	*Click*	OK

The list is filtered. Your screen should look similar to Figure 8-10.

FIGURE 8-10
Filtered List

Colored row header indicates a filter is applied

Colored filter arrow indicates filter is applied

You can use wildcards in your custom filters. A **wildcard** is used in place of other characters. Suppose you want to filter a list for all last names starting with R. You could enter R* in the Custom AutoFilter dialog box, where the asterisk (*) represents any characters after the R. The question mark (?) can be used in place of a single character. If you used the filter r?n on a list of words, for example, you would see *ran*, *ron*, and *run*. You need to clear the previous filter first unless you want to filter only the records showing from the previous filter. To apply a wildcard filter:

Step 1	***Click***	Data
Step 2	***Point to***	Filter
Step 3	***Click***	Show all
Step 4	***Click***	the Last Name filter arrow
Step 5	***Click***	(Custom...)
Step 6	***Verify***	that equals is selected in the operator list on the left
Step 7	***Enter***	m* in the value box on the right
Step 8	***Click***	OK

The list is filtered to show all last names beginning with M.

Step 9	***Turn off***	AutoFilter
Step 10	***Save***	the workbook

Creating Custom Filters with Multiple Operators

Another way to filter records is to use advanced filters. Advanced filters allow you to work with multiple AND and OR operators in each field to filter a list. These types of filters are more difficult to set up than AutoFilters, however. To take advantage of advanced filters, you must establish a criteria range in the worksheet. The column labels in the criteria range must match the column labels of your list. Rows beneath the column labels in the criteria range indicate the filter criteria. You should follow these guidelines when using advanced filtering:

- Place the criteria range above or below the rows containing your list data. Do not set up the range in the same rows as the list, because filtered rows remain hidden from view.

- The first row of the criteria range identifies the columns to be filtered. Although its formatting does not have to match that of the column labels in the list you are filtering, the spelling must match exactly.
- Adding multiple criteria in the same row creates an AND condition. For example, to list employees who have an annual salary greater than $40,000 AND who work in the Central division, you would enter ">40000" under the column heading Salary and "Central" under the column label Division; both entries would appear in the same row.
- Entering criteria in subsequent rows specifies an OR condition. For example, if you wanted to find all employees who made more than $40,000 OR less than $30,000 per year, you would enter ">40000" in one row under the Salary column label and "<30000" in the next row under the column label. Each time you add another row to the criteria, you specify another OR condition.

To create a criteria range:

Step 1	***Insert***	six blank rows above row 1
Step 2	***Enter***	Last Name in cell D1
Step 3	***Enter***	Salary in cell E1

The criteria range appears above your list. Next, enter the criteria you want to use in the filter. To add criteria to a criteria range:

Step 1	***Enter***	a* in cell D2

This sets up a filter that displays records starting with the letter "A" in the Last Name field.

Step 2	***Enter***	m* in cell D3
Step 3	***Enter***	>40000 in cell E3

This multiple-column condition displays records that start with the letter "M" in the Last Name field AND have a salary greater than $40,000.

Step 4	***Enter***	g* in cell D4

This complex filter displays records for all employees whose last name starts with A or G, as well as records for any employee whose last name starts with M and whose salary is more than $40,000. To apply the advanced filter:

Step 1	*Click*	cell A8

You must select a cell within the list that you want to filter. Excel automatically searches for the header row.

Step 2	*Click*	Data
Step 3	*Point to*	Filter
Step 4	*Click*	Advanced Filter

QUICK TIP

You can use named ranges as references in the Advanced Filter dialog box.

The Advanced Filter dialog box on your screen should look similar to Figure 8-11. You can select the list range and criteria range and specify whether you want to create a copy of the filtered records or filter the list in place. The default is to filter the list in place. The list range is selected automatically.

FIGURE 8-11
Advanced Filter Dialog Box

Step 5	*Click*	in the Criteria range: text box
Step 6	*Key*	D1:E4
Step 7	*Click*	OK

The filtered list displays only records that meet the criteria specified in the criteria range D1:E4. Your screen should look similar to Figure 8-12.

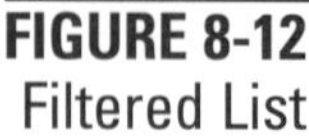

FIGURE 8-12
Filtered List

Step 8	***Clear***	the filter

Extracting Data

When you use the advanced filter copy option, you leave the original list of data unfiltered and **extract** the records meeting your filter criteria, which are copied to a new location. You want to extract a list of all employees who make more than $35,000 per year. To extract data:

> **QUICK TIP**
>
> To learn about other advanced filtering techniques, use online Help to search for information about advanced filters and examples of advanced filter criteria.

Step 1	***Delete***	the contents of cells D2:E4
Step 2	***Enter***	>35000 in cell E2
Step 3	***Click***	any cell in the list
Step 4	***Open***	the Advanced Filter dialog box
Step 5	***Select***	all the text in the Criteria range: text box
Step 6	***Key***	D1:E2
Step 7	***Click***	the Copy to another location option button
Step 8	***Click***	in the Copy to: text box
Step 9	***Click***	cell I1 in the worksheet

Note that you can copy filtered data only to the active worksheet. Once you have extracted the records, you can move or copy them to wherever you like.

Step 10	***Click***	OK
Step 11	***Scroll***	the worksheet to view the extracted data
Step 12	***Increase***	the width of columns J and L to show the data

The filtered records, including the column headings, are copied to the new location, starting in cell I1. Your screen should look similar to Figure 8-13.

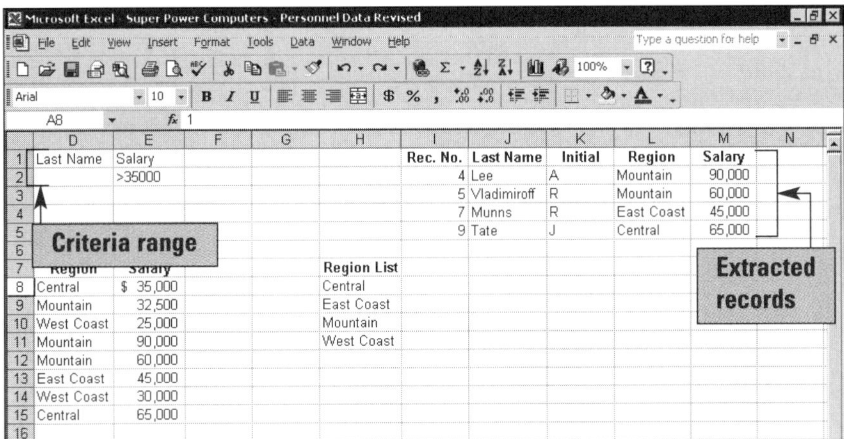

FIGURE 8-13
Extracted Records

Step 13	***Save***	and close the workbook

QUICK TIP

It may take you some time to become comfortable with working with data lists and filters, but these features represent powerful tools for storing and retrieving data.

8.e Performing Single and Multilevel Sorts

The *Super Power Computers - Sales Rep Data* workbook contains gross sales data for each salesperson. Before you can create a meaningful report, the data needs to be sorted. First open the workbook containing the data. To open the workbook:

Step 1	***Open***	the *Super Power Computers - Sales Rep Data* workbook on the Data Disk
Step 2	***Save***	the workbook as *Super Power Computers - Sales Rep Data Revised*

Column A contains the column label Region. This column label acts as your sort **criteria**, indicating the type of data you want to sort by. If you place the active cell in this column, Excel will know which column to sort. To sort the sales representative data:

Step 1	***Activate***	cell A4
Step 2	***Click***	the Sort Ascending button on the Standard toolbar

QUICK TIP

To sort on four to six columns, first sort on the columns of least importance. Then, using the sorted data, sort on the other three columns.

The column is sorted in ascending order (alphabetically) by region. When Excel works with lists, it assumes that the top row of the list contains the column labels and does not sort that row. Using the Sort dialog box, you can sort by as many as three criteria. To sort on multiple columns:

Step 1	*Click*	Data
Step 2	*Click*	Sort

Your Sort dialog box should look similar to Figure 8-14. When you open the Sort dialog box, Excel scans for the header row of the active list and adds the column headings to the criteria list boxes. It also assumes that the first sort criterion is the column containing the active cell.

FIGURE 8-14
Sort Dialog Box

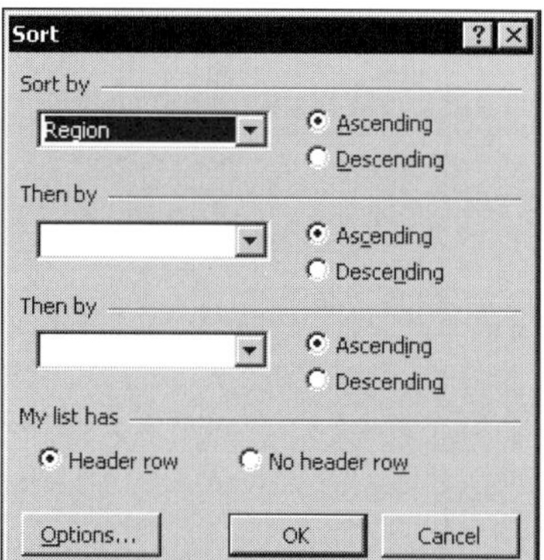

Step 3	*Verify*	that Region is selected in the Sort by list box
Step 4	*Click*	the Then by list arrow in the middle of the dialog box
Step 5	*Click*	Gross Sales in the list
Step 6	*Click*	the Descending option button next to Gross Sales
Step 7	*Click*	OK

The list is sorted alphabetically by region, then from highest to lowest by gross sales within each region.

8.f Using Grouping and Outlines to Create Subtotals

Outlines offer a powerful option for viewing data in a worksheet. An **outline** shows data in hierarchies, or levels, up to eight levels.

An easy way to create outlines is to use the Subtotals command. When you create subtotals, you specify at what points subtotals should be calculated. Excel automatically inserts the SUBTOTAL function at the specified points, then creates a grand total at the end. The information appearing above each subtotal is called **detail data**. Applying the Subtotals command automatically creates an outline, and a set of outline symbols appears on the left of the worksheet, providing the controls to display or hide detail data.

You can calculate the subtotals for each region as well as obtain totals for the company as a whole. To create a subtotal outline:

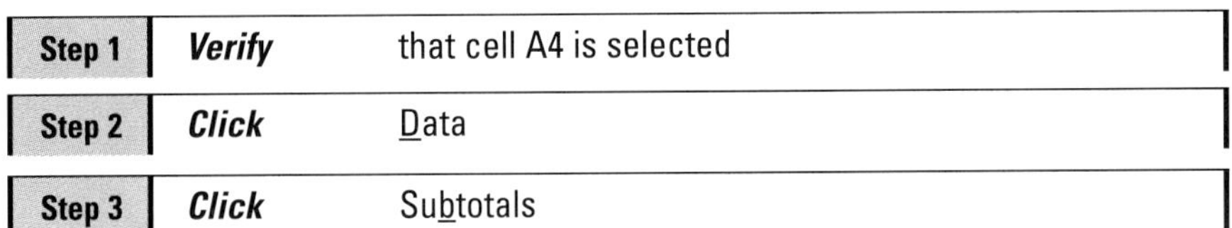

Step 1	*Verify*	that cell A4 is selected
Step 2	*Click*	Data
Step 3	*Click*	Subtotals

The Subtotal dialog box on your screen should look similar to Figure 8-15. Region—the first column in the data set—is automatically selected in the At each change in: list. The Region column is sorted alphabetically. Whenever a new value appears in the Region column, a subtotal will be calculated. In the Add subtotal to: list, Gross Sales—the last column in the data set—is selected.

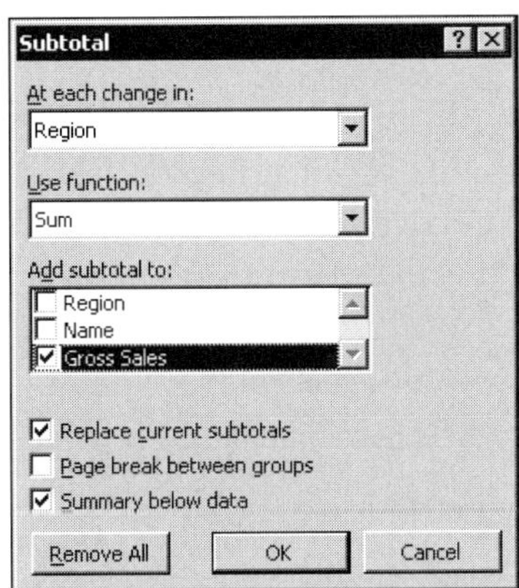

FIGURE 8-15
Subtotal Dialog Box

QUICK TIP

You can create an outline by clicking the Data menu, pointing to Group and Outline, then clicking Auto Outline. Use Group and Ungroup to create single levels of data. Your worksheet must be set up properly for this function to work. See online Help for more information about creating an outline manually.

CAUTION TIP

Leaving the Replace current subtotals check box *checked* will replace your current outline with a new one. If you want to add another level of detail to an existing outline, you must remove the check mark.

Step 4	*Click*	OK
Step 5	*Scroll*	the worksheet to view row 71

New rows are inserted at each change in the Region column, and Excel calculates a subtotal for each region. Outline symbols showing a two-level outline appear on the left. At the bottom of the list, a grand total is calculated. Your screen should look similar to Figure 8-16.

FIGURE 8-16
Outline Created Using the Subtotals Command

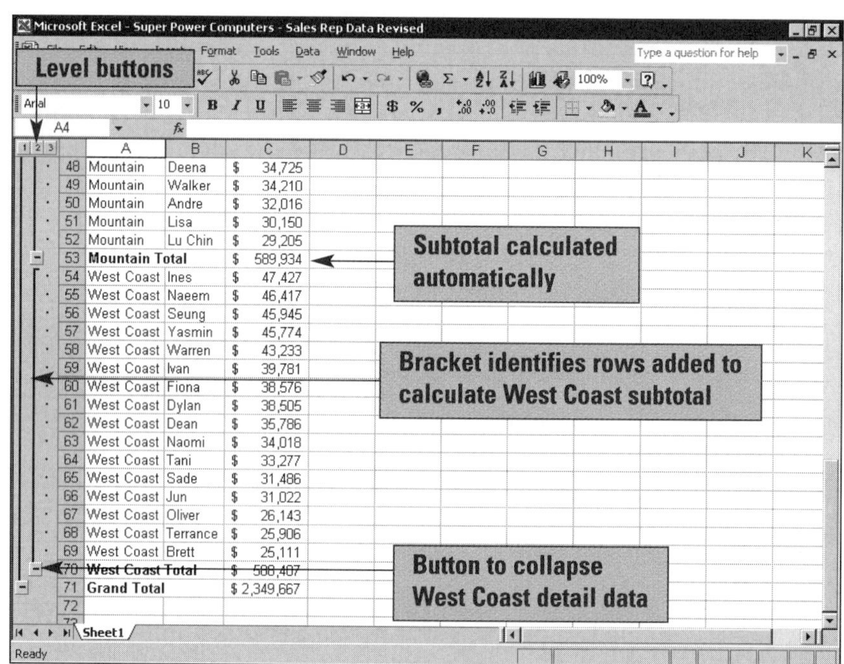

You can hide detail data by collapsing the outline. To collapse outline levels:

Step 1	*Click*	the Collapse Level button to the left of row 70

The detail data for the West Coast Region becomes hidden, and only the subtotal for that category appears. The Collapse Level button changes to an Expand Level button.

Step 2	*Click*	the 2 Level button at the top of the outline to display only subtotals for each region
Step 3	*Scroll*	to the top of the worksheet to view all of the subtotals
Step 4	*Save*	the workbook and close it

QUICK TIP

To remove the subtotals and the outline, open the Subtotal dialog box, then click the Remove All button.

Summary

- You can identify the main components of a list, including field, field name, header row, and record.
- Data validation criteria ensure that users enter the proper data in each field of a record.
- You can use the data form to add, modify, locate, and delete records.
- Custom filters allow you to build complex filters using AND and OR operators.
- You can extract records from a list to move or copy them to another location.
- You can sort data by using as many as three levels of sort criteria.
- You can use subtotals to create outlines automatically. You can add as many as eight levels of subtotals. Select outline symbols to hide or reveal detail.

Commands Review

Action	Menu Bar	Shortcut Menu	Toolbar	Task Pane	Keyboard
Set data validation	Data, Validation				ALT + D, L
Use a data form to enter records	Data, Form				ALT + D, O
Apply an AutoFilter	Data, Filter, AutoFilter				ALT + D, F, F
Apply an advanced filter	Data, Filter, Advanced Filter				ALT + D, F, A
Show all records	Data, Filter, Show All				ALT + D, F, S
Sort data	Data, Sort		A↓Z Z↓A		ALT + D, S
Use subtotals	Data, Subtotals				ALT + D, B
Expand an outline level	Data, Group, Show detail		1 2 3 +		ALT + D, G, S
Collapse an outline level	Data, Group, Hide detail		1 2 3 −		ALT + D, G, H

Concepts Review

Circle the correct answer.

1. A field name:
[a] is a collection of characters or numbers that make up one part of a record.
[b] is the collection of fields that make a complete entry.
[c] identifies the contents of each column.
[d] can appear anywhere on the worksheet.

2. A record:
[a] is a collection of characters or numbers that make up one part of a record.
[b] is the collection of fields that make a complete entry.
[c] identifies the contents of each column.
[d] can appear anywhere on the worksheet.

3. Why should you leave one column and one row blank on all sides of a list?
[a] This approach makes it easier to return the list to its original sort order.
[b] Excel can detect list boundaries more easily.
[c] You should not leave blank rows or columns, because spaces affect the sort order of a list.
[d] It does not matter, as long as you format each field in the same way.

4. Data validation is used to:
[a] sort fields using criteria you define.
[b] restrict the data that can be entered in each field.
[c] search for records containing certain characters.
[d] make a copy of filtered records in another location.

5. A data form can be used to:
[a] add records to a list.
[b] locate records meeting specific criteria in a list.
[c] delete records from a list.
[d] all of the above

6. Multiple criteria in the same row in an advanced filter criteria range indicate:
[a] an AND condition.
[b] an OR condition.
[c] a wildcard character.
[d] the inclusion of additional fields in the result.

7. Criteria in additional rows beneath a criteria column heading indicate:
[a] an AND condition.
[b] an OR condition.
[c] a wildcard character.
[d] the inclusion of additional records in the result.

8. Extracted data refers to records:
[a] meeting filter criteria that are moved from the list.
[b] meeting filter criteria that are copied from the list.
[c] not meeting filter criteria.
[d] that are randomly removed from the database.

9. You can create outlines with as many as:
[a] five levels of detail.
[b] six levels of detail.
[c] seven levels of detail.
[d] eight levels of detail.

10. One drawback of a data form is that:
[a] you cannot delete records from a list.
[b] the data validation criteria are not active.
[c] you cannot move from record to record.
[d] you cannot edit records once they are entered.

Circle **T** if the statement is true or **F** if the statement is false.

T F 1. Column headings for advanced filter criteria must be spelled exactly like the column headings in the list you are filtering.

T F 2. "Part No." would be a likely field name in a warehouse database.

T F 3. The terms "record" and "field" refer to the same thing.

T F 4. Clicking one of the Sort buttons performs a sort based on the column of the active cell.

T F 5. Spaces at the beginning of a field entry affect the sort order of a list.

T F 6. You cannot specify AND or OR conditions using AutoFilters.

T F 7. The header row can be placed anywhere in a list, as long as it is formatted differently from the rest of the list.

T F 8. Filters allow you to work with a subset of records in a list.

T F 9. When you apply a filter to a list, you hide all other records that don't meet the criteria.

T F 10. A wildcard is used in place of other characters.

Skills Review

Exercise 1 C

1. Create a new workbook.

2. Use the following field names to create a product list for use in the warehouse: "Part No."; "Description"; "Manufacturer"; "Cost"; "Quantity"; and "Value."

3. Select 15 rows per column. Use data validation to set the rules in the table below, using the following instructions:

a. Do not allow blank entries for any fields.

b. The valid manufacturer names are: Price Mfg., Sunrise Products Inc., Watershed Mfg., and Irontown Mfg.

c. Use a formula in the Value column to calculate the value of stock on hand by multiplying the quantity of each item times the cost.

Field Name	Validation Characteristic	Input Message	Error Alert Type
Part No.	Whole number between 1,000 and 4,999	Yes	Stop
Description	Text limited to 20 characters	Yes	Information
Manufacturer	Use list of four manufacturer names (see Step b)	Yes	Stop
Cost	Decimal number limited to less than $100.00	Yes	Information
Quantity	Whole number limited to less than 1,000	Yes	Stop

4. Review your list setup to make sure that it fits the list guidelines discussed in this chapter.

5. Save the workbook as *Warehouse Parts*, and then print and close it.

Exercise 2 

1. Open the *Warehouse Parts* workbook that you created in Exercise 1, change the data validation for the Description column to a maximum of 30 characters.
2. Enter the data shown in the table below. Calculate the Value column by using a formula.

Part No.	Description	Manufacturer	Cost	Quantity	Value
1010	Sugar, 50 lb	Price Mfg.	19.95	333	(use a formula)
1020	Sugar, 125 lb	Price Mfg.	39.95	693	(use a formula)
1030	Molasses	Watershed Mfg.	45.95	282	(use a formula)
2100	Sprinkles, 1,000 gross	Sunrise Products Inc.	70.95	314	(use a formula)
2200	Rainbow Sprinkles, 10 gross	Watershed Mfg.	6.95	838	(use a formula)
3001	Flour, 25 lb	Irontown Mfg.	12.95	940	(use a formula)
3002	Flour, 5 lb	Irontown Mfg.	5.95	412	(use a formula)
3003	Wheat flour, 150 lb	Price Mfg.	99.95	758	(use a formula)
4020	Honey, 30 gallons	Sunrise Products Inc.	89.95	687	(use a formula)
4030	Honey, 2 gallons	Sunrise Products Inc.	6.95	769	(use a formula)
4040	Honey, 1 quart	Watershed Mfg.	1.95	930	(use a formula)

3. Resize columns to fit, as necessary.
4. Format columns D and F using the Accounting format, two decimal places.
5. Save the workbook as *Warehouse Parts Inventory*, and then print and close it.

Exercise 3 

1. Open the *Warehouse Parts Inventory* workbook that you created in Exercise 2.
2. Use a data form to edit part number 3002. Change the description to Wheat Flour, 7 lb.
3. Use a data form to delete part number 4040.
4. Use a data form to add a new record using the information in the following table.

Part No.	Description	Manufacturer	Cost	Quantity
4041	Honey, 25 gallons	Price Mfg.	35.95	750

5. Apply AutoFilters to the list.
6. Using the AutoFilter list arrows, filter the list to find all items manufactured by Price Mfg.
7. Print the filtered list, save the workbook as *Warehouse Parts Inventory Filter 1*, and then close it.

Exercise 4

1. Open the *Warehouse Parts Inventory Filter 1* workbook that you created in Exercise 3.
2. Clear any active filters. Create an advanced filter criteria that will find any records with a quantity of more than 500 items, or any item that costs less than $30.00 (be sure you don't create an "AND" condition).
3. Filter the list with the criteria you set in Step 2.

4. Sort the list in ascending order by Quantity.
5. Print the list, save the workbook as *Warehouse Parts Inventory Filter 2*, and then close it.

Exercise 5 C

1. Open the *Sweet Tooth Sales to Stores* workbook located on the Data Disk.
2. Apply AutoFilters to the list.
3. Filter the list to show only items sold in quantities greater than 200.
4. Save the workbook as *Sweet Tooth Sales to Stores Filter1*, and then print and close it.

Exercise 6 C

1. Open the *Sweet Tooth Sales to Stores Filter1* workbook that you created in Exercise 5.
2. Remove the filter you created in Exercise 5, then create a new advanced filter to find records of employees whose Total Sales were less than $500 or more than $2000.
3. Filter the list using the filter you created in the previous step.
4. Print the filtered list, save the workbook as *Sweet Tooth Sales to Stores Filter 2*, and then close it.

Exercise 7 C

1. Open the *Sweet Tooth Sales to Stores Filter 2* workbook that you created in Exercise 6.
2. Display all records.
3. Click any cell in the data list, then use a data form to add the following record to the list:

   East Coast *New York* *Jungle Planet* *124* *240* *6.95* *Kaili Muafala*
4. Save the workbook as *Sweet Tooth Sales Data 2*, and then print and close it.

Exercise 8 C

1. Open the *Employee Time* workbook located on the Data Disk.
2. Sort the data by Project (ascending order), and then by Hours (descending order).
3. Create an outline of the data by creating subtotals for each Project.
4. Collapse the outline to level 2.
5. Change the title in cell A1 to Time by Project.
6. Save the workbook as *Project Time Subtotals*, and then print and close it.

Case Projects

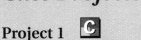

Project 1 C

You have just been promoted to programming director at the radio station where you work. The station manager wants to completely reorganize the way in which the station keeps track of which songs are played. Prepare a workbook that can sort songs by the number of times played in a week, duration, artist, and musical classification. Be sure to format the cells so that they display the correct units. Add the titles of at least 10 songs, and create fictitious data for the number of times played and duration. Save the workbook as *Record Tracker*, and then print and close it.

Project 2 

As the personnel director for a small retail sales company, you are in charge of tracking personnel information. Create a list of 15 employees. Include a unique record number for each employee, starting at 1. Each record should include a record number, last name, first initial, hire date (within the last five years), date of last pay increase, current salary, and department (use at least three departments). Use appropriate data validation for each field. Prepare and print a series of sorted reports showing employees sorted by record number, alphabetically by last name, by hire date, by department (alphabetically by last name within each department), and by current salary. Use subtotals to prepare a pie chart showing salary percentages by department. Print the chart. Save the workbook as *Personnel Information*, and then close it.

Project 3

Use the Ask A Question Box to find out how to locate cells that have data validation rules applied. Write a step-by-step summary of this process. Save the document as *Find Data Validation Cells.doc*, and then print and close it.

Project 4  

You are a serious baseball card collector. Create a worksheet to organize your card collection by player, card manufacturer, or value. Connect to the Internet and search for Web sites devoted to baseball card collectors. Create a workbook containing the names, card manufacturers, card years, and values for 20 cards. Include at least three different cards for three of the players. Organize the data so that it can be sorted by player name, card manufacturer, year, or value. Filter the data to display only those cards with a worth greater than or equal to $100 and manufactured by Topps or Upper Deck. Save the workbook as *Baseball Card Collection*, and then print and close it.

Project 5 

Programmers sometimes add "Easter Eggs" to a program: If a user follows a certain sequence of commands, they might see a special message containing the names of the programmers or something else fun. Connect to the Internet and search the Web for Excel Easter Eggs. See if any of them work with Excel 2002. You also could try searching for Easter Eggs in other programs you use. Print at least one page explaining how to display an Easter Egg.

Project 6 

You are the data manager at a shipping company. Create a workbook to track shipping dates, company names, addresses, and four-digit item numbers. Use a data form to add five records to the list. Print the list, save the workbook as *Shipping*, and then close it.

Project 7  

Your marketing firm is preparing a commercial that it would like to release in the 10 largest cities in the United States. Connect to the Internet and search the Web for a list of populations of cities in the United States. Create a new workbook, and set up field names for each city, its state, and its population. Apply data validation to each column. Limit the data in the city field to a text length of 15 characters and the state field to a text length of 2 characters. Limit the population field to a whole number greater than 1,000,000 with a Warning message if a number less than this is entered. Enter the data for the 10 largest cities you can find. Save the workbook as *Population*, and then print and close it.

Project 8

You work at a telemarketing company. Create a list to log the date, time, and duration of each call. Use data validation to restrict the data entry for each cell to the appropriate type of data (limit call length to less than 60 minutes). Enter fictitious data for five calls. Save the workbook as *Phone Log*, and then print and close it.

Increasing Productivity with Macros, Templates, and Custom Toolbars and Menus

Chapter Overview

Many tasks you perform in Excel, such as common formatting tasks, are very repetitive. Macros can record these steps then replay them much more rapidly than you can perform them, and as often as you like. In this chapter, you learn to record, edit, and run macros. Another time-saving strategy is to create and use templates, special workbooks with formatting and formulas already in place. You learn to create, edit, and use templates to become more productive.

Case profile

Every time you create a new worksheet for Super Power Computers, you spend precious time keying worksheet and column titles, adding formulas, and formatting the worksheet titles same way you do all the other worksheet titles. By using macros to automate repetitive tasks, you can save a lot of time. Saving a formatted workbook as a template also increases your productivity. To work even more efficiently, you can customize the menus and the toolbars.

Learning Objectives

- Use macros to automate repetitive tasks
- Edit a macro
- Use workbooks containing macros
- Create and edit templates
- Customize toolbars and menus

chapter nine

9.a Using Macros to Automate Repetitive Tasks

A **macro** is a group of instructions that automatically executes a set of commands. By using macros, you can automate repetitive tasks. For example, you usually format Super Power Computers' worksheet titles with the Impact font, 16-point size, blue color, and centered across several cells. The task described is a perfect candidate for a simple macro: repetitive, specific commands that you use over and over again. Other good candidates for macros include tasks such as adding headers and footers to a print report, creating charts, sorting lists, and setting up worksheets.

Macros are written or recorded in a programming language called Visual Basic, which is used in all of the Office applications. Visual Basic is fairly easy to learn. If you learn its basics, you can create macros that work in Word, Access, PowerPoint, or Excel.

Now, take a deep breath. Yes, we said "programming." And yes, you're going to do it. Keep a few things in mind: (1) programming is not just for geeks anymore, and (2) by learning how to do a little bit of programming (deep breath), you can actually lighten your workload and free yourself to do other things.

QUICK TIP

The Personal Macro Workbook is a hidden workbook that opens automatically each time Excel opens. This makes the macros contained in the Personal Macro Workbook, called "global macros," available for use with any open workbook. An example of a global macro is a print macro.

If you work on a shared computer or network, consider storing macros in the workbook in which you created them to ensure that others don't accidentally modify or delete your macros. You can copy macros from one workbook to another.

Recording a Macro

The simplest way to create a macro is to record it. When you record a macro, Excel takes note of every command you use and every keystroke you press. To start recording a macro:

Step 1	***Create***	a new, blank workbook
Step 2	***Save***	the workbook as *Super Power Computers - Title Macro*
Step 3	***Click***	Tools
Step 4	***Point to***	Macro
Step 5	***Click***	Record New Macro

The Record Macro dialog box opens. Macro names cannot contain spaces, so use the underscore (_) character instead. You can choose to store a macro in the workbook in which you created it or in a global workbook called the Personal Macro Workbook. Macros stored in a workbook are only available when that workbook is open. Macros stored in the Personal Macro Workbook are available whenever you are working in Excel. You store the SPC_Title macro in the open workbook.

Step 6	***Key***	SPC_Title in the Macro name: text box
Step 7	***Verify***	that This Workbook is selected in the Store macro in: list box
Step 8	***Drag***	to select all of the text in the Description: text box
Step 9	***Key***	Create and format a worksheet title

Your dialog box should look similar to Figure 9-1.

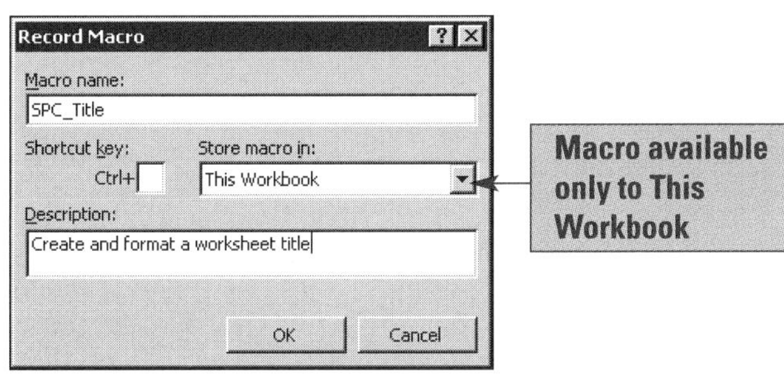

FIGURE 9-1
Record Macro Dialog Box

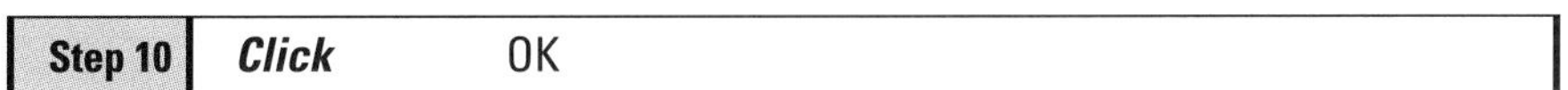

Step 10	***Click***	OK

The Stop Recording toolbar appears, and Recording appears in the status bar. Your screen should look similar to Figure 9-2.

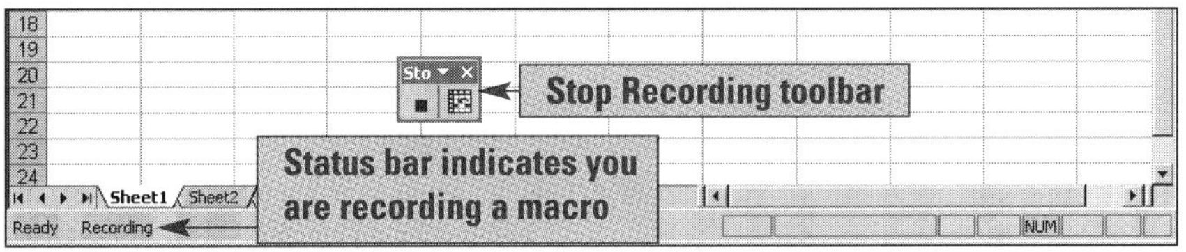

FIGURE 9-2
Stop Recording Toolbar

Next, you enter and format the titles you want on your worksheet. To enter the titles:

Step 1	***Enter***	Super Power Computers in cell A1
Step 2	***Enter***	<Add a subtitle in cell A2> in cell A2 (include the brackets)
Step 3	***Select***	the range A1:F1
Step 4	***Click***	the Merge and Center button on the Formatting toolbar
Step 5	***Repeat***	Steps 3 and 4 with the range A2:F2
Step 6	***Select***	the range A1:A2

QUICK TIP

When creating macros, a very helpful technique is to write down or practice each step in the task you want to automate. When you are sure that you have written down all of the steps involved, begin recording your macro.

Step 7	***Open***	the Font tab in the Format Cells dialog box
Step 8	***Click***	Impact in the Font: list
Step 9	***Click***	16 in the Size: list
Step 10	***Click***	the Blue box in the Color: palette
Step 11	***Click***	OK
Step 12	***Activate***	cell A1
Step 13	***Click***	the Stop Recording button on the Stop Recording toolbar

The macro is saved as part of the workbook, and the Stop Recording toolbar closes.

Running a Macro

You must run the macro to test it. You can use the Macro dialog box to run macros stored in any currently open workbook or macros stored in your Personal Macro Workbook. To run the macro:

Step 1	***Click***	the Sheet2 sheet tab
Step 2	***Click***	Tools
Step 3	***Point to***	Macro
Step 4	***Click***	Macros to open the Macro dialog box
Step 5	***Click***	SPC_Title in the available macros list

The description you keyed when you recorded the macro appears at the bottom of the dialog box. Your Macro dialog box should look similar to Figure 9-3.

FIGURE 9-3
Macro Dialog Box

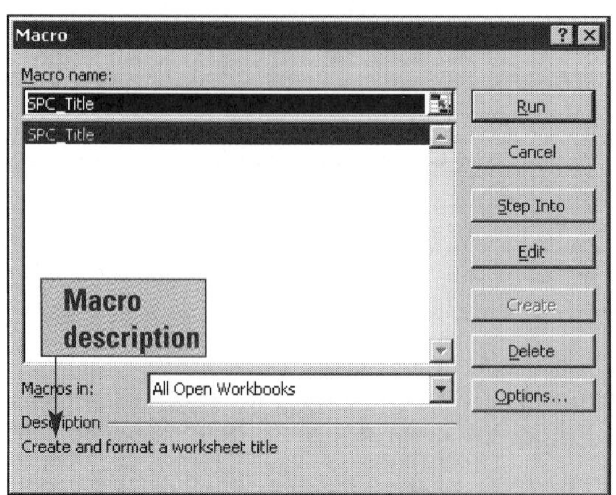

Step 6	*Click*	Run

The macro performs the steps that you recorded earlier. Your screen should look similar to Figure 9-4.

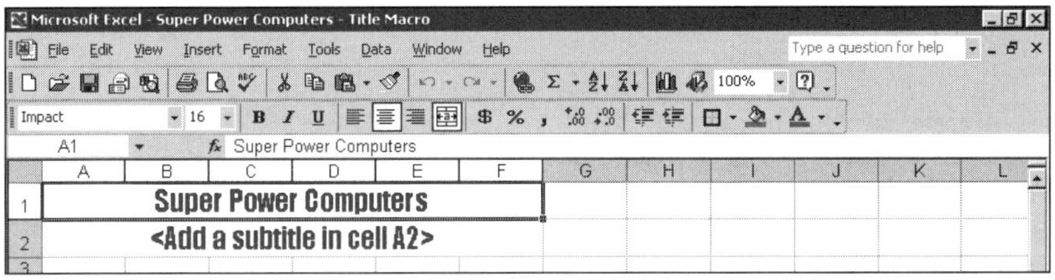

FIGURE 9-4
SPC_Title Macro Results

9.b Editing a Macro

Using the Visual Basic Editor, you can edit macros that you've previously recorded or written. The Visual Basic Editor is a separate program that runs in its own window, outside of Excel, and provides toolbars and menus specifically intended for working with Visual Basic programming code. To edit the SPC_Title macro:

Step 1	*Open*	the Macro dialog box and select the SPC_Title macro
Step 2	*Click*	Edit
Step 3	*Click*	the Maximize button in the Code window, if necessary

Your screen should look similar to Figure 9-5. The selected macro is open in the right side of the Visual Basic Editor. The Visual Basic Editor program button appears in the taskbar.

On the left side of the Visual Basic Editor window, the Project Explorer window displays a hierarchical list of all open projects and each of the items associated with each particular project. A **project** includes objects in the workbook, such as the worksheets, **modules** (where macro code is stored), and **forms** (custom dialog boxes). Projects also can contain other items, such as ActiveX controls, class modules, and references to other projects.

The Properties window, located beneath the Project Explorer window, is used to modify the properties for selected objects. For example, the code module has a (Name) property that you can change. Other types of objects, such as buttons or controls used on forms (dialog boxes), have many additional properties. The Code window to the right contains the macro code for the SPC_Title macro.

QUICK TIP

You can write new macros, test, debug, and delete macros from the Visual Basic Editor.

If you want additional information about recording macros and items that can be included in projects, use Microsoft Visual Basic Help in the Visual Basic Editor.

FIGURE 9-5
Visual Basic Editor

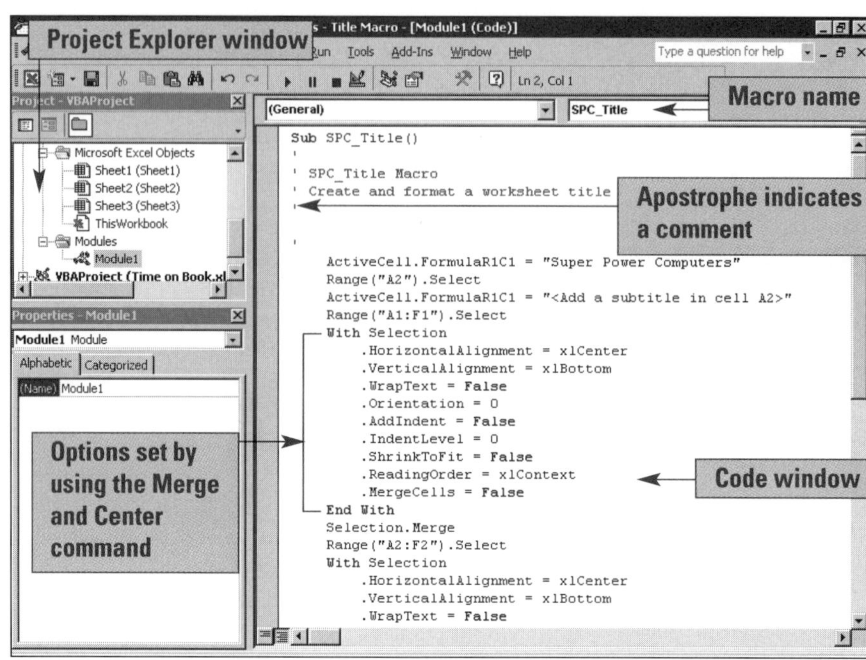

Step 4	*Scroll*	the Code window to review the code

Table 9-1 describes different sections of the code.

TABLE 9-1
Macro Code Description

Macro Line	Description
Sub SPC_Title()	Sub appears in blue text and defines the beginning of a macro (sometimes called a subroutine). The title of the macro appears on the Sub line and appears in black text.
Green text lines	Green text that appears after an apostrophe is a comment line. Comments are used to explain the steps in your macro. Notice that the description you entered in the Record Macro dialog box appears at the top of your code.
ActiveCell.FormulaR1C1 = "Super Power Computers"	Enters the text "Super Power Computers" in the current cell (using R1C1 style cell references—use online Help to learn more about this topic)
Range("A2").Select	Selects cell A2
All lines starting with Range("A1:F1").Select to Selection.Merge	Merges and centers cells A1:F1
All lines beginning with Range("A1:F2").Select to End With	Selects cells A1:F2 and sets the font options
End Sub	Indicates the end of the macro

Whenever a Super Power Computers employee uses this macro, the current date should be added, in a blue font, to cell A3. To modify the code:

Step 1	***Locate***	the line that reads Range ("A1:F1").Select near the end of the macro
Step 2	***Drag***	to select the range reference A1:F1
Step 3	***Key***	A3
Step 4	***Press***	the END key to move to the end of the line
Step 5	***Press***	the ENTER key
Step 6	***Key***	ActiveCell.FormulaR1C1 = "=TODAY()"

After you key "ActiveCell." a list appears with options belonging to the ActiveCell object. As you continue keying "FormulaR1C1," that option is selected in the list. When the correct option is highlighted, you can press the SPACEBAR or the TAB key, and Visual Basic will finish the typing for you. This feature not only saves time, but also helps reduce errors when you are creating and modifying macro code.

The completed line will enter the TODAY date formula in the current cell, A3, when you run the macro.

Step 7	***Press***	the ENTER key
Step 8	***Key***	Selection.Font.ColorIndex = 5

This line sets the font color to 5, which is the color index code for the color blue.

Step 9	***Press***	the ENTER key
Step 10	***Key***	Range("A1").
Step 11	***Scroll***	down the list until you see Select
Step 12	***Double-click***	Select

Your screen should look similar to Figure 9-6.

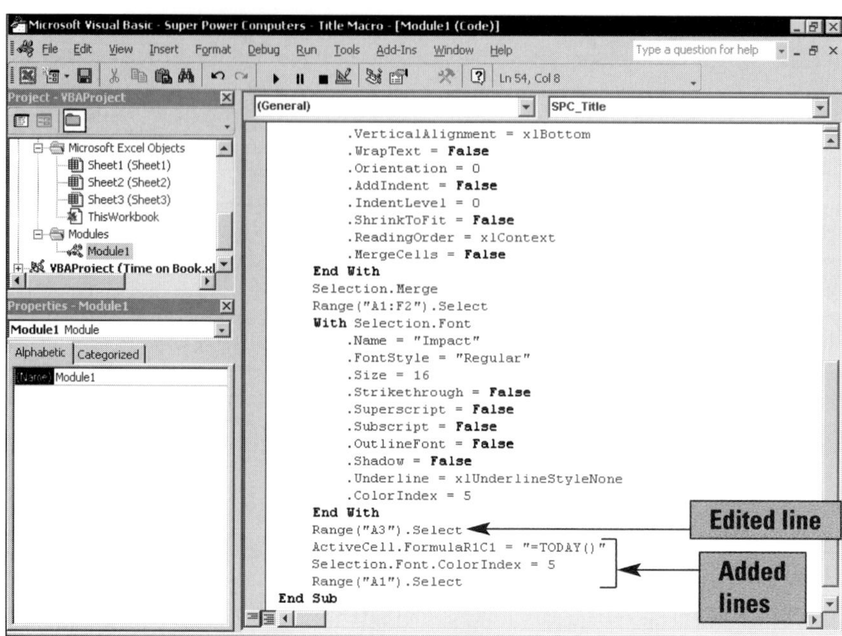

FIGURE 9-6
Edited Macro

Before you run your macro, it is a good idea to save the workbook. You can save the workbook in the Visual Basic Editor, or in Excel. Then you run your revised macro. To save the workbook and run the revised macro:

Step 1	***Click***	the Save button in the Visual Basic Editor window
Step 2	***Switch to***	the Excel program window using the taskbar
Step 3	***Click***	the Sheet3 sheet tab
Step 4	***Open***	the Macro dialog box
Step 5	***Verify***	that SPC_Title is selected in the macros list
Step 6	***Click***	Run to run the SPC_Title macro

Your screen should look similar to Figure 9-7.

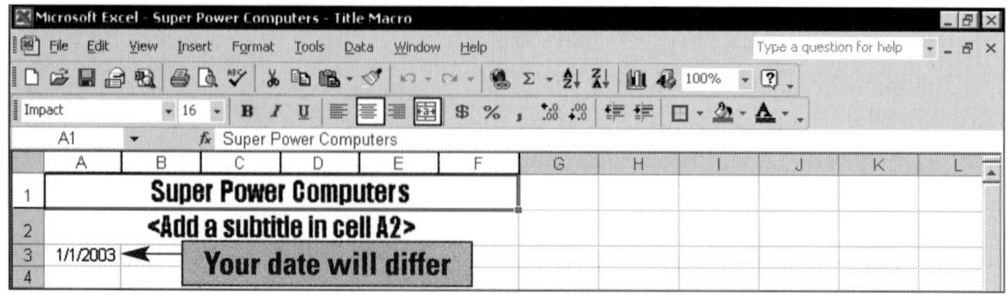

FIGURE 9-7
Results of the Revised Macro

To print the macro code and close the Visual Basic Editor:

Step 1	*Switch to*	the Visual Basic Editor program using the taskbar
Step 2	*Click*	File
Step 3	*Click*	Print
Step 4	*Click*	OK to print the current module
Step 5	*Click*	File
Step 6	*Click*	Close and Return to Microsoft Excel

The Visual Basic Editor closes, and the Excel window becomes the active window.

Step 7	*Save*	the workbook and leave it open

9.c Using Workbooks Containing Macros

Whenever you share workbooks with other users or download files from the Internet, your file(s)—or the downloaded files—could be infected with viruses. Viruses are malicious programs that can destroy files and data. **Macro viruses** are a special class of viruses that embed themselves in macros. Whenever you open a workbook containing a macro virus, the virus can replicate itself to other workbooks, destroy files on your hard drive, and do other types of damage. Because of this threat, Excel prompts you before opening any file containing macros.

Opening a Workbook with Macros

The *Super Power Computers - Header Macro* workbook contains a previously recorded macro that sets up a header, and you want to edit it. Macros will only run if the Excel security setting is set to Medium or lower. To set the Excel security setting to Medium:

Step 1	*Click*	Tools
Step 2	*Click*	Options
Step 3	*Click*	the Security tab

CAUTION TIP

If cell A3 displays TODAY(), click the Visual Basic taskbar button, click before the T in TODAY, and key an equal sign (=). Switch back to Excel and run the macro again.

Step 4	***Click***	Macro Security
Step 5	***Click***	the Medium option button, if necessary
Step 6	***Click***	OK
Step 7	***Click***	OK

To open a workbook containing a macro:

Step 1	***Open***	the *Super Power Computers - Header Macro* workbook on your Data Disk

The warning dialog box on your screen should look similar to Figure 9-8.

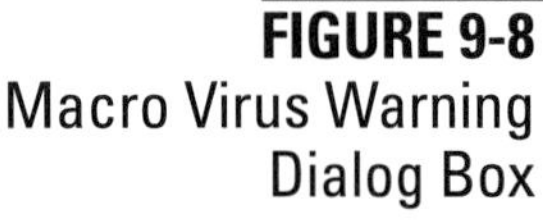

FIGURE 9-8
Macro Virus Warning Dialog Box

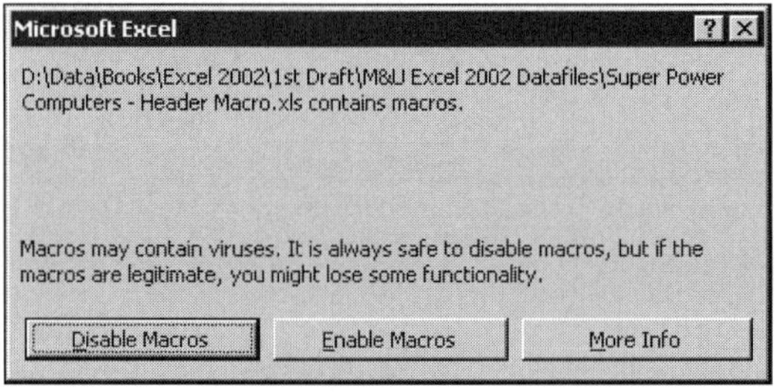

QUICK TIP

To scan your files for viruses, you must purchase special antivirus software capable of scanning your files, hard drive(s), and floppy drive(s). Most newer antivirus programs can scan files containing macros for macro viruses. For more information about macro viruses, refer to online Help.

Excel cannot determine whether a macro is actually a macro virus. If you are not sure about the origins of the workbook, you should select Disable Macros. The contents of the workbook can still be edited, but any special macros stored in the workbook cannot be executed. If possible, contact the person who created the workbook to find out which macros should appear in the workbook. Once you've determined that the source of this workbook is safe, you can open the file with macros enabled.

Step 2	***Click***	Enable Macros

Copying Macro Code to Another Workbook

You want to copy the macro in this workbook to the *Super Power Computers - Title Macro* workbook you created earlier. To copy macro code:

Step 1	***Click***	Tools
Step 2	***Point to***	Macro
Step 3	***Click***	Visual Basic Editor

The Project Explorer window contains a new VBAProject (Super Power Computers - Header Macro.xls).

Step 4	*Click*	the + sign next to VBAProject (Super Power Computers - Header Macro.xls) in the Project Explorer window, if necessary

If a – (minus sign) appears next to VBAProject (Super Power Computers - Header Macro.xls), do not click it.

Step 5	*Click*	the + sign next to Modules, if necessary
Step 6	*Double-click*	Module1
Step 7	*Press*	the CTRL + A keys to select all the code
Step 8	*Click*	the Copy button on the Visual Basic Editor Standard toolbar

In the Project Explorer window, you can expand the view for the Super Power Computers Title project.

Step 9	*Scroll*	the Project Explorer window, if necessary
Step 10	*Click*	the + sign next to VBAProject (Super Power Computers - Title Macro.xls), if necessary
Step 11	*Right-click*	the Modules folder indented under VBAProject (Super Power Computers - Title Macro.xls)
Step 12	*Point to*	Insert
Step 13	*Click*	Module

A blank macro module opens with the name of the Title Macro worksheet in the title bar.

Step 14	*Click*	Paste button on the Visual Basic Editor standard toolbar
Step 15	*Close*	the Visual Basic Editor
Step 16	*Click*	Window
Step 17	*Click*	Super Power Computers - Title Macro
Step 18	*Save*	the *Super Power Computers - Title Macro* workbook

Step 19	***Switch to***	the *Super Power Computers - Header Macro* workbook
Step 20	***Close***	the *Super Power Computers - Header Macro* workbook

The macro from *Super Power Computers - Header Macro* is pasted into the *Super Power Computers - Title Macro* workbook. To reset the security setting to its default value of High:

Step 1	***Open***	the Options dialog box
Step 2	***Click***	Macro Security on the Security tab
Step 3	***Click***	the High option button
Step 4	***Click***	OK
Step 5	***Click***	OK

9.d Creating and Editing Templates

Templates are designed to save you time and effort. You know how to open a new workbook based on one of the Excel predesigned templates. You can also create templates from scratch, save existing workbooks as templates, and modify existing templates.

Creating a Workbook Template

At Super Power Computers, you generate a lot of sales reports. To save time formatting the worksheets, you create a template from an existing workbook. To create a workbook template:

Step 1	***Verify***	that the *Super Power Computers - Title Macro* workbook is open
Step 2	***Open***	the *Super Power Computers - Store 2 Sales* workbook located on the Data Disk
Step 3	***Select***	the range A5:E8
Step 4	***Press***	the DELETE key to clear the data cells
Step 5	***Clear***	cell A2

The template should contain as much information as you are likely to reuse, but not data that is likely to change.

CAUTION TIP

Be sure *not* to click the Save button on the Standard toolbar when you intend to save the workbook as a template. Remember, the Undo list starts over after each save!

Step 6	*Click*	File
Step 7	*Click*	Save As
Step 8	*Click*	the Save as type: list arrow
Step 9	*Click*	Template

Notice that the Save in: folder changes to the default Templates folder. Generally, you should save your templates to the default template folder to make them available when you click the General Templates link in the New Workbook task pane. If you save them to another location, as you do here, you click the New from existing workbook link on the task pane, which makes all workbooks *and* templates act as templates.

Step 10	*Change*	the Save in: location to the folder where you store your completed files
Step 11	*Key*	*Super Power Computers - Store Sales Template* in the File name: text box
Step 12	*Click*	Save
Step 13	*Close*	the template

To find more template examples, open the New Workbook task pane, then click the Templates on Microsoft.com link.

Once you save a template, you can create new workbooks from this template by clicking the General Templates link in the task pane, then selecting the template you want to use.

Editing a Template

You can modify both templates that you created and the Excel built-in templates. To edit a template, you must open it as a template (instead of as a new workbook). To modify the template you just created:

QUICK TIP

Creating a new workbook from a template is different from opening the template file itself.

Step 1	*Open*	the Open dialog box
Step 2	*Change*	the Look in: list box to the folder where you store your completed files, if necessary
Step 3	*Click*	*Super Power Computers - Store Sales Template*
Step 4	*Click*	Open

Any changes you make and save to the template will be added to new workbooks you create in the future.

Step 5	*Enter*	Store # in cell A2
Step 6	*Save*	and close the template

9.e Customizing Toolbars and Menus

Another way to boost your productivity is to create your own custom toolbars and menus. Excel features many commands that can be added to toolbars or menus, and you can add macros you have recorded as well. You can even add menus to toolbars.

Creating a Custom Toolbar

If there is a set of commands that you use often, it can be more efficient to create your own toolbar. To create a custom toolbar:

Step 1	*Verify*	that the *Super Power Computers - Title Macro* workbook is the active workbook
Step 2	*Right-click*	any toolbar
Step 3	*Click*	Customize
Step 4	*Click*	the Toolbars tab

MOUSE TIP

You can move a menu from a toolbar to the menu bar, or vice versa, as long as the Customize dialog box remains open. Just drag the menu item from the toolbar to the menu bar or from the menu bar to the toolbar.

You can remove items from a toolbar or menu while the Customize dialog box remains open. Drag the item from the toolbar or menu and drop it anywhere on the worksheet.

Your Customize dialog box should look similar to Figure 9-9. The Toolbars tab helps you create, rename, and delete toolbars.

FIGURE 9-9
Toolbars Tab in the Customize Dialog Box

Step 5	*Click*	New
Step 6	*Key*	My Custom Toolbar in the Toolbar name: text box in the New Toolbar dialog box

Step 7	*Click*	OK
Step 8	*Observe*	the small empty toolbar, named My Custom Toolbar, that appears on your screen

You can see only the M of the toolbar name in the title bar. Next, you add buttons or menus to your toolbar. To add a button to a toolbar:

Step 1	*Click*	the Commands tab in the Customize dialog box
Step 2	*Click*	Edit in the Categories: list
Step 3	*Scroll*	down the Commands: list until you see Paste Formatting
Step 4	*Drag*	Paste Formatting from the Commands: list to your new toolbar

This button is a shortcut for clicking the Paste Special command on the Edit menu, and clicking Formatting.

Creating a Custom Menu

You can modify menus by adding or removing existing commands, or you can create your own menus. You want to create a menu with commands to run your macros. To create a new menu:

Step 1	*Verify*	that the Commands tab in the Customize dialog box is open
Step 2	*Scroll*	the Categories: list to locate New Menu
Step 3	*Click*	New Menu
Step 4	*Drag*	New Menu from the Commands: list to the new toolbar
Step 5	*Right-click*	the New Menu menu on the toolbar
Step 6	*Drag*	in the Name: text box to select all of the text
Step 7	*Key*	My Macros
Step 8	*Press*	the ENTER key
Step 9	*Click*	Macros in the Categories: list in the Customize dialog box
Step 10	*Drag*	Custom Menu Item to the My Macros menu you added to your custom toolbar, but do not release the mouse button

QUICK TIP

You can assign a macro to a toolbar button. Open the Customize dialog box, and click the Commands tab. Right-click a custom button that you've added to a toolbar, then click Assign Macro. Select the desired macro, then click the OK button.

CAUTION TIP

Toolbars and custom menus are usually saved on your computer. If you want a toolbar to "travel" with a workbook or template, you need to attach it. Open the Customize dialog box, then click Attach on the Toolbars tab. Select an available toolbar in the Custom toolbars: list, then click Copy>>. Click the OK button, then click the Close button, and save the workbook or template.

When you open a workbook with an attached custom toolbar, that toolbar is automatically added to the Toolbars: list in the Customize dialog box. You must delete the toolbar if you don't want it stored on your computer.

MENU TIP

You can key & in front of a menu item character in the Name: text box to create an ALT + *key* shortcut. For example, key "&My Menu" to create the ALT + M shortcut to access the My Menu menu.

CAUTION TIP

The SPC_Title and SPC_Header macro shortcuts on the custom menu will not run the associated macros unless one of the workbooks that contains the macro is open.

A small menu pop-out appears below the My Macros menu name. Dropping a button or macro on this area adds it as a menu item. A black line appears to indicate where the menu item will be placed.

Step 11	***Drop***	the menu item on the menu pop-out
Step 12	***Right-click***	Custom Menu Item
Step 13	***Click***	Assign Macro
Step 14	***Click***	SPC_Title
Step 15	***Click***	OK
Step 16	***Rename***	the menu item as Title
Step 17	***Follow***	Steps 10 through 15 to add the SPC_Header macro to the My Macros menu
Step 18	***Rename***	the menu item as Header
Step 19	***Click***	Close
Step 20	***Save***	the workbook and close it

Occasionally, you need to delete a toolbar. To delete a toolbar:

Step 1	***Open***	the Customize dialog box
Step 2	***Click***	the Toolbars tab
Step 3	***Click***	My Custom Toolbar in the Toolbars: list
Step 4	***Click***	Delete
Step 5	***Click***	OK
Step 6	***Close***	the Customize dialog box

The toolbar is removed from Excel. There are many ways to customize Excel to increase your productivity. Macros, templates, and custom toolbars and menus can help you make short work of many common tasks.

Summary

- A macro is a set of instructions that executes several commands automatically. Macros can be simple recorded steps, or they can be complex programs capable of making decisions based on user input.
- Recording a macro is the simplest way to create a macro. During the recording process, Excel records exactly what you do.
- Once a macro is recorded, it must be run to perform the desired task.
- You can edit macros using the Visual Basic Editor. Visual Basic is the programming language used by Excel and other Office programs. The Visual Basic Editor is a separate application used to create, edit, delete, and test Visual Basic modules or macros.
- Some macros can contain viruses, or programs that can damage files on your computer system. If you are unsure of a workbook's origin, disable macros when you open the workbook. You can still view and edit data in the workbook.
- You can copy macro code between Visual Basic projects (other workbooks) by using the Cut and Paste commands.
- You can create templates from scratch or by saving existing workbooks as templates. To save a workbook as a template, click Template in the Save as type: list in the Save As dialog box.
- To edit a custom template you created or a built-in template, open it as a template instead of as a new workbook.
- You can create custom toolbars and menus by dragging command buttons onto the toolbar or menu.
- You can drag items from a toolbar or menu to remove them.

Commands Review

Action	Menu Bar	Shortcut Menu	Toolbar	Task Pane	Keyboard
Record a macro	Tools, Macro, Record New Macro				ALT + T, M, R
Run or edit a macro	Tools, Macro, Macros, then Run or Edit button				ALT + T, M, M ALT + F8
Open the Visual Basic Editor	Tools, Macro, Visual Basic Editor				ALT + T, M V ALT + F11
Save a template	File, Save As, then change file type to Template				ALT + F, A
Open a template for editing	File, Open, then change file type to Template				ALT + F, O
Customize a toolbar or menu	Tools, Customize	Right-click toolbar, then Customize			ALT + T, C

Concepts Review

Circle the correct answer.

1. **Macros:**
   [a] are much too difficult for the average user to program.
   [b] can waste time because they run every time you open a workbook.
   [c] consist of a set of instructions that automatically executes a set of commands.
   [d] can never be modified.

2. **Which of the following tasks can be performed by macros?**
   [a] printing worksheets
   [b] creating and modifying charts
   [c] sorting lists
   [d] all of the above

3. **To make a macro available in all workbooks, you should save it:**
   [a] in every workbook you use.
   [b] in the Personal Macro Workbook.
   [c] on a floppy disk.
   [d] to the All Macros folder on your hard drive.

4. **You edit macros in the:**
   [a] Excel application window.
   [b] Macro dialog box.
   [c] Visual Basic Editor program window.
   [d] Record Macro dialog box.

5. **Visual Basic is the programming language used by:**
   [a] only Microsoft Excel.
   [b] only Microsoft Word.
   [c] only Microsoft Access.
   [d] all Office applications.

6. **An apostrophe (') in Visual Basic, signifies a:**
   [a] shortened version of the REMOVE command.
   [b] blank line follows.
   [c] comment section.
   [d] shortened version of REMEMBER, preceding a programmer's reminder section.

7. **When you record a macro, you:**
   [a] must write all the actions you want to perform, then key them in the Visual Basic Editor program window.
   [b] start recording, then Excel automatically records every keystroke.
   [c] must open the Visual Basic Editor first, before Excel will record your keystrokes.
   [d] click the Record button after each keystroke so that mistakes are not recorded.

8. **If you see a message telling you that a workbook contains macros, you should:**
   [a] always click Disable Macros because the workbook contains a virus.
   [b] always click Enable Macros because the workbook will not display all the data unless you do.
   [c] cancel the operation quickly because the macro may contain a virus.
   [d] decide whether the workbook comes from a reliable source, then click either Disable or Enable Macros.

9. **Templates:**
   [a] save time by eliminating repetitious formatting and setup tasks.
   [b] are difficult to create.
   [c] cannot be modified.
   [d] can be used by clicking the New button on the Standard toolbar.

10. **To create a custom toolbar:**
    [a] drag buttons off the Standard toolbar.
    [b] drag the name of the toolbar from the Toolbars list in the Customize dialog box.
    [c] right-click an open toolbar, then click New Toolbar.
    [d] click the New button on the Toolbars tab of the Customize dialog box.

Circle **T** if the statement is true or **F** if the statement is false.

T F 1. Macros save a lot of time.

T F 2. You can save any workbook as a template by using the File menu, then clicking Save As and setting the Save As type: list to Template.

T F 3. Custom menus can be added to the menu bar, but not to custom toolbars.

T F 4. You can write macros that work across several Office applications.

T F 5. Learning the basics of Visual Basic can help you write macros in all of the Office applications.

T F 6. The easiest way to create a macro is to open the Visual Basic Editor and key the code by hand.

T F 7. If you make a mistake when recording a macro, you have to record a new macro.

T F 8. Whenever you see the macro virus warning when opening an Excel workbook, the workbook must contain a macro virus and should not be opened.

T F 9. Macro viruses are usually harmful programs embedded in a macro, capable of copying themselves to other files and destroying data.

T F 10. A module is the basic storage unit for macro code.

Skills Review

Exercise 1

1. Create a new workbook.

2. Create a new toolbar named "Special Edit."

3. Add the following Edit category commands: Paste Formatting, Paste Values, Clear Contents, Clear Formatting, and Select Current Region.

4. On the Toolbars tab, select the Special Edit toolbar, click Attach, select Special Edit in the Custom toolbars: list, click Copy>>, then click OK to attach the toolbar to the workbook.

5. Save the workbook as *Special Edit* and close it.

6. Delete the Special Edit toolbar (the toolbar will still be available when you open the *Special Edit* workbook because you attached it).

Exercise 2

1. Open the *Sort List* workbook located on the Data Disk.

2. Click any cell within the list of data on Sheet1.

3. Record a new macro called "Sort1" and save it in the current workbook.

4. Sort the list by name in ascending order.

5. Stop recording the macro.

6. Record a second macro called "Sort2" and save it in the current workbook.

7. Sort the list by region and then by name in ascending order.

8. Stop recording the macro.

9. Save the workbook as *Sort List with Macros,* and then print and close it.

Exercise 3 C

1. Create a new expense statement workbook, using the Expense Statement template on the Spreadsheet Solutions tab.
2. Enter the following data. Name: "Luis Alvarez," Position: "Owner."
3. Save the workbook as a template named *Sweet Tooth Owner Expenses* and then print and close it.

Exercise 4 C

1. Open the *Video Rental* workbook located on the Data Disk.
2. Bold and center the column headings in row 2.
3. Use a red cell fill with white text in row 2.
4. Select the range B3:G7 and add All Borders to the selection.
5. Select the range G3:G10 and add a Thick Box Border to the selection.
6. Select the range B1:G10 and add a Thick Box Border to the selection.
7. Set the print area to this selection and print it.
8. Activate cell B3.
9. Save the workbook as a template named *Video Rental*, and then close it.

Exercise 5 C

1. Create a new workbook using the *Video Rental* template that you created in Exercise 4.
2. Enter fictitious data on the form for two video rentals. Enter today's date in the Check Out Date column for each video. Enter a video title for each video.
3. Print the Video Rental form, save the workbook as *Video Rental1*, and then close it.

Exercise 6 C

1. Open the *Central Region Sales 2* workbook located on the Data Disk.
2. Record a macro called "Chart." Store the macro in This Workbook.
3. Select the range A4:E8 on the Central Region Summary worksheet, and click the Chart Wizard button on the Standard toolbar.
4. Create a Clustered Column chart with a 3-D visual effect chart subtype. Enter "Central Region Summary" as the Chart title. Create the chart as a new sheet named "Central Region Summary Chart."
5. When the chart appears, click the Stop Recording button to stop recording the macro.
6. Delete the new chart sheet tab.
7. Run the macro to verify that it works correctly.
8. Save the workbook as *Central Region Sales 2 Chart Macro*, and then print and close it.

Exercise 7

1. Open the *Central Region Sales 2 Chart Macro* workbook that you created in Exercise 6.
2. Open the Macro dialog box, and select the Chart macro for editing.
3. In the Visual Basic Editor, edit the macro code as follows (insert the text in bold):
   a. Insert **NM = ActiveSheet.Name** before the line Range("A4:E8").Select
   b. Use Replace (press the CTRL + H keys) to replace "Central Region Summary" (including the quotation marks) with **NM**
   c. Use Replace to replace all occurrences of "Central Region Summary Chart" (including the quotation marks) with **NM & " Summary Chart"** (include a space between the first quotation mark and the letter S).
   d. In the line .ChartTitle.Characters.Text = "Central Region Summary Chart" replace "Central Region Summary Chart" with **NM & " Summary Chart"**

   These changes find the current sheet tab name and assign it to the variable NM. The macro then uses this variable to create and automatically give a title to a new chart on a new chart sheet that it also names automatically.
4. Switch to Excel using the taskbar.
5. Click the South Division tab.
6. Run the Chart macro.
7. Create charts for each of the Division pages of your workbook, using the Chart macro.
8. Print the charts, save the workbook as *Central Region Sales 2 Chart Revised*, and then close it.

Exercise 8

1. Open the *Central Region Sales 2 Chart Revised* workbook that you created in Exercise 7.
2. Create a new toolbar called "Macros."
3. Add the Chart macro to the toolbar.
4. Attach the toolbar to the workbook.
5. Save the workbook as *Central Region Sales 2 Chart Revised 2.*
6. Delete the Macros toolbar from the Toolbars: list in the Customize dialog box.

Case Projects

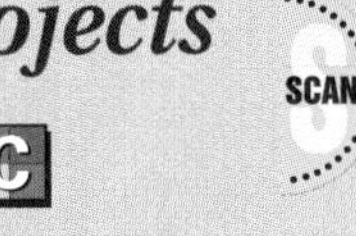

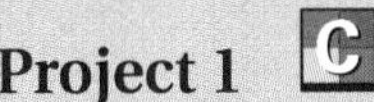

Project 1

As a busy student who uses Excel for many homework assignments, you find it tedious to constantly add your name, class, and date to your workbooks before you turn them in. In a new workbook, record a macro to insert three rows at the top of your workbook, and insert your name in cell A1, the class name in cell A2, and today's date in cell A3. Name the macro "NameStamp." Test your macro on Sheet2 of the workbook. Save the workbook as *Name Stamp Macro* and then print and close it.

Project 2

Connect to the Internet and search the Web for information about Visual Basic and Visual Basic for Applications. Focus your search on tutorials, especially those intended for beginners. Print at least two beginner tutorials, and save five links in your browser's Favorites or Bookmarks.

Project 3  

As the manager of a retail music store, you create a chart every week listing the bestselling CDs. Use the Internet to search for the Top 15 Bestselling CDs for the current week. Create a new workbook containing each album's title, artist's name, and the number of CDs sold. Create records for at least 15 CDs by your favorite bands, or other popular titles. Generate fictitious sales data (for your store) for each CD. Record a macro to do the following: (1) sort the list by number of CDs sold, then by album title, (2) create a chart selecting the top 10 bestselling albums, (3) create a centered header with your store's name, (4) create a footer with the date on the left and the time on the right, (5) change the page layout to landscape orientation, and (6) print the chart. Then, randomly change the number of albums sold, and run the macro again. Save the workbook as *Record Sales,* and then print and close it.

Project 4 

As an accountant who deals with a high volume of clients every day, you want to see the current date and time when you switch between clients. Create a new, blank workbook, and save it as *Time Clock.* Open the Visual Basic Editor and double-click Module 1 of the Time Clock.xls project in the Project Explorer window. Use Visual Basic Help to create a message dialog box that displays the current date and time. (*Hint:* Search for the MsgBox, Date, and Time functions.) Assign the macro to your clock object. Print the module code, then save the workbook as *Time Clock.*

Project 5 

As an office manager, you receive a large volume of phone calls each day. Create a custom phone message template. Include cells to record the time and date of the call, the name of the person whom the message is for, the message text, the caller's phone number, and the requested response. Be creative in your use of borders, shading, drawing objects, font styles, and so on. Apply number formats as appropriate. Set print settings to print messages correctly. Save the template as *Phone Message,* and then print and close it.

Project 6 

As the owner of a small bookstore, you want to create a receipt template to record sales. The template should include the current date and time of the transaction, a place to enter the title of the book(s) purchased, and the price of each book. It also should include formulas to calculate the subtotal of items sold, sales tax, and the total sale amount. Save the template as *Book Sales Receipt,* and then print and close it.

Project 7 

You are worried about the security of workbooks that you share with other people over the Internet. Connect to the Internet and search the Web for information about Excel macro viruses. Print at least one page identifying one existing Excel macro virus, explaining what it does, and describing how you can eliminate it.

Project 8 

You own a retail computer store. In addition to selling custom computers, you service computers that aren't working. You need a template to enter service order information. In the client information section, you need to enter the client's name, address, city, state, ZIP code, phone number, and e-mail address. In the computer information section, you need to enter the CPU speed, amount of RAM, hard drive space, and operating system. In the problem description section, you need to enter a description of the problem as explained by the client. In the estimate section, you need to enter an estimate of the number of hours it will take a technician to repair the problem, plus the estimated cost of any parts that may need to be replaced. Create formulas to: (1) multiply the number of estimated hours by the current rate of $45/hour, (2) add the estimated technician cost to the estimated parts cost, (3) calculate the sales tax on the estimate, and (4) add the subtotal and the calculated sales tax to provide a total. Create a new template named *Service Order* that includes all these sections, and then print and close it.

Using Problem-Solving Tools

Chapter Overview

Finding solutions to complex business problems is one of the things that Excel does best. You can create data tables to replace the values used in formulas with variables. Data tables allow you to quickly see the results that occur from changing one or two variables. Goal Seek modifies one variable in a formula to create a desired outcome. Solver allows you to arrive at a desired outcome by changing the values of multiple cells and placing constraints as to what changes can take place. Scenarios let you store multiple sets of values for selected cells, allowing you to quickly view the results of several different situations. Finally, you can add trendlines to a chart to show projected values based on existing data.

Case profile

To be successful in business, you must know how to analyze information and how to make decisions based on the analysis of that information. This month, Super Power Computers is looking to expand its fleet of cars and needs to know how much the company can afford to borrow. The warehouse division is also seeking a solution to some scheduling problems. You use a variety of what-if analysis tools to resolve each of these problems.

Learning Objectives

- Create data tables
- Use Goal Seek and Solver
- Create scenarios
- Create a trendline

notes

Several of the tools presented in this chapter require certain Excel Add-In components to be activated. To activate the necessary add-ins, click the Add-Ins command on the Tools menu. Click the Solver Add-In check box and the Analysis ToolPak check box to insert check marks, if necessary. Click the OK button to activate the add-ins.

10.a Creating Data Tables

One of the key strengths of Excel is its ability to help you perform what-if analyses. In a **what-if analysis**, you change data values and then observe the effect on calculations—for example, what if I change the value in cell A2? To make this kind of trial-and-error process easier, you can use **data tables** to show the results of a formula by replacing one or two of the variables with several different values. **One-variable data tables** can be created to show the results of changing one variable in several formulas at once. **Two-variable data tables** can show the results of changing two variables in a single formula.

Creating a One-Variable Data Table

A **variable** is like a container, or placeholder, for a value. When you create formulas in Excel using cell references, the cell reference acts as a variable. As you change the value of the referenced cell, the formula automatically displays the new result. A **one-variable data table** uses a variable to replace one of the arguments in a given formula and then calculates results using several different values for that argument.

Super Power Computers is considering purchasing a fleet of automobiles for its sales representatives. The purchase amount of each car is $25,000, with a loan interest rate of 9.5%. The company wants to determine the monthly payment per car, and the amount of interest to be paid depending on the term of the loan. In this case, the term argument is the variable. To open the workbook and set up a one-variable data table:

Step 1	***Open***	the *Super Power Computers - Interest Calculator* workbook located on the Data Disk
Step 2	***Save***	the workbook as *Super Power Computers - Interest Calculator Revised*

One of the financial functions, CUMIPMT, calculates the cumulative interest paid over the course of a loan. Another related function, PMT, calculates the monthly payment on a loan. Both of these financial functions share common arguments, including the *rate* (percentage), *nper* (number of periods in the life of the loan), and *pv* (present value of the loan). The syntax of the CUMIPMT function is:

=CUMIPMT(rate,nper,pv,start_period,end_period,type)

In this workbook, the loan information has already been entered. Cell B5 holds the value representing the *nper* argument used in both the CUMIPMT and the PMT functions. This value will be replaced by the values in the range C5:C8, which are shaded in green. (In this case, the period of time for the *nper* argument is months.) The payment (PMT) calculation takes place in column D. The cumulative interest (CUMIPMT) is calculated in column E.

Step 3	***Enter***	=PMT(B4/12,B5,B6) in cell D4 on the One Variable worksheet
Step 4	***Enter***	=CUMIPMT(B4/12,B5,B6,1,B5,1) in cell E4

Your screen should look similar to Figure 10-1.

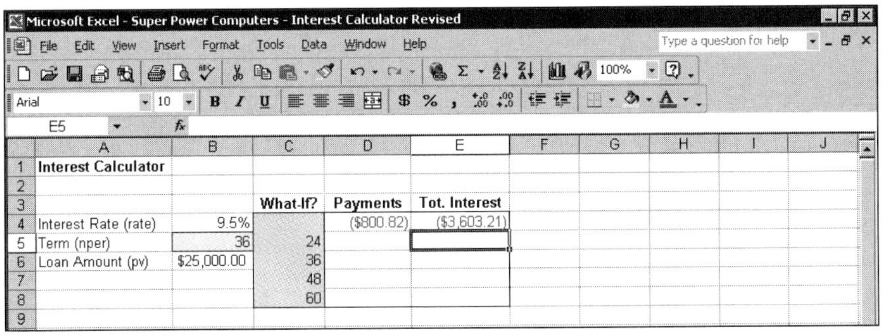

	A	B	C	D	E
1	Interest Calculator				
2					
3			What-If?	Payments	Tot. Interest
4	Interest Rate (rate)	9.5%		($800.82)	($3,603.21)
5	Term (nper)	36	24		
6	Loan Amount (pv)	$25,000.00	36		
7			48		
8			60		

FIGURE 10-1
One-Variable Data Table

QUICK TIP

For more information about financial functions, use online Help.

To automatically open a Help window with information about a function you entered, click the function in the Formula Bar to display its ScreenTip, then click the function name link in the ScreenTip.

Next you calculate what happens when you change the term of the loan. To perform a what-if analysis using a one-variable data table:

Step 1	***Select***	the range C4:E8
Step 2	***Click***	Data
Step 3	***Click***	Table

The Table dialog box opens. The value that you want to change in the formula is stored in the input cell. Because the replacement values you will use are arranged in a column, you use a Column input cell.

Step 4	***Click***	in the Column input cell: text box
Step 5	***Click***	cell B5

The data table replaces the value in cell B5 with each of the values in the leftmost column of the selected data table. First, Excel calculates the PMT function using the value 24 (the first value in column C) instead of the current value of cell B5. Then, Excel calculates the PMT function again, using the next value in column C, 36, in place of the current value of cell B5. Excel continues this process until it reaches the end of the table you selected. Your screen should look similar to Figure 10-2.

FIGURE 10-2
Choosing the Variable in a One-Variable Data Table

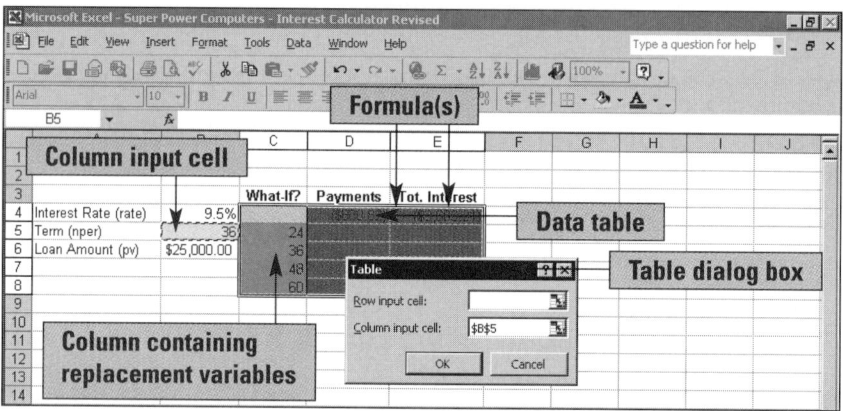

Step 6	*Click*	OK
Step 7	*Click*	cell A1

The monthly payment and cumulative interest for each term length are calculated. Your screen should look similar to Figure 10-3.

FIGURE 10-3
One-Variable Data Table Calculated

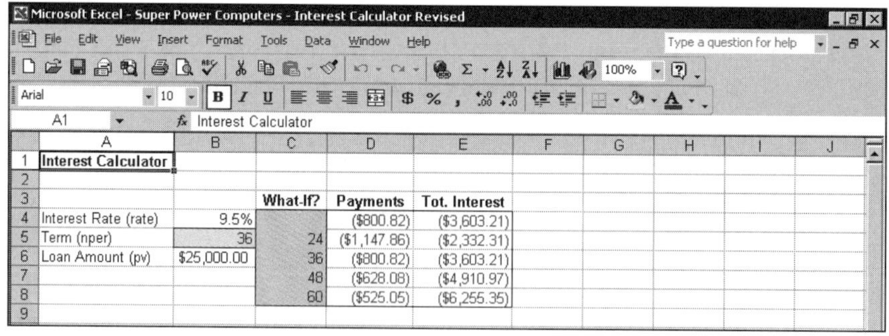

Step 8	*Save*	the workbook

Creating a Two-Variable Data Table

Two-variable data tables allow you to see the results of a formula that uses two different variables. You want to calculate the monthly payments on the auto loan for various terms at different interest rates. To set up a two-variable data table:

Step 1	*Activate*	the Two Variable worksheet
Step 2	*Enter*	=PMT(B4/12,B5,B6) in cell C4

Two-variable data tables can use only one formula at a time, and this formula must be located in the cell directly above the column of the first replacement values and to the right of the second replacement values. The result of the formula, ($800.82), appears in cell C4.

Now you can perform the what-if calculations. To create a two-way data table:

Step 1	*Select*	the range C4:G8
Step 2	*Click*	Data
Step 3	*Click*	Table
Step 4	*Click*	cell B4 so that it appears as an absolute reference in the Row input cell: text box
Step 5	*Click*	in the Column input cell: text box
Step 6	*Click*	cell B5
Step 7	*Click*	OK
Step 8	*Click*	cell A1

Your final data table should look similar to Figure 10-4.

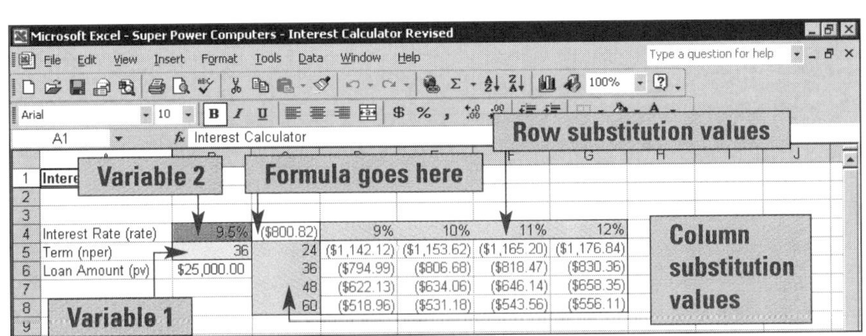

			9%	10%	11%	12%
Interest Rate (rate)	9.5%	($800.82)	9%	10%	11%	12%
Term (nper)	36	24	($1,142.12)	($1,153.62)	($1,165.20)	($1,176.84)
Loan Amount (pv)	$25,000.00	36	($794.99)	($806.68)	($818.47)	($830.36)
		48	($622.13)	($634.06)	($646.14)	($658.35)
		60	($518.96)	($531.18)	($543.56)	($556.11)

FIGURE 10-4
Two-Variable Data Table

Step 9	*Save*	the workbook

chapter ten

C

10.b Using Goal Seek and Solver

Excel includes several tools to help you solve complex problems. When you know the desired result of a formula but the values currently used in the formula don't produce the correct result, you can use the Goal Seek tool to change a variable in the formula and obtain the correct result. Goal Seek can modify only one variable. Solver works in much the same way, but it allows you to change the values of several variables; at the same time, it sets constraints on how much you can alter those variables.

Using Goal Seek

Super Power Computers has decided to purchase 40 new cars for the company, at a total cost of $1,000,000. The company wants to pay off the loan in 36 months, but it has a budget of only $30,000 per month available to make payments. The board of directors needs to know how much money Super Power Computers can borrow at 10% to meet this budget limitation. To set up the workbook:

Step 1	*Activate*	the Car Purchase worksheet
Step 2	*Enter*	=PMT(B8/12,B9,B10) in cell B13

The monthly payment is calculated at $32,032.95. You need to adjust the loan amount so that the monthly payment fits the budget of $30,000. To use Goal Seek:

Step 1	*Activate*	cell B13
Step 2	*Click*	Tools
Step 3	*Click*	Goal Seek
Step 4	*Click*	in the To value: text box

The company will pay this amount, so you use a negative number to indicate an expense.

Step 5	*Key*	-30000
Step 6	*Press*	the TAB key to move to the By changing cell: text box

Step 7	*Click*	cell B10

Your Goal Seek dialog box should look similar to Figure 10-5. Goal Seek finds the solution and displays the Goal Seek Status dialog box. When you click OK, Excel changes the value of the variable cell—B10 in this case—so that the formula in cell B13 meets your goal.

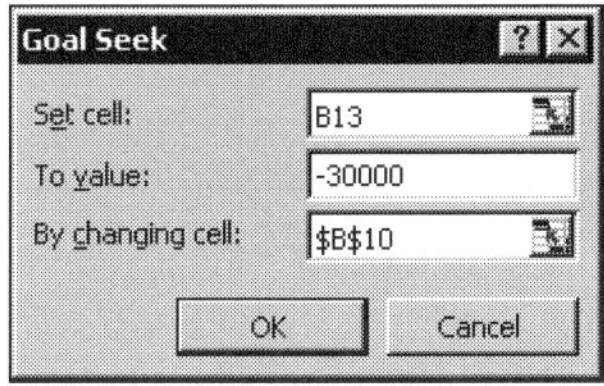

FIGURE 10-5
Goal Seek Dialog Box

Step 8	*Click*	OK

Figure 10-6 shows the results of the Goal Seek operation. To meet the budgeted payment amount of $30,000 per month, Super Power Computers can borrow a maximum of $936,536.

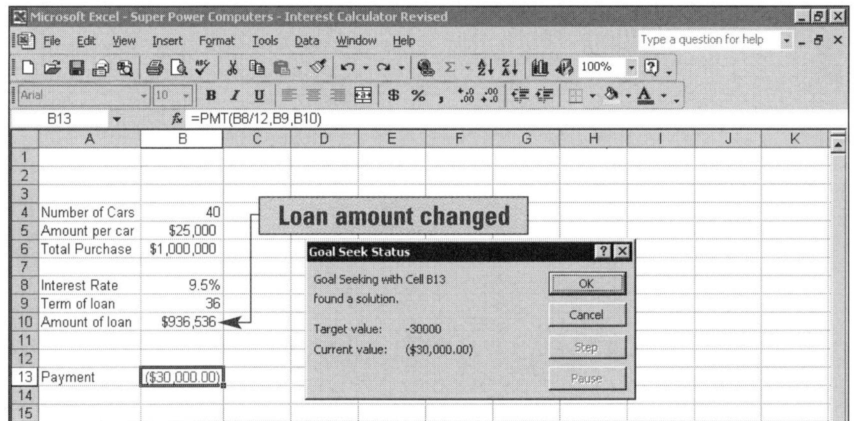

FIGURE 10-6
Goal Seek Status Dialog Box

Step 9	*Click*	OK
Step 10	*Save*	the workbook and leave it open

Using Solver

Luis Alvarez, president of Super Power Computers, has requested that all divisions of the company study ways to save the company money. Many departments are overstaffed, but some departments are understaffed or are not scheduling employees efficiently. The warehouse has especially serious scheduling problems.

The warehouse division currently employs 64 employees and runs seven days a week. Each employee works a schedule of five days on, two days off. Under the current schedule, approximately 45 employees are scheduled each day, but this system creates problems. More employees are needed during the week, when the warehouse is at its busiest. The goal is to minimize the amount of payroll paid out each week, by reducing the staff required to meet the demand for each day. Sound like a complicated problem? It is, and that's why Solver is so useful. To open the workbook and save it with a new name:

Step 1	***Open***	the *Super Power Computers - Warehouse Personnel Scheduling* workbook located on the Data Disk
Step 2	***Save***	the workbook as *Super Power Computers - Warehouse Personnel Scheduling Solution*

This worksheet shows the scheduling for employees in the warehouse. The number of employees currently assigned to each shift appears in the range C5:C11, with the total number of employees being displayed in cell C13. The range D13:J13 calculates the number of employees working each day by multiplying the number of employees on each shift by the on value of 1 or the off value of 0 for each day on the schedule. The range D15:J15 indicates the actual numbers of employees that the warehouse needs on staff each day. Cells C18 and C19 calculate the payroll total for each week. Each warehouse employee is paid $100 per day. To use Solver to create the most efficient schedule:

Step 1	***Click***	Tools
Step 2	***Click***	Solver

The Solver Parameters dialog box on your screen should look similar to Figure 10-7.

FIGURE 10-7
Solver Parameters Dialog Box

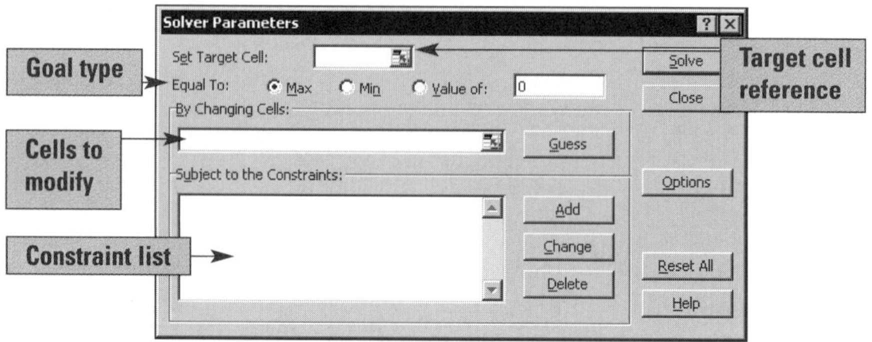

The goal of this exercise is to reduce the total payroll, so cell C19 is the target. To set the Solver target:

Step 1	*Click*	cell C19
Step 2	*Click*	the Min option button next to Equal To:

Solver will look for the solution that results in the lowest possible value for the target cell C19. Next, you need to specify which cells can be changed to reach the goal. To identify which cells can be changed:

Step 1	*Click*	the Collapse dialog button in the By Changing Cells: text box
Step 2	*Select*	the range C5:C11
Step 3	*Click*	the Expand dialog button

Solver changes the number of employees on each shift so as to best reduce the amount of payroll paid each week. To ensure that Solver does not eliminate the entire warehouse staff, you must apply some constraints. The first constraint is that the number of employees on each shift must be greater than or equal to the total demand for each day. The second constraint is to force Excel to use whole numbers—after all, it's difficult to get 0.58 of a worker to appear at work on any given day. To add constraints:

Step 1	*Click*	Add

The Add Constraint dialog box opens with the insertion point in the Cell Reference: text box.

Step 2	*Select*	the range D13:J13
Step 3	*Click*	>= in the constraint type list (in the middle of the dialog box)
Step 4	*Select*	the range D15:J15 in the Constraint: list box

This constraint requires the values in the range D13:J13 to be greater than or equal to the values in the range D15:J15. You need the number of employees on each schedule to be a whole number, so you also apply an integer constraint. Your Add Constraint dialog box should look similar to Figure 10-8.

FIGURE 10-8
Add Constraint Dialog Box

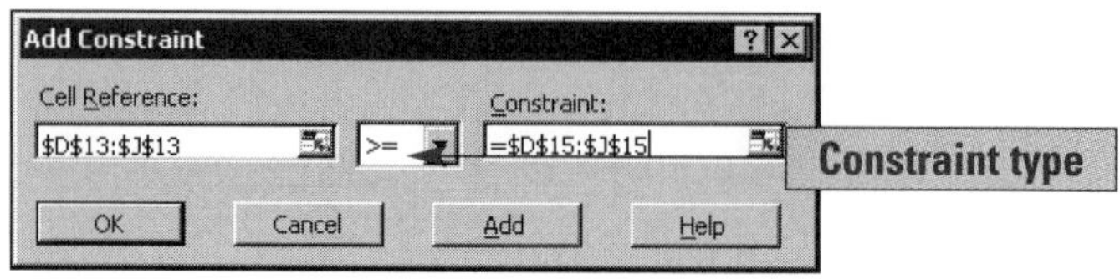

> **QUICK TIP**
>
> The Options button provides settings to optimize the calculation methods in Solver; it also allows you to save and load Solver models for use in other worksheets. If you want to change the way that Solver calculates solutions, open the Solver dialog box, then click Options. Use the online Help to learn more about the Solver Options dialog box.

You need to add the constraint you just defined. You also want the result—the number of employees on each schedule—to be a whole number, so you need to define and add an integer constraint.

Step 5	***Click***	Add
Step 6	***Select***	the range C5:C11
Step 7	***Click***	int in the type of constraint list
Step 8	***Click***	OK
Step 9	***Click***	Solve

Depending on the worksheet and the speed of your computer, Solver may take a few seconds to perform its calculations. Solver figures out the solution, displays the results on your worksheet, and opens the Solver Results dialog box. Your screen should look similar to Figure 10-9.

FIGURE 10-9
Solver Results Dialog Box

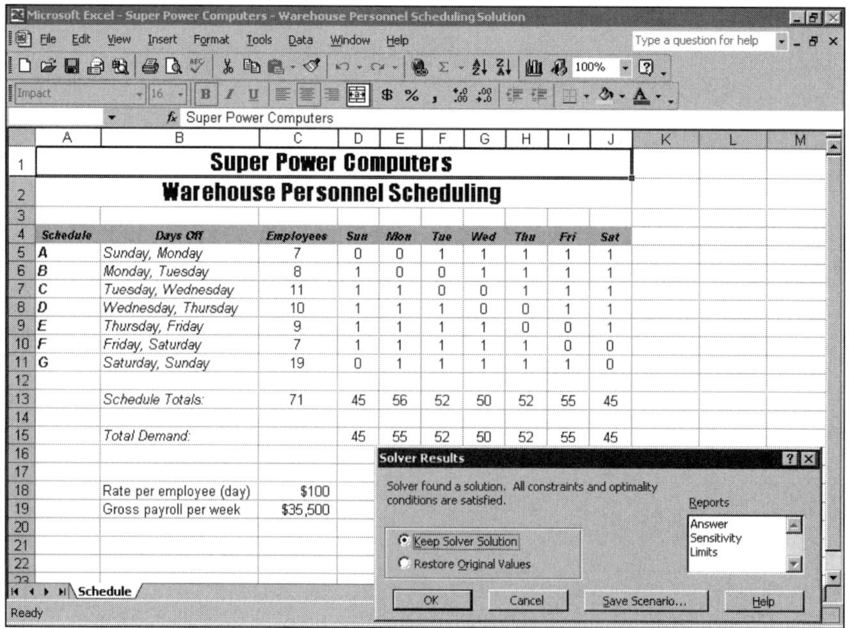

Interestingly, the best solution for the warehouse is to add more employees. By doing so, Solver came up with a scheduling solution that provides the correct number of employees for each day of the week. Only once does the number of employees exceed the required number of employees.

Step 10	***Click***	Answer in the Reports list box
Step 11	***Click***	OK
Step 12	***Click***	the Answer Report 1 sheet tab

CAUTION TIP

Once you complete the Solver operation, you cannot undo it. Before closing the Solver Results dialog box, you have the option of restoring the original values. To do that, click the Restore Original Values option button, then click OK.

Excel generates The Answer Report shown in Figure 10-10. The Answer Report provides information about the calculations and constraints used by Solver to generate the solution. It displays information about the date on which this solution was created, and provides all data used in the solution, including the target cell, adjustable cells, and constraints. Original cell values are shown adjacent to the final cell values after Solver is run.

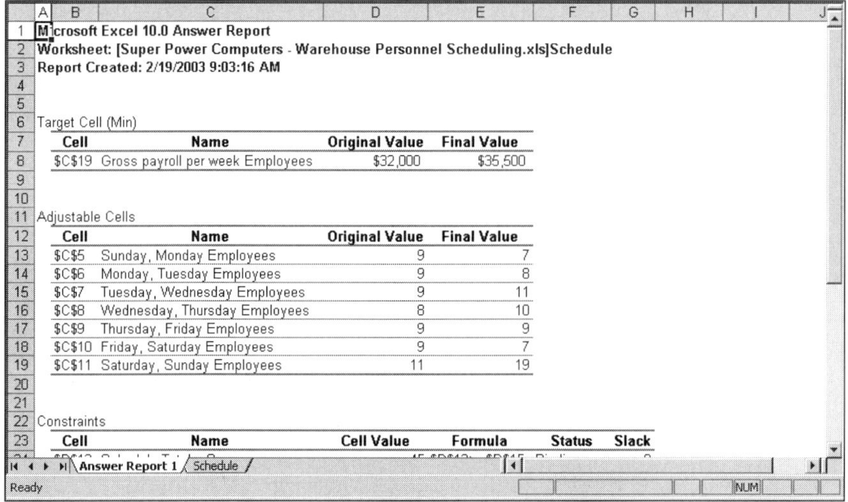

Microsoft Excel 10.0 Answer Report
Worksheet: [Super Power Computers - Warehouse Personnel Scheduling.xls]Schedule
Report Created: 2/19/2003 9:03:16 AM

Target Cell (Min)

Cell	Name	Original Value	Final Value
$C$19	Gross payroll per week Employees	$32,000	$35,500

Adjustable Cells

Cell	Name	Original Value	Final Value
$C$5	Sunday, Monday Employees	9	7
$C$6	Monday, Tuesday Employees	9	8
$C$7	Tuesday, Wednesday Employees	9	11
$C$8	Wednesday, Thursday Employees	8	10
$C$9	Thursday, Friday Employees	9	9
$C$10	Friday, Saturday Employees	9	7
$C$11	Saturday, Sunday Employees	11	19

Constraints

Cell	Name	Cell Value	Formula	Status	Slack

Answer Report 1 / Schedule /

Ready NUM

FIGURE 10-10
Solver Answer Report

QUICK TIP

To find out more information about the Limits and Sensitivity reports, use online Help.

Step 13	***Save***	the workbook

10.c Creating Scenarios

The tools introduced in this chapter—data tables, Goal Seek, and Solver—are designed to allow you maximum flexibility in asking the question, "What if?" Many times, you will need to quickly see the results of several "What if?" situations. For example, what if the current level of activity in the warehouse drops off? What if the current level of activity in the warehouse increases, as it always does during the holiday season?

The demand values in cells D15:J15 indicate how many employees are needed on a given day. By using scenarios, you can change the values contained in these cells and run Solver using the new set of values to find a solution that satisfies the constraints of the given scenario.

Creating Scenarios

Scenarios allow you to quickly replace the values in several cells with another set of values, which you can then use in formulas throughout the worksheet. To create scenarios:

Step 1	***Click***	the Schedule sheet tab
Step 2	***Select***	the range D15:J15
Step 3	***Click***	Tools
Step 4	***Click***	Scenarios

Your Scenario Manager dialog box should look similar to Figure 10-11.

FIGURE 10-11
Scenario Manager Dialog Box

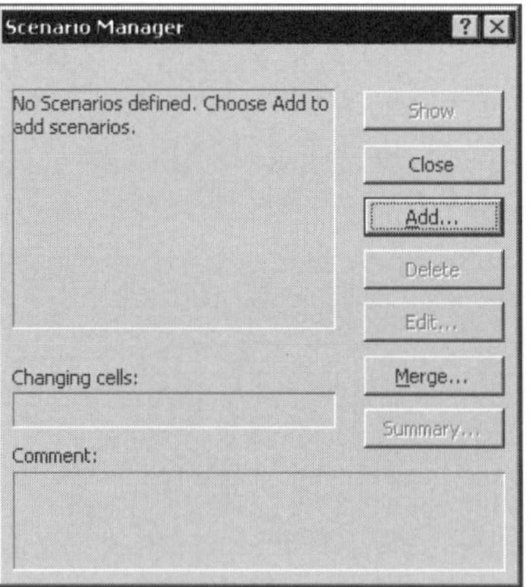

Step 5	***Click***	Add

The Add Scenario dialog box opens. In this dialog box, you can name your scenario, select the cells to be changed under the new scenario, and add descriptive comments about your scenario.

Step 6	***Key***	Normal Demand in the Scenario name: text box
Step 7	***Verify***	that the Changing cells: box references D15:J15

Step 8	***Click***	at the end of the Created by...on MM/DD/YY comment in the Comment: text box
Step 9	***Press***	the ENTER key
Step 10	***Key***	Normal demand covers April-September.
Step 11	***Click***	OK

MOUSE TIP

You can drag the scroll box down to see the rest of the cells you selected.

The Scenario Values dialog box on your screen should look similar to Figure 10-12. You can enter different values for each of the changing cells in this dialog box. Because the values currently in those cells are the Normal Demand values, you can leave them alone.

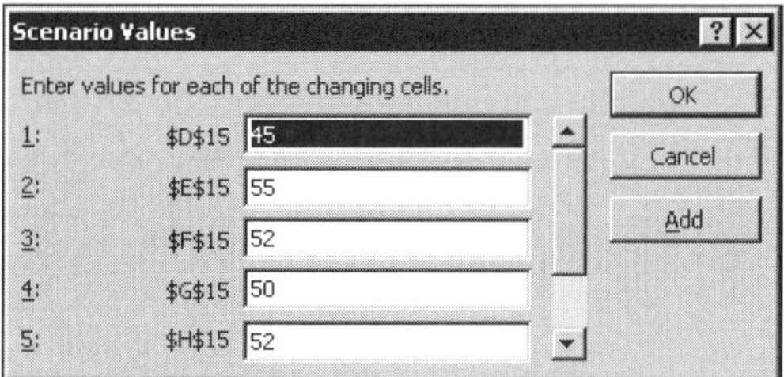

FIGURE 10-12
Scenario Values Dialog Box

Step 12	***Click***	OK to return to the Scenario Manager dialog box
Step 13	***Click***	Add and create another scenario named Low Demand that covers January-March
Step 14	***Click***	OK in the Add Scenario dialog box
Step 15	***Key***	20 in the 1: text box next to $D$15
Step 16	***Press***	the TAB key
Step 17	***Continue***	replacing the values with those listed in Table 10-1

QUICK TIP

Press the TAB key to move from box to box in the Scenarios Values dialog box.

$D$15	$E$15	$F$15	$G$15	$H$15	$I$15	$J$15
20	45	45	40	45	50	20

TABLE 10-1
Low Demand Values

Step 18	***Add***	a scenario named High Demand that covers October-December and uses the values listed in Table 10-2

$D$15	$E$15	$F$15	$G$15	$H$15	$I$15	$J$15
40	60	60	60	60	65	40

TABLE 10-2
High Demand Values

Displaying Scenarios

Once you've created different scenarios, you can display each one so as to replace the values in row 15, then run Solver to calculate the number of employees needed for each scenario. To display different scenarios:

Step 1	***Click***	Low Demand in the Scenarios: list box in the Scenario Manager dialog box
Step 2	***Click***	Show

> **QUICK TIP**
>
> To show your scenario as a PivotTable, click the Scenario PivotTable option button. You also must select Result cells that perform calculations on the cells saved in your scenario(s).

The values in the range D15:J15 change to display the scenario values you created.

Step 3	***Show***	the High Demand scenario

> **MOUSE TIP**
>
> Click the Outline symbols to expand the outline and view the comments for each scenario.

A scenario report displays the values contained in each scenario.

Step 4	***Click***	Summary
Step 5	***Verify***	that the Scenario summary option button is selected
Step 6	***Click***	OK

A scenario summary is created and inserted on a new worksheet named Scenario Summary, which automatically becomes the active worksheet. Your summary should look similar to Figure 10-13. This scenario summary lists the current values of the changing cells as well as the values for each of the defined scenarios.

FIGURE 10-13
Scenario Summary

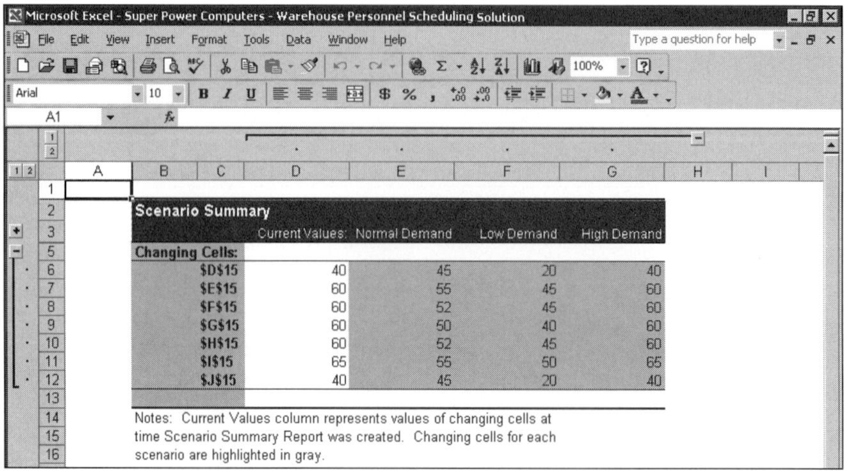

Microsoft Excel - Super Power Computers - Warehouse Personnel Scheduling Solution

Scenario Summary

	Current Values:	Normal Demand	Low Demand	High Demand
Changing Cells:				
$D$15	40	45	20	40
$E$15	60	55	45	60
$F$15	60	52	45	60
$G$15	60	50	40	60
$H$15	60	52	45	60
$I$15	65	55	50	65
$J$15	40	45	20	40

Notes: Current Values column represents values of changing cells at time Scenario Summary Report was created. Changing cells for each scenario are highlighted in gray.

Step 7	*Save*	the workbook and close it

Using these different scenarios, you can run Solver to find the best solution for each period of the year.

10.d Creating a Trendline

C

Another type of what-if analysis involves forecasting trends. For example, by analyzing previous sales figures, Super Power Computers can project future growth potential. In a way, forecasting trends is like predicting the weather. Based on existing (past) data, a prediction, or forecast can be made for future events. **Trendlines** are often added to charts to provide a graphical illustration of the direction in which a set of data is headed. Excel can add a trendline to a chart based on the existing data. When you also need to see the actual values associated with a trendline, you use a special group of statistical functions. To add a trendline to a chart:

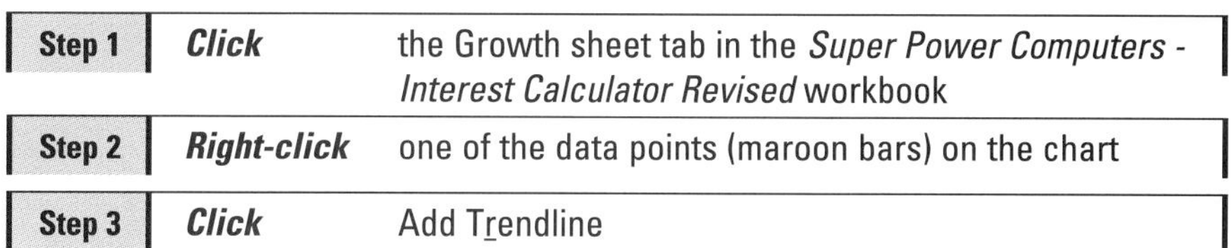

Step 1	*Click*	the Growth sheet tab in the *Super Power Computers - Interest Calculator Revised* workbook
Step 2	*Right-click*	one of the data points (maroon bars) on the chart
Step 3	*Click*	Add Trendline

The Add Trendline dialog box that opens should look similar to Figure 10-14. Each option in the Trend/Regression type uses a different formula to predict the trend in the data provided. The linear trend averages the differences over the data you supply, then calculates the trend as a straight line continuation of the trend over the number of periods you specify. You want to project a linear trend four months into the future.

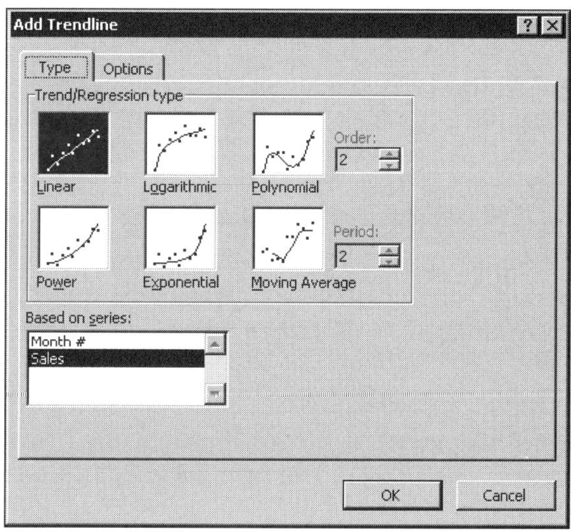

FIGURE 10-14
Add Trendline Dialog Box

chapter ten

Step 4	***Verify***	that Linear is selected
Step 5	***Click***	the Options tab
Step 6	***Double-click***	the Forward: text box
Step 7	***Key***	4
Step 8	***Click***	OK
Step 9	***Resize***	the chart to match the one shown in Figure 10-15

QUICK TIP

For more information about the different types of trends, refer to online Help.

The chart is updated to show a trendline and four additional months. No extra data points are added to the chart. Your chart should look similar to Figure 10-15. To add the projected data points, you need to use a statistical function to calculate the values.

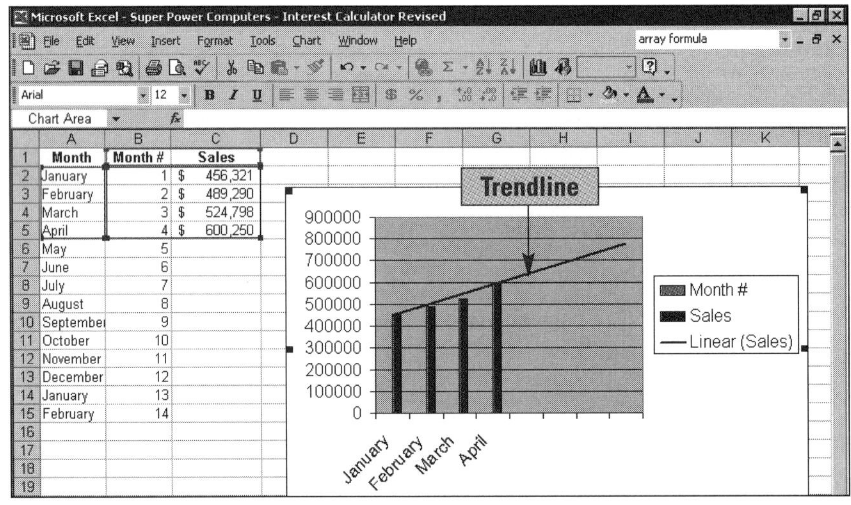

FIGURE 10-15
Chart with Trendline

The TREND function returns values reflecting a linear trend, and uses the following syntax:

=**TREND(known_y's**, known_x's, new_x's,const)

The **known_y's** are the actual data that indicate some sort of trend or pattern. In this workbook, the known_y's are the sales amounts. To create the trend, the y values change over time, so the **known_x's** represent an increment in establishing a time frame for the trend. In this workbook, the known_x's are the months corresponding to the known sales figures. The months are represented by their numeric value because the formula calculates a numerical increment. Your task is to project the future sales values (y), for the months ahead.

To have this formula calculate values for several months at a time, you must change it to an **array formula**. An array formula can use a single formula to perform multiple calculations and return multiple results. In this case, you want the TREND function to return values in the range C6:C15, based on the data in the range B2:C5, and projecting across the periods indicated by the range B6:B15. To calculate the sales trend using an array formula:

Step 1	*Select*	the range C6:C15 to automatically enter the array formula in each of these cells
Step 2	*Key*	=TREND(C2:C5,B2:B5,B6:B15
Step 3	*Press*	the CTRL + SHIFT + ENTER keys simultaneously

This special key combination enters the formula as an array formula. In the Formula Bar, an array formula is surrounded by curly braces, {**=TREND(C2:C5,B2:B5,B6:B15)**}. The array formula calculates a new value in each row of column C based on the value of the adjacent cell in column B. In other words, the TREND function "predicts" the sales for months 5–14 based on the existing data in cells B2:C5. Now, you update your chart.

Step 4	*Click*	in a blank area of the chart object
Step 5	*Drag*	the blue Range Finder handle in the worksheet so that it includes the range A2:C15
Step 6	*Double-click*	the trendline on the chart

The Format Trendline dialog box opens. Because your chart now includes the projected data (as calculated by the TREND function), you want to eliminate the extra four months of projection.

Step 7	*Click*	the Options tab
Step 8	*Key*	0 in the Forward: text box
Step 9	*Click*	OK
Step 10	*Resize*	the chart as necessary to display the first four months

Your chart displays the additional data points.

Step 11	*Save*	the workbook and close it

The "What-if" tools presented in this chapter offer powerful ways for businesses to analyze trends and make important financial decisions that often have long-term implications.

Summary

- Use a one-variable data table to replace one variable of a formula(s) with multiple values.
- Use a two-variable data table to replace two variables of a single formula with multiple values.
- Use Goal Seek to change the values of variables used in a formula to obtain a certain result.
- Use Solver to change the values of multiple cells and apply constraints to limit the changes of those cells so as to obtain a certain result.
- Use scenarios to store cell values for different situations.
- Add a trendline to charts to project future data.
- Create data points on a trendline using a variety of statistical functions, including the TREND function.

Commands Review

Action	Menu Bar	Shortcut Menu	Toolbar	Task Pane	Keyboard
Create a data table	Data, Table				ALT + D, T
Use Goal Seek	Tools, Goal Seek				ALT + T, G
Activate an add-in	Tools, Add-Ins				ALT + T, I
Use Solver	Tools, Solver				ALT + T, V
Create scenarios	Tools, Scenarios				ALT + T, E
Add a trendline to a graph	Click data point, then Chart, Add Trendline	Right-click data point, Add Trendline			ALT + C, R
Create an array formula					Key formula, then CTRL + SHIFT + ENTER to accept entry

Concepts Review

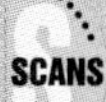

Circle the correct answer.

1. If you want to see how different interest rates and different terms affect the payment of a loan, which of the following tools would you use?
- [a] one-variable data table
- [b] two-variable data table
- [c] Solver
- [d] Goal Seek

2. Solving complex business problems often requires you to:
- [a] look at a problem several ways.
- [b] know the expected outcome of a formula.
- [c] perform a what-if analysis.
- [d] all of the above

3. When you need to calculate values for predicting future sales, you should:
- [a] add a trendline to a graph.
- [b] use the Draw toolbar to draw lines based on your best guess.
- [c] average the difference between each of the known sales amounts, then add that to the last known sales amount.
- [d] use a statistical function such as TREND.

4. Which of the following is not a setting used by Solver?
- [a] Target
- [b] Changing cells
- [c] Constraints
- [d] Summary

5. Goal Seek is useful when you:
- [a] know the outcome and have to change only one variable.
- [b] know the outcome and have to change multiple variables.
- [c] don't know the outcome, but know one of the variables.
- [d] don't know the outcome, but know two of the variables.

6. Constraints:
- [a] cannot be modified.
- [b] set limits regarding how much a cell's value can be changed.
- [c] help Solver run faster.
- [d] set limits regarding the speed at which Solver runs.

7. A what-if analysis can show you:
- [a] how changing data affects various calculations.
- [b] how to set up one-variable data tables if you don't know the value of any of the variables.
- [c] which feature is the better choice to solve your problem—Goal Seek or Solver.
- [d] which calculations will change if you change a variable.

8. In a two-variable data table, you can replace:
- [a] two variables in more than one formula.
- [b] two variables in a single formula.
- [c] one variable in two formulas.
- [d] one variable in one formula.

9. The Scenario Manager allows you to:
- [a] add a new scenario.
- [b] delete a scenario.
- [c] merge scenarios from other workbooks.
- [d] all of the above

10. If you know the outcome you want for a given formula and can change multiple values, which tool should you use?
- [a] scenarios
- [b] Solver
- [c] one-variable data table
- [d] Goal Seek

Circle **T** if the statement is true or **F** if the statement is false.

T F 1. You can use more than one formula in a one-variable data table.

T F 2. You can use more than one formula in a two-variable data table.

T F 3. You can create a what-if analysis by manually changing the values of cells referenced in a formula.

T F 4. Goal Seek can create a report when it finds a solution.

T F 5. Solver is the best tool to use whenever you're trying to do a what-if analysis.

T F 6. Solver can create three different reports when it has found a solution.

T F 7. You can save a scenario from Solver.

T F 8. The formula for a two-variable data table must appear immediately above the column variables and immediately to the right of row variables.

T F 9. Once you run Solver, you cannot retrieve your original data.

T F 10. When you add a trendline to a chart, the type of formula used makes no difference; all the trendlines come out the same.

Skills Review

Exercise 1 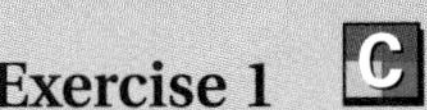

1. Open the *Warehouse Personnel Scheduling 2* workbook located on the Data Disk.

2. Set up constraints in the Solver Parameters dialog box to accomplish the following:

a. The goal is to reduce the value of cell C19 to a minimum.

b. The values in the range C5:C11 can change, but must be integers and must be greater than or equal to 1.

c. The values in the range D13:J13 must meet or exceed the total demand in the range D15:J15.

3. Run Solver on the workbook and create an Answer Report.

4. Print the schedule and the Answer Report.

5. Save the workbook as *Warehouse Personnel Scheduling Solution 1*, and close it.

Exercise 2 

1. Open the *Warehouse Personnel Scheduling Solution 1* workbook that you created in Exercise 1.

2. Create four scenarios called "1st Quarter," "2nd Quarter," "3rd Quarter," and "4th Quarter" by changing the range D15:J15 on the Schedule tab. Values for each scenario are listed below:

1st Quarter—use the values currently set

2nd Quarter—D15 = 37, E15 = 54, F15 = 56, G15 = 56, H15 = 60, I15 = 52, J15 = 40

3rd Quarter—D15 = 35, E15 = 52, F15 = 52, G15 = 50, H15 = 55, I15 = 48, J15 = 37

4th Quarter—D15 = 45, E15 = 55, F15 = 55, G15 = 55, H15 = 60, I15 = 55, J15 = 45

3. Save the workbook as *Warehouse Personnel Scheduling Scenarios*, and close it.

Exercise 3 

1. Open the *Warehouse Personnel Scheduling Scenarios* workbook that you created in Exercise 2.
2. Rename the Answer Report 1 sheet tab to "1st Quarter Answer."
3. Show the 2nd Quarter scenario.
4. Run Solver and create an Answer Report.
5. Rename the sheet tab "2nd Quarter Answer."
6. Follow Steps 3 through 5 to show the 3rd and 4th Quarter scenarios, run Solver and generate an Answer Report, and rename each Answer Report sheet tab.
7. Print the Answer Reports.
8. Save the workbook as *Warehouse Personnel Scheduling Scenarios 2*, and then print and close it.

Exercise 4 

1. Open the *Projected Portfolio* workbook located on the Data Disk.
2. In cell E4, enter the formula =FV(B4/12,B5,B6).
3. Select the range D4:E7.
4. Create a one-variable data table using cell B6 as the Column input cell.
5. Save the workbook as *Projected Portfolio Final*, and then print and close it.

Exercise 5 

1. Open the *Home Purchase* workbook located on the Data Disk.
2. Use Goal Seek to find the maximum amount of a loan according to the following parameters:
   a. Use cell B8 as the goal, with a value of 650.
   b. Change the value in cell B5.
3. Save the workbook as *Home Purchase Loan*, and then print and close it.

Exercise 6 

1. Open the *System Purchase* workbook located on the Data Disk.
2. Use Solver to find the optimum purchasing solution, given the following parameters:
   a. Seek the minimum total purchase price in cell D7.
   b. Change the range C4:C6.
   c. Use the following constraints:
      - C4:C6 must be integers.
      - You need to buy at least 65 new computers.
      - At least 15 computers need to be P-4 1.4s.
      - At least 20 computers need to be P-III 850s.
      - The total number of Duron 700s cannot exceed 20.

3. Generate an Answer Report.
4. Print your solution and the Answer Report.
5. Save the workbook as *System Purchase Solution* and close it.

Exercise 7 C

1. Open the *Manufacturing Production* workbook located on the Data Disk.
2. Use Solver to find a solution to maximize total profit (cell H8). Use the following constraints:
   a. The number of cases must be an integer.
   b. The number of cases for each product must be at least 1.
   c. The minimum number of cases of product A-123 to produce is 100.
   d. The maximum number of cases of product A-128 to produce is 25.
   e. The minimum number of cases of product A-128 to produce is 10.
   f. The total storage space must not exceed 25,000.
   g. The maximum production hours is 80.
3. Create an Answer Report.
4. Print the Answer Report and the solution.
5. Create a scenario using the constraint values in the range B11:B17. Name it "Normal Production Schedule."
6. Save the workbook as *Manufacturing Production Solution*, and then print and close it.

Exercise 8 C

1. Open the *North Region 2003 Sales* workbook located on the Data Disk.
2. Select the range B9:E9.
3. Create a Column chart according to the following parameters:
   a. In Step 2 of the Chart Wizard, click the Series tab, then select the range B4:E4 as the Category (X) axis labels.
   b. In Step 4 of the Chart Wizard, create the chart as an embedded chart.
4. Add a trendline to the chart projecting forward four quarters.
5. Insert two columns between columns E and F.
6. Change the column labels in the range B4:G4 to 1, 2, 3, 4, 5, 6.
7. In cell F9, enter the TREND formula using cells B9:E9 as known_y, B4:E4 as known_x, and F4:G4 as new_x.
8. Select the range F9:G9.
9. Press the F2 key to edit cell F9, then press the CTRL + SHIFT + ENTER keys to enter the formula as an array formula.
10. Click the chart.
11. Use the Range Finder to include the range F9:G9 in the chart.
12. Save the workbook as *North Region 2004 Projected Sales*, and then print and close it.

Case Projects

Project 1

You want to buy a new house. To buy the house you want, you need a loan of $140,000. You've been shopping for loans and have found one offering an interest rate of 9.5% with a 15-year term, 8.5% with a 20-year term, 7.5% with a 25-year term, and 7% with a 20-year term. Use a data table(s) to calculate your monthly payments for each interest rate, and what your total interest would be for each loan. Save the workbook as *Home Loan Calculator*, and print and close it.

Project 2

Connect to the Internet and search the Web for Excel Solver tutorials. Locate at least one tutorial and print the Web page(s) containing the tutorial.

Project 3

You want to buy a car for $28,500. The car dealer has offered to finance your purchase at 8.5% for 48 months. You can afford to make payments of $400.00 per month. Use Goal Seek to find the maximum amount you can borrow at this interest rate. Save the workbook as *Car Loan*, print the solution, and close the workbook.

Project 4

Connect to the Internet and search for stock prices for a company that interests you. Find a closing price on the same day for the last six months. (*Hint:* Search for historical data.) Record these six closing prices in a new workbook. Create a column chart of this data, then add a trendline covering the next six months. Save the workbook as *Stock Trend*, and print and close it.

Project 5

Set up a budget for a sales company with an estimated gross sales income of $25,000 per month. Figure an amount for rent of $5,000, utilities and overhead of $5,000, payroll of $8,500, and advertising costs of $2,500. Set up a workbook to calculate the net profit or loss using these figures. Save the gross sales income, payroll, and advertising costs as a scenario called "Best Case." Create a second scenario called "Worst Case," with the following amounts: income = $17,500, rent = $5,000, utilities/overhead = $5,000, payroll = $5,000, advertising = $1,000. Show the worst-case scenario values, then save the workbook as *Best and Worst Case Sales*, and print and close it.

Project 6

You are deciding between two jobs located in different cities. Job offer #1 provides a salary of $35,000 per year. Job offer #2 includes a salary of $40,000 per year. Create a workbook to calculate a budget based on each scenario. In your budget, you estimate that 30% of your salary can be spent on house payments, 10% can be spent on car payments, 30% on living expenses, and 10% for savings. Also include a formula to sum the total budgeted expenses, then subtract this amount from the salary. Create a scenario summary worksheet and print it. Save the workbook as *Job Offers*, then print and close it.

Project 7

You would like to reduce the length of time needed to pay off your car loan. Instead of paying off the $10,000 loan (at 9%) in 48 months, you want to see what your monthly payments would be if you paid off the loan in 42, 36, and 30 months. Create a one-variable table to calculate these payments. Save the workbook as *Quick Payoff*, and print and close it.

Project 8

You are a broker for an investment firm. Your job is to analyze companies to see whether you should invest in them. Create a fictitious company with sales data for the last seven months. Create a graph with a trendline with data points showing the projected growth for the next seven months. Indicate projected months by shading the cells. Save the workbook as *Growth Analysis*, and print and close it.

Excel 2002

Using Auditing Tools

Chapter Overview

Auditing tools help you identify relationships between cells. The Formula Auditing toolbar provides tools to identify precedents and dependents, trace errors to their source, and locate invalid data. In this chapter, you use Range Finder to check and review data, identify data between precedent and dependent cells, use error checking, and identify invalid data.

Learning Objectives

- Use Range Finder to check and review data
- Identify relationships between precedent and dependent cells
- Use error checking
- Identify invalid data

Case profile

Many Super Power Computers employees use the Excel workbooks you create as well as create their own. As you share workbooks with coworkers, you occasionally notice their errors (and find your own *rare* errors) or need to review the sources of values referenced by a certain formula. The Excel auditing tools help you quickly track down the source of errors or identify locations where values are used throughout even the most complex worksheets.

11.a Using Range Finder to Check and Review Data

Whenever you open a workbook created by someone else, it is a good idea to review the worksheet's assumptions and calculations before you begin editing data. Previously, you used Range Finder to adjust which cells were used for chart data. Here, Range Finder helps you track down references used in formulas.

The *Super Power Computers - Projected Profit with Errors* workbook contains several errors that should be corrected. To open the workbook and save it with a new name:

Step 1	***Open***	the *Super Power Computers - Projected Profit with Errors* workbook located on the Data Disk
Step 2	***Save***	the workbook as *Super Power Computers - Projected Profit Revised*

The Projected Profit worksheet contains projections for income and expenses for the coming year. Rows 17–22 contain multipliers used in some of the formulas on the worksheet to calculate expense amounts. Because the information for the third and fourth quarters consists of projected data, it is italicized.

Excel tools can help you pinpoint errors in formulas and correct them. Several of the cells contain small green triangles in the upper-left corner. Excel automatically checks for errors, and these triangles indicate possible errors in those cells. When you click a cell containing a detected error, the Trace Errors button appears. Clicking that button opens a menu of commands that can help you in fixing the error.

To use Range Finder to revise a formula:

QUICK TIP

You can disable automatic error checking by clicking the Options command on the Tools menu. Click the Error Checking tab, then click Enable background error checking check box. Several other error-checking options are available on this tab.

Step 1	***Click***	cell E13 on the Projected Profit worksheet

The Trace Errors button appears to the left of cell E13. The formula in cell E13 is supposed to calculate the projected profit for the third quarter, but it currently shows a value of zero (shown as a dash in the Accounting format).

Step 2	***Click***	the Trace Errors button
Step 3	***Click***	Edit in Formula Bar

Your screen should look similar to Figure 11-1. The formula highlights each cell or range reference, using a different color for each reference to make it easier to identify the reference.

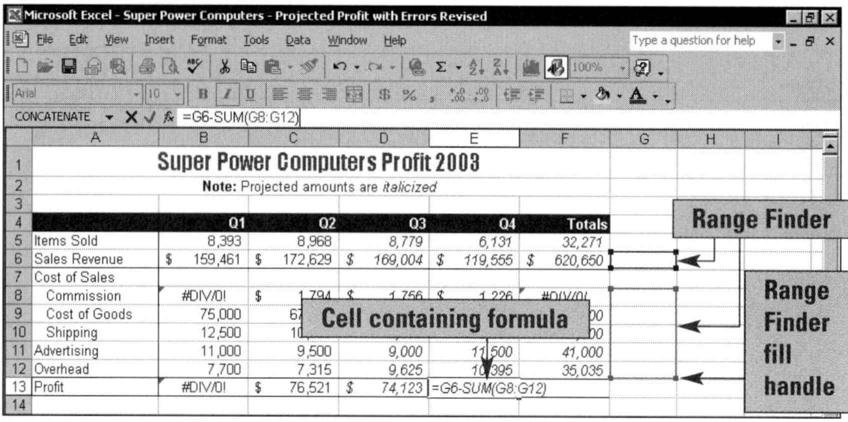

FIGURE 11-1
Using Range Finder to Locate References

As shown by the Range Finder, the formula refers to empty cells G6 and G8:G12. To adjust a reference, you drag the border of the Range Finder to the correct location in column E. If necessary, you can drag the Range Finder fill handle to increase or decrease the size of the range.

Step 4	***Drag***	the blue Range Finder border to cell E6
Step 5	***Observe***	that as you drag the border, the formula in the Formula Bar adjusts automatically
Step 6	***Drag***	the green Range Finder border to cells E8:E12
Step 7	***Click***	the Enter button on the Formula Bar
Step 8	***Observe***	that the total $11,434 appears in cell E13
Step 9	***Save***	the workbook

11.b Identifying Relationships Between Precedent and Dependent Cells

As workbooks grow larger and more complex, it becomes increasingly difficult to locate and review relationships between cells. Excel provides auditing features to simplify this job.

Tracing Precedents

Precedents are the cells referred to by a formula. You can locate precedents by using the Formula Auditing commands on the Tools menu and on the Formula Auditing toolbar. To show the Formula Auditing toolbar:

Step 1	***Click***	Tools
Step 2	***Point to***	Formula Auditing
Step 3	***Click***	Show Formula Auditing Toolbar

MENU TIP

To trace precedents, point to Formula Auditing on the Tools menu, then click Trace Precedents.

The formula in cell F6 adds the total Sales Revenue figures for each quarter. To trace the precedents for this formula:

Step 1	***Click***	cell F6
Step 2	***Click***	the Trace Precedents button [icon] on the Formula Auditing toolbar

MOUSE TIP

You can jump to a referenced cell by using the tracer arrow lines. Double-click an arrow line, and the active cell moves back and forth between the referenced cells and the formula.

A heavy blue tracer arrow identifies the precedent(s) for this formula. When the precedent consists of a range of cells, the tracer arrow is indicated with a heavy line, and the range is highlighted with a blue border. When the precedent consists of a single cell, the tracer arrow is indicated with a thin line. Your screen should look similar to Figure 11-2.

FIGURE 11-2
Tracing Precedents

Many times, the results of a formula are not based on a single level of precedents. For example, the formula in cell F6 refers to the range B6:E6, but the values in this range are derived from still other formulas.

To view a second level of precedents:

Step 1	*Click*	the Trace Precedents button on the Formula Auditing toolbar a second time

Your screen should look similar to Figure 11-3.

FIGURE 11-3
Tracing Multiple Levels of Precedents

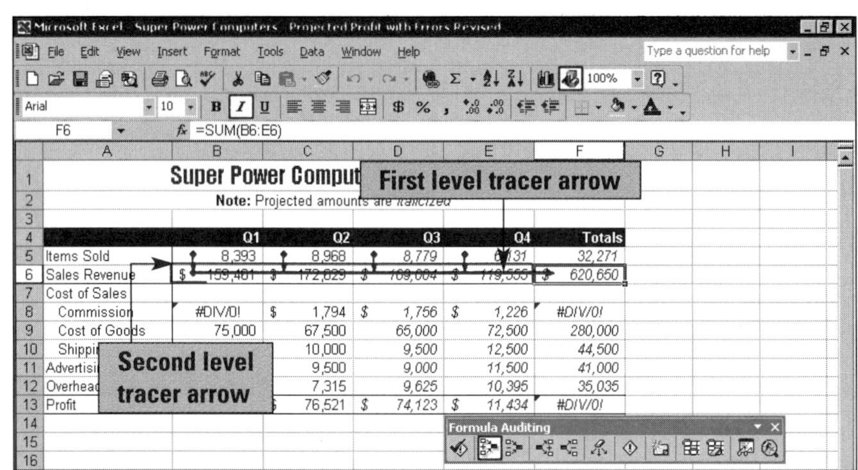

Step 2	*Click*	the Trace Precedents button on the Formula Auditing toolbar

QUICK TIP

You can preview and print tracer arrows.

An alert sound indicates that Excel has reached the last level of precedents. Once you have finished viewing the precedents for a cell, you may want to clear the precedent arrows to view your worksheet more easily. To clear all precedent arrows:

Step 1	*Click*	the Remove All Arrows button on the Formula Auditing toolbar to remove the arrows

Tracing Dependents

Dependents are cells containing formulas that rely on the value of another cell. A cell may be referenced by one or several formulas throughout a workbook. You can locate dependents in the same manner that you located precedents. To trace dependents:

Step 1	*Click*	cell B5
Step 2	*Click*	the Trace Dependents button on the Formula Auditing toolbar

Thin blue tracer arrows point to cells B6, B8, and F5. Each of these cells contains a formula that references cell B5. Your screen should look similar to Figure 11-4.

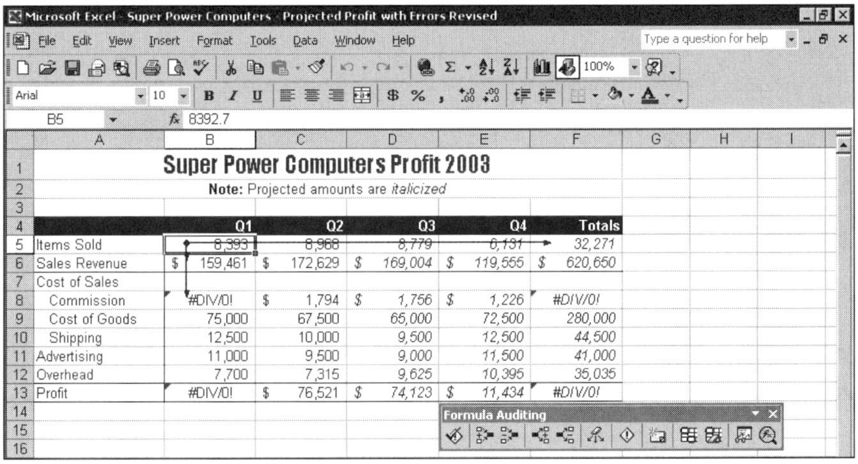

	Q1	Q2	Q3	Q4	Totals
Items Sold	8,393	8,968	8,779	6,131	32,271
Sales Revenue	$ 159,461	$ 172,629	$ 169,004	$ 119,555	$ 620,650
Cost of Sales					
Commission	#DIV/0!	$ 1,794	$ 1,756	$ 1,226	#DIV/0!
Cost of Goods	75,000	67,500	65,000	72,500	280,000
Shipping	12,500	10,000	9,500	12,500	44,500
Advertising	11,000	9,500	9,000	11,500	41,000
Overhead	7,700	7,315	9,625	10,395	35,035
Profit	#DIV/0!	$ 76,521	$ 74,123	$ 11,434	#DIV/0!

FIGURE 11-4
Tracing Dependents

You can identify multiple levels of dependents by continuing to click the Trace Dependents button on the Formula Auditing toolbar. The number of items sold, which appears in cell B5, is referenced by the formula in cell B8, which calculates the commission expense. This amount is then referenced by still other formulas. Cell B5 is also referenced by the formula in cell B6, which is then referenced by cell F6.

Step 3	***Click***	the Trace Dependents button on the Formula Auditing toolbar a second time

A second level of tracer arrows is added to the display. A blue tracer arrow now points to cell F6. Because the formula in cell B8 contains an error, red tracer arrows point to the two cells that use cell B8 in their formulas. You fix this error in the next section.

You can remove a single level of arrows rather than removing all arrows at once. To remove a single level of arrows:

Step 1	***Click***	the Remove Dependent Arrows button on the Formula Auditing toolbar
Step 2	***Observe***	that the second level of tracer arrows disappears
Step 3	***Click***	the Remove Dependent Arrows button on the Formula Auditing toolbar
Step 4	***Observe***	that the first level of tracer arrows disappears

MENU TIP

To remove all precedent and dependent tracer arrows, click Tools, point to Formula Auditing, then click Remove All Arrows.

Tracing Cell Relationships Between Worksheets

As you learned in previous chapters, you can reference cells located on other worksheets as well as those on the current worksheet. The Excel auditing tools help you trace references to these cells. To trace precedents between worksheets:

Step 1	***Click***	cell B12
Step 2	***Click***	the Trace Precedents button on the Formula Auditing toolbar

A worksheet icon and a black tracer arrow appear, indicating that a reference in cell B12 is located on another worksheet. Check the formula in the Formula Bar to verify this relationship. Your screen should look similar to Figure 11-5. You can quickly jump to the referenced cell.

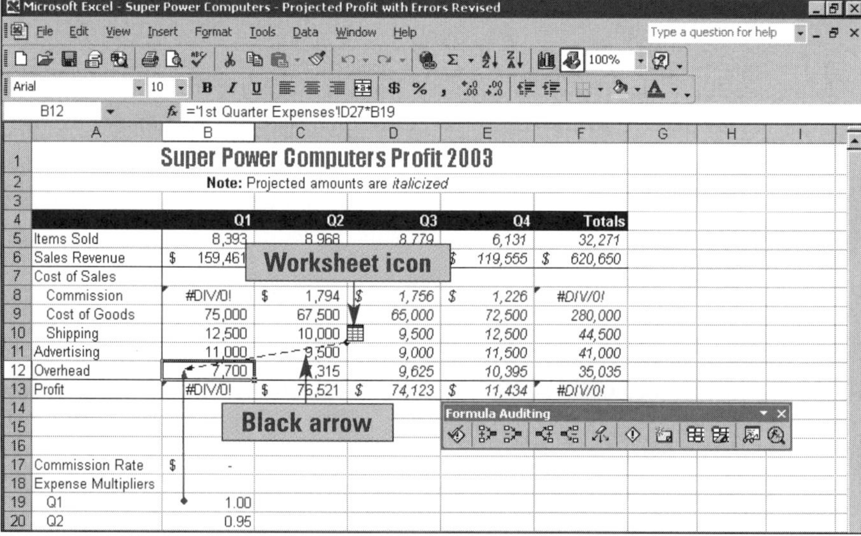

FIGURE 11-5
Tracing Relationships Between Worksheets

> **CAUTION TIP**
>
> Make sure the mouse pointer is in the shape of an arrow and not the cross when you double-click the black tracer arrow.

Step 3	***Double-click***	the black tracer arrow

The Go To dialog box opens.

Step 4	***Click***	the reference listed at the top of the Go to: list
Step 5	***Click***	OK

The 1st Quarter Expenses worksheet is activated, and the active cell moves to cell D27. The total in cell D27 is used in cell B12 on the Projected Profit worksheet.

Step 6	***Click***	the Projected Profit sheet tab
Step 7	***Click***	the Remove All Arrows button on the Formula Auditing toolbar
Step 8	***Save***	the workbook

11.c Using Error Checking

Excel features several tools to help you pinpoint errors in formulas and correct them. As you've seen, Excel tags cells with detected errors with a small green triangle in the upper-left corner, and when you click a cell containing a detected error, the Trace Errors button appears. Another tool, Error Checking, helps you locate and resolve common errors by scanning the worksheet for errors. When it finds one, the error is flagged, and Error Checking suggests ways to fix it. You can display tracer arrows from a cell containing a formula with errors to identify all cells referenced in the formula.

The formulas in cells B8, F8, B13, and F13 display the #DIV/0! error. This error indicates that at least one of these cells contains a formula that attempts to divide a value by zero. To trace and correct the source of this error:

Step 1	***Activate***	cell F8
Step 2	***Click***	the Error Checking button on the Formula Auditing toolbar
Step 3	***Click***	Trace Error in the Error Checking dialog box

The formula in cell F8 refers to the range B8:E8. Because an error occurs in cell F8, you see a red error arrow, as shown in Figure 11-6. Cell B8, however, is also displaying the #DIV/0! error. Clicking Edit in Formula Bar in the Error Checking dialog box won't do any good, because the source of the error isn't in cell F8, so you keep going to let the Error Checker find the source of the problem.

QUICK TIP

Select a cell, then click the Show Watch Window button on the Formula Auditing toolbar to open the Watch Window toolbar to watch the value in the cell.

MENU TIP

You can trace errors by clicking, pointing to the Formula Auditing command on the Tools menu, and then clicking Trace Error.

FIGURE 11-6
Tracing Errors

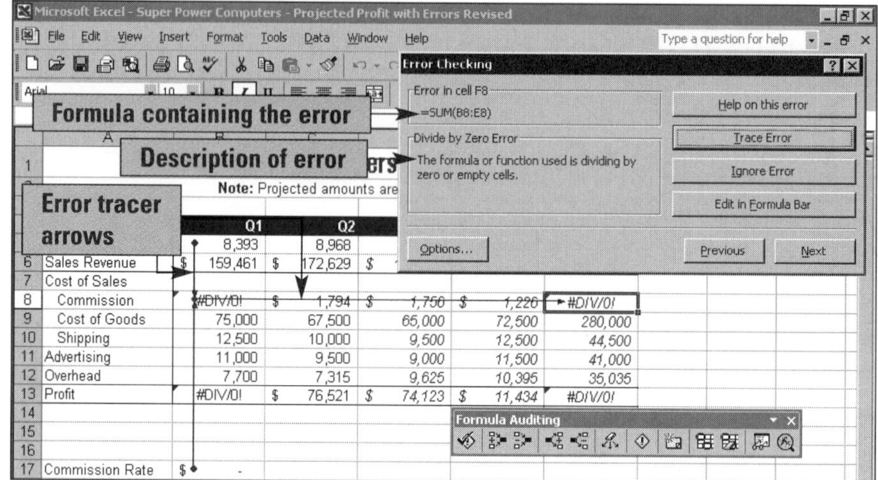

MOUSE TIP

Use the Trace Error button on the Formula Auditing toolbar to display trace arrows from a cell containing an error. This is equivalent to clicking Trace Error in the Error Checking dialog box.

Step 4	***Click***	Next to move to the next error
Step 5	***Click***	Trace Error
Step 6	***Observe***	that this error in cell B13 again points to cell B8
Step 7	***Click***	Next
Step 8	***Click***	Trace Error
Step 9	***Observe***	that this error in cell F13 also points to cell B8
Step 10	***Click***	Next

QUICK TIP

Clicking Options in the Error Checking dialog box opens a dialog box in which you can select or deselect the rules that the Error Checker uses to check your workbooks.

This time, the command in the Error Checking dialog box changes to Show Calculation Steps. This is because the error originates in this cell, cell B8. Your dialog box should look similar to Figure 11-7.

FIGURE 11-7
Error Checking Dialog Box

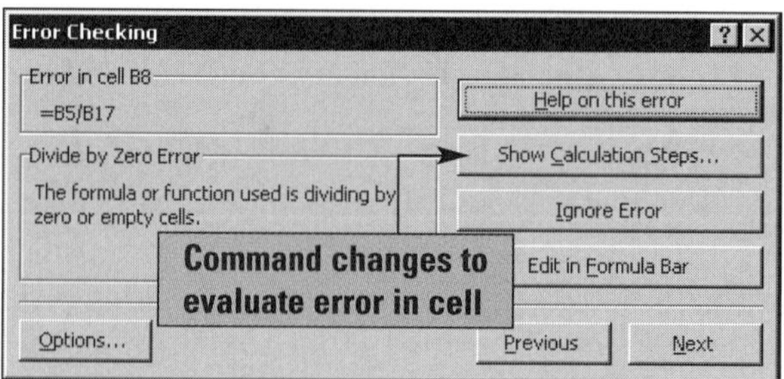

Step 11	***Click***	Show Calculation Steps

The Evaluate Formula dialog box opens, displaying the actual calculation that takes place. In this case, you are trying to divide the value in cell B5, 8392.7, by the value in cell B17, which is currently 0.

Step 12	*Click*	Evaluate

This results in an error. Cell B17 is the source of all four errors; it contains a value of 0.

Step 13	*Click*	Close
Step 14	*Click*	Next
Step 15	*Click*	OK in the dialog box that opens, telling you that error checking is complete
Step 16	*Enter*	5 in cell B17

MENU TIP

Another way to track down errors is to display the formulas in the cells instead of the values. To do this, point to the Formula Auditing command on the Tools menu, then click Formula Auditing Mode.

This correction solves the "divide by 0" error in cell B8, and consequently eliminates the problems in cells B13, F8, and F13. The red error arrows are replaced by blue tracer arrows.

Step 17	*Click*	the Remove All Arrows button on the Formula Auditing toolbar
Step 18	*Save*	the workbook

11.d Identifying Invalid Data

In Chapter 8, you learned how to use data validation when creating lists of data. You also learned about the three different types of error alert messages. Two of the error alert messages—Information and Warning—allow a user to input invalid data, even though the user is informed that the information is invalid. To help you identify cells in a list that contain data violating data validation rules, you can use an auditing command.

The 1st Quarter Expenses worksheet has been prepared using data validation. However, several errors were made. To find invalid data:

Step 1	*Click*	the 1st Quarter Expenses sheet tab
Step 2	*Click*	the Circle Invalid Data button on the Formula Auditing toolbar

Step 3	*Scroll*	the worksheet up until you can see row 1

All cells containing invalid data are circled in red. Your screen should look similar to Figure 11-8.

FIGURE 11-8
Identifying Invalid Data

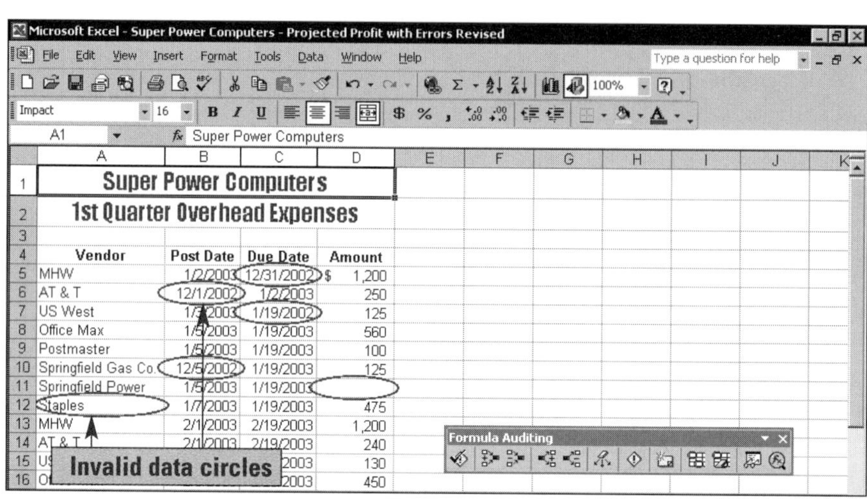

MOUSE TIP

You can turn off the circles by clicking the Clear Validation Circles button on the Formula Auditing toolbar.

Step 4	*Click*	cell B6
Step 5	*Enter*	1/2/03 in cell B6
Step 6	*Enter*	1/5/03 in cell B10
Step 7	*Enter*	1/31/03 in cell C5
Step 8	*Enter*	1/19/03 in cell C7
Step 9	*Enter*	185 in cell D11
Step 10	*Click*	the list arrow in cell A12
Step 11	*Click*	Office Max
Step 12	*Click*	the Circle Invalid Data button on the Formula auditing toolbar to double-check for additional errors
Step 13	*Close*	the Formula Auditing toolbar
Step 14	*Save*	the workbook and close it

The Formula Auditing toolbar can be helpful when your worksheets include complicated formulas that use many precedents.

Summary

- You can use Range Finder to quickly edit cell references in a formula. Click and drag Range Finder borders to move a reference. The Range Finder fill handle enables you to "resize" a range reference.
- Precedents are cells or ranges referenced by a specific formula. You can select a cell containing a formula, then use the Trace Precedents tool to identify cells and ranges referenced in that particular formula.
- Dependents are cells containing formulas that depend on the value of a certain cell. You can select a cell containing a value or formula, then use the Trace Dependents tool to identify other cells containing formulas that reference that particular cell.
- You can use the Error Checker tool to quickly locate and resolve the source of a formula error.
- You can locate data that violates data validation rules by using the Circle Invalid Data auditing tool.

Commands Review

Action	Menu Bar	Shortcut Menu	Toolbar	Task Pane	Keyboard
Trace precedents	Tools, Formula Auditing, Trace Precedents				ALT + T, U, T
Trace dependents	Tools, Formula Auditing, Trace Dependents		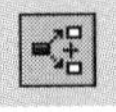		ALT + T, U, D
Error checking					
Trace errors	Tools, Formula Auditing, Trace Error				ALT + T, U, E
Remove all arrows	Tools, Formula Auditing, Remove All Arrows				ALT + T, U, A
Circle invalid data					
Clear validation circles					

Concepts Review

Circle the correct answer.

1. Precedents are cells that:
[a] are referred to by a formula.
[b] depend on the value of another cell.
[c] have blue arrow lines showing the relationship between two cells.
[d] have red arrow lines showing the source of an error.

2. Dependents are cells that:
[a] are referred to by a formula.
[b] depend on the value of another cell.
[c] have blue arrow lines showing the relationship between two cells.
[d] have red arrow lines showing the source of an error.

3. Traced errors are indicated by a:
[a] blue arrow.
[b] black arrow.
[c] red arrow.
[d] blinking cell border.

4. A black tracer arrow indicates a:
[a] serious error.
[b] multiple-cell reference.
[c] single-cell reference.
[d] reference on another worksheet.

5. A green triangle in a cell indicates a:
[a] comment placed by you.
[b] possible error detected by Excel.
[c] comment placed by another user.
[d] precedent.

6. To locate data that violates data validation, use the:
[a] Trace Precedents tool.
[b] Trace Error tool.
[c] Trace Dependents tool.
[d] Circle Invalid Data tool.

7. To quickly jump to a precedent or dependent in another worksheet that has been traced:
[a] click the worksheet icon that appears in the worksheet.
[b] double-click the black tracer arrow.
[c] drag the black tracer arrow to the sheet tab.
[d] double-click the cell to which the black tracer arrow points.

8. You can trace errors in worksheet formulas by:
[a] clicking the Trace Error button on the Formula Auditing toolbar.
[b] double-clicking the tracer arrows until they point to the errors.
[c] clicking the Find Errors button on the Formula Auditing toolbar.
[d] dragging the red tracer arrows to the precedent cell.

9. If data in a worksheet has a red circle around it, you should:
[a] fix the precedent cells.
[b] reenter the value currently in the cell.
[c] enter a valid entry in the cell.
[d] erase the red circles using the Eraser button on the Drawing toolbar.

10. Range Finder can help you:
[a] adjust the data used in a chart.
[b] change cell references in a formula.
[c] locate which cell references are used in a formula.
[d] all of the above

Circle **T** if the statement is true or **F** if the statement is false.

T F 1. You can view multiple levels of precedents and dependents.

T F 2. It is a good idea to review the relationships between cells when using a workbook prepared by someone else or when using a workbook with which you haven't worked on for a long time.

T F 3. You can jump between ends of a tracer arrow by double-clicking the arrow line.

T F 4. You can open the Formula Auditing toolbar by right-clicking the toolbar and clicking Auditing.

T F 5. The #DIV/0! error indicates a number that Excel cannot display.

T F 6. Red arrows indicate precedents and dependents.

T F 7. If a cell containing a formula that results in an error is a precedent of a formula in another cell, both cells display the error.

T F 8. To move a range with Range Finder, click and drag the Range Finder fill handle.

T F 9. You can use the Trace Error tool to find invalid data entered in a list.

T F 10. As you correct invalid entries in a list, the validation circles disappear.

Skills Review

Exercise 1

1. Open the *Warehouse Inventory Errors* workbook located on the Data Disk.
2. Use the Formula Auditing toolbar to locate cells containing invalid data.
3. Select rows 17–24.
4. Use the Clear All command (open the Data Validation dialog box) to clear data validation settings from rows 17–24.
5. Click the Circle Invalid Data button on the Formula Auditing toolbar again.
6. Print the worksheet with the circles displayed.
7. Correct the errors using data that is compatible with the validation rules.
8. Save the workbook as *Warehouse Inventory Errors Fixed* and print and close it.

Exercise 2

1. Open the *Fee Calculator Errors* workbook located on the Data Disk.
2. Start the Error Checker.
3. Evaluate the first suggestion. Because this formula is not in error, click Next to move to the next error.
4. Trace the #NAME? error to its source.
5. The formula in cell C3 refers to a named range, percentage, that does not exist in the worksheet. Edit the formula to properly refer to cell C2. If necessary, check the formula in the cell to the right.
6. Close Error Checking.
7. Save the workbook as *Fee Calculator Errors Fixed 1* and print and close it.

Exercise 3 C

1. Open the *Fee Calculator Errors Fixed 1* workbook that you created in Exercise 2.
2. Click cell H7.
3. Use the Trace Precedents button, and then use the Range Finder to correct the formula so that it adds the range H3:H6.
4. Save the workbook as *Fee Calculator Errors Fixed 2* and print and close it.

Exercise 4 C

1. Open the *Fee Calculator Errors Fixed 2* workbook that you created in Exercise 3.
2. Trace the source of the #DIV/0! error in cell B10.
3. Remove the arrows.
4. Change the value of the erroneous cell to 5.
5. Print the worksheet.
6. Save the workbook as *Fee Calculator Errors Fixed 3,* and close it.

Exercise 5 C

1. Open the *XYZ Accounting* workbook located on the Data Disk.
2. Click cell B2 and trace its precedents.
3. Print the worksheet with the arrows displayed.
4. Double-click the black arrow line.
5. Select the reference to the San Diego tab and click OK.
6. Print the worksheet.
7. Save the workbook as *XYZ Accounting 1* and close it.

Exercise 6 C

1. Open the *XYZ Accounting 1* workbook that you created in Exercise 5.
2. Click cell E5.
3. Display the first-level precedents for cell E5.
4. Display the second-level precedents for cell E5.
5. Print the worksheet.
6. Save the workbook as *XYZ Accounting 2* and close it.

Exercise 7 C

1. Open the *XYZ Accounting 2* workbook that you created in Exercise 6.
2. Activate cell B2 on the Summary tab.
3. Trace all dependents of cell B2.
4. Print the worksheet.
5. Save the workbook as *XYZ Accounting 3* and close it.

Exercise 8

1. Open the *Day Off* workbook located on the Data Disk.
2. Use Error Checking to help you determine the cause of the error in cell B4.
3. Change the IF function to see if cell B2="Monday."
4. Change the width of column A.
5. Save the workbook as *No Day Off* and print and close it.

Case Projects

Project 1

Use the Ask A Question Box to look up the topic "Find and correct errors in formulas." Using the information you find, create a new workbook and try to create one of each type of error. In another column enter a description of how you "caused" each error (there are several ways to create almost all errors; just describe the one you used). Save the workbook as *Errors* and print and close it.

Project 2

Some of your clients work with other spreadsheet applications that use the R1C1 cell reference style. Use the Ask A Question Box to research the R1C1 reference style. Write a description of the differences between the R1C1 and the A1 reference styles, and how to use absolute and relative cell references in the R1C1 style. Include instructions on how to change Excel to use the R1C1 reference style. Save the document as *R1C1 Instructions.doc* and print and close it.

Project 3

Use the Ask A Question Box to research "circular references." In Word, write a two-paragraph memo explaining what a circular reference is, how to turn on the Circular Reference toolbar, and how to resolve the problem. Save the document as *Circular References.doc* and print and close it.

Project 4

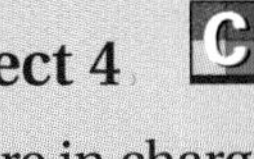

You are in charge of hiring new employees for the Accounting Division. Part of your hiring procedure is to test applicants using a workbook containing several errors, to see how they resolve the problems. Create a workbook similar to the one used in this chapter, using your own row and column headings, and data. Create erroneous formulas using incorrect references, named ranges that don't exist, circular references, and a divide by 0 error. Save your workbook as *Error Test* and print and close it.

Project 5

History hunt! Connect to the Internet and search the Web to find out who invented the first spreadsheet application. Print a Web page explaining who invented it, why (s)he invented it, and what (s)he named it.

Project 6

You are the manager of a retail goods store. Create a template that can be used for calculating a typical sales transaction. Use a formula to add the sum of several items (minimum of five cells), then calculate a sales tax of 7% and add that to the previously calculated sum and display the total for the sale. Save the template as *Sales Transaction Template*. Create a new workbook from this template, enter fictitious sales data, then turn on Trace Precedents to trace the source of the total formula. Print the worksheet, save the workbook as *Sample Sales Transaction*, and then close it.

Summarizing Data with Data Analysis, PivotTables, and PivotCharts

LEARNING OBJECTIVES

- Use data analysis
- Create PivotTable reports
- Modify a PivotTable report
- Format a PivotTable report
- Create PivotChart reports

Chapter Overview

Excel provides many ways to analyze and summarize data. Data analysis tools help you to prepare reports based on selected data, using a variety of statistical calculations. Using PivotTables and PivotCharts, you can prepare data reports by dragging and dropping report fields. PivotTables are very powerful, allowing you to quickly reorganize data as necessary.

Case profile

Lately, you have been inundated with requests for information from every department in Super Power Computers. The warehouse needs to know which items are the best-sellers so that it knows how much to keep in stock. Shipping needs to know which stores are selling the most so that it can prepare orders accordingly. Personnel wants to know which sales representatives are ready to be promoted based on their sales performance. You can use data analysis tools, PivotTables, and PivotCharts to make short work of all these requests.

12.a Using Data Analysis

Data analysis tools comprise a set of statistical analysis tools used to quickly generate reports based on a given set of data. Excel offers nearly 20 such analysis tools. In this section, you learn about the descriptive statistics and the rank and percentile tools. These tools generate statistics using several of the statistical functions with which you are already familiar.

The **descriptive statistics** tool creates a table of statistical data based on a range of numerical data. Statistics generated include Sum, Count, Minimum, Maximum, Range, Median, Mean, and Standard Deviation. By analyzing these types of statistics generated over a certain period of time, Super Power Computers can spot trends in the growth of the company. This information can be very helpful when the company president must make decisions about Super Power Computers' future. To generate a descriptive statistics report:

Step 1	*Open*	the *Super Power Computers - Store Sales Ranking* workbook located on the Data Disk
Step 2	*Save*	the workbook as *Super Power Computers - Store Sales Ranking Revised*
Step 3	*Click*	Tools
Step 4	*Click*	Data Analysis to open the Data Analysis dialog box
Step 5	*Double-click*	Descriptive Statistics in the Analysis Tools list (you may need to scroll up the list)

The Descriptive Statistics dialog box on your screen should look similar to Figure 12-1. You use this dialog box to select the input range and set output options for the statistical report.

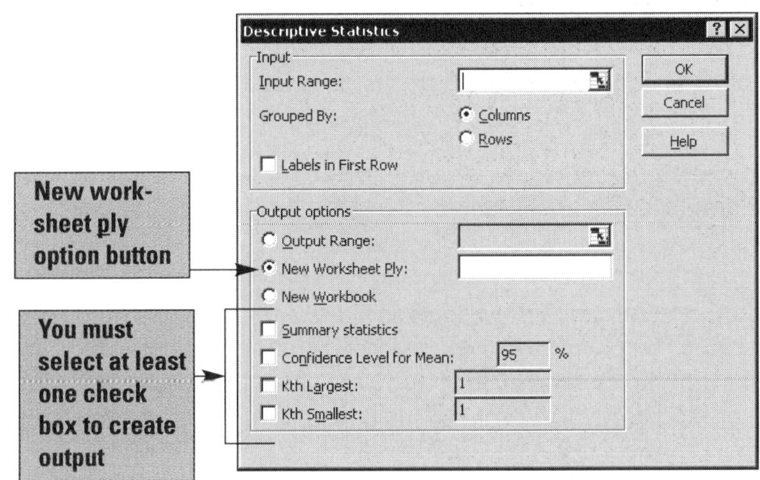

FIGURE 12-1
Descriptive Statistics Dialog Box

chapter twelve

> **CAUTION TIP**
>
> When you use data analysis tools, you do not actually insert formulas in the reports. Instead, creating these reports is analogous to taking a snapshot of the data at a given point in time. Having such a fixed reference point is important when you must evaluate statistical trends over a period of time. If the source data changes, you must create a new statistical report.

Step 6	***Click***	in the Input Range: text box, if necessary
Step 7	***Drag***	to select the range B1:B17
Step 8	***Click***	the Labels in First Row check box

You want to generate the statistical report on a new worksheet named Statistics.

Step 9	***Click***	in the New Worksheet Ply: text box
Step 10	***Key***	Statistics
Step 11	***Click***	the Summary statistics check box to insert a check mark
Step 12	***Click***	OK

A new worksheet named Statistics is inserted in your workbook.

Step 13	***AutoFit***	columns A and B
Step 14	***Click***	cell A1 to deselect the cells

Your worksheet should look similar to Figure 12-2.

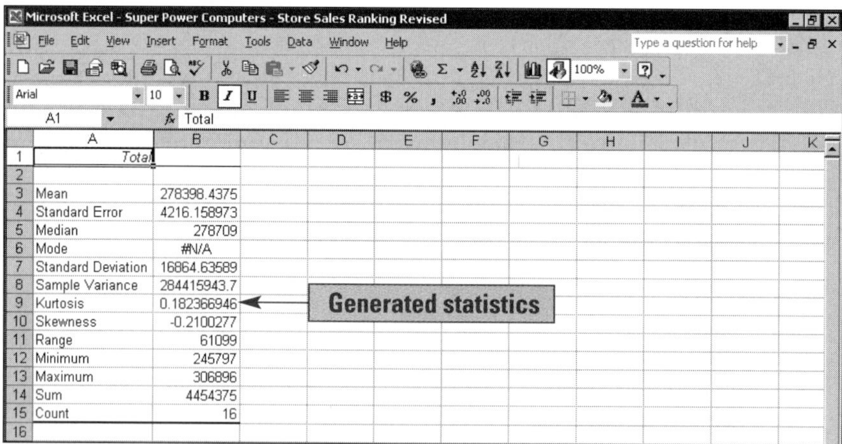

	A	B
1	Total	
2		
3	Mean	278398.4375
4	Standard Error	4216.158973
5	Median	278709
6	Mode	#N/A
7	Standard Deviation	16864.63589
8	Sample Variance	284415943.7
9	Kurtosis	0.182366946
10	Skewness	-0.2100277
11	Range	61099
12	Minimum	245797
13	Maximum	306896
14	Sum	4454375
15	Count	16
16		

FIGURE 12-2
Report Generated Using the Descriptive Statistics Analysis Tool

Many of the statistics in this report could be derived from statistical functions you already know, such as SUM, MIN, MAX, and COUNT.

The **rank and percentile** tool creates a ranking table that sorts values in order from largest to smallest and provides a percentage based on each item's ranking. You can use this type of table to analyze the relative standing of values in a data set.

To generate a rank and percentile report:

Step 1	***Click***	the Summary sheet tab
Step 2	***Click***	Tools
Step 3	***Click***	Data Analysis
Step 4	***Double-click***	Rank and Percentile (scroll down the list) to open the Rank and Percentile dialog box
Step 5	***Select***	the range B1:B17 as the Input range:
Step 6	***Click***	the Labels in First Row check box to insert a check mark
Step 7	***Enter***	Rank & Percentile in the New Worksheet Ply: text box
Step 8	***Click***	OK to insert a new worksheet named Rank & Percentile in your workbook
Step 9	***Click***	cell A1 to deselect the selected cells

QUICK TIP

To find out more about any of the other descriptive statistics generated or other data analysis tools, use the Ask A Question Box.

Your worksheet should look similar to Figure 12-3. The rank and percentile report includes four columns of information. The Point column identifies the original position, or order, of the data "point" in the source data (the Summary worksheet). The Total column displays the actual values, or points, from the raw data. The totals for the points are sorted in descending order, from highest to lowest, and placed in the Rank in Ascending order from first to last. The final column, Percent, gives the percentage of each item in terms of its rank.

Microsoft Excel - Super Power Computers - Store Sales Ranking Revised

	A	B	C	D
1	Point	Total	Rank	Percent
2	15	$306,896.00	1	100.00%
3	7	$306,146.00	2	93.30%
4	13	$292,733.00	3	86.60%
5	1	$286,235.00	4	80.00%
6	12	$285,615.00	5	73.30%
7	14	$285,571.00	6	66.60%
8	8	$285,307.00	7	60.00%
9	6	$281,050.00	8	53.30%
10	10	$276,368.00	9	46.60%
11	16	$274,313.00	10	40.00%
12	3	$273,377.00	11	33.30%
13	11	$272,649.00	12	26.60%
14	5	$267,164.00	13	20.00%
15	9	$265,445.00	14	13.30%
16	4	$249,709.00	15	6.60%
17	2	$245,797.00	16	.00%

Percentage of item
Current order based on totals
Actual value of data in descending order
Original order of source data

FIGURE 12-3
Report Generated Using Rank & Percentile Analysis Tool

Step 10	***Save***	the workbook and close it

12.b Creating PivotTable Reports

Excel is often used to maintain lists of data. You've already learned how to sort lists and create outlines using lists. **PivotTables** are a special kind of table that you create to summarize unsorted data stored in lists. Using PivotTables, you can quickly rearrange how data is displayed and select different data sets to use.

You receive requests for data from Super Power Computers' many departments every day. Rather than maintaining separate lists of data for each department, which increases the chance of introducing errors in your data lists, you can maintain a single list of data. Then, using PivotTable reports, you can quickly display the exact data requested. The *Super Power Computers - Sales* workbook contains a portion of the sales data for the company's Central and East Coast Regions. To respond to the many requests for these data, you construct PivotTables. To create PivotTables:

Step 1	***Open***	the *Super Power Computers - Sales* workbook located on the Data Disk
Step 2	***Save***	the workbook as *Super Power Computers - Sales Revised*

This workbook includes several columns of unsorted data. Sorting allows you to readily retrieve certain information for lists. For example, you can easily sort the list by Region and Store, and then add subtotals to generate a summary of sales by store. However, suppose that you were asked to generate a report identifying how many units of Item 123 were sold at Store #7. Or maybe you want to find the quantity of each item sold by a certain sales rep. Gathering this type of information is not easily accomplished through simple sorting. These complex sorting and filtering tasks are easily accomplished using a PivotTable report.

Step 3	***Click***	in the Name Box
Step 4	***Enter***	A1:H97 to quickly select that range, which includes all of the data
Step 5	***Click***	Data
Step 6	***Click***	PivotTable and PivotChart Report

The PivotTable and PivotChart Wizard guides you through three steps to create your PivotTable or PivotChart report. In Step 1 of the PivotTable and PivotChart Wizard, you can select the source of your data and the type of report you wish to create. Because you're using data in the current workbook and creating a PivotTable, you leave the settings in this step at their defaults. Your dialog box should look similar to Figure 12-4.

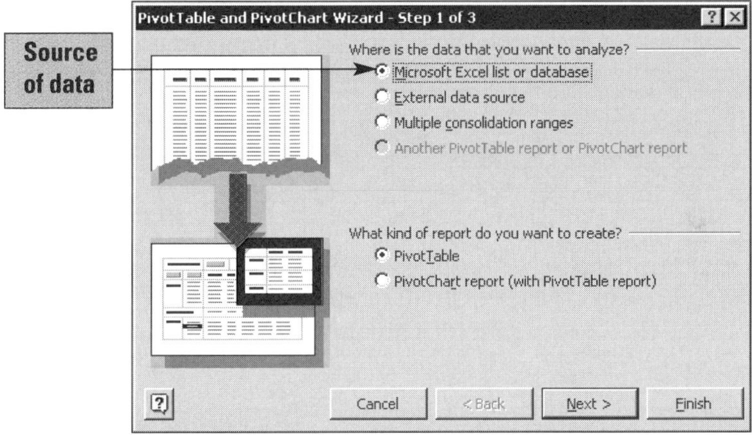

FIGURE 12-4
Step 1 of PivotTable and PivotChart Wizard

Step 7	*Click*	Next >

Step 2 of the wizard should look similar to Figure 12-5. In this dialog box, you specify the data to use in your report. You've already selected the range, so accept the range indicated in this step.

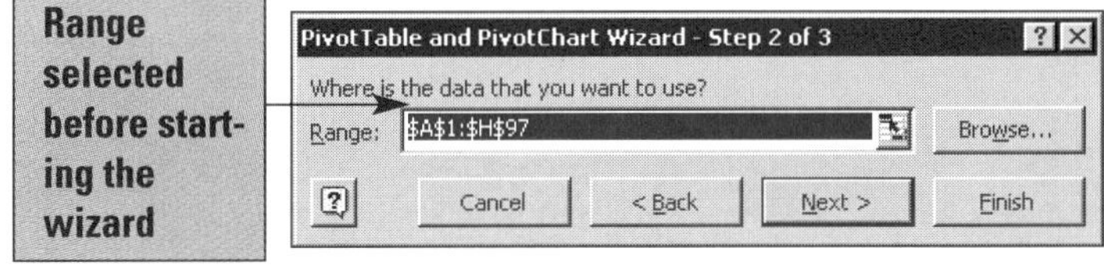

FIGURE 12-5
Step 2 of PivotTable and PivotChart Wizard

Step 8	*Click*	Next >

Step 3 of the wizard should look similar to Figure 12-6.

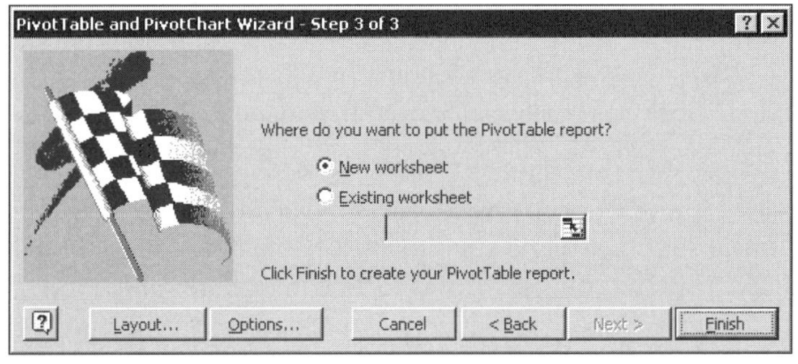

FIGURE 12-6
Step 3 of PivotTable and PivotChart Wizard

chapter twelve

MOUSE TIP

Clicking Layout in Step 3 of the wizard lets you preselect a layout for your data, but you can also make this selection directly on the worksheet when the wizard is finished. Clicking Options lets you set format and data options for your report. You can also change these settings later.

In this dialog box, you specify the report destination as either a new worksheet or an existing worksheet. You want the default settings—to insert the report on a new worksheet.

Step 9	*Click*	Finish
Step 10	*Drag*	the PivotTable toolbar by its title bar to the bottom of the screen so it "docks" into place below the sheet tabs, if necessary

Your screen should look similar to Figure 12-7. A new worksheet containing an empty PivotTable is inserted in your workbook and the PivotTable Field List appears with buttons matching the column labels of your worksheet. You create the PivotTable report by dragging field buttons from the field list to different areas of the PivotTable.

FIGURE 12-7
Empty PivotTable

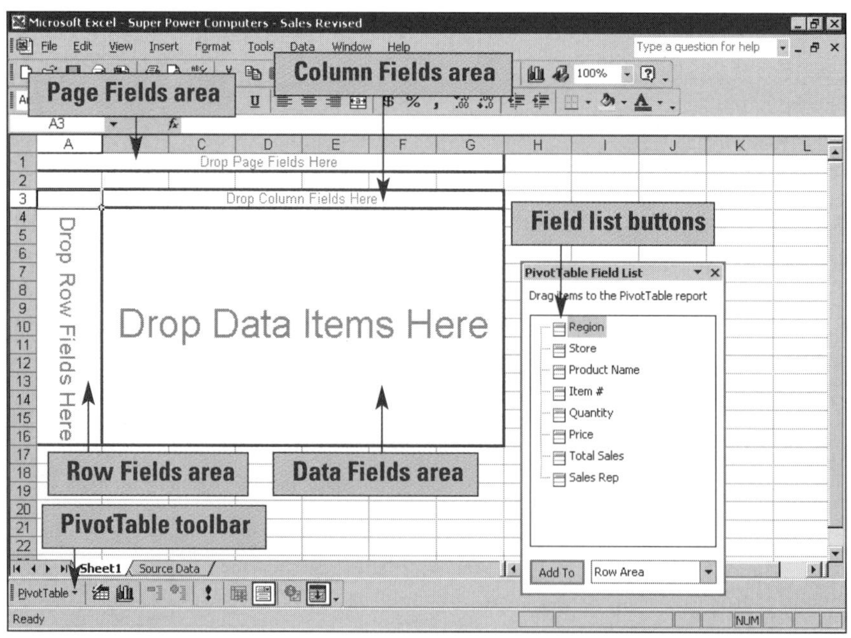

CAUTION TIP

If you click anything outside the PivotTable area, the Field list and the PivotTable toolbar close.

You want to find out the quantity of items sold by each sales rep. working at Store #2. To create this report:

Step 1	*Drag*	the Store button in the PivotTable Field List to the Drop Page Fields Here area at the top of the worksheet

The Page Fields area is used when you need to limit the data displayed in the report. Cell A1 displays the Store button. Cell B1 contains a filter list arrow that allows you to filter the data displayed in the report. This list includes each unique name found in the Store column (column B) of the Source Data tab. For this report, you limit the display of data to only Store #2, one of the company stores, after you've added the other fields to the report.

Your report should include the names of the items that were sold. You add this field to the row area of the PivotTable report.

Step 2	*Drag*	the Product Name button in the PivotTable Field List to the Drop Row Fields Here area at the left of the worksheet

The Product Name button appears in cell A4 with a filter list arrow. This list includes each unique product name found in the Product Name column (column C) of the Source Data tab. When the report is complete, you can use this filter to display data for all products or only a selected group of products.

Next you add the Sales Rep field to the column field area of the report.

Step 3	*Drag*	the Sales Rep button in the PivotTable Field List to the Drop Column Fields Here area in rows 3 and 4 of the worksheet

The Sales Rep button appears in cell B3 with a filter list arrow. This list includes each unique name found in the Sales Rep column (column H) of the Source Data tab. As with the other buttons in your report, you can filter the values displayed in the Item # field in your report by using the filter list arrow.

The last item needed in your report is the quantity of items sold to each store. This data is found in the Quantity column (column E) of the Source Data tab. Add the Quantity field to the data area of the report.

Step 4	*Drag*	the Quantity button in the PivotTable Field List to the Drop Data Items Here area on the worksheet

The final step in creating your report is to filter the list of stores so that only data for Store #2 is displayed.

Step 5	*Click*	the Store filter list arrow in cell B1 (the Page fields area)
Step 6	*Click*	Store #2
Step 7	*Click*	OK

The filtered data on your screen should look similar to Figure 12-8.

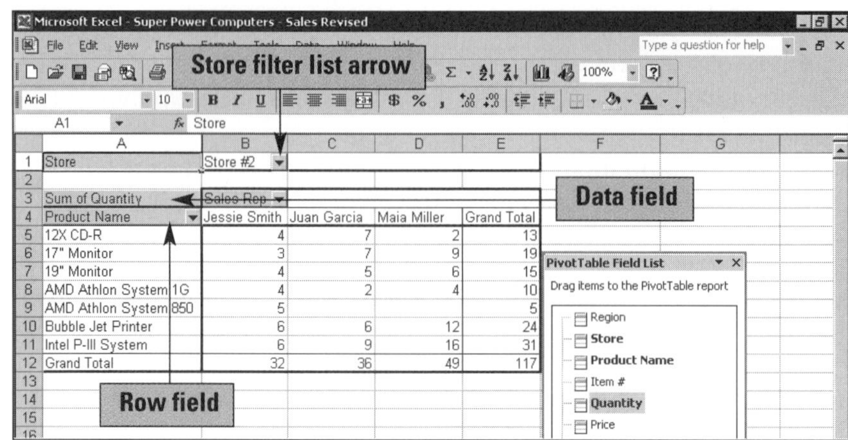

FIGURE 12-8
Filtered PivotTable Report

Step 8	***Rename***	the sheet tab PivotTable
Step 9	***Save***	the workbook

An employee from Super Power Computers' Sales Department has just called and asked for the total sales by store. You can quickly gather this information by modifying your PivotTable report.

12.c Modifying a PivotTable Report

The real power of a PivotTable report lies in the variety of ways in which you can quickly display data by rearranging fields included in the report. You also can format PivotTable results easily. Now you want to view the total sales by each employee. To modify the PivotTable report:

MOUSE TIP

Access the PivotTable Field dialog box by right-clicking any cell in the PivotTable or a field name button and selecting Field Settings.

Step 1	***Drag***	the Sum of Quantity button off the PivotTable to a blank area of the worksheet

This field is not necessary for the new report you want to create. As you drag button off the PivotTable, a Remove Field pointer appears to indicate that you are removing the field from your report.

Step 2	***Drag***	the Total Sales button to the Drop Data Items Here area

The PivotTable displays the total sales by each sales rep. You want to display this information in the Accounting format.

Step 3	*Verify*	that cell A3 is selected
Step 4	*Click*	the Field Settings button on the PivotTable toolbar

The PivotTable Field dialog box opens and should look similar to Figure 12-9.

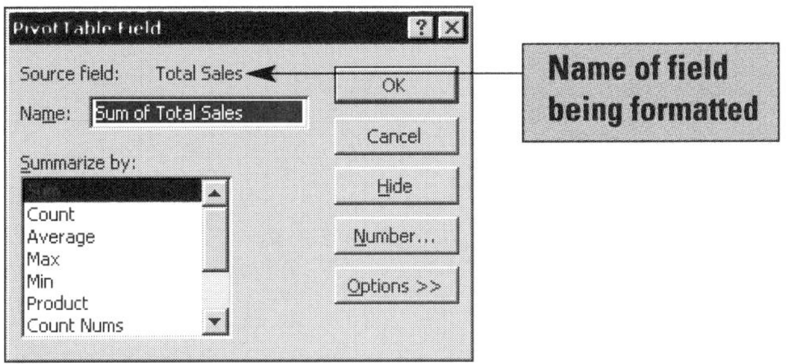

FIGURE 12-9
PivotTable Field Dialog Box

Step 5	*Click*	Number to open the Number tab of the Format Cells dialog box
Step 6	*Click*	Accounting in the Category: list

Applying this number format affects only the data in the Total Sales field. If you change the data in the report, the numerical format changes back to the default setting.

Step 7	*Click*	OK
Step 8	*Click*	OK

Rather than displaying the sales by sales rep, you want to show the total sales of each product by store.

Step 9	*Drag*	the Sales Rep field button off the PivotTable

When you remove the Sales Rep field, the Total column displays only the sum of all sales made at Store #2.

Step 10	*Drag*	the Store field from cell A1 (the Page Fields area) to cell B3 (the Column Fields area)

Using this report, it's easy to spot the leader in sales for a given product. Your screen should look similar to Figure 12-10.

QUICK TIP

You can change the type of summary from Sum to Count, Min, Max, or Average or alter a number of other statistical summaries by selecting an item in the Summarize by list. The Options button allows you to change the way that data is displayed. For example, you might want to show the difference between sales amounts through a store-to-store comparison.

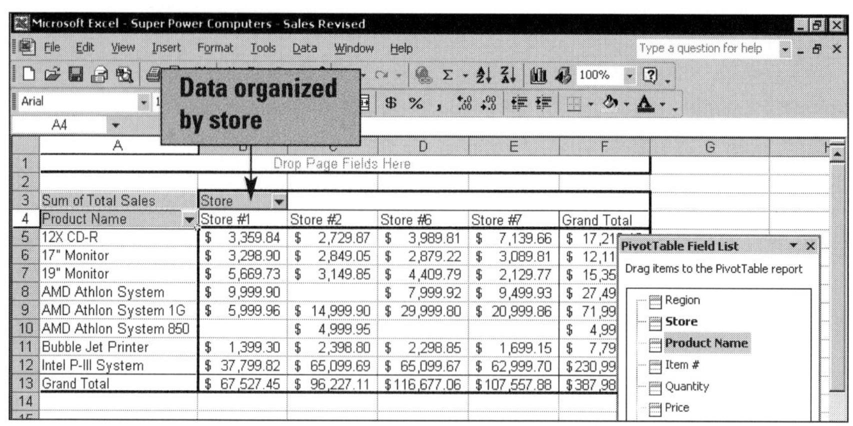

FIGURE 12-10
Column Fields Organized by Store

Step 11	*Drag*	the Store field to the left of the Product Name field (cell A4)

You have successfully reorganized the report, providing a different view of the same data. This view is organized more like an outline, with the Store names appearing in column A and the products sold at each store listed in column B. Your screen should look similar to Figure 12-11.

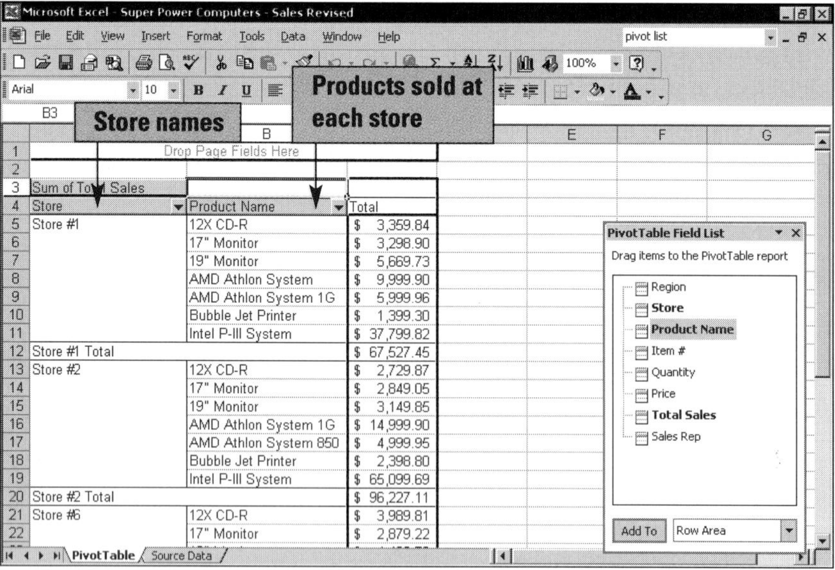

FIGURE 12-11
Row Fields Organized by Store with Subtotals

Displaying and Hiding Detail in a Field

Excel provides many ways to display selected data in a PivotTable report. One feature allows you to extract selected data into a new table on a new worksheet. The manager of Store #2 would like to see a detailed report of 12X CD-R sales for her store. Using your PivotTable report, you can quickly extract the desired data to a new worksheet.

To show detailed data:

Step 1	***Click***	cell C13
Step 2	***Click***	the Show Detail button on the PivotTable toolbar
Step 3	***Click***	cell A1 in the new worksheet
Step 4	***Rename***	the sheet tab Store #2 CD-R

The new worksheet contains a detailed summary of 12X CD-R sales at Store #2. Your worksheet should look similar to Figure 12-12.

Region	Store	Product Name	Item #	Quantity	Price	Total Sales	Sales Rep
East Coast	Store #2	12X CD-R	130	3	209.99	629.97	Juan Garcia
East Coast	Store #2	12X CD-R	130	4	209.99	839.96	Jessie Smith
East Coast	Store #2	12X CD-R	130	2	209.99	419.98	Maia Miller
East Coast	Store #2	12X CD-R	130	4	209.99	839.96	Juan Garcia

FIGURE 12-12
Detail Data Extracted from PivotTable

MENU TIP

You can hide data from the Data menu. Point to Group and Outline on the Data menu, then click Hide Detail.

You also can alter the display of data so as to hide selected records. For example, suppose you want to see only a summary of Store #1 and Store #2, but detailed reports for Store #6 and Store #12. The process used to modify the PivotTable is similar to collapsing levels in an outline. To hide data:

Step 1	***Click***	the PivotTable sheet tab
Step 2	***Click***	cell A11

You can actually click any cell in the range A5:B11. The PivotTable has a format similar to that of an outline. Each of the cells in the range belongs to Store #1. Selecting Hide Detail while any of these cells is active hides the details for the entire level.

MOUSE TIP

You can hide data using a shortcut menu. Right-click any of the cells whose data you want to hide to access the PivotTable shortcut menu. Point to Group and Show Detail, then click Hide Detail.

Step 3	***Click***	the Hide Detail button on the PivotTable toolbar
Step 4	***Click***	cell A6
Step 5	***Click***	the Hide Detail button on the PivotTable toolbar

Unlike outlines, hiding data in a PivotTable does not simply hide rows. The data is actually removed from the PivotTable until you choose to display the data again. To show the details for Store #2:

Step 6	*Verify*	that cell A6 is still the active cell
Step 7	*Click*	the Show Detail button on the PivotTable toolbar
Step 8	*Click*	cell A5
Step 9	*Click*	the Show Detail button on the PivotTable toolbar

Show Detail acts differently when used to show the detail of a row or column field. Rather than extracting the data to a new worksheet, it includes additional data within the PivotTable report. As you can see, Excel offers a variety of ways in which to organize data with PivotTables. Fortunately, rearranging reports is a simple drag-and-drop matter that has no effect on your source data. As a result, you can experiment, worry-free, with as many different combinations as you can dream up.

Step 10	*Save*	the workbook

Your PivotTable report will be used in a presentation to the Sales Department. Next, you apply AutoFormats to a PivotTable report.

12.d Formatting a PivotTable Report

Recall that AutoFormats enable you to quickly format tables. PivotTables can also be formatted similarly to other tables. For PivotTables, AutoFormat provides 10 report styles and 10 table styles. Applying AutoFormats rearranges the field layouts to a preset scheme. To format the PivotTable with an AutoFormat:

Step 1	*Click*	the Format Report button on the PivotTable toolbar to open the AutoFormat dialog box
Step 2	*Scroll*	down the list of AutoFormats
Step 3	*Click*	Table 8

Step 4	*Click*	OK

The report is reorganized and formatted using different font, border, and text orientation settings to emphasize the store names and grand totals in row 13. Table AutoFormat styles arrange the data horizontally in the worksheet.

Step 5	*Click*	cell A1

The PivotTable is deselected, and the Page Fields area disappears because the current report does not require its presence. The field buttons on the PivotTable toolbar are not active while the active cell remains outside the PivotTable report. Your screen should look similar to Figure 12-13.

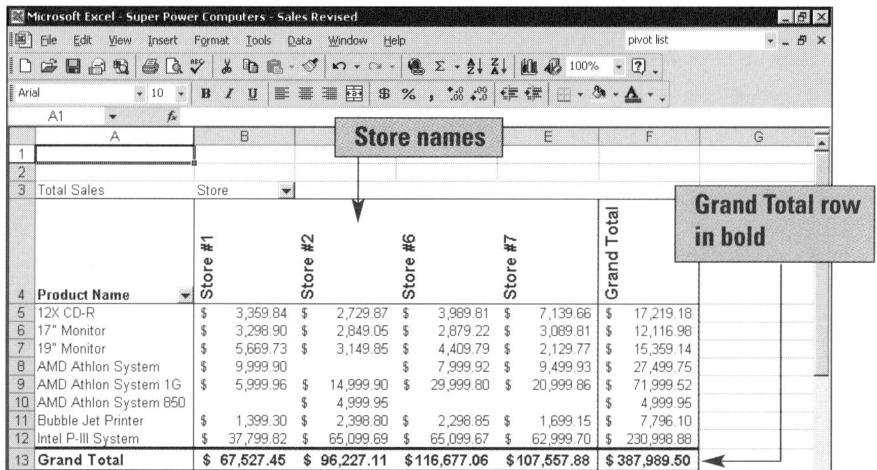

Total Sales	Store				
Product Name	Store #1	Store #2	Store #6	Store #7	Grand Total
12X CD-R	$ 3,359.84	$ 2,729.87	$ 3,989.81	$ 7,139.66	$ 17,219.18
17" Monitor	$ 3,298.90	$ 2,849.05	$ 2,879.22	$ 3,089.81	$ 12,116.98
19" Monitor	$ 5,669.73	$ 3,149.85	$ 4,409.79	$ 2,129.77	$ 15,359.14
AMD Athlon System	$ 9,999.90		$ 7,999.92	$ 9,499.93	$ 27,499.75
AMD Athlon System 1G	$ 5,999.96	$ 14,999.90	$ 29,999.80	$ 20,999.86	$ 71,999.52
AMD Athlon System 850		$ 4,999.95			$ 4,999.95
Bubble Jet Printer	$ 1,399.30	$ 2,398.80	$ 2,298.85	$ 1,699.15	$ 7,796.10
Intel P-III System	$ 37,799.82	$ 65,099.69	$ 65,099.67	$ 62,999.70	$ 230,998.88
Grand Total	**$ 67,527.45**	**$ 96,227.11**	**$116,677.06**	**$107,557.88**	**$ 387,989.50**

FIGURE 12-13
AutoFormat Table Style Arranges Data Horizontally

MOUSE TIP

You can turn the Fields display (the blue borders around the PivotTable field areas) on and off by clicking the Hide/Show Field List button on the PivotTable toolbar.

Rather than view your data in a simple table layout, you would rather examine the data in a report format.

Step 6	*Activate*	cell A4 in the PivotTable report
Step 7	*Click*	the Format Report button on the PivotTable toolbar
Step 8	*Click*	Report 4
Step 9	*Click*	OK
Step 10	*Click*	cell A1 to deselect the PivotTable report

The PivotTable is rearranged in a report style with a new color format. Report AutoFormat styles arrange the data vertically in the worksheet. Your screen should look similar to Figure 12-14.

FIGURE 12-14
AutoFormat Report Style Arranges Data Vertically

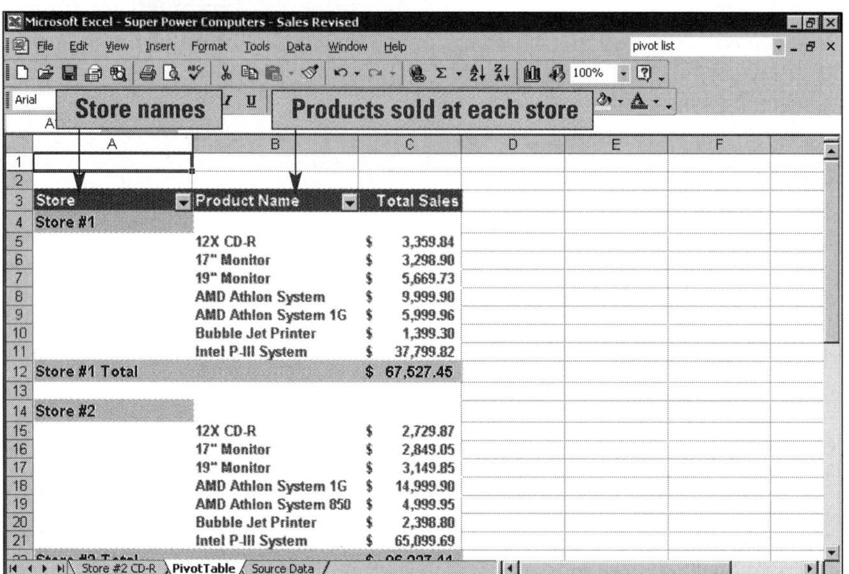

Step 11	***Preview***	the worksheet
Step 12	***Print***	the worksheet
Step 13	***Save***	the workbook

This report will be very useful to the Sales Department. You also can organize the data in a PivotChart, based on the PivotTable report.

12.e Creating PivotChart Reports

PivotCharts present another option for summarizing data. **PivotCharts** combine the features of both charts and PivotTable reports. Field buttons, which you can rearrange to modify how data is grouped and displayed, appear on the PivotChart. When you reorganize PivotChart fields, you also alter the underlying PivotTable structure. In constructing a PivotChart, you can either use an existing PivotTable report or create a new PivotTable report when you create a PivotChart.

To create a PivotChart from an existing PivotTable:

Step 1	***Activate***	any cell within the PivotTable
Step 2	***Click***	the Chart Wizard button on the Standard or PivotTable toolbar

A PivotChart is created on a new worksheet named Chart1. When you use the Chart Wizard to create a chart from a PivotTable, the Chart Wizard makes all decisions for you.

Step 3	***Rename***	the chart tab PivotChart
Step 4	***Close***	the PivotTable Field List by clicking the Close button in the title bar, if necessary
Step 5	***Drag***	the Chart toolbar by its title bar so it docks next to the PivotChart toolbar

The Chart Wizard creates the new chart, which should look similar to Figure 12-15. The field buttons employed in the PivotTable are automatically placed on the chart. You can rearrange the field buttons on the chart to modify the data display.

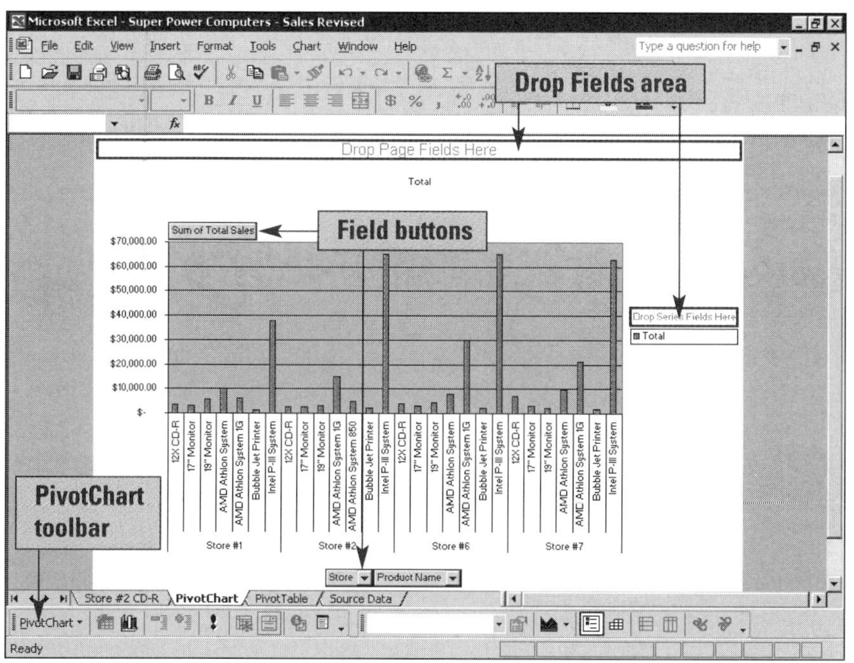

FIGURE 12-15
PivotChart

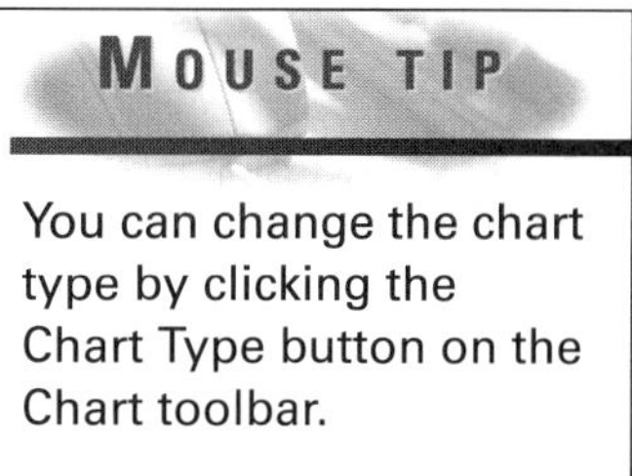

You can change the chart type by clicking the Chart Type button on the Chart toolbar.

You decide to change the chart to show total sales for stores located in New York.

Step 6	***Drag***	the Store field button to the Page Fields area at the top of the chart (you may need to scroll)
Step 7	***Click***	the Store field button list arrow
Step 8	***Click***	Store #6
Step 9	***Click***	OK
Step 10	***Click***	in the gray area outside the chart to deselect the chart

The updated chart on your screen should look similar to Figure 12-16.

FIGURE 12-16
Modified PivotChart

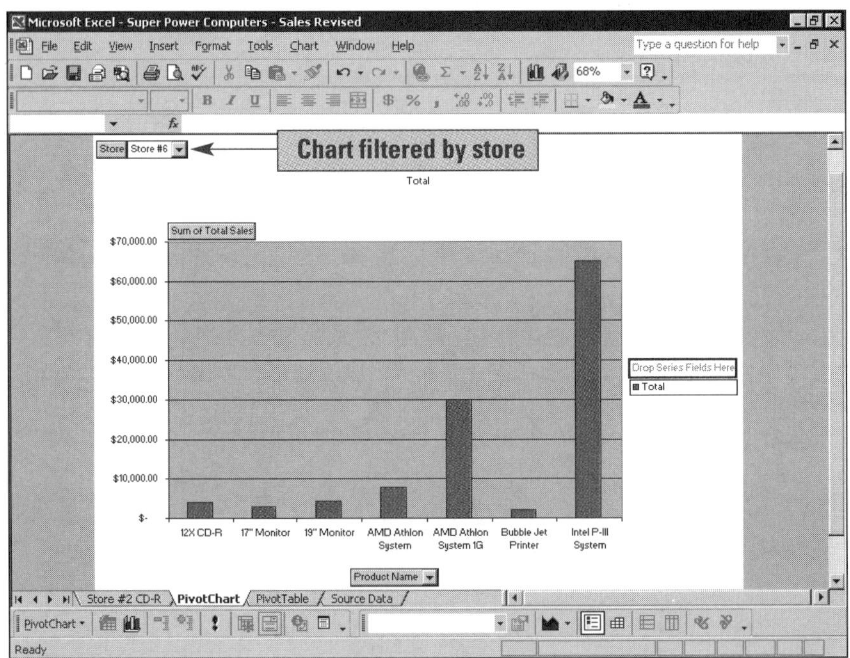

Step 11	***Print***	the PivotChart
Step 12	***Click***	the PivotTable sheet tab

When you modify a PivotChart, you also change the PivotTable on which the chart is based. Thus the PivotTable now shows the total sales for stores in New York.

Step 13	***Save***	the workbook and close it

PivotTables and PivotCharts are very powerful tools for quickly summarizing data.

Summary

- Data analysis tools enable you to examine data from a variety of angles using statistical calculations.
- You can create PivotTable reports with the PivotTable and PivotChart Wizard to quickly display data in a variety of report layouts.
- You can modify PivotTables by dragging and dropping fields at different locations on the PivotTable report.
- You can extract data from a PivotTable by using Show Detail on a Data Field item.
- You can hide and display data in row and column field items organized into an outline.
- You can use AutoFormats to format a PivotTable report with preset report and table styles.
- You can create a PivotChart based on a PivotTable report. Drag and drop fields on the PivotChart to modify the chart's data display.

Commands Review

Action	Menu Bar	Shortcut Menu	Toolbar	Task Pane	Keyboard
Use data analysis tools	Tools, Data Analysis				ALT + T, D
Create a PivotTable or PivotChart report	Data, PivotTable and PivotChart Report	Right-click a PivotTable, then PivotChart	Select a PivotTable, then PivotTable		ALT + D, P
Show detail	Data, Group and Outline, Show Detail	Group and Outline, Show Detail			ALT + D, G, S
Hide detail	Data, Group and Outline, Hide Detail	Group and Outline, Hide Detail			ALT + D, G, H
Format a PivotTable		Format Report			
Change field settings of a PivotTable		Field Settings			
Refresh data in a PivotTable or PivotChart	Data, Refresh Data	Refresh Data			ALT + D, R

Concepts Review

Circle the correct answer.

1. Clicking the Show Detail button on the PivotTable toolbar while the selected cell is in detail data:
- [a] extracts the supporting data to a new worksheet.
- [b] shows the supporting data in the PivotTable.
- [c] hides the supporting data in the PivotTable.
- [d] extracts the supporting data to the same worksheet as the PivotTable.

2. Which of the following is *not* calculated using the Descriptive Statistics analysis tool?
- [a] mean
- [b] median
- [c] sum
- [d] average

3. Fields that you specify in a PivotTable or PivotChart report are represented by:
- [a] field buttons.
- [b] field icons.
- [c] data labels.
- [d] field menus.

4. PivotTables can be created from:
- [a] only the current workbook.
- [b] only an external file, such as a workbook or database.
- [c] only another PivotTable or PivotChart report.
- [d] the current workbook, an external file, or another PivotTable or PivotChart report.

5. When you modify a PivotChart, the underlying PivotTable:
- [a] is not affected.
- [b] disappears.
- [c] is reorganized to match the PivotChart changes.
- [d] is copied to prevent unwanted changes.

6. Field buttons can be removed from a PivotTable or PivotChart by:
- [a] double-clicking the field button.
- [b] right-clicking the field button and selecting Delete.
- [c] dragging the field button off the report or chart.
- [d] clicking Delete Field Button on the Edit menu.

7. To summarize data for one item at a time, drag the field button to the:
- [a] Column Fields area.
- [b] Row Fields area.
- [c] Data Items area.
- [d] Page Fields area.

8. When you want to show a field as a column header of a PivotTable, drag the field button to the:
- [a] Column area.
- [b] Row area.
- [c] Data area.
- [d] Page area.

9. To see any data in a PivotTable, you need to drag a minimum of:
- [a] one item.
- [b] two items.
- [c] three items.
- [d] four items.

10. To change the number format in a PivotTable report, use the:
- [a] Format Report button.
- [b] PivotTable Wizard button.
- [c] Field Settings button.
- [d] Format Cells dialog box.

Circle **T** if the statement is true or **F** if the statement is false.

T F 1. Rearranging PivotTable fields has no effect on the data used to create the PivotTable report.

T F 2. Rearranging PivotChart fields has no effect on the PivotTable used to create the PivotChart.

T F 3. Using an AutoFormat Report style has no effect on the PivotTable layout, other than changing attributes like colors, borders, and number formatting.

T F 4. Using an AutoFormat Table style has no effect on the PivotTable layout, other than changing attributes like colors, borders, and number formatting.

T F 5. Data analysis reports contain formulas that are automatically updated when the data is changed.

T F 6. The PivotTable and PivotChart Wizard has a total of four steps.

T F 7. PivotTables and PivotCharts are created on new sheets by default.

T F 8. When you are placing multiple field buttons in a row or column, the arrangement of the field buttons does not affect the display of the data.

T F 9. You can change the name of a field button.

T F 10. To remove a field button from a PivotTable or PivotChart, drag it off the report or chart.

Skills Review

Exercise 1

1. Open the *Sweet Tooth Sales to Stores Q2* workbook located on the Data Disk.

2. Sweet Tooth's warehouse Store needs to know the quantity of each item being sold, so that it can keep adequate supplies in the warehouse. Create a new PivotTable report based on the data in cells A1:H97 using the PivotTable Wizard.

a. Use default settings for all three steps of the wizard.

b. Rename the tab PivotTable Report.

c. Drag the Item # field button to the Row fields area.

d. Drag the Quantity field button to the Data Items area.

3. Format the report using the Table 5 AutoFormat style.

4. Print the PivotTable report.

5. Save the workbook as *Sweet Tooth Sales to Stores Warehouse*, and then close it.

Exercise 2

1. Open the *Sweet Tooth Sales to Stores Warehouse* workbook that you created in Exercise 1.

2. Shipping needs to know the quantity of each item being shipped to stores in Minnesota. Using the PivotTable Report tab, do the following:

a. Remove all field buttons from the PivotTable report.

b. Drag the Division field button to the Page Fields area.

c. Select Minnesota from the filter list.

d. Drag the Item # field button to the Row area.

e. Drag the Store field button to the Row area and drop it to the left of the Item # field button.

f. Drag the Quantity field button to the Data area.

3. Format your report using Report 4 style.
4. Print the report.
5. Save the workbook as *Sweet Tooth Sales to Stores Shipping*, and then close it.

Exercise 3 C

1. Open the *Sweet Tooth Sales to Stores Shipping* workbook that you created in Exercise 2.
2. Marketing has asked you to figure out which stores are buying the most in each region.

   a. Remove all field buttons from the PivotTable.

   b. Drag the Store field button to the Columns area.

   c. Drag the Total Sales field button to the Data area.

   d. Drag the Region field button to the Rows area.
3. Print your report.
4. Save the workbook as *Sweet Tooth Sales to Stores Marketing* and then close it.

Exercise 4 C

1. Open the *Sweet Tooth Sales to Stores Marketing* workbook that you created in Exercise 3.
2. Create a PivotChart based on the PivotTable report.
3. Change the chart type to Clustered Column with a 3-D visual effect.
4. Drag the Store field button to the Drop Page Fields Here area at the top of the chart.
5. Drag the Region button off the PivotTable.
6. Drag the Sales Rep field button from the PivotTable Field List to the Drop Category Fields Here area at the bottom of the chart.
7. Change the chart title to "Sales by Rep."
8. Change the chart title's font size to 20 and the style to Bold.
9. Rename the chart sheet tab to "Sales Rep Chart," then print the chart.
10. Save the workbook as *Sweet Tooth Sales to Stores Marketing 2* and then close it.

Exercise 5 C

1. Open the *Sweet Tooth Sales to Stores Marketing 2* workbook that you created in Exercise 4. Management would like to see a breakdown of sales by sales representative within each store.
2. Click the PivotTable Report sheet tab.
3. Format the PivotTable using the Accounting number format.
4. Drag the Division Field button to the left of the Sales Rep field in the Row Fields area.
5. Print the report.
6. Save the workbook as *Sweet Tooth Sales to Stores Management* and then close it.

Exercise 6 

1. Open the *Sweet Tooth Sales to Stores Management* workbook that you created in Exercise 5.
2. Drag the Sales Rep field button off the PivotTable.
3. Drag the Store field button to the right of the Division button in the Row Fields area. (*Hint:* Position the mouse pointer below the Division button to the right.)
4. Format the report using the Table 2 style.
5. Print the report.
6. Save the workbook as *Sweet Tooth Sales to Stores Management 2* and then close it.

Exercise 7 

1. Open the *Sweet Tooth Sales to Stores Management 2* workbook that you created in Exercise 6.
2. Click the Source Data tab.
3. Generate a Descriptive Statistics report using cells G1:G97 as your source.
4. Place the report on a new worksheet called Stats, using Summary Statistics.
5. AutoFit columns A and B.
6. Print the report.
7. Save the workbook as *Sweet Tooth Sales to Stores Accounting* and then close it.

Exercise 8 

1. Open the *Sweet Tooth Sales to Stores Accounting* workbook that you created in Exercise 7.
2. Click the PivotTable Report sheet tab.
3. Display the PivotTable toolbar, if necessary.
4. Drag the Sales Rep field button to the Page Fields area.
5. Filter the Sales Rep to show data for Portia Greene only.
6. Print the worksheet.
7. Save the workbook as *Sweet Tooth Sales to Stores Personnel* and then close it.

Case Problems

Problem 1 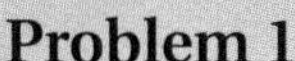  

You own a computer retail store. Connect to the Internet and search the Web for computer component prices. Find at least three items in the following categories: hard drive, RAM, monitors, printers. Using the prices and product descriptions that your search turns up, create a table of information using the following column headings: Category, Item Description, Price, Q1 Quantity, Q2 Quantity, Q3 Quantity, Q4 Quantity, and Total Sales (use a formula to multiply Price by the sum of the quantity columns). Use fictitious sales data for the each quarter's quantities. Create a PivotTable that shows total sales for each item by category. Save the workbook as *Computer Sales*, and then print and close it.

Problem 2

You own a successful catering business. Create a table to keep track of your clients. Include column headings for party name, menu item, quantity, price, and total sale. Create a menu of four items with prices for each item. Create fictitious data for three separate parties and indicate how many of each menu item were ordered for each of the parties. Enter a price for each item, then use a formula to calculate the total sales for each item. Create a PivotChart showing which items are bestsellers. Save the workbook as *Catering*, and then print and close it.

Problem 3

You are in charge of recordkeeping at a local veterinarian's office. You must keep track of owner names, pet names, pet visit dates, treatment, and treatment cost. Create five pet/owner combinations. Use fictitious data to show each pet visiting the veterinarian's office at least twice for different treatments. Create a PivotTable showing each pet, the treatments the animal received, and the amount due for treatments provided. Save the workbook as *Veterinarian*, and then print and close it.

Problem 4 

Connect to the Internet and search the Web for PivotTable tutorials. Print at least one tutorial you find on the Web.

Problem 5 

You work at a busy convenience store. Create a workbook to keep track of sales for 20 items grouped in four different categories. Use fictitious sales data for seven days. Create a PivotTable showing the total items sold each day by category. Save the workbook as *Convenience Store*, and then print and close it.

Problem 6 

Connect to the Internet and search the Web for information about the latest trends in spreadsheet applications and/or office suites. Print Web pages containing reviews of at least two competing products.

Problem 7

You are a teacher analyzing the latest test scores. Create a workbook with 30 scores between 40 and 100. Use data analysis to generate a Rank and Percentile report. Save the workbook as *Test Scores*, and then print and close it.

Problem 8

You are analyzing sales made by sales representatives in your company. Create a workbook with fictitious sales figures for 10 sales reps. Use data analysis to generate a Descriptive Statistics report. Save the workbook as *Sales Statistics*, and then print and close it.

Working with Charts and the Drawing Tools

Chapter Overview

You've already learned to create and print charts. In this chapter, you explore advanced chart types, such as the XY scatter and area charts, and features such as combining two chart types on one chart. Charts are not the only way to dress up a workbook. Using the drawing tools, you can create conceptual and organizational diagrams. You can use the drawing tools to insert company logos and even create newsletters and design colorful visual worksheets.

Learning Objectives

- Create special charts
- Modify charts
- Use the drawing tools
- Create and edit a conceptual diagram

Case profile

At Super Power Computers, company sales are analyzed each quarter to see which stores are selling the highest quantity of goods and which stores are bringing in the most revenue. You are to analyze this data using special types of charts to determine which stores are generating the most income on the fewest sales. You also need to create an organizational chart to show the various leadership positions at Super Power Computers.

13.a Creating Special Charts

Charts are a way to visually represent numerical data. For most people, charts make data easier to understand. In this section, you learn about two special types of charts, area and XY scatter charts.

Creating an Area Chart

Area charts are used to show the magnitude of change over time. In the workbook *Super Power Computers - Sales Comparison*, data for all 16 stores is listed. Among this data is the percentage of each store's sales for the last three quarters. An area chart illustrates this data more clearly than looking at the numerical data. You have a worksheet that lists the total number of sales transactions and the total income from those transactions. You need to create an area chart to illustrate these percentages for the last two quarters. To create an area chart:

Step 1	***Open***	the *Super Power Computers - Sales Comparison* workbook located on the Data Disk
Step 2	***Save***	the workbook as *Super Power Computers - Sales Comparison Revised*

The percentages calculated in columns D:F indicate the percentage of each store's contribution to the company's total sales.

Step 3	***Select***	the range D5:E21
Step 4	***Click***	the Chart Wizard button on the Standard toolbar
Step 5	***Click***	Area in the Chart type: list
Step 6	***Verify***	that Stacked Area is selected in the Chart sub-type: area (first row, second column)
Step 7	***Click***	Next >

You want to show the store numbers as the Category (X) labels. You can do this in Step 2 of the Chart Wizard using the Series tab.

Step 8	***Click***	the Series tab
Step 9	***Click***	in the Category (X) axis labels: text box
Step 10	***Select***	A6:A21
Step 11	***Click***	Next >

Step 12	***Click***	Next >
Step 13	***Click***	the As new sheet: option button
Step 14	***Key***	Percentage Chart in the As new sheet: box
Step 15	***Click***	Finish

Your workbook should look similar to Figure 13-1.

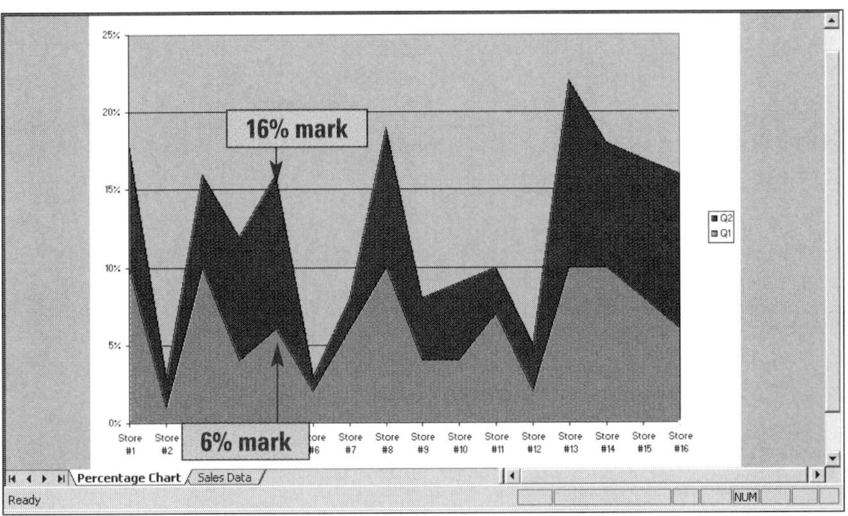

FIGURE 13-1
Area Chart

This chart makes it easy to see each store's contribution to the company's overall sales for the past two quarters. By examining the area chart, you can see that store #5, which accounted for approximately 6% of the company's sales in the first quarter, had a good second quarter, accounting for 10% of the company's sales.

Creating an XY Scatter Chart

Another special type of chart is the XY scatter chart. XY scatter charts are useful for graphing clusters of data. A common example of this use in the computer industry is determining the overall value of a computer system by charting the system cost against the overall system speed. This type of evaluation enables customers to determine whether they are getting a good deal. You use the scatter chart to evaluate which stores are generating the most revenue on the fewest sales. To create an XY scatter chart:

Step 1	***Select***	the range B5:C21 on the Sales Data worksheet
Step 2	***Open***	the Chart Wizard
Step 3	***Click***	XY (Scatter) in the Chart type: list

Step 4	*Verify*	that Scatter is selected in the Chart sub-type: area (first row)
Step 5	*Click*	Next >
Step 6	*Click*	Next >
Step 7	*Click*	the Titles tab, if necessary
Step 8	*Key*	Total Revenue by Number of Sales in the Chart title: text box
Step 9	*Key*	Number of Sales in the Value (X) axis: text box
Step 10	*Key*	Revenue in the Value (Y) axis: text box

Next, you want to place the data from column B next to each point in the chart to make identification easier.

Step 11	*Click*	the Data Labels tab
Step 12	*Click*	the X Value check box to insert a check mark
Step 13	*Click*	Next >
Step 14	*Add*	the chart as a new sheet named Revenue by Sales
Step 15	*Click*	Finish

The XY scatter chart is added to the worksheet, as shown in Figure 13-2. This chart makes it relatively easy to find a few standouts.

FIGURE 13-2
XY Scatter Chart

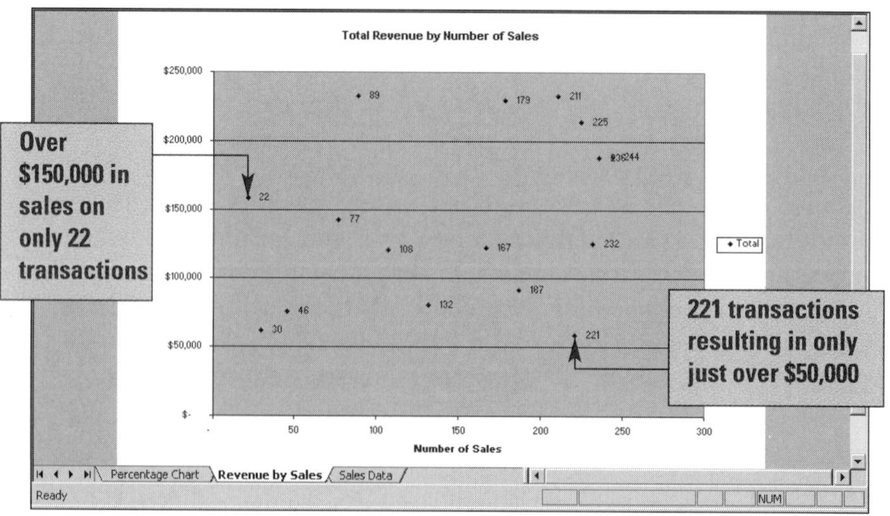

13.b Modifying Charts

There are many ways to modify charts in Excel. You can add a data series to or remove it from a chart after it has been created. You also can combine chart types to show different kinds of data on the same chart.

Adding, Deleting, and Moving a Data Series

Once a chart is created, you may want to add, remove, or change the data series used in the chart. In the area chart, you are currently displaying two data series. You want to add a third. To add a data series:

Step 1	***Right-click***	the area chart on the Percentage Chart sheet tab
Step 2	***Click***	Source Data
Step 3	***Click***	the Series tab

Your Source Data dialog box should look similar to Figure 13-3. You use the Series tab to add, remove, or change the location of data series used in a chart. Q1 and Q2 are already listed. You need to add another series for the Q3 data in column F.

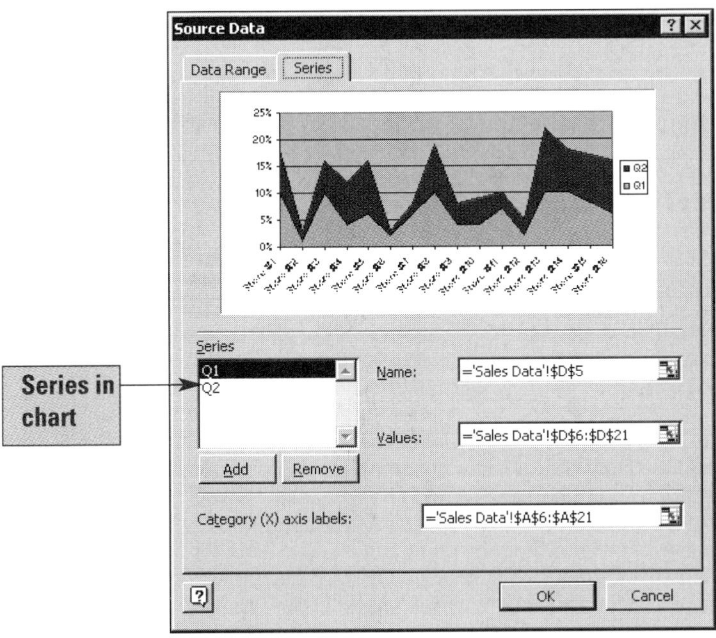

FIGURE 13-3
Series Tab of the Source Data Dialog Box

> **QUICK TIP**
>
> To remove a series, select the series name on the Series tab in the Source Data dialog box, then click Remove. To move a series, highlight the series name, collapse the dialog box in the Values text box, select a new range in your worksheet, expand the dialog box again, and click OK.

Step 4	*Click*	Add
Step 5	*Click*	the Collapse dialog button in the Name: text box
Step 6	*Click*	cell F5 on the Sales Data worksheet
Step 7	*Click*	the Expand dialog button in the Source Data - Name: text box
Step 8	*Click*	the Collapse dialog button in the Values: text box:
Step 9	*Select*	the range F6:F21 on the Sales Data worksheet
Step 10	*Click*	the Expand dialog button in the Source Data - Values: text box
Step 11	*Click*	OK

The chart is updated to include the new series. To make the data clearer, you decide to add value data labels to the chart.

Step 12	*Right-click*	in a gray area in the chart
Step 13	*Click*	Chart Options
Step 14	*Click*	the Data Labels tab, if necessary
Step 15	*Click*	the Value check box to insert a check mark
Step 16	*Click*	OK

The percentage values are added beneath each data point in the chart.

Combining Chart Types on One Chart

Combining chart types can be a good way to compare data. The Store Sales sheet tab includes some other data that can be effectively shown using a combination chart. To combine chart types:

Step 1	*Verify*	that the range B5:C21 on the Sales Data worksheet is selected
Step 2	*Open*	the Chart Wizard
Step 3	*Click*	the Custom Types tab
Step 4	*Click*	Line - Column on 2 Axes in the Chart type: list (you may need to scroll)
Step 5	*Click*	Next >

Step 6	***Click***	the Series tab
Step 7	***Click***	in the Category (X) labels: text box
Step 8	***Select***	the range A6:A21
Step 9	***Click***	Next >
Step 10	***Click***	Next >
Step 11	***Add***	the chart as a new sheet called Revenue by Sales 2
Step 12	***Click***	Finish

The chart, shown in Figure 13-4, makes it easy to see that Stores #12 and #16 had great total sales on relatively few sales transactions.

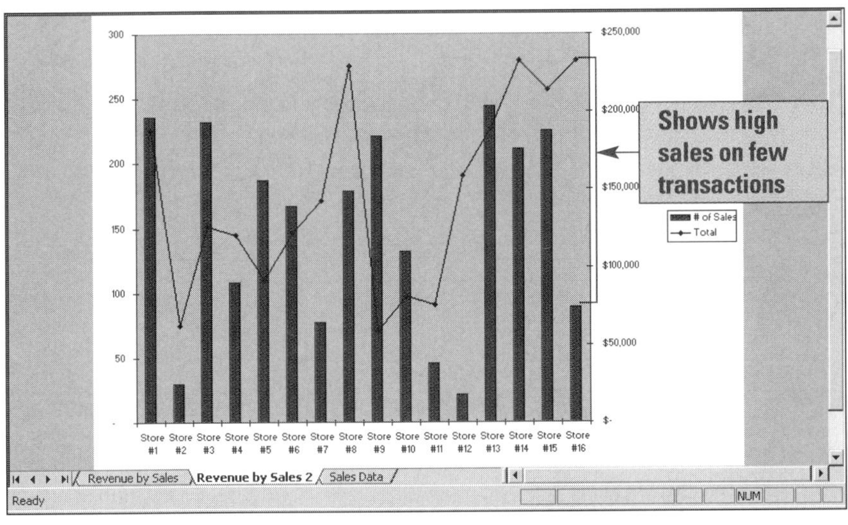

FIGURE 13-4
Combination Chart

Step 13	***Save***	the workbook and close it

13.c Using the Drawing Tools

The Excel drawing tools help you create a variety of useful diagrams and enhance worksheets and charts. **Clip art** is ready-made graphics you can insert in a worksheet. Office XP includes the **Clip Organizer**, a feature that indexes clip art on your computer and on the Web, making it easier to find the graphic you want to use. **AutoShapes** are simple outlined shapes, such as squares, circles, arrows, and banners, that you can insert in your worksheet. The AutoShape called a connector line helps you create diagrams.

MOUSE TIP

You can use the Zoom button list box on the Standard toolbar to zoom a worksheet from 10% to 400%.

Inserting Clip Art Objects

Using clip art, you create a network diagram for Super Power Computers' central office. A network diagram is useful as a map showing how computers on the network communicate with one another. You want to add a network diagram to a workbook that contains information about the computer equipment used in Super Power Computers' central office. To open the workbook:

Step 1	***Open***	the *Super Power Computers - Computer Equipment Inventory* workbook located on the Data Disk
Step 2	***Edit***	cell A1 to read "Central Office Computer Equipment Diagram"
Step 3	***Save***	the file as *Super Power Computers - Computer Equipment Diagram*

This file has been zoomed to 75% to allow you to view more of the worksheet area. Several objects are already inserted in this worksheet, but you need to add a printer and a laptop to the diagram. You insert a printer by using the Clip Organizer. To open the Clip Organizer and search for appropriate clips art:

Step 1	***Click***	the Drawing button on the Standard toolbar to display the Drawing toolbar if necessary
Step 2	***Click***	the Insert Clip Art button on the Drawing toolbar

CAUTION TIP

You might see a message asking if you want to catalog the media on your computer. This process takes a while, as your computer is searched for media that can be added to the Clip Organizer. If this message appears, click the Later button.

The Insert Clip Art task pane appears with search options to help you search through the Clip Organizer.

Step 3	***Key***	printer in the Search text: text box in the Insert Clip Art task pane

The Search in: list under Search Options allows you to specify which collections you search. These collections include Office Collections (clip art that comes with Office), My Collections (media on your computer that you have catalogued), and Web Collections (clip art available online). The Results should be: list allows you to limit the type of media searched, such as clip art, photographs, movies, or sounds.

Step 4	***Click***	the Search in: list arrow

Step 5	*Click*	the Web collections check box to remove the check mark, if necessary
Step 6	*Click*	anywhere in the task pane to close the list
Step 7	*Click*	the Results should be: list arrow
Step 8	*Click*	the Clip Art and Photographs check boxes to insert check marks, if necessary
Step 9	*Click*	the Movies and Sounds check boxes to remove the check marks, if necessary
Step 10	*Click*	anywhere in the task pane to close the list
Step 11	*Click*	Search in the task pane

MENU TIP

You can insert clip art from the Insert menu. Point to Picture, then click Clip Art to open the Insert ClipArt dialog box.

Any clips found that match the keyword are displayed in the task pane, and similar to the ones shown in Figure 13-5. (The clips on your screen may not match the one in the figure exactly.)

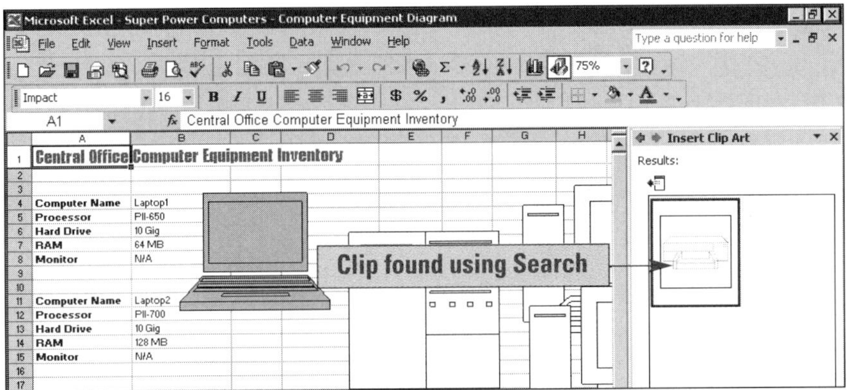

FIGURE 13-5
Insert Clip Art Task Pane

You can drag clips from the task pane right into your worksheet. When you point to a clip, a ScreenTip appears displaying information about the clip art, such as the file size and file type. To drag clip art from the task pane to the worksheet:

Step 1	*Point to*	the clip resembling a drawing of a printer in the task pane (if you don't have the printer clip art, drag a similar clip instead)
Step 2	*Drag*	the line art drawing of a printer clip art onto the worksheet near cell H26

As you drag the clip, a large dotted outline appears in your worksheet. Your clip will probably be much smaller than the outline seems to indicate. It may be difficult to accurately position the clip art with the task pane in the way. You can reposition a clip later.

You may want to browse for clip art rather than searching by keywords. The Clip Organizer indexes clip art by allowing you to add categories and keyword information to a media file. Its categories display related clips. For example, the Networking category displays clip art of several computers and computer peripherals, such as printers, scanners, and a CD-ROM drive.

Step 3	***Click***	the Clip Organizer link in the task pane
Step 4	***Click***	the + sign next to the Office Collections folder in the Collection List
Step 5	***Click***	the + sign next to the AutoShapes folder in the Collection List
Step 6	***Click***	the Networking folder

Clip Organizer categorizes clip art into categories and subcategories, and displays them as folders, even though the clip art might be stored in different locations on your computer. Your Clip Organizer should look similar to Figure 13-6.

FIGURE 13-6
Clip Organizer

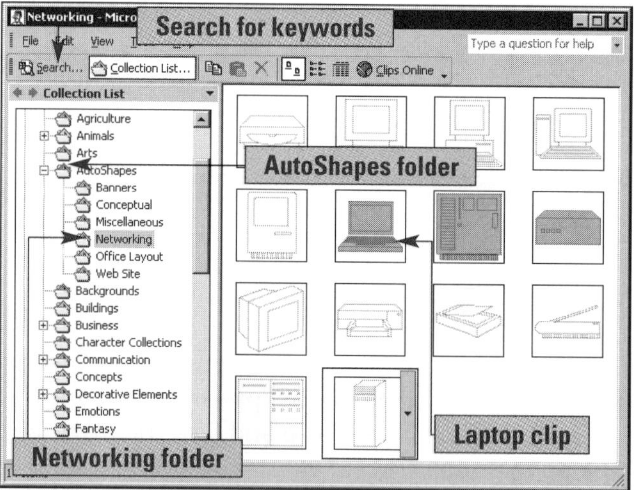

Step 7	***Point to***	the clip resembling a laptop computer
Step 8	***Drag***	the clip art image onto your worksheet near cell C13

The laptop images may overlap because they are too large, but you scale and reposition them later. After you drop the clip art, Clip Organizer minimizes itself on the taskbar.

Step 9	*Right-click*	the Clip Organizer button on the taskbar
Step 10	*Click*	Close
Step 11	*Close*	the Insert Clip Art task pane

QUICK TIP

You can switch between Clip Organizer and Excel or other open applications by pressing the ALT + TAB keys.

The Picture toolbar appears when you select a clip.

Scaling and Moving Objects

You can reposition and resize drawing objects. At present, the clips are too large for the area on your worksheet. You can select multiple objects for editing, by holding down the SHIFT key as you click each object. To select and resize the objects:

Step 1	*Press & hold*	the SHIFT key
Step 2	*Click*	each of the clips on the worksheet (a total of six) to select them (observe the sizing handles)
Step 3	*Right-click*	one of the objects
Step 4	*Click*	Format Object to open the Format Object dialog box
Step 5	*Click*	the Size tab

MOUSE TIP

If you need to remove an object from a multiple object selection, press and hold the SHIFT key as you click the object again.

The dialog box on your screen should look similar to Figure 13-7. When you modify the height or width of an object with lock aspect ratio turned on, the object scales equally in the other dimension.

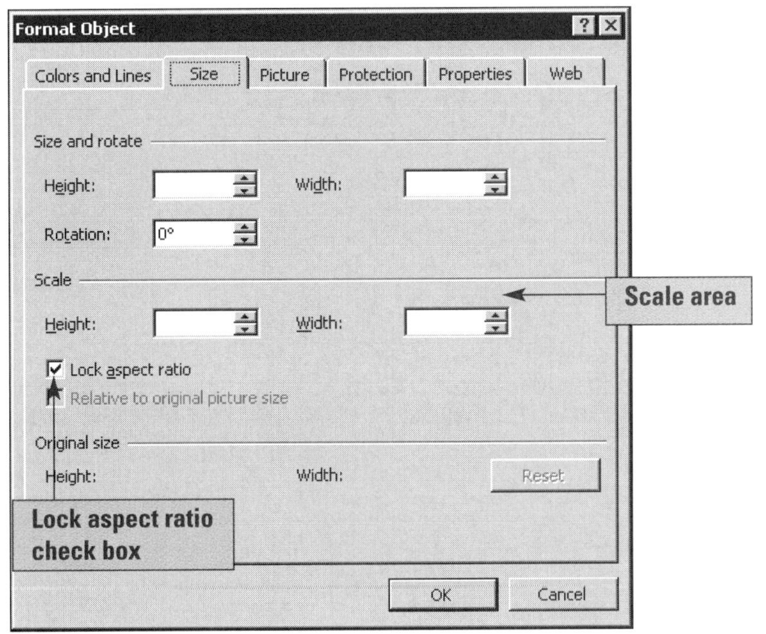

FIGURE 13-7
Size Tab in the Format Object Dialog Box

chapter thirteen

Step 6	***Click***	the Lock aspect ratio check box to insert a check mark, if necessary
Step 7	***Key***	65 in the Height: text box in the Scale group
Step 8	***Press***	the TAB key to move to the Width: text box and automatically adjust the width to 65%

The width automatically adjusts to the same percentage as the height because the Lock aspect ratio check box is checked.

Step 9	***Click***	OK
Step 10	***Observe***	that all of the objects are scaled to 65% of their original size
Step 11	***Press***	the ESC key to deselect the drawing objects

To move the printer object above its description in cells G26:H26:

Step 1	***Move***	the mouse pointer over the printer clip until it changes to a four-headed arrow move pointer
Step 2	***Drag***	the clip above row 26 in columns G and H

As you drag the clip, a dashed box matching the width and length of the actual clip appears, helping you to position the clip more precisely.

Step 3	***Follow***	Steps 1 and 2 to reposition the other objects as necessary to match Figure 13-8

FIGURE 13-8
Scaling and Moving Objects

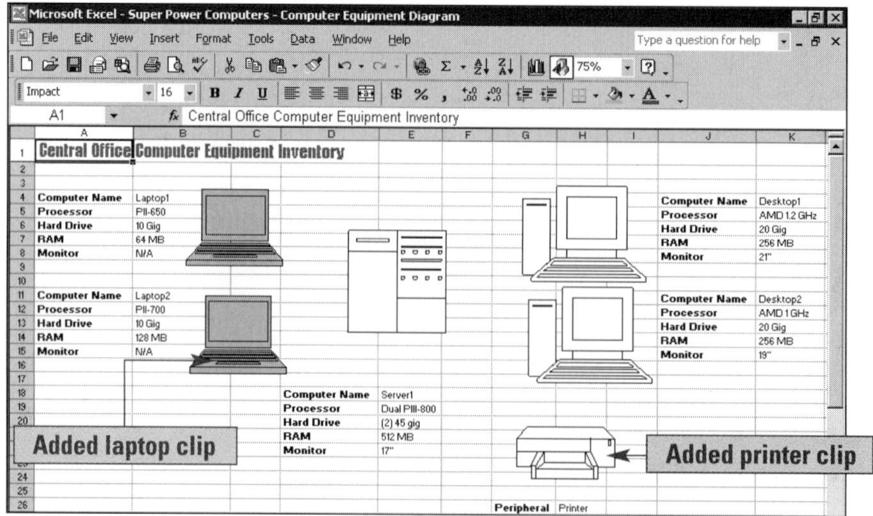

Using an AutoShape

AutoShapes come in a variety of styles and shapes, making it easy to add interest to your diagrams. Shapes are grouped into categories such as arrows, callouts, and banners and include everything from ovals, rectangles, and triangles to stars, lightning bolts, and smiley faces.

To diagram Super Power Computers' network properly, you must connect the clips using connector lines. A **connector line** is a special type of AutoShape that automatically snaps to connection points on an object. When you move objects connected with connector lines, the line stays attached. To add connector lines:

Step 1	***Click***	the AutoShapes button on the Drawing toolbar

There are several AutoShapes categories, which you may want to spend a few minutes exploring. As you move your pointer across the displayed AutoShape styles, a ScreenTip description appears.

Step 2	***Point to***	Connectors
Step 3	***Point to***	a button on the Connectors submenu
Step 4	***Observe***	the ScreenTip description
Step 5	***Click***	Elbow Double-Arrow Connector
Step 6	***Move***	the mouse pointer close to the top laptop clip (Laptop #1)

Near a clip, the mouse pointer changes to a connection pointer, and blue connection points surround the edges of the clip. Your screen should look similar to Figure 13-9.

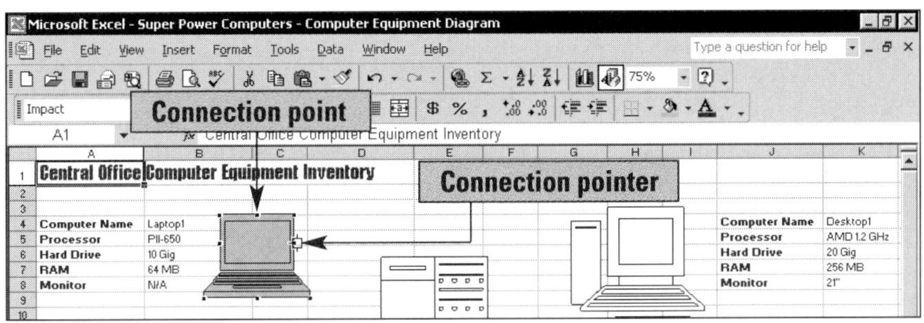

FIGURE 13-9
Using Attachment Points

Step 7	***Click***	the middle-right connection point on the first laptop clip

MENU TIP

You can use the AutoShapes toolbar to insert AutoShapes. To display the AutoShapes toolbar, click the Insert menu, point to Picture, then click AutoShapes.

chapter thirteen

> **MOUSE TIP**
>
> You may find it difficult to draw on top of cells while the gridlines remain on. You can turn gridlines on or off by using the Options dialog box. Click Options on the Tools menu, click the View tab, click the Gridlines check box in the Window options group, then click the OK button.

Step 8	***Move***	the mouse pointer to the server clip
Step 9	***Observe***	that as you drag across the worksheet, a dotted line extends from the point you clicked to the mouse pointer position
Step 10	***Click***	the middle-left connection point on the server clip

Your screen should look similar to Figure 13-10. When a connector line is attached, a red circle appears at the end of the line. When a connector line is unattached, a green circle is displayed. You can drag the yellow adjustment handle to change the position of the line.

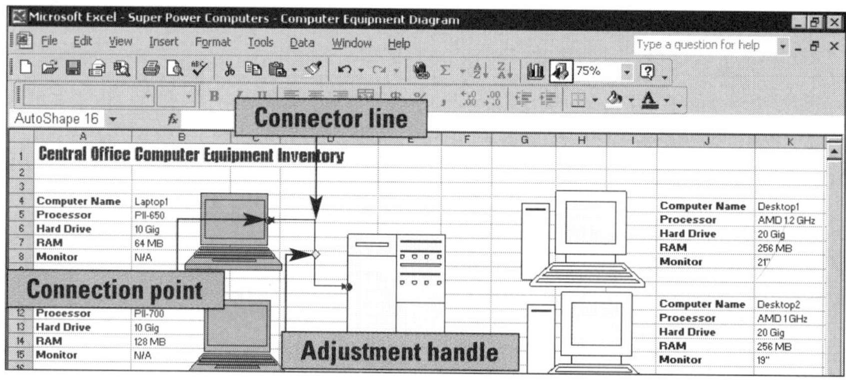

FIGURE 13-10
Completed Connector Line

Step 11	***Follow***	Steps 1 through 10 to attach each of the clips to the server clip
Step 12	***Drag***	the yellow adjustment handle to reposition any lines if necessary

Your screen should look similar to Figure 13-11.

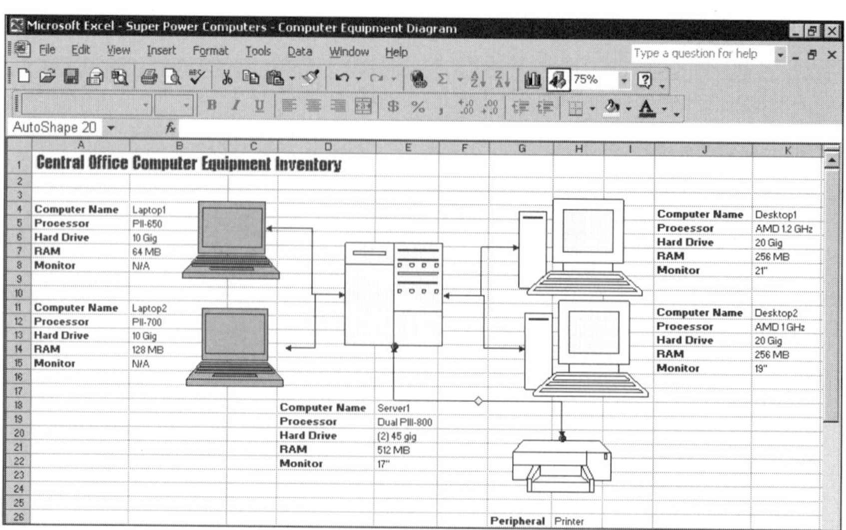

FIGURE 13-11
Final Diagram

Step 13	*Press*	the ESC key to deselect the connector line
Step 14	*Save*	the workbook and close it

13.d Creating and Editing a Conceptual Diagram

Conceptual diagrams are used for showing different types of relationships. One example of this is an organization chart, which is a hierarchical diagram of a company's management structure.

Creating an Organization Chart

Organizational charts show the reporting structure of employees in a company. To create a diagram:

Step 1	*Create*	a new, blank workbook
Step 2	*Save*	the workbook as *Super Power Computers - Management Diagram*
Step 3	*Click*	the Insert Diagram or Organization Chart button on the Drawing toolbar

The Diagram Gallery dialog box on your screen should look similar to Figure 13-12. This dialog box allows you to select the type of chart you wish to create.

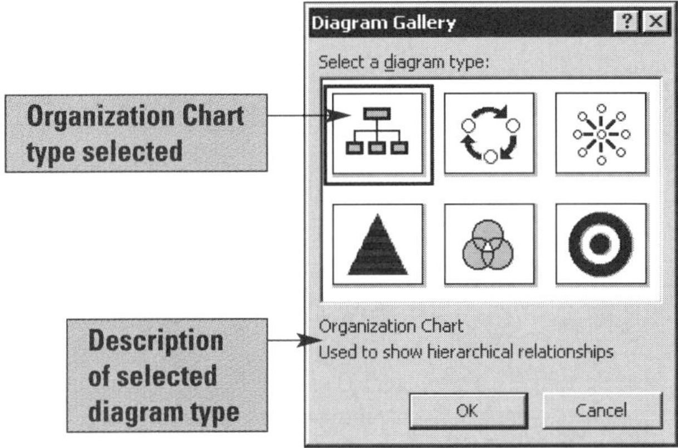

FIGURE 13-12
Diagram Gallery Dialog Box

Step 4	*Verify*	that Organization Chart is selected
Step 5	*Click*	OK

The Organization Chart is added to your worksheet. Your worksheet should look similar to Figure 13-13. The area inside the border is the drawing space.

FIGURE 13-13
Organization Chart

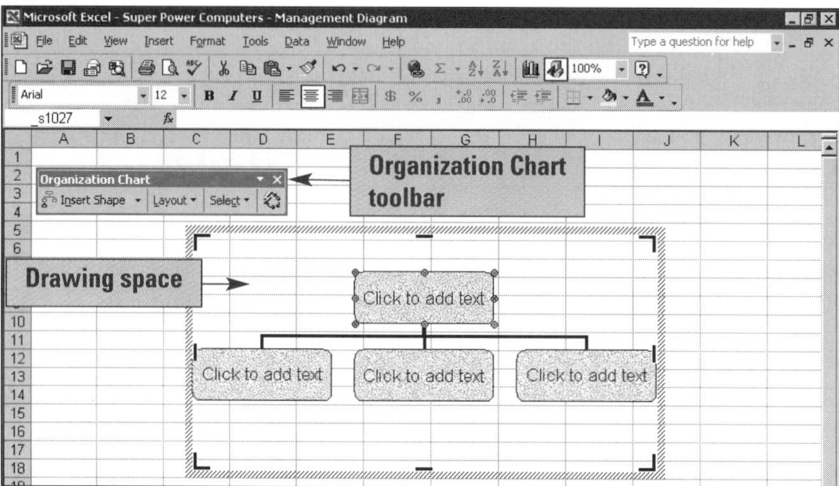

Editing an Organization Chart

Editing a conceptual diagram involves entering text in different boxes, and adding and deleting coworkers, assistants, or subordinates. To edit the organization chart:

Step 1	***Click***	the box at the top of the organization chart
Step 2	***Key***	President
Step 3	***Press***	the ESC key
Step 4	***Right-click***	the President box border
Step 5	***Click***	Assistant

A new assistant box is inserted.

Step 6	***Click***	the new box
Step 7	***Key***	Assistant
Step 8	***Click***	the left box on the bottom row
Step 9	***Key***	Regional Manager
Step 10	***Right-click***	the Regional Manager box border
Step 11	***Click***	Subordinate

QUICK TIP

You can click the Insert Shape button on the Organization Chart toolbar, then click an option on the list that appears to add boxes to an organization chart.

A new subordinate box is placed beneath the Regional Manager box.

Step 12	*Click*	the new box
Step 13	*Key*	Store Manager
Step 14	*Right-click*	the Store Manager box border
Step 15	*Click*	Coworker
Step 16	*Click*	the new box
Step 17	*Key*	Store Manager
Step 18	*Change*	the other two boxes on the third level to Regional Manager
Step 19	*Add*	two Subordinate Store Manager boxes to each Regional Manager box

As you add the new items, the font sizes will adjust to odd sizes. To readjust font sizes in an organization chart:

Step 20	*Click*	in the organization chart drawing space
Step 21	*Click*	8 in the Font size list

Selecting the entire organization chart and changing font settings sets all boxes to use the same settings. Your chart should look similar to Figure 13-14.

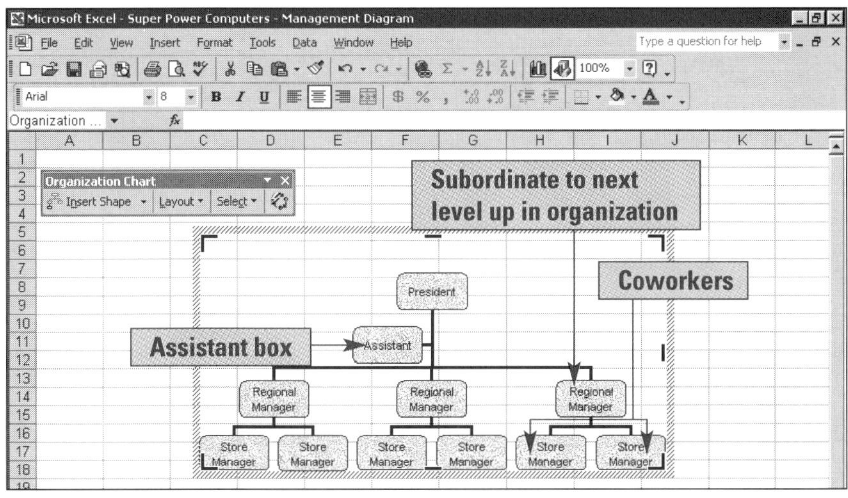

FIGURE 13-14
Completed Organization Chart

chapter thirteen

MOUSE TIP

You can add text to most AutoShapes, not just to text boxes. To add text to an AutoShape, right-click the AutoShape, then click Add Text.

QUICK TIP

You can use the Format Object dialog box to change Font settings for text added to AutoShapes, or you can click buttons on the Formatting toolbar to accomplish the same task. For example, if you want the text in an AutoShape object to be bold, select the object, then click the Bold button on the Formatting toolbar.

Inserting a Text Box Object

Text boxes are useful in diagrams because you can freely reposition the box so it doesn't interfere with other objects in your diagram. To add a text box:

Step 1	*Click*	the Text Box button on the Drawing toolbar
Step 2	*Drag*	from cell A2 to cell C10
Step 3	*Key*	Super Power Computers Organizational Diagram
Step 4	*Drag*	one of the text box corner handles to resize the text box so it is not so tall
Step 5	*Click*	the Center button on the Formatting toolbar
Step 6	*Click*	the Bold button on the Formatting toolbar
Step 7	*Press*	the ESC key to deselect the Text Box object

Printing a Worksheet with Drawing Objects

Drawing objects are printed along with anything else on the worksheet. You can preview and change the page setup of the worksheet with a drawing object. To preview and print the worksheet:

Step 1	*Click*	the Print Preview button on the Standard toolbar
Step 2	*Click*	the Setup button on the Print Preview toolbar
Step 3	*Click*	the Landscape option button on the Page tab
Step 4	*Click*	the Horizontally and Vertically check boxes on the Margins tab to insert check marks
Step 5	*Click*	OK
Step 6	*Print*	the worksheet
Step 7	*Save*	the workbook and close it

The drawing objects enhance your printed workbook.

Summary

- Area and XY scatter charts show complex relationships between data.
- You can add, delete, or modify data series to change the information shown in a chart.
- Custom chart types enable you to combine chart types on one chart.
- The Clip Organizer allows you to insert clip art symbols. You can locate clip art by browsing categories or by searching for keywords either in Clip Organizer or on the Insert Clip Art task pane.
- You can scale objects by dragging their resize handles or by using the Size tab of the Format AutoShape dialog box.
- Connector lines connect objects. Connector lines automatically route around objects and stay attached when you move either connected object. You can choose from a variety of connector styles, including straight, elbow, and curved.
- The Insert Diagram or Organizational Chart tool enables you to create conceptual and organizational diagrams. These types of diagrams simplify the illustration of complex hierarchical relationships.
- You can insert drawing objects, such as text boxes, to further enhance diagrams and worksheets.
- You print a worksheet with drawing objects as you would any other worksheet.

Commands Review

Action	Menu Bar	Shortcut Menu	Toolbar	Task Pane	Keyboard
Use the Chart Wizard	Insert, Chart				ALT + I, H
Change chart type	Chart, Chart Type	Chart Type			ALT C + Y
Change chart options	Chart, Chart Options	Chart Options			ALT C + O
Add a data series	Chart, Add data				ALT + C, A
View Drawing toolbar	View , Toolbars, Drawing				ALT + V, T
Open Insert ClipArt dialog box	Insert, Picture, Clip Art			Insert Clip Art	ALT + I, P, C
Switch between applications					ALT + TAB

Action	Menu Bar	Shortcut Menu	Toolbar	Task Pane	Keyboard
Open Format AutoShape dialog box	Format, AutoShape	Format AutoShape			ALT + O, O CTRL + 1
View AutoShapes toolbar	Insert, Picture, AutoShape				ALT + I, P, A
Insert AutoShapes			AutoShapes		
Insert Text box					
Change AutoShape			Draw, then Change AutoShape		
Insert line object					
Insert arrow object					
Change line color					
Change line style					
Change dash style					
Change arrow style					
Deselect objects					ESC
Rotate objects			Draw, then Rotate or Flip		
Flip objects			Draw, then Rotate or Flip		
Insert WordArt	Insert, Picture, WordArt				ALT + I, P, W
Add or modify color fill					
Add shadow to an object					
Create 3-D objects					
View 3-D Drawing toolbar			, then 3-D Settings		
Change stack order		Order	Draw, then Order		
Group objects		Grouping, Group	Draw, then Group		
Ungroup objects		Grouping, Ungroup	Draw, then Ungroup		
Zoom	View, Zoom		100%		ALT + V, Z

Concepts Review

Circle the correct answer.

1. To select multiple objects for editing, press and hold the:
- [a] SHIFT key while selecting objects.
- [b] END key while selecting objects.
- [c] CTRL key while selecting objects.
- [d] ALT key while selecting objects.

2. Area charts are used to:
- [a] show the magnitude of change over time.
- [b] compare pairs of values.
- [c] compare values across categories.
- [d] show trends in values across two dimensions.

3. To deselect an object, press the:
- [a] SHIFT key.
- [b] ESC key.
- [c] CTRL key.
- [d] ALT key.

4. Connection lines are more useful than line objects when diagramming because:
- [a] you can't change the arrow style of a line object.
- [b] connection lines stay attached even when objects are moved.
- [c] connection lines reroute around the objects to which they are attached.
- [d] connection lines stay attached when objects move, and also reroute around the objects to which they are attached.

5. XY scatter charts are used to:
- [a] show the magnitude of change over time.
- [b] compare values across categories.
- [c] compare pairs of values.
- [d] show trends in values across two dimensions.

6. A data table is used:
- [a] in place of a chart.
- [b] to override chart data.
- [c] as a different type of chart.
- [d] to show numerical data along with the chart.

7. Which of the following media types can be catalogued in Clip Organizer?
- [a] images
- [b] sounds
- [c] movies
- [d] images, sounds, and movies

8. Connector lines are a type of:
- [a] AutoShape.
- [b] line.
- [c] rectangle.
- [d] WordArt.

9. An organizational diagram shows:
- [a] a foundation-based relationship.
- [b] a continuous cycle process.
- [c] relationships of a core element.
- [d] a hierarchical organization.

10. Adding a coworker to an organization chart places a new element:
- [a] above the currently selected element.
- [b] below the currently selected element.
- [c] adjacent to the currently selected element.
- [d] between the selected element and the next lower level element.

Circle **T** if the statement is true or **F** if the statement is false.

T F 1. You must turn off gridlines before using drawing tools.

T F 2. Once you create a chart you cannot add or remove data series from the chart.

T F 3. When you are adding connector lines, tiny blue connection points appear when the pointer is moved close to an object.

T F 4. A green handle on a connector indicates that the connector is attached to a connection point.

T F 5. A red handle on a connector indicates that the connector is attached to a connection point.

T F 6. To change the font settings for an entire diagram, select the diagram object and change the font settings using the Formatting toolbar.

T F 7. AutoShapes can be resized.

T F 8. You can add media collected on your computer to the Clip Organizer.

T F 9. You cannot print diagrams or drawings created using drawing tools.

T F 10. Clip Organizer can look for clip art on the Web.

In the following Skills Review Exercises, several drawing tools are used that were not explicitly covered in the chapter. Use the Drawing toolbar and watch the status bar for instructions on using the tools.

Skills Review

Exercise 1

1. Create a new, blank workbook.

2. Use AutoShapes to do the following:

a. Click the Rectangle AutoShape on the Drawing toolbar, then drag to create a rectangle about 2½ inches by 3 inches.

b. Click the Oval AutoShape on the Drawing toolbar, then drag to create an oval about 4 inches wide.

c. Click AutoShapes on the Drawing toolbar, point to Basic Shapes, click the Isosceles Triangle shape (fourth column, second row), then drag to create a triangle about 3 inches tall.

d. Click AutoShapes on the Drawing toolbar, point to Basic Shapes, click the Cross shape (third column, third row), then drag to create a cross about 4 inches tall.

3. Double-click the triangle.

4. On the Colors and Lines tab, change the fill color to Bright Green.

5. Double-click the rectangle.
6. Change the fill color to Blue.
7. Change the transparency to 50%.
8. Click the Cross shape.
9. Click the Dash Style button on the Drawing toolbar to change the dash style to Square Dot.
10. Save the workbook as *Drawing Objects*, and then print and close it.

Exercise 2

1. Create a new, blank workbook.
2. Open the Clip Organizer.
3. Search for clips related to sports.
4. Insert three clips representing sports you enjoy (playing or watching).
5. Add a drop shadow to the clips by selecting all three clips, then clicking the Shadow Style button on the Drawing toolbar.
6. Save the workbook as *Sports*, and then print and close it.

Exercise 3

1. Open the *Computer Price Chart* workbook located on the Data Disk.
2. Add cells A3:A9 on Sheet1 to the Category (X) axis labels using the Source Data dialog box.
3. Display the Drawing toolbar, if necessary.
4. Click AutoShapes on the Drawing toolbar, point to Callouts, click the Rectangular Callout shape (first row, first column), then drag the callout shape over the AMD 900 MHz system.
5. With the callout object selected, key "Biggest Price Drop!" and then click the Center button on the Formatting toolbar to center the text.
6. With the callout object selected, click the Fill Color list arrow on the Drawing toolbar and change the fill color to Red.
7. Drag the yellow object handle to point the callout to the "Now" price of the AMD 900 MHz system.
8. Save the workbook as *Computer Price Chart Revised*, and then print and close it.

Exercise 4

1. Open the *Business Transactions* workbook located on the Data Disk.
2. Zoom in on the worksheet, if necessary.
3. Click the Line button on the Drawing toolbar, then drag to draw a line between the Total Income in cells C22 and F16.
4. Draw a line between the Total Distributions in cells K15 and F17.
5. Draw a line between the Total Expenses in cells D42 and F18.
6. Select all three lines, then change the line style of the lines to 3 pt by clicking the Line Style button on the Drawing toolbar.

7. With all three lines selected, change the line color to lavender by clicking the Line Color button list arrow on the Drawing toolbar.
8. Change the arrow style of all three lines to Arrow Style 7 by clicking the Arrow Style button on the Drawing toolbar, then clicking the seventh style in the list.
9. Zoom the worksheet to 50% if you changed it earlier.
10. Save the workbook as *Business Transactions Revised*, and then print and close it.

Exercise 5

1. Open the *Temperature Data* file located on the Data Disk.
2. Create an XY Scatter chart using all the data shown on Sheet1.
3. Use Chart Options to:
   a. Add the title "Recorded Temperatures."
   b. Add the Value (X) axis title "Date."
   c. Add the Value (Y) axis title "Temperature."
4. Save the workbook as *Temperature Data Chart*, and then print and close it.

Exercise 6

1. Open the *Half Marathon Mile Splits 2* workbook located on the Data Disk.
2. Select the range B3:B15.
3. Open the Chart Wizard.
4. Create an area type chart as an embedded chart in Sheet1.
5. Right-click the Y-axis on the left side of the chart, then click Format Axis.
6. On the Scale tab, set the Minimum to 0.004 and click OK.
7. Save the workbook as *Half Marathon Mile Splits Chart*, and then print and close it.

Exercise 7

1. Open a new, blank workbook.
2. Using the Rectangle button on the Drawing toolbar, draw a box representing a house.
3. Click the Fill Color button list arrow on the Drawing toolbar, click Fill Effects, click the Pattern tab, then select a brick pattern to add to the house.
4. Using more rectangles, add windows to the house with a light blue fill color.
5. Add another rectangle and a circle for a door.
6. Using a triangle AutoShape, add a roof with a brown fill color.
7. Add a rectangle for a tree trunk with dark red fill color.
8. Click AutoShapes on the Drawing toolbar, point to Stars and Banners, then click the Explosion 2 AutoShape (first row, second column) and create the top of the tree with a green fill color.
9. Print the drawing, save the workbook as *House Drawing*, and then close it.

Exercise 8

1. Open the *Product Quantities* workbook located on the Data Disk.
2. Select the range A1:B4, then use the Chart Wizard to create a Line - Column on 2 Axes chart.
3. Insert the chart on the worksheet.
4. Save the workbook as *Product Quantities Chart,* and then print and close it.

Case Projects

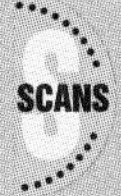

Project 1

You work for a mortgage company that is seeking ways to promote its low interest rates on home loans. Open the *Interest* workbook located on the Data Disk. Using AutoShapes with text and clip art, create a newsletter-type document in Excel advertising a 6.9% interest rate. To add an eye-catching title, draw an AutoShape, then add text. Select the text and format it, then add a fill color to the shape. Target your newsletter toward first-time homebuyers. Try searching for clip art associated with homes, saving money, and families. Save the workbook as *Interest Advertisement,* and then print and close it.

Project 2

You own a successful restaurant. You train your employees to always follow a four-step system to serve clients. The steps are as follows: (1) Greet Customers, (2) Take the Order, (3) Prepare the Order, and (4) Collect the Amount Due. Using AutoShapes with text, add each of the steps to a new workbook. Then use curved connector lines to create a flow chart that you can use in training meetings to emphasize this system. You may need to resize the objects to fit on-screen. Save the worksheet as *Serve System,* and then print and close it.

Project 3

Connect to the Internet and search the Web for a food pyramid. Using the Excel organizational charts, recreate the food pyramid. Save the workbook as *Food Pyramid,* and then print and close it.

Project 4

This one's just for fun but might prove useful in Algebra class. Open a new, blank workbook. Select cells A1:B21 and create an XY scatter chart using smoothed lines (one of the chart subtypes). In column A, enter the following values (leave cells empty when you see EMPTY): X, 0.5, 0.75, 0.5, 0.25, 0.5, EMPTY, -0.5, -0.75, -0.5, -0.25, -0.5, EMPTY, 0, -0.25, 0.25, 0, EMPTY, -1, 0, 1. In column B, place the following values: Y, 0.5, 0.25, 0, 0.25, 0.5, EMPTY, 0.5, 0.25, 0, 0.25, 0.5, EMPTY, 0, -0.5, -0.5, 0, EMPTY, -0.2, -0.8, -0.2. Save the completed workbook as *XY Fun,* and then print and close it.

Project 5

Prediction time! Randomly select five classmates. In a new workbook, predict what score you think they earned on a recent assignment (do this before you find out their actual score). Next, record the actual score they earned. Create a Line-Column on 2 Axes chart to show how well you were able to predict their scores. To maintain anonymity, be sure to assign each student a number instead of using his or her name in the workbook. Save the workbook as *Score Prediction,* and then print and close it.

Project 6

Your cookie company has been tremendously successful. You want to find out which cookies have been contributing most to your success. Create fictional sales data for five types of cookies. Include quantities for each of the last four quarters. Create an area chart with a data table to illustrate the data. Save your workbook as *Cookie Sales Chart*, and then print and close it.

Project 7

You work for an interior design company creating layouts of office furniture. Use Clip Organizer to insert clip art of office furniture (*Hint:* Use the Office Layout category or search for furniture). Save your workbook as *Office Layout*, and then print and close it.

Project 8

You work as a technical support engineer. Each day you receive calls from customers who are having problems opening Excel workbooks. To make it easier for you to do your job, create a troubleshooting flow chart of questions you can ask to determine the source of the problem. Each question should have a Yes or No answer. If the answer is Yes, you ask the next question on your list; if the answer is No, include steps to solve the problem. Place each question and each solution set in its own text box, then connect the boxes using connectors. Save the workbook as *Troubleshooting*, and then print and close it.

Importing and Exporting Data from Other Applications

Chapter Overview

Excel worksheets and charts can be used in a variety of ways outside of Excel. For example, you can create reports in Word using Excel data, and you can enhance PowerPoint presentations with Excel data and charts. In addition, you can create Access tables from existing Excel lists or query Access databases from Excel to analyze data. You can paste or link workbook data to documents created in other programs. You can also embed workbooks within other documents to share the functionality of Excel with other programs.

Case profile

You are responsible not only for gathering data from each store at Super Power Computers, but also for distributing the data to regional and store managers. For example, you periodically write memos to regional managers, distribute reports to management, and prepare presentations for potential investors. By integrating Excel-based data into other Office documents, and by querying existing Access databases for information, you can save time and ensure accurate data.

Learning Objectives

- Integrate Excel data with Word and PowerPoint
- Integrate Excel with Access
- Import data from text files

chapter fourteen

It is assumed that you have a basic knowledge of the Word, Access, and PowerPoint applications. Your instructor may provide additional instructions as you complete the activities in this chapter.

14.a Integrating Excel Data with Word and PowerPoint

Excel data can be integrated with other applications, such as Word, PowerPoint, and Access. In Word and PowerPoint documents, worksheets and charts can be linked or embedded. Alternately, you can create a "table" from within Word or PowerPoint, using Excel features.

There are several ways to integrate Excel data with Word documents and PowerPoint presentations. First, you can insert an Excel file (the **source file**) in a Word document or PowerPoint presentation (the **target file**). Second, you can embed an Excel object in a Word document or PowerPoint presentation. Third, you can create a link between an Excel workbook and a Word document or PowerPoint presentation.

When you **insert** Excel data into a Word document, you place the data in a Word table that can be edited using the Word table editing commands. When you insert Excel data into a PowerPoint presentation, the data is inserted as a graphic object, similar to a picture of the data, which cannot be edited. All links to the original data are lost. Thus, if you modify the data in the target file, the original Excel workbook is not updated. Likewise, if you update the Excel workbook, the target file is not updated. Because you can use the Copy and Paste commands to insert Excel data into the target file, this method is very fast.

Embedding an Excel object in a target file creates a connection between the target application and Excel. When you double-click an embedded worksheet object to edit it, the target application's menu bar and toolbars are replaced with the Excel menu bar and toolbars. Using an embedded worksheet is like opening a window in the target application to the Excel application. Although you use the familiar Excel menu bar and toolbars to edit the data, you are not actually altering the original data. That is, your changes are not reflected in the original Excel workbook. When you do not need to maintain a link to the original data, but do want access to Excel features to format and edit data, use this method.

When you **link** an Excel worksheet to a target file, you create a reference to the original Excel worksheet. Double-clicking a linked object opens the original file. Because the workbook is linked to the target file, any changes you make in Excel are reflected in your target file. Linking files saves hard drive space, because you do not create a second copy of the data in the target file. If having up-to-date data in the target file is essential, linking is your best option.

Integrating Excel with Access involves sharing data normally used in a database. Data stored in lists in Excel can be used to create new data tables in Access, and data stored in an Access database can be queried and extracted into an Excel workbook.

Embedding Excel Data in a Word Document

You need to send a memo to the management personnel at Super Power Computers showing the sales totals for 2003. You wrote the memo in Word, and you collected the data in Excel. You want to embed the Excel data, so the managers can correct the data if necessary. To embed Excel data in a Word document:

Step 1	***Start***	Word
Step 2	***Open***	the *Memo to Store 3 Manager* document located on the Data Disk
Step 3	***Save***	the Word document as *Memo to Store 3 Manager with Embedded Data*
Step 4	***Click***	the Show/Hide button ¶ on the Standard toolbar to display the nonprinting formatting marks in Word, if necessary
Step 5	***Key***	your name on the From: line, replacing Your Name
Step 6	***Press***	the CTRL + END keys to move the insertion point to the end of the document
Step 7	***Press***	the ENTER key to create a new line
Step 8	***Start***	Excel
Step 9	***Open***	the *Super Power Computers - Mountain Region Sales* workbook located on the Data Disk
Step 10	***Click***	the Store #3 sheet tab
Step 11	***Select***	the range A1:F9
Step 12	***Click***	the Copy button on the Standard toolbar
Step 13	***Click***	the Word button on the taskbar
Step 14	***Click***	Edit
Step 15	***Click***	Paste Special

The Paste Special dialog box opens in Word.

> **QUICK TIP**
>
> You can click the Paste link: option button to link the worksheet to the document. Then you can change the data from either file.

Step 16	*Click*	Microsoft Excel Worksheet Object in the As: list box
Step 17	*Verify*	that the Paste: option button is selected
Step 18	*Click*	OK

The worksheet is embedded in the document as an object. When a worksheet is embedded in the target file, you must change it from within the Word target file. To edit the embedded Excel object in the Word document:

Step 1	*Double-click*	the embedded worksheet object to edit it with Excel tools

Your screen should look similar to Figure 14-1.

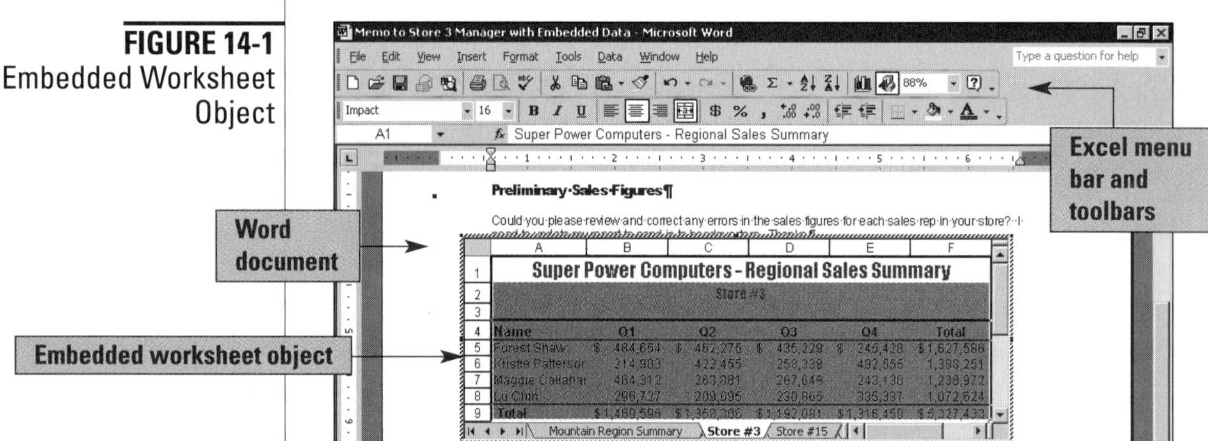

FIGURE 14-1
Embedded Worksheet Object

Step 2	*Select*	the range A4:F4
Step 3	*Click*	the Fill Color button list arrow on the Formatting toolbar
Step 4	*Click*	the Gray-25% square
Step 5	*Activate*	cell A1
Step 6	*Click*	anywhere in the Word document to deactivate the Excel object

You can drag the object in Word to reposition it or align it on the page using the Formatting toolbar. To center the embedded object:

Step 1	*Click*	the embedded worksheet object to select it

Step 2	***Click***	the Center button on the Formatting toolbar
Step 3	***Click***	in a blank area of the document to deselect the object

Your document should look similar to Figure 14-2.

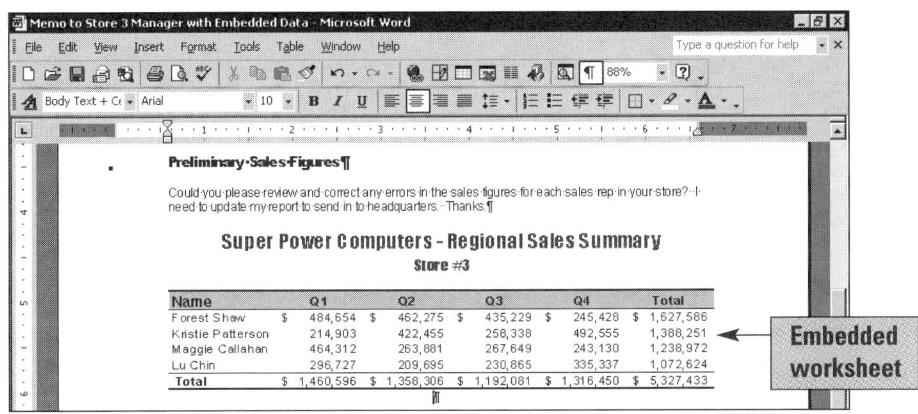

Name	Q1	Q2	Q3	Q4	Total
Forest Shaw	$ 484,654	$ 462,275	$ 435,229	$ 245,428	$ 1,627,586
Kristie Patterson	214,903	422,455	258,338	492,555	1,388,251
Maggie Callahan	464,312	263,881	267,649	243,130	1,238,972
Lu Chin	296,727	209,695	230,865	335,337	1,072,624
Total	$ 1,460,596	$ 1,358,306	$ 1,192,081	$ 1,316,450	$ 5,327,433

FIGURE 14-2
Embedded Worksheet Object after Formatting

Step 4	***Save***	the Word document

Creating a Chart in Word Using Excel Data

An alternate method of creating charts in Word is to use Excel data along with the Microsoft Chart Object. To create a chart in Word using Excel data:

Step 1	***Click***	the Excel button on the taskbar
Step 2	***Copy***	the range A4:F8 on the Store #3 sheet tab
Step 3	***Click***	the Word button on the taskbar
Step 4	***Press***	the ENTER key to move the insertion point below the embedded worksheet object
Step 5	***Click***	Insert
Step 6	***Click***	Object
Step 7	***Click***	Microsoft Graph Chart in the Object type: list
Step 8	***Click***	OK

The Microsoft Graph Chart object appears in your document, along with the Datasheet window. Your screen should look similar to Figure 14-3.

The datasheet contains sample data, on which the chart is. In the datasheet, you can paste and modify data used in the chart.

FIGURE 14-3
Microsoft Graph Chart Object

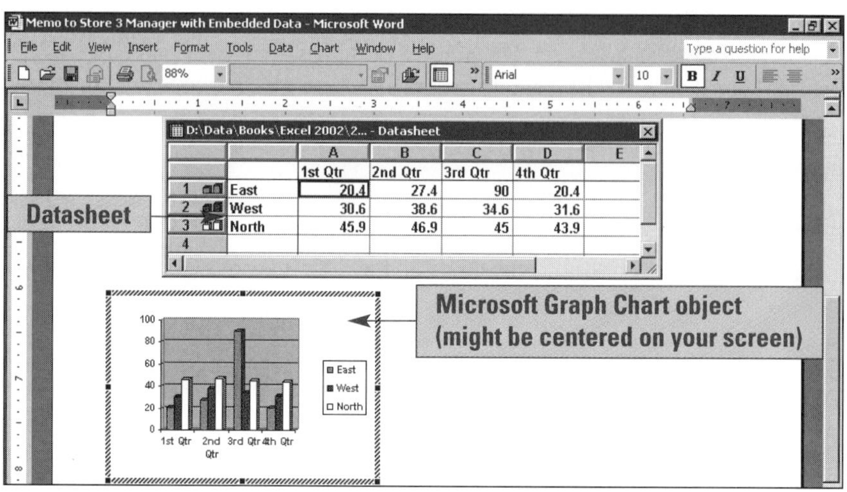

> **CAUTION TIP**
>
> If you double-click a column head rather than a column divider in the Datasheet window, you may deactivate the column. If the data in a column is gray, double-click the column header again to reactivate it.

Step 9	***Right-click***	the upper-left cell in the datasheet, the blank cell to the left of 1st Qtr
Step 10	***Click***	Paste
Step 11	***Double-click***	the boundaries between each column to AutoFit each column, if necessary

You added the Total column to the chart, which you want to deactivate. To modify the chart:

Step 1	***Double-click***	the column E header to deactivate the column

The Total data disappears from the chart and appears grayed out in the Datasheet window.

> **CAUTION TIP**
>
> If you make the chart too large, it may slip onto the next page. If this happens, resize the chart, making it a little smaller until it returns to the first page of the document.

Step 2	***Click***	outside the chart object to deselect it and close the Datasheet window
Step 3	***Click***	the chart object once to select it
Step 4	***Drag***	the sizing handle at the lower-right corner to make the chart as large as possible without jumping to the next page
Step 5	***Save***	the Word document and close it
Step 6	***Exit***	Word
Step 7	***Close***	the *Super Power Computers - Mountain Region Sales* workbook

Linking an Excel Worksheet to a PowerPoint Presentation

You are working on a PowerPoint presentation showing sales data for the South Region. You want to include a chart showing this year's data in the presentation. You know that the worksheet will be updated later, so you decide to link it to the presentation. You then can update the chart right before your presentation. To add a link to the data:

Step 1	***Open***	the *Super Power Computers - Store #10 Summary* workbook located on the Data Disk
Step 2	***Start***	PowerPoint
Step 3	***Open***	the *Super Power Computers - Store #10 Presentation* file located on the Data Disk
Step 4	***Save***	the presentation as *Super Power Computers - Store #10 Presentation Final*
Step 5	***Click***	the Excel button on the taskbar
Step 6	***Verify***	that the Summary Chart sheet is active
Step 7	***Click***	the Copy button on the Standard toolbar

Excel automatically selects and copies the chart on the Summary Chart worksheet.

Step 8	***Click***	the PowerPoint button on the taskbar
Step 9	***Click***	the Slide 2 slide icon in the Outline tab to move to the second slide
Step 10	***Click***	Edit
Step 11	***Click***	Paste Special
Step 12	***Click***	the Paste link option button
Step 13	***Click***	OK

The chart is linked to the PowerPoint presentation, but you need to resize it so it fits on the slide. When you press and hold the CTRL key while you resize an object, the object resizes proportionally toward or from the center of the object. To resize the chart object:

Step 1	***Press & hold***	the CTRL key

Step 2	*Drag*	a corner sizing handle until the object fits nicely on the slide
Step 3	*Move*	the object so it is visually centered on the slide
Step 4	*Press*	the ESC key to deselect the object
Step 5	*Save*	the presentation

Your screen should look similar to Figure 14-4.

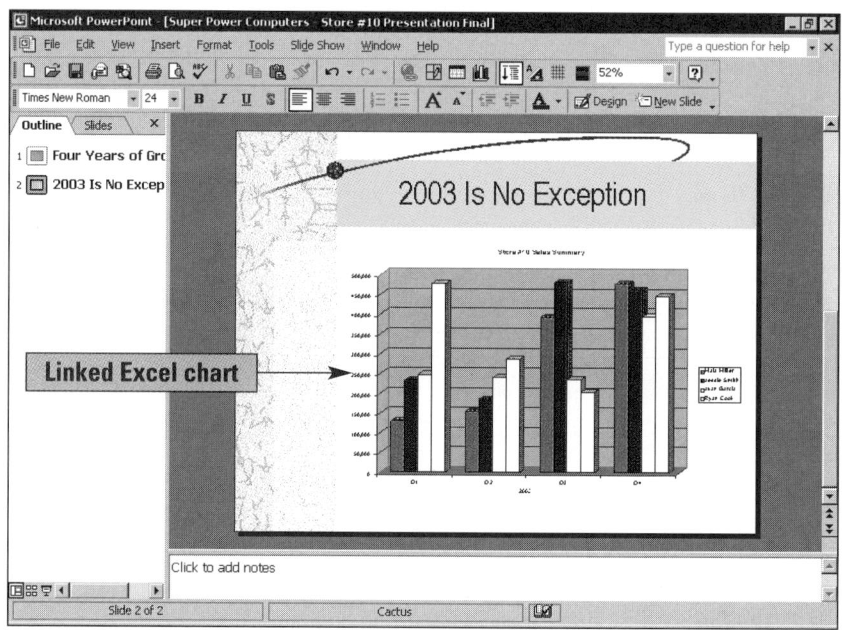

FIGURE 14-4
Excel Data Linked to PowerPoint Slide

> **CAUTION TIP**
>
> If you move or rename a workbook that has been linked to other files, the link must be corrected for the data to be updated. However, the most recently updated data (before the link was broken) is displayed until you update the link. For more information about breaking and reestablishing links in a PowerPoint presentation, refer to PowerPoint online Help.

Step 6	*Close*	the *Super Power Computers - Store #10 Summary* workbook in Excel

The chart is linked to the PowerPoint presentation. When an Excel worksheet is linked to a target file, double-clicking the Excel object takes you directly to Excel and opens the linked file, if necessary. As you edit the linked data, the target file is updated automatically. To modify the worksheet object:

Step 1	*Click*	the PowerPoint button on the taskbar, if necessary
Step 2	*Double-click*	the linked chart object

Excel becomes the active program, and the workbook containing the chart object appears in the active window.

Step 3	***Maximize***	the Excel workbook window, if necessary
Step 4	***Save***	the workbook as *Super Power Computers - Store #10 Summary Revised*
Step 5	***Right-click***	the taskbar
Step 6	***Click***	Tile Windows Vertically to display both program windows
Step 7	***Click***	in the Excel window to make it active

Your screen should look similar to Figure 14-5.

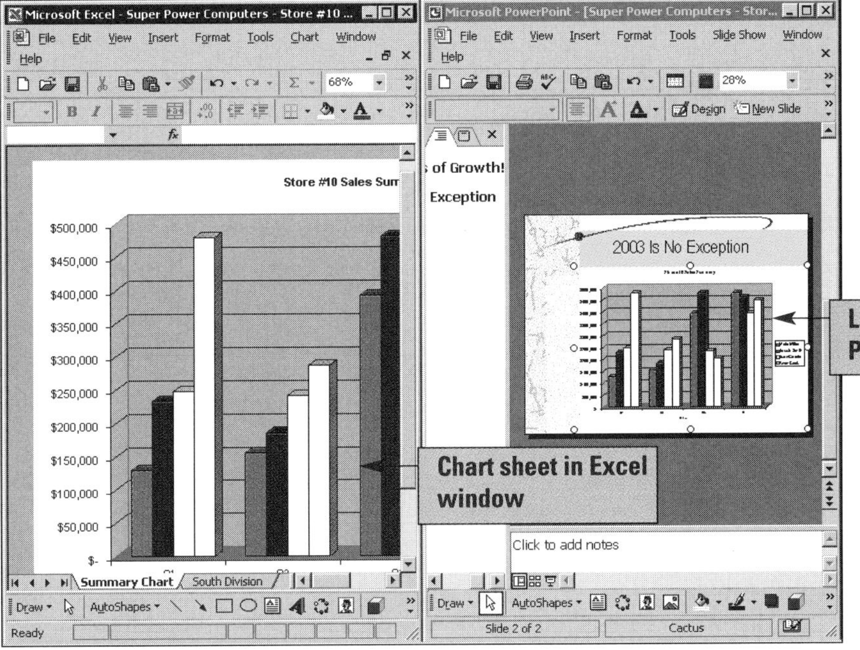

FIGURE 14-5
PowerPoint and Excel Windows Tiled Vertically

Step 8	***Select***	the Chart Title object in Excel
Step 9	***Press***	the DELETE key to delete the Chart Title object in the Excel window
Step 10	***Click***	in the PowerPoint window to make it active
Step 11	***Right-click***	the Chart object in PowerPoint
Step 12	***Click***	Update Link

The chart title no longer appears on the PowerPoint slide.

Step 13	***Maximize***	the PowerPoint program window
Step 14	***Save***	the PowerPoint presentation and close it

Step 15	*Exit*	PowerPoint
Step 16	*Maximize*	the Excel program window
Step 17	*Save*	the workbook and close it

QUICK TIP

Even though databases store large amounts of data efficiently, Excel still offers advantages when it comes to performing calculations on that information. As a result, you may prefer to import data from Access databases to Excel to perform more complex calculations and create charts.

14.b Integrating Excel with Access

Although Excel can store a large volume of data in list form, a database application—such as Access—is better suited to holding large amounts of this type of data. As your Excel lists grow in size, you can export them to create Access tables.

Exporting Excel Data to an Access Database

You can use existing lists of Excel data to build data tables in Access. The *Sales Rep Data* workbook contains a variety of information about the sales for each of Sweet Tooth's divisions. You think it would be a good idea to store the data in a database rather than in Excel. Before you import Excel-based data into Access, however, you need to prepare the information. To prepare the Excel data:

Step 1	*Open*	the *Super Power Computers - Sales Rep Data 2* workbook located on the Data Disk
Step 2	*Save*	the workbook as *Super Power Computers - Sales Rep Data to Import*

You should delete any worksheet titles and blank rows that appear above the data to be imported into Access. The labels in the first row become the field names in the database, so you want the column headings in the first row.

Step 3	*Delete*	rows 1 through 4
Step 4	*Verify*	that the column headings appear in the first row of the worksheet you want to import
Step 5	*Activate*	cell A1
Step 6	*Delete*	the PivotTable and PivotChart worksheets
Step 7	*Save*	the workbook and close it

To start Access and create a new database:

Step 1	*Start*	Access
Step 2	*Click*	the Blank Database link in the New File task pane
Step 3	*Switch to*	the drive and folder containing your completed files
Step 4	*Key*	Super Power Computers - Sales Rep Data in the File name: text box
Step 5	*Click*	Create

To import data from Excel:

Step 1	*Click*	File
Step 2	*Point to*	Get External Data
Step 3	*Click*	Import
Step 4	*Click*	the Files of type: list arrow in the Import dialog box
Step 5	*Click*	Microsoft Excel
Step 6	*Click*	*Super Power Computers - Sales Rep Data to Import*
Step 7	*Click*	Import

The Import Spreadsheet Wizard opens. The first row of data in the workbook contains the column headings.

Step 8	*Click*	the First Row Contains Column Headings check box to insert a check mark

Notice that in the bottom half of the dialog box the column headings from the worksheet become the field headings for the new Access table. Below those headings, you see how the data divides into records (horizontally) and fields (vertically).

Step 9	*Click*	Next >
Step 10	*Click*	Next > to accept the default option of creating the database in new table
Step 11	*Click*	Next > to accept the default information about each of the fields you are importing

In a database, a primary key is used to uniquely identify each record in a table and to speed up data retrieval in large databases. Access adds a primary key by default in Step 4 of the Wizard.

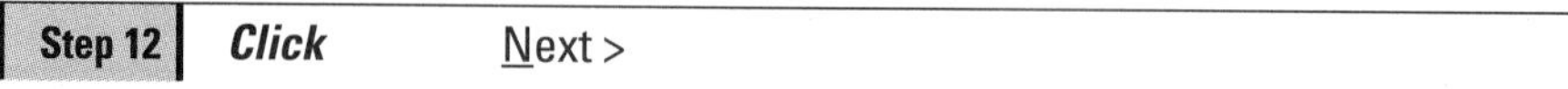

Step 12	*Click*	Next >

The next step names the new Access database table.

Step 13	*Verify*	Sales Report Data is entered in the Import to Table: text box
Step 14	*Click*	Finish
Step 15	*Click*	OK to close the message dialog box

The new table name appears in the Database window.

Step 16	*Double-click*	the Sales Report Data table icon

Your screen should look similar to Figure 14-6.

FIGURE 14-6
Access Table Created Using an Excel List

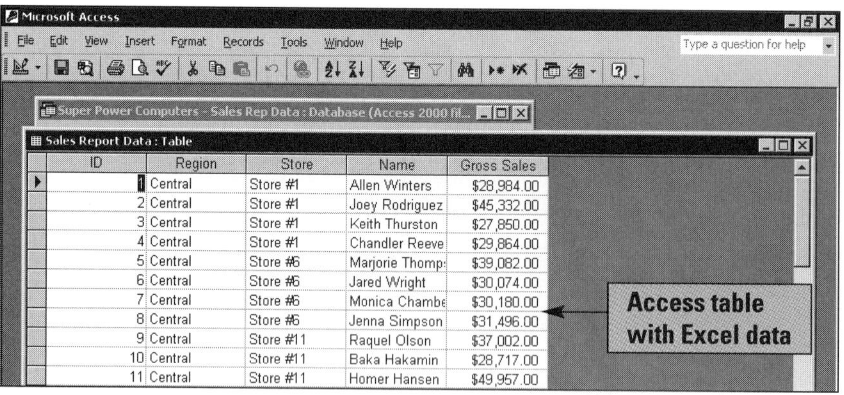

Step 17	*Exit*	Access

Querying Data from an Access Database

A **query** is a method of extracting information from a database. You can use Excel to query data stored in Access and search for records meeting certain criteria. Then, you can import only those records that meet your criteria into Excel so as to create charts, develop PivotTable reports, or perform statistical analysis. To query a database, you use Microsoft Query in Excel.

To query the database:

Step 1	*Create*	a new workbook in Excel
Step 2	*Click*	Data
Step 3	*Point to*	Import External Data
Step 4	*Click*	New Database Query
Step 5	*Click*	MS Access Database* in the Choose Data Source dialog box
Step 6	*Verify*	that the Use the Query Wizard to create/edit queries check box contains a check mark
Step 7	*Click*	OK
Step 8	*Switch to*	the drive and folder containing your completed files
Step 9	*Click*	*Super Power Computers - Sales Rep Data.mdb* in the Database Name list box in the Select Database dialog box
Step 10	*Click*	OK

Once you have selected a database source, the Query Wizard starts. In Step 1 of the wizard, you select which columns you want to include from your table in your query. If you omit a column, the data in that column is not extracted from the database. To add columns to your query:

Step 1	*Click*	the + next to Sales Report Data in the Available tables and columns: list box
Step 2	*Verify*	that Sales Report Data is selected
Step 3	*Click*	the > button to add the entire table to the Columns in your query: list box
Step 4	*Click*	Next >

Step 2 of the Query Wizard enables you to set query filters. **Filters** allow you to view only records meeting criteria you define. For this query, you want to extract only the records of sales representatives who work in the West Coast Region and whose gross sales exceed $35,000. To set query filters:

Step 1	*Click*	Gross Sales in the Column to filter: list box
Step 2	*Click*	the Operator list arrow in the active box on the right
Step 3	*Click*	is greater than in the list of operators
Step 4	*Key*	35000 in the Value list box on the right

Your query extracts all records in which the value of the Gross Sales column exceeds $35,000, as shown in Figure 14-7.

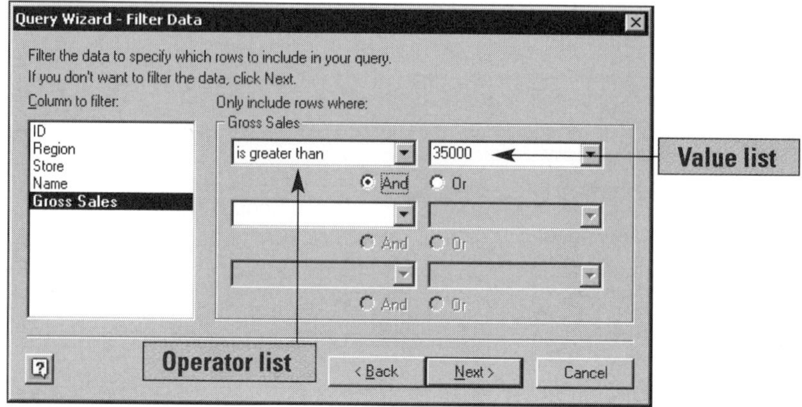

FIGURE 14-7
Step 2 of the Query Wizard

QUICK TIP

If you plan to reuse this query to update data at a later time, you can save it by clicking the Save Query button in the last step of the Query Wizard.

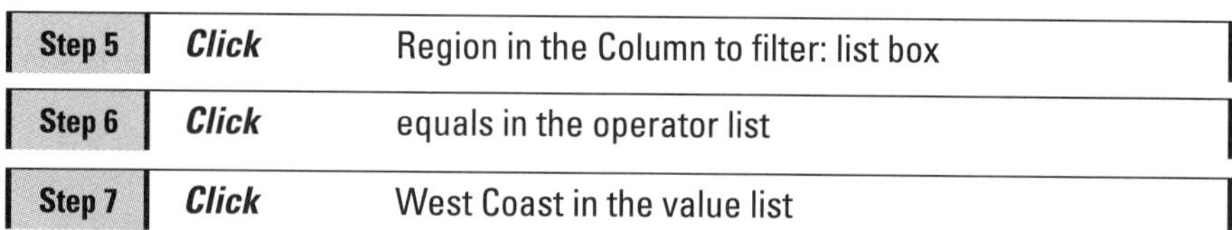

Step 5	***Click***	Region in the Column to filter: list box
Step 6	***Click***	equals in the operator list
Step 7	***Click***	West Coast in the value list

Notice that both Region and Gross Sales are highlighted in the Column to filter: list box. This indicates that both columns have a filter applied. The query extracts all records where the value in the Gross Sales column is greater than $35,000 *and* where the region equals West Coast.

Step 8	***Click***	Next >

The third step of the Query Wizard allows you to define a sort order for the records. To set the sort order:

Step 1	***Click***	the Sort by list arrow
Step 2	***Click***	Gross Sales
Step 3	***Click***	the Descending option button
Step 4	***Click***	Next >

The final step of the Query Wizard allows you to specify where the data should appear. You want to create a new list in Excel.

To specify the output option of your query results:

Step 1	***Verify***	that the Return Data to Microsoft Excel option button is selected
Step 2	***Click***	Finish

The Import Data dialog box opens. You need to select a location where the data will be placed. Cell A1 (the default) is just fine.

MOUSE TIP

The External Data toolbar appears after you run a query. Using this toolbar, you can refresh the data source, modify the query to extract other records, or modify the data range properties.

Step 3	***Click***	OK
Step 4	***Save***	the workbook as *Super Power Computers - Database Query*

Your query results should look similar to Figure 14-8.

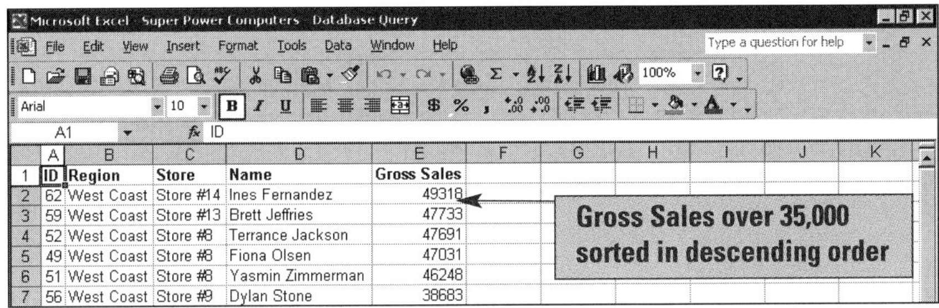

	A	B	C	D	E
1	ID	Region	Store	Name	Gross Sales
2	62	West Coast	Store #14	Ines Fernandez	49318
3	59	West Coast	Store #13	Brett Jeffries	47733
4	52	West Coast	Store #8	Terrance Jackson	47691
5	49	West Coast	Store #8	Fiona Olsen	47031
6	51	West Coast	Store #8	Yasmin Zimmerman	46248
7	56	West Coast	Store #9	Dylan Stone	38683

FIGURE 14-8
Results of Database Query

Step 5	***Close***	the workbook

14.c Importing Data from Text Files

A common method of exchanging data between applications involves **comma-separated** or **tab-delimited** text files. These files can be created in any text editor and use commas, tabs, or other characters to separate columns of data. You can import these files into an open workbook, or you can create a new workbook using the text file. You have located an old document containing financial data that was exported from an accounting program. This file uses tabs to separate information into columns. To import data from a text file into Excel:

QUICK TIP

You could use other characters as well, including commas, semicolons, or even spaces, to separate columns of data.

Step 1	***Create***	a new workbook
Step 2	***Click***	Data

Step 3	***Point to***	Import External Data
Step 4	***Click***	Import Data

The Select Data Source dialog box opens.

Step 5	***Click***	the Files of type: list arrow
Step 6	***Click***	Text Files
Step 7	***Select***	*Monthly Cash Flow* located on the Data Disk
Step 8	***Click***	Open

QUICK TIP

Virtually any character can be used as a delimiter, so Excel permits you to specify a character in the Other box. If the data is not divided into columns automatically, you need to specify a character other than a tab.

Step 1 of the Text Import Wizard appears. This wizard walks you through three steps to help you import and properly separate the text file into columns of data. Because the data is delimited, you can leave the settings at their defaults.

Step 9	***Click***	Next > to go to Step 2
Step 10	***Click***	Next > to accept the default choice of tabs as delimiters
Step 11	***Click***	Finish to accept the default settings for specifying how columns of data are formatted
Step 12	***Click***	OK in the Import Data dialog box

You can format and rearrange the imported data as necessary. Because Super Power Computer's file is a plain text file, it cannot carry formulas with it; thus all totals and subtotals are included only as values. Upon reviewing the information, you notice that the totals in the workbook are not correct. You decide to correct the totals by replacing them with functions. To replace values with functions:

Step 1	***Activate***	cell B10
Step 2	***Click***	the AutoSum button Σ on the Standard toolbar
Step 3	***Press***	the ENTER key
Step 4	***Follow***	Steps 1 through 3 to sum the total outflows in cells B14:B28 in cell B30
Step 5	***Enter***	=B10-B30 in cell B33
Step 6	***Save***	the workbook as *Old Monthly Cash Flow* and close it

Importing and exporting data enables you to accurately and quickly use Excel data in other Office applications.

Summary

- You can paste Excel data into a Word document to use the Word table tools.
- You can embed Excel data to use the functionality of Excel without providing for data to be updated from the source.
- You can create charts in Word using Excel data and the Microsoft Graph Chart object.
- You can link Excel documents when data must be kept up to date.
- You can embed or link charts and data to PowerPoint slides to enhance presentations.
- You can use Excel lists to create tables in Access. You also can query Access databases from Excel to create charts, reports, and statistical analysis.
- You can import data from different types of files using the Import Text Wizard.

Commands Review

Action	Menu Bar	Shortcut Menu	Toolbar	Task Pane	Keyboard
Insert a copy of Excel data in a Word document	Insert, File				ALT + I, L
Place Excel data in a Word document as a Word table	Edit, Copy Edit, Paste	Right-click selected data, Copy Right-click, Paste			ALT + E, C ALT + E, P CTRL + C CTRL + V
Embed Excel data in a Word document	Insert, Object Edit, Copy Edit, Paste Special, Paste				ALT + I, O ALT + E, C ALT + E, S ALT + P
Link Excel data in a Word document	Edit, Copy Edit, Paste Special, Paste link	Right-click Excel range, Copy			ALT + E, C ALT + E, S ALT + L CTRL + C
Link Excel worksheet data or chart to PowerPoint slide	Edit, Copy Edit, Paste Special, Paste link	Right-click Excel range, Copy			ALT + E, C ALT + E, S ALT + L CTRL + C
Embed Excel worksheet data or chart in PowerPoint slide	Edit, Copy Edit, Paste Special, Paste	Right-click Excel range or chart, Copy Right-click PowerPoint slide, Paste			ALT + E, C ALT + E, S ALT + P CTRL + C CTRL + V

Concepts Review

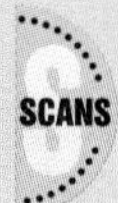

Circle the correct answer.

1. To embed worksheet data in a Word document:
[a] use Copy and Paste.
[b] use Copy and Paste Special.
[c] press the CTRL key and drag a selection from Excel to Word.
[d] use Copy and Paste Special or drag a selection from Excel to Word.

2. Integrating Excel with other applications:
[a] is difficult and creates outdated copies of data.
[b] is unnecessary because Excel can format a worksheet any way you want.
[c] increases your productivity and enhances your options for presenting data.
[d] cannot be done.

3. Embedding an Excel file in Word or PowerPoint:
[a] creates a link to the Excel application and the source data.
[b] creates a link to the Excel application but not to the source data.
[c] makes a copy of the Excel data using a Word table structure.
[d] makes a picture object of the data that can be only resized or moved.

4. When creating a Word document with integrated Excel data that might change later, you should use:
[a] embedded data.
[b] linked data.
[c] inserted data.
[d] copied data.

5. If you need to keep a "snapshot" of Excel data in another document at a given time, you should:
[a] use embedded data.
[b] use linked data.
[c] use a screen shot.
[d] save the workbook using a different filename.

6. Text files can use which of the following characters as delimiters?
[a] comma
[b] tab
[c] semicolon
[d] comma, tab, or semicolon

7. When Excel lists become very large, a better option may be to:
[a] remove infrequently used records.
[b] create a second workbook and move half the records there.
[c] convert the worksheet to an Access database.
[d] condense the data by abbreviating names and other information.

8. You can output the results of a query to:
[a] the Microsoft Query window.
[b] an Excel worksheet.
[c] the Excel Query dialog box.
[d] all of the above

9. A comma-delimited file uses what character as a delimiter?
[a] ,
[b] ;
[c] TAB
[d] `

10. Which application is best suited to storing large lists of data?
[a] Excel
[b] Word
[c] PowerPoint
[d] Access

Circle **T** if the statement is true or **F** if the statement is false.

T F 1. Inserting and embedding data create copies of the data that are not linked to the source data.

T F 2. Linking Excel data to a Word document requires more disk space than embedding, because it creates an additional copy of the Excel workbook.

T F 3. You cannot create a simultaneous link to the same data in both a Word document and a PowerPoint presentation.

T F 4. The Paste Special dialog box can be used to embed or link data.

T F 5. Right-click and drag an object from Excel to a Word document to create a linked object.

T F 6. When editing embedded or linked Excel data in a Word document, you stay "in" the Word document, but the Excel menu and toolbars appear.

T F 7. Double-clicking the column head in the Datasheet window of a Microsoft Graph Chart object toggles the column on and off.

T F 8. Double-clicking a linked worksheet opens the linked worksheet document in Excel.

T F 9. Double-clicking an embedded worksheet opens the linked worksheet document in Excel.

T F 10. Learning to use the right software tool for the job can save time and effort.

Skills Review

Exercise 1

1. Create a new, blank workbook.

2. Use Microsoft Query (Data, Import External Data, New Database Query) to query the *Excel List.mdb* database located on the Data Disk.

3. Create a query to extract records from the Mountain or Central regions where the gross sales exceed $40,000.

4. Sort the results by gross sales in descending order.

5. Output the results to Excel.

6. Create a chart on a new sheet listing the top 10 sales representatives and their gross sales totals.

7. Add a title to your chart that describes its contents.

8. Print the chart.

9. Save the workbook as *Top 10*, and close it.

Exercise 2

1. Open the *Top 10* workbook that you created in Exercise 1.

2. Open the *Top 10 Sales Representatives.ppt* presentation located on the Data Disk using PowerPoint.

3. Save the presentation as *Top 15.ppt*.

4. Link the Top 10 Chart to the first slide in the presentation by using Copy and Paste Special, then selecting the Paste link option.

5. Resize and reposition the chart as necessary.

6. Click the Excel button on the taskbar.
7. Modify the Chart Source Data to include the top 15 sales representatives.
8. Remove the chart title.
9. Click the PowerPoint button on the taskbar and update the link.
10. Rename the Slide title as "Top 15 Sales Representatives."
11. Print the PowerPoint slide, then save the PowerPoint presentation and exit PowerPoint.
12. Save the workbook as *Top 15* and close it.

Exercise 3 

1. Open the *Warehouse Inventory* workbook located on the Data Disk.
2. Sort the list by Part No., then save the workbook as *Warehouse Inventory Modified.*
3. Select the range A4:F16 and click the Copy button on the Standard toolbar, then close the workbook.
4. Open the Word application.
5. Open the *Letter to Warehouse Division Manager.doc* document located on the Data Disk.
6. Save the Word document as *Letter with Data.doc.*
7. Insert a blank line between the first and second paragraphs of the letter.
8. Use the Paste Special command on the Edit menu to embed the data as a Microsoft Excel worksheet object.
9. Resize and reposition the embedded object as necessary.
10. Double-click the embedded object to make the following modifications:
    a. Change the cost of item 1020 to $29.95.
    b. Change the quantity of item 3001 to 500.
    c. Center the data in the range E5:E16. (*Hint:* If you scroll the worksheet so that the visible range changes, scroll it back so that the visible range is again A4:F16.)
    d. Turn off the display of gridlines by using the Options dialog box.
11. Print, save, and close the letter.

Exercise 4 

1. Open the *Letter with Data.doc* document that you created in Exercise 3, and delete the embedded object.
2. Open the file *Warehouse Inventory Modified* workbook that you created in Exercise 3, then save it as *Warehouse Inventory Modified 2.*
3. Copy the range A4:F16.
4. Use the Paste Special command in Word to create a linked worksheet object in the document, then resize it and reposition the object as necessary.
5. Double-click the linked object to edit the data as follows:
    a. Center the range E5:E16.
    b. Change the cost of item 1020 to $35.95.
    c. Change the quantity of item 3001 to 750.
    d. Select the range A5:A16 and left-justify the range.

6. Save the workbook.
7. In Word, right-click the linked object and click Update Link.
8. Save the Word document as *Letter with Linked Data.doc*.
9. Print and close the workbook and the Word document.

Exercise 5 

1. Create a new, blank workbook.
2. Create a database query using the *Excel List.mdb* database located on the Data Disk to extract all records where the gross sales exceed $45,000.
3. Sort the results by gross sales in descending order.
4. Output the results to Excel.
5. Copy the data.
6. Start a new Word document.
7. Embed the data as a Microsoft Excel worksheet object in a new Word document.
8. Save the Word document as *Sales Above 45000.doc* and close it.
9. Save the workbook as *Sales Above 45000* and close it.

Exercise 6

1. Create a new, blank workbook.
2. Use Import Data (Data, Import External Data, Import Data) to import the tab-delimited text file *Movie Times.txt.*
3. Save the workbook as *Movie Times Imported*, then print and close it.

Exercise 7

1. Create a new, blank workbook.
2. Create a database query using the *Sales Data.mdb* database located on the Data Disk.
3. Extract records from the West Coast Region whose Q1 sales and Q2 sales each exceeded $2,000.
4. Sort the records by Name in ascending order.
5. Format columns E and F with Currency format.
6. Hide column A.
7. Rename the sheet tab as "West Coast."
8. Save the workbook as *Sales Data Extracted*, then print and close it.

Exercise 8

1. Open the *Sales Data Extracted* workbook that you created in Exercise 7.
2. On Sheet2 create another database query using the *Sales Data.mdb* database located on the Data Disk.
3. Extract records from the North subregions whose Q1 sales are not more than $1,500.
4. Sort the records by Region in ascending order.
5. Format columns E and F with Currency format.

6. Hide column A.
7. Rename the sheet tab to "North Subregions."
8. Save the workbook as *Sales Data Extracted 2*, then print and close it.

Case Projects

Project 1

You work for a framing company that builds houses. You are preparing a bid on a new job. In a new workbook, create categories for materials, labor, and markup. Include fictitious data for the materials and labor costs. Calculate the markup as 10% of the sum total of materials and labor costs. Calculate the grand total of your bid. Save the workbook as *Framing Bid*. In a new Word document, write a letter explaining your proposal. Embed the workbook data in the Word document. Save the document as *Final Bid.doc*, then print and close it. Close the workbook.

Project 2  

You are a busy stockbroker. In an effort to drum up investment business, you decide to send a letter to your clients showing the recent results of several stocks that have been performing well lately. Use the Internet to research two or three companies that might pique your clients' interest. Create a workbook to record high/low/close prices for each stock over the last week. Save the workbook as *Recent Stock Prices*. Create a chart for each stock and link the charts to your letter. If you are having problems positioning the linked charts, turn on the Drawing toolbar in Word, then use the Text Wrapping button to change the wrapping (Top and Bottom or Square work pretty well). Print the letter and save the document as *Stock Letter.doc*. Close the document and the workbook.

Project 3

You are the assistant to the president of a large advertising company. One of your responsibilities is to prepare a monthly report showing the amounts collected from your five largest clients. Create a workbook with fictitious data for 10 clients over the last three months. Sort the data by totals for the quarter to find your five largest clients. Create a pie chart of the data for these clients. Save the workbook as *Client Data*. Working in PowerPoint, create a new presentation. Link the chart from your workbook to the first slide. Link the data, including all 10 clients, to the second slide. Save the presentation as *Clients.ppt*, then print and close it. Close the workbook.

Project 4

You are the personnel director for a large firm. You have been keeping a list of employee data, including first and last names, ages, phone extensions, and departments in an Excel workbook. Because the list keeps growing larger, you decide to maintain this information in an Access database. Create a workbook containing data for 20 fictitious employees. Save the workbook as *Personnel Data*. In Access, create a new blank database called *Personnel Data.mdb* and import the data from this newly created workbook. Print the database table, then close the table and the database. Close the workbook.

Project 5

Your sales company has been forced to release some of its sales staff. Using the *Excel List* database located on the Data Disk, create a new workbook using a database query. Query the database for records in the Central Region whose gross sales are less than $30,000. Sort the results by gross sales in descending order. Save the workbook as *Cutback*, then print and close it.

Project 6 

You are in charge of application licensing for your firm. Create a new workbook in which you can record the application name, version number, and upgrade cost for each application installed on your computer. Using your own computer, add information for as many applications installed on your computer as you can. Try and find upgrade prices for each of the applications by looking at the vendor's Web site. Save the workbook as *Application Licensing*. Create a Word document addressed to management explaining which applications you think need to be upgraded in the near future and why. Link the data from your workbook to this document and save it as *Application Licensing.doc*. Print the letter, then close the document. Close the workbook.

Project 7 

As a travel broker, you use "open house" presentations to encourage your existing clients to travel more often. This month, you are featuring a special on travel to Europe. Use the Internet to look up the current exchange rate between U.S. dollars and the euro. Record this information in a workbook and save the workbook as *Travel to Europe*. Embed this data in a PowerPoint slide. Save the PowerPoint presentation as *Travel to Europe.ppt*, then print and close it. Close the workbook.

Project 8 

You are a columnist for the local newspaper covering the NBA (or another sport that interests you or is in season). Prepare a workbook covering the score of a recent game, including a column for each team, column labels for four quarters (periods, or innings, depending on the sport you chose), plus a total column. Add a formula in the total column that sums the total number of points scored by each team. Save the workbook as *Sports Scores.ppt*. Create a chart, then embed the chart in a Word document. Save the document as *Embedded Sports Scores.doc*, then print and close it. Close the workbook.

Sharing Workbooks with Others

Chapter Overview

Changes in today's software reflect the way the business world works. Documents are shared between departments and among coworkers and can be edited simultaneously by many people connected to a network. During the editing process, Excel tracks all changes made to a workbook. Workbooks can be distributed electronically, then merged into a single workbook after several people make modifications. You can add comments to cells to clarify results or add an informative note. You can customize by creating custom number formats, then using lookup functions to create highly specialized workbooks.

Learning Objectives

- Create and apply custom number and conditional formats
- Use lookup and reference functions
- Use workgroup features

Case profile

Super Power Computers uses Excel to look up and track inventory. Using custom number formats and special reference functions in this workbook saves a lot of time during data entry and retrieval. Working efficiently often requires several people to collaborate, or work together in a workbook. The Excel collaboration features make this a simple task.

chapter fifteen

15

15.a Creating and Applying Custom Number and Conditional Formats

Number formats speed data entry by inserting symbols, text, or extra zeroes in entries to maintain a consistent look to data entered on a worksheet. These number format styles don't change the value entered in the cell; they just add special formatting and symbols, such as monetary symbols, comma separators, and so on. You have seen these formats at work when applying the Currency, Percent, and Accounting styles to cells. Excel also provides other specialized number formats such as ZIP codes, telephone numbers, and Social Security numbers. In addition to the number formats provided, you can create and apply your own specialized number formats. You also can apply number formats to a cell or cells based on the value or condition of another cell's content.

Creating Custom Number Formats

At the Super Power Computers warehouse, each item receives a special sorting code made up of a mixture of letters and numbers, to make it easier to locate specific items. The *Super Power Computers - Warehouse Receiving Log* keeps track of all merchandise received at the warehouse. To start:

Step 1	***Open***	the *Super Power Computers - Warehouse Receiving Log* workbook located on the Data Disk
Step 2	***Save***	the workbook as *Super Power Computers - Warehouse Receiving Log Revised*

The January 2003 worksheet contains a list of items received at the warehouse in January. You see an example of the number format that the warehouse department would like to apply in the Item # column. These entries are text values and therefore are not recognized as numbers. Each character must be entered by hand. Correct entries use the ##-SPC-#### format, where # represents a significant digit. Your worksheet, which includes several incorrect entries, should look similar to Figure 15-1.

FIGURE 15-1
Incorrect Data Entry

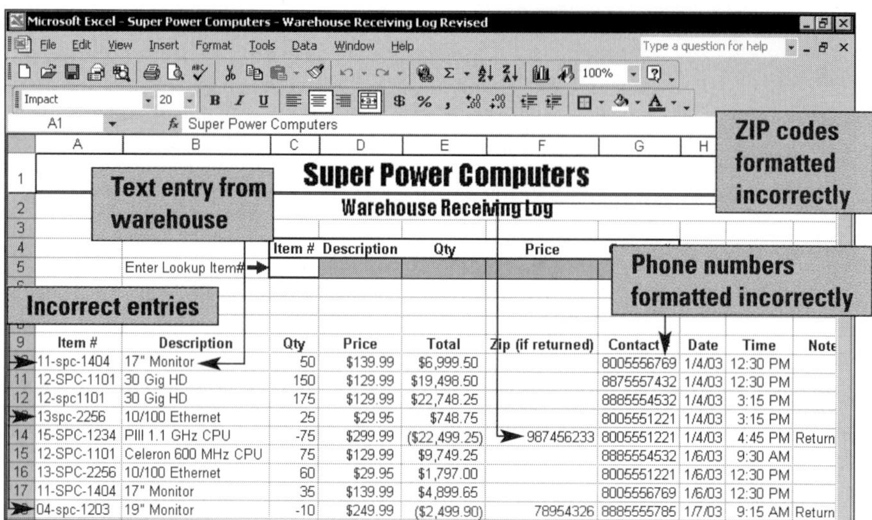

As part of an effort to reduce data entry errors, you create a custom numeric format that corresponds to the company's existing system. To create a custom number format:

Step 1	*Key*	111404 in cell A10, replacing the previous entry

This value is the numerical portion of the item number.

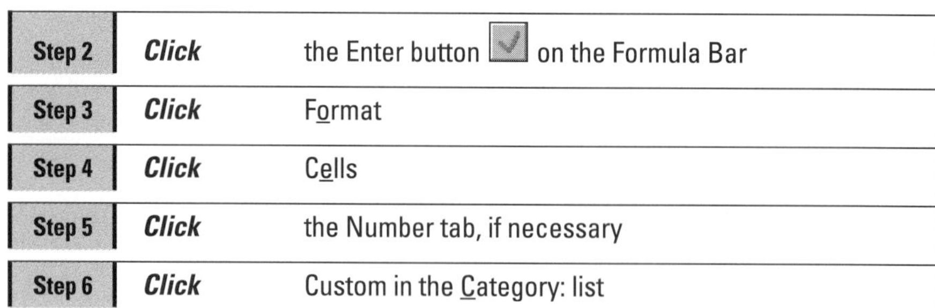

Step 2	*Click*	the Enter button on the Formula Bar
Step 3	*Click*	Format
Step 4	*Click*	Cells
Step 5	*Click*	the Number tab, if necessary
Step 6	*Click*	Custom in the Category: list

You can set the color of the entry, and you can determine how and where the numerical data will be placed. The formats listed in the Type: list can serve as starting points for your own custom format. The formats use special codes to specify various types of formatting. Table 15-1 describes these codes.

TABLE 15-1
Custom Number Format Codes

Format Code	Use
#	Displays significant digits, but not insignificant zeroes
0	Displays insignificant zeroes if a number has fewer digits than the number of zeroes specified in the format
?	Adds spaces for insignificant zeroes to line up decimals; also used for fraction formats with varying numbers of digits
,	Thousands separator
*	Repeats the next character in the format code to fill any blank spaces in a cell
"text"	Inserts any text within the quotes as part of the number format
\	Displays a single character as part of the number format
_	Inserts a space character in the number format
;	Separates sections of a custom number format; each format can have four sections to format positive, negative, zero, and text values
<=, <, >=, >, <>, =	Conditional operators that apply the custom format only if a numerical value meets the specified condition
[Color]	Use one of eight colors (Black, Blue, Cyan, Green, Magenta, Red, White, and Yellow) to display values; colors must be listed first in a section
@	Used as the last entry in a custom number format to display text; if this symbol is omitted from the custom format, any text entered is not displayed

QUICK TIP

Significant digits on the left of a decimal point start with the number farthest to the left that is not a zero. Significant digits to the right of the decimal point do not include ending zeroes.

For each custom number format you define, you can specify four formats in the following order: positive numbers, negative numbers, zero values, and text. Each section is separated by a semicolon. If you omit the negative and zero value formats from the style definition, those values are displayed in the same way as the positive number format. If you omit the text style from the style definition, text entered in the cell is stored but not displayed.

Step 7	***Double-click***	the Type: text box to select the previous entry
Step 8	***Key***	[Blue]00-"SPC"-0000

The Custom category of the Number tab should look similar to Figure 15-2. As you enter the code, the preview displays the formatted number the way it will appear in your worksheet. The first part of this number format, **[Blue]**, sets the text color of the entry to blue. The rest of the code determines how and where numerical data is placed. The first two digits are separated by **-SPC-** followed by the last four digits.

FIGURE 15-2
Creating a Custom Number Format

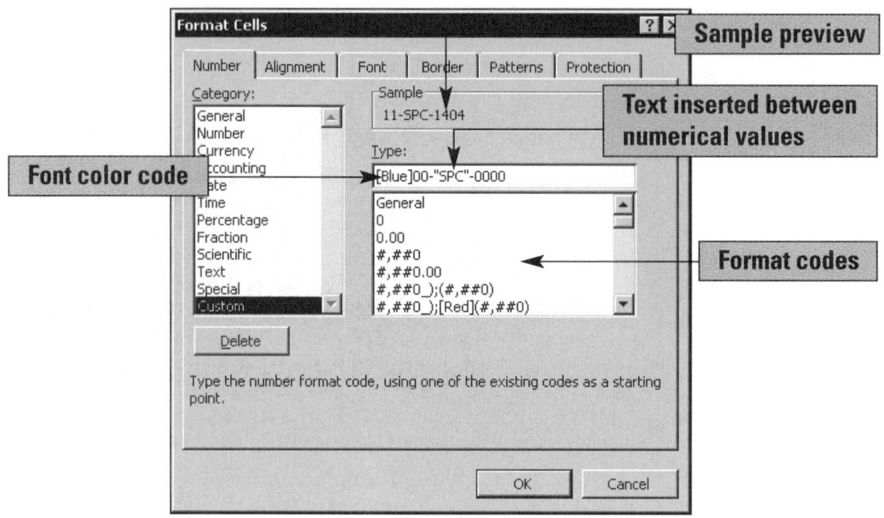

Step 9	*Click*	OK

The formatting applied to cell A10 of your worksheet should look similar to Figure 15-3.

FIGURE 15-3
Custom Format Applied to Cell A10

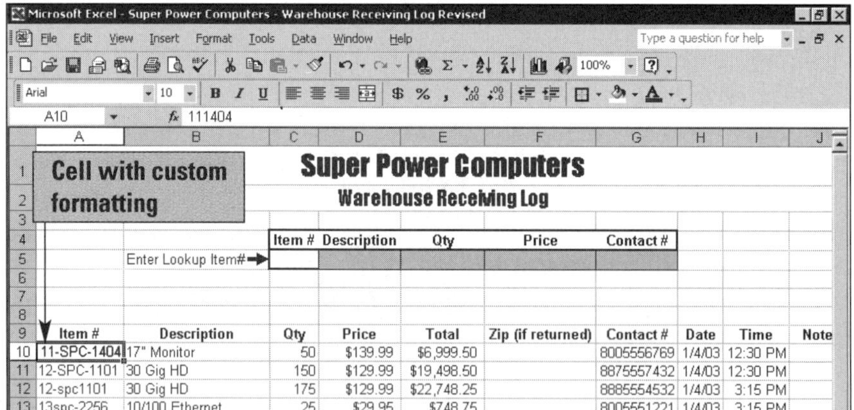

Applying Custom Number Formats

Once you've created a custom number format, it is added to the Type: list. You apply that format by selecting the cell and then selecting the format in the list. To apply custom number formats:

Step 1	*Select*	the range A11:A21
Step 2	*Open*	the Number tab in the Format Cells dialog box
Step 3	*Click*	Custom in the Category: list

Step 4	*Scroll*	down the Type: list
Step 5	*Click*	[Blue]00-"SPC"-0000
Step 6	*Click*	OK

Even though the number format has been applied, the data in the cell doesn't match the "picture" Excel expects to find. You need to reenter the numerical portion of each entry.

Step 7	*Enter*	121101 in cell A11

Notice that the font changes to blue, and the extra information is inserted into the middle of the numerical data.

Step 8	*Repeat*	Step 7 to reenter the numerical values only in cells A12:A21

Next you finish formatting the workbook.

Step 9	*Select*	the range F10:F21
Step 10	*Open*	the Number tab in the Format Cells dialog box
Step 11	*Click*	Special in the Category: list box
Step 12	*Click*	Zip Code + 4 in the Type: list box
Step 13	*Click*	OK
Step 14	*Apply*	the Special format "Phone Number" to column G
Step 15	*Save*	the workbook

CAUTION TIP

When applying the Zip Code + 4 format, double check to make sure the Locale is set to English (United States).

Applying Conditional Formatting

Conditional formatting evaluates the value of a cell for a true or false condition and applies different formatting to the cell based on the results of that evaluation. For example, you can apply a conditional format to the cell containing the quantity of an item in the warehouse so that the format changes when inventory levels in the warehouse fall below a certain level.

When you apply conditional formatting to a cell, you can test for as many as three conditions by using cell-to-cell comparisons or a logical function; you can then apply shading and borders to the cell itself, in addition to changing the font style and color. You can use conditional formatting to apply as many as three different formatting styles, based on either a comparison of the cell value to another value or the results of a logical function.

In the worksheet, you want to flag the quantity when the inventory falls to certain levels. To apply conditional formatting:

Step 1	***Activate***	cell C10
Step 2	***Click***	Format
Step 3	***Click***	Conditional Formatting

The Conditional Formatting dialog box on your screen should look similar to Figure 15-4.

FIGURE 15-4
Conditional Formatting Dialog Box

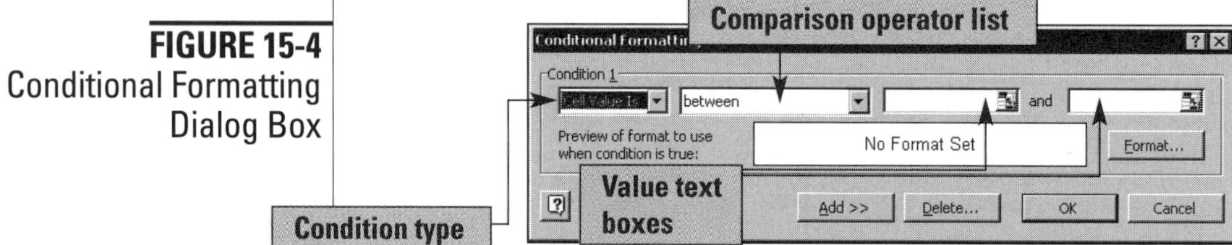

When the quantity of any item falls below 50, you want the cell to show a red background.

Step 4	***Press***	the TAB key
Step 5	***Select***	less than from the list
Step 6	***Press***	the TAB key
Step 7	***Key***	50 in the value text box
Step 8	***Click***	Format
Step 9	***Change***	the font color to White (you must select the White box instead of the default Automatic)
Step 10	***Click***	the Border tab
Step 11	***Click***	Outline
Step 12	***Click***	the Patterns tab
Step 13	***Click***	the red box
Step 14	***Click***	OK

You want to add another condition in case the inventory of an item falls between 50 and 75.

Step 15	*Click*	Add >>
Step 16	*Press*	the TAB key twice
Step 17	*Key*	50
Step 18	*Press*	the TAB key
Step 19	*Key*	75
Step 20	*Change*	the font color to blue and the cell shading color to yellow
Step 21	*Click*	OK twice
Step 22	*Observe*	the formatting in cell C10

To copy the conditional formatting to the range C11:C21:

Step 1	*Click*	the Format Painter button on the Standard toolbar
Step 2	*Select*	the range C11:C21 to apply the conditional formatting to all the quantity cells
Step 3	*Select*	A1

Your worksheet should look similar to Figure 15-5.

9	Item #	Description	Qty	Price	Total	Zip (if returned)	Contact #	Date	Time	N
10	11-SPC-1404	17" Monitor	50	$1			-6769	1/4/03	12:30 PM	
11	12-SPC-1101	30 Gig HD	150	$1			-7432	1/4/03	12:30 PM	
12	12-SPC-1101	30 Gig HD	175	$129.99	$22,748.25		(888) 555-4532	1/4/03	3:15 PM	
13	13-SPC-2256	10/100 Ethernet	25	$29.95	$748.75		(800) 555-1221	1/4/03	3:15 PM	
14	15-SPC-1234	PIII 1.1 GHz CPU	-75	$299.99	($22,499.25)	98745-6233	(800) 555-1221	1/4/03	4:45 PM	Ret
15	12-SPC-1101	Celeron 600 MHz CPU	75	$129.99	$9,749.25		(888) 555-4532	1/6/03	9:30 AM	
16	13-SPC-2256	10/100 Ethernet	60	$29.95	$1,797.00		(800) 555-1221	1/6/03	12:30 PM	
17	11-SPC-1404	17" Monitor	35	$139.99	$4,899.65		(800) 555-6769	1/6/03	12:30 PM	
18	04-SPC-1203	19" Monitor	-10	$249.99	($2,499.90)	07895-4326	(888) 555-5785	1/7/03	9:15 AM	Ret
19	13-SPC-2256	10/100 Ethernet	60	$29.95	$1,797.00		(800) 555-1221	1/7/03	9:15 AM	
20	11-SPC-1404	17" Monitor	-45	$139.99	($6,299.55)	12435-6803	(800) 555-6769	1/7/03	1:45 PM	Ret
21	04-SPC-1203	19" Monitor	45	$249.99	$11,249.55		(888) 555-5785	1/8/03	4:30 PM	
22										

Inventory between 50-75

Inventory below 50

January 2003

Ready

NUM

FIGURE 15-5
Conditional Formatting Applied to Worksheet

Step 4	*Save*	the workbook

15.b Using Lookup and Reference Functions

Lookup functions are a special class of functions that can be used to locate information in a workbook. Certain lookup functions can be used to lookup and retrieve associated data. For example, when you search for an ISBN number at an online bookseller, information about the book's title, author, number of pages, and the price are returned.

The **VLOOKUP** function searches for a value in the leftmost column of an array, an arrangement or list of items, usually in columns and rows.

The VLOOKUP function has the following syntax:

=VLOOKUP(lookup_value,table_array,col_index_num,range_lookup)

The lookup_value is the Item # you will input in cell A2. The table_array is the list set up in cells A5:E11. When VLOOKUP finds a match to the Item #, it retrieves the value located in the same row as the matching Item # and in the column number in the array specified as the col_index_num argument.

VLOOKUP searches for an exact match. The default value of the optional range_lookup argument is TRUE, which means that if VLOOKUP cannot find an exact match, it returns the next largest value that is less than the lookup value. Using the default range_lookup setting requires your data to be sorted in ascending order. If you set the range_lookup argument to FALSE, VLOOKUP returns only an exact match.

The Inventory worksheet contains a list of items available in the warehouse. As this list grows, it will become more difficult to quickly look up information. By adding the VLOOKUP formula to cells B2:E2, an item number can be entered in cell A2, and data from the list matching the item # will be returned. To use the VLOOKUP function:

MOUSE TIP

If you drag to select a range as an argument, the Function Arguments dialog box automatically collapses when you start your selection and expands when you release the mouse button.

Step 1	***Activate***	cell D5
Step 2	***Click***	the Insert Function button to the left of the Formula Bar
Step 3	***Double-click***	the VLOOKUP function in the Lookup & Reference function category
Step 4	***Key***	C5 in the Lookup_value argument text box
Step 5	***Key***	A10:J21 in the Table_array argument text box

QUICK TIP

In practice, you would probably key a row number well beyond row 21 so that additional items could be entered into the lookup array without adjusting the formulas.

Next, you want to retrieve the value located in the second column of the array, the Description.

Step 6	***Key***	2 in the Col_index_num text box
Step 7	***Key***	FALSE in the Range_lookup text box
Step 8	***Click***	OK

Cell D5 displays the #N/A error because cell C5 does not yet contain a value to look up.

Step 9	*Enter*	111404 in cell C5

Cell D5 displays the correct product description, 17" Monitor. Now finish adding VLOOKUP formulas to the remaining cells.

Step 10	*Enter*	=VLOOKUP(C5,A10:J21,3,false) in cell E5
Step 11	*Enter*	=VLOOKUP(C5,A10:J21,4,false) in cell F5
Step 12	*Enter*	=VLOOKUP(C5,A10:J21,7,false) in cell G5

Now look up another Item #.

Step 13	*Enter*	151234 in cell C5

The information is retrieved from the list and displayed in cells D5:G5. Your worksheet should look similar to Figure 15-6.

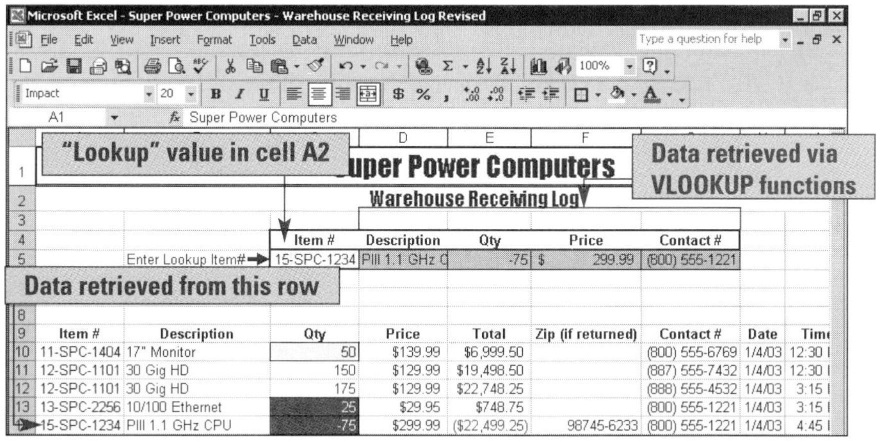

FIGURE 15-6
Using the VLOOKUP Reference Function

Step 14	*Save*	the workbook

The HLOOKUP function works similarly to the VLOOKUP function, but searches for values in a row rather than a column. When it finds a match, the HLOOKUP function retrieves data located in a specified row of the column where the match was found. This allows for flexibility in the way you set up your worksheets. The syntax of the HLOOKUP function is the same as that of the VLOOKUP function except that you supply a row index number to return instead of a column index number.

CAUTION TIP

The #VALUE! error occurs when you use the wrong type of argument or operand. For example, entering "hello" as the range_lookup argument in the VLOOKUP function would produce this error. Supply the correct type of argument required by the function to fix this error.

The #N/A! error occurs when a value is not available to a function or formula.

QUICK TIP

Excel provides more than 15 lookup and reference functions. To find out more about functions not covered in this section, use online Help.

15.c Using Workgroup Features

Often, you need to create a workbook that many people will have access to. The Warehouse Receiving Log will be used by many people. You are still developing the format of the workbook, and you want to collect input from several other people at Super Power Computers. You also want to allow warehouse workers to use the lookup function you added to find the current inventory of any product, but you don't want someone to inadvertently change a formula. You can protect the formulas in the workbook from changes, then put the workbook on the company network and allow many people to access it and make any changes they want to the unprotected cells. You can collect their revisions and then merge the results.

Protecting Cells, Worksheets, and Workbooks

When a workbook is used by many people, you may want to prevent other users from changing the data or formatting in that workbook. You accomplish this task by enabling workbook protection. If security is a concern, you can add a password to your workbooks as well.

Excel provides two ways to protect individual cells from being altered. **Hiding** cells prevents the formula from appearing in the Formula Bar when a user clicks the cell, but still calculates the result as usual. **Locking** cells prevents other users from changing them. To set these options, you use the Format Cells dialog box, then enable worksheet protection.

You want to protect the cells containing the VLOOKUP functions you just entered. To set cell protection options:

Step 1	*Select*	the range D5:G5
Step 2	*Open*	the Format Cells dialog box
Step 3	*Click*	the Protection tab
Step 4	*Click*	the Hidden check box to insert a check mark

The Locked check box is selected by default. When checked, the Hidden option prevents other users from seeing formulas in the Formula Bar. Neither option affects the selected cells until you protect the worksheet.

Step 5	*Click*	OK

You want warehouse personnel to be able to add new entries, as well as use cell D5 for data entry. You need to unlock these cells specifically, then apply worksheet protection.

Step 6	*Click*	cell C5
Step 7	*Press & hold*	the CTRL key
Step 8	*Select*	the range A10:J35
Step 9	*Open*	the Format Cells dialog box
Step 10	*Click*	the Locked check box on the Protection tab to remove the check mark
Step 11	*Click*	OK

To apply worksheet protection:

Step 1	*Click*	Tools
Step 2	*Point to*	Protection
Step 3	*Click*	Protect Sheet

The Protect Sheet dialog box on your screen should look similar to Figure 15-7. It allows you to protect cell contents, formatting, drawing objects, scenarios, and more. If security is an issue, you can apply a password to prevent anyone who does not have that password from changing the settings.

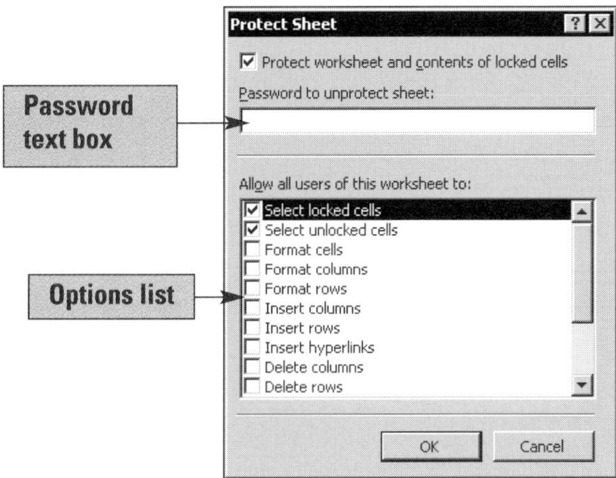

FIGURE 15-7
Protect Sheet Dialog Box

CAUTION TIP

Be sure to remember your password. If you forget it, you may not be able to access your workbook.

To apply a password:

Step 1	*Enter*	your first name in the Password to unprotect sheet: text box (use lowercase letters)

As you enter your password, an asterisk (*) replaces each letter you type, as a security measure.

Step 2	*Click*	OK

Excel prompts you to reenter your password to ensure that you entered it correctly. Passwords are case-sensitive, so *Your Name* is not the same password as *your name.*

Step 3	*Enter*	your first name again, exactly as you entered it before
Step 4	*Click*	OK
Step 5	*Click*	cell D5
Step 6	*Observe*	that you can no longer see the formula in the Formula Bar
Step 7	*Press*	any letter key to change the contents of the cell

Excel notifies you that the cell is protected.

Step 8	*Click*	OK

In the Protect Workbook dialog box, you are given two options. Checking the Structure check box prevents users from deleting, moving, renaming, or inserting worksheets into a workbook. Checking the Windows check box prevents users from resizing, minimizing or restoring the document window. This option is useful for a specially formatted workbook designed to work as a form for entering data, such as a sales receipt. To turn on workbook protection:

Step 1	*Click*	Tools
Step 2	*Point to*	Protection
Step 3	*Click*	Protect Workbook
Step 4	*Key*	your first name in lowercase letters in the Password (optional): text box

Step 5	*Click*	OK
Step 6	*Key*	your first name in lowercase letters again
Step 7	*Click*	OK
Step 8	*Right-click*	the January 2003 sheet tab

Most of the options normally available, such as Rename, Insert, and Delete, are disabled now that workbook protection is enabled. When you no longer need the workbook or worksheet protection, you can disable them. To remove worksheet and workbook protection:

Step 1	*Click*	Tools
Step 2	*Point to*	Protection
Step 3	*Click*	Unprotect Sheet
Step 4	*Key*	your password (your first name) exactly as you entered it previously
Step 5	*Click*	OK
Step 6	*Observe*	that the formula contained in cell D5 reappears in the Formula Bar
Step 7	*Click*	Tools
Step 8	*Point to*	Protection
Step 9	*Click*	Unprotect Workbook
Step 10	*Key*	your password
Step 11	*Click*	OK
Step 12	*Save*	the workbook

Sharing a Workbook

You can share a workbook by routing it to other users via e-mail or by working simultaneously with other users on a network. When you collaborate with others via a network, each user is notified when another user has saved changes.

The warehouse personnel need to begin using the workbook, even though you are still finalizing the workbook features. Sharing the workbook allows multiple users to work on the same workbook at the same time. To share a workbook:

Step 1	*Click*	Tools

MENU TIP

You can change your user name in the Options dialog box. Click the Options command on the Tools menu. On the General tab, key your name in the User name box, then click OK.

QUICK TIP

The Advanced tab of the Share Workbook dialog box includes advanced tracking options. For more information about these settings, click the Help button, then click the setting about which you want to learn.

Step 2	*Click*	Share Workbook to open the Share Workbook dialog box
Step 3	*Click*	the Allow changes by more than one user at the same time check box to insert a check mark

The Share Workbook dialog box on your screen should look similar to Figure 15-8.

FIGURE 15-8
Share Workbook Dialog Box

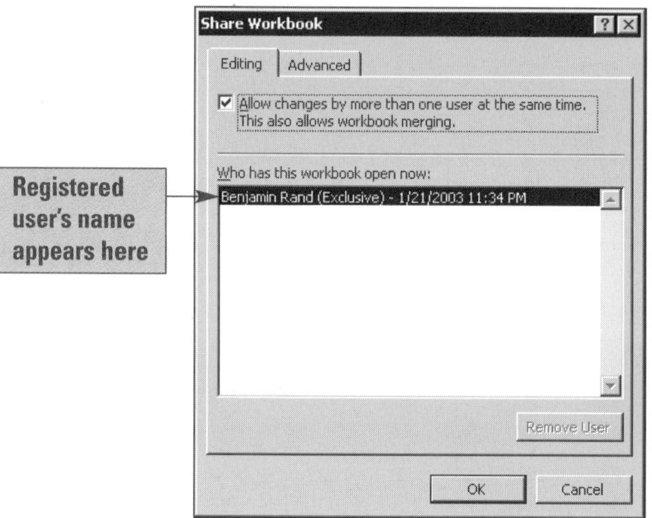

CAUTION TIP

When you share a workbook, certain limitations exist regarding what changes can and cannot be made to it. For example, all elements in place before the workbook is shared, such as charts, conditional formatting, and drawing objects, can be viewed by others, but not edited. Once you turn off workbook sharing, you can edit the workbook as usual. To obtain a complete list of these limitations, use online Help.

Step 4	*Click*	OK
Step 5	*Click*	OK to save changes to the workbook

The workbook is saved automatically, and the title bar reflects the fact that the workbook is [Shared].

Tracking Changes

When you share a workbook, you can track modifications to it. When you track changes, highlighted borders quickly identify cells whose contents have been edited. When several people work together on the same workbook, each user's changes are assigned a different color, making it easy to see who made changes to various cells. Note that the color assigned to each user's changes may differ each time you open the workbook. To highlight changes:

QUICK TIP

A quick way to enable workbook sharing and to track changes simultaneously is to open the Track Changes dialog box, then click the Track changes while editing check box.

Step 1	*Click*	Tools
Step 2	*Point to*	Track Changes
Step 3	*Click*	Highlight Changes

The Highlight Changes dialog box should look similar to Figure 15-9. In this dialog box, you select which changes to show.

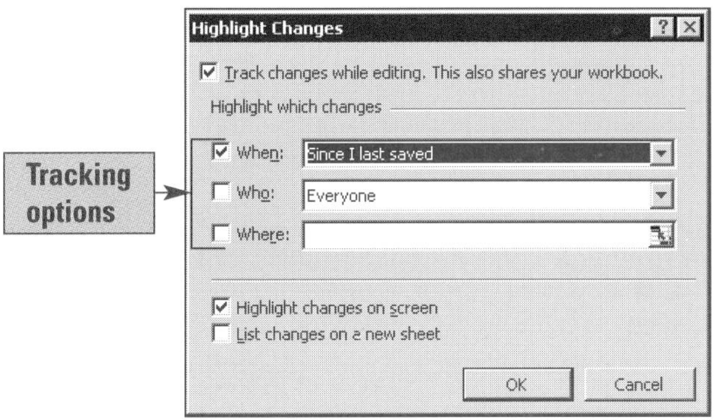

FIGURE 15-9
Highlight Changes Dialog Box

Step 4	*Click*	the When: list arrow
Step 5	*Click*	All
Step 6	*Click*	OK

Excel notifies you that it did not find any changes since the last time the workbook was saved.

Step 7	*Click*	OK
Step 8	*Enter*	10250 in cell A14
Step 9	*Move*	the mouse pointer over cell A14

Your worksheet should look similar to Figure 15-10.

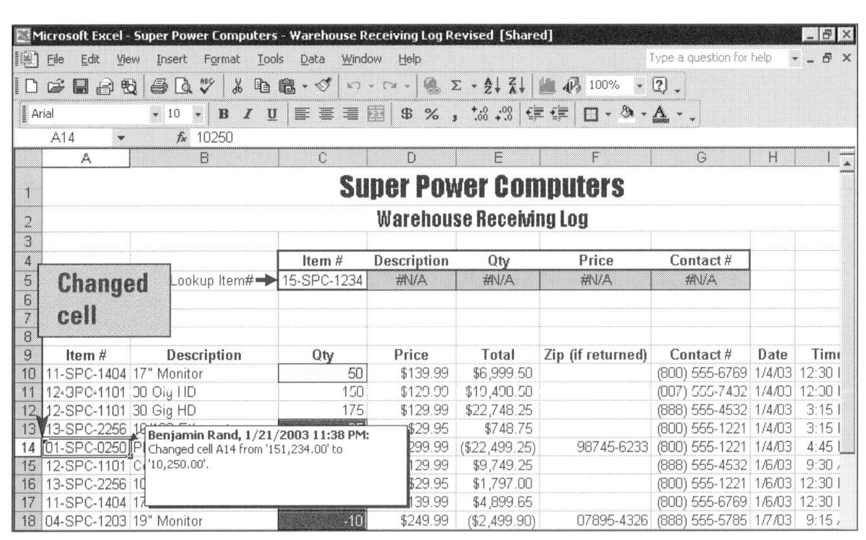

FIGURE 15-10
Changes to a Shared Workbook

MOUSE TIP

Excel keeps track of changes on a separate worksheet. Normally, this worksheet remains hidden from view, but you can display it by clicking the List changes on a new sheet check box in the Highlight Changes dialog box. This history list displays detailed information about all changes made to the workbook since the "track changes" feature was enabled.

A ScreenTip indicates the user name of the person who made the change, the date and time when the change was made, and the modification that was made to the cell. The border of the cell changes to a colored border and a small triangle is added in the upper-left corner, indicating that the cell's contents have changed.

Step 10	*Enter*	19.95 in cells D13, D16, and D19

You can accept or reject any change to the workbook. To accept or reject changes:

Step 1	*Click*	Tools
Step 2	*Point to*	Track Changes
Step 3	*Click*	Accept or Reject Changes
Step 4	*Click*	OK to save the changes to the workbook

QUICK TIP

When working simultaneously with multiple users, conflicting changes may occur. Excel can either save the latest changes—known as the "whoever saves last, wins" rule—or it can open the Resolve Conflicts dialog box to allow you to select which change to accept. This option appears on the Advanced tab of the Share Workbook dialog box.

The Select Changes to Accept or Reject dialog box opens. This dialog box allows you to filter the changes made since a certain date, changes made by a certain user, or changes affecting certain cells. The default is to select changes that you haven't reviewed yet.

Step 5	*Click*	OK

MOUSE TIP

Click Accept All or Reject All to quickly accept or reject all cells currently being reviewed.

When you click the OK button, the Accept or Reject Changes dialog box opens, allowing you to accept or reject individual or group changes. Your dialog box should look similar to Figure 15-11.

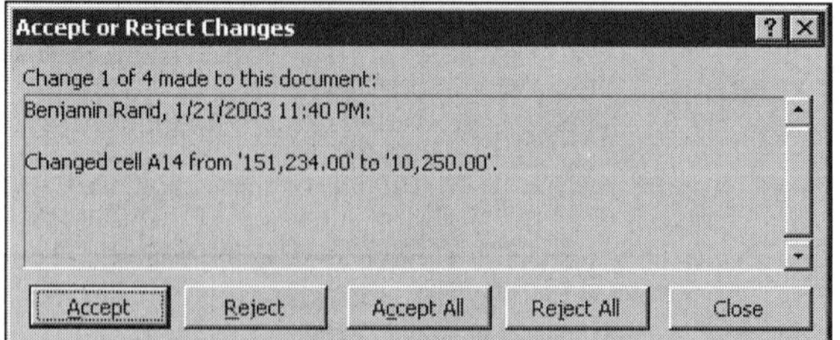

FIGURE 15-11
Accept or Reject Changes Dialog Box

Step 6	*Click*	Accept to accept the first change
Step 7	*Click*	Reject three times to reject the second, third, and fourth changes

The values in cells D13, D16, and D19 return to their original values, and the colored triangle and border that indicated a change disappears from each cell.

Step 8	*Save*	the workbook

Merging Workbooks

When you merge workbooks, you must follow several rules. First, you must create copies of a workbook for which the sharing and track changes features are enabled. Second, each copy must have a unique filename. Third, all workbooks must have a common password or no password. Fourth, when you enable workbook sharing, you can specify the length of time for which you want to track changes on the Advanced tab of the Share Workbook dialog box (the default is 30 days). You must merge the copies within this period. For example, if you set the "keep change" history to 30 days, and the workbook copies were made 45 days ago, you can no longer merge the workbooks. If necessary, you can set the "keep change" history to 32,767 days (about 90 years), which should give you plenty of time to merge workbooks.

When you perform the merge, only the destination (workbook receiving the changes) can be open. Your workbook should still be open, with track changes and sharing enabled. To create a copy and merge changes:

QUICK TIP

Occasionally, you may need to distribute copies of a shared workbook to users who do not have access to your network. Although you can route the workbook via e-mail, if you must continue editing the workbook simultaneously, this option may not work. In this case, you can save copies of the workbook and distribute them. When other users return these copies to you with their changes, you can incorporate the additional changes into the original workbook by using the Merge workbooks command.

Step 1	*Save*	the workbook as *Super Power Computers - Warehouse Receiving Log Warehouse Copy*
Step 2	*Save*	the workbook again as *Super Power Computers - Warehouse Receiving Log Office Copy*
Step 3	*Enter*	89.95 in cell D11
Step 4	*Enter*	20 in cell C10
Step 5	*Save*	the *Office Copy* workbook and close it
Step 6	*Open*	the *Super Power Computers - Warehouse Receiving Log Warehouse Copy* workbook
Step 7	*Open*	the Highlight Changes dialog box
Step 8	*Select*	All in the When: list
Step 9	*Click*	OK
Step 10	*Enter*	80 in cell C10
Step 11	*Save*	the *Warehouse Copy* workbook and close it
Step 12	*Open*	the *Super Power Computers - Warehouse Receiving Log Revised* workbook
Step 13	*Click*	Tools

Step 14	*Click*	Compare and Merge Workbooks
Step 15	*Press & hold*	the CTRL key
Step 16	*Click*	the *Office Copy* and the *Warehouse Copy* workbooks you saved earlier
Step 17	*Click*	OK

The changes in the revised (source) workbook are merged into the target workbook.

Step 18	*Open*	the Highlight Changes dialog box
Step 19	*Select*	All in the When: list
Step 20	*Click*	OK

The colored border indicates the changed cells. Your screen should look similar to Figure 15-12.

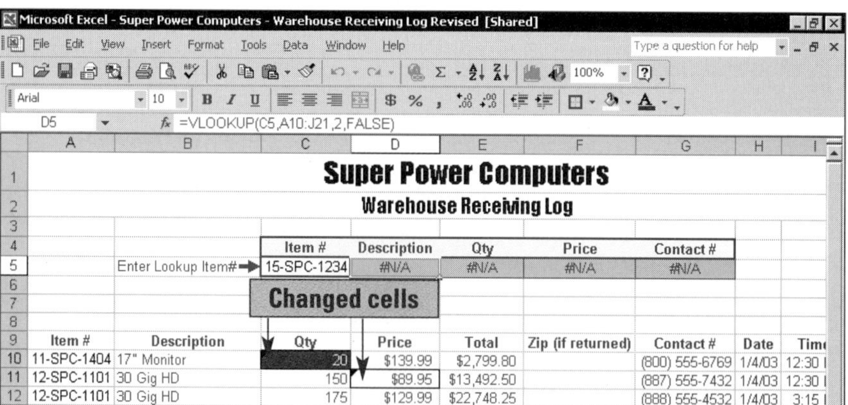

FIGURE 15-12
Merging Workbooks

Step 21	*Save*	the workbook

Changing Workbook Properties

Workbook **properties** comprise information about the workbook that can be stored with the workbook. This information includes file size, creation date, company and author name, and date that the workbook was last modified or accessed. You can change some of this information in the workbook Properties dialog box. Before you can change properties, you need to turn off workbook sharing. To disable workbook sharing:

Step 1	*Open*	the Share Workbook dialog box

Step 2	***Click***	the Allow changes check box to remove the check mark
Step 3	***Click***	OK
Step 4	***Click***	Yes after reading the warning about turning off the sharing feature

CAUTION TIP

When you disable workbook sharing, you also turn off the track changes feature and erase the History list.

Now you can change the workbook's properties. To change a workbook's properties:

Step 1	***Click***	File
Step 2	***Click***	Properties
Step 3	***Key***	your name in the Author: text box
Step 4	***Key***	Super Power Computers in the Company: text box

Your dialog box should look similar to Figure 15-13.

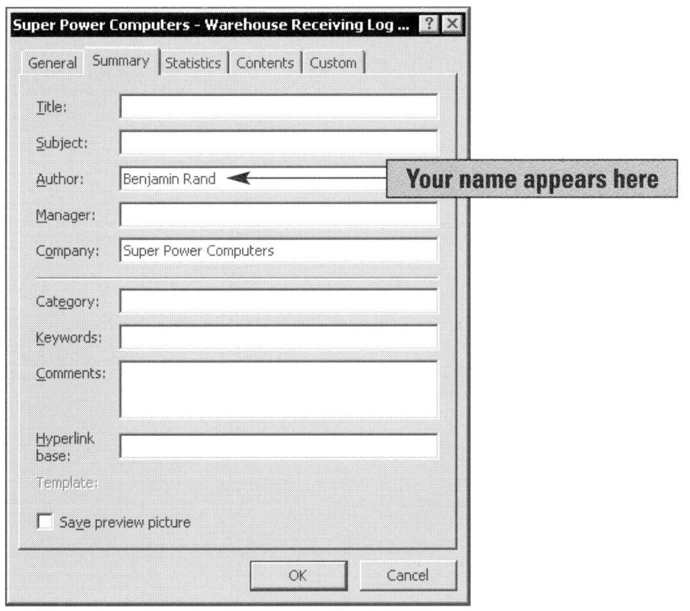

FIGURE 15-13
Workbook Properties Dialog Box

MOUSE TIP

You can view a workbook's properties without opening the workbook. In Windows Explorer or in the Open dialog box, right-click any workbook, then click Properties on the shortcut menu.

Step 5	***Click***	OK
Step 6	***Save***	the workbook and close it

Sharing workbooks and tracking changes can be a good way to boost productivity by allowing multiple users to work on and modify the same workbook simultaneously. Protecting cells, worksheets, or entire workbooks ensures that critical data and formulas are not changed.

Summary

- Number formats change the manner in which numerical values are displayed; they do not change the underlying values.
- You can create custom number formats to display additional characters, text, comma styles, and decimal options.
- You can apply conditional formatting to cells. You use cell value comparisons or logical formula evaluations to determine which formatting should be applied to a cell. You can assign as many as three conditions with which to test a cell.
- Lookup functions, including VLOOKUP and HLOOKUP, search for a value in a row or column, then return another value in the table or array, depending on the arguments supplied.
- You can protect a workbook from changes by enabling protection. You also can add a level of security by providing password protection to a worksheet or workbook.
- Multiple users can edit a workbook simultaneously on a network. While a workbook is shared, certain features remain unavailable, such as chart and drawing tools.
- You can track changes to see which modifications have been made and who made them.
- You can merge workbooks to combine information from multiple copies of a shared workbook.
- You can add comments to clarify information or to act as a reminder.

Commands Review

Action	Menu Bar	Shortcut Menu	Toolbar	Task Pane	Keyboard
Format cells	Format, Cells	Right-click cell, Format Cells			CTRL + 1 ALT + O, E
Apply conditional formatting	Format, Conditional Formatting				ALT + O, D
Protect a worksheet	Tools, Protection, Protection Sheet				ALT + T, P, P
Unprotect a worksheet	Tools, Protection, Unprotect Sheet				ALT + T, P, P
Protect a workbook	Tools, Protection, Protect Workbook				ALT + T, P, W
Unprotect a workbook	Tools, Protection, Unprotect Workbook				ALT + T, P, W
Share a workbook	Tools, Share workbook				ALT + T, H
Highlight changes	Tools, Track changes, Highlight changes				ALT + T, T, H
Accept or reject changes	Tools, Track changes, Accept or Reject changes				ALT + T, A
Merge workbooks	Tools, Merge Workbooks				ALT + T, W
Modify Workbook	File, Properties				ALT + F, I

Concepts Review

Circle the correct answer.

1. When you hide formulas using worksheet protection:

[a] formulas are not calculated.
[b] the formula is displayed but not the calculated value.
[c] formulas are calculated but are not displayed in the Formula Bar.
[d] formulas appear and are calculated as usual.

2. You can identify modified cells when using Track Changes by a colored:

[a] border and triangle in the upper-right corner.
[b] border and triangle in the upper-left corner.
[c] triangle in the upper-right corner.
[d] triangle in the upper-left corner.

3. The 0 symbol in a custom number format code:

[a] displays an @ symbol in the cell.
[b] acts as a repeat code; the character following it will be repeated to fill a cell.
[c] allows the displaying of text in a cell formatted with a number format.
[d] displays nonsignificant zeroes.

4. To select view options for changes, click Tools, then:

[a] Merge Workbook.
[b] Share Workbook.
[c] Track Changes, Highlight changes.
[d] Track Changes, Accept or Reject changes.

5. Conditional formatting (*not* conditional number format) can check a maximum of:

[a] one condition.
[b] two conditions.
[c] three conditions.
[d] four conditions.

6. When merging workbooks:
- [a] both workbooks can be open.
- [b] only the target workbook can be open.
- [c] only the source workbook can be open.
- [d] neither of the workbooks has to be open.

7. Given a value of 9995551234, what is displayed when the cell is formatted using the following custom number format code: (###) ###-####?
- [a] 9995551234
- [b] 999 555 1234
- [c] (999) 555-1234
- [d] (###) ###-####

8. Workbook properties:
- [a] cannot be modified.
- [b] contain fields of additional data that are stored with the workbook.
- [c] cannot be displayed unless the workbook is open.
- [d] can be displayed only outside of Excel.

9. The VLOOKUP function:
- [a] searches for a specific value in the left-most column of a table or an array.
- [b] searches for a specific value in the top-most row of a table or an array.
- [c] returns the relative position of an item in a table or an array that matches a specific value.
- [d] returns a value or the reference to a value from within a table or an array.

10. In Excel, you can protect:
- [a] worksheets, but not workbooks.
- [b] only selected cells.
- [c] selected cells, entire worksheets, or entire workbooks.
- [d] only worksheets in which changes are highlighted.

Circle **T** if the statement is true or **F** if the statement is false.

T F 1. Changing a cell's number format alters the actual value of the cell.

T F 2. You must enable sharing before multiple users can access a workbook simultaneously.

T F 3. You can track changes without enabling workbook sharing.

T F 4. You can view a workbook's properties in Windows Explorer.

T F 5. ###-####[Yellow] is a valid custom number format.

T F 6. Excel automatically saves a workbook before enabling the sharing feature.

T F 7. The logical test of a conditional format can only test the cell to which the formatting is applied.

T F 8. The VLOOKUP function looks in any column of a data array to find a match.

T F 9. You can protect a worksheet or workbook without applying a password.

T F 10. You can set all font options, including font size, when setting conditional formatting options.

Skills Review

Exercise 1

1. Create a new, blank workbook.
2. Enter "Division" in cell A1, "Sales Rep" in cell B1, and "Total Sales" in cell C1. Enter "East" in cells A2:A5, enter "West" in cells A6:A9, enter "North" in cells A10:A13, and enter "South" in cells A14:A17.
3. Save the workbook as *Divisional Sales*.
4. Share the workbook.
5. Save the workbook, then print and close it.

Exercise 2

1. Open the *Divisional Sales* workbook that you created in Exercise 1.
2. Save the workbook as *Divisional Sales 1*.
3. Enable Track Changes and set the When option to All.
4. In column B, add fictitious sales representative names for each division. Resize the column as necessary.
5. Replace the text in cell A14 with "North."
6. Reject the change in cell A14; accept the rest of your changes.
7. In column C, create fictitious sales data between $1,000 and $5,000. Resize the column as necessary.
8. Save the workbook, then print and close it.

Exercise 3

1. Open the *Divisional Sales 1* workbook that you created in Exercise 2.
2. Open the Highlight Changes dialog box, check the box next to List changes on a new sheet, and set the When option to All.
3. Print the History worksheet.
4. Save the workbook. Note that when you save the workbook, the History list becomes hidden again.
5. Close the workbook.

Exercise 4

1. Open the *Divisional Sales 1* workbook that you created in Exercise 2.
2. Save the workbook as *Divisional Sales 2*.
3. Change the column heading "Sales Rep" to "Rep Name."
4. Save and close the workbook, then open the *Divisional Sales* workbook you created in Exercise 1.
5. Compare and merge the *Divisional Sales 1* and *Divisional Sales 2* workbooks with the open workbook. Click OK in the alert dialog box that appears.
6. Disable workbook sharing.

7. Add a title to the workbook properties, change the Author name to your name, and change the company name to Sweet Tooth.

8. Save the workbook as *Divisional Sales Merged,* then print and close it.

Exercise 5

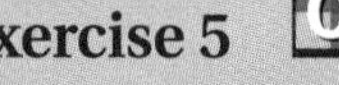

1. Create a new, blank workbook.

2. Create a table containing tax rates for the following income levels: 0–12,000 = 12%; $12,001–$18,000 = 15%; $18,001– $30,000 = 21%; $30,001–$42,000 = 28%; >$42,000 = 39%.

3. Create a formula using the VLOOKUP function to multiply a given income by the proper tax percentage.

4. Save the workbook as *Choose Tax,* then print and close it.

Exercise 6

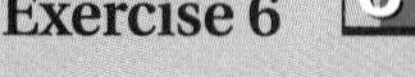

1. Open the *Warehouse* workbook located on the Data Disk.

2. Create a custom number format to display the Part No. as shown, using only numerical entries. All part numbers start with the letter *A* and end with the letter *B.*

3. Create a custom number format to display the Storage location as shown, using only numerical entries.

4. Reenter the data in cells A2 and B2 as the numerical values 1240 and 1125, respectively, to test your number format.

5. Enter four other four-digit numbers in each column, and apply the correct number format to each column.

6. Print the worksheet.

7. Save the workbook as *Warehouse Numbers,* and close it.

Exercise 7

1. Create a new, blank workbook.

2. Enter five different times in column A.

3. Enter five different dates in column B.

4. Select the values in column A.

5. Create a new time format that inserts the text string "Time: " in front of the time format. (*Hint:* Look at the custom number formats for illustrations of custom date and time formats.)

6. Select the values in column B.

7. Create a new time format that inserts the text string "Date: " in front of the time format. (*Hint:* Look at the custom number formats for illustrations of custom date and time formats.)

8. Protect the range A1:B5 to hide the formulas, protect the sheet, then protect the workbook.

9. Save the workbook as *Custom Date and Time,* then print and close it.

Exercise 8 

1. Open the *Semi-Annual Results* workbook located on the Data Disk.
2. Apply a conditional format to cell B2 that does the following:
   a. If the value in the cell is less than 100, format the cell with red and italics.
   b. If the value in the cell is equal to or greater than 100, format the cell with a yellow fill.
3. Use Format Painter to format cells B3:B6 with the same format as cell B2.
4. Deselect the cells.
5. Print the worksheet.
6. Save the workbook as *Semi-Annual Results Formatted*, and close it.

Case Projects

Project 1 

You are the personnel manager for a small company. You maintain information about the company's employees using a worksheet. Create a workbook with fictitious names, home phone numbers, and Social Security numbers for 10 employees. You want to prevent unauthorized users from viewing the contents of this workbook. In addition to protecting worksheets and workbooks, you can add a password to keep users from opening a workbook, when you save the file. Use the Save As command on the File menu to save your workbook as *Employee Info*. Before clicking Save, click the Tools menu button, then click General Options. Add a password consisting of your first name in uppercase letters in the Password to open text box. Print and close the workbook.

Project 2

Your boss is concerned about securing information contained in some workbooks that you are sharing with other staff members. Use the Ask A Question Box to research how to limit what others can see and change in a shared workbook. Write a half-page summary of your findings, including any steps necessary to hide or protect portions of a workbook from other users. Name your document *Securing Workbook Information*, then print and close it.

Project 3 

As a small business owner just learning Excel, you want to take a class to help you become familiar with this program more rapidly. Connect to the Internet and search the Web for organizations offering Excel training in your area. Print a Web page containing contact information for an organization near you.

Project 4 

You are looking for a new job where you can apply your Excel skills. Connect to the Internet and search the Web for jobs where Excel is a required skill. (*Hint:* Search for Job Sites first.) Print at least two job descriptions that sound intriguing.

Project 5

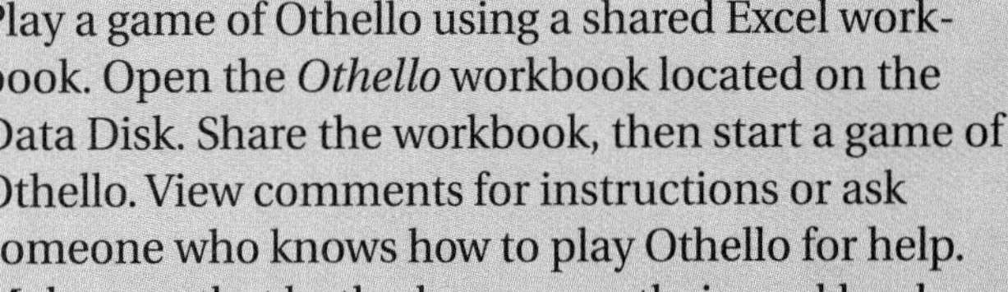

Play a game of Othello using a shared Excel workbook. Open the *Othello* workbook located on the Data Disk. Share the workbook, then start a game of Othello. View comments for instructions or ask someone who knows how to play Othello for help. Make sure that both players save their workbooks after each player's turn ends.

Project 6 

You are in charge of keeping track of donations to a local charity. Create a workbook with five fictitious donors and amounts between $50 and $1,000. Use column headings and widen columns to fit the data as necessary. Create and apply a number format that inserts the text "Gift:" in front of the gift amount, displays a $ symbol in front of the amount, and uses a decimal and two zeros after the decimal. Apply a conditional format that highlights donations exceeding $500 with red text and a border around the cell. Save the workbook as *Donations*, then print and close it.

Project 7 

You are a sales manager who is evaluating cell phone calling plans for the sales representatives who you manage. You want to see if your usage in the last year warrants changing your cellular calling plan. Create a worksheet with columns for local and long-distance minutes. Randomly generate numbers between 0 and 400 for each month for local airtime, and numbers between 0 and 150 for long-distance airtime. Use conditional formatting to identify total airtimes exceeding 500 minutes for any given month. Copy the cells containing the airtime data, then use the Paste Special command to paste only the values (not the formulas) in the same cells from which you copied. Save the workbook as *Cell Phone*, then print and close it.

Project 8 

You work for a retail company that uses a special inventory numbering system. If the inventory number is less than 1000, the inventory number is entered in the form: "A-0999-B"; if the inventory number is greater than or equal to 1000, the inventory number is entered in the form: "C-1001-D." Create a new workbook with a custom number format that allows you to enter just the numerical portion of the entry. Add 20 inventory numbers between 0 and 2000. Save the workbook as *Part Numbers*, then print and close it.

Integrating Excel with the Internet or an Intranet

Chapter Overview

Integrating Excel with the Internet enables a whole new level of communication. Worksheets and workbooks can be published as interactive Web pages, allowing users to check data and perform calculations via the Internet. Data can be exchanged easily between Web pages and Excel workbooks through importing, Web queries, and XML. You can look up important up-to-the-minute financial data, such as stock quotes. You can distribute workbooks via e-mail to other users.

Case profile

You need to monitor local competitors of Super Power Computers by checking their Web pages for current pricing. You can do this by copying the data to an Excel worksheet. You also can use Web queries to monitor the major stock market indices, and keep tabs on individual stock prices. In addition, you need to set up a process that allows customers to "create" a custom computer from a list of available options, and to compute the price. You can do this by using interactive Web pages.

Learning Objectives

- Import data from the Internet
- Work with XML
- Publish worksheets and workbooks to the Web
- Send a workbook via e-mail

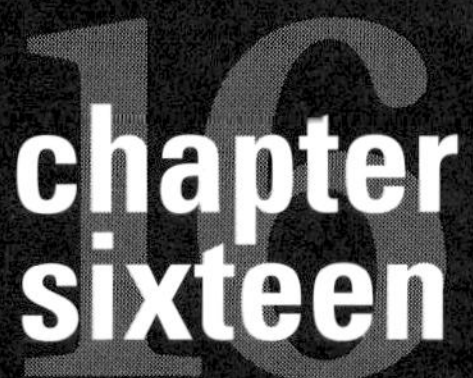

16.a Importing Data from the Internet

The Internet is a gold mine of data that can be imported directly into Excel. Tables in Web pages can be copied and pasted into worksheets. Using Web queries, dynamic data can be updated continually. In this section, you learn to make the most of the Internet and Excel.

Copying Data from a Web Page

Many Web pages use tables to display information in columns and rows, much like a worksheet. You can select this data in your Web browser, then use the Copy and Paste features or the drag-and-drop process to import the information directly into Excel.

Once a month, you visit the Web sites of competitors to check their current prices. You prepare a report of your findings for Luis Alvarez, the president of Super Power Computers. For this activity, you use a Web page located on the Data Disk. To copy data from a Web page:

Step 1	***Create***	a new, blank workbook
Step 2	***Save***	the workbook as *Competitor Pricing*
Step 3	***Close***	the New Workbook task pane, if necessary

notes

This activity requires Internet Explorer 5.0 and higher. If you are using another browser, your instructor may modify the steps or provide additional information.

Step 4	***Start***	Internet Explorer
Step 5	***Click***	File
Step 6	***Click***	Open
Step 7	***Click***	Browse
Step 8	***Click***	the Look in: list arrow
Step 9	***Switch to***	the disk drive and folder where your Data Files are stored
Step 10	***Double-click***	*MegaComputers*
Step 11	***Click***	OK

Step 12	*Press*	the CTRL + A keys to select the entire Web page
Step 13	*Right-click*	anywhere on the selected data in the browser window
Step 14	*Click*	Copy
Step 15	*Click*	the Excel button on the taskbar
Step 16	*Right-click*	cell A1
Step 17	*Click*	Paste

The data is copied into the worksheet, but is difficult to read. You reformat the data for better legibility.

Step 18	*Click*	Format
Step 19	*Point to*	Column
Step 20	*Click*	AutoFit Selection
Step 21	*Activate*	cell A1
Step 22	*Rename*	the Sheet1 tab as Mega Computers' Prices

Your workbook should look similar to Figure 16-1. The Excel worksheet isn't formatted exactly the same as the data on the Web page, but the data is identical.

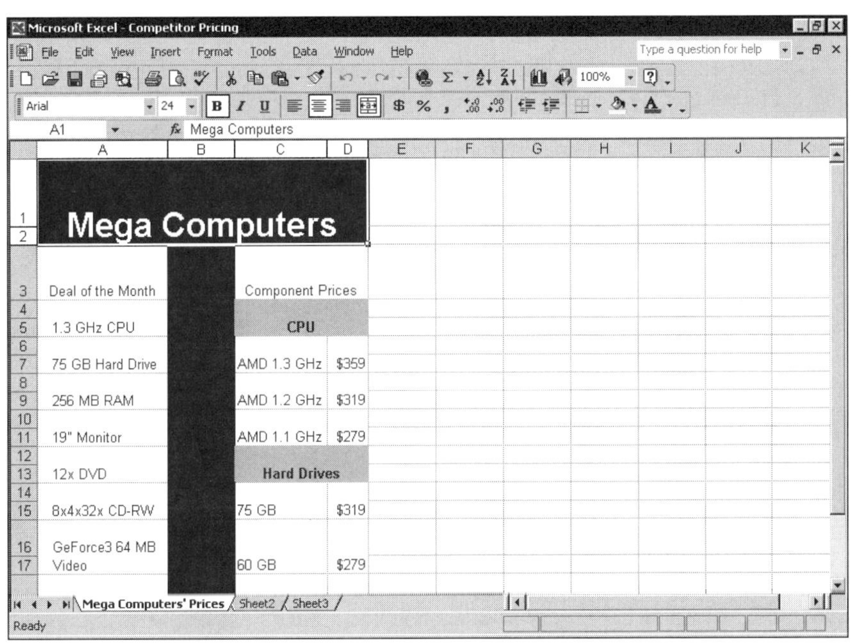

FIGURE 16-1
Data Copied from a Web Page

MOUSE TIP

Once you've selected data in your Internet browser, you can drag-and-drop it into Excel. If Excel is open but you can't see it, drag the information to the Excel button on the Windows taskbar, but do not release the mouse button. After a few seconds, the Excel window moves to the front, and you can drag the information into place on the worksheet.

Step 23	*Save*	the workbook

Importing Data from External Sources

In Chapter 14, you learned to import data from database and text file sources. In the fast-paced business climate, these sources may not be updated quickly enough. Excel can import real-time information from the Internet, helping you to stay up to date on important events.

Super Power Computers invests a portion of its income in the stock market. Tracking the stock market indices and major companies within the computer industry helps you evaluate the investments currently held by the company. In your monthly report to Luis, you also need to report on the major stock indices and your competitors' stock prices. You can set up a Web query that keeps track of major market indices or individual stock quotes.

notes

You must be connected to the Internet to complete these steps. If you are not, you can read the steps, but you won't be able to complete them.

To set up a Web query:

Step 1	*Click*	the Sheet2 sheet tab
Step 2	*Rename*	the sheet tab as Market Indices
Step 3	*Click*	Data
Step 4	*Point to*	Import External Data
Step 5	*Click*	Import Data

QUICK TIP

You can add data sources to this list by clicking New Source in the Select Data Source dialog box. The Data Connection Wizard starts and takes you through the steps necessary to set up a connection to a database server.

The Select Data Source dialog box opens, allowing you to choose from a variety of data sources.

Step 6	*Click*	MSN MoneyCentral Investor Major Indices
Step 7	*Click*	Open
Step 8	*Click*	OK in the Import Data dialog box to accept cell A1 in the existing worksheet as the destination

After a few moments, data from the major stock indices appears, as shown in Figure 16-2. The External Data toolbar is also displayed. The imported data on your screen will differ from that shown in the figure because stock prices fluctuate constantly.

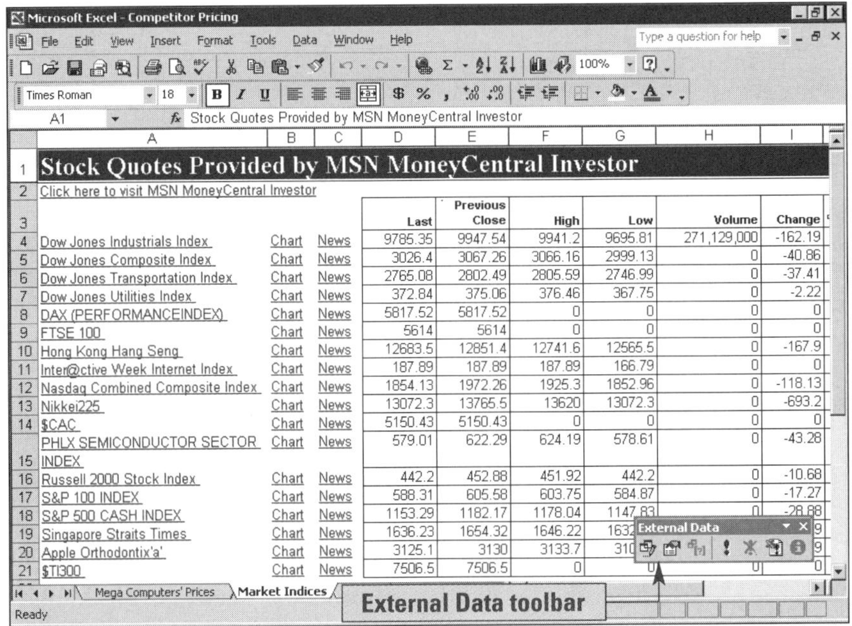

	A	B	C	D	E	F	G	H	I
1	Stock Quotes Provided by MSN MoneyCentral Investor								
2	Click here to visit MSN MoneyCentral Investor								
3				Last	Previous Close	High	Low	Volume	Change
4	Dow Jones Industrials Index	Chart	News	9785.35	9947.54	9941.2	9695.81	271,129,000	-162.19
5	Dow Jones Composite Index	Chart	News	3026.4	3067.26	3066.16	2999.13	0	-40.86
6	Dow Jones Transportation Index	Chart	News	2765.08	2802.49	2805.59	2746.99	0	-37.41
7	Dow Jones Utilities Index	Chart	News	372.84	375.06	376.46	367.75	0	-2.22
8	DAX (PERFORMANCEINDEX)	Chart	News	5817.52	5817.52	0	0	0	0
9	FTSE 100	Chart	News	5614	5614	0	0	0	0
10	Hong Kong Hang Seng	Chart	News	12683.5	12851.4	12741.6	12565.5	0	-167.9
11	Inter@ctive Week Internet Index	Chart	News	187.89	187.89	187.89	166.79	0	0
12	Nasdaq Combined Composite Index	Chart	News	1854.13	1972.26	1925.3	1852.96	0	-118.13
13	Nikkei225	Chart	News	13072.3	13765.5	13620	13072.3	0	-693.2
14	$CAC	Chart	News	5150.43	5150.43	0	0	0	0
15	PHLX SEMICONDUCTOR SECTOR INDEX	Chart	News	579.01	622.29	624.19	578.61	0	-43.28
16	Russell 2000 Stock Index	Chart	News	442.2	452.88	451.92	442.2	0	-10.68
17	S&P 100 INDEX	Chart	News	588.31	605.58	603.75	584.87	0	-17.27
18	S&P 500 CASH INDEX	Chart	News	1153.29	1182.17	1178.04	1147.83	0	-28.88
19	Singapore Straits Times	Chart	News	1636.23	1654.32	1646.22	1632	[illegible]	9
20	Apple Orthodontix'a'	Chart	News	3125.1	3130	3133.7	310	[illegible]	9
21	$TI300	Chart	News	7506.5	7506.5	0	0	0	0

FIGURE 16-2
Results of Web Query

As you can see, the data displayed includes indices for stock markets around the world. You want to narrow the report by selecting indices that better reflect conditions in the U.S. stock market as a whole. The Dow Jones Industrials, the Nasdaq and the S&P 500 are considered leading indicators of the stock market conditions in the United States. To edit the Web query:

Step 1	***Verify***	that cell A1 is the active cell
Step 2	***Click***	the Edit Query button on the External Data toolbar

The Edit Web Query window opens, as shown in Figure 16-3. The query is listed in the Address text box at the top of the dialog box.

The Edit Web Query window is a special, enhanced browser that displays the portions of a Web page that show the result of your query. The small yellow squares that contain a black arrow are the areas on the Web page that you can query.

FIGURE 16-3
Edit Web Query Window

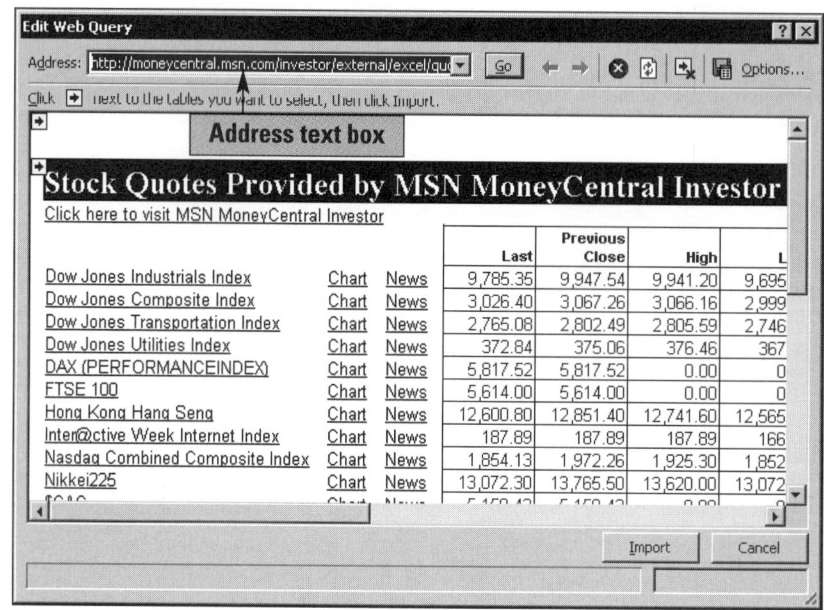

Step 3	*Click*	in the Address: text box

Near the end of the Web address, you should see "symbol=" followed by several index symbols such as "$INDU,$COMP..." Each variable listed after the = sign is a symbol of a market index that is listed in the table in the window; for example, $INDU is the symbol for the Dow Jones Industrial index, and $COMP is the symbol for the Dow Jones Composite index. You need to edit the Web query to show only the Dow Jones Industrial, Nasdaq, and S&P 500 indices. First, you need to position the insertion point immediately following the equal sign.

Step 4	*Press*	the RIGHT ARROW key until the insertion point is to the right of the = sign

The first symbol after the equal sign should be "$INDU," the symbol for the Dow Jones Industrial index. You still want to display that index.

Step 5	*Press*	the RIGHT ARROW key six times to position the insertion point after the comma
Step 6	*Press*	the SHIFT + END keys to select the remaining text
Step 7	*Press*	the DELETE key

$COMPX is the symbol for the Nasdaq, and $INX is the symbol for the S&P 500 index.

Step 8	*Key*	$COMPX,$INX
Step 9	*Click*	Go to update the table
Step 10	*Click*	Import

After a few moments, the worksheet displays the results of the revised query. Over the course of a day, this data can be refreshed to keep you informed up to the minute. The data can be refreshed periodically throughout the day while the major markets are open. After a few minutes, you want to update the data. To update a Web query:

Step 1	*Click*	the Refresh Data button  on the External Data toolbar

The data is refreshed after a few seconds.

Step 2	*Save*	the workbook

16.b Working with XML

C

XML, short for eXtensible Markup Language, is fast emerging as a standard language for exchanging data on the Internet and between applications. In this section, you learn what XML is, how to create XML documents using Excel, and how to create Web Queries that take advantage of XML.

Understanding XML

Years ago, a special computer language was invented called Hypertext Markup Language, or HTML. HTML uses a system of format codes, or tags, to describe the visual appearance of content in a document. As the Internet expanded, people began to recognize some serious limitations of HTML. HTML tags describe how information should *look*, they don't describe what that information *means*, so although HTML is great for creating pages that are "pretty" to look at, it is not very good at exchanging data with other applications, such as databases.

Databases are often used to collect data in a table. A good example of this is a phone directory. Each entry in the phone book is a record, and within each record are the fields: name, address, and phone number. These fields define the meaning of the data in the record. The number 8005551234 could mean many things, but when identified as a member of the phone number field, the meaning becomes clear: (800) 555-1234. Data stored this way is called **structured data**.

XML uses a system of tags, similar to the formatting tags in HTML, to describe the meaning and structure, or organization, of data. Applications can easily process and analyze structured data, because it has meaning.

XML provides a way for different applications, including Web browsers, to exchange structured data. For example, data stored in a database can be extracted and analyzed, then formatted and displayed on the Internet. Information obtained from a Web site can be formatted as an XML document and fed directly into a database. Figure 16-4 shows an XML file displayed in a Web browser. This file contains data about a computer system at Super Power Computers.

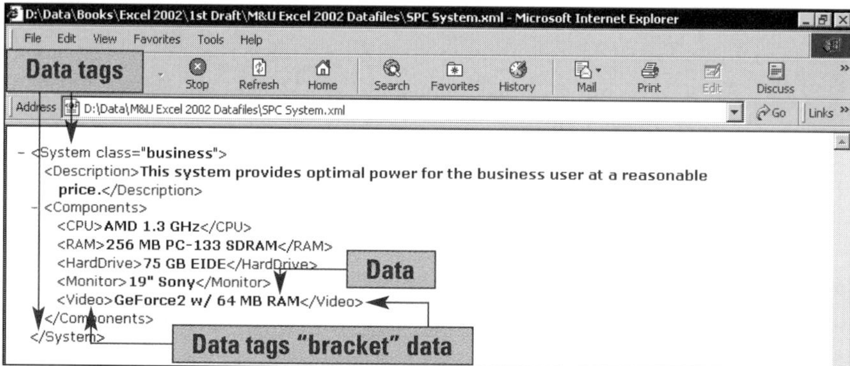

FIGURE 16-4
Sample XML File

For an XML file to be displayed on the Web in a meaningful way, a style sheet is used to describe how the data should be formatted.

It is important to realize that XML does not do anything by itself. It is a storage container for data that shows the relationship, or organization, of the data. The way it stores data makes it easy for other applications to use the data.

Using XML to Share Excel Data on the Web

How does XML apply to Excel? Worksheets store data in columns and rows, very similarly to the way databases store data in tables. You know how to store data in lists in Excel, which also could be described as structured data. You can save Excel files as XML documents. An XML version of an Excel workbook describes the data in the workbook in such a way that other applications can be written to make use of this data.

You can save the data in the *Competitor Pricing* workbook as an XML file. To save a workbook as an XML file:

Step 1	***Open***	the Save As dialog box
Step 2	***Click***	the Save as type: list arrow
Step 3	***Click***	XML Spreadsheet

Step 4	***Key***	Competitor Pricing XML File in the File name: text box
Step 5	***Click***	Save

Now you can view the file in your Web browser.

Step 6	***Switch to***	the Internet Explorer window
Step 7	***Click***	File
Step 8	***Click***	Open
Step 9	***Click***	Browse
Step 10	***Click***	the Look in: list arrow
Step 11	***Switch to***	the disk drive and folder where you store your completed files
Step 12	***Click***	the Files of type: list arrow
Step 13	***Click***	All Files
Step 14	***Click***	*Competitor Pricing XML File*
Step 15	***Click***	Open
Step 16	***Click***	OK

Your screen should look similar to Figure 16-5.

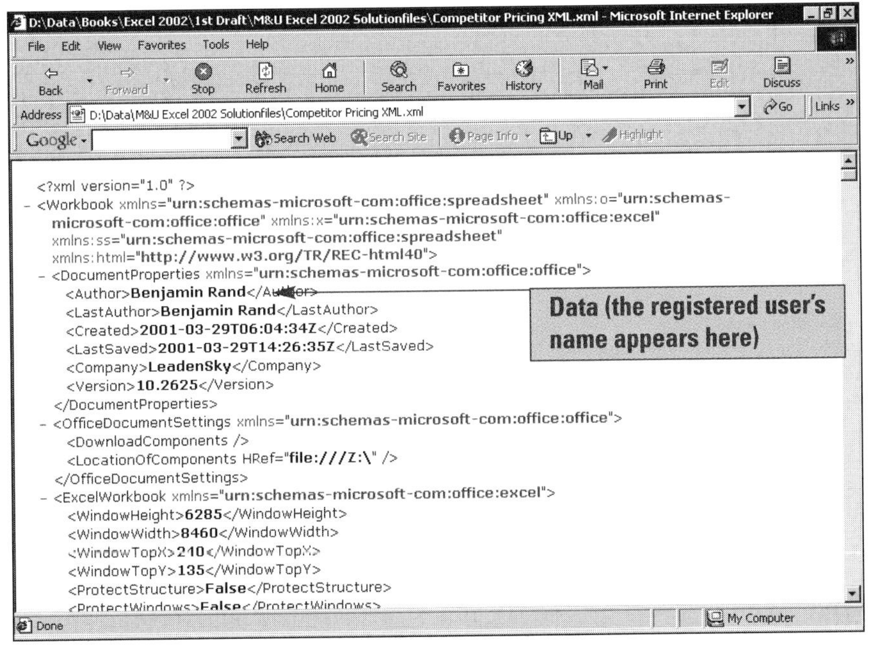

FIGURE 16-5
XML Spreadsheet Data

Remember that the XML file does not look like a reproduction of the workbook. Instead, it provides a description of the structure of the workbook, including the data it holds. Although XML files are stored as text files and are meant to be simple in nature, they are really intended to be read and processed by computers.

Before continuing, you need to close the XML workbook in Excel and reopen the Excel workbook.

Step 17	***Click***	the Close button [X] in the browser application window
Step 18	***Close***	the *Competitor Pricing XML File* workbook in Excel
Step 19	***Open***	the *Competitor Pricing* workbook

Creating XML Queries

An XML query is a special type of Web query you can use to keep track of important, dynamic data, such as stock prices. Fortunately, this sounds a lot more difficult than it really is. Creating an XML query is as simple as starting the New Web Query command and selecting a specific area of a Web page to query (or link to) using a specially modified browser.

As part of your efforts to track information to use to help Super Power Computers set computer prices, you watch the stock prices of some of the leading technology companies. You decide to use an XML query to make Excel do the work for you, allowing you to update the current stock prices with the click of a button. You add this query to your workbook. To create an XML query:

Step 1	***Activate***	cell A20 on the Market Indices worksheet
Step 2	***Click***	Data
Step 3	***Point to***	Import External Data
Step 4	***Click***	New Web Query

The New Web Query dialog box opens. You want to set up a query to update stock prices, so you need to locate a site that displays up-to-date stock quotes.

Step 5	***Key***	moneycentral.msn.com in the Address: text box

Step 6	*Click*	Go

The New Web Query window opens. This window is similar to the Edit Query window you saw earlier in this chapter.

Before linking to this site, you want to locate the exact information you are looking for, in this case, the current stock quotes for Microsoft and Intel Corporation. Companies are listed on the stock market by unique three or four letter names, such as MSFT for Microsoft and INTC for Intel Corporation.

CAUTION TIP

If a dialog box opens, telling you that it might be possible for others to see the information you are sending over the Internet and asking if you want to continue, click Yes.

Step 7	*Key*	intc,msft in the Enter Symbol(s): text box on the Web page
Step 8	*Click*	Go next to the Enter Symbols(s): text box on the Web page (not at the top of the New Web Query window)

The returned data should look similar to Figure 16-6.

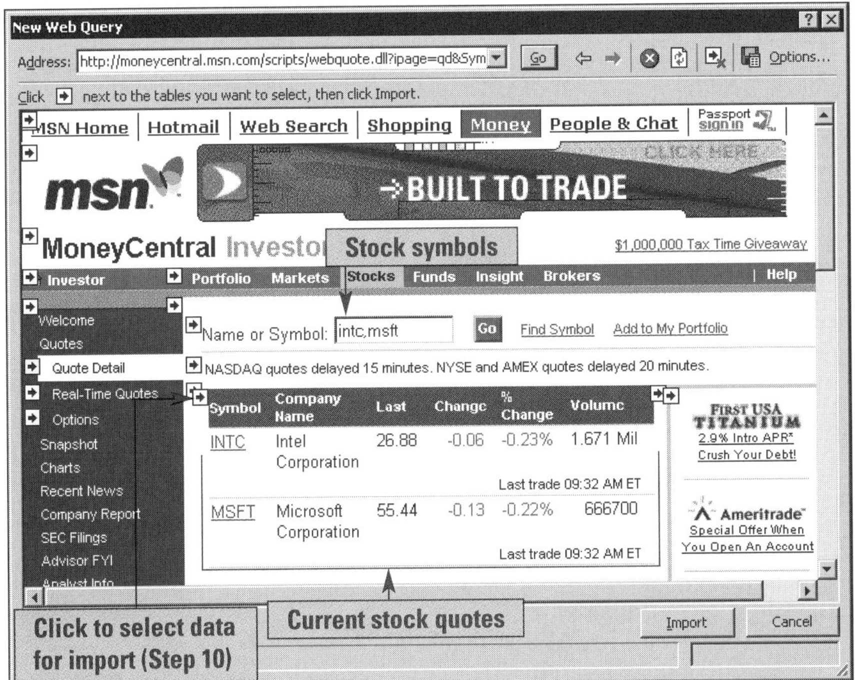

FIGURE 16-6
Located Stock Prices

Step 9	*Move*	the mouse pointer over the yellow square with the arrow symbol in the top left corner of the stock quotes as shown in Figure 16-6 (the yellow square becomes a green square when the mouse point is positioned over it)

A border appears around the data.

Step 10	*Click*	the green square with the arrow symbol to select the stock quotes

The green square contains a check mark, and the selected area is shaded. Your screen should look similar to Figure 16-7.

FIGURE 16-7
Web Data Selected for Import

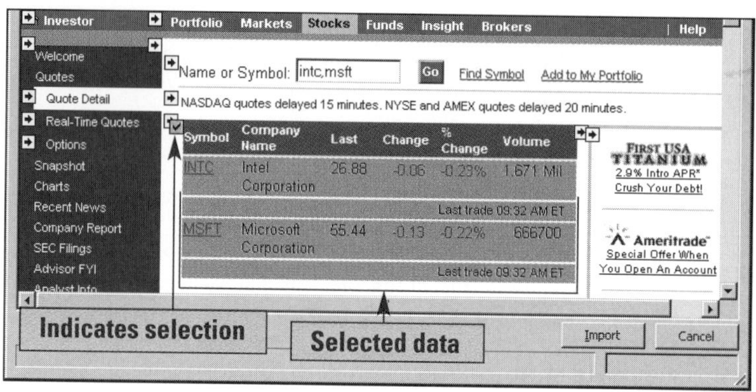

Step 11	*Click*	Import
Step 12	***Verify***	that =$A$20 is entered in the Existing worksheet: text box
Step 13	***Click***	OK
Step 14	***Scroll***	the worksheet to view rows 20 through 24

After a moment, the data is downloaded to your worksheet. Your screen should look similar to Figure 16-8. This query can be updated when needed by using the Refresh button on the External Data toolbar.

FIGURE 16-8
Data Imported into Excel

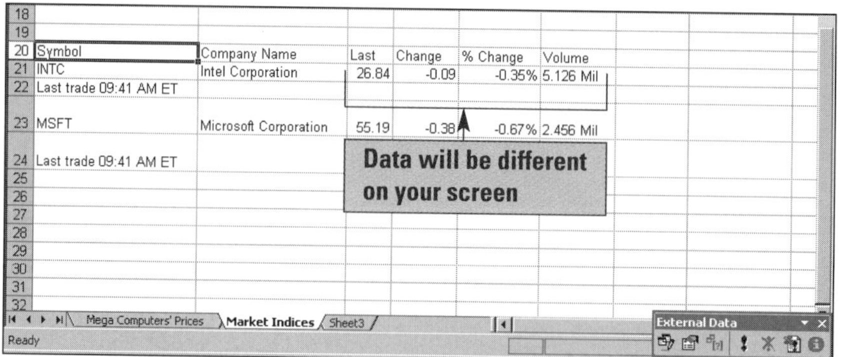

Step 15	*Save*	the workbook and close it

16.c Publishing Worksheets and Workbooks to the Web

In just a few short years, businesses around the world have embraced the Internet as an essential part of doing business. The ability of a Web site to attract potential customers from around the world is just one of the many benefits. Information can also be communicated more readily to employees, customers, and other business partners in a fraction of the time it once took.

Preparing a Workbook to Be Used as an Interactive Web Page

Super Power Computers sells several different computer system packages. Each package requires the same components: a CPU, RAM, a hard drive, a monitor, a video card, and so forth. For each component, there are many options. For example, the monitor selection includes several manufacturers, sizes, and types. You have created a worksheet to help sales reps when they fill out orders for new computers. You realize that by providing this worksheet as an interactive Web page, customers could create and price their own custom systems on the Web, providing a valuable service to customers and speeding up the sales process. To prepare a workbook to be used as an interactive Web page:

Step 1	***Open***	the *Super Power Computers - Build System* workbook located on the Data Disk
Step 2	***Save***	the workbook as *Super Power Computers - Build System Complete*

This workbook allows customers to "build" a custom computer by entering item numbers of their choice of available components. Item numbers are entered in the white cells in column B. The Invoice area at the bottom of the page uses the VLOOKUP formula to automatically create an invoice using the items selected by the customer.

Step 3	***Scroll***	to row 33
Step 4	***Activate***	cell B25

In the Formula Bar, you see the formula =VLOOKUP(B5,$C$5:$E$7,2). The #N/A error appears because a value has not been entered in cell B5. If a value is entered and located in the first column of the range C5:E7, the matching description in the second column of the array (D5:D20) will be returned.

Step 5	*Activate*	cell B17

The formula =IF(OR(B11=200,B11=201),400,401) appears in the Formula Bar. This special logical formula uses the IF function to evaluate the condition of cell B11 and select the correct motherboard for the selected CPU. The nested OR function is used to test cell B11 for either of two conditions, item 200 OR item 201. If the item number in cell B11 is 200 or 201, then the value of cell B17 will be set to item 400, otherwise the value of cell B17 will be set to item 401. Notice that the value of B17 is already 401, even though cell B11 is currently blank. A blank cell fails either of the criteria in the OR statement, so the IF statement evaluates to the FALSE condition.

Before saving your workbook as a Web page, you should verify that everything works correctly.

Step 6	*Enter*	122 in cell B5
Step 7	*Enter*	131 in cell B8
Step 8	*Enter*	201 in cell B11
Step 9	*Enter*	301 in cell B14
Step 10	*Enter*	500 in cell B19
Step 11	*Scroll*	the worksheet to row 33 again

The Invoice total should be $1,064.35, as shown in Figure 16-9.

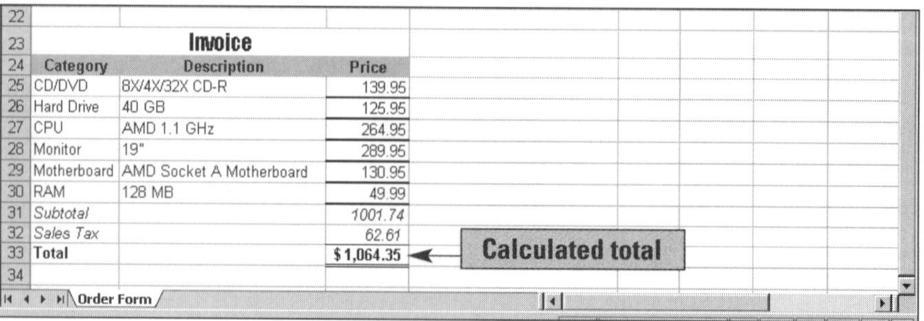

	Invoice		
24	Category	Description	Price
25	CD/DVD	8X/4X/32X CD-R	139.95
26	Hard Drive	40 GB	125.95
27	CPU	AMD 1.1 GHz	264.95
28	Monitor	19"	289.95
29	Motherboard	AMD Socket A Motherboard	130.95
30	RAM	128 MB	49.99
31	*Subtotal*		*1001.74*
32	*Sales Tax*		*62.61*
33	**Total**		**$1,064.35**

FIGURE 16-9
Tested Worksheet

Step 12	*Delete*	the contents of cells B5, B8, B11, B14, and B19
Step 13	***Save***	the workbook

Using Web Page Preview

Previewing a workbook as a Web page is a simple task. To preview your workbook:

Step 1	*Click*	File
Step 2	***Click***	Web Page Preview

Your browser opens with the workbook in HTML format.

Step 3	*Maximize*	the browser window, if necessary

Your screen should look similar to Figure 16-10. Although you prepared the worksheet to be used as an interactive Web page, the preview is not interactive.

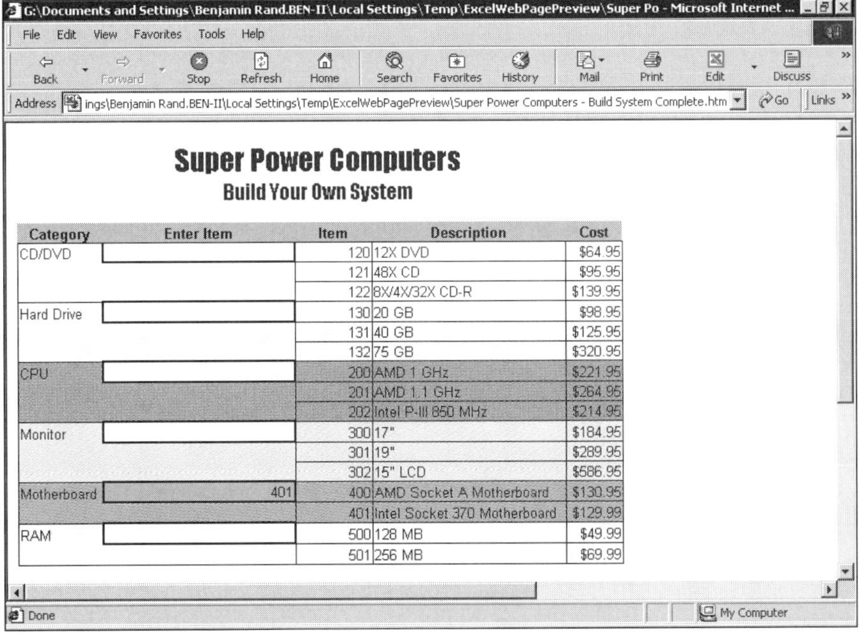

Category	Enter Item	Item	Description	Cost
CD/DVD		120	12X DVD	$64.95
		121	48X CD	$95.95
		122	8X/4X/32X CD-R	$139.95
Hard Drive		130	20 GB	$98.95
		131	40 GB	$125.95
		132	75 GB	$320.95
CPU		200	AMD 1 GHz	$221.95
		201	AMD 1.1 GHz	$264.95
		202	Intel P-III 850 MHz	$214.95
Monitor		300	17"	$184.95
		301	19"	$289.95
		302	15" LCD	$586.95
Motherboard	401	400	AMD Socket A Motherboard	$130.95
		401	Intel Socket 370 Motherboard	$129.99
RAM		500	128 MB	$49.99
		501	256 MB	$69.99

FIGURE 16-10
Web Page Preview of a Workbook

Step 4	*Close*	the browser window

Publishing a Worksheet or Workbook to the Web

Publishing a worksheet or a workbook is also easy. When a worksheet or workbook is published, new options are available in the Save As dialog box. These options allow you to choose which portions of the workbook are published, where the finished documents are saved, and whether to add interactivity.

notes

The interactivity feature only works with Internet Explorer version 4.01 or higher.

To publish your worksheet:

Step 1	***Click***	File
Step 2	***Click***	Save as Web Page

The Save As dialog box on your screen should look similar to Figure 16-11.

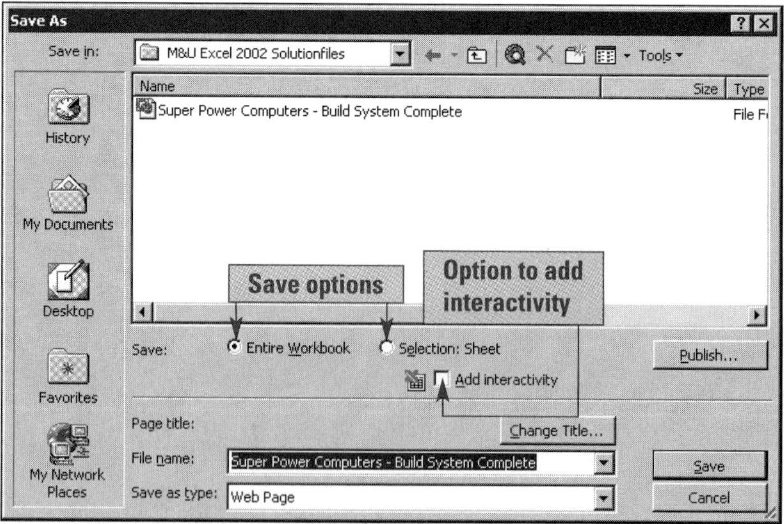

FIGURE 16-11
Save As Dialog Box with Web Page Options

Publishing the workbook differs from saving it by providing additional options. Using this feature, you can choose to automatically republish the workbook every time you save it, select specific areas of the workbook to publish, and select the interactive functionality (spreadsheet or PivotTable).

Step 3	*Click*	Publish

The Publish as Web Page dialog box on your screen should look similar to Figure 16-12.

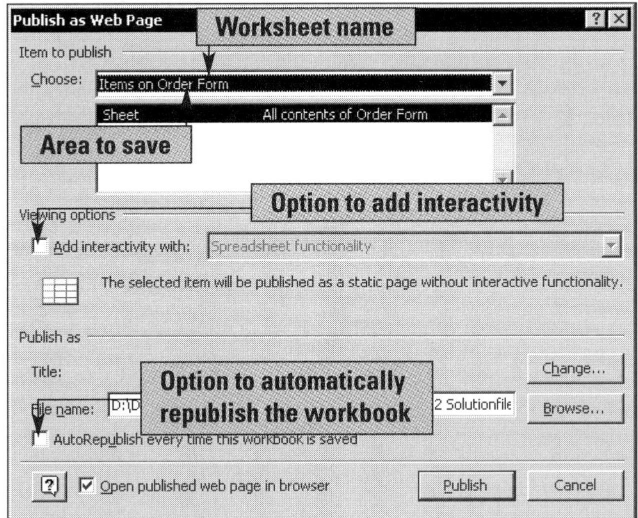

FIGURE 16-12
Publish as Web Page Dialog Box

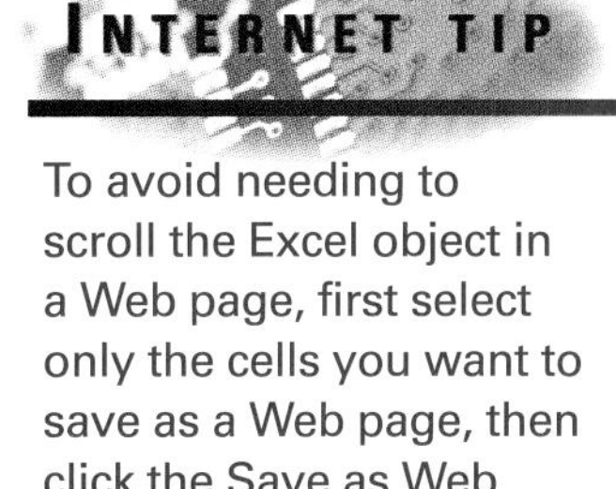

To avoid needing to scroll the Excel object in a Web page, first select only the cells you want to save as a Web page, then click the Save as Web Page on the File menu.

Step 4	*Verify*	that Items on Order Form is selected in the Choose: list
Step 5	*Click*	the Add interactivity with: check box to insert a check mark
Step 6	*Verify*	that Spreadsheet functionality is selected in the Add interactivity with: list
Step 7	*Click*	the Open published web page in browser check box to insert a check mark, if necessary
Step 8	*Click*	Browse
Step 9	*Key*	Super Power Computers - Build System Complete in the File name: text box
Step 10	*Verify*	that the Save in: list box lists the folder in which you store your completed files
Step 11	*Click*	OK
Step 12	*Click*	Publish

QUICK TIP

To publish an entire workbook, you would click Entire Workbook in the Choose: list.

The workbook is published and your browser opens. Because this workbook was saved with interactivity, you can use the workbook as though you were working in Excel.

Step 13	*Enter*	121 in cell B5
Step 14	*Enter*	130 in cell B8
Step 15	*Enter*	202 in cell B11
Step 16	*Enter*	300 in cell B14
Step 17	*Enter*	500 in cell B19
Step 18	*Scroll*	the Excel object window to view the Invoice section

Your screen should be similar to Figure 16-13.

FIGURE 16-13
Interactive Workbook

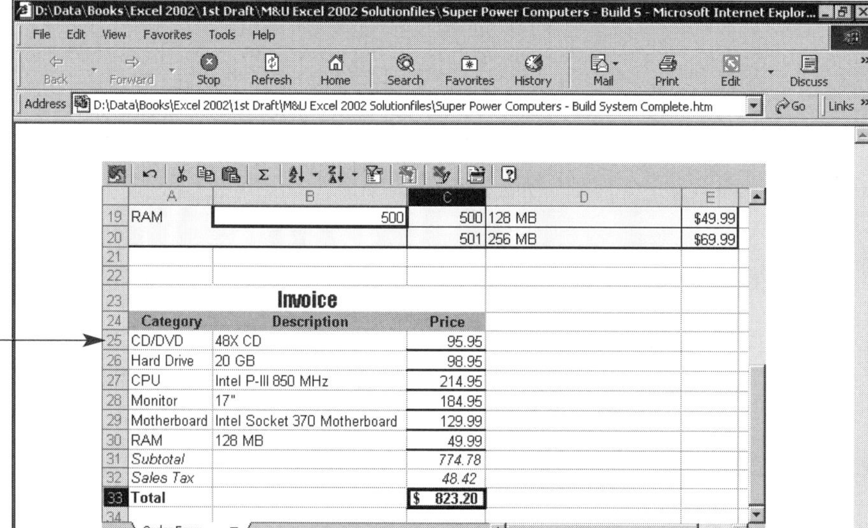

Interactive worksheet

Step 19	*Close*	the browser window

16.d Sending a Workbook via E-mail

Using e-mail capabilities built in to Excel, you can quickly send a worksheet or an entire workbook to a colleague. You can transmit a single worksheet as an HTML-formatted mail message—an option that allows the recipient to see all the formatting of the original message. The recipient can select the data in his or her message and drag it into Excel. When you need to send an entire workbook, you can transmit it as an attachment. **Attachments** accompany a regular e-mail message and allow you to send any type of document or program.

This section describes how to send workbooks via e-mail using Microsoft Outlook as the e-mail application. If you are using a different e-mail application, your instructor may modify the steps.

Sending a Worksheet as HTML Mail

HTML mail is a newer form of e-mail that allows you to send a Web page as the body of an e-mail message. All the formatting, alignment, and drawing objects can be sent and viewed in HTML mail-enabled mail readers. Microsoft Outlook, which is part of the Office suite, can receive and display HTML mail. To test this method, you send the *Super Power Computers - Build System Complete* workbook to yourself.

You must have Internet access and an e-mail account to complete these steps. Otherwise you can read the steps but you cannot complete them.

To send a worksheet as part of a message:

Step 1	*Activate*	cell A1
Step 2	*Click*	the E-mail button on the Standard toolbar

Your screen should look similar to Figure 16-14.

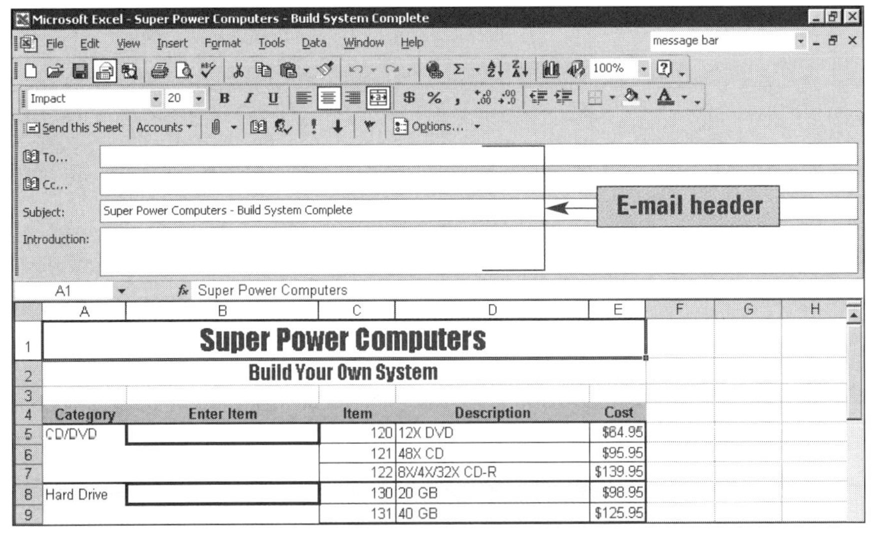

FIGURE 16-14
E-mailing a Workbook

MENU TIP

You can send a worksheet by pointing to Send to on the File menu, and then clicking Mail recipient.

To send the entire workbook as an attachment, point to Send to on the File menu, then click Mail Recipient (as Attachment). When you send a workbook as an attachment, the recipient can then open the file in Excel.

MOUSE TIP

If you want to use the Address Book to fill in e-mail addresses, click the To button or the Address Book button on the toolbar.

Step 3	*Enter*	your e-mail address in the To text box
Step 4	*Click*	the Send this Sheet button

The message is sent to the Outbox. You need to start Outlook, connect to your ISP, and send the message.

Step 5	*Start*	Outlook
Step 6	*Click*	the Send/Receive button to send the message
Step 7	*Open*	the message you sent yourself

If your e-mail program can display HTML mail, your message should look similar to Figure 16-15.

FIGURE 16-15
Viewing HTML Mail

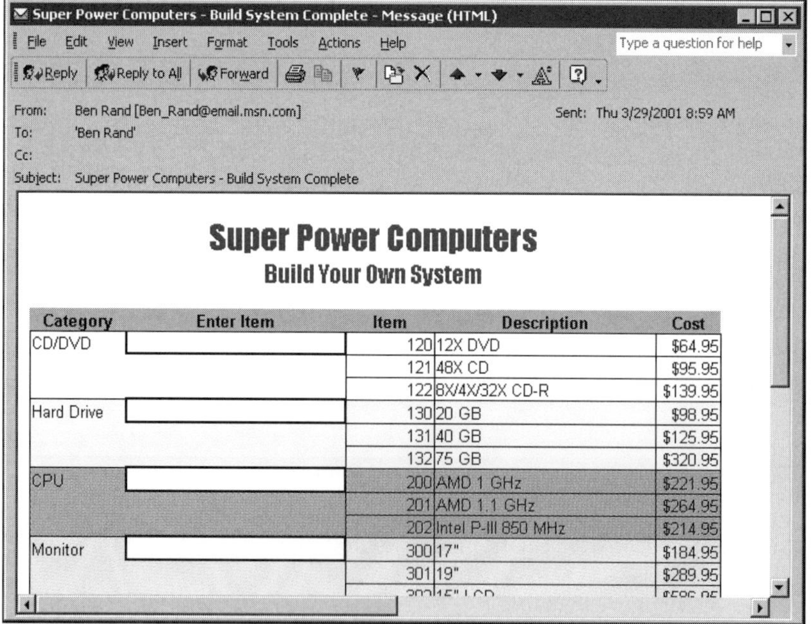

QUICK TIP

Change your mind about sending a worksheet? To turn off the messaging toolbar without sending the message, click the E-mail button on the Standard toolbar again.

Step 8	*Close*	the e-mail message
Step 9	*Switch to*	the Excel application window

Sending a Workbook as an Attachment

Often, you need to send a copy of an entire workbook so that it can be opened and edited directly in Excel. To do this, you need to send the workbook as an attachment. To send a workbook as an e-mail attachment:

Step 1	***Click***	File
Step 2	***Point to***	Send to
Step 3	***Click***	Mail Recipient (as Attachment)

A new message is created with the workbook attached, and should look similar to Figure 16-16.

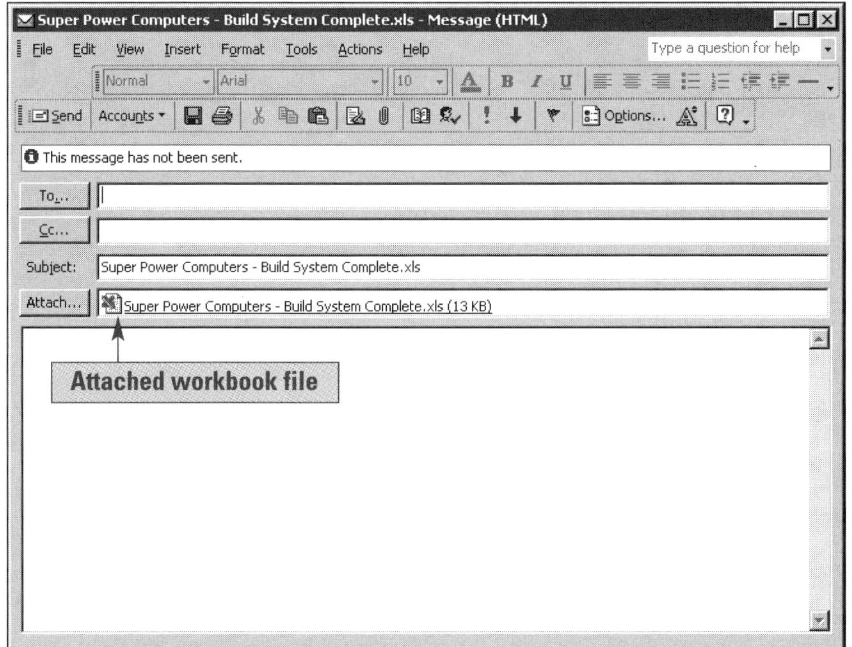

FIGURE 16-16
Workbook Attached to E-mail Message

CAUTION TIP

While most newer e-mail applications can properly display HTML mail, many older applications cannot. If this is the case with your system, you should be able to send the message but may not be able to view it properly when you receive it.

At this point, you fill in the recipient address and send the message as you would normally. For this activity, you don't send the message.

Step 4	***Close***	the e-mail message
Step 5	***Close***	the Outlook window, if necessary
Step 6	***Save***	the workbook and close it

Excel makes it easy to share workbook information with others via e-mail.

Summary

- You can copy data from Web pages and paste it into Excel. You also can select information on a Web page, then drag and drop it directly onto a worksheet.
- You can import data from a variety of sources, including the Internet. Use Web queries to extract data and update dynamic data, such as stock quotes and market indices.
- XML makes it easier for applications to share data, such as that found in databases, with the Web.
- Excel can save XML-formatted workbooks.
- You create custom XML queries by selecting areas of a Web page using the New Web Query dialog box.
- You can use Web Page Preview to preview a workbook or worksheet you want to publish to the Web. Previews are not interactive.
- You can publish a worksheet or workbook to the Web to share data. AutoPublish automatically updates the published Web page each time the workbook is modified and saved. Published workbooks can be interactive, allowing users to input data while the Web page correctly calculates the results.
- You can send worksheets or workbooks to others without leaving Excel by e-mailing worksheets as HTML mail, or sending workbooks as e-mail attachments.

Commands Review

Action	Menu Bar	Shortcut Menu	Toolbar	Task Pane	Keyboard
Import external data	Data, Import External Data, Import Data				ALT + D, D, D
Create a Web query	Data, Import External Data, New Web Query				ALT + D, D, W
Edit a Web Query	Data, Import External Data, Edit Query				ALT + D, D, E
Refresh data in a Web query	Data, Refresh Data	Refresh Data			ALT + D, R
Preview a workbook as a Web page	File, Web Page Preview				ALT + F, B
Publish a workbook as a Web page	File, Save as Web Page				ALT + F, G
Send a workbook as HTML mail	File, Send to, Mail Recipient				ALT + F, D, M
Send a workbook as an attachment	File, Send to, Mail Recipient (as Attachment)				ALT + F, D, A

Concepts Review

Circle the correct answer.

1. You can import data into Excel from:
[a] databases.
[b] text files.
[c] the Internet.
[d] databases, text files, and the Internet.

2. A Web query:
[a] must be recreated every time you want to update the data.
[b] requires in-depth programming knowledge.
[c] can be refreshed easily whenever you want.
[d] cannot be edited.

3. XML is short for:
[a] hyper teXt Markup Language.
[b] eXtended Markup Language.
[c] Standardized General Markup Language.
[d] structured data.

4. XML is not used to:
[a] display data.
[b] store data.
[c] exchange data between applications.
[d] describe structured data.

5. When you refresh the data in a Web query:
[a] the new data overwrites the old data.
[b] the new data is appended after the old data.
[c] the new data is inserted before the old data.
[d] You can't refresh Web queries.

6. XML files are intended to be:
[a] displayed in Web browsers without any additional files.
[b] read by human beings.
[c] extremely complex.
[d] processed and analyzed by computer applications.

7. A worksheet sent as HTML mail:
[a] can be edited directly in the e-mail message.
[b] is a good way to transfer a workbook file.
[c] can be copied and pasted into Excel for editing.
[d] can have interactivity enabled.

8. To send a workbook as an e-mail attachment:

[a] you must first save and close the document.
[b] you must first open your e-mail program.
[c] click the Attachment button in Excel.
[d] click the E-mail button, then choose to send the workbook as an attachment.

9. The OR function is used to evaluate:

[a] whether a single condition is true.
[b] whether any of several conditions are true.
[c] whether all of several conditions are true.
[d] a set of conditions, then return one value if the conditions are true, and another value if the conditions are false.

10. HTML is used on the Internet to:

[a] describe how data should appear.
[b] define what data means.
[c] exchange data between applications.
[d] store structured data.

Circle **T** if the statement is true or **F** if the statement is false.

T F 1. Enabling AutoPublish in the Publish dialog box means that the Web page will be updated every time the workbook is saved.

T F 2. Once you turn on the messaging (e-mail) toolbar, you cannot turn it off until you send the file.

T F 3. You can send most types of documents or computer files as attachments.

T F 4. Interactive worksheets allow users to enter data, but formulas are disabled and do not calculate results.

T F 5. An XML spreadsheet in a Web browser looks just like an Excel worksheet.

T F 6. XML uses tags to describe the way data should appear when it is viewed.

T F 7. Sending a workbook as an e-mail attachment and sending a workbook as HTML mail are identical operations.

T F 8. You can enable interactivity in a Web page preview.

T F 9. Interactive Web pages enable users to interact with the Web page's data.

T F 10. Although you can copy and paste data from a Web page into Excel, you cannot drag and drop selected data from a Web page into Excel.

Skills Review

Exercise 1

1. Create a new, blank worksheet.

2. Create a new Web Query.

3. In the Address box, go to *www.msnbc.com.*

4. Click the headlines link and wait for the headlines to appear.

5. Move the pointer over the box next to News (all the headlines should be highlighted). Click the box to select the headlines area.

6. Click Import and place the results in cell A1.

7. Save the workbook as *Today's News*. Print the workbook and close it.

Exercise 2 C

1. Open the *Annual Sales by Country* workbook located on the Data Disk.
2. Create an Area Blocks chart (*Hint:* look on the Custom Types tab) with the following settings:
   a. Chart title should be "Annual Sales by Country."
   b. Turn on the legend.
   c. Turn on the data table.
   d. Create the chart as a new chart sheet.
3. Save the workbook as *Annual Sales by Country with Chart.*
4. E-mail the workbook as an attachment to a classmate.
5. You should also receive a workbook from your classmate via e-mail. Open the workbook in the e-mail message.
6. Change the value of cell B4 to 2,500,000, then print the chart.
7. Save the workbook as *Annual Sales by Country with Chart Revised.* Print the workbook and close it.

Exercise 3 C

1. Open the *Annual Sales by Country with Chart Revised* workbook you created in Exercise 2.
2. You cannot save a workbook as an XML spreadsheet if it contains a chart, so delete the chart sheet.
3. Save the workbook as an XML spreadsheet named *Annual Sales by Country XML*, and then close the workbook.
4. Open the *Annual Sales by Country XML* file in your browser.
5. Print the XML document, then close your browser.

Exercise 4 C

1. Create a new, blank workbook.
2. In cell A1, enter the text "Enter Stock Symbol". Shade the cell with Gray-25%.
3. From the Data menu, point to Import External Data, then click Import Data.
4. Select MSN MoneyCentral Investor Stock Quotes, then click Open.
5. Click the Parameters button.
6. Click the Get the value from the following cell option button, click the box underneath the option button, then click cell B1 in the worksheet.
7. Click the Refresh automatically when cell value changes check box to insert a check mark.
8. Click OK.
9. Click cell A4 as the output cell.
10. Click OK.
11. Enter the stock symbol for Dell computers, dell, in cell B1.
12. Save the workbook as *Stock Lookup.*
13. Print the worksheet and close the workbook.

Exercise 5 

1. Open the *Car Loan Payments* workbook located on the Data Disk.
2. Select cells E1:E2.
3. Open the Format Cells dialog box, click the Protection tab, and click the Locked check box to remove the check mark.
4. Click Tools, point to Protection, and click Protect Sheet.
5. Turn off Select locked cells and make sure Select unlocked cells is on.
6. Select the range A1:I20, click Save as Web Page on the File menu, then save the selection as an interactive Web page named *Car Loan Payment Calculator*.
7. Open the *Car Loan Payment Calculator* in your Web browser.
8. Enter 12,500 as the loan amount in cell E1.
9. Enter 2.5% as the interest rate in cell E2.
10. Print the Web page from your browser, then close the browser.
11. Save the workbook as *Car Loan Payment Calculator* and close it.

Exercise 6 

1. Use the *Month Calendar* template located on the Data Disk to create a new calendar workbook. (*Hint:* In the Open dialog box, click All Microsoft Excel files in the Files of type: list box.)
2. Enter the correct dates for the current month.
3. Modify the calendar title in cell A1 to display the current month.
4. Modify the cell shading to correspond to the current month.
5. Select the calendar area.
6. Save the calendar as a Web page with interactivity. Name the Web page *Calendar Web Page.htm*.
7. Print the Web page and close your browser.
8. Close the workbook without saving it and close the custom Calendar toolbar, if necessary.

Exercise 7 

1. Open the *Calendar Web Page.htm* file in ycur browser.
2. Add at least five appointments to the calendar.
3. Click the Export to Excel button in the browser to create a copy of the appointments.
4. Save the workbook as an Excel workbook named *Calendar Export*, and print it.
5. Close the browser and the workbook.

Exercise 8 

1. Open the *Calendar Export* workbook that you created in Exercise 7.
2. Send the workbook as an HTML message to a classmate.
3. You should receive a similar message from a classmate. View the e-mail message in Outlook, and then print the HTML mail message.
4. Close the workbook without saving changes.

Case Projects

SCANS

Project 1

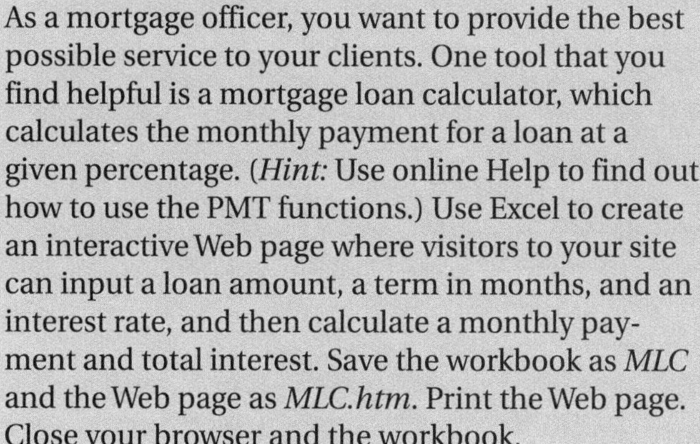

As a mortgage officer, you want to provide the best possible service to your clients. One tool that you find helpful is a mortgage loan calculator, which calculates the monthly payment for a loan at a given percentage. (*Hint:* Use online Help to find out how to use the PMT functions.) Use Excel to create an interactive Web page where visitors to your site can input a loan amount, a term in months, and an interest rate, and then calculate a monthly payment and total interest. Save the workbook as *MLC* and the Web page as *MLC.htm*. Print the Web page. Close your browser and the workbook.

Project 2

Connect to the Internet and search the Web for a table of data displaying current stock prices for Microsoft (stock symbol: MSFT). Select the table in your browser and drag it into a new Excel workbook. Save the workbook as *Imported Stock Price*, and then print and close it.

Project 3

As an investment advisor for a small mutual fund that caters to first-time investors, you want to help your clients see how ups and downs in the stock market have affected their investments. Create a worksheet with an initial investment of 250 shares purchased at a price of $40 per share. Create a formula to calculate the value of the investment. Save the workbook as *Investment*. Next, save only the cells you use as an interactive Web page called *Investment Interactive*. Change the title to “Enter Share Price” in the Publish Web Page dialog box. Test your Web page in a browser by changing the price of the shares (the calculated value of the investment should change). Print the Web page and close your browser. Close the workbook.

Project 4

You are a busy stockbroker with clients who are very interested in technology stocks. Create a worksheet with a Web query that looks up stocks for the following companies: Microsoft, Intel Corporation, IBM, Dell, Gateway, AMD, and Apple. (*Hint:* Most financial sites help you locate company stock symbols by entering the company name in a lookup box.) After you import the data, use the Data Range Properties button on the External Data toolbar to refresh the data every 30 minutes. Save the workbook as *Technology Stock Updates*. Print the workbook and close it.

Project 5

You and some friends are planning an outdoor activity, but your plans depend on the weather. Connect to the Internet and search for a Web site that forecasts the local weather four or five days in advance. Select the forecast and drag and drop (or copy and paste) it into a new, blank workbook. Add a hyperlink in your workbook to the site from which you copied the forecast. Save the workbook as *Weather Forecast*, then print and close it.

Project 6

COMDEX is one of the computer industries biggest trade shows. You decide you want to attend, but first, you need to find out when and where the event takes place this year. Connect to the Internet and search for the COMDEX Web site. Search the Web site to find out when and where the show is being held this year, then copy the information into a new workbook. Next search the Web for plane fares to and from your city to the site of the event, and copy the results into your workbook. Save the workbook as *Plane Fares to COMDEX*, then e-mail the workbook as HTML mail to a colleague who is interested in attending. Print the workbook and close it.

Project 7 C

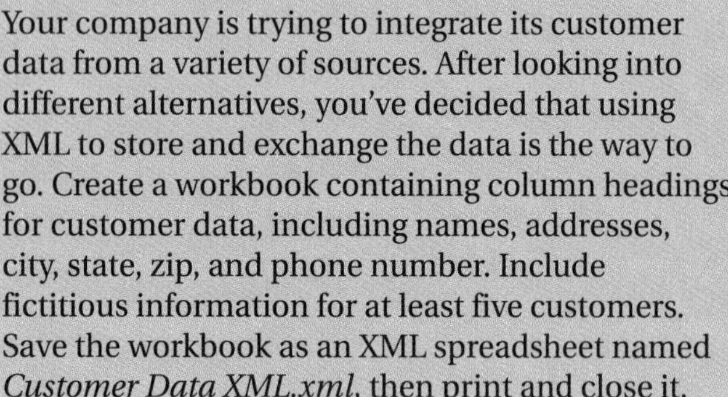

Your company is trying to integrate its customer data from a variety of sources. After looking into different alternatives, you've decided that using XML to store and exchange the data is the way to go. Create a workbook containing column headings for customer data, including names, addresses, city, state, zip, and phone number. Include fictitious information for at least five customers. Save the workbook as an XML spreadsheet named *Customer Data XML.xml*, then print and close it.

Project 8 C

You work in the Marketing Department for Widgit, Inc. To help increase sales, you need to create a Web page that allows clients to input the number of Widgits they want to order and then the worksheet calculates the total price of the transaction. To encourage customers to buy more Widgits, the company is offering special pricing based on the quantity purchased. If the customer buys between 1 and 50 Widgits, they cost $19.95 each; if a customer buys between 51 and 100 Widgits, they cost $17.95 each; and if a customer buys more than 100 Widgits, they cost $14.95 each. In the price cell, use a formula to display the correct price based on the number entered in the quantity cell. Unlock the quantity cell then protect the worksheet to prevent data being entered in any cell except the quantity cell. Save the workbook as *Widgits*, then print it. Select the cells that make up your "form" and save them as an interactive web page named *Widgits.htm*. Close the workbook and the Web page files.

Working with Windows 2000

Appendix

Appendix Overview

The Windows 2000 operating system creates a workspace on your computer screen, called the desktop. The desktop is a graphical environment that contains icons you click with the mouse pointer to access your computer system resources or to perform a task such as opening a software application. This appendix introduces you to the Windows 2000 desktop by describing the default desktop icons and showing how to access your computer resources, use menu commands and toolbar buttons to perform a task, and review and select dialog box options.

Learning Objectives

- Review the Windows 2000 desktop
- Access your computer system resources
- Use menu commands and toolbar buttons
- Use the Start menu
- Review dialog box options
- Use Windows 2000 shortcuts
- Understand the Recycle Bin
- Shut down Windows 2000

A

appendix

A.a Reviewing the Windows 2000 Desktop

Whenever you start your computer, the Windows 2000 operating system automatically starts. You are prompted to log on with your user name and password, which identify your account. Then the Windows 2000 desktop appears on your screen. To view the Windows 2000 desktop:

Step 1	*Turn on*	your computer and monitor

The Log On to Windows dialog box opens, as shown in Figure A-1.

FIGURE A-1
Log On to Windows Dialog Box

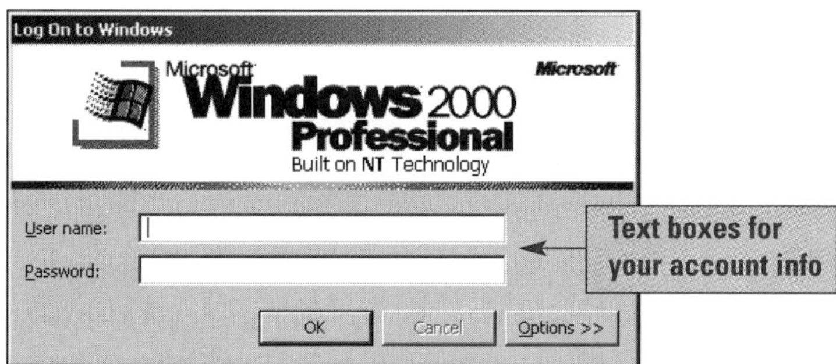

Step 2	*Key*	your user name in the User name: text box
Step 3	*Key*	your password in the Password: text box
Step 4	*Click*	OK
Step 5	*Click*	the Exit button in the Getting Started with Windows 2000 dialog box, if necessary
Step 6	*Observe*	the Windows 2000 desktop work area, as shown in Figure A-2

QUICK TIP

If you don't see the Log On to Windows dialog box, you can open the Windows Security window at any time by pressing the CTRL + ALT + DELETE keys. From this window, you can log off the current user and log back on as another user. You can also change passwords, shut down Windows 2000 and your computer, and use the Task Manager to shut down a program.

The Windows 2000 desktop contains three elements: icons, background, and taskbar. The icons represent Windows objects and shortcuts to opening software applications or performing tasks. Table A-1 describes some of the default icons. The taskbar, at the bottom of the window, contains the Start button and the Quick Launch toolbar, and tray. The icon types and arrangement, desktop background, or Quick Launch toolbar on your screen might be different.

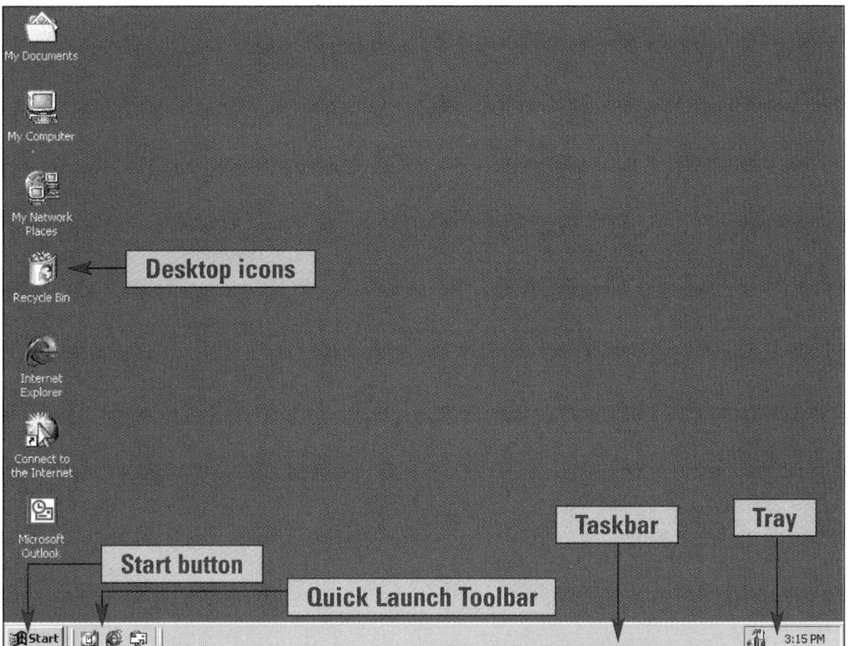

FIGURE A-2
Windows 2000 Desktop

TABLE A-1
Common Desktop Icons

Icon	Name	Description
	My Computer	Provides access to computer system resources
	My Documents	Stores Office documents (by default)
	Internet Explorer	Opens Internet Explorer Web browser
	Microsoft Outlook	Opens Outlook 2002 information manager software
	Recycle Bin	Temporarily stores folders and files deleted from the hard drive
	My Network Places	Provides access to computers and printers net worked in your workgroup

The Start button on the taskbar displays the Start menu, which you can use to perform tasks. By default, the taskbar also contains the **Quick Launch toolbar**, which has shortcuts to open the Internet Explorer Web browser and Outlook Express e-mail software, and to switch between the desktop and open application windows. You can customize the Quick Launch toolbar to include other shortcuts.

QUICK TIP

An **active desktop** can contain live Web content. You can create an active desktop by adding windows to the desktop that contain automatically updated Web pages. To add Web pages to your desktop, right-click the desktop, point to Active Desktop, click Customize my Desktop, and click the Web tab in the Display Properties dialog box. For more information on Active Desktop features, see online Help.

A.b Accessing Your Computer System Resources

The My Computer window provides access to your computer system resources. Double-click the My Computer desktop icon to open the window. To open the My Computer window:

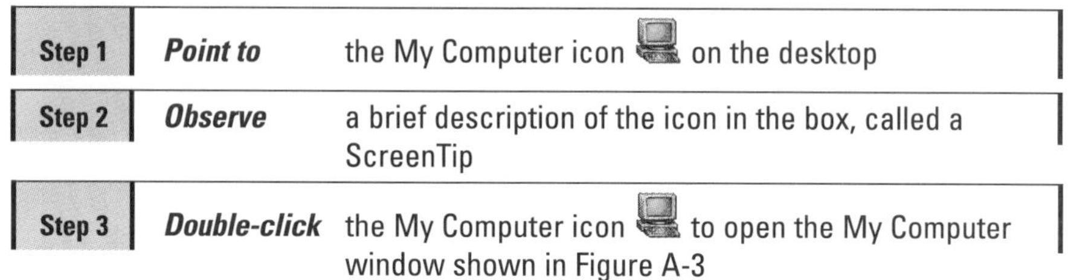

Step 1	*Point to*	the My Computer icon on the desktop
Step 2	*Observe*	a brief description of the icon in the box, called a ScreenTip
Step 3	*Double-click*	the My Computer icon to open the My Computer window shown in Figure A-3

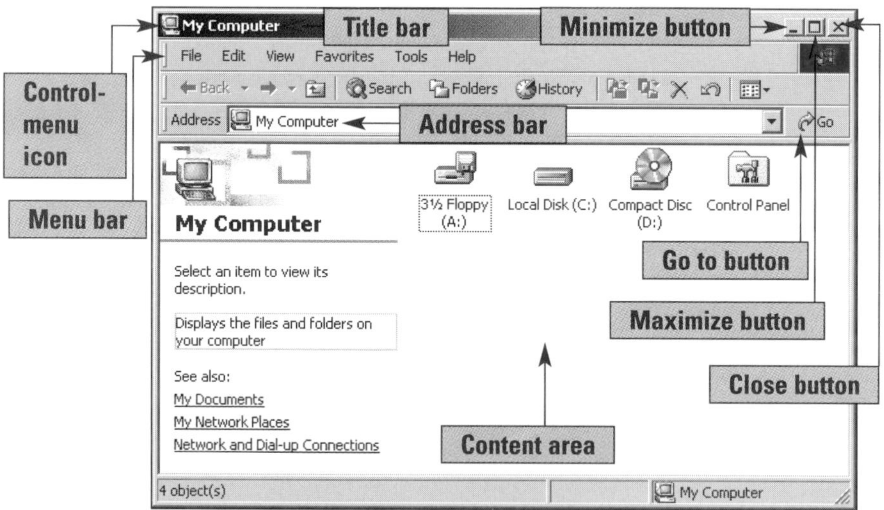

FIGURE A-3
My Computer window

A window is a rectangular area on your screen in which you view operating system options or a software application, such as Internet Explorer. Windows 2000 has some common window elements. The **title bar**, at the top of the window, includes the window's Control-menu icon, the window name, and the Minimize, Restore (or Maximize), and Close buttons. The **Control-menu icon**, in the upper-left corner of the window, accesses the Control menu that contains commands for restoring, moving sizing, minimizing, maximizing, and closing the window. The **Minimize** button, near the upper-right corner of the window, reduces the window to a taskbar button. The **Maximize** button, to the right of the Minimize button, enlarges the window to fill the entire screen viewing area above the taskbar. If the window is already maximized, the Restore button appears in its place. The **Restore** button reduces the window size. The **Close** button, in the upper-right corner, closes the window. To maximize the My Computer window:

Step 1	*Click*	the Maximize button on the My Computer window title bar
Step 2	*Observe*	that the My Computer window completely covers the desktop

When you want to leave a window open, but do not want to see it on the desktop, you can minimize it. To minimize the My Computer window:

Step 1	*Click*	the Minimize button on the My Computer window title bar
Step 2	*Observe*	that the My Computer button remains on the taskbar

The minimized window is still open but not occupying space on the desktop. To view the My Computer window and then restore it to a smaller size:

Step 1	*Click*	the My Computer button on the taskbar to view the window
Step 2	*Click*	the Restore button on the My Computer title bar
Step 3	*Observe*	that the My Computer window is reduced to a smaller window on the desktop

You can move and size a window with the mouse pointer. To move the My Computer window:

Step 1	*Position*	the mouse pointer on the My Computer title bar
Step 2	*Drag*	the window down and to the right approximately ½ inch
Step 3	*Drag*	the window back to the center of the screen

Several Windows 2000 windows—My Computer, My Documents, and Windows Explorer—have the same menu bar and toolbar features. When you size a window too small to view all its icons, a vertical or horizontal scroll bar may appear. A scroll bar includes scroll arrows and a scroll box for viewing different parts of the window contents.

QUICK TIP

This book uses the following notations for mouse instructions. **Point** means to place the mouse pointer on the command or item. **Click** means to press the left mouse button and then release it. **Right-click** means to press the right mouse button and then release it. **Double-click** means to press the left mouse button twice very rapidly. **Drag** means to hold down the left mouse button as you move the mouse pointer on the mouse pad. **Right-drag** means to hold down the right mouse button as you move the mouse pointer on the mouse pad. **Scroll** means to use the application scroll bar features or the IntelliMouse scrolling wheel.

MOUSE TIP

You can display four taskbar toolbars: Address, Links, Desktop, and Quick Launch. The Quick Launch toolbar appears on the taskbar by default. You can also create additional toolbars from other folders or subfolders and you can add folder or file shortcuts to an existing taskbar toolbar. To view other taskbar toolbars, right-click the taskbar, point to Toolbars, and then click the desired toolbar name.

To size the My Computer window:

Step 1	*Position*	the mouse pointer on the lower-right corner of the window
Step 2	*Observe*	that the mouse pointer becomes a black, double-headed sizing pointer
Step 3	*Drag*	the lower-right corner boundary diagonally up until the horizontal scroll bar appears and release the mouse button
Step 4	*Click*	the right scroll arrow on the horizontal scroll bar to view hidden icons
Step 5	*Size*	the window to a larger size to remove the horizontal scroll bar

You can open the window associated with any My Computer icon by double-clicking it. The windows open in the same window, not separate windows. To open the Control Panel Explorer-style window:

Step 1	*Double-click*	the Control Panel icon
Step 2	*Observe*	that the Address bar displays the Control Panel icon and name, and the content area displays the Control Panel icons for accessing computer system resources

A.c Using Menu Commands and Toolbar Buttons

You can click a menu command or toolbar button to perform specific tasks in a window. The **menu bar** is a special toolbar located below the window title bar that contains the File, Edit, View, Favorites, Tools, and Help menus. The **Standard Buttons toolbar**, located below the menu bar, contains shortcut "buttons" you click with the mouse pointer to execute a variety of commands. You can use the Back and Forward buttons on the Standard Buttons toolbar to switch between My Computer and the Control Panel. To view My Computer:

Step 1	*Click*	the Back button on the Standard Buttons toolbar to view My Computer
Step 2	*Click*	the Forward button on the Standard Buttons toolbar to view the Control Panel
Step 3	*Click*	View on the menu bar
Step 4	*Point to*	Go To
Step 5	*Click*	the My Computer command to view My Computer

Step 6	*Click*	the Close button on the My Computer window title bar

A.d Using the Start Menu

The **Start button** on the taskbar opens the Start menu. You use this menu to access several Windows 2000 features and to open software applications, such as Word or Excel. To open the Start menu:

Step 1	*Click*	the Start button on the taskbar to open the Start menu, as shown in Figure A-4

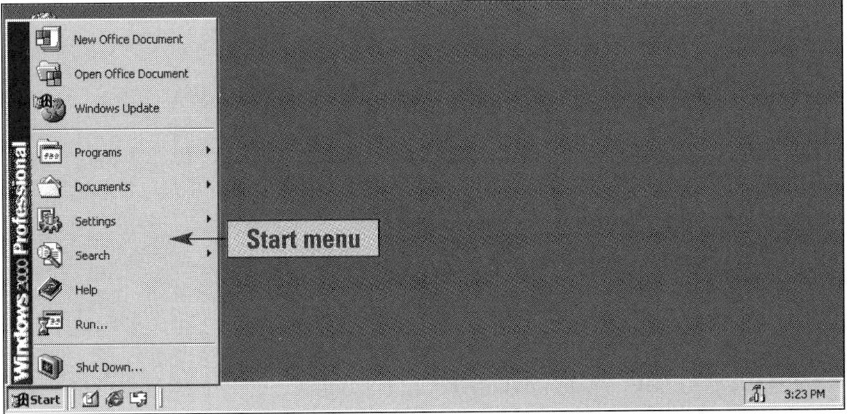

FIGURE A-4
Start Menu

Step 2	*Point to*	Programs to view the software applications installed on your computer
Step 3	*Click*	the desktop outside the Start menu and Programs menu to close them

A.e Reviewing Dialog Box Options

A **dialog box** is a window that contains options you can select, turn on, or turn off to perform a task. To view a dialog box:

Step 1	*Right-click*	the desktop
Step 2	*Point to*	Active Desktop

QUICK TIP

You can use Start menu commands to create or open Office XP documents, connect to the Microsoft Web site to download operating system updates, open software applications, open a favorite folder or file, or open one of the last fifteen documents you worked on. You can also change the Windows 2000 settings, search for files, folders, and resources on the Internet, get online Help, run software applications, log off a network, and shut down Windows 2000.

> **QUICK TIP**
>
> Many dialog boxes contain sets of options on different pages organized on **tabs** you click. Options include drop-down lists you view by clicking an arrow, text boxes in which you key information, check boxes and option buttons you click to turn on or off an option, and buttons that access additional options.

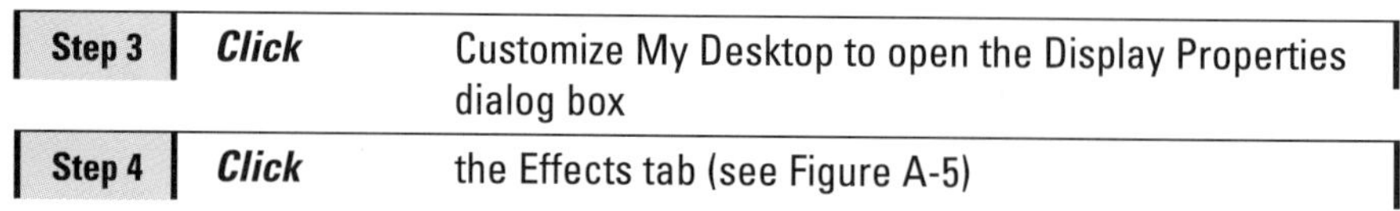

Step 3	***Click***	Customize My Desktop to open the Display Properties dialog box
Step 4	***Click***	the Effects tab (see Figure A-5)

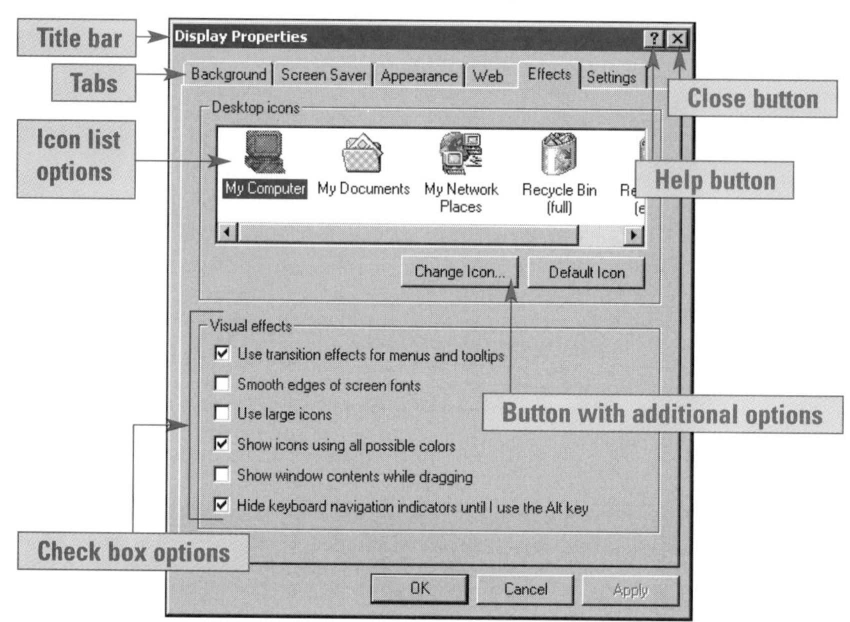

FIGURE A-5
Effects Tab in the Display Properties Dialog Box

Step 5	***Click***	each tab and observe the different options available *(do not change any options unless directed by your instructor)*
Step 6	***Right-click***	each option on each tab and then click What's This? to view its ScreenTip
Step 7	***Click***	Cancel to close the dialog box without changing any options

> **MOUSE TIP**
>
> One way to speed up tasks is to single-click (rather than double-click) a desktop icon just like you single-click a Web page hyperlink. You can create a Web-style, single-click environment by opening the Folder Options dialog box from the Tools menu in any Windows 2000 window or the Control Panel from the Settings command on the Start menu. The Single-click to open an item (point to select) and Underline icon titles consistent with my browser options add an underline to icon titles, similar to a hyperlink.

A.f Using Windows 2000 Shortcuts

You can use the drag-and-drop method to reposition or remove Start menu commands. You can also right-drag a Start menu command to the desktop to create a desktop shortcut. To reposition the Windows Update item on the Start menu:

Step 1	***Click***	the Start button Start on the taskbar
Step 2	***Point to***	the Windows Update item
Step 3	***Drag***	the Windows Update item to the top of the Start menu

To remove the Windows Update shortcut from the Start menu and create a desktop shortcut:

Step 1	*Drag*	the Windows Update item to the desktop
Step 2	*Observe*	that the desktop shortcut appears after a few seconds
Step 3	*Verify*	that the Windows Update item no longer appears on the Start menu

To add a Windows Update shortcut back to the Start menu and delete the desktop shortcut:

Step 1	*Drag*	the Windows Update shortcut to the Start button Start on the taskbar and then back to its original position when the Start menu appears
Step 2	*Close*	the Start menu
Step 3	*Drag*	the Windows Update shortcut on the desktop to the Recycle Bin

You can close multiple application windows at one time from the taskbar using the CTRL key and a shortcut menu. To open two applications and then use the taskbar to close them:

Step 1	*Open*	the Word and Excel applications (in this order) from the Programs menu on the Start menu
Step 2	*Observe*	the Word and Excel buttons on the taskbar (Excel is the selected, active button)
Step 3	*Press & hold*	the CTRL key
Step 4	*Click*	the Word application taskbar button (the Excel application taskbar button is already selected)
Step 5	*Release*	the CTRL key
Step 6	*Right-click*	the Word or Excel taskbar button
Step 7	*Click*	Close to close both applications

You can use the drag-and-drop method to add a shortcut to the Quick Launch toolbar for folders and documents you have created. To create a new subfolder in the My Documents folder:

Step 1	*Double-click*	the My Documents icon on the desktop to open the window
Step 2	*Right-click*	the contents area (but not a file or folder)

Caution Tip

Selecting items in a single-click environment requires some practice. To **select** (or highlight) one item, simply point to the item. *Be careful not to click the item; clicking the item opens it.*

You can use the SHIFT + Click and CTRL + Click commands in the single-click environment. Simply *point to* the first item. Then press and hold the SHIFT or CTRL key and *point to* the last item or the next item to be selected.

Menu Tip

In the Windows environment, clicking the right mouse button displays a **shortcut menu** of the most commonly used commands for the item you right-clicked. For example, you can use a shortcut menu to open applications from the Programs submenu. You can right-drag to move, copy, or create desktop shortcuts from Start menu commands.

Step 3	***Point to***	New
Step 4	***Click***	Folder
Step 5	***Key***	Example
Step 6	***Press***	the ENTER key to name the folder
Step 7	***Drag***	the Example folder to the end of the Quick Launch toolbar (a black vertical line indicates the drop position)
Step 8	***Observe***	the new icon on the toolbar
Step 9	***Close***	the My Documents window
Step 10	***Position***	the mouse pointer on the Example folder shortcut on the Quick Launch toolbar and observe the ScreenTip

You remove a shortcut from the Quick Launch toolbar by dragging it to the desktop and deleting it, or dragging it directly to the Recycle Bin. To remove the Example folder shortcut and then delete the folder:

Step 1	***Drag***	the Example folder icon to the Recycle Bin
Step 2	***Open***	the My Documents window
Step 3	***Delete***	the Example folder icon using the shortcut menu
Step 4	***Click***	Yes
Step 5	***Close***	the My Documents window

MENU TIP

You can open the Recycle Bin by right-clicking the Recycle Bin icon on the desktop and clicking Open. To restore an item to your hard drive after opening the Recycle Bin, click the item to select it and then click the Restore command on the File menu. You can also restore an item by opening the Recycle Bin, right-clicking an item, and clicking Restore.

To empty the Recycle Bin, right-click the Recycle Bin icon and then click Empty Recycle Bin.

A.g Understanding the Recycle Bin

The **Recycle Bin** is an object that temporarily stores folders, files, and shortcuts you delete from your hard drive. If you accidentally delete an item, you can restore it to its original location on your hard drive if it is still in the Recycle Bin. Because the Recycle Bin takes up disk space you should review and empty it regularly. When you empty the Recycle Bin, its contents are removed from your hard drive and can no longer be restored.

A.h Shutting Down Windows 2000

It is very important that you follow the proper procedures for shutting down the Windows 2000 operating system when you are finished, to allow the operating system to complete its internal "housekeeping" properly. To shut down Windows 2000 correctly:

Step 1	***Click***	the Start button [Start] on the taskbar
Step 2	***Click***	Shut Down to open the Shut Down Windows dialog box shown in Figure A-6

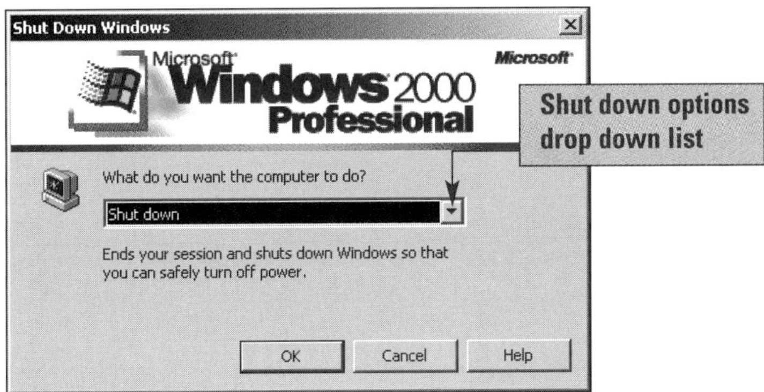

FIGURE A-6
Shut Down Windows Dialog Box

You can log off, shut down, and restart from this dialog box. You want to shut down completely.

Step 3	***Click***	the Shut down option from the drop-down list, if necessary
Step 4	***Click***	OK

appendix A

Appendix

Formatting Tips for Business Documents

Appendix Overview

Most organizations follow specific formatting guidelines when preparing letters, envelopes, memorandums, and other documents to ensure the documents present a professional appearance. In this appendix you learn how to format different size letters, interoffice memos, envelopes, and formal outlines. You also review a list of style guides and learn how to use proofreader's marks.

Learning Objectives

- Format letters
- Insert mailing notations
- Format envelopes
- Format interoffice memorandums
- Format formal outlines
- Use style guides
- Use proofreader's marks

B appendix

B.a Formatting Letters

Most companies use special letter paper with the company name and address (and sometimes a company logo or picture) preprinted on the paper. The preprinted portion is called a **letterhead** and the paper is called **letterhead paper**. When you create a letter, the margins vary depending on the style of your letterhead and the length of your letter. Most letterheads use between 1 inch and 2 inches of the page from the top of the sheet. There are two basic business correspondence formats: block format and modified block format. When you create a letter in **block format**, all the text is placed flush against the left margin. This includes the date, the letter address information, the salutation, the body, the complimentary closing, and the signature information. The body of the letter is single spaced with a blank line between paragraphs.[1] Figure B-1 shows a short letter in the block format with standard punctuation.

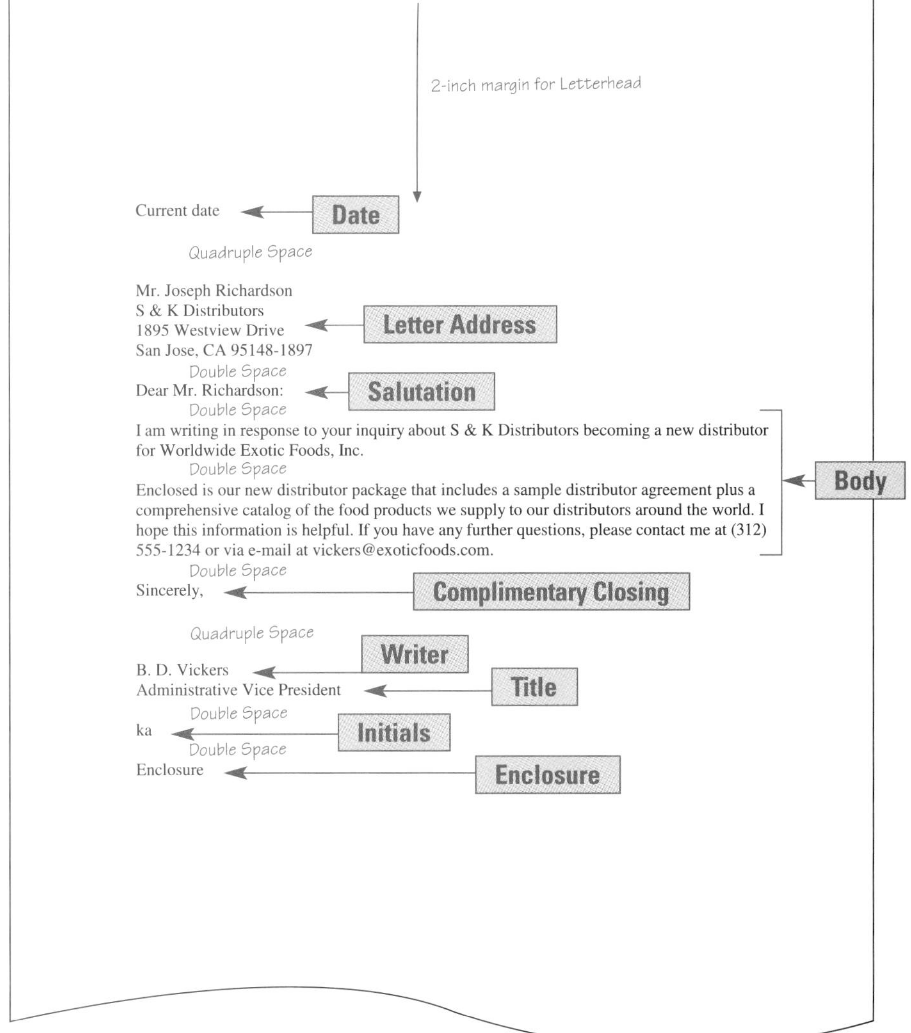

FIGURE B-1
Block Format Letter

QUICK TIP

The quality and professionalism of a company's business correspondence can affect how customers, clients, and others view a company. That correspondence represents the company to those outside it. To ensure a positive and appropriate image, many companies set special standards for margins, typeface, and font size for their business correspondence. These special standards are based on the common letter styles illustrated in this section.

appendix B

In the **modified block format**, the date begins near the center of the page or near the right margin. The closing starts near the center or right margin. Paragraphs can be either flush against the left margin or indented. Figure B-2 shows a short letter in the modified block format with standard punctuation.

FIGURE B-2
Modified Block Format Letter

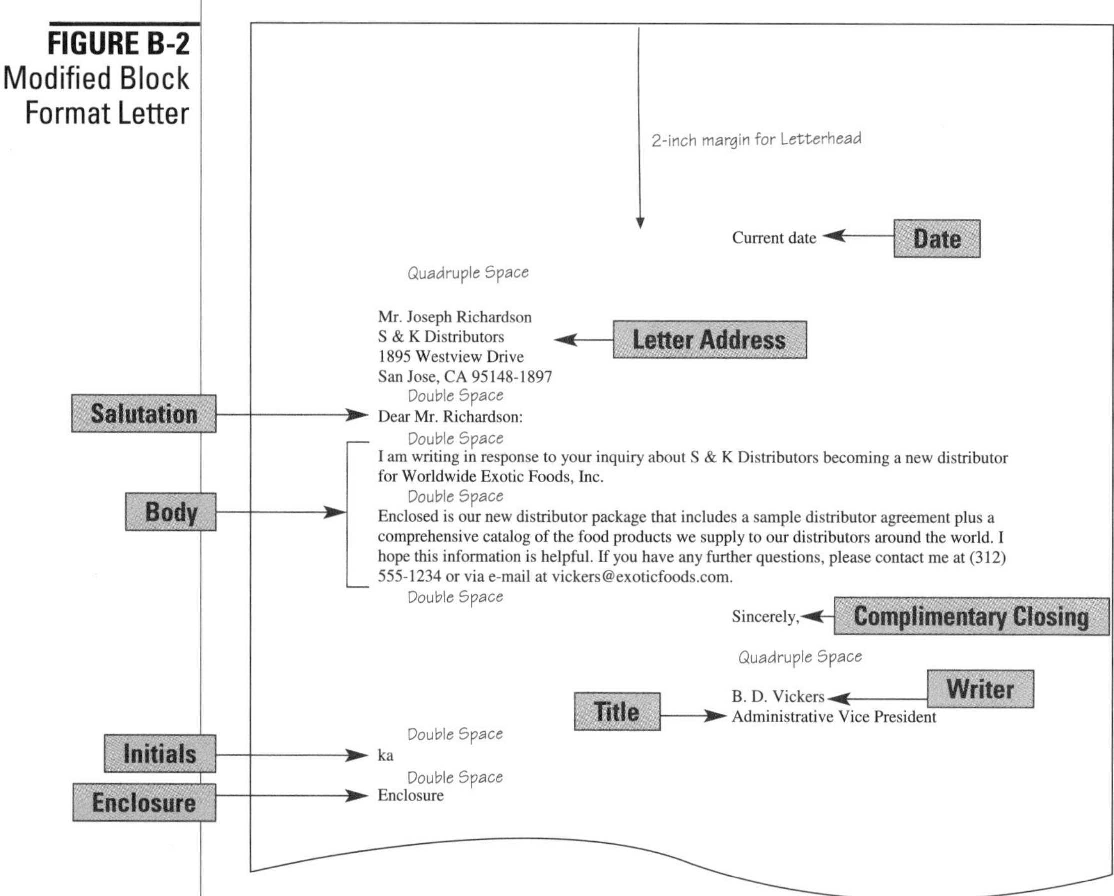

QUICK TIP

When you key a letter on plain paper in the modified block format, the return address usually appears near the right margin and above the date, with one blank line between the return address and the date.

Both the block and modified block styles use the same spacing for the non-body portions. Three blank lines separate the date from the addressee information, one blank line separates the addressee information from the salutation, one blank line separates the salutation from the body of the letter, and one blank line separates the body of the letter from the complimentary closing. There are three blank lines between the complimentary closing and the writer's name. If a typist's initials appear below the name, a blank line separates the writer's name from the initials. If an enclosure is noted, the word "Enclosure" appears below the typist's initials with a blank line separating them. Finally, when keying the return address or addressee information, one space separates the state and the postal code (ZIP+4).

B.b Inserting Mailing Notations

Mailing notations add information to a business letter. For example, the mailing notations CERTIFIED MAIL or SPECIAL DELIVERY indicate how a business letter was sent. The mailing notations CONFIDENTIAL or PERSONAL indicate how the person receiving the letter should handle the letter contents. Mailing notations should be keyed in uppercase characters at the left margin two lines below the date.[2] Figure B-3 shows a mailing notation added to a block format business letter.

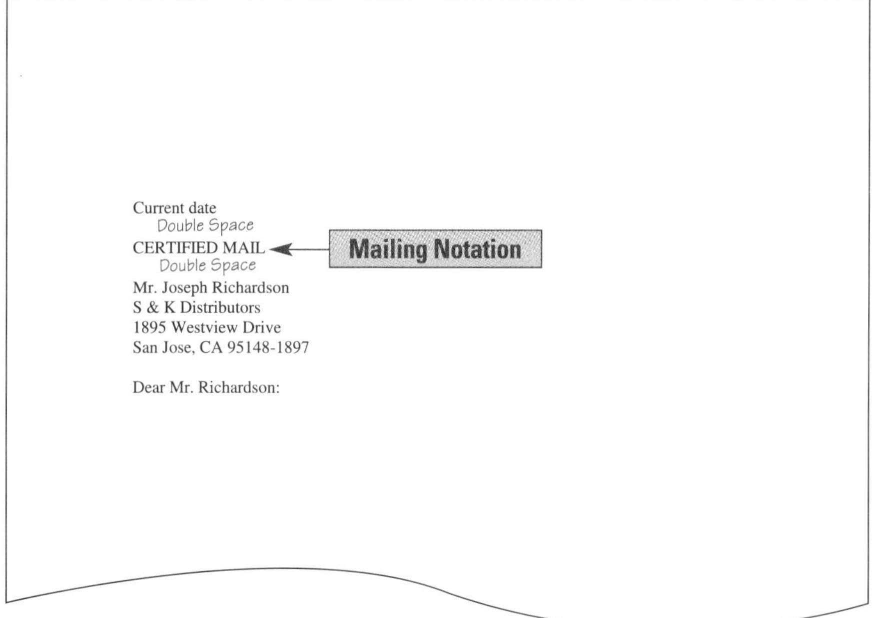

FIGURE B-3
Mailing Notation on Letter

B.c Formatting Envelopes

Two U.S. Postal Service publications, *The Right Way* (Publication 221), and *Postal Addressing Standards* (Publication 28) available from the U.S. Post Office, provide standards for addressing letter envelopes. The U.S. Postal Service uses optical character readers (OCRs) and barcode sorters (BCSs) to increase the speed, efficiency, and accuracy in processing mail. To get a letter delivered more quickly, envelopes should be addressed to take advantage of this automation process.

Table B-1 lists the minimum and maximum size for letters. The post office cannot process letters smaller than the minimum size. Letters larger than the maximum size cannot take advantage of automated processing and must be processed manually.

TABLE B-1
Minimum and Maximum Letter Dimensions

Dimension	Minimum	Maximum
Height	3½ inches	6⅛ inches
Length	5 inches	11½ inches
Thickness	.007 inch	¼ inch

The delivery address should be placed inside a rectangular area on the envelope that is approximately ⅝ inch from the top and bottom edge of the envelope and ½ inch from the left and right edge of the envelope. This is called the **OCR read area**. All the lines of the delivery address must fit within this area and no lines of the return address should extend into this area. To assure the delivery address is placed in the OCR read area, begin the address approximately ½ inch left of center and on approximately line 14.[3]

The lines of the delivery address should be in this order:

1. any optional nonaddress data, such as advertising or company logos, must be placed above the delivery address
2. any information or attention line
3. the name of the recipient
4. the street address
5. the city, state, and postal code (ZIP+4)

The delivery address should be complete, including apartment or suite numbers and delivery designations, such as RD (road), ST (street), or NW (northwest). Leave the area below and on both sides of the delivery address blank. Use uppercase characters and a sans serif font (such as Arial) for the delivery address. Omit all punctuation except the hyphen in the ZIP+4 code.

Figure B-4 shows a properly formatted business letter envelope.

QUICK TIP

Foreign addresses should include the country name in uppercase characters as the last line of the delivery address. The postal code, if any, should appear on the same line as the city.

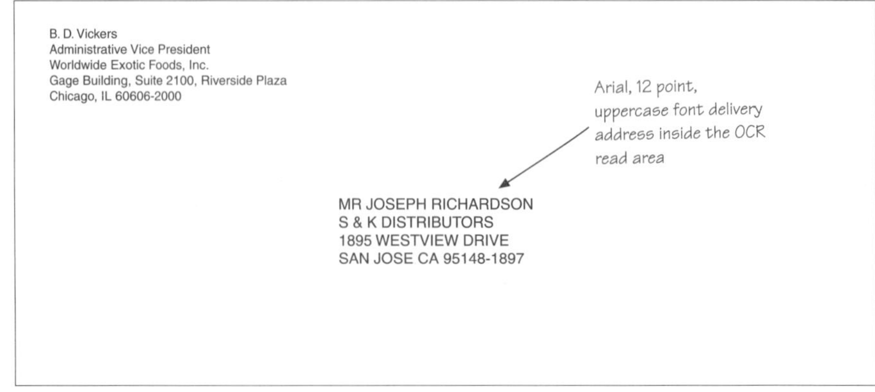

FIGURE B-4
Business Letter Envelope

B.d Formatting Interoffice Memorandums

Business correspondence that is sent within a company is usually prepared as an **interoffice memorandum**, also called a **memo**, rather than a letter. There are many different interoffice memo styles used in offices today, and word processing applications usually provide several memo templates based on different memo styles. Also, just as with business letters that are sent outside the company, many companies set special standards for margins, typeface, and font size for their interoffice memos.

A basic interoffice memo should include lines for "TO:", "FROM:", "DATE:", and "SUBJECT:" followed by the body text. Memos can be prepared on blank paper or on paper that includes a company name and even a logo. The word MEMORANDUM is often included. Figure B-5 shows a basic interoffice memorandum.

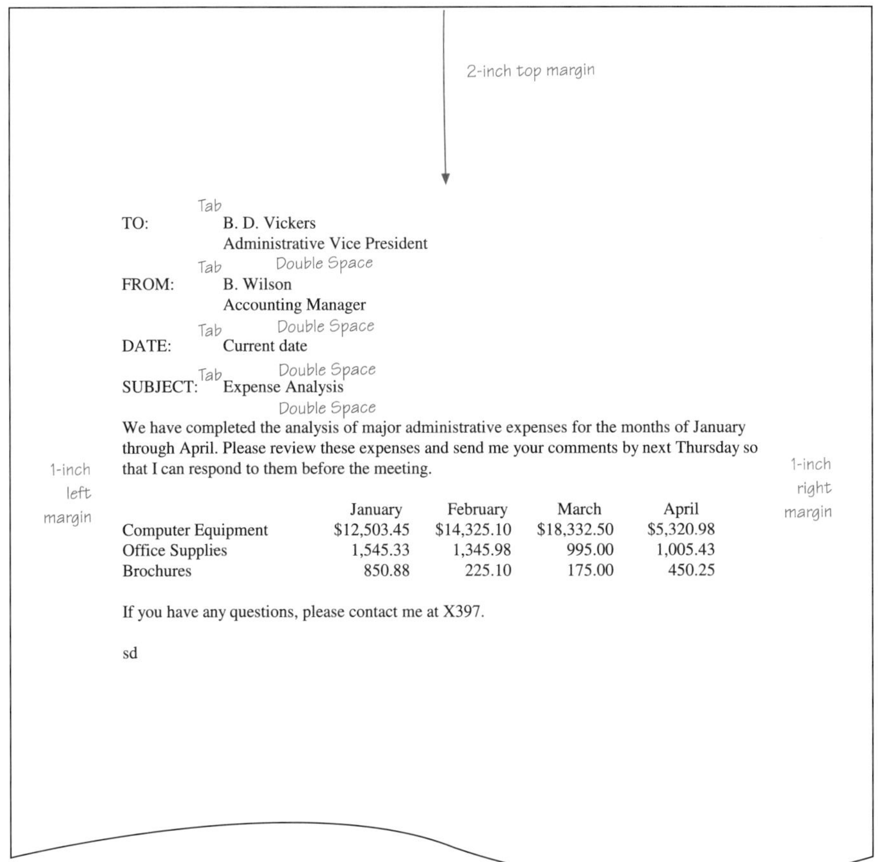

TO: B. D. Vickers
Administrative Vice President

FROM: B. Wilson
Accounting Manager

DATE: Current date

SUBJECT: Expense Analysis

We have completed the analysis of major administrative expenses for the months of January through April. Please review these expenses and send me your comments by next Thursday so that I can respond to them before the meeting.

	January	February	March	April
Computer Equipment	$12,503.45	$14,325.10	$18,332.50	$5,320.98
Office Supplies	1,545.33	1,345.98	995.00	1,005.43
Brochures	850.88	225.10	175.00	450.25

If you have any questions, please contact me at X397.

sd

FIGURE B-5
Interoffice Memorandum

appendix B

B.e Formatting Formal Outlines

Companies use outlines to organize data for a variety of purposes, such as reports, meeting agenda, and presentations. Word processing applications usually offer special features to help you create an outline. If you want to follow a formal outline format, you may need to add formatting to outlines created with these special features.

Margins for a short outline of two or three topics should be set at 1½ inches for the top margin and 2 inches for the left and right margins. For a longer outline, use a 2-inch top margin and 1-inch left and right margins.

The outline level-one text should be in uppercase characters. Second-level text should be treated like a title, with the first letter of the main words capitalized. Capitalize only the first letter of the first word at the third level. Double space before and after level one and single space the remaining levels.

Include at least two parts at each level. For example, you must have two level-one entries in an outline (at least I. and II.). If there is a second level following a level-one entry, it must contain at least two entries (at least A. and B.). All numbers must be aligned at the period and all subsequent levels must begin under the text of the preceding level, not under the number.[4]

Figure B-6 shows a formal outline prepared using the Word Outline Numbered list feature with additional formatting to follow a formal outline.

B.f Using Style Guides

A **style guide** provides a set of rules for punctuating and formatting text. There are a number of style guides used by writers, editors, business document proofreaders, and publishers. You can purchase style guides at a commercial bookstore, an online bookstore, or a college bookstore. Your local library likely has copies of different style guides and your instructor may have copies of several style guides for reference. Some popular style guides are *The Chicago Manual of Style* (The University of Chicago Press), *The Professional Secretary's Handbook* (Barron's), *The Holt Handbook* (Harcourt Brace College Publishers), and the *MLA Style Manual and Guide to Scholarly Publishing* (The Modern Language Association of America).

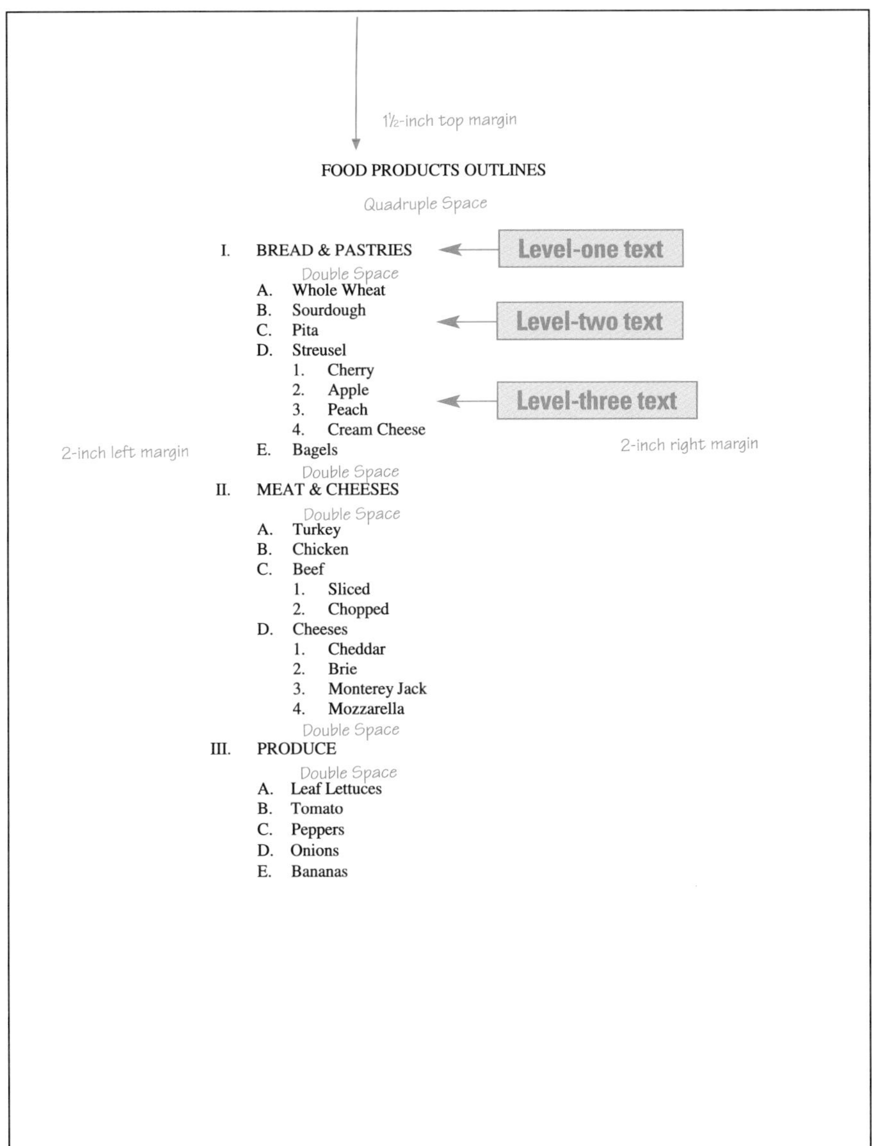

FOOD PRODUCTS OUTLINES

I. BREAD & PASTRIES
  A. Whole Wheat
  B. Sourdough
  C. Pita
  D. Streusel
    1. Cherry
    2. Apple
    3. Peach
    4. Cream Cheese
  E. Bagels

II. MEAT & CHEESES
  A. Turkey
  B. Chicken
  C. Beef
    1. Sliced
    2. Chopped
  D. Cheeses
    1. Cheddar
    2. Brie
    3. Monterey Jack
    4. Mozzarella

III. PRODUCE
  A. Leaf Lettuces
  B. Tomato
  C. Peppers
  D. Onions
  E. Bananas

FIGURE B-6
Formal Outline

B.g Using Proofreader's Marks

Standard proofreader's marks enable an editor or proofreader to make corrections or change notations in a document that can be recognized by anyone familiar with the marks. The following list illustrates standard proofreader's marks.

Defined		Examples
Paragraph	¶	¶ Begin a new paragraph at this
Insert a character	^	point. Insrt a letter here.
Delete	ℓ	Delete these words. Disregard
Do not change	stet or . . .	the previous correction. To
Transpose	tr	transpose is to around turn.
Move to the left	[	[Move this copy to the left.
Move to the right	]	]Move this copy to the right.
No paragraph	No ¶	No ¶ Do not begin a new paragraph
Delete and close up		here. Delete the hyphen from pre-empt and close up the space.
Set in caps	Caps or ≡	a sentence begins with a capital
Set in lower case	lc or /	letter. This Word should not
Insert a period	⊙	be capitalized. Insert a period⊙
Quotation marks	" "	"Quotation marks and a comma
Comma	^	should be placed here he said.
Insert space	#	Space between thesewords. An
Apostrophe	'	apostrophe is whats needed here.
Hyphen	=	Add a hyphen to Kilowatthour. Close
Close up	⁀	up the extra spa ce.
Use superior figure	1	Footnote this sentence.[1] Set
Set in italic	Ital. or ___	the words, sine qua non, in italics.
Move up	⊓	This word is too low. That word is
Move down	⊔	too high.

Endnotes

[1] Jerry W. Robinson et al., *Keyboarding and Information Processing* (Cincinnati: South-Western Educational Publishing, 1997).
[2] Ibid.
[3] Ibid.
[4] Ibid.

Appendix

Using Office XP Speech Recognition

Appendix Overview

You are familiar with using the keyboard and the mouse to key text and select commands. With Office XP, you also can use your voice to perform these same activities. Speech recognition enables you to use your voice to perform keyboard and mouse actions without ever lifting a hand. In this appendix, you learn how to set up Speech Recognition software and train the software to recognize your voice. You learn how to control menus, navigate dialog boxes, and open, save, and close a document. You then learn how to dictate text, including lines and punctuation, correct errors, and format text. Finally, you learn how to turn off and on Speech Recognition.

LEARNING OBJECTIVES

- Train your speech software
- Use voice commands
- Dictate, edit, and format by voice
- Turn Microsoft Speech Recognition on and off

C.a Training Your Speech Software

Speech recognition is an exciting new technology that Microsoft has integrated into its XP generation of products. Microsoft has been working on speech recognition for well over a decade. The state-of-the-art is advancing. If you haven't tried it before, this is a great time for you to experience this futuristic technology.

Voice recognition has important benefits:

- Microsoft's natural speech technologies can make your computer experience more enjoyable.
- Speech technology can increase your writing productivity.
- Voice recognition software can greatly reduce your risk for keyboard- and mouse-related injuries.

In the following activities, you learn to use your voice like a mouse and to write without the aid of the keyboard.

Connecting and Positioning Your Microphone

Start your speech recognition experience by setting up your microphone. There are several microphone styles used for speech recognition. The most common headset microphone connects to your computer's sound card, as shown in Figure C-1. Connect the microphone end to your computer's microphone audio input port. Connect the speaker end into your speech output port.

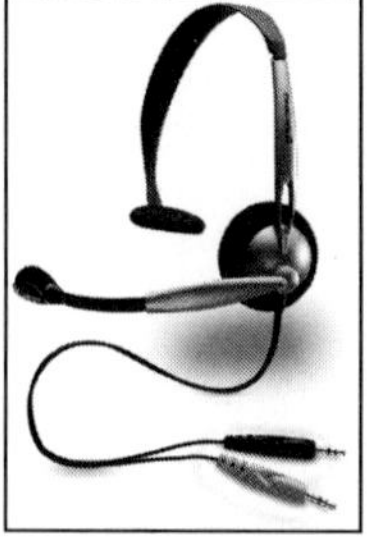

FIGURE C-1
Standard Sound Card Headset (Courtesy Plantronics Inc.)

USB speech microphones, such as the one shown in Figure C-2, are becoming very popular because they normally increase performance and accuracy. USB is short for Universal Serial Bus. USB microphones bypass the sound card and input speech with less distortion into your system.

USB microphones are plugged into the USB port found in the back of most computers. Windows automatically installs the necessary USB drivers after you start your computer with the USB microphone plugged into its slot.

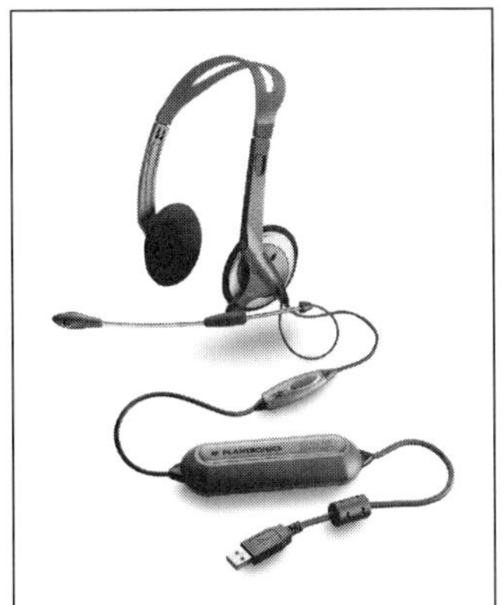

FIGURE C-2
A USB Headset (Courtesy Plantronics Inc.)

After your headset has been installed, put on your headset and position it comfortably. Remember these two important tips:

- Place the speaking side of your microphone about a thumb's width away from the side of your mouth, as shown in Figure C-3.
- Keep your microphone in the same position every time you speak. Changing your microphone's position can decrease your accuracy.

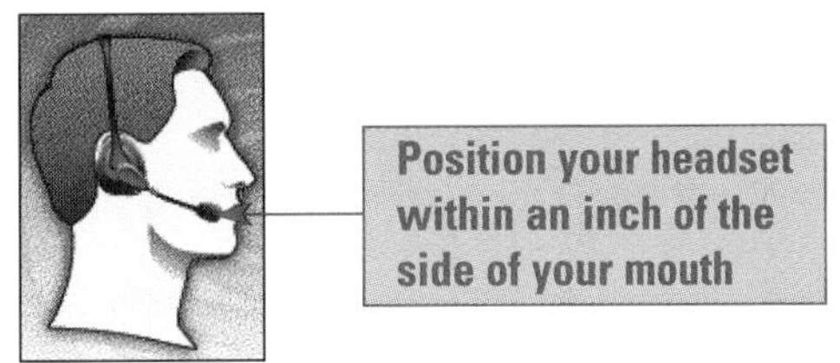
Position your headset within an inch of the side of your mouth

FIGURE C-3
Proper Headset Position

CAUTION TIP

If you see additional buttons on the Language Bar than shown in Figure C-4, click the Microphone button to hide them.

Installing Microsoft Speech Recognition

Open Microsoft Word and see if your speech software has already been installed. As Word opens, you should see either the floating Language Bar, shown in Figure C-4, or the Language Bar icon in the Windows Taskbar tray, as shown in Figure C-5.

Correction | Microphone | Tools | Write | Lined Paper | ?

FIGURE C-4
Floating Language Bar

Show the Language bar
Click the Language Bar icon and click Show the Language Bar

FIGURE C-5
Language Bar Icon

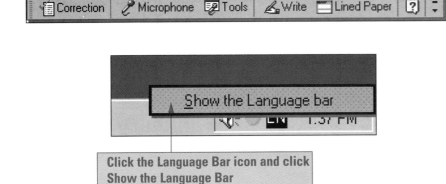

appendix C

If you can open and see the Language Bar, jump to Step-by-Step C.2. However, if this essential tool is missing, proceed with Step-by-Step C.1.

Step-by-Step C.1

Step 1 To install Microsoft speech recognition, open Microsoft Word by clicking **Start**, **Programs**, **Microsoft Word**.

Step 2 Click **Tools**, **Speech** from the Word menu bar, as shown in Figure C-6.

FIGURE C-6
Click Speech from the Tools menu

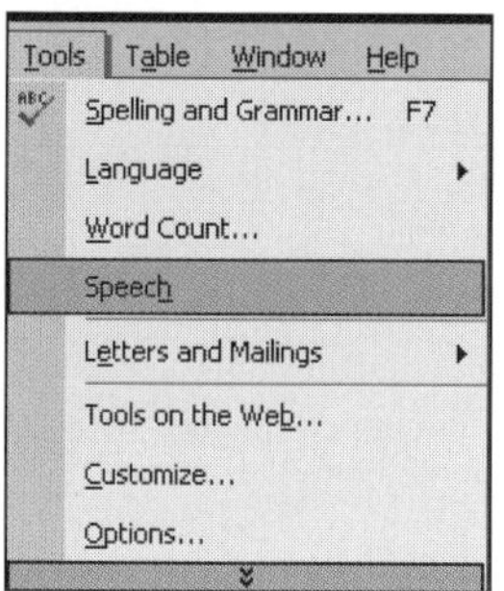

Step 3 You are prompted through the installation procedure. The process is a simple one. Follow the onscreen instructions.

Training Your System

Microsoft speech recognition can accommodate many different voices on the same computer. In order to work properly, your Microsoft Office Speech Recognition software must create a user **profile** for each voice it hears—including your voice.

If you are the first user and have just installed your speech software, chances are the system is already prompting you through the training steps. Skip to Step 3 in Step-by-Step C.2 for hints and help as you continue. However, if you are the second or later user of the system, you need to create a new profile by starting with Step 1.

Step-by-Step C.2

Step 1 To create your own personal speech profile, click the **Tools** button on the Language Bar and click **Options**, as shown in Figure C-7. This opens the Speech Properties dialog box.

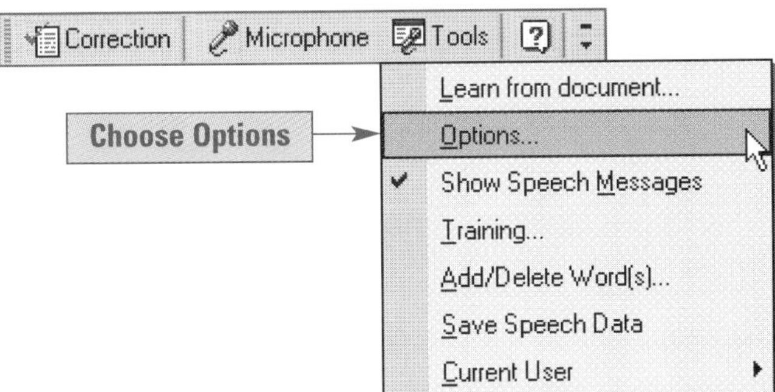

FIGURE C-7
Language Bar's Tools Menu

Step 2 In the Speech Properties dialog box, click **New**, as indicated in Figure C-8.

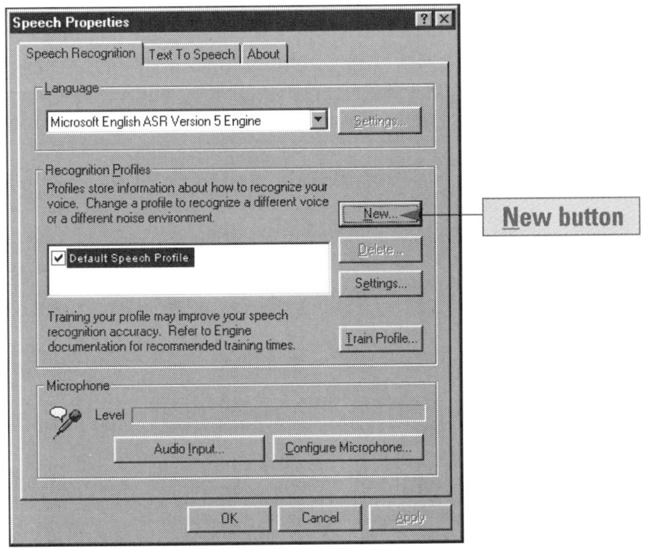

FIGURE C-8
Speech Properties Dialog Box

Step 3 Enter your name in the Profile Wizard, as shown in Figure C-9, and click **Next>** to continue. (*Note:* If you accidently click Finish instead of Next>, you must still train your profile by clicking Train Profile in the Speech Properties dialog box.)

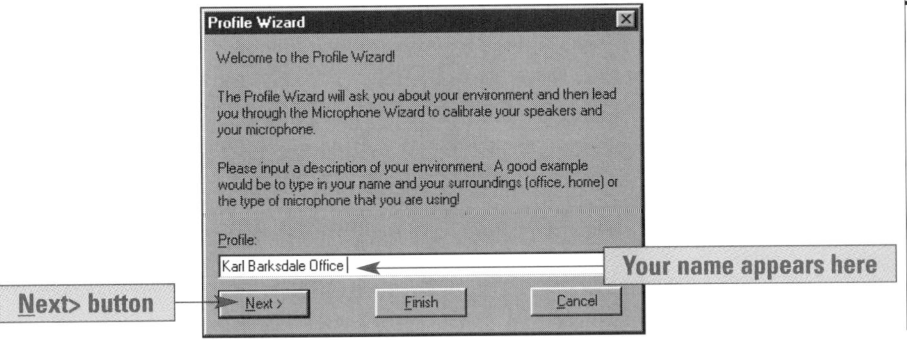

FIGURE C-9
New Profile Dialog Box

appendix C

Step 4 Adjust your microphone, as explained on the Microphone Wizard Welcome dialog box, as shown in Figure C-10. Click **Next>** to begin adjusting your microphone.

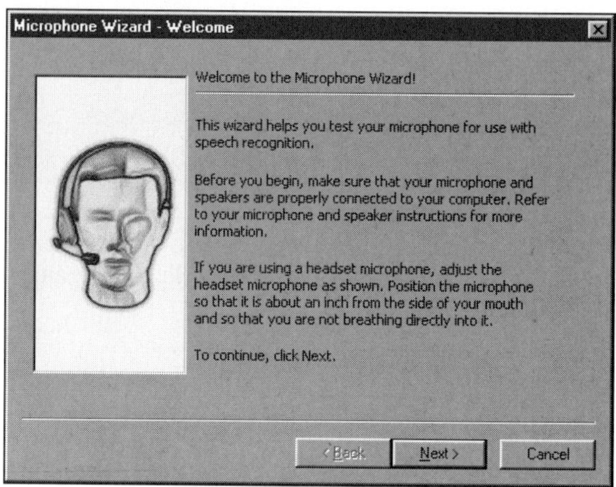

FIGURE C-10
Correctly Position Your Microphone

Step 5 Read the test sentence indicated in Figure C-11 until the volume adjustment settings appear consistently in the green portion of the volume adjustment meter. Your volume settings are adjusted automatically as you speak. Click **Next>** to continue.

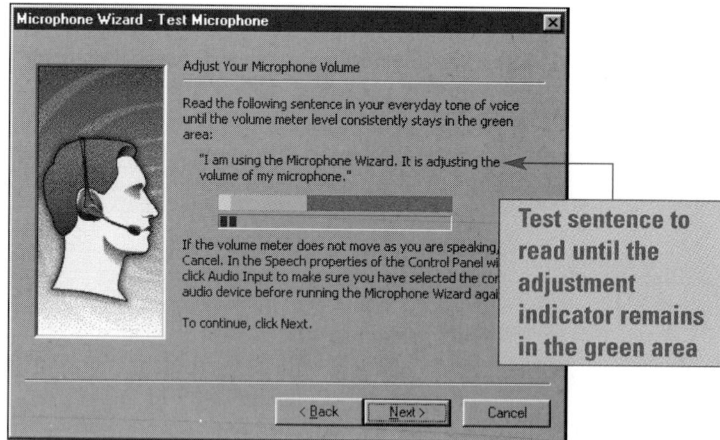

FIGURE C-11
Read Aloud to Adjust Your Microphone Volume

QUICK TIP

Microsoft Office Speech Recognition tells you if your microphone is not adequate for good speech recognition. You may need to try a higher quality microphone, install a compatible sound card, or switch to a USB microphone. Check the Microsoft Windows Help files for assistance with microphone problems.

Step 6 The next audio check tests the output of your speakers. Read the test sentence indicated in Figure C-12 and then listen. If you can hear your voice, your speakers are connected properly. Click **Finish** and continue.

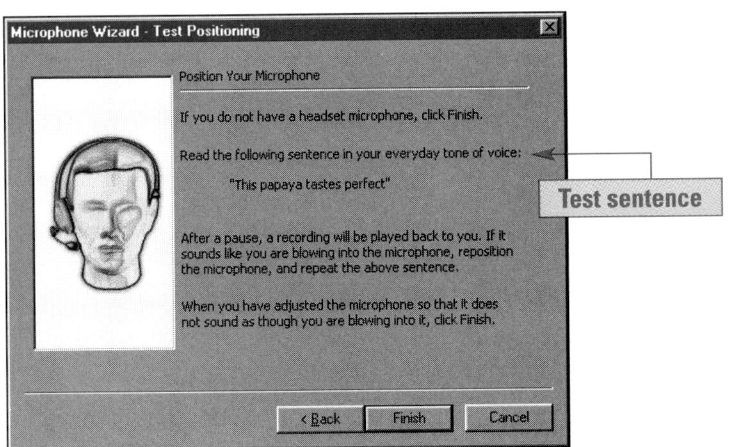

FIGURE C-12
Read Aloud to Test Your Sound Output

Training Your Software

Next, you are asked to train your software. During the training session, you read a training script or story for about 10 to 15 minutes. As you read, your software gathers samples of your speech. These samples help the speech software customize your speech recognition profile to your way of speaking. As you read, remember to:

- Read clearly.
- Use a normal, relaxed reading voice. Don't shout, but don't whisper softly either.
- Read at your normal reading pace. Do not read slowly and do not rush.

Step-by-Step C.3

Step 1 Microsoft Office Speech Recognition prepares you to read a story or script. Read the instruction screen shown in Figure C-13 and click **Next>** to continue.

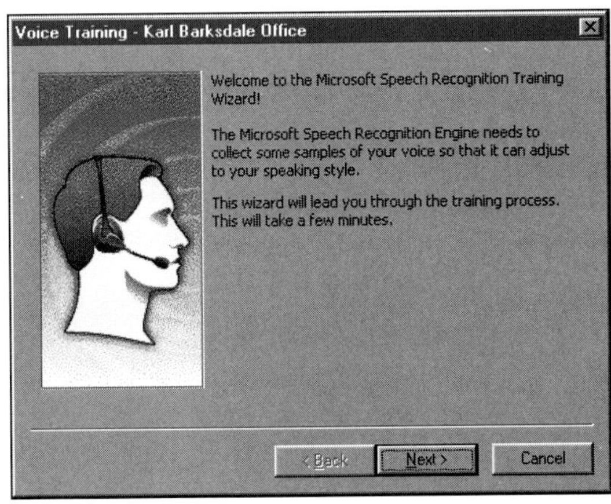

FIGURE C-13
Read the Onscreen Instructions Carefully

Step 2 Enter your gender and age information (see Figure C-14) to help the system calibrate its settings to your voice. Click **Next>** to continue.

QUICK TIP

Your user file will remember your microphone settings from session to session. However, if others use the system before you, you may need to readjust the audio settings by clicking **Tools, Options, Configure Microphone.**

CAUTION TIP

Never touch any part of your headset or microphone while speaking. Holding or touching the microphone creates errors.

FIGURE C-14
Enter Your Gender and Age Information

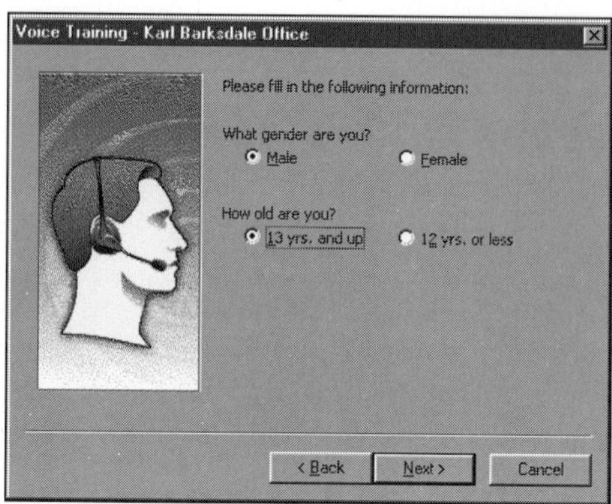

Step 3 Click **Sample** and listen to a short example of how to speak clearly to a computer. See Figure C-15. After the recording, click **Next>** to review the tips for the training session, and then click **Next>** to continue.

FIGURE C-15
Listen to the Speech Sample

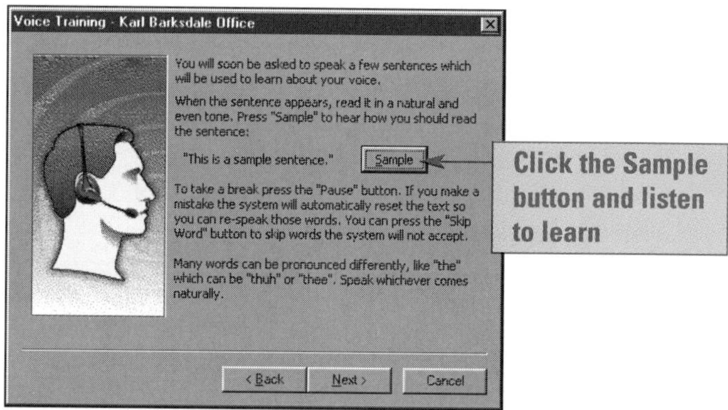

Step 4 Begin reading the training session paragraphs, as shown in Figure C-16. Text you have read is highlighted. The Training Progress bar lets you know how much reading is left. If you get stuck on a word, click **Skip Word** to move past the problem spot.

FIGURE C-16
Software Tracks Your Progress

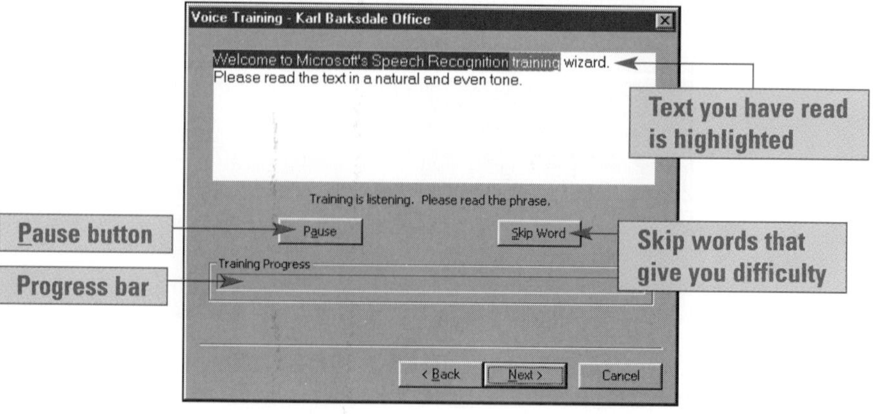

Step 5 The screen shown in Figure C-17 appears after you have finished reading the entire first story or training session script. You now have a couple of choices. Click **More Training**, click **Next>**, and continue reading additional scripts as explained in Step 6 (or you can click Finish and quit for the day).

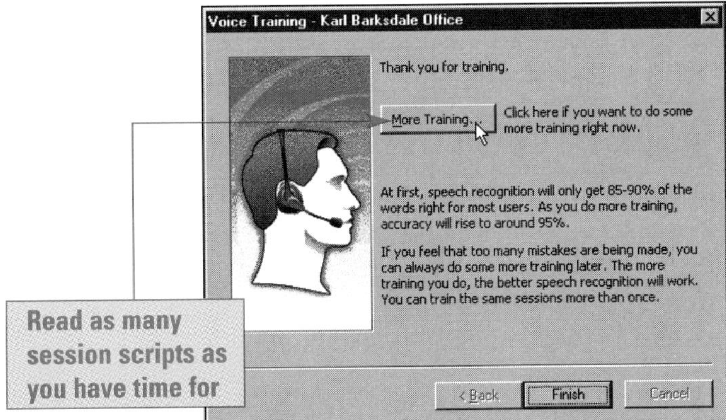

FIGURE C-17
First Training Script Completed

Step 6 Choose another training session story or script from the list, as shown in Figure C-18, and then click **Next>**.

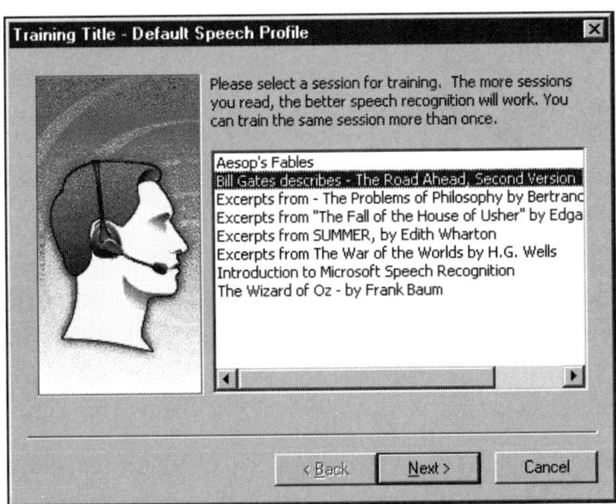

FIGURE C-18
Choose Another Story or Training Script to Read

Step 7 At the end of the training process, Microsoft Office Speech Recognition shows you a multimedia training tutorial (you may need to install Macromedia Flash to view the tutorial). Enjoy the tutorial before continuing.

QUICK TIP

The more stories you read, the better. Users with thick accents, or accuracy below 90 percent, must read additional stories. You can read additional training session scripts at any time by clicking **Tools**, **Training** on the Language Bar.

CAUTION TIP

You must read until Microsoft Office Speech Recognition has a large enough sample of your voice to process and adjust to your unique way of speaking. Click **Pause** to take a break. However, it is best to read the entire session training script in one sitting.

C.b Using Voice Commands

Microsoft makes it easy to replace mouse clicks with voice commands. The voice commands are very intuitive. In most cases, you simply say what you see. For example, to open the File menu, you can simply say **File**.

Microsoft Office XP voice commands allow you to control dialog boxes and menu bars, and to format documents by speaking. You can give your hands a rest by speaking commands instead of clicking them. This can help reduce your risk for carpal tunnel syndrome and other serious injuries.

Before you begin using voice commands, remember that if more than one person is using speech recognition on the same computer, you must select your user profile from the Current Users list. The list is found by clicking the Language Bar Tools menu, as shown in Figure C-19.

FIGURE C-19
Current Users List

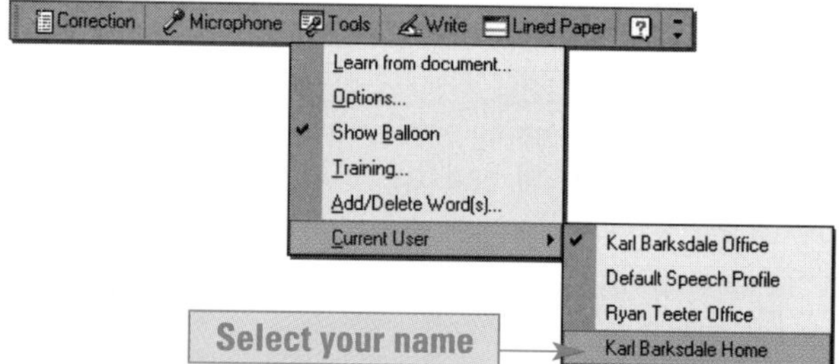

MENU TIP

After you have selected your user profile, you may wish to refresh your audio settings by clicking **Tools, Options, Configure Microphone.** This will help adjust the audio settings to the noise conditions in your current dictation environment.

Switching Modes and Moving the Language Bar

Microsoft Office Speech Recognition works in two modes. The first is called **Dictation mode**. The second is called **Voice Command mode.** Voice Command mode allows you to control menus, give commands, and format documents.

When using Voice Command mode, simply *say what you see on the screen or in dialog boxes.* You see how this works in the next few exercises. In Step-by-Step C.4, you learn how to switch between the two modes.

Step-by-Step C.4

Step 1	Open **Microsoft Word** and the **Language Bar**, if necessary.
Step 2	The Language Bar can appear collapsed (see Figure C-20) or expanded (see Figure C-21). You can switch between the two options by clicking the **Microphone** button.

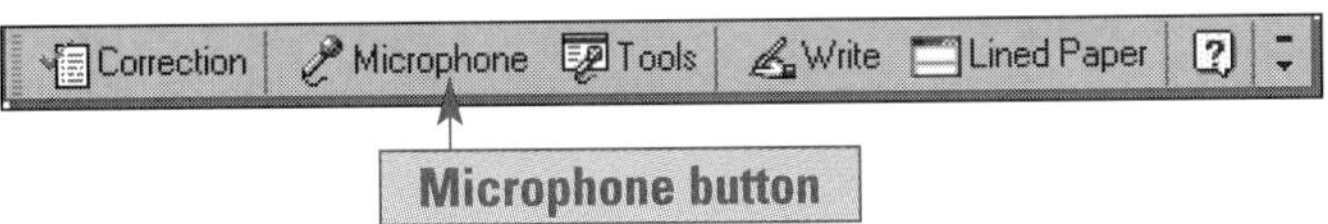

FIGURE C-20
Collapsed Language Bar

Clicking the Microphone button with your mouse turns on the microphone and expands the Language Bar.

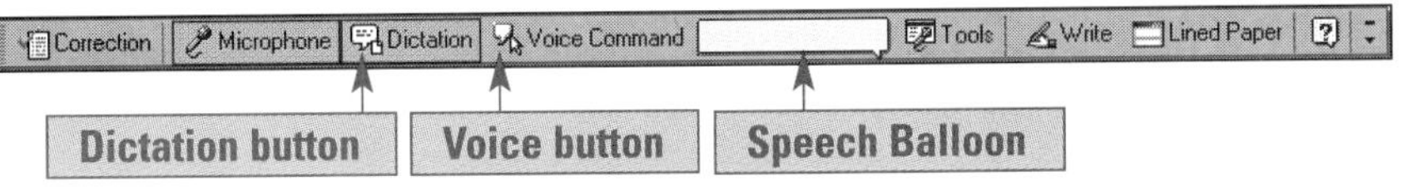

FIGURE C-21
Expanded Language Bar

Step 3 Compare the tools found on the expanded Language Bar with those in the collapsed Language Bar. You see several new features on the expanded bar, including the Dictation, Voice Command, and Speech Balloon options.

Step 4 Switch between **Dictation** mode (used for dictating words) and **Voice Command** mode (used for giving commands) by saying the following commands clearly. Make sure you pause momentarily after you say each command.
Turn on the Microphone and say:

Voice Command ***<pause>***
Dictation ***<pause>***
Voice Command ***<pause>***
Dictation ***<pause>***

Step 5 Practice turning off the microphone with your voice (thereby collapsing the Language Bar) by saying:
Microphone

Step 6 Click and drag the Language Bar to various parts of the screen by clicking the markers found on the left end of the Language Bar (see Figure C-22).

QUICK TIP

The Language Bar can float anywhere on the screen. Move the Language Bar to a spot that is convenient and out of the way. Most users position the Language Bar in the title bar or status bar when using speech with Microsoft Word.

FIGURE C-22
Move the Language Bar to a Convenient Spot

Giving Menu Commands

When you use Microsoft Office Voice Commands, your word will be obeyed. Before you begin issuing commands, take a few seconds and analyze Figure C-23. The toolbars you will be working with in the next few activities are identified in the figure.

FIGURE C-23
Customize Microsoft Word with Your Voice

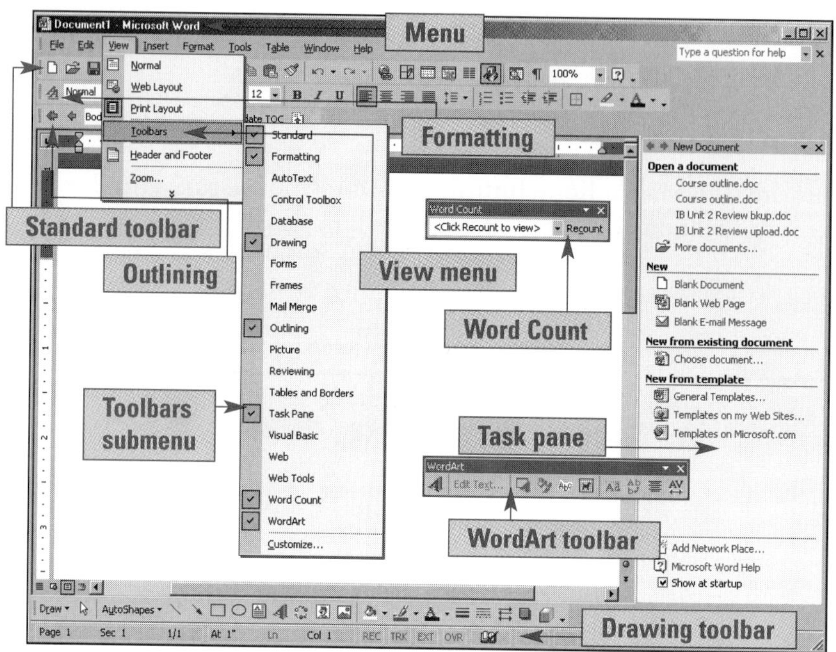

QUICK TIP

In Voice Command mode, you can say almost any command you would click with your mouse, and achieve the same result. For the most part, simply say what you see on the screen. Voice Commands are very easy to learn.

QUICK TIP

The Escape and Cancel commands are like pressing the ESC key on the keyboard. These commands cancel whatever menu you have voice-selected.

Step-by-Step C.5

Step 1 Switch on the **Microphone** from the Language Bar.

Step 2 Switch to Voice Command mode by saying:
Voice Command

Step 3 Open and close several menus by saying:
File *(Pause briefly between commands)*
Escape
Edit
Cancel
View
Escape

Step 4 Close or display a few of the popular toolbars found in Microsoft Word by saying the following commands:
View
Toolbars
Standard
View
Toolbars
Formatting
View
Toolbars
Drawing

Step 5 Close or redisplay the toolbars by saying the following commands:
View
Toolbars
Drawing
View
Toolbars
Formatting
View
Toolbars
Standard

Step 6 Practice giving voice commands by adding and removing the Task Pane and WordArt toolbar. Try some other options. When you are through experimenting, turn off the microphone and collapse the Language Bar by saying:
Microphone

Navigating Dialog Boxes

Opening files is one thing you do nearly every time you use Microsoft Office. To open files, you need to manipulate the Open dialog box (Figure C-24). A dialog box allows you to make decisions and execute voice commands. For example, in the Open dialog box you can switch folders and open files by voice.

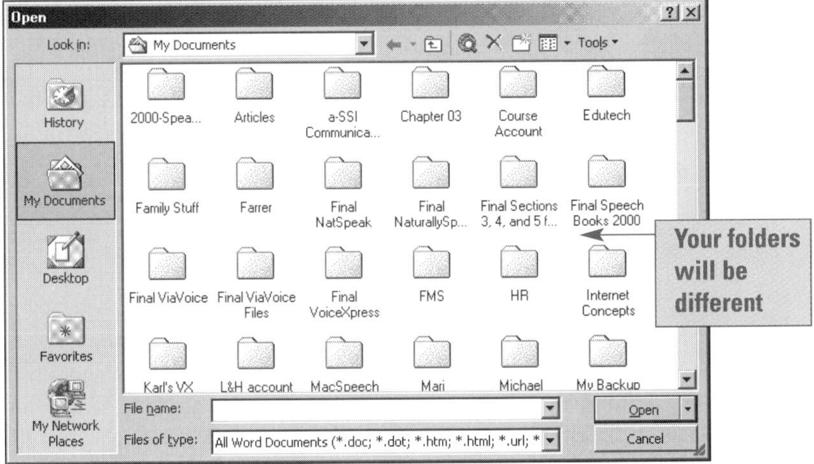

FIGURE C-24
Open Dialog Box

Step-by-Step C.6

Step 1 Turn on the **Microphone**, switch to Voice Command mode, and access the Open dialog box, as shown in Figure C-25, using the following commands:
Voice Command
File
Open

FIGURE C-25
Say File, Open

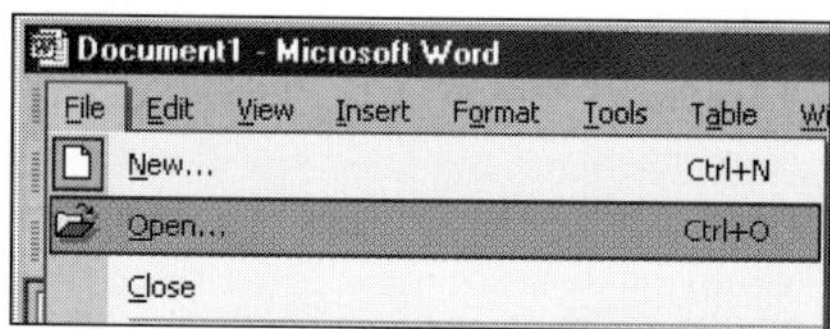

Step 2

Switch between various folder locations with your voice. In this case, you're going to switch between the Desktop, My Documents, and other folders located on the side of the Open dialog box, as shown in Figure C-26. Say the following voice commands to switch between folder locations. Pause slightly after saying each command:

Desktop
My Documents
History
Desktop
Favorites
My Documents

FIGURE C-26
Switch Between Various Folder Locations

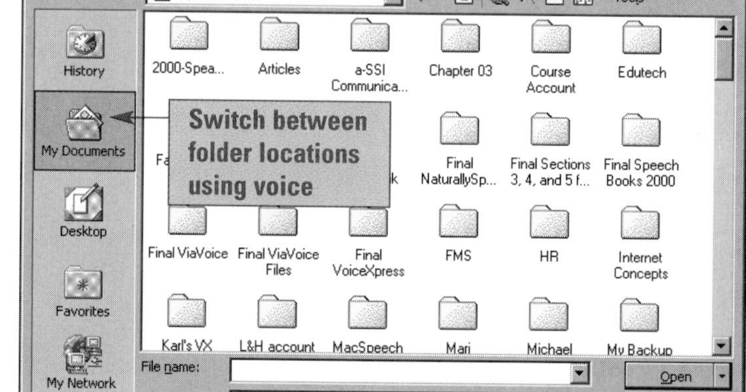

QUICK TIP

Any time a button in a dialog box appears dark around the edges, the button is active. You can access active buttons at any time by saying the name of the button or by saying **Enter**. You can also move around dialog boxes using the **Tab** or **Shift Tab** voice commands, or move between folders and files by saying **Up Arrow, Down Arrow, Left Arrow**, and **Right Arrow**. When selecting files, you'll probably find it much easier to use your mouse instead of your voice.

Step 3

You can change how your folders and files look in the Open dialog box by manipulating the Views menu, as shown in Figure C-27. Say the following voice commands to change the look of your folders and files:

Views
Small Icons
Views
List
Views
Details
Views
Thumbnails
Views
Large icons
Views
List

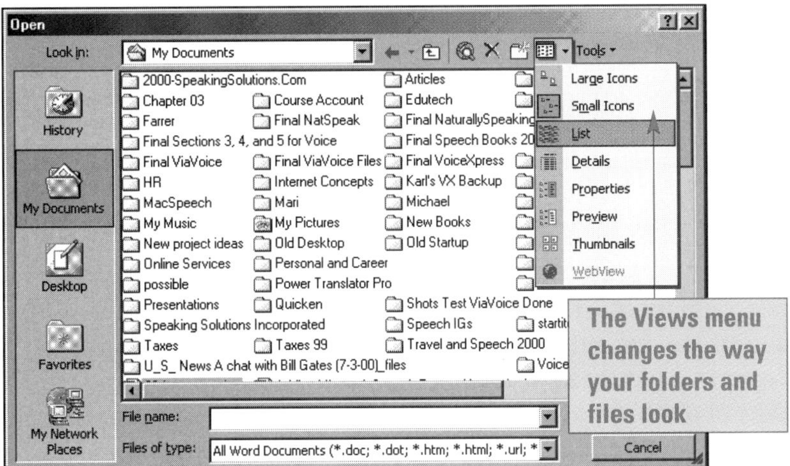

FIGURE C-27
Change the Look of Folders with the Views Menu

Step 4	Close the Open dialog box by using the Cancel command. Say: ***Cancel***

Open and Count a Document

In Step-by-Step C.7, you combine your traditional mouse skills with voice skills to accomplish tasks more conveniently. Use your skills to open a file. Then, use your menu selecting technique to open the Word Count toolbar and count the number of words in a document.

Step-by-Step C.7

Step 1	Using your voice, say ***File, Open*** and select the **My Documents** folder (or the location of your Data Disk). View the folders and files in **List** view. (Review Step-by-Step C.6 if you have forgotten how to make these changes in the Open dialog box.)
Step 2	Scroll through the list of files with your mouse until you see the file called ***Prevent Injury***. To open the file, select it with your mouse and say: ***Open*** (or you also may say ***Enter***)
Step 3	As the file opens, notice that the document title is PREVENT INJURY WITH SPEECH. Speech recognition can help you avoid serious keyboarding and mouse injuries. Count the words in the article. Open the Word Count toolbar by saying the following: ***View*** ***Toolbars*** ***Word Count***
Step 4	With the Word Count toolbar open, say the following command to count the words: ***Recount***

QUICK TIP

To complete Step-by-Step C.7, the *Prevent Injury* document should be moved from the Data Disk to the My Documents folder on your computer.

Step 5	How many words are contained in the article?
Step 6	Leave the *Prevent Injury* document open for the next activity.

Save a Document and Exit Word

Saving a file will give you a chance to practice manipulating dialog boxes. Switching from the keyboard and mouse to your voice has several benefits. For example, have you heard of carpal tunnel syndrome and other computer keyboard-related injuries caused by repetitive typing and clicking? By using your speech software even part of the time, you can reduce your risk for these long-term and debilitating nerve injuries.

In Step-by-Step C.8, you change the filename *Prevent Injury* to *My prevent injury file* using the Save As dialog box.

Step-by-Step C.8

Step 1	Make sure the ***Prevent Injury*** document appears on your screen. If you closed the document, repeat Step-by-Step C.7.
Step 2	Open the **Save As** dialog box. Notice that it is a lot like the Open dialog box. Try the following commands: ***Voice Command*** *(if necessary)* ***File*** ***Save as***
Step 3	Switch to the **My Documents** folder and display the folder in **List** view as you learned to do in Step-by-Step C.7.
Step 4	Click your mouse in the **File name:** text box and type the filename or switch to Dictation mode and name the file with your voice by saying: ***Dictation*** ***My prevent injury file***
Step 5	Save your document and close the Save As the box by saying: ***Voice Command*** ***Save***
Step 6	Close the **Word Count** toolbar using the steps you learned earlier.
Step 7	Close Microsoft Word and collapse the Language Bar with the following commands: (When asked whether to save other open documents, say ***No***.) ***File*** ***Close*** ***Microphone***

C.c Dictating, Editing, and Formatting by Voice

If you have always dreamed of the day when you could sit back, relax, and write the next great American novel by speaking into a microphone, well, that day has arrived. It is possible to write that novel, a report, or even a simple e-mail message at speeds of 130–160 words per minute. However, it takes practice to achieve an acceptable level of accuracy. This section is designed to help you build accuracy.

Microsoft Office Speech Recognition is not made for complete handsfree use. You still need to use your keyboard and mouse much of the time. But, if you're willing to put in some effort, you can improve your speaking accuracy to the point that you can dramatically improve your output.

Dictating

Microsoft Speech Recognition allows you to work in **Dictation** mode when voice writing words into your documents. Switching from Voice Command mode to Dictation mode is as easy as saying ***Dictation***.

In Dictation mode, don't stop speaking in the middle of a sentence—even if your words don't appear immediately. The software needs a few seconds to process what you're saying. Microsoft Office Speech Recognition lets you know it is working by placing a highlighted bar with dots in your document, as shown in Figure C-28. A few seconds later, your words appear.

QUICK TIP

The best way to improve dictation accuracy is to read additional training session stories to your computer. You should read at least three to five stories. Do this by clicking **Tools, Current User**, and double-checking to see if your user profile name has a check mark by it. Then, click **Tools, Training** from the Language Bar and follow the onscreen instructions.

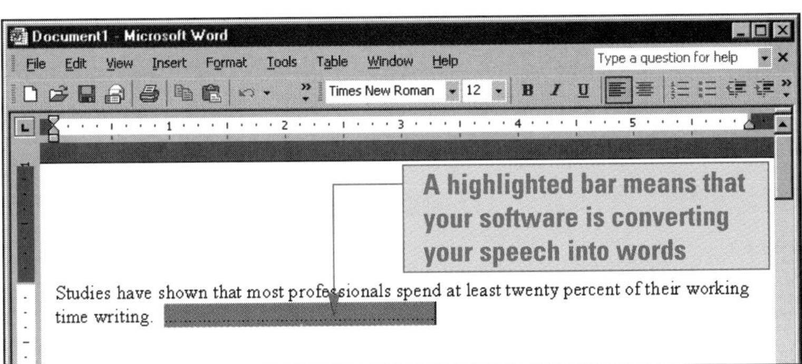

FIGURE C-28
Continue Talking Even If Your Words Don't Appear Instantly

appendix C

QUICK TIP

Think about the following as you begin voice writing:

- Speak naturally, without stopping in the middle of your sentences.
- Don't speak abnormally fast or slow.
- Say each word clearly. Don't slur your words or leave out sounds.

QUICK TIP

You'll need to dictate punctuation marks. Say the word ***Period*** to create a (.), say ***Comma*** to create a (,), say ***Question Mark*** for a (?), and ***Exclamation Mark/Point*** for (!).

During the next steps, don't be overly concerned about making mistakes. You learn some powerful ways to correct mistakes in the next few exercises. For now, experiment and see what happens.

Step-by-Step C.9

Step 1	Open **Microsoft Word** and the **Language Bar**, if necessary. Don't forget to select your user profile.
Step 2	Turn on the **Microphone**, switch to **Dictation mode**, and read this short selection into Microsoft Word. ***Dictation*** ***Studies have shown that most professionals spend at least twenty percent of their working time writing <period> You can use speech recognition software to help you in any career you choose <period> Microsoft speech can be used in the medical <comma> legal <comma> financial <comma> and educational professions <period>*** ***Microphone***
Step 3	Examine your paragraph. How well did you do? Count the mistakes or word errors. How many errors did you make?
Step 4	Now delete all the text on your screen. Start by turning on the **Microphone** and then switching to **Voice Command** mode by saying (remember to pause briefly after each command): ***Voice Command*** ***Edit*** ***Select All*** ***Backspace***
Step 5	Repeat the selection from Step 2. This time, say any word that gave you difficulty a little more clearly. See if your computer understands more of what you say this time around.
Step 6	Did you improve? Yes/No
Step 7	Delete all the text on your screen again before you continue, using the ***Voice Command, Edit, Select All, Backspace*** commands.

Using the New Line and New Paragraph Commands

In this next set of exercises, you have a chance to use the New Line and New Paragraph commands to organize text. These essential commands allow you to control the look and feel of your documents. (See Figure C-29.) It helps to pause briefly before and after you say each command.

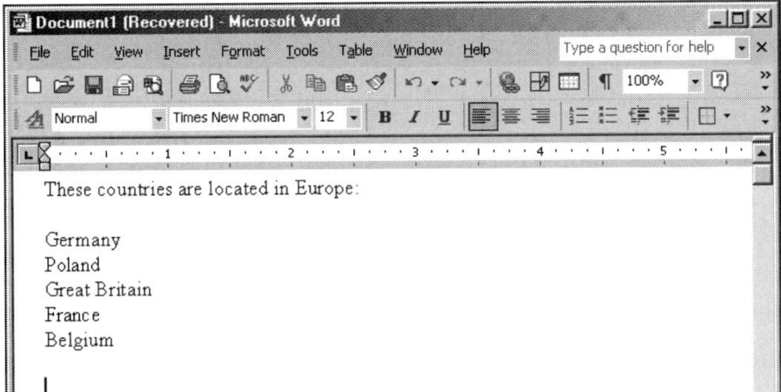

FIGURE C-29
New Line and New Paragraph Commands Organize Text

Step-by-Step C.10

Step 1 The New Line and New Paragraph commands help organize lists of information. Dictate the following list of European countries. Turn on the **Microphone**, if necessary, and say:

Dictation

These countries are located in Europe <colon> <New Paragraph>

Germany	***<New Line>***
Poland	***<New Line>***
Great Britain	***<New Line>***
France	***<New Line>***
Belgium	***<New Paragraph>***

Step 2 Save the file in the Save As dialog box with the ***Voice Command, File, Save As*** commands.

Step 3 Click your mouse in the **File name:** text box and enter ***Countries of Europe*** as the filename. (*Note:* If you speak the filename, remember to switch to Dictation mode.)

Step 4 Close the Save As dialog box with the ***Voice Command, Save*** commands, and then clear your screen by saying ***Edit, Select All, Backspace.***

QUICK TIP

Say the word ***Colon*** to create a (:).

QUICK TIP

When dictating words in a list, it helps to pause slightly before and after saying the commands, as in ***<pause> New Line <pause>*** and ***<pause> New Paragraph <pause>***.

Using Undo

Microsoft Office Speech Recognition offers powerful ways to make corrections and train the software to recognize difficult words, so they appear correctly when you say them again. For example, erasing mistakes is easy with the Undo command. That's the first trick you learn in this section.

The Undo command works like pressing the Undo button or clicking Edit, Undo with your mouse. You can quickly erase the problem when you misspeak. All you need to do is switch to Voice Command mode and say ***Undo***.

CAUTION TIP

A common speech mistake occurs when speakers break words into syllables. For example, they may say **speak keen clear lee** instead of **speaking clearly.**

QUICK TIP

A key to great accuracy in speech recognition is to speak in complete phrases and sentences. Complete sentences and phrases make it easier for the software to understand what you're trying to say. The software makes adjustments based on the context of the words that commonly appear together. The more words you say as a group or phrase, the more information your software has to work with.

Step-by-Step C.11

Step 1 In this step, say the name of the academic subject, then erase it immediately with the Undo command and replace it with the next subject in the list. Erase the subject regardless of whether it is correct. Switch to Voice Command mode before saying Undo.

Dictation

Biology	***Voice Command***	***Undo***	***Dictation***
French	***Voice Command***	***Undo***	***Dictation***
American history	***Voice Command***	***Undo***	***Dictation***

Step 2 The Undo command deletes the last continuous phrase you have spoken. Say each of the following phrases, then use Undo to erase them.

To infinity and beyond	***Voice Command***	***Undo***	***Dictation***
The check is in the mail	***Voice Command***	***Undo***	***Dictation***
Money isn't everything	***Voice Command***	***Undo***	

Microphone

Correcting Errors

Correcting mistakes is obviously important. There are several ways to make corrections effectively.

Because speech recognition software recognizes phrases better than individual words, one of the best ways to correct a mistake is to use your mouse to select the phrase where the mistake occurs and then repeat the phrase. For example, in the sentence below the software has keyed the word ***share*** instead of the word ***sure***. Select the phrase (like the boldface example) with your mouse, then say the phrase again:

What you should select: You sound **very share of yourself**.
What you would repeat: **very sure of yourself**

If you still make a mistake, select the misspoken word with your mouse and take advantage of the power of the **Correction** button on the Language Bar. Carefully read through these steps and then practice what you learned in Step 5.

Step-by-Step C.12

Step 1 If you make an error, select the mistake, as shown in Figure C-30.

Step 2 With your microphone on, say ***Correction*** or click the Correction button with your mouse.

Step 3 If the correct alternative appears in the correction list, click the correct alternative with your mouse.

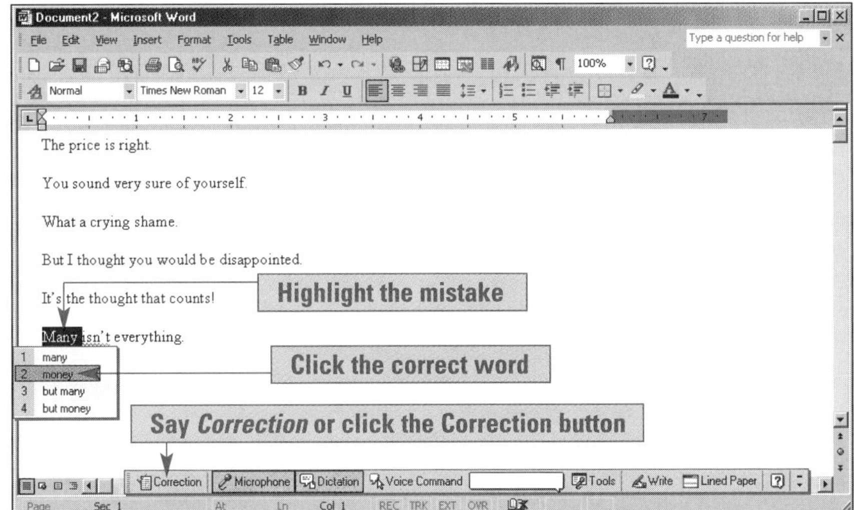

FIGURE C-30
Select the Mistake and Say *Correction*

Step 4 If the correct word does not appear, as in Figure C-31, key the correct response with your keyboard.

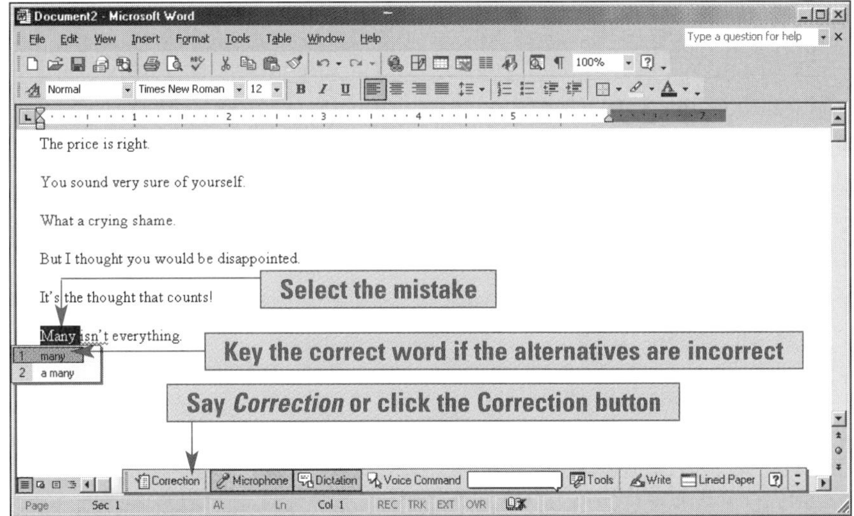

FIGURE C-31
If the Correct Word Doesn't Appear, Key the Word

Step 5 Now give it a try. Speak the following sentences. (*Hint:* Say the complete sentence before you make any corrections.) Try to correct the error first by repeating the phrase. Then, select individual word errors and use the Correction button to help you fix any remaining mistakes:

The price is right.
You sound very sure of yourself.
What a crying shame.
But, I thought you would be disappointed.
It's the thought that counts!
Money isn't everything.

appendix C

Formatting Sentences

After you dictate text, you can format it, copy it, paste it, and manipulate it just like you would with a mouse. In this exercise, you dictate a few sentences, and then you change the font styles and make a copy of the sentences. That is a lot to remember, so take a look at what you are about to accomplish. Review Figure C-32 to get a sneak preview of this activity.

FIGURE C-32
Dictate, Format, and Copy and Paste These Lines

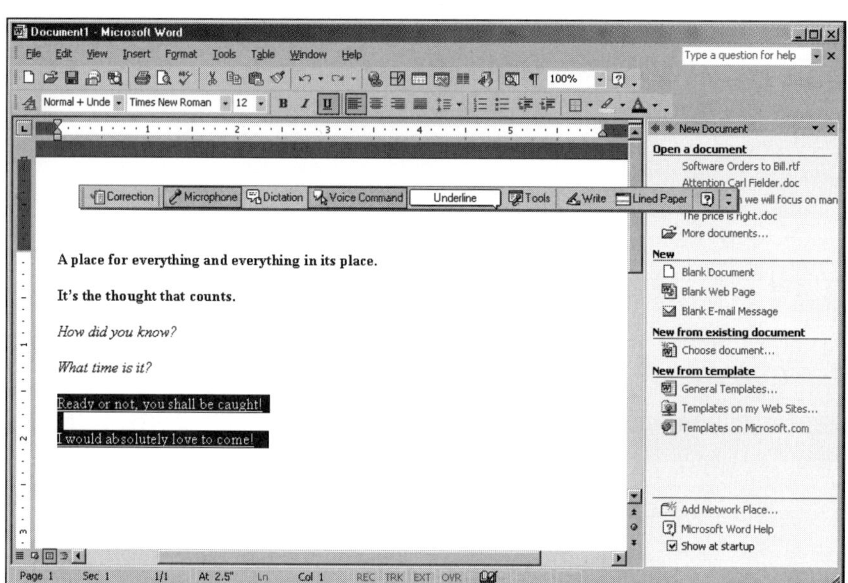

MOUSE TIP

When you correct a mistake using the Correction button, Microsoft Office Speech Recognition plays back what you said and remembers any corrections that you make. This helps to ensure that the software won't make the same mistake the next time you say the same word or phrase. Use the Correction button as often as you can. This helps to improve your speech recognition accuracy.

A few quick reminders before you begin:

- Use your mouse and voice together to bold, italicize, and underline text.
- Say the basic punctuation marks, exclamation point/mark (!), period (.), comma (,), question mark (?), semicolon (;), colon (:).
- Start a new line with the New Paragraph command.

Step-by-Step C.13

Step 1 Speak the following sentences, using the New Paragraph command to space between each. Do not pause in the middle of any sentence. If you make mistakes, correct them using the Correction button, as explained in Step-by-Step C.12.

Dictation
A place for everything and everything in its place.
It's the thought that counts.
How did you know?
What time is it?
Ready or not, you shall be caught!
I would absolutely love to come!

Step 2 With your mouse, select the first two sentences and make them bold with the following commands:
Voice Command
Bold

Step 3 Select the two questions and italicize them by saying:
Italic

Step 4 Select the final two exclamatory sentences and underline them by saying:
Underline

Step 5 Copy all the text on your screen and paste a copy at the bottom of your document by saying:
Edit
Select All
Copy
Down Arrow
Paste

Step 6 Print your document with the following commands:
File
Print
OK

Step 7 Close your document without saving using the ***File, Close*** command and then say ***No*** when you are asked to save.

Step 8 Open a new document with your voice with the ***File, New, Blank Document*** commands and turn off your ***Microphone*** before you continue.

Adding and Training Names

Your speech software can remember what you teach it as long as you follow these simple steps. When you click Add/Delete Word(s) from the Tools menu, the Add/Delete Word(s) dialog box opens. This is a very powerful tool. It allows you to enter a name or any other word or phrase, click the **Record pronunciation** button, and record your pronunciation of the word or phrase.

Step-by-Step C.14

Step 1 Click **Tools, Add/Delete Word(s)** from the Language Bar, as shown in Figure C-33.

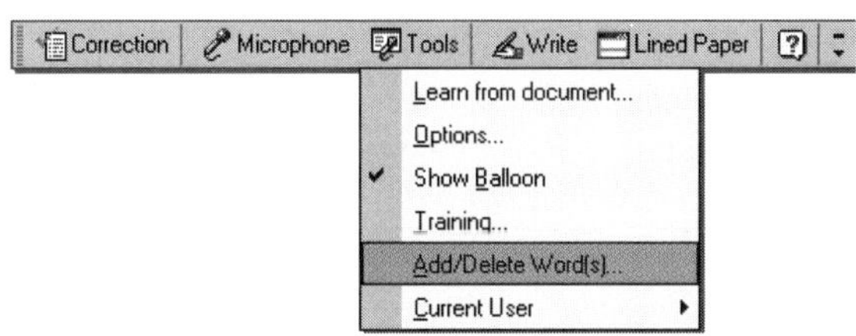

FIGURE C-33
Click the Add/Delete Word(s) Option

appendix C

Step 2 Enter your name into the **Word** text box as shown in Figure C-34.

FIGURE C-34
Enter Your Name in the Word Text Box

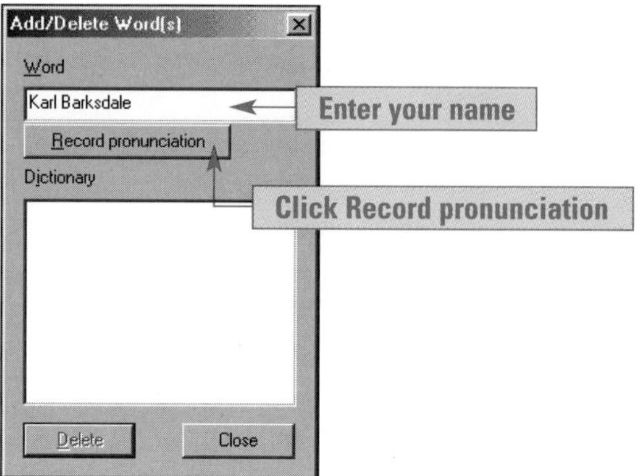

QUICK TIP

If your speech recognition software doesn't hear you properly, your name does not appear in the Dictionary. If this happens, try again. When the system has accepted your pronunciation of the word, the name appears in the Dictionary.

Step 3 Click the **Record pronunciation** button and say your name aloud.

Step 4 Your name appears in the Dictionary list. Double-click your name to hear a digitized voice repeat your name. (See Figure C-35.)

FIGURE C-35
Add/Delete Word(s) Dialog Box

CAUTION TIP

If your name doesn't appear properly when you say it, return to the Add/Delete Word(s) dialog box, select your name, then click the **Record pronunciation** button and re-record the correct pronunciation of your name.

Step 5 Close the Add/Delete Word(s) dialog box by clicking the **Close** button.

Step 6 Return to Microsoft Word, turn on your **Microphone**, switch to **Dictation** mode. Say your name several times and see if it appears correctly.

Step 7 To improve your accuracy, it's important to add troublesome words to your dictionary. Pick five words that have given you difficulty in the past. Train the software to recognize these words as explained in Steps 1 through 6. As you add and train for the pronunciation of those words, your accuracy improves bit by bit.

C.d Turning Microsoft Speech Recognition On and Off

Microsoft Office Speech Recognition isn't for everybody—at least not in its present form. It requires a powerful CPU and a lot of RAM. It also takes a quality headset. If you don't have the necessary hardware, chances are speech recognition isn't working very well for you.

Perhaps you are simply uncomfortable using speech software. You may be an expert typist with no sign of carpal tunnel syndrome or any other repetitive stress injury. Whatever your reason for choosing not to use Microsoft speech software, it is important to know how to disable the feature.

There are two ways to turn off your speech software. You can minimize the toolbar and place it aside temporarily, or you can turn it off entirely. If you decide you want to use speech recognition at a later time, you can always turn it back on again.

Turning Off Speech Recognition

Microsoft Speech Recognition allows you to minimize the Language Bar, putting it aside temporarily. Minimizing places the Language Bar in the taskbar tray in the form of the Language Bar icon. After the Language Bar has been minimized, it is then possible to turn the system off altogether. To see how this is accomplished, follow Step-by-Step C.15.

Step-by-Step C.15

Step 1	Open **Microsoft Word** and the **Language Bar**, if necessary.
Step 2	Click the **Minimize** button on the Language Bar, as shown in Figure C-36.

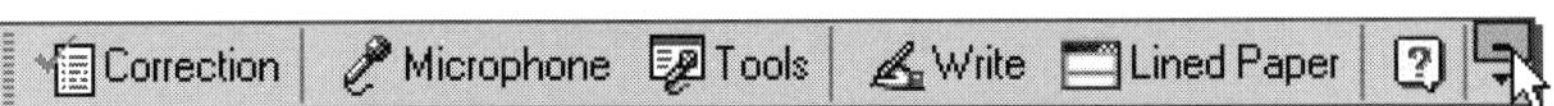

FIGURE C-36
Click the Minimize Button on the Language Bar

appendix C

Step 3 When you minimize for the first time, a dialog box explains what is going to happen to your Language Bar, as shown in Figure C-37. Read this dialog box carefully, then click **OK**.

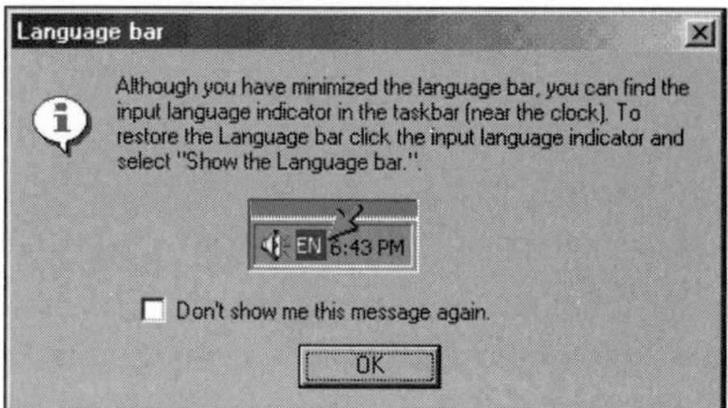

FIGURE C-37
Read This Information Carefully

Step 4 Right-click the **Language Bar** icon in the taskbar. Several options appear, as shown in Figure C-38. Click **Close the Language Bar**.

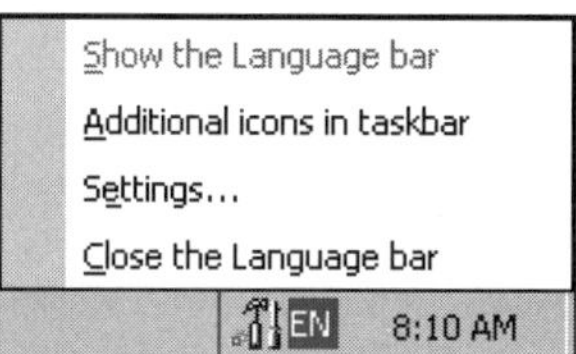

FIGURE C-38
Right-Click the Language Bar Icon

Step 5 Another dialog box opens to explain a process you can follow for restoring your speech operating system after you have turned it off. Click **OK**. The system is turned off and your language tools disappear, as shown in Figure C-39. Close Word. (*Note:* If you click **Cancel**, you return to normal and can continue using the speech recognition system by opening the Language Bar.)

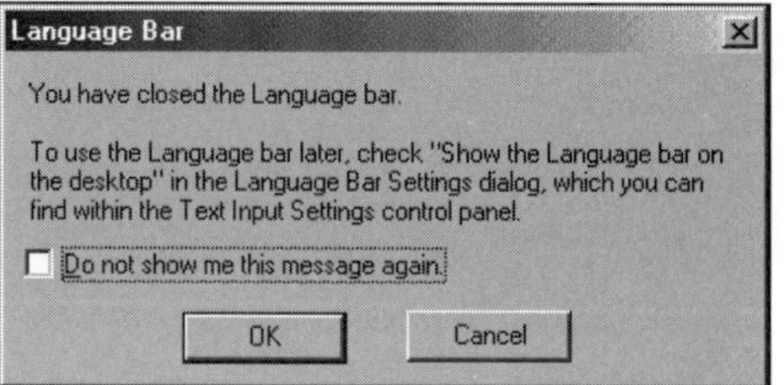

FIGURE C-39
Click OK to Turn Off Speech Recognition

Turning On Speech Recognition

There are several ways to turn your speech recognition system back on. Follow Step-by-Step C.16.

Step-by-Step C.16

Step 1 Open **Microsoft Word** and click **Speech** on the **Tools** menu, as shown in Figure C-40. Your speech recognition software is restored and you can begin using it again.

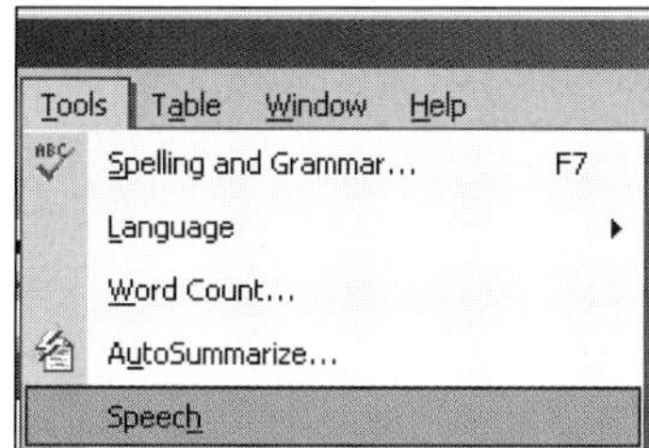

FIGURE C-40
Click Speech on the Tools Menu

If your speech software did not restore itself after Step 1, continue with Steps 2 through 5.

Step 2 Click the **Start** button, **Settings**, **Control Panel**. Then double-click the **Text Services** icon to open the Text Services dialog box, as shown in Figure C-41.

FIGURE C-41
Click Language Bar in the Text Input Settings Dialog Box

appendix C

Step 3 Click **Language Bar** in the Text Services dialog box.

Step 4 In the Language Bar Settings dialog box, click the **Show the Language bar on the desktop** check box to insert a check mark, as shown in Figure C-42.

FIGURE C-42
Language Bar Settings Dialog Box

Step 5 Click **OK**, then exit and restart your computer. The speech software should be restored and you can begin speaking again. (*Note:* If the Language Bar is still missing after you launch Word, try selecting Tools, Speech one more time.)

Mastering and Using Microsoft Excel 2002

APPROVED COURSEWARE

Core MOUS Objectives

Standardized Coding Number	Skill Sets and Skills Being Measured	Chapter Number	Chapter Pages	Exercise Pages	Exercises
Ex2002-1	***Working with Cells and Cell Data***				
Ex2002-1-1	Insert, delete, and move cells	3 4	EI 46–49 EI 68, 84	EI 66 EI 91–96	Skills Review 8 Skills Review 1, 2, 4, 6, 7 Case Projects 1, 3–7
Ex2002-1-2	Enter and edit cell data including text, numbers, and formulas	2 3 4	EI 28–32 EI 43–44, 50, 52, 53–57 EI 72–75	EI 38–41 EI 62–66 EI 91–96	Skills Review 1, 2, 4–8 Case Projects 1–8 Skills Review 1–4, 6, 7 Case Projects 1, 2, 5, 6, 8 Skills Review 1–4, 6, 7 Case Projects 1, 3–7
Ex2002-1-3	Check spelling	5	EI 99–101	EI 117	Skills Review 3
Ex2002-1-4	Find and replace cell data and formats	5 6	EI 98–99 EI 136–137	EI 117 EI 141–142	Skills Review 3 Skills Review 1, 3
Ex2002-1-5	Work with a subset of data by filtering lists	4	EI 86–87	EI 91, 96	Skills Review 1 Case Project 6
Ex2002-2	***Managing Workbooks***				
Ex2002-2-1	Manage workbook files and folders	1	EI 6–7, 13	EI 23–25	Skills Review 1, 2, 4–8 Case Project 2
Ex2002-2-2	Create workbooks using templates	1	EI 17–19	EI 23, 25	Skills Review 3 Case Project 4
Ex2002-2-3	Save workbooks using different names and file formats	1	EI 14–15, 17	EI 23–25	Skills Review 1–8 Case Project 4

Standardized Coding Number	Skill Sets and Skills Being Measured	Chapter Number	Chapter Pages	Exercise Pages	Exercises
Ex2002-3	***Formatting and Printing Worksheets***				
Ex2002-3-1	Apply and modify cell formats	4	EI 70–79	EI 91–96	Skills Review 1–8 Case Projects 1–7
Ex2002-3-2	Modify row and column settings	4	EI 82, 84–86	EI 92, 94–96	Skills Review 2, 7 Case Projects 3, 4, 6
Ex2002-3-3	Modify row and column formats	4	EI 72, 82–84	EI 91–96	Skills Review 1, 2, 4–8 Case Projects 1–7
Ex2002-3-4	Apply styles	4	EI 80–82	EI 94–95	Skills Review 8
Ex2002-3-5	Use automated tools to format worksheets	4	EI 70–71	EI 92	Skills Review 3
Ex2002-3-6	Modify Page Setup options for worksheets	5	EI 102–112	EI 116–119	Skills Review 1–4, 6–8 Case Projects 2–4, 6–8
Ex2002-3-7	Preview and print worksheets and workbooks	1 5	EI 16–17 EI 102, 108–113	EI 23–24 EI 116–119	Skills Review 1–5, 8 Skills Review 1–4 Case Projects 2–4, 6–8
Ex2002-4	***Modifying Workbooks***				
Ex2002-4-1	Insert and delete worksheets	1	EI 11, 13	EI 23–24	Skills Review 4, 5, 6
Ex2002-4-2	Modify worksheet names and positions	1 2	EI 11–13 EI 34–35	EI 23–24 EI 39–41	Skills Review 2, 6 Skills Review 3, 6, 7 Case Projects 3, 4, 8
Ex2002-4-3	Use 3-D references	3	EI 58–59	EI 64–65	Skills Review 7, 8
Ex2002-5	***Creating and Revising Formulas***				
Ex2002-5-1	Create and revise formulas	3	EI 43–44, 49–51	EI 62–66	Skills Review 1, 4, 7 Case Projects 1, 8
Ex2002-5-2	Use statistical, date and time, financial, and logical functions in formulas	3	EI 50–59	EI 62–66	Skills Review 1, 7 Case Projects 1, 2, 6
Ex2002-6	***Creating and Modifying Graphics***				
Ex2002-6-1	Create, modify, position, and print charts	6	EI 121–127, 129–132	EI 141–144	Skills Review 1, 3–8 Case Projects 1, 3–8
Ex2002-6-2	Create, modify, and position graphics	6	EI 127–128	EI 141–144	Skills Review 3 Case Project 3
Ex2002-7	***Workgroup Collaboration***				
Ex2002-7-1	Convert worksheets into Web pages	6	EI 135–136	EI 142, 144	Skills Review 6 Case Project 7
Ex2002-7-2	Create hyperlinks	6	EI 133–134	EI 143, 144	Skills Review 8 Case Project 4
Ex2002-7-3	View and edit comments	6	EI 132–133, 134–135	EI 143–144	Skills Review 7 Case Projects 1, 8

Expert MOUS Objectives

Standardized Coding Number	Skill Sets and Skills Being Measured	Chapter Number	Chapter Pages	Exercise Pages	Exercises
Ex2002a-1	***Importing and Exporting Data***				
Ex2002e-1-1	Import data to Excel	16	EA 214–219	EA 237–239	Skills Review 4, 7 Case Projects 2, 4, 5, 6
Ex2002e-1-2	Export data from Excel	16	EA 220, 224	EA 238, 240	Skills Review 5, 6, 7 Case Project 7
Ex2002e-1-3	Publish worksheets and workbooks to the Web	16	EA 228–230	EA 238–240	Skills Review 5, 6, 8 Case Projects 1, 3, 6, 8
Ex2002e-2	***Managing Workbooks***				
Ex2002e-2-1	Create, edit, and apply templates	9	EA 64, 65	EA 72, 74	Skills Review 3, 4, 5 Case Projects 5, 6, 8
Ex2002e-2-2	Create workspaces	7	EA 16–17	EA 21	Skills Review 3
Ex2002e-2-3	Use Data Consolidation	7	EA 9–11	EA 20, 22–24	Skills Review 1, 6 Case Projects 1, 3
Ex2002e-3	***Formatting Numbers***				
Ex2002e-3-1	Create and apply custom number formats	15	EA 187–191	EA 210, 212	Skills Review 6, 7 Case Projects 6, 8
Ex2002e-3-2	Use conditional formats	15	EA 191–193	EA 210, 212	Skills Review 8 Case Projects 6, 7
Ex2002e-4	***Working with Ranges***				
Ex2002e-4-1	Use named ranges in formulas	7	EA 6-9	EA 22	Skills Review 6
Ex2002e-4-2	Use Lookup and Reference functions	15	EA 193–195	EA 210	Skills Review 5
Ex2002e-5	***Customizing Excel***				
Ex2002e-5-1	Customize toolbars and menus	9	EA 66–68	EA 71, 73	Skills Review 1, 8
Ex2002e-5-2	Create, edit, and run macros	9	EA 54–61	EA 71–74	Skills Review 2, 6, 7 Case Projects 1, 3, 4
Ex2002e-6	***Auditing Worksheets***				
Ex2002e-6-1	Audit formulas	11	EA 100–103	EA 112–113	Skills Review 3, 5, 6, 7 Case Projects 4, 6
Ex2002e-6-2	Locate and resolve errors	11	EA 99–100, 105–107	EA 111–113	Skills Review 2, 4, 8 Case Project 4
Ex2002e-6-3	Identify dependencies in formulas	11	EA 100–107	EA 111–113	Skills Review 2, 4, 7, 8 Case Project 4

Standardized Coding Number	Skill Sets and Skills Being Measured	Chapter Number	Chapter Pages	Exercise Pages	Exercises
Ex2002e-7	***Summarizing Data***				
Ex2002e-7-1	Use subtotals with lists and ranges	8	EA 45–46	EA 51–52	Skills Review 8 Case Project 2
Ex2002e-7-2	Define and apply filters	8	EA 37–43	EA 50–52	Skills Review 4, 5, 6 Case Project 4
Ex2002e-7-3	Add group and outline criteria to ranges	8	EA 45–46	EA 51	Skills Review 8
Ex2002e-7-4	Use data validation	8	EA 27–34	EA 49–50, 52	Skills Review 1, 2 Case Projects 2, 7, 8
Ex2002e-7-5	Retrieve external data and create queries	16	EA 220–222	EA 237, 240	Skills Review 3 Case Project 7
Ex2002e-7-6	Create Extensible Markup Language (XML) Web queries	16	EA 222–224	EA 236, 239	Skills Review 1 Case Project 4
Ex2002e-8	***Analyzing Data***				
Ex2002e-8-1	Create PivotTables, PivotCharts, and PivotTable/PivotChart Reports	12	EA 118–122, 128–130	EA 133–136	Skills Review 1–6, 8 Case Projects 1, 2, 3, 5
Ex2002e-8-2	Forecast values with *what-if* analysis	10	EA 76–79, 80–85, 89–91	EA 94–97	Skills Review 1, 4–8 Case Projects 1, 3, 4, 7, 8
Ex2002e-8-3	Create and display scenarios	10	EA 85–89	EA 94–97	Skills Review 2, 3, 7 Case Projects 5, 6
Ex2002e-9	***Workgroup Collaboration***				
Ex2002e-9-1	Modify passwords, protections, and properties	15	EA 196–199	EA 210–211	Skills Review 7 Case Project 1
Ex2002e-9-2	Create a shared workbook	15	EA 199–200	EA 209–211	Skills Review 1, 4 Case Project 5
Ex2002e-9-3	Track, accept, and reject changes to workbooks	15	EA 200–202	EA 209–210	Skills Review 2, 3, 4
Ex2002e-9-4	Merge workbooks	15	EA 203–204	EA 209–210	Skills Review 4

Index

E

F

G

H

I

N

O

P

Q

R

S

V

W

X

Y

Z